Also by Mark Bowden:

Black Hawk Down

Killing Pablo

Road Work

Finders Keepers

GUESTS OF THE AYATOLLAH

THE FIRST BATTLE IN THE WEST'S WAR WITH MILITANT ISLAM

MARK BOWDEN

Atlantic Books
London

First published in hardback in the United States of America in 2006
by Grove/Atlantic Inc.

First published in Great Britain in 2006 by Atlantic Books,
an imprint of Grove/Atlantic, Inc.

This paperback edition published in Great Britain in 2007
by Atlantic Books.

9 8 7 6 5 4 3 2 1

A CIP catalogue record for this book is available from the British Library.

ISBN 978 1 84354 496 8

Printed and bound in Great Britain by Bookmarque Ltd, Croydon

Atlantic Books
An imprint of Grove/Atlantic Ltd.
Ormond House
26–27 Boswell Street
London
WC1N 3JZ

To Aaron, Beth, Anya, BJ, Dan, and Ben

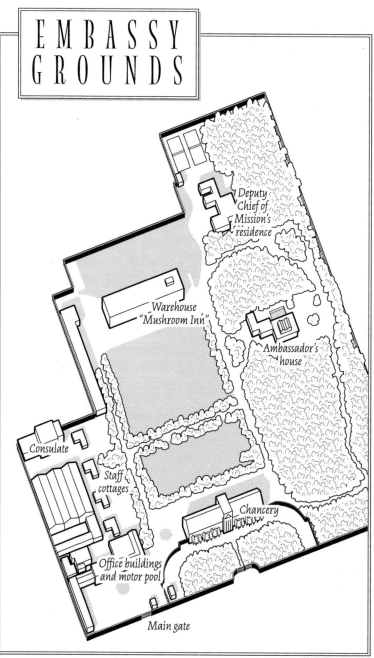

EMBASSY GROUNDS

Deputy Chief of Mission's residence

Warehouse "Mushroom Inn"

Ambassador's house

Consulate

Staff cottages

Chancery

Office buildings and motor pool

Main gate

MATTHEW ERICSON

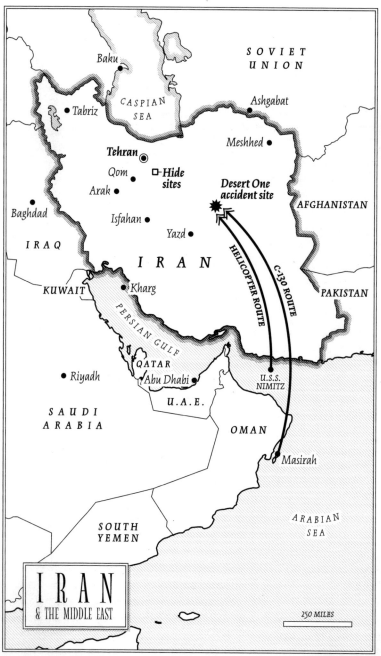

MATTHEW ERICSON

CONTENTS

The terror of the unforeseen is what the science of history hides, turning a disaster into an epic.

—Philip Roth

PART ONE

THE
"SET-IN"

(Tehran, November 4, 1979)

Students storming the U.S. embassy in Tehran, November 4, 1979.
(Courtesy: Russ Kick, thememoryhole.org)

Jerry Miele paraded to the embassy gate, November 11, 1979. The man on
Miele's left is believed by some to be Mahmoud Ahmadinejad, the current
president of Iran. *(Courtesy: AP)*

1

THE DESERT ANGEL

Before dawn Mohammad Hashemi prepared himself to die. He washed according to ritual, then knelt in his dormitory room facing southwest toward Mecca, bent his head to the floor, and prayed the prayer for martyrdom. After that the stout, bushy-haired young man with the thick beard tucked a handgun in his belt, pulled on a heavy sweater, and set out through the half darkness for the secret meeting.

It was, in Iran, the thirteenth day of Aban in the year 1358. The old Zoroastrian calendar had been resurrected a half century earlier by the first self-appointed shah in the Pahlavi line, Reza Khan, in an effort to graft his royal pretensions to the nation's ancient traditions. That flirtation with Persia's gods and bearded prophets had backfired, sprung up like an uncorked genie in the previous ten months to unseat his son and the whole presumptuous dynasty. Aban is Persia's old water spirit, a bringer of rebirth and renewal to desert lands, and the mist wetting the windows of high-rises and squeaking on the windshields of early traffic in this city of more than five million was a kept promise, an ancient visitation, the punctual return of a familiar and welcome angel. As it crept downhill through the sprawling capital and across the gray campus of Amir Kabir University, where Hashemi hurried to his meeting, Iran was in tumult, in mid-revolution, caught in a struggle between present and past. Towering cranes posed like skeletal birds at irregular intervals over the city's low roofline, stiff sentinels at construction sites stranded in the violent shift of political climate. The fine rain gently blackened concrete and spotted dust in the canals called *jubes* on both sides of every street, fanning out like veins. Moisture haloed the glow from streetlamps.

Hashemi was supposed to be a third-year physics major, but for him, as for so many of Tehran's students, the politics of the street had supplanted study. He hadn't been to a class since the uprising had begun more than a year ago. It was a heady time to be young in Iran, on the front lines of change. They felt as though they were shaping not only their own futures but the future of their country and the world. They had overthrown a tyrant. Destiny or, as Hashemi saw it, the will of Allah was guiding them. The word on campus was, "We dealt with the shah and the United States is next!"

Few of the hundred or so converging from campuses all over the city on Amir Kabir's School of Mechanics that morning knew why they were gathering. Something big was planned, but just what was known only to activist leaders like Hashemi. Shortly after six, standing before an eager crowded room, he spread out on a long table sketches of the U.S. embassy, crude renderings of the mission's compound just a few blocks west. He and others had been scouting the target for more than a week, watching from the rooftops of tall buildings across the side streets, riding past on the upper floor of two-decker buses that rolled along Takht-e-Jamshid Avenue in front, and waiting in the long lines outside the embassy's newly opened consulate. The drawings showed the various gates, guard posts, and buildings, the largest being the chancery, the embassy's primary office building; the bunkerlike consulate; and the airy two-story white mansion that served as home for the American ambassador. There was a murmur of satisfaction and excitement in the crowd as Hashemi announced they were going to lay siege to the place.

In retrospect, it was all too predictable. An operating American embassy in the heart of revolutionary Iran's capital was too much for Tehran's aroused citizenry to bear. It had to go. It was a symbol of everything the nascent upheaval hated and feared. Washington's underestimation of the danger was just part of a larger failure; it had not foreseen the gathering threat to its longtime Cold War ally Mohammad Reza Pahlavi, the now reviled, self-exiled shah. A CIA analysis in August 1978, just six months before Pahlavi fled Iran for good, had concluded that the country "is not in a revolutionary or even a prerevolutionary situation." A year and a revolution later America was still underestimating the power and vision of the mullahs behind it. Like most of the great turning points in history, it was obvious and yet no one saw it coming.

The capture of the U.S. embassy in Tehran was a glimpse of something new and bewildering. It was the first battle in America's war against militant Islam, a conflict that would eventually engage much of the world. Iran's revolution wasn't just a localized power struggle; it had tapped a subterranean ocean of Islamist outrage. For half a century the tradition-bound peoples of the Middle and Near East, owning most of the world's oil resources, had been regarded as little more than valuable pawns in a worldwide competition between capitalist democracy and communist dictatorship. In the Arab states, the United States had thrown its weight behind conservative Sunni regimes, and in Iran behind Pahlavi, who stood as a bulwark against Soviet expansionism in the region. As the two great powers saw it, the Cold War would determine the shape of the world; all other perspectives, those from the so-called Third World, were irrelevant, or important only insofar as they influenced the primary struggle. An ignored but growing vision in the Middle East, nurtured in mosque and madrasah but considered quaint or backward by the Western world and even by many wealthy, well-educated Arabs and Persians, saw little difference between the great powers. Both were infidels, godless exploiters, uprooting centuries of tradition and trampling sacred ground in heedless pursuit of wealth and power. They were twin devils of modernity. The Islamist alternative they foresaw was an old twist on a familiar twentieth-century theme: totalitarianism rooted in divine revelation. It would take many years for the movement to be clearly seen, but the takeover of the embassy in Tehran offered an early glimpse. It was the first time America would hear itself called the "Great Satan."

How and why did it happen? Who were the Iranian protesters who swarmed over the embassy walls that day, and what were they trying to accomplish? Who were the powers behind them, so heedless of age-old privileges of international diplomacy? What were their motives? Why was the United States so surprised by the event and so embarrassingly powerless to counter it? How justified were the Iranian fears that motivated it? How did one of the triumphs of Western freedom and technology, a truly global news media, become a tool to further an Islamo-fascist agenda, narrowly focusing the attention of the world on fifty-two helpless, captive diplomats, hijacking the policy agenda of America for more than a year, helping to bring down the presidency of Jimmy Carter, and leveraging a radical fundamentalist regime in Iran into lasting power?

The U.S. embassy in Tehran stood behind high brick walls midway down the city's muscular slope, where the land flattened into miles of low brown slums and, beyond them, the horizon-wide Dasht-e Kavir salt desert. Inside the enclosure was a parklike campus, a twenty-seven-acre oasis of green in a smoggy world of concrete and brick. Its primary structure, the chancery, bathed now in the swirling mist of the water angel, stood fifty or so feet behind the front gate, a blocks-long structure two tall stories high built in the dignified art deco style typical of American public buildings at midcentury. It looked like a big American high school, which is why years ago it had been dubbed "Henderson High," after Loy W. Henderson, the first U.S. ambassador to use it, in the early fifties. Scattered beneath a grove of pine trees behind the chancery were the new concrete consulate buildings; the white Ambassador's Residence, a two-story structure with a wraparound second-story balcony; a smaller residence for the deputy chief of mission; a warehouse; a large commissary; a small office building and motor pool; and a row of four small yellow staff cottages. There were tennis courts, a swimming pool, and a satellite reception center.

When the embassy opened more than four decades previously, Tehran had been a different place, a small but growing city. The United States was then just one among many foreign powers with diplomatic missions in Iran. Before the chancery stood a low, decorative wooden fence that allowed an unobstructed view of the beautiful gardens from Takht-e-Jamshid, which was then just a quiet side street, paved with cobblestones. In those days, the new embassy's openness and its distance from the row of major missions on busy Ferdowsi Avenue contributed to America's image as a different kind of Western power, one that had no imperial designs.

In the years since, Tehran itself had grown noisy and crowded, a bland, featureless, unplanned jumble of urgent humanity that flowed daily in great rivers of cars through uninteresting miles of low, pale brown and gray two- and three-story boxlike buildings. Takht-e-Jamshid's quaint cobblestones had long since been paved and the avenue widened. In daylight it was clogged with cars, motorbikes, and buses. The embassy's main entrance, Roosevelt Gate, was named after Franklin D. Roosevelt, whose distant cousin CIA officer Kermit Roosevelt, Theodore's grandson, had helped engineer the 1953 coup d'état that toppled an elected Iranian government and replaced it with the shah. At the time, the coup had powerful Iranian backers and was welcomed by many in the country, but today it was seen simply as a tawdry American stunt, another example of cynical CIA meddling in the Third World.

By the fall of 1979, in the receding tide of the revolution, the old embassy had become a provocation. It was moored like an enemy battleship just a stone's throw from the street, a fact demonstrated repeatedly. For a country in a fit of Islamist, nationalist, and increasingly anti-American fervor, such a grand and central presence in the capital city was a daily thumb in the eye. Lately most of the harassment had been relatively minor. The walls that now surrounded Henderson High and its campus were covered with insults and revolutionary slogans and were topped by three feet of curved and pointed steel bars. A few days earlier a band of young men had sneaked into the compound and were caught shinnying up the big pole in front of the chancery to take down the American flag. The marines had since greased the pole. As a defense against rocks and an occasional gunshot from passing motorists, all of the windows facing front had been layered with bulletproof plastic panels and sandbags. The chancery looked like a fort.

While the Americans inside saw these changes as purely defensive, the picture they presented strongly encouraged suspicion. The embassy was an enemy foothold behind the lines of the revolution. Washington had been the muscle behind the shah's rule, and a big part of throwing off the monarchy had been the desire to break Iran's decades-long fealty to Uncle Sam. Yet here the embassy still stood. Those Iranians who supported the United States—and there were many still among the prosperous middle and upper classes—prayed that its obdurate presence meant the game wasn't over, that the free world was not really going to abandon them to the bearded clerics. But these were an embattled, endangered minority. To the great stirred mass of Iranians, afire with the dream of a perfect Islamist society, the embassy was a threat. Surely the architects of evil behind those walls were plotting day and night. What was going on inside? What plots were being hatched by the devils coming and going from its gates?

Why was no one stopping them?

2

WOULD THE
MARINES SHOOT?

A big demonstration was already in the works that morning, which had been proclaimed National Students Day, in honor of collegiate protesters who had been gunned down by the shah's police the year before. The numbers of those massacred had been wildly inflated, from a few score to "thousands," which played to Shia Islam's obsession with martyrdom. In addition to honoring the slain students, this rainy Sunday had also been declared an official day of mourning for more than forty *pasdoran,* Revolutionary Guards, who had been killed in a clash with Kurdish separatists the week before. There would be thousands of people in the streets. Hashemi and the others planned to launch their surprise from inside this larger crowd.

Standing before a crowded room he explained that the assaulters would be divided into five groups, one for each of the embassy's larger buildings. The initial thrust would be through Roosevelt Gate. Local police would not interfere—their support had been quietly enlisted—but there was no telling what the Americans would do. If they opened fire, then the bodies of those martyred in the vanguard would be passed out to the crowd and carried aloft through the streets, sure to incite rage. When the planning session ended, the students drifted across town to the rallying point, the corner of Takht-e-Jamshid and Bahar Street, several blocks west of the embassy. Thousands had already begun to assemble in groups of twos and threes, in cars and on foot.

The plan had been hatched by a dozen young Islamist activists, representatives from each of Tehran's major universities, who had formed just weeks before a group that called itself Muslim Students Following the Imam's Line, to differentiate itself from factions with agendas that varied from the teachings of Imam Ruhollah Khomeini. Hashemi was the son of an Isfahan cleric and had been raised in the devout traditions of Shia Islam. Unlike the city's other large universities, Amir Kabir was strictly Islamist. Classes were conducted as though teachers and students were together in a mosque, and prayer was a big part of every day and night. Robed women students did not speak to men other than family members unless the situation required it, such as working together in a lab. While Marxist and other leftist groups tended to dominate on the bigger, more secular campuses such as Tehran University, where the religious students were often still an unpopular minority, Amir Kabir was known as a center for Islamist radicals, young people strictly allied with Khomeini and the new mullah establishment.

All men in the Islamic organizations called each other "brother," but Hashemi was part of a smaller, militant inner circle called the Brethren— "brothers who were more brothers than others," was how one would later explain it. Most of those recruited for the takeover effort were simply students, but the Brethren were something more. They would eventually form the nucleus of the new Iran's intelligence ministry. They were armed at all times and had connections with the powerful clergy and with high-ranking officials in the police and the provisional government who had sympathy for their political agenda. Hashemi had not been one of the instigators of the plot to seize the American embassy that day, but when those plans were formed he was naturally one of the first approached for help.

The plan was the brainchild of three young men, Ibrahim Asgharzadeh, an engineering student from Sanati Sharif University, Mohsen Mirdamadi from Amir Kabir University, and Habibullah Bitaraf from Technical University. Asgharzadeh was the first to suggest it. They would storm the hated U.S. embassy, a symbol of Western imperial domination of Iran, occupy it for three days, and from it issue a series of communiqués that would explain Iran's grievances against America, beginning with the overthrow of Mohammed Mossadeq in 1953 and decades of support for the shah, now a wanted man in Iran accused of looting the nation's treasure and torturing and killing thousands. America's imperialist designs had not ended when the shah fled Iran the previous February. The criminal tyrant had recently been allowed to fly to America on the pretense of needing medical treatment and was being sheltered there with his stolen fortune. America was stirring up political opposition to the imam, instigating ethnic uprisings in the various enclaves that made up the border regions of their country, and had recently begun secretly collaborating with the provisional government to undermine the revolution. A clandestine meeting in Algiers between secular members of the provisional government and White House National Security Adviser Zbigniew Brzezinski had been revealed to dramatic effect in Tehran. All of it added up to only one thing in the students' eyes: America was determined to hang on to its colony and restore the shah to his throne. The danger was pressing. The provisional government had sold out; it was nothing more than a group of old men wedded to Western decadence bent on tamping down the ardor of the Islamist uprising. One thing the revolution had taught the students was the folly of waiting for something to happen. They had seen the fruits of bold, direct action. Seizing the embassy would stop the American plot in its tracks and would force the provisional government to show its hand. Any move against the heroic embassy occupiers would expose acting Prime Minister Mehdi Bazargan and his administration as American stooges. The students believed that if they did not act soon to expose him if his government weathered its first year, then the United States would have its hooks back in Iran for good, and their dream of sweeping, truly revolutionary change would die.

When Asgharzadeh had proposed the move two weeks earlier at a meeting of an umbrella activist group called Strengthen the Unity, it was opposed by two students, Mahmoud Ahmadinejad from Tarbiat Modarres University and Mohammed Ali Seyyedinejad from Elm-o-Sanat University. Both preferred targeting the Soviet embassy instead. Asgharzadeh, Mirdamadi, and Bitaraf voted them down and then had expanded their planning cell by inviting activists from various local schools, including Hashemi, Abbas Abdi, Reza Siafullahi, and Mohammad Naimipoor, all young men experienced with street demonstrations and organizing. These Brethren were both students and members of the fledgling intelligence services. All of these men, including Ahmadinejad and Seyyedinejad, eventually joined ranks behind the seizure of the American embassy. They were all committed to a formal Islamic state and were allied, some of them by family, with the clerical power structure around Khomeini. Several, including Asgharzadeh, had been closely associated with the Keramat Mosque, home base for Ayatollah Ali Khamenei, one of the most powerful young clerics in the country (and the man who would ultimately succeed Khomeini as supreme leader). The revolution was shaping up as a struggle between leftist nationalists who wanted a secular, socialist-style democracy and young Islamists like these who wanted something the world had not yet seen, an Islamic Republic.

The mullahs' ideas about Iran and the world had merged with the naive idealism of students like these over the previous years to create a simple powerful vision. For years the banned writings of the philosopher-activist Ali Shariati had been circulating underground on Iran's campuses, firing the imagination and national pride of students who dreamed of creating a new kind of Iranian state and of seizing center stage in the dreamy "revolution" of world youth that was raging in America and Europe. Shariati had embraced the leftist rhetoric of the era without endorsing the Soviet Union and regarded capitalism as a root evil. He saw in Islam a third path toward utopia, one that was neither communist nor capitalist but founded on "authentic," divine principles. The philosopher saw the materialism of the West as the biggest threat to the purity of an Islamic state, and his writings had spawned a whole school of thought that interpreted the freedoms and excesses of America and western Europe as a plot to ensnare the virtuous and enslave the world in a capitalist, godless dystopia. Shariati himself had not been impressed with Iran's clerical establishment, and much of what he had written was critical of old mullahs such as Khomeini, but in the heat of the revolution those differences had been forgotten. The idea of the third path, one rooted in the rich history of the Shia faith, dovetailed in most ways with the vision of the mullahs. The clerics lived a cloistered existence; their knowledge of history and current events was grounded exclusively in the Koran's prerenaissance, seventh-century ideology. Theirs was a world suspended in an eternal struggle between good and evil, and one where neither was just an abstract concept. To the devout, Allah was alive in the world and so was satan, working with superhuman powers of deception and ruthless application of force. Only one superpower fit that description, and that was the godless, mercantile, devious monster known as the United States of America. To them, America was quite literally the embodiment of evil, the Great Satan, and their ultimate enemy. Young activists like Asgharzadeh, Mirdamadi, and the others were among the brightest of their generation—competition for places at Tehran's universities was fierce—but most of them had excelled in math, engineering, or science. Few were well traveled or well read. It was easy for them to see the U.S. embassy behind its high walls as, quite simply and literally, the source of all evil.

In sessions during the previous week at Amir Kabir, they had divided up the work into six committees: Documents, Operations, Public Relations, Logistics, Hostage Control, and Information. They would need about four hundred students to carry out the assault and thousands more to rally in support outside the embassy walls. Preparations were made to feed the occupiers and the hostages for three days. Others worked on organizing mass demonstrations in support of the siege on the streets around the embassy. Given the anti-Americanism in Tehran, one of the group's biggest fears was that opposition camps would either get wind of the idea and execute it first or move in and take over the demonstration once it had started, muddying the intended political message; they were primarily worried about the well-organized, militant leftist factions such as Mujahedin-e Khalgh and Fadaeian-e Khalgh. They knew the provisional government would move against them if it could, so it was critical that right from the start they be recognized as a strictly Islamic organization, one loyal to Khomeini, which is why they had come up with the name Muslim Students Following the Imam's Line, to make their allegiance perfectly clear. At first it was just Students Following the Imam's Line but then it was decided to add "Muslim" to distinguish theirs from the more secular student groups that also professed allegiance to Khomeini, most notably the well-organized communist Tudeh party. To make clear their affiliation on the day of the action they formed a committee to copy a photograph of their inspiration, the white-bearded, brooding imam, and prepare plastic-covered placards that would be hung around their necks on a length of string. "Muslim Students Following the Imam's Line" was written on each photo, and armbands were made with the slogan "Allahuakbar" (God Is Great) and featuring a picture of the imam. This would also help them recognize one another in the confusion of the first hours. Hashemi had been charged with planning the assault. He figured there were about one hundred Americans working at the embassy. One of his subcommittees had prepared strips of cloth to bind and blindfold that many.

The planners had also dispatched several of their members to tip off in advance a member of the Assembly of Experts, the body drafting Iran's new constitution, and four more of the student leaders, Bitaraf, Mirdamadi, Siafullahi, and Asgharzadeh, had called on Mousavi Khoeniha, a young, black-bearded radical cleric whose preaching they admired. A slight man who spoke softly outside the pulpit, Khoeniha was considerably to the left of the conservative mullah establishment, and he was popular with the Islamist youth organizations at the universities who shared his more free-form, interpretive take on Koranic doctrine. Khoeniha immediately endorsed the idea of the takeover. He agreed with the planners that the devilish practices inside the U.S. embassy needed to be derailed, and that its emerging secret ties with the provisional government needed to be broken. The young cleric saw clearly that seizing the American embassy would also put great pressure on Prime Minister Bazargan and his government. They would be obliged to protect their American friends. Yet if the embassy was seized correctly, and by what was seen to be a group of pious, nonviolent youth allied to Khomeini, then it would make it virtually impossible for Bazargan to act without an order from the imam himself. The planners asked him to take their plan to Khomeini, but on this the radical mullah demurred. Why ask permission? In the years of building a movement against the shah, students and more radical clerics many times had successfully pressured the more powerful and moderate mullahs simply by acting without asking. Khomeini had a stake in preserving the provisional government; after all, he had appointed it. Asking him to approve an act that could topple it might invite disapproval. But if the embassy were occupied by his own professed supporters, and a large crowd was massed around the wall cheering them on, it would make it very hard, perhaps even impossible, even for the imam to oppose it, which would paralyze Bazargan and his traitorous administration.

The students had also secured the support of the Revolutionary Guards through Mohsen Razaee, one of the young leaders of that organization (he would become its head in two years). With the quiet backing of both the police and Razaee, they were confident that no authority would chase them from the grounds before they had a chance to seize the Americans and make a statement.

Everyone involved knew this could be a deciding moment in the revolution. If Khomeini condemned the takeover and ordered the students out of the embassy, it would signal his firm support for the provisional government and would likely mean that the clerical establishment would not directly run the state. If he supported the takeover, it would most likely collapse the Bazargan administration and the hopes of those who preferred at least some separation of church and state. To the students, the former course meant nothing less than total defeat, since they saw Bazargan as an American collaborator. They felt the weight of history and saw a chance to change the world.

Days after the plan was hatched, Khomeini gave a speech urging "all grade-school, university, and theological students to increase their attacks against America." Asgharzadeh thought at first that the imam had been told of their plan and was signaling his support. He was elated, and then surprised and disappointed to learn from Khoeniha that the imam had not been consulted and knew nothing of the takeover plan. The remarks may have been coincidental, but they certainly suggested that Khomeini would support the assault.

Now, as Hashemi moved among the throng just blocks away from the embassy, he could see all the pieces coming together as planned. He would be one of the first through the gates. Abbas Abdi carried a loudspeaker from which he would issue the command to begin. Asgharzadeh was there too. He would stay back and try to make sure that those entering were members of his own group, and then see that the gates were locked behind them—if they were going to maintain control of the action they needed to prevent rival political organizations from storming inside. Mohammad Naimipoor had his large group of protesters assigned with forming a giant human ring around the chancery. Some of the chador-wearing women carried bolt cutters under their robes, for the chains on the gates, and also new chains and locks with which to secure the gates behind them. In addition to the laminated photos and armbands, all carried cards identifying their organization. Some carried the strips of cloth to bind and blindfold their American captives. It was both thrilling and daunting. Many saw the fine Aban rain that morning as heavenly approval, a symbol of Iran purifying itself, washing itself clean of its relationship with the Great Satan.

Hashemi's concealed weapon was more to deal with rival factions than with the Americans. A short-lived takeover of the embassy in February had devolved into gunfights between competing militias. The students had decided that their assault would be strictly nonviolent. They would not harm the Americans, even if they opened fire. But there was also a chance things would get out of control. Would the marines shoot? If they did, and the bloodied bodies of martyrs were passed out to the crowd, what would happen then?

3

THE MORNING MEETING

Walking down the wide corridor that ran the length of the chancery's second floor, John Limbert mapped out his day in hopes of finding an hour to slip out for a haircut. He was on his way to the meeting that officially began each workday at the embassy. The second secretary in the political section, he had been traveling the week before in southern Iran, and it occurred to him that his thick brown hair, which now fell over the tops of his ears, must look pretty shaggy.

Ordinarily Limbert did not attend the morning meeting, which was chaired by the acting ambassador, Bruce Laingen, the chargé d'affaires, and included the various embassy departmental heads. Today he had been invited to sit in for his boss, First Political Secretary Ann Swift, who was coming in late. Everyone was eager to hear about his swing through the cities of Abadan and Shiraz. Limbert was an ambitious foreign service officer, but about him there was nothing pushy or abrasive. He was a loose-limbed, affable man with a narrow face and a nose so ample, starkly framed by dark-rimmed glasses above and by a heavy brown mustache below, that it ruled his face. Behind stylish, lightly tinted lenses were the playful eyes of an intensely curious and fun-loving soul. The loose cut of his suit advertised that he had lived primarily outside of the United States in recent years. This assignment to Iran had been ideal for him, one for which he was particularly well suited. He had spent years in the country, first in the Peace Corps and later as a teacher working on his doctorate in Middle Eastern studies, and he spoke Farsi so well that when he wore locally made clothes he passed for Iranian. That wasn't necessarily a good thing in an American embassy, where there was an institutional suspicion of foreign service officers who had "gone native," but Iran was suddenly of utmost importance in Washington, and Limbert's set of skills and experience was rare. He had been at this job for only a few months and was still conscious of making the right impression. He wished he'd gotten the haircut earlier.

Limbert was one of two political officers who worked with Swift. The other was Michael Metrinko, whom Limbert had known before this assignment. Metrinko had partly learned his Farsi from Limbert's Iranian wife, Parvaneh, who had taught him when he was a Peace Corps volunteer; she considered him to have been her best student. Along with the head of that section, Victor Tomseth, who was also acting deputy chief of mission, these three were among a very small number of fluent Farsi-speaking Iran experts in the State Department. With their years in the country and language skills, they were prized sources of information in the embassy, which even at its highest levels was filled with newcomers. Limbert, Tomseth, and Metrinko formed an especially sharp contrast to the three-man CIA station, which had no Farsi speakers and a combined experience in Iran of fewer than five months. This tour was a chance for all three to shine. Because they could read the local newspapers, listen to the radio and TV, and talk to a wide variety of Iranians, they were the only ones with a real feel for the place.

The morning meeting was held around a long table in the "The Bubble," a bizarre room with walls made of clear plastic, a complete enclosure inside a normal room on the second-floor front of the chancery that was designed to avoid electronic eavesdropping. The clear plastic walls insulated the space and prevented the hiding of listening devices in the walls, floor, or ceiling. At the head of the table, the compact, athletic, and tanned chargé d'affaires was feeling upbeat, as was his way. A Minnesota farm boy, Laingen had retained his youthful appearance well into middle age, with stray locks of dark hair that fell casually across his forehead. Laingen had been in Tehran since June, dispatched on short notice to fill in after the new regime had summarily rejected Walter Cutler, the man President Carter had appointed ambassador. No new ambassador had been named, so Laingen was the top American official in Tehran. He was no Iran expert, but he had served in the city more than a quarter century earlier as a young foreign officer in the heady days after Kermit Roosevelt's legendary coup, when he had learned enough Farsi to hold simple conversations. Languages did not come as easily to Laingen as they did to some of those on his staff. His assignment now was to begin a dialogue with the country's new rulers and convince them that the despised United States, despite its close ties to the toppled monarchy, was ready to accept the new Iran. He felt a big part of his job was to project confidence and cheer into this small American community, which was reduced to a fraction of its normal size, having sent home all nonessential personnel and family members of those who stayed. A more cautious leader might have spent more time preparing for the worst, destroying files and further paring down the staff, but Laingen had a constitutional bias toward hope; he believed things were getting better and heading back toward normal. He worked hard to improve morale, arranging a number of social outings for the staff, such as a tennis tournament against other embassies and softball games, and had even allowed a slight easing of security restrictions—he had approved, for instance, opening a new drinking club for the marines in their apartment building just off embassy grounds, which, given the revolution's abhorrence of alcohol, might have been considered needlessly provocative. His efforts were working. The mood at the embassy had noticeably lifted since his arrival, and Laingen was popular with his coworkers and staff, and although some saw his chipper outlook as distinctly rose-tinted, even the skeptics had to admit there were encouraging signs. Despite daily torrents of rhetorical venom, the revolutionary powers had chased away the group that had invaded and briefly occupied the embassy in February, and had cooperated in the construction of the compound's new consulate, a modern concrete structure designed to more efficiently handle the thousands of Iranian visa seekers who still lined up outside the embassy every day—voting with their feet. Khomeini had recently denounced such Western-yearning Iranians as "traitors," and as "America-loving rotten brains who must be purged from the nation." Vitriol like this and the imam's recent encouragement of "attacks" on America were so commonplace now that they had ceased to cause alarm. It was just considered the climate. John Graves, the flamboyant United States Information Agency chief, had cabled Washington that week that the mood in Tehran had improved sufficiently to resume his program and increase his staffing. Laingen had even recommended allowing some family members of those working at the embassy to return to Tehran on a case by case basis.

The decision to allow the shah to fly to New York City for cancer treatment had threatened to undo everything. In a meeting weeks earlier with Foreign Minister Ibrahim Yazdi to inform him that the shah was being admitted to the United States, Yazdi had promised to do what he could to protect the embassy, but warned that it would be a tall order—he had doubted they would be able to do it. In an equivocating cable to Washington at the end of September, Laingen had predicted that the move would be a setback, but gave little hint that it might mean serious trouble for the mission itself. He had written of an overall improvement in American-Iran relations—itself a very rosy estimate—but admitted that progress was slow. "It is not yet of the substance that would weather very well the impact of the shah entering the United States." He noted the ascendancy of the clerics, which "I fear worsens the public atmosphere as regards any gesture on our part toward the shah," who was being denounced as a traitor and criminal whom justice demanded be returned to Iran to stand trial and, presumably, join the general parade of former regime officials to the killing grounds. "Given that kind of atmosphere and the kind of public posturing about the shah by those who control or influence public opinion here, I doubt that the shah being ill would have much ameliorating effect on the degree of reaction here." In the next sentence he slightly backed off that assertion. "It would presumably make our own position more defensible if we were seen to admit him under demonstrably humanitarian conditions." In other words: they won't like it but, if it is well handled, the effect shouldn't be catastrophic.

It was one of several factors that weighed in favor of allowing the shah to come to New York for surgery. In October, Carter had polled his top advisers on the question, and most of them supported letting the shah in.

"What are you guys going to advise me to do if they overrun our embassy and take our people hostage?" asked the president. No one had answered.

The embassy had braced itself for the worst. Just three days earlier, fearing violent demonstrations, Laingen had ordered all nonessential personnel off the compound and had placed the entire complement of embassy marines on alert. But the protests, which turned out an estimated two million people at nearby Tehran University, had resulted in nothing more than some additional spray-painted graffiti on the compound walls. Friday and Saturday, the Iranian weekend, had been calm, and that Sunday morning there was a palpable sense of relief in the building, the sense that they had weathered the worst.

In its heyday the embassy staff had numbered nearly a thousand; now it was down to just over sixty. Even in its stripped-down state it remained a complex enterprise with scores of objectives and tasks. Laingen and his small political and economics sections were busily trying to give Washington fresh insight into current conditions in the country. The defense attaché and newly organized military liaison staff were sifting through what remained of the two countries' long-standing defense ties, and the small staff of information officers had begun the challenging task of convincing Iran that America was not the enemy. The consular section was coping with a flood tide of applications for visas from the substantial number of Iranians who needed no convincing—a line a quarter of a mile long had begun forming days before the new consulate opened that summer. There was the small CIA presence at the embassy, three officers who were trying to make sense of shifting conditions and to make friends with anyone close to the new centers of power. Administering the compound, buildings, and employees, managing security operations and the embassy's commissary, was a big job with scores of employees, many of them Iranian. In the mix were foreign service officers concerned with cultural ties, some of them working on site and others scattered around Tehran. It was a busy mission, like that of any large country with wide-ranging interests. The faces in Laingen's conference room represented all of the facets of this ongoing effort, serious professionals who in some cases had been doing their jobs in one country or another for decades.

Malcolm Kalp, a CIA officer who had arrived only four days before, told the group of meeting with David Rockefeller shortly before he had left the States. Rockefeller had been one of the powerful Americans who, along with former Secretary of State Henry Kissinger, had lobbied hard for President Carter to admit the shah. Kalp said that Rockefeller had told him, "I hope I haven't caused you all too many problems." From around Laingen's conference table came the laugh of the powerless. Clearly this group lacked the clout to compete with the combined influence of Kissinger and Rockefeller, and the latter's belated words of concern for them rang hollow. But few in this room felt bitter about it. Most of those now stationed in Tehran, especially professionals like Limbert, Tomseth, Metrinko, CIA station chief Tom Ahern, and his two officers, Kalp and Bill Daugherty, as well as the military liaisons and aides, were comfortable with risk. Some were motivated by patriotism, some by ambition, and some, especially the lower-level State Department communicators and staffers, for the danger pay—Tehran was a 25 percent differential post, meaning one earned a full fourth more than the usual pay. For some it was a chance to escape a failing marriage or family obligations that had become too onerous. Many of them were in Tehran precisely because they sought exotic or dangerous postings. The tension created esprit among those who could rise above it; it made everyone's job seem all the more vital and rare. Yet not everyone could rise above it.

Some of those in this room periodically approached youthful, muscular Al Golacinski, the embassy's security chief, to ask for his assessment of the risk, weighing whether to stay on or quit and clear out. He was always reassuring. Golacinski felt they had turned the corner. After the violent February invasion, the compound had been patrolled for months by a band of roguish local gunmen whom he had finally managed to ease out. Anxiety remained, but he felt events were coming under control. Golacinski expected continued demonstrations and thought there might even be occasional, isolated assassination attempts—a German diplomat had been gunned down in Tehran weeks earlier. But these were low-percentage risks. He personally assured everyone who asked that another invasion was unlikely and advised them to ride it out. To buttress his argument he made a point of keeping up a brave, confident front.

Just that morning he had averted a potential showdown. A local *khomiteh*, a gang of armed young men who dispensed revolutionary justice in the neighborhood, had shown up to complain about the removal of a large Khomeini poster that had been hung on Roosevelt Gate during the big demonstration. Golacinski had defused the encounter by tracking down the poster—it had been taken down by Navy Commander Donald Sharer, who thought it would make a nifty wall decoration for the marines' new bar. Golacinski returned it and extracted a promise that it would not be hung where it obscured the view of embassy guards. He told the story at the morning meeting, the point being that confrontation, if well handled, could be peacefully resolved.

Limbert then talked about his trip south, promising a more complete written report, and the discussion turned to the "Students Day" demonstration planned for that morning. Some of those present thought that the embassy should be closed for the day to avoid trouble, but others argued against it. Tomseth wanted to keep the embassy open.

"If we close the embassy down every time there's a demonstration in Tehran we would be closing down just about every day," he said.

This opinion prevailed. There was some debate over whether to acknowledge the day of official mourning by flying the Stars and Stripes at half-mast before the chancery, and it was decided not to do so. In light of the attempt to steal the flag off the pole, lowering it halfway might tempt another try. Golacinski briefed the meeting on what to expect. There was already a crowd of about 150 to 200 people outside Roosevelt Gate, and they had been peaceful so far. The big rally was expected to draw together various rival elements among the revolutionary student groups, the more numerous religious conservatives from various universities around the city, and the smaller but better-organized leftists who were centered mostly at the University of Tehran. Because the street out front led directly to the university, large crowds of students marching toward the rally would be passing by the embassy all morning, which would mean more noise and the usual chanting and nastiness. Still, Golacinski said, the protest "is not aimed at us."

To Iranians, Aban the thirteenth had an additional significance that went unnoted by the American staff. It was the fifteenth anniversary of the day the shah had exiled the Ayatollah Khomeini.

Laingen concluded the meeting by announcing that he had an appointment at the Foreign Ministry that morning, so he and Tomseth would be away for a few hours. Golacinski advised his assistant, Howland, who would accompany Laingen to the Ministry, to avoid streets around the University of Tehran on their way.

As he walked back down the corridor to his office, Limbert decided against visiting the barber. It would keep him from his office for several hours and he didn't feel right getting a haircut on government time. Instead, he would start writing up his report of the trip.

Michael Metrinko was just arriving for work. He ignored the larger-than-usual crowd outside the east-side entrance. The protests were often worse later in the morning. Metrinko was a night owl and was customarily one of the last to show up. He did his real work after hours, meeting with Iranians, eating, drinking, smoking, and talking, trying to figure things out. As he saw it, that's what his job was about. And what a fascinating job it was.

For a student of politics, being in Tehran just then was like being a geologist camped on the rim of an active volcano. Iran had gone temporarily insane. Revolution gives ordinary people the false belief that they can remake not just themselves, their country, and the whole wide world but human nature itself. That such grand designs always fail, that human nature is immutable, that everyone's idea of perfection is different—these truths are all for a time forgotten. Those in the grip of righteousness saw the opportunity—no, the *need*—to weed the impure from their new and glorious garden. It started as always with the officials of the overthrown regime, authors of the criminal past, who were given show trials and marched out in the streets or to rooftops to be shot or hanged. With the taste of blood, the executioners then turned on those who had merely collaborated with the old order or its foreign sponsors or allies. Next, as former revolutionary brothers vied for permanent power, the killing turned inward.

This was where things had arrived after nine months. Various political and religious streams had joined in the exciting years before, Islamist fanatics, nationalist democrats, European socialists, Soviet-sponsored communists . . . they had all allied to bring down the shah. Now they were eyeing one another dangerously. The competition was not academic; it was a matter of life and death. The losers were being imprisoned, assassinated, or marched to the rooftop shooting galleries, outmaneuvered and denounced as traitors and spies. Tehran was a cauldron of intrigue, mysterious factions, uprisings, plots, clandestine maneuvers. Clerics considered too liberal were being gunned down in the streets by their more radical brothers, and some considered too conservative were being killed by violent leftists; Khomeini was cracking down on women who ignored the new mandates for *hijab*, traditional Islamic dress; the Kurds were rebelling in the northwest. This was the big leagues, people playing politics for keeps, reinventing themselves and their country, borrowing from Marx, from Jefferson, from Muhammad. And Metrinko wasn't on the sidelines, either, he was right in the middle of things. While others studied the dynamics of political upheaval in libraries, he was present for one, and this revolution was particularly intriguing and original. He would describe it to his friends at home as "Delightful chaos with lots of blood!"

At thirty-three he was still a young man in the State Department, that ponderous, mysterious, plodding bureaucracy that could be, depending on the time and place, brilliant or utterly blind. It was an organization that respected age and tradition to a fault, and while it cultivated worldly expertise, grooming young officers like Metrinko to become expert in their region of the world, it was famous for ignoring or distrusting them. It had a mission to explore and understand foreign politics and cultures, but the farther afield its officers wandered the more suspect they became, as though distance from Foggy Bottom meant distance from the truth. The more one's reports deviated from the venerated status quo and challenged established policy, the more readily they were dismissed. There was an institutional fear of going native.

Metrinko was aware of this but undaunted. He was *working* Iran. He was ambitious, but not for promotion or pay. His ambitions were intellectual and personal. He was from a small town in Pennsylvania, from a family of eccentrics. The Metrinkos owned a huge, rambling apartment and tavern complex of more than fifty rooms in Olyphant, a coal-mining town about an hour and a half north of Philadelphia. Growing up surrounded by the immigrants and travelers who wandered through the family home had broadened his horizons, and he had grown to be a man more at home abroad than anywhere else. He had wide-set blue eyes and a broad forehead, with the thickening features of his Pennsylvania Slav ancestry. A mustache partly framed his full lips. His wide wire-rimmed glasses were stylish, but he kept his brown hair well trimmed in a way that was out of step with the shaggier fashion of the day. Metrinko did things his own way. He was stout but solid; he studied judo with an Iranian policeman, but efforts at fitness were no match for his nightly bull sessions with food, wine, and tobacco. He held forth in such sessions with a peculiarly proud, precise way of speaking, building long complex sentences that came out fully sanded and polished, like he had written them down beforehand and memorized them. They sounded like comments delivered between long thoughtful puffs on a pipe, except Metrinko's vice was cigarettes, which he smoked habitually. He sometimes found it hard to mask his impatience with others, which could make him seem high-toned and superior. He dealt with Iranians daily who knew their own history and language less well than he did, and with Americans, in both Tehran and distant Washington, most of them his bosses, who lacked his language skills, his experience in the country, and his complete absorption in the work. He was used to knowing more than anyone around him about the subject matter at hand.

The way he had it figured, Iran was about the size of a big state back home. It held about thirty-eight million people, the vast majority of whom would never play even a slight role in deciding the country's fate. Decisions were made, as they were in any state back home or in any small country, by a tiny fraction of the educated and well connected. In a country the size of Iran, he figured, it was theoretically possible to know most of those people. He had collected hundreds of names and profiles, a vast network of acquaintanceship. He preferred not to meet with people in their offices but in restaurants, or in their homes, where they relaxed and said what they really felt. And nothing bad ever came of unburdening oneself to Michael Metrinko, because his reports were never published inside or outside Iran. He was a sponge and a valuable contact. He offered people a perfectly neutral, sympathetic sounding board. He listened well, asked questions, empathized, and almost never argued, unless it was to better flesh out his subject's feelings and ideas. A person like that is rare anywhere, but in a society as notoriously closed and fearful as Iran's—and things had gotten worse even in that respect since the overthrow of the shah— Metrinko was addictive. People sought him out, trying to glean intelligence as they positioned themselves on ever shifting grounds. He reaped fascinating insights nightly and wrote incisive, well-grounded, and reasoned reports for the department, reports that would be thrown into the mix with all the others that guided American policy. Metrinko had no illusions that the brilliance of his fieldwork and insights would outshine those of the CIA, military, press, and various other foreign service departments at work in the field. He was content to play his part. His reports floated off into the mists of Foggy Bottom. He loved the work for its own sake, for giving him a chance to live well overseas. If he could serve the United States at the same time, all the better. In the deepest sense, though, Metrinko was working for himself.

Most American staffers overseas lived in carefully constructed American cocoons, safe inside the walls of the embassy grounds or at home in apartment clusters with their coworkers. They shopped for the usual American foods at the well-stocked embassy commissary, watched American TV, and hung out with other staffers after hours. Not Metrinko. He was the opposite of that kind of foreign service officer, a man fully and warmly immersed in the local culture. He was thoroughly familiar with Iran, having worked in the country off and on for three years in the Peace Corps before joining the State Department. He took pride in his ability to blend. It was his special talent. To the other Americans at the embassy he was considered a loner, an oddball, and even something of an elitist. Joan Walsh, a secretary in his section, thought he was strange, a man whose idea of a good time was sitting up all night smoking scented tobacco with a bunch of mullahs. More than any of the other places he had worked—Syria and Israel—Metrinko had fallen in love with the place, with its language, its bazaars, its quaint, courtly customs, its food, its art, and its spirit. His nightly dinner outings were a chance to show off this passion, especially rare for an American, and they usually lasted until the wee hours.

This morning he was the last in, but he was much earlier than usual. He had set his alarm for eight. Two sons of the Ayatollah Mahmoud Taleghani, the city's onetime Friday prayer leader who had died under fishy circumstances weeks earlier, had urged Metrinko to meet with them early that Sunday. The sons were convinced that their father, a revered figure in Iran (the street in front of the embassy would eventually be renamed for him), had been murdered by clerics loyal to Khomeini, but there was no proof. Nobody really knew what was going on in Tehran, but it was assumed that around Khomeini was a circle of men—sometimes called "the Bureau"—that was pulling strings behind the scenes. In Tehran there was the provisional government, headed by Bazargan, which was managing things until a constitution was written. Writing the new consti-tution was the Assembly of Experts, made up of select members of the Revolutionary Command Council, but beyond all this there were further layers of power and connection, shadowy factions, plots, and maneuvers that no one could fully fathom. Taleghani was the most recent prominent victim of these treacherous, shifting waters. He had advocated keeping mosque and state separate, a concept now opposed by the imam. Because he was widely revered, his opinion was dangerous. His family insisted his murder had been arranged by the clergy, but nothing was certain. They were now reaching out to him. One of the sons, Mehdi, had said he was about to leave the country for a meeting with Yasir Arafat, the Palestinian Liberation Organization (PLO) leader. Metrinko was both surprised and a little pleased that Mehdi and his brother wanted to confer with him be-forehand. A PLO connection would make an intriguing addition to his next report.

So Metrinko paid little heed to the crowd he passed that morning. It was just the usual rabble, young men with beards, women in loose black manteaus, white-bearded old men with stained teeth, most of them carry-ing signs, chanting slogans both triumphant and hateful, shaking their fists in the air, burning American flags and giant dolls of President Carter and other Western leaders—the standard background noise. Metrinko didn't underestimate what these mobs could do; he had been in Tabriz during the riots that followed the shah's exit and he had seen the bodies dangling from trees. He had come close to a similar fate. But what he felt for the rabble was more contempt than fear. The way he saw it, they were nothing more than the tools of more powerful men.

Entering the relatively calm green enclosure, he was met with the familiar scent of pine. He walked up the chancery's rear steps and mounted the stairs to his office on the second floor, where he poured himself a cup of coffee, lit another cigarette, and waited for the call from the guards to tell him the Taleghani brothers had arrived. He had a full schedule that day. After meeting with the brothers, a University of Tehran official was coming by to pick up a passport. Metrinko then planned to lunch with friends from Tabriz, including the former mayor of that city. An old roommate from the Peace Corps was in town and they planned to meet for dinner. As he looked through the milky plastic over the sandbags in his window, he was startled to see some people scaling the walls out front, forty or so feet away.

Picturing the job faced by the embassy guards, he watched amused as the protesters darted across the front yard.

4

WE ONLY WISH TO SET-IN

Kevin Hermening, who at nineteen was the youngest of the marines assigned to the embassy, woke up in the seven-story apartment building
across Bijan Alley from the back wall of the embassy, where he lived with
the other marines. Hermening had worked from afternoon to eleven o'clock
the night before, so he was not assigned guard duty that morning. He got
up at eight, late for him, and did his laundry in the apartment building basement. Then he decided to tackle some paperwork. One of his jobs was
to account for the copious amounts of food and drink he and the other
marines consumed, documenting the money collected for meals, and planning menus for the coming week. So instead of putting on one of his uniforms, he donned his "office clothes," a powder blue suit with a vest, and
strode across the empty alley, entered the compound, and walked toward
the chancery.

He was stopped at the front door by his boss, Al Golacinski, who had
been trying in vain to raise on his walkie-talkie the Iranian police captain
who was stationed at the motor pool just inside the front gate. Golacinski
asked the marine to find him. When Hermening stepped back outside he
was surprised to hear the volume of crowd noise jump. The mob was re-
acting to him, which was unnerving. He noticed for the first time that
some of the protesters had gotten inside the walls. Instead of walking, he
trotted in the direction of the motor pool, where he found the Iranian
captain.

"Al wants you to call him," Hermening said.

"Fine," the captain said.

When Hermening turned to go back, the masses outside the gate
seemed to lurch toward him, so he broke into a run, which provoked gleeful cheering. As he bounded up the front steps he saw the big front doors
of the chancery closing and heard panic in his voice as he shouted, "I'm
coming in! Don't close the doors yet!"

He took the rest of the steps three at a time and made it back into the building before the doors were closed and locked.

Inured to months of angry public displays, the Tehran embassy staff was slow to recognize that this one was different. It was late morning when Tom Ahern first noticed that there were young Iranians in the compound. The CIA station chief was a tall, slender man with a concave face, deep-set eyes, and straight, thin, brown hair. The Eagle Scout son of a Wisconsin plumbing contractor, Ahern had earned a degree in journalism from the University of Notre Dame before joining the agency. He had a studious, retiring manner and a wry sense of humor and worked in a complex of offices behind an unmarked door on the east end of the chancery's second floor. He usually started early, reading through the cables collected overnight and chatting with people in the political section. Early that morning he had encountered Laingen on the front steps conferring with a gardener and, pausing to say hello, had quipped, "Sorry to interrupt a meeting of the Fine Arts Committee."

When he saw protesters inside the walls he called downstairs to alert the marines, but when he looked back out the window a few minutes later the number of invaders had grown. He checked with the political folks across the hall, who seemed unconcerned. They demurred when Ahern suggested they might want to consider destroying sensitive files.

Given his position, it made sense that Ahern would be more sensitive about protecting sources and files than the others. At that moment, all of his office papers fit into a file only three inches thick. This was partly because the spy agency was cautious about keeping written records on site in a precarious post, but it also reflected the paucity of CIA activity in the country. Ahern himself had arrived only four months earlier and the two officers on his staff, Bill Daugherty and Malcolm Kalp, had even less time in the country. Daugherty had arrived fifty-three days earlier and Kalp just a few days ago. They had been focusing their efforts on trying to sort out the political mess and find sympathetic Iranians from the ranks of the more moderate mullahs and nonreligious factions in the emerging power structure. They had plans. They wanted to get back up and running the vital Tacksman sites, telemetry collection centers along the northern Iran border that had been essential for monitoring Soviet missile tests, but which had been shut down by *khomitehs* earlier that year. If the current unrest and instability continued, they hoped eventually to figure out how to influence events in a more America-friendly way. But they were still a long way from making these things happen.

The difficulty excited Ahern, who at forty-eight was an old agency pro. He had held posts throughout Southeast Asia, including Vietnam, during the long years of conflict there, and he had signed on for Tehran knowing that its future would be tumultuous and uncertain. He didn't have much to work with, however, only his two officers, neither of whom spoke Farsi, and no real agents to speak of, only a handful of prospects. The language barrier invited misadventure. Once, Ahern had gone to a high-rise apartment house to meet with an informant. The two men stepped into an elevator to go upstairs and their car abruptly halted in mid-ascent. It went completely black inside. Trapped for more than an hour, they held their meeting right there in the dark. Ahern learned only later that he had walked past a large sign in Farsi on the apartment house front door warning of a power shutdown at that hour. In the four months since he'd arrived, he had mostly managed to reestablish links with people who had spied for the agency in the past. His file was thin, but it was important that none of it fall into the wrong hands. The information was ruinous to his own meager efforts, embarrassing to the United States, and potentially catastrophic (even fatal) to the Iranians involved. Ahern walked down the hall to the other end of the building, to the communications vault, and began feeding his files into the disintegrator, a drum-shaped device with a metal feeding chute like a mail slot. It had blades, grinders, and chemicals inside that tore, pulverized, and deconstructed documents and electronic parts, rendering all into a fine, dry, gray-blue ash. The machine made such a terrible racket that users were supposed to wear earplugs to protect their hearing. For now, Ahern began feeding short stacks of paper into it. The machine worked methodically but slowly, and kept jamming, so Ahern started feeding some of his files into a shredder that cut the paper into long, thin, vertical strips.

In his office over by the motor pool, Barry Rosen, the embassy's press attaché, was closest to the demonstration and among the first to see Iranians coming over the walls. He was working on a ridiculous directive from his superiors in the International Communications Agency (ICA) in Washington, who wanted him to draw up a chart of the current power structure in Iran. Were they kidding? Nobody he knew had a clear idea of what was going on. Rosen had a better fix than most Americans; he spoke Farsi and had worked in Iran as a Peace Corps volunteer a decade ago. He had networks of friends all over the country. He had been in Tehran on this ICA tour for nearly a year, through the fall of the shah, the return of Khomeini, the February siege of the U.S. embassy, when he had briefly been held hostage, to the current provisional government phase and ongoing struggle to form a more permanent state. This year on the ground had made him, like Metrinko and Limbert, one of the old heads at the embassy at age thirty-five. But the little he knew only underscored how much he didn't. Iran was like the intricate designs on its famous Persian rugs: the closer you looked the harder it was to discern a pattern.

Nevertheless, after attending the morning meeting, he dutifully inserted paper in his typewriter and started banging out a response. When the demonstration outside grew louder he got up from his desk and went into his outer office to stand with his secretary and watch out the window. The demonstrators were all very young, and he noticed many of them had plastic-covered placards around their necks with photos of Khomeini. As he watched, the mob swelled rapidly.

Then a few of the young men began scaling the front gates. Rosen locked the door to his outer office and slid a locking metal bar into place. He told his secretary, Mary, not to open the door for anyone.

Then he ran back to his inner office and began flipping through his files looking for classified documents to destroy. Things were happening fast. He heard some of his colleagues being taken from their offices down the hall. Rosen was not unduly concerned. When it had happened nine months earlier he had been convinced as he was led out into the tear-gas-filled compound that he was going to be shot. When he had not been, along with the enormous sense of relief came a reduced fear of the demonstrators. Their bark was worse than their bite. He assumed this would be another rude interruption; his biggest concern was that it might convince Washington to close the embassy and bring everyone home. He hoped that didn't happen. He was enjoying the work too much to go home now.

Rosen figured the bar on the outer door would buy him enough time to destroy the most vital papers, so he was surprised when he heard the scrape of metal. His secretary, an Armenian woman apparently frightened by threats from behind the door, was removing the metal bar.

"Don't!" Rosen shouted.

It was too late. He was at once surrounded by young Iranians, boys and girls, the girls in manteaus and the boys carrying clubs, many of them with kerchiefs wrapped around their faces.

"Get out!" he shouted in Farsi.

"Either you move out of this room or we are going to drag you out," one of the invaders said.

"This is United States property. Get out of this building immediately."

Rosen's defiance was not simply bravado. He found it hard to take this bunch seriously. They were so young, for one thing, shabbily dressed and clearly nervous. He was more angry than frightened.

The growing crowd in his office didn't budge. Some of them began pulling open drawers to his desk and file cabinets and removing his files. His secretary was curled in the corner, frightened.

"Leave this room immediately or you will be hurt," one of the demonstrators ordered Rosen. "This is no joke. We're now in control of this place. You are flouting the will of the Iranian people."

"*You* leave immediately," said Rosen. "You have no right to set foot in here, any of you. You are violating diplomatic immunity. It is totally illegal."

When a club was waved in his face, Rosen relented. He was led out of his office.

Inside the front door to the chancery, Golacinski felt events slipping out of control. He flipped the switch on his radio and with unmistakable urgency in his voice ordered, "Recall! Recall! All marines to Post One!"

The plan Golacinski and Mike Howland had put together in case of an invasion, which was designed to prevent Americans from being taken hostage, involved locking down part of the workforce and encouraging others to flee. The second floor of the chancery could be closed off behind a steel door, so employees had been instructed to congregate there in an emergency and wait for help from the provisional government. If the door to the second floor were breached, the communication vault on the west end was a final fallback position. It was large enough to accommodate dozens of people and was well stocked with food and water, so theoretically it could protect the chancery staff long enough for help to arrive. Those working in the buildings spread out across the campus would be told to move toward the relatively quiet back gates, where protesters rarely gathered, and slip out toward the British, Canadian, or Swiss embassies. Ordinarily Howland would have helped coordinate this response, but he had gone to the Foreign Ministry with Laingen and Tomseth. By radio, Golacinski told his assistant to stay there and press for an immediate local rescue force.

Several of the young Iranians who had climbed the gate now severed its chains with bolt cutters and swung the doors open wide. Protesters flooded in. On his radio, Golacinski heard reports from the various marine guard posts.

"They're coming over the walls!" shouted Corporal Rocky Sickmann from another spot on the compound.

This was clearly a coordinated action.

Golacinski's emergency call had awakened four marines who had worked the night shift and were asleep in the apartment building behind the compound. They quickly dressed but, as they prepared to leave the building, saw protesters and Iranian police massed around their building.

"Stay where you're at," said Golacinski.

Usually there would have been only three or four marines in the chancery at that hour, but today there were about a dozen. Some had come in to get paid and others had been attending a language class. Corporals Billy Gallegos and Sickmann had just come running through the front door, having abandoned their guard posts, as instructed. Gunnery Sergeant Mike Moeller, the top-ranking marine at the embassy, gathered his force together and couldn't contain his enthusiasm.

"All right, guys," he said with a grin. "Let's go for it."

Sickmann noticed that his hands were trembling as he fed rounds into his shotgun and .38 pistol. Outside, the protesters were now ramming a long wooden pole into the large, locked front doors. Inside, every impact shook bits of plaster off the frame. He watched this until the frame was almost completely shattered and then called Sergeant Moeller on his walkie-talkie to tell him that the doors were not going to last much longer.

Outside the door, demonstrators with bullhorns were repeating re-assurances in both Farsi and English, "We do not wish to harm you. We only wish to set-in."

Staffers throughout the building were standing on chairs in their offices, watching the drama unfold. The security barriers on the windows blocked the view on the lower half, so they had to climb to see outside. Joan Walsh, the blond-haired secretary in the political section, was fright-ened as she watched the now dozens of protesters running around the building. She knew the chancery was virtually a fortress but also that one of the windows on the basement floor was not barred like the others. It had been secured only by a single lock to provide ready egress in case of fire. Seeing some of the protesters with bolt cutters, she assumed it would be only a matter of time before they were in the building.

Gallegos ran to the front door duty station and changed clothes quickly, donning fatigues. He was annoyed because he had polished his combat boots the night before and had left them in his apartment. He had reported to work in the regulation short-sleeve tan shirt, blue pants, and black dress shoes, but the dress shoes looked stupid with the cammies, and it bugged him, but there was nothing to do. He pulled on his emergency gear and ran to his post upstairs, which was in the ambassador's spacious office. There were floor-to-ceiling windows looking south over the compound. Gallegos saw that the safe doors were still open in Laingen's office—his secretary, Liz Montagne, had not finished emptying them—and ordered them shut and locked. He stretched himself prone on the floor pointing his weapon out the window. It was a great spot. If he were ordered to shoot, he could pick off targets all day. He kept cocking and aiming his empty rifle at the demonstrators below, pretending to shoot. Corporal Greg Persinger saw this and worried that his buddy, always a little too gung ho, was going to get them all killed.

Golacinski pulled on riot gear and watched images of disorder on an array of closed-circuit TV screens. There were easily thousands of pro-testers on the grounds now. Four of his marines had surrendered to the mob, and he suspected correctly that Rosen, Graves, and the others in the motor pool office building had also been taken. He had told the marines still in the Bijon Apartments to stay there.

Laingen phoned.

"I'm coming back," he told Golacinski.

"No, you won't be able to get near the embassy," Golacinski said. He could picture the chargé d'affaires' limo engulfed in a sea of hostile Iranians. Laingen, Howland, and Tomseth might be torn limb from limb. He advised them to turn right around and go back into the Foreign Ministry building and stay there.

Laingen said that under no circumstances were the guards to open fire on the demonstrators. Golacinski asked if, as a last resort, they could use tear gas.

"Only as a last resort," Laingen said.

In earlier discussions, when they had expected trouble immediately after the shah had been allowed to enter the United States, they agreed that tear gas was not to be used anywhere on the embassy grounds, only inside the buildings. Tehran's protesters were accustomed to tear gas and had learned how to cope with it during the months of their uprising—that explained the kerchiefs many of them wore wrapped across their faces. Using it would only further incite them. Given that the grounds were completely overrun, the buildings were now the line of defense. Most areas of the second floor were off-limits to those without the highest levels of security clearance, so Golacinski ordered all the local employees to the basement and all Americans to the top floor. Howland came up on the radio seeking an update.

"Look, I can't talk to you right now," Golacinski told him. "I'm trying to get this under control."

At the Foreign Ministry, an impressive collection of large ornate buildings several miles east, Laingen and Tomseth implored Deputy Foreign Minister Kamal Kharrazi to send help to their besieged embassy. Only a short while earlier they had concluded a polite lower-level meeting over sugary tea, in which Laingen had officially thanked the provisional government for its help in controlling the large demonstrations outside the embassy the week before. They had discussed obtaining diplomatic immunity—a touchy subject in Iran—for the embassy's new military liaison group, commanded by Army Colonel Chuck Scott. After leaving that meeting, Laingen had gone out to the courtyard to his car, where Howland told him what was going on. They had driven only about two blocks from the ministry when Golacinski advised them to turn back. The chargé and his deputy had raced back into the ministry building, where they first confronted the chief of protocol. He was a gentle, nervous man, who immediately began wringing his hands with anxiety. He was sympathetic but powerless. He had led them back in to Kharrazi.

Ibrahim Yazdi, the foreign minister, and Mehdi Bazargan, the prime minister, had been away for a few days to attend the conference in Algiers, where the informal meeting with President Carter's national security adviser Zbigniew Brzezinski had set off alarms in Tehran. Yazdi was due back that day but had not returned to his office.

So Laingen and Tomseth listened impatiently as Kharrazi phoned various police and security officials trying to get some force over to the embassy to restore order. It was clear from the tenor of his conversations that no one was eager to intervene. The police had their hands full dealing with the mass demonstrations at Tehran University. Help would come eventually, Kharrazi said, but it would take more time.

5

MICHAEL, I'M REALLY SORRY

Inside the consulate, on the east side of the compound, there were a small number of staff and about sixty Iranians who had made appointments that day to discuss their visa applications. Consul general Richard Morefield had closed the building to the normal flood of applicants while the graffiti painted on the new walls was removed, but scheduled appointments were being honored and most of the staff was at work. Among them was Bob Ode, a retired foreign service officer who had taken a temporary assignment to help out in Tehran. He had a backlog of about three hundred visas to review and hoped that a quiet morning would allow him to put a dent in it. Another was Richard Queen, a lanky, shy, bookish vice consul with big glasses, who was working with three other consulate officers typing data into AVLOS, the building's new computer system. Assisted by four of his colleagues, he was pulling from the files of rejected visa applicants those who had been convicted of crimes or who had been turned down within the past year and entering that information into the computer, which was linked to American consulates around the world. That way, if the same applicant popped up at an office in a different country, there would be a record of what the Tehran office had discovered. It was boring work, and Queen was looking forward to finishing early and spending some time exploring Tehran.

Ode was helping a pretty young American woman, married to an Iranian, who wanted to check on her mother-in-law's passport. He got up from his desk with the passport number and was flipping through his files when outside his office he heard Morefield urgently announce, "All right, everybody upstairs! Everybody upstairs!"

"What's the matter?" the young woman asked.

"I don't know," said Ode.

"Does this sort of thing happen often?" she asked.

"I have no idea," said Ode. "It's never happened before since I've been here, but I've only been here a short time."

Ode cleared the paperwork off his desk and locked it in a small safe, which contained his personal things, passport, travel orders, American money, and some letters and other items that he thought were more secure in the office safe than at the apartment where he had been staying. Then he accompanied the young woman upstairs.

"Stay away from the windows," Morefield said as people filed past him. Queen saw clumps of young Iranians milling around in the compound below, and noted the curious laminated photos of Khomeini that hung from their necks. They didn't look too menacing, but some had makeshift weapons. One carried nunchucks, another had what looked like a croquet mallet, and another held a length of broken board.

Downstairs, demonstrators were breaking windows and reaching in through the bars trying to grab anything inside they could reach. Marine Sergeant Jimmy Lopez moved from window to window, whacking arms and hands with his nightstick, then herding everyone up to the second floor. If they turned off the lights on the first floor and everyone stayed upstairs, it was hoped the protesters outside would assume the building was empty. The Iranians were asked to sit on the floor of the visa processing room and stay low.

Lopez and Morefield were discussing what to do next when the power went out. Then they heard footsteps on the roof.

In his second-floor chancery office, Michael Metrinko's amusement at the activity outside quickly soured. As the numbers of intruders grew, he realized that the demonstration was now severe enough to disrupt the busy day he had planned. When the embassy had been overrun in February—he was in Tabriz—he heard it had screwed things up for days. He wondered how much this fracas would set them back.

Staff members from the lower floors were massed in the hallway outside his door. When word came that the basement had been breached, Metrinko phoned his friend Mehdi Taleghani.

A security guard answered and there was a delay before he came back on the line.

"Michael, he won't talk to you," the guard said.

"Do you know what is happening here at the embassy?" Metrinko asked.

"Yes, we know," the guard said, and then, "Michael, I'm really sorry." He hung up.

Metrinko thought, *So much for Persian friendship*. He felt set up.

Golacinski was losing his TV cameras. One by one the monitors in the chancery front guard post went blank. The invading protesters were either destroying the cameras or tilting them up to the ceiling. There were four marines lined up behind the front door, each down on one knee with his weapon up. The door shook more with each impact from the wooden ram. Then, abruptly, it stopped. Sickmann looked through one of the thick Plexiglas windows and saw that the group on the porch had dropped its battering ram and gone off.

Then Gallegos radioed the news that protesters had broken through a basement window. The front side of the building had a sunken concrete porch that ran its full length, letting sunlight in the basement windows. It looked like an empty moat. The protesters had found the one window that had not been completely secured. It had a steel mesh over it and a lock but it was clearly a weak point. Golacinski wondered if they had known about it in advance.

Downstairs, Gallegos confronted the intruders at the foot of the basement stairs. He cocked his shotgun when he saw the first three enter the hallway and they all retreated. Behind Gallegos crouched Persinger, who was handed a tear gas grenade by army Sergeant Joe Subic, a pudgy young man with dirty-blond hair and glasses who worked as a clerk in the defense attaché's office and whom the marines regarded as a wannabe. Persinger had no use for the grenade, which he did not yet have permission to use. So he set it down on the step next to him and then heard a *tink!* When he looked down he noticed the grenade's pin was missing and that the safety lever had popped open. Before handing it over, Subic must have pulled the pin! It went off as he bent to pick it up, blasting a scalding stream of gas into his lower leg. He screamed in pain and the tear gas sprayed off into the basement.

Upstairs, Golacinski smelled the gas. He shooed the remainder of the staff up the stairs. Persinger arrived on a run from downstairs and pulled off his tear-gas-covered pants, uncovering a nasty burn on the outside of his calf. He stripped down to a T-shirt, pulled on cammie pants and boots, then ran upstairs with everyone else. At the bottom of the steps, Gallegos had been joined by Sickmann. Before the two marines was a growing crowd of Iranians, crying and choking from the gas, all with the Khomeini placards, some hand-lettered in English, "Don't be afraid. We just want to set-in." Those in the back were pushing and those in front were shouting, "Don't shoot! Don't shoot!" and inching forward.

Sickmann and Gallegos had donned gas masks. The blood was pounding in their ears and they heard only the whoosh of their own breathing inside the masks, misting up the glass visors. The marines would pump their shotguns and the crowd would jump back. That was the scene Golacinski encountered as he descended the stairs with his Browning 9mm pistol drawn. He joined the protesters in shouting at the marines, "Don't shoot!"

"No, no, no," coaxed a woman in the crowd. "We don't mean any harm."

More armed marines appeared behind Golacinski on the steps.

One of the young men seemed to be the leader, so Golacinski grabbed him by the arm and asked if he spoke English. When he nodded, Golacinski told him that they all had to get out.

"We are not going to stand for this," he said, angrily. "Maybe you didn't realize it but we are prepared to defend this place."

"Yes, yes," the young man said. "We don't want problems. We just want a peaceful demonstration. That's all we want."

"You can't do a peaceful demonstration *in* the embassy," Golacinski said. "Now you all are going to have to get out of here."

The young man nodded. He told the others in Farsi to go back out the window, and the crowd complied. Golacinski directed Gallegos and the other marines to head upstairs.

Golacinski watched until all of the trespassers except the ringleader were out the window. He then took the young Iranian up the stairs, leading him by the arm. Perhaps he could be useful.

On the radio, Howland reported that Laingen and Tomseth had obtained assurances from officials in the Foreign Ministry that help was on the way.

"Just hold out as long as you can," Howland said. "We are trying to contact the chief of police."

"That's fine," Golacinski said, "but we have a force of police over by the motor pool and they're not doing anything!"

Upstairs, the hallway was crowded now with American and Iranian staffers. Marines were handing out gas masks and the mood was still calm, although some of the Iranian workers were crying. They knew how ugly these revolutionary confrontations could get. The sting of tear gas was in the air. Joan Walsh walked up and down the hall with a wooden box offering to take any valuables the staffers wanted to secure—during the February takeover, people had been robbed. Up and down the hall staffers dropped jewelry, watches, and wallets into the box, which Walsh then locked in her safe.

Limbert found his boss Ann Swift in the anteroom outside Laingen's empty office standing before a bank of phones. She was supposed to have gone with Laingen that morning to the Foreign Ministry, but she had been out late the night before and been delayed getting in that morning, so she had asked Tomseth to take her place. Now, with the two ranking diplomats across town, she was in charge. She seemed calm and decisive.

She asked Limbert to call Washington and talk to the State Department watch officer—it was about three o'clock in the morning there. He waited as a secretary placed the call, and when it got through he learned that the department had already received word of what was happening. He handed the phone to Swift and listened to one end of a conversation about what the marines should do, how far they should go in trying to fend off the protesters. In the February episode there had been a lot of shooting before the provisional government provided a local thug, Mashallah Khashani, to drive out the invaders. Khashani had then camped with his gang at the embassy for months, collecting protection fees and running it like his own private concession. That was what they wanted to avoid. Limbert started phoning local Iranian authorities to plead for official assistance.

Both he and Metrinko had done a lot of favors for officials in the provisional government, mostly helping them to obtain visas. It was payback time. Limbert tried to reach a friend at the prime minister's office. He got a secretary on the phone, introduced himself hurriedly, and began to explain to her what was going on.

"Oh, Mr. Metrinko!" the woman said, mistaking him for his colleague. "It's so nice to hear from you! Tell me, are those visas we sent over ready?"

Limbert explained that he was not Mr. Metrinko, and that if she didn't find him some help soon she could kiss her visa applications good-bye. He explained what was going on at the embassy.

"Oh, don't worry about it," the woman said dismissively. "We have a relief force of Revolutionary Guards and police on the way over. You have nothing to worry about. In twenty minutes or so they should be there."

"I'm happy to hear it," Limbert told her. "I hope what you say is true."

"All the students want to do is read a declaration that they have, and leave."

"Fine," said Limbert. "We have no problem with their reading a declaration. Our concern is that there be no blood shed. We're glad you have a group on the way. They should get these people off the embassy grounds as soon as possible or something might happen for which we feel your government would be responsible."

Limbert hung up the phone, and when Swift took a break he got on the phone to Washington and explained to Assistant Secretary of State Harold Saunders what had been promised.

Downstairs, Golacinski was preoccupied with the radio. He knew that the marines he had told to stay at the Bijon Apartments had been captured there, and that those in the small office building off the motor pool, most notably ICA staffers John Graves and Barry Rosen and their staffs, had also been taken. The only hope of restoring order was for the provisional government to act, so his hopes rested with Laingen and Tomseth at the Foreign Ministry. He requested permission from the chargé to send Washington a "flash" message, the highest emergency protocol, and the chargé authorized it.

The wiry young Iranian Golacinski had taken by the arm kept insisting that all he and the others wanted was to stage a sit-in, and that he wanted to speak directly to Laingen. Golacinski relayed this to Howland, but they all agreed that the chargé d'affaires shouldn't get on the phone with an Iranian protester. Golacinski asked for permission to go outside with the guy and face the crowd himself, acting as a go-between on the radio for Laingen.

"This can't go on," he told the young Iranian. "If somebody breaks through these doors we're going to have to defend ourselves, and people are going to get hurt."

"We must stop this," the young man agreed.

"Yes," said Golacinski.

Laingen told the security chief that he could go out so long as his personal security was assured. There wasn't much chance of that. Golacinski felt responsible for the embassy staffers who had already fallen into the hands of the demonstrators. He believed somebody had to do something to turn this around, and he wasn't nicknamed "Bulldog" for nothing. He loped up the staircase to the top floor and told Bert Moore, an administrative consul, about the authorization to send a flash message, and that Laingen had authorized him to go outside. That meant that decisions regarding security inside the embassy, including supervising the marines, were now Moore's responsibility.

As he went back downstairs, Golacinski got a radio call from Sergeant Lopez at the consulate.

"Sit tight," he told Lopez. "You have a very secure building. I'm going outside to try and get this thing resolved."

Upstairs in the chancery's communications vault monitoring events on the radio, State Department communicator Bill Belk thought Golacinski was nuts. The vault was the embassy's most sensitive and secure spot, and Belk had been at work since early that morning, downloading messages from the satellite and sorting through them. Being in the vault gave him a sense of distance from the events just downstairs, which were increasingly compelling. He had stepped out to look out a window at the demonstrators, and back in the vault later he heard someone gasp into the radio, "My God, they are in the basement!" Then he heard people shouting, evidently at a marine downstairs, "Don't shoot! Don't shoot!"; and then "Don't throw any more tear gas!" It sounded pretty hairy. When he heard that Golacinski was going out he thought, *Great, give them a hostage!*

Golacinski handed his weapon to Gallegos and removed his flak jacket. He wanted to appear nonthreatening.

"I've got to talk to these people," he said. "I know what's going on."

"Al, don't go out there," Gallegos said.

"I'll be all right," he said.

The security chief had made up his mind. Gallegos followed him and the Iranian back downstairs to the open window. Golacinski sent the Iranian out first and then said to Gallegos, somewhat dramatically, "Cover me," and climbed out himself.

Hermening, the young marine who was still wearing his blue suit, watched the security chief go out alone with amazement and admiration. He wouldn't want to go out there for the world. But he had seen Golacinski intervene several times in tense situations and resolve them. That's what this situation needed.

6

HOSTAGE TO WHOM?
FOR WHAT?

As soon as he stepped out into the gray drizzle, Golacinski was surrounded. With the wiry Iranian by his side translating, he demanded that everyone leave. Some of the leaders of the crowd quieted the others, which heartened him. They were listening.

His handheld radio crackled with the voice of a State Department communicator upstairs.

"Should we start destroying files?" he asked.

"No, hold off," Golacinski said. "I think we're going to get this under control."

Sergeant Lopez radioed again to say that protesters were now on the consulate roof and were trying to get through windows, so Golacinski began moving in that direction. The crowd tried to stop him.

"Look!" Golacinski complained. "I've got to go over there and get that calmed down. You want to help me or not?"

So they all followed him through the rain. He felt like the pied piper, leading a train of placard-wearing demonstrators across the compound, their number swelling as they moved. At the consulate, Golacinski was let inside by Lopez, and they ran upstairs to confer with Morefield.

At the top of the stairs, Lopez moved quickly to deal with a protester who was climbing in through the second-floor bathroom window, having lowered himself from the roof. The marine handed his shotgun to Gary Lee, the senior general services officer.

Lee held it awkwardly. He was not used to guns and couldn't tell if the safety was on or off.

Lopez popped a tear gas grenade and entered the bathroom with pistol in hand. The intruder saw him approaching and backed out the window, and Lopez flipped the grenade out after him. Then he popped the pin on another grenade, dropped it and closed the bathroom door behind him. He went to work securing the handles to both the men's and women's bathrooms from the outside with a length of electrical cord, which he tied to a post between the two doors.

One of the secretaries passed around candy. Invaders were banging hard on the roof, trying to break through, but Lee assured those around him with a smile that the roof was solid concrete. "They'll never break through," he said.

Golacinski and Morefield agreed that those trapped in the consulate should choose a moment to head over and take shelter on the second floor of the chancery with everyone else. The security chief then went back outside to lead his growing entourage of Iranians away from the building. His radio crackled to life. Protesters were coming through the chancery basement window again. Golacinski started jogging in that direction with his retinue, which now numbered almost one hundred.

As he approached the motor pool he saw Bill Keough, a giant of a man who stood six-six and weighed almost three hundred pounds, towering in the fine rain over a small mob of chanting protesters. Keough was a school headmaster who had come to Tehran for only a few days to sort out the records from the closed American school. He looked down on his tormentors like a bemused Gulliver.

One of the young men in the crowd around Golacinski was filming him now with a small 8mm camera, and it slowly dawned on the soggy security chief that he was no longer so much leading this crowd as being led by it. He heard Farsi coming from his walkie-talkie; the protesters had evidently grabbed some of the marines' radios.

His own was then snatched from him. The wiry young man he had seized in the basement had melted off into the crowd. He was now addressed by a bigger man with a gruff voice, who appeared to have taken charge. Golacinski recognized him as one of the Revolutionary Guards who had chased off Mashallah, and was at first relieved. Then the man said, "No more on the radio."

"Okay, but I told you, I've got to get permission for you people to be on the compound here. If not, something bad is going to happen." His bluff sounded lame.

He was led toward the motor pool office building. Looking over his left shoulder, Golacinski saw that the chancery was now ringed by thousands of protesters, who were holding hands and chanting. It looked like they were performing an exorcism, and it reminded him of the Pentagon demonstration more than a decade ago when flaky antiwar protesters had tried to levitate the building.

"Let me have a cigarette," he asked one of the Iranians. A young man handed him one and then lit it for him.

At the motor pool garage, he phoned Sergeant Wesley Williams, a marine guard at the chancery's main post inside the front door.

"Look, things are starting to turn here, Williams," Golacinski told him. "It's absolutely essential that you get Laingen on the phone for me."

From the speaker on his radio in the Iranian's hand he could hear Williams—the systems were linked—talking to someone at the Foreign Ministry, trying in vain to track down the chargé. The consulate was still holding on. Someone grabbed Golacinski by the arm and steered him in that direction. As he was being pulled out, he caught the gaze of the Iranian police captain, who was sitting with his men, watching. The captain looked at Golacinski apologetically and shrugged his shoulders, as if to say, *What can I do?*

Inside the consulate, Sergeant Lopez had gotten a similar response from the local police. His contact at headquarters listened politely as the marine described what was going on and responded with a simple, "Thank you." No help was coming from that front. The battery on his radio was going dead, and he was no longer getting a response from the guard post in the chancery. The bulk of the crowd outside the building had left with Golacinski, but there were still protesters beating on the windows with sticks and some had come in through the open second-floor bathroom window again and were trying to break through the cords he had used to secure them. Morefield ordered the visa plates destroyed. Vice consul Don Cooke and Richard Queen got them out of a safe and began whacking them to bits with a steel bar.

"Well, no matter what happens, we won't have any work to do now for five or six weeks," said Morefield. "It will take that long to get new plates, and we can't issue new visas without them."

Lopez collected embassy ID cards from the Iranian employees, which they handed over readily—none of them wanted to be caught on the streets and identified as American collaborators. Morefield and Lopez decided they would let the visa applicants go first, and then the American staffers would walk together over to the chancery. The women were told to walk together.

"Be prepared for a mob," said Lopez. "If anyone grabs for your purse, let them have it. Let them take whatever they want."

As they prepared to leave they noticed that the demonstrators outside the consulate had suddenly vanished. Lopez heard on the radio that the chancery had been breached again. Apparently all the protesters had rushed off in that direction, so instead of going that way themselves, Morefield decided they would all leave in the opposite direction, out the consulate's front door and into the side street. From there maybe they could melt into the city.

One of the marines at the chancery radioed, "You're on your own. Good luck."

Lopez destroyed his shotgun and pistol. Then he, Morefield, Queen, and the other American staff waited until the east-side alley looked clear before peeking out of the garage door. Traffic barred by the mob on Takht-e-Jamshid Avenue was trying to get around the embassy on their side, so it was jammed with cars. Outside were two *pasdoran,* but they seemed to have their hands full with the traffic. Morefield let the Iranian visa applicants go first. One embassy worker stood at the door, looking out, and another at the top of the stairs. When the street was clear, the door would open and ten of the Iranians would be let down the stairs and out the door. They did this until all sixty or so of them, including the young American woman, had gotten away. Bob Ode came down the steps holding the arm of a terrified, elderly Iranian man who was nearly blind. "God bless you, my son," the man kept saying, patting Ode on the wrist. "God bless you, God bless you." Ode led him out the door into the side street alongside the embassy, which was fairly quiet. A car was waiting there to pick up the old man, and Ode helped him into the car and saw him safely off.

Then the first of the American workers walked out, accompanied by the Iranian staff.

Cora and Mark Lijek, Joe and Kathy Stafford, Bob Anders, and Kim King, a tourist who had stopped by the consulate that morning, walked across the street and proceeded at a brisk pace down a road that paralleled Takht-e-Jamshid. They went straight ahead for four blocks, then turned left toward the British embassy. Mark Lijek felt odd walking in a three-piece suit in the light rain with no coat or umbrella. He was getting soaked. King separated from them and headed for a local police station; he was trying to work out a passport problem prior to his scheduled departure. The Americans offered to bring the Iranian employees with them to the British embassy, still a few blocks away, but all but one of them decided to melt off on their own. So the Lijeks and Staffords proceeded with Anders and the remaining Iranian staffer, who said she would show them the way—they were not used to walking the streets in Tehran.

They came upon a square crowded with demonstrators, so the Iranian woman offered to take them to her house. They thanked her but decided it was a bad idea, that it might place her in a dangerous position. But they agreed that they needed to get off the street. People were beginning to stare at them. Anders suggested they go to his apartment. They turned around and headed back in the direction from which they'd come. They made their way circuitously, searching out streets that were relatively quiet, and crossing them in staggers, two at a time. About an hour after leaving the consulate they arrived safely. Anders cooked chicken curry for a late lunch.

After helping the old man, Ode had not followed the Lijek group but had gone back to the remaining staffers. He was carrying a briefcase that Mark Lijek had handed him for some reason, no doubt expecting him to come with them. As he made his way back toward the door, one of the armed *pasdoran* grabbed at the briefcase. Ode didn't know what was in it but he wasn't going to give it up that easily, and even though the Iranian was armed Ode shoved him backward and pulled the briefcase out of his grasp.

"Keep your hands off me!" Ode said. The startled gunman backed off.

Ode was joined then by Morefield, Lopez, Queen, and several other staffers. The marine pulled the door shut behind them, inserted keys in the locks, and broke them off. He had taken off his uniform shirt, torn the red stripes from his blue uniform trousers, and replaced his Marine Corps belt with its shiny buckle with Queen's plain black one. He was wearing an old army fatigue jacket and still carrying his two-way radio. Queen grabbed his pipe, tobacco, lighter, briefcase, and a flashlight. They chose a direction at random and started walking fast. They could not have been more conspicuous. Morefield looked like an American businessman, a short, wide, balding pale man in a business suit who had turned fifty the month before. Lopez had the standard high-and-tight marine haircut, and the others were wearing ties and suits or sport jackets and carrying briefcases. The streets were crowded with excited demonstrators. Someone shot at them. Lopez heard the snap of a round close by, and then the loud report of the gun. They encountered some local police, who eyed them dubiously, and one demanded the radio. Lopez smashed it hard against the side of a building and then handed it over, broken. The police scowled at them and walked off.

Morefield proposed they go to his house, which was nearby. Others wanted to try the Swiss embassy, only a few blocks away. There was some question about whether the Swiss mission was open on Sunday. Lopez wished they'd stop arguing and make a decision.

"I've got a radio at my house," said Morefield.

So the six of them started toward there, spreading out so that they would be less of a target. They made it a few blocks without being noticed, but then one young man began running alongside, shouting, "See-ah! See-ah! [CIA! CIA!]" His alarm summoned others, and soon a crowd had formed around them. Some were shouting in English, "Go back! Go back!" The Americans ignored the mob and tried to push on through, but then they heard another shot and suddenly Morefield was surrounded by armed men carrying pipes, clubs, pistols, and automatic rifles.

"Look, the embassy is yours, do what you want with it," the consul said.

"No, you are a hostage!" one of the armed men answered.

"What do you mean, *hostage*? Hostage to whom? For what?" Morefield asked.

All six of the Americans were roughly steered back to the embassy, and then were marched through the misty rain across the compound through mobs of jeering protesters. At first they were told to put their hands over their heads. Ode held up his, including the briefcase, and hung on to it even when one of his captors tried to pull it away. They walked for a while this way, then were ordered to put their hands down.

"Make up your minds," complained Ode. He didn't get far before the briefcase was finally wrested from him. It was opened on the spot, and Ode leaned in for a look, as curious about it as his captors. All that it held were some in-house newsletters and press releases. *Why on earth had Lijek wanted me to carry that?*

A cameraman filmed them as they made their way toward the ambassador's residence.

7

SHOOT ME, DON'T BURN ME!

On the top floor of the chancery, inside the thick metal walls of the communications vault, Rick Kupke had only a vague notion of what was happening outside. He was a State Department communicator and was busily feeding papers into the raucous disintegrator. The vault had a heavy steel door like the ones on bank safes. It had been open all morning and news of the excitement outside had been drifting in, reaching him secondhand. He knew they wouldn't be destroying everything unless the circumstances were dire. This was confirmed when Bert Moore stepped in and told him to send Foggy Bottom a flash message.

"Tell them the demonstrators have entered the compound and the embassy," he said.

Kupke didn't usually write messages himself, he just copied them.

"Do you want *me* to write it?" he asked.

Moore nodded, hurrying away, so Kupke sat down before the teletype and composed his own short message. He began with five *Z*s, which would cause alarm bells to ring in the relay centers.

Kupke typed: "Demonstrators have entered embassy compound and have entered the building."

Then he went back to destroying the piles of cables and messages that had been accumulating for months. Helping him were Bill Belk and Charles Jones, the other State Department communicators, Army Sergeant Regis Regan, and CIA communicators Phil Ward, Cort Barnes, and Jerry Miele. Air Force Captain Paul Needham had joined them.

All along Kupke had figured it was just a matter of time. A few weeks ago he had watched on a monitor at the guard station downstairs as one or two intrepid locals had scaled the front gate, and he and the guards had placed bets then on whether the whole mob was going to come over. Kupke was from rural Indiana and spoke with a slow country drawl. He was on temporary duty in Tehran, in part because he was ambitious and had made a point of accepting difficult assignments, and in part because of an act of kindness. His primary posting was to an isolated outpost in the Sinai Desert, where staffers were rotated out periodically on temporary jobs to give them a break. The temporary duty was usually in Athens or Rome, and when one of his married colleagues drew Tehran instead, a hardship post where he could not be reunited with his wife and children, Kupke offered to take it instead. He was single and, besides, he knew that hardship posts were a short path to promotion in the department. He had arrived two months ago and by now was accustomed to the low cloud of anxiety that hung over the embassy, the fear of being taken hostage or of being torn apart by one of the bombs that were occasionally lobbed over the walls. When he and his buddies played poker in one of the small cottages near the east wall, and gunfire outside grew close, they would just duck their heads under the table and keep playing. Kupke originally had been scheduled to leave in October but had extended his stay after discovering that, hidden beneath their dark robes, Iranian girls had the same charms as girls at home. He was particularly interested in a spirited young woman he had met at a party thrown by the marines a few weeks earlier. Once inside the door she had lifted off her black manteau to reveal an amazing skin-tight silver dress. Some of the girls at the marine parties were as wild as any girls they had ever met back home. Kupke had been scheduled to leave tomorrow, November fifth, and even had seven crisp hundred-dollars bills in his pocket for that travel, but he wasn't eager to return to the desert and had asked to be extended a second time. He fully expected that his request would be approved, as it wasn't easy at that point to find Americans who wanted to work in Tehran.

When he heard on the radio that protesters were in the building, Kupke put down his papers for a moment and stepped out in the hall for a look. People were sitting on the floor on both sides of the hallway, and some of the female Iranian staffers were wailing. Walking down the corridor, tear gas stinging his eyes and nose, he stepped into Laingen's office to listen as Swift, Limbert, and the others worked the phones. He quickly gathered that help was not on the way. Phone lines were being kept open to a number of places, and at one point Kupke was handed a phone with an open line to the crisis operations center at the State Department. He was holding it to his ear when a voice came on and asked, "Have you started destroying files?"

"We are now," Kupke told him.

"Have you destroyed the back channel?" This was the highest-level State Department information kept at the embassy, kept in a separate safe.

"No," said Kupke.

"Can you confirm to me that you've destroyed it and get right back to me?" the crisis center man asked.

Kupke put down the phone and ran to the safe that contained those files. He scooped them up, mostly papers concerning the shah's travel to the United States, and carried them back to the disintegrator. Kupke hurriedly fed this stack in, bunching the papers more thickly than before. The blades of the machine began loudly tearing at the pile. Then he ran back down the corridor and picked up the phone.

"Yeah, all the back channel stuff on the shah is gone," he said.

Seeing Kupke arrive with that pile of documents sent Belk down the crowded corridor to ask the chargé's secretary, Liz Montagne, if there were any more classified documents in Laingen's office that had to go. She said she had already handed over everything, but the chargé's personal safe was locked—Gallegos had earlier demanded that it be closed—and she didn't know the combination.

Trying to escape the gas thickening in the hall, some of the staff began crowding into the vault. Kupke began handing out gas masks and bottled water. One woman gave Kupke her diamond ring and a wad of cash, saying, "Here, hold this for me, Rick." When others who had not given their valuables to Walsh saw this they began pulling off their rings and producing more wads of money. Soon Kupke's right front pocket bulged with money and jingled with jewelry. One Iranian woman became hysterical and began to hyperventilate inside the gas mask; Kupke noticed that she had not taken a tape off the air filter at the bottom and so was suffocating herself; he gently removed the mask and tried to calm her. An American woman, one of the secretaries, was sobbing. Kupke put his arm around her and assured her that it would be okay.

"We're diplomats, they don't just murder diplomats," he said. He hoped it was true.

Not all the women were distraught. Terri Tedford, who worked on the clerical staff, was very poised.

"You're not worried, are you?" Belk asked her.

"Oh, no," she said. "I'm fine." She was working to encourage the others to stay calm.

For some reason the tear gas didn't bother Belk that much; it only made his eyes water a little, so he didn't bother putting on a mask. He brought a small fan out to the hallway and started it in order to blow the gas away from the vault, but it quickly shorted out.

Until that point, the communicators had been picking out for destruction only the classified material from the piles, but now Kupke sensed that time was running out. He had seen how easily the machine had handled the stack of back channel files, and noticing that Barnes and Miele had finished feeding their CIA documents into the device he suggested, "Let's just start destroying everything." He felt odd giving directions, but nobody else was.

At the foot of the basement stairs, Corporal Gallegos heard a crash, and when he went to investigate he saw Iranians climbing back in through the broken window. He pulled the pin on another tear gas grenade, threw it, and backed up toward the stairs, calling for help on his handheld radio.

"If we can get somebody down there, we will," said Sergeant Moeller.

Then Gallegos heard the order, "Everybody upstairs." He opened the weapons cabinets at the foot of the stairs, wrapped both arms around shotguns and rifles, and started up the stairs. He got to the small landing on the second floor and the big door was already closed. It had a wood veneer but was steel inside, and it hurt his foot when he kicked it. He was wishing all the more he had his boots on. "It's me! It's me!" he shouted. "Open up!"

"Go downstairs," someone shouted through the door. "Get the guns in the cabinets."

Gallegos already had as many as he could carry, but he knew there were more radios and weapons in the lockers at the guard post. So he set down the weapons he had and ran back down to the first floor. Hermening was struggling with the combination locks. Gallegos knew the combination, but in his excitement he couldn't make it work. So he found a pair of bolt cutters and severed the locks. He and Hermening pulled radios and weapons from the lockers.

The odor of tear gas was now mingled with smoke. The protesters downstairs were burning paper to ward off the sting of the gas. They would be coming up the steps any minute. The two marines broke the closed-circuit TV monitors, grabbed all the weapons they could carry, and ran up the stairs to the second floor. The door was opened for them and then slammed shut and locked. A barricade was pulled back into place against it, a table with a refrigerator on top and a couch wedged behind both.

Gallegos was surprised to find all the marines on the top floor unarmed.

"What the hell is going on?" he asked Moeller.

"Put your weapons up," the sergeant said.

"You're crazy!" said Gallegos. "I'm not giving up my weapon."

Moeller yelled at him to obey orders, and then Ann Swift stepped out into the hallway, angry, harried, and not in the mood for discussion.

She pointed to all the weapons Gallegos and Hermening had hauled upstairs and said, "Put them away!"

Looking down from an upstairs chancery window through a determined gray drizzle, Hermening saw his boss, Al Golacinski, being led across the compound by a small mob of young Iranians. The security chief looked soaked and defeated. One of the protesters had a pistol pointed at his head.

Someone from another window shouted down, "Al, are you okay?"

"Yes, I'm okay!" he shouted back.

It was midafternoon, almost two hours since the protesters had come over the walls. Hermening leveled his weapon nervously and surveyed the chaos below. The spacious compound was now swarming with protesters, thousands of young bearded men, most of them in blue jeans and many wearing green khaki army jackets, and young women draped in long tunics and wearing head scarves like the nuns he had known as a boy back in Wisconsin. Golacinski's decision to go out and reason with them now appeared to have been a mistake.

A muscular man with a thick mop of dark hair that now clung wetly to his head, Golacinski's vision was blurry and his eyes stung from tear gas. He yelled up at the windows, "Have you gotten hold of Laingen?"

There was no answer. Golacinski bellowed up that he needed a phone number there. The ones who had taken him were demanding that he get the chargé d'affaires on the phone.

"Look, this is just like February fourteenth!" Golacinski shouted up, referring to the brief invasion of the grounds nine months earlier. He wanted to reassure those inside that this was going to be over shortly, that they should sit tight. He was then led to the front of the building, where one of the protesters demanded that he tell the others to open up and come out.

"They can't hear me inside," Golacinski said.

Someone held a bullhorn up to his face.

"Tell them to come out," he was told. "If not, you are going to see what we are going to do."

Golacinski's amplified voice echoed off the orange brick of the front wall. "These people say if you come out they won't hurt you. This is just like February fourteenth," he said.

The militant with the gun was growing irate. He spoke in Farsi to two of the others, who ran off toward the motor pool just east of the chancery.

"They are going to get the rope!" explained a young man in a rugby shirt who spoke fluent English.

Golacinski gathered from this that they intended to string him up, a fear quickened by the jeering multitude behind him, both inside and outside the embassy walls, which had been roaring thunderously ever since he had been led around to the front of the building, thrilled to see a hated American captured. He felt a sudden quiver in his knees and bowels.

One of the other protesters pounded on the door and shouted in English, "Open these doors! You will see what we do to your brother!"

Nothing happened. The doors stayed shut and the gunman returned without a rope. Golacinski was relieved, and also struck by the apparent confusion among these protesters. There seemed to be violent ones, like the one with the gun, more moderate ones, like the one in the rugby shirt, and others who just seemed to be going with the flow. No one appeared to be in charge.

One of the Iranians tied a cloth strip over his eyes.

"Okay," the gunman said. "We are going to go in there. You are going to go in first. If anything happens, you die."

They walked him down to the concrete moat and, with the gunman holding the pistol to the back of his head, he was directed to climb
back down the same opened window he had climbed up and out of an
hour earlier. Held by both arms and blindfolded, Golacinski eased himself down awkwardly, feeling his way. They had rigged a chair on top of
a table that he had to negotiate blind. The air inside was choked with
tear gas and smoke. Right behind him was the gunman, and Golacinski
knew it didn't take much pressure on the trigger. A sudden slip by either of them might end his life. When he got both feet on the floor
he was grateful. The Iranians who followed then pushed him through
the basement hallway, advancing warily past the office doors on either
side.

"Tell them, no shoot!" the gunman said.

Golacinski knew that by now everyone was upstairs, but nevertheless he shouted, "Don't shoot! Don't shoot!" as they made their way up the
steps to the first floor and then up the steps to the second-floor landing.
The door had a cipher lock by the handle. Tear gas had pooled in the stairwell, which was now crowded with invaders.

The blindfolded captive's nerves were about shot, and when one of
his captors rolled up a magazine and lit it and he felt the flame near his
face, he panicked.

"Don't burn me!" he screamed. "Shoot me, don't burn me!"

"No, no, no," one of the Iranians told him. "For the gas. For the gas."

Another demanded, "Open the door."

"Open the door or you will see what we will do!" shouted several of
the men around him.

"They have eight of us!" yelled Golacinski, referring to the others
he knew were being held by the protesters outside.

Behind the door he heard one of his colleagues shouting, "They're
trying to burn it down!"

After seeing Golacinski outside with a gun to his head, it was clear that
this demonstration had aims beyond simply the reading of a "declaration,"
which is what the aide in the prime minister's office had assured Limbert
would happen.

He phoned the provisional government once more and this time spoke with an assistant in the office of Mahdi Chamran, a deputy minister. Limbert explained the situation with more vehemence, and once again was told not to worry.

"Everything is under control," the assistant said.

Limbert said that things didn't look under control from his vantage point. There was no sign of the force that had been promised earlier.

"What is being done?" Limbert asked. "What are you going to do?"

"What we are going to do is have a meeting this afternoon to decide what to do about this problem," the assistant said peevishly.

Limbert understood that they were on their own. The government was neither inclined to nor capable of coming to their rescue, so delay wasn't going to solve anything. The goal now was to protect the embassy personnel and employees, which could probably best be accomplished by surrender. His greatest fear was that one of the marines would shoot a protester. He could imagine the frenzy a martyr's blood would ignite. They would all surely be killed.

He spoke to the demonstrators on the radio. They had taken walkie-talkies from the marines and from the security chief, and Limbert could hear them talking back and forth, trying to figure out how the equipment worked.

The smell of smoke sent a ripple of alarm through the crowd of Americans and embassy workers in the corridor upstairs. The downside of being locked on the top floor was that there was no way out. Now smoke began to curl up from underneath the furniture piled against the door. Limbert tried to get someone on the other side to talk to him. He spoke briefly to Golacinski, who told him that there was a gun to his head and that if the door wasn't opened they would shoot him. Limbert told them all to stand back.

"We're going to open the door and I'm going to come out to talk," he said.

It was a decision Limbert made on the spot. Once he learned that help was not coming, it was clear that someone who spoke Farsi would have to try talking to the protesters. If he could find what they wanted, perhaps they could work out an arrangement where nobody would get hurt. Two of the marines pulled back the barricade and one of them opened the door enough for Limbert to slip out to the landing. The door slammed shut behind him.

Crowded on the staircase before him leading down to the first floor were fifty or more very excited young Iranian men, unshaven, wet, and wearing rumpled, worn clothing. Limbert knew immediately that he was going to get nowhere with this bunch. As the door closed behind him he thought, *Of all the stupid things you have ever done, this is the topper.*

Golacinski was four or five steps down. Limbert rubbed his tearing eyes and felt his nose begin to run from the pungent stab of gas and smoke. He tried to speak calmly. He introduced himself and adopted a scolding professorial tone—he had taught students exactly like these years before at Shiraz University.

"You really need to get out of here before someone gets hurt," he told them in Farsi. "We have been in contact with the authorities. They are sending police to clear the compound. You have no business here. If someone is hurt it's going to be your responsibility. You are going to be responsible for the bloodshed."

His words stunned the crowd momentarily. The last thing they had expected from the top floor of the American embassy was a stern lecture from someone in fluent, unaccented Farsi.

"You're not an American," one of the students protested. "You're a Persian speaker."

"Yes, but I am an American," Limbert said. He pushed ahead, asking questions: "Who are you?" and "What do you want?"

"Are you armed in there?" one of the militants asked.

"That's no business of yours," said Limbert. "What do you care?"

"We want to get in."

"Is there somebody here from the government?" he asked.

"We don't care about the government," came the answer.

"What about the Revolutionary Council?" Limbert asked.

"We don't care about the Revolutionary Council," one of the young men said.

The Iranians were now arguing among themselves. They kept referring to their own "five-man council" that made decisions, but apparently no one from that controlling group was here on the steps. So they quarreled.

"Let's go in now!" said one.

"No, we've got to discuss this."

"Let's just knock the door down!" shouted another.

"We do what the council says!" another answered.

As Limbert saw it, to the extent that the crowd on the steps had a leader, it was a young man with a thick Isfahani accent. He was bouncing with excitement and anxiety, capable of anything.

"Tell them if they don't come out we're going to kill everybody," he said.

From inside the door Metrinko bellowed in Farsi, "We just heard on the radio that Khomeini has ordered the Revolutionary Guards to clear the embassy!"

The mob on the stairs wasn't buying it. Limbert was grabbed and blindfolded. One of the Iranians shouted at the door, "Look, if you don't come out in fifteen minutes, we are going to shoot both of these people!"

Now Limbert was even more frightened. He judged that this crowd would carry out the threat. He wondered if his colleagues would open the door; he wondered if they *should* open it. He had volunteered to come out and he had to accept the consequences. He expected this to end badly, for him and for everyone else.

8

ANN, LET THEM IN

On the other side of the heavy door, Ann Swift was on the line to Washington, while Colonel Chuck Scott, the military liaison officer, and Colonel Tom Schaefer, the defense attaché, were talking to Laingen at the Foreign Ministry, giving him running reports on the situation.

The whole point of holding out on the second floor was to protect personnel and documents until local authorities arrived and restored order. Clearly that wasn't going to happen. With so many Americans already in the hands of the protesters, and with the threats to kill Golacinski and Limbert, a consensus was emerging that holding out further was pointless. That's what Laingen told Scott, and when the colonel handed the phone to Swift the chargé said, "Ann, let them in."

They prepared to open the door. The stash of weapons was carried down to the coms vault, where Bert Moore stepped in and announced, "We're going to surrender."

"Mr. Moore, I've got more documents to destroy," Kupke said. "We'll surrender when we can."

He had no intention of giving up, although he didn't say that.

"I'm going to close the door," Kupke shouted. "Anybody who wants to surrender, leave now."

All of the embassy staffers and Iranian employees filed out, and as Kupke swung the heavy door shut he saw that his tall friend Bill Belk was among those in the hallway. He thought about holding the door and trying to get his attention, but the marines had begun pulling apart the barricade down the hall. He closed the vault door and locked it.

One of the marines shouted through the main stairwell door, "Do not shoot! We are not armed. We are letting you in."

Then the door swung open.

Belk felt more disgusted than angry or frightened. He had gone to retrieve more files for the disintegrator, and when he saw that the vault door was shut he knew he was stuck. Why were they surrendering? They had water and some food. Belk figured they could easily have held out for a few days or more, long enough for these yahoos to give up and go away.

But it was too late for that. Protesters swarmed into the corridor, men and women, all young, draped with their Khomeini placards, wet and excited. Some of them were armed. They began to charge off down the hallway but stopped abruptly when one of their leaders raised his hands over his head and bellowed, "We are going to do this in a well-organized way! You will come out one at a time."

The invaders resumed moving down the hallway, more methodically now, ignoring those seated against the walls and moving instead from room to room. Swift was still on the phone giving Washington a blow-by-blow when an Iranian grabbed it from her hand.

Scott was talking to Mike Howland, who was with Laingen at the Foreign Ministry.

"Surrender with your head held high," Howland said.

Scott didn't get to respond. An angry young Iranian grabbed the phone out of his hand.

"Who were you talking to?" he demanded.

"Ayatollah Khomeini," said Scott. "He told me to tell you all to leave here and let us go."

The Iranian hit Scott across the face with the back of his hand.

Everyone was herded into the halls. They were ordered to line up single file and their captors started binding their hands and blindfolding them with the prepared strips of white cloth.

Behind the closed door of the vault, standing before the still loudly grinding disintegrator, Kupke watched the surrender on the black-and-white closed-circuit monitor. He saw Iranians running from office to office, carrying out drawers and files. His colleagues, including poor Belk, were being herded out the door. Kupke watched until an Iranian, young and bearded like the rest, peered up curiously at the camera that was mounted outside the vault in the hallway and then removed his jacket and tossed it upward. The screen went blank.

There were eleven others with Kupke in the vault: CIA chief Tom Ahern and his agency communicators Phil Ward, Jerry Miele, and Cort Barnes, Army Sergeant Regan, foreign service officer Steve Lauterbach, two marines, Hermening and Persinger, Air Force Captain

Paul Needham, Navy Commander Bob Englemann, and another State Department communicator, Charles Jones. So far, the Iranians didn't know they were there.

Golacinski was hustled down the stairs and captives were led out the chancery door one by one. Word of the successful storming of the embassy spread throughout the city and soon enraged masses roared outside its walls like some mindless, insatiable, million-throated monster, screaming for American blood. It was as though an impregnable fort had been breached and taken. It was a great victory, a cleansing, an exorcism. A deafening cheer rose as each blindfolded, bound American emerged.

One of the marines who came down the steps asked Golacinski, "What's going on?"

"Just stay cool," Golacinski said. "Stay cool." He said it as much to himself.

As he emerged the crowd chanted joyfully, *"Allahuakbar! Allahuakbar!"*

After the smoke and tear gas, it was a relief to breathe fresh air. The rain seemed to be coming harder and colder.

Air Force Lieutenant Colonel Dave Roeder was led down the staircase, held gently on both sides by young Iranian men. Immediately outside the door they had placed a partly burned American flag, which he was made to walk over on his way out.

The strip of cloth tied tightly around navy Commander Don Sharer's eyes burned like hell. It felt like it had been soaked in tear gas.

As Morehead Kennedy, the embassy's chief economics officer, was being led down the stairs, the Iranian who had hold of his arm kept repeating with each step, "Vietnam, Vietnam, Vietnam . . ."

Belk was grabbed and blindfolded. His hands were bound with a nylon rope. When the young man tying the rope used a knife to cut off a strip he had inadvertently jabbed Belk with it in the side.

"Oh, I'm sorry," he said. "I'm sorry."

The tall State Department technician was led down the stairs and out the front door. He towered over his captors, a middle-aged father of two boys back in South Carolina, with longish hair and sideburns wrapped in a cloth blindfold, wearing an open-collared shirt, hands bound in front, surrounded by triumphant students. His captor kept telling him, "Don't be afraid, don't be afraid," but with a multitude screaming for his blood it was hard not to feel like he was being led to his death. "We will teach you," his captors said. "We will bring to you Khomeini's thoughts." He was surprised by how gentle they were. In the din he heard camera shutters clicking. Photographs of Belk emerging from the chancery would be transmitted around the world and would become emblematic. He was urging himself to maintain his dignity. *If they are going to kill me, then at least I'll keep my head up.* He squared his shoulders and held high his blindfolded head.

Bruce German was convinced that he was being led to his execution. He had been asked before leaving the building if he would make a statement to cameras outside denouncing President Carter.

"I won't say anything," he said.

As marine guard Rocky Sickmann was being led through the fine rain he heard the protesters around him making hissing sounds. Some would come right up to him and hiss loudly in his ear. He didn't know what it meant. It sounded like they were shushing him, telling him not to say anything. He had nothing to say. The large angry crowd outside the embassy was apparently being held back, and inside the compound there were photographers snapping pictures of him and everyone else. One of the protesters came up to him and held a knife to his temple, which made the others around him laugh. Someone snapped a picture of it.

Joe Hall felt oddly elated. A young army warrant officer from Oklahoma with a broad forehead, dark straight hair, and mustache, he had never liked the idea of being stationed in Tehran and had arrived with great reluctance that summer to work in the defense attaché's office. He and his wife, Cherlynn, had worked together for four years at the U.S. embassy in Athens, and it had been the best four years of Hall's life. This assignment meant they would have to live apart for a full year. They had been missing each other terribly. Hall had taken the post only because the army had tied it to the warrant officer promotion he felt he had earned, and he had resented it from the start. He had found Tehran to be dusty, dry, hot, crowded, and hostile. Now, bound and blindfolded, reeling under the waves of hatred from the Iranian mob, he walked with captors holding him on either side, feeling the drizzle on his face, the first rain he remembered since he had arrived, convinced that this meant his stay in Tehran would be over a lot sooner than planned. So his first reaction to being taken hostage was delight. He figured it meant they would all be evacuated as soon as the local authorities got things in hand. This was going to be the shortest assignment of his career. He would be back home with Cheri soon!

John Limbert was delighted to get out of the tear gas and smoke. The rain felt soothing. He felt a sudden enormous rush of relief at having escaped death on the staircase and he was overjoyed just to be alive.

In answer to the chanting crowd he shouted, "*Allahuakbar!*" in agreement, rejoicing.

They must have thought he was nuts, an American official, a "spy" flushed from the very bowels of America's espionage machine, blindfolded, shouting earnestly with them in the rain, "*Allahuakbar!*"

President Jimmy Carter was awakened at Camp David with news of trouble at the embassy in Tehran. It was four-thirty in the morning and the call was from Zbigniew Brzezinski, his crisply efficient national security adviser. Carter then spoke briefly with his secretary of state, Cyrus Vance. The hostage takers were demanding the return of the shah, which was, of course, out of the question. Brzezinski was optimistic. So far none of the hostages had been shot, he said, which was a good sign, because such actions were usually the most violent in the first hours. But before he went back to sleep the president had an awful vision of hostages being executed, one a day, for his refusal to be blackmailed. What would he do then?

As Carter tried to get back to sleep, word flew from phone to phone throughout the highest levels of the American government. White House staffers, generals, and diplomats were awakened before dawn. Word reached out and down to those who would need to know immediately. The train of early morning calls eventually found U.S. Army Colonel Charlie Beckwith in a hotel room in Hinesville, Georgia.

He was awakened by Delta's CIA liaison, Burr Smith.

"I thought you'd like to know, Boss," he said. "The American embassy in Iran has gone down. The entire staff is being held hostage."

Beckwith, who had slept only two or three hours, got dressed, checked out, and pointed his car north on Interstate 95. It was a five-hour drive to Fayetteville, to the Stockade, the unit's headquarters at Fort Bragg, North Carolina. As he drove through sunrise over the spectacular fall display, the colonel, who had once been a lineman at the University of Georgia, thought, *What a great day for football!*

9

I TOLD YOU SO

Farouz Rajaeefar was elated. An engineering student at Amir Kabir University, she had been among the first wave into the compound. Raised in a secular family, she had spent time in the United States and in fact had been enrolled earlier that year at the University of Texas. But she hadn't made it back to the States for classes. Swept up by the revolutionary and religious fervor at Amir Kabir, she had joined the embassy invaders as a translator. Her English was fluent.

She was thrilled with their success. The demonstration was similar to ones she had heard about in the United States and in Europe, where young people had seized campus or government buildings in order to publicize their grievances. She marched that morning dressed in a long pullover and blue jeans, with her Khomeini picture pinned to her chest, waving her fist in the air and chanting anti-American slogans. The takeover had gone more smoothly than they had dared to hope. Many of the men felt sure there would be shooting, and that there would be martyrs, but the whole invasion had succeeded without anyone firing a shot, so far as she knew.

On the chancery second floor, in the heart of the evil beast, she and the others stared in amazement at the piles of shredded documents they found on the floor of some offices. What more proof of American plotting and trickery was needed? What were these spies trying so desperately to hide? This would be the students' next great task, to piece together not just these documents but the whole place, who was who, what work was going on in these offices, what secrets were hidden in these files. They would study this den of espionage and piece it all back together and reveal its evil machinations to Iran and to the world.

But first Rajaeefar had to call home. How should she tell her parents that she had taken part in invading and occupying a foreign embassy, and not just any embassy but a superpower's?

She picked up one of the embassy phones and dialed home. Her mother answered.

"Where are you?" she asked.

"Listen to the radio," Rajaeefar said triumphantly, and, with a good-bye, she hung up.

Other excited occupiers were using the phones in the chancery, calling family and friends to boast of their success. One of the young women involved phoned a local radio station, which at first refused to believe her when she said she was calling from "the former American embassy, the present Den of Spies." She directed them to phone the main number for the U.S. embassy and ask for the extension of the phone she was using.

The students had prepared a communiqué, which was read over the phone to the radio station. It reflected the full idealistic and naive sweep of the students' intentions, which were nothing less than to ignite a world-wide spiritual uprising of the virtuous oppressed masses.

"In the name of God the Merciful, the Compassionate," it began, and then quoted from the imam's recent speech urging students throughout Iran to "forcefully expand their attacks against America and Israel."

> The Islamic Revolution of Iran represents a new achievement in the ongoing struggle between the peoples and the oppressive superpowers. It has kindled hope in the hearts of the enchained nations and has set an example and created a legend of self-reliance and ideological stead-fastness for a nation contending with imperialism. This was in reality a conquest over the curse of blindness that the superpowers had imposed so that even the intellectuals of the oppressed world could not conceive of any other freedom than under the benediction of another superpower.
>
> Iran's revolution has undermined the political, economic, and strategic hegemony of America in the region.

It went on to explain that "the world-devouring America," which for years had been exploiting Iran's resources, was now engaged in "spiteful attempts" to regain power.

> We Muslim students, followers of Imam Khomeini, have occupied the espionage embassy of America in protest against the ploys of the

imperialists and the Zionists. We announce our protest to the world;
a protest against America for granting asylum and employing the
criminal Shah while it has on its hands the blood of tens of thousands
of women and men in this country. . . . And, finally, for its undermining and destructive role in the face of the struggle of the peoples for
freedom from the chains of imperialism, wherein thousands of revolutionary and faithful humans have been slaughtered.

It was signed, "Muslim Students Following the Imam's Line."

A few miles away from the embassy compound, a furious Bruce Laingen
was finally allowed to see the foreign minister Ibrahim Yazdi, a gentle,
professorial man with a sparse, graying beard who had been out of sight—
conspicuously, Laingen thought—throughout the ongoing siege. Laingen
unloaded on the minister, protesting the seizure of his embassy and reminding Yazdi of his obligation and promise to protect it under long-
standing rules of international diplomacy.

Yazdi heard this out patiently. He seemed troubled, acknowledged
his government's responsibility to protect the embassy, and apologized for
what had happened. He was surprised by how agitated Laingen seemed.
After all, this sort of thing had happened before. The foreign minister
spoke English fluently; his exile during the shah's years had been spent
primarily in Waco, Texas, where he had worked as a medical researcher
and had been Khomeini's man in America in the years leading up to the
revolution.

"Calm down," he told Laingen, and couldn't keep from adding, "I told
you so."

Yazdi had warned weeks ago that there would be consequences he
might not be able to control if the United States admitted the shah. In a
meeting with the State Department's top Iran hand Henry Precht, the
foreign minister had likened welcoming the shah to "opening a Pandora's
box." Yazdi was in a position that both Laingen and Vic Tomseth, the
chargé's acting deputy, recognized as precarious. Tomseth thought now
that he had not fully appreciated how precarious. The foreign minister was
one of a group of primarily secular intellectuals who had formed a brain
trust around Khomeini when he was in the last months of his exile in Paris.
Along with Prime Minister Bazargan, he was part of a practical political

faction that wanted to see the new Iran form a Western-style democracy. They wanted to show the world that postrevolutionary Iran was not some renegade nation of religious fanatics but a serious country, one that understood its obligations in the world, and one that was led by sober, practical, well-educated people. But he was increasingly under attack, as was Bazargan, by hard-line clerics who claimed the revolution for Allah alone and who wanted a radical Islamist state. These street demonstrations, and the rampant anti-Americanism, were tools in the mullahs' arsenal. Any politician who dared step up to defend the need for continued ties with the Great Satan before the pious mob put not only his political goals and career in jeopardy but his freedom and quite possibly his life. Yazdi had warned that admitting the shah would play right into the hands of these powerful forces, who fully embraced the fantasy of devilish American omnipotence. They would tell the people that President Carter was plotting to restore the monarchy, and if that happened Yazdi and his government were in trouble. Yazdi had answered Precht, "The responsibility is yours if you let him in." It was not a threat. He knew what the mullahs would make of such a gesture, and he suspected his fragile government would not survive the storm that followed.

When it happened, they had considered severing relations with America but had dismissed the idea as impractical. Even Khomeini and the Revolutionary Council had agreed. There were too many outstanding issues—military contracts, the shah's vast bank accounts in the United States—that needed resolution. It was decidedly not in Iran's interest, at least in any short-term sense, to completely shun America.

The foreign minister had earned some credibility with his American guests. He had personally defused the February takeover, when as deputy prime minister he had gone to the embassy as the invaders were chased off and the compound restored to the American mission. It had taken courage. But much had changed in nine months. Yazdi's current position as foreign minister was a less powerful post, and Carter's decision to admit the shah had badly eroded his authority. Just as he had predicted, the mullahs had been fanning fears of an American countercoup. Yazdi believed this was nonsense, but politics is based not on reality but on perception. Leaked reports of the private meeting with Brzezinski in Algiers days before had worsened matters. It had provoked wild speculation in Tehran. Now he and Bazargan were openly branded as sellouts and traitors. This was intensely serious business. Yazdi had a better appreciation of the dangers than did his American guests, who had not fully grasped the fury of suspicion in Iran.

Laingen brought up Yazdi's contribution in February, as though nothing had changed. Yazdi was tactful. He tried to explain.

"Then, there was a risk of violence," he said. This situation, from all accounts, was peaceful. It involved university students. It would take a little time, he said, but the situation was at least "under control." To Yazdi, living in a world of firing squads, a sit-in at the American embassy was not a crisis.

He allowed the Americans to use the phones at a table in his own office. Laingen got on the line with the small group of his colleagues still holed up in the vault, and to his superiors in Washington. Yazdi was also working the phones, including a special red one, which was a direct line to Khomeini's offices in Qom.

After some time at this, Yazdi said confidently, "We will solve this tonight. I have just had some good news."

He explained that high-level discussions were under way between the provisional government, the Revolutionary Council, and the imam himself. None of the Americans had been harmed, he said. The embassy had not been seriously damaged and tomorrow, at the latest, Laingen's staff would be released and the embassy returned.

10

I'M GOING TO CUT
OUT THIS EYE FIRST

Inside the chancery vault, Rick Kupke continued to feed documents into the clamorous disintegrator. The other communicators set about destroying their communications equipment. This was not as simple as banging things with a hammer. They had a list instructing them step by step. First they had downloaded a program called "Terminal Equipment Replacement," which would enable them to get most of their electronics back up and running quickly in case the invaders were chased off and the crisis suddenly ended. Then they began taking apart the machines in a selective, nondestructive way, but one that would make it exceedingly difficult for anyone unused to them to restart them. A telex machine in pieces that could not be readily reassembled by anyone but an expert was preferable to a broken telex machine. So it was very deliberate work, and because some of the machines, like the teletype, had been in use all day, they were hot. Barnes would read off the serial number of the selected piece and Regan would write it down. The list was prioritized, so that the last items to go were the secure teletypes that kept them connected to Washington. When it was decided to begin destroying them, selected parts were culled from the various bits and either smashed with a hammer or cut in half with a saw. Miele held the computer list and would cross off items one by one as they were destroyed. Some of the people in the vault didn't work there and were unfamiliar with the equipment, but everyone pitched in. Those who knew what they were doing gave instructions to those who didn't. The center of all this activity was the overstressed disintegrator, which kept churning and banging away.

Tear gas came through the air-conditioning vent, so Phil Ward put on a gas mask. He wore it for only a few minutes and then took it off.

"I can't breathe in this," he said. Cort Barnes inspected the mask and saw that Ward, like the Iranian woman earlier, had not removed the tape at the bottom that covered the airholes. They got a laugh out of that. Barnes tried the gas mask for a few minutes but he had to remove his glasses to wear it and he couldn't see well enough to do his work. So he also discarded it and just fought through the discomfort. They had earlier donned blue and yellow flak jackets, but took those off, too. Barnes thought the colors looked silly.

About two hours after Kupke closed the vault door they were finished. They performed a complete check of the master list, and then took a careful look around, pulling open drawers and safes, making sure that nothing had been accidentally left behind. They left open only the one or two phone lines to Washington. The vault was a mess; strewn across the floor were papers and broken equipment. When they were done they broke open some of the stock of C rations and snacked on peanut butter and chocolate.

Kupke then noticed the weapons. He had been stepping over them for hours but hadn't looked down. Kevin Hermening had brought them into the vault and dumped them on the floor. There were long rifles, Uzis, handguns, and shotguns and boxes of ammo.

Tom Ahern was talking on the phone with Mike Howland, the assistant security chief, who was at the Foreign Ministry with Laingen and Tomseth. Howland was concerned about the weapons falling into the hands of the Iranians, which had happened during the February crisis.

"Get rid of them," he advised.

Ahern passed along this instruction to Hermening. More than turning over the weapons, the CIA station chief was worried about how it might look for this mob of fired-up protesters to find them holed up in a vault armed to the teeth.

They set to work breaking the weapons down and stashing the parts in the now empty safes. They had planned to leave the safes open to show that there was nothing inside, but now they decided to lock away the remains of the guns. They tossed in the handguns and Uzis. Most of the guns fit into the safe's drawers. The ammo was placed in the main chamber. The shotguns were too long to fit, so Kupke looked around for another way of getting rid of them. The vault consisted of two small rooms, divided by a wall of electronic equipment, power panels, wires, and transmitters. One of the chambers had a steep, narrow spiral metal ladder that led up to the roof.

"I'm going to take some of these guns and stick them up there," he said.

At the top of the ladder was a flat steel door about a quarter of an inch thick on rollers. With an armful of shotguns under one arm, Kupke used the other to slide the door open. He swung the weapons out to the roof and then climbed up after them. Toward the center of the building was a wooden shed, which he crawled to on his belly, being careful to keep his body below the eighteen-inch lip of wall around the roof. Kupke wasn't worried about being seen from below—the roof was about fifty feet up—but he was concerned about being seen from the window of one of the multistory buildings that ringed the compound. He was wearing a yellow shirt, so he would have been easy to spot. With the shotguns, he feared that if he was seen someone might start shooting at him. He stayed close to the wall.

As Kupke was disposing of the guns, Ahern wanted a better idea of what was happening outside so he and Hermening climbed up to the attic that ran the length of the building and, using a flashlight, eased out along the ceiling studs. They walked stooped in the darkness, stepping over crossbeams. At one point they had to balance their way along a beam for about fifteen feet—falling would most likely have meant crashing through the ceiling and into the middle of the occupied hallway underneath. At each end of the building were triangular windows that had big fans in them. They were both badly startled by a loud bang from overhead—Kupke was dropping weapons up there but they didn't know that. They assumed that somehow the invading Iranians had made their way to the roof. They eased out to the window, shut off the fan, and Ahern had a good look around the compound. There were Iranians everywhere.

Above them, Kupke peeked over the rim and saw the same scene. Some of his colleagues were blindfolded and being led across the compound toward the ambassador's residence at the south end. There were still mobs of excited Iranians running in all directions; outside the walls was a growing mass of cheering people, urged on by protesters with megaphones. He placed the shotguns on a short pile of wooden planks beside the shed, crawled back to the sliding door, and backed down the ladder. He got on the phone with the State Department.

"I was just on the roof," he said. "There are hundreds of demonstrators on the grounds."

"Did you see any Americans?" asked the man on the other end.

"I saw some Americans blindfolded."

When he returned to the disintegrator, he found Barnes smoking a cigarette and looking worried. Barnes's hands were shaking. He had been evacuated from the roof of the American embassy in Saigon only four years earlier. Now that the documents had all been destroyed, they were feeding circuit boards from the computers and encryption devices into the disintegrator, which was hot and roaring. Both Kupke and Barnes were sweating profusely.

The State Department communicator screamed to his CIA friend over the noise, "Cort, when you were flown off that embassy, were you more scared then, or are you more scared now?"

"Now," he said.

"I didn't want to hear that," Kupke said.

Barnes fed a thick piece of circuit board into the machine and, abruptly, it came to a halt. The blades stopped and wouldn't move. Kupke picked up a two-by-four and prepared to give the blades a whack.

"Don't do that!" Barnes protested.

Kupke slammed the two-by-four into the blades and they started to turn so quickly that the machine bit the end of his two-by-four right off, then sputtered to a stop again. Kupke next found a four-by-four, whacked at the blades with that, and the machine once more began churning.

There were still shotguns on the floor; some time later Kupke took a break and carried more of them up to the roof.

The phone lines started to go inside the vault. The Iranian invaders had control of the main switchboard. Soon, the only ones functioning were local lines: one to the Foreign Ministry, where Howland had stayed on the line, and another across town to the Iran-America Society offices, where the director, Kathryn Koob, and her assistant Bill Royer were acting as go-betweens for Washington. Royer stayed on the line to the vault and Koob would relay questions or instructions from Washington to him, then he would pass them to Jones.

"I think it's just a sit-in that got out of hand," said Jones. "They said they were just going to sit-in, but it sounds as if they've gone wild."

At the Foreign Ministry, Laingen remained optimistic.

"Help is coming," Howland told Ahern.

The station chief still had a direct teletype link to his supervisors at CIA headquarters in Langley, Virginia. There wasn't anything headquarters could do, of course, except to wish him well and ask for frequent updates. So the agency's station chief decided there was no point holding out further. Files and sensitive material had all been destroyed or shredded and the weapons had been broken down and removed. The Iranians outside were working on the vault door with a sledgehammer and would eventually break through. Refusing to open it would only further antagonize them, and any attempt they made to blow open the door would probably injure those inside.

At the Foreign Ministry, Howland was urging Ahern to hang on.

"Tom, we think you're more valuable not surrendering," he said.

Then, outside the vault, the Iranian invaders produced Howland's boss, Golacinski.

The security chief had been marched through the rain with the others to the ambassador's residence, where he had briefly been tied to a chair in the dining room with a large number of other captives. The residence was a mansion, with huge rooms designed for entertaining on a grand scale. The dining room was furnished like an old French palace. The Iranian invaders had removed cushions from the chairs and placed them on the floor, where they lounged with their weapons. The hostages all sat on the hard, straight-backed chairs, which in time grew quite uncomfortable. Still, the mood had been surprisingly light. Everyone was talking and joking. The protesters were a little giddy with success. Both they and their captives assumed that government forces would arrive shortly to restore order. But then Golacinski had been taken from his chair and led back out across to the chancery and upstairs to the vault door at the west end of the second floor, the final holdout. He figured that the men inside were still destroying documents and resolved to buy them as much more time as he could.

His captors took off his blindfold and one who spoke English told him to talk his colleagues inside into opening the door.

"There's nobody in there," he said, but then they distinctly heard someone shouting on the other side of the door.

"Look, it's a very thick door," Golacinski said. "They'll never hear me."

He suggested that instead of him shouting through the door that they use a phone.

"No," said his lead captor.

"Then I can't talk to them."

They relented and took him into an office a few steps down the hall. Golacinski said he didn't remember the phone number, so they searched for an in-house phone book. The guards opened drawers and poked through bookshelves. They could not find anything. Finally, disgusted, they led Golacinski back out to the vault door. They banged on the door and Golacinski shouted in.

He heard Hermening's voice inside saying, "It's Mr. Golacinski out there!"

"Al, are you okay?" Hermening asked through the door.

"I'm okay. Everybody is over at the ambassador's house. These people want you to come out, and they say they won't hurt you."

"Do we have some time, Al?" he heard Tom Ahern shout.

"I don't know," Golacinski said.

At the Foreign Ministry, where Howland had been talking to Ahern on a phone in a small office downstairs, Howland set the phone down on the desk in order to keep the line open and ran upstairs to Yazdi's office to confer with Laingen.

He explained that Ahern was ready to open the door and the reasons why he thought it should not be done.

"No, I agree," said Laingen. "Tell them to hold on."

Howland ran back downstairs, but when he got there he found the phone on the cradle. Someone had seen it off the hook and hung it up. Howland dialed the number for the vault but he didn't get through. It was about four o'clock.

He hung up the phone, and seconds later it rang. Howland picked it up and heard an American voice. It was a sergeant calling from Germany who had somehow, in all this confusion, tracked him down to this office inside the Iranian Foreign Ministry.

"How did you—" he started to ask, but the sergeant cut him off. "Hold on for just a minute, sir."

Then a four-star general was on the phone, asking for a full situation report. Howland was shocked and impressed. He began explaining things to the general.

On his end, when the line went dead, Ahern decided to wait another five minutes and then instructed everyone to make one last check of all the drawers, files, and equipment. Hermening went to work helping Jones and the others destroy heavy "core boards" from the computers. They were as thick as books and had to be cut into pieces with a knife before being fed into the disintegrator, which would loudly break them down further.

Kupke made one more trip to the roof to get rid of the last four shotguns. He slid open the door, pulled himself back up, and sat squatting with two shotguns under each arm. His yellow shirt was wet and filthy, covered with dirt and tar from his belly-crawls on the roof. He dropped down again and moved along the edge of the low wall. There was a din of thousands outside the embassy walls, urged on by voices amplified with loudspeakers.

Downstairs, unaware that Kupke was alone on the roof, Ahern swung open the vault door. On the other side stood an angry, excited, but dumbfounded crowd of young Iranians, one of whom stepped up and drove an elbow hard into Ahern's ribs. He managed to keep his feet, then was quickly blindfolded and bound. Golacinski was thrown to one side and cracked his head on the wall. He heard the sounds of his colleagues being beaten. Bob Englemann's black-rimmed glasses were broken and he doubled over with his hands up, trying to protect himself from the blows.

Hermening made one last pass through the vault, gathering up anything left on the tables and floor and throwing them down the disintegrator chute. As he did this he was grabbed from behind by both arms. Two Iranians had hold of him, and one demanded that he put his hand down the chute and retrieve whatever he had thrown in. He refused and was then roughly hauled out of the vault to the hallway.

Barnes saw a tiny Iranian man waving a big gun. As the line of Americans filed out of the vault, the tiny one kicked and punched at them, so Barnes flicked his cigarette to the floor and scooted over as close behind Ward as he could, figuring it would make it harder for Tiny to land a clean blow. It worked.

Hermening was not so fortunate. Held from behind by both arms, one of his captors slapped him hard across the face. The young marine was determined not to cry out or complain. He took the blow and stared furiously back at his attacker, which earned him another hard slap. Out of the corner of his eye he saw Golacinski and some of the others lined up on the floor against one wall. Some were blindfolded and some had bags over their heads. He was pushed down in the same line between Ward and Paul Needham, who thought the bag over his head was a very bad sign. For months they had been seeing pictures of executions, and in most the victims had bags over their heads. There was a lot of shouting in the hallway; the Iranians were going down the line demanding that their newest captives identify themselves and their jobs. Hermening wondered what he should say. He thought, *name, rank, and serial number,* but he could see right away that this answer was going to get him in trouble. If he didn't tell them he was a marine guard, they were going to make other damaging assumptions about him. He hadn't been caught with the other marines, he wasn't in uniform, and he had been hiding in the secret vault. Was he allowed to tell them his job at the embassy? To his relief, Needham, the air force captain, promptly told them who he was and described his position with the military liaison group. Hermening thought, if an officer can do that, then it's okay for me to do it, too. When they asked him he said his name and then, "I'm a marine security guard."

"What's that?" his questioner shouted.

He did his best to explain, but because he was wearing a blue suit with a vest, he could see that they didn't believe him.

Still alone on the roof, Kupke was startled when the loud incinerator downstairs suddenly went silent. He hurried back to the door and, looking down, saw a group of Iranian men gathered below. Ahern had opened the door!

He slowly slid the door to the roof shut and sat alone, perplexed. Should he give himself up? He looked around him on the roof and saw the shotguns alongside him and those piled next to the shed. Kupke didn't know what to do. He didn't want to be discovered on the roof with weapons; they would probably assume he had been preparing to open fire. He looked across the compound and saw people in the windows of the tall building across the street. Surely they could see him. It was only a matter of time before they alerted someone.

He cracked open the door to the vault again and listened. *If there's gunfire,* he thought, *I'm staying put.* It was quiet. He reluctantly and slowly descended.

The burn room was empty so he stood there alone for a moment. He tiptoed over to peer into the adjacent room. At the far end were two Iranian men in green army jackets sitting with their backs to him before the destroyed radio equipment. He raised his hands and walked up behind them.

"Excuse me," he said.

The two jumped up when they heard him and began shouting at him in Farsi.

"Americano," he said.

One of the two smashed his fist into Kupke's glasses, right between the eyes. *There's got to be an easier way to surrender,* Kupke thought. He dropped to one knee and reached for his glasses, which had broken and scratched him under the eye. He shoved the pieces into his pocket, an instinctive move for which he would later be very glad. Suddenly the small room was filled with irate Iranians. They surrounded him, pulled him to his feet, and began pushing him back and forth. Some took swings at him, hitting him in the back and face. Kupke covered his head and ducked, trying to remember the protective moves he had learned in tae kwon do class. One of the men in the circle was leaning back on one leg and had the other elevated, trying to aim a kick. He was taking up so much space that it allowed Kupke room to dive into a corner with his back to the wall, fending off blows. He was pulled to his feet and dragged back out into the middle of the room, where the beating resumed until somebody slammed him hard from behind, probably with the same two-by-four he had used on the incinerator. It struck him more in the neck than in the head, but the force of the blow momentarily blacked him out. He came to with everything around him swirling in slow motion. He felt no pain.

He could hear the men speaking in Farsi. Most were young, although a few looked middle-aged. With their beards it was hard to tell. Most had guns. Kupke immediately doubted that they would shoot him. There were too many people in the room, for one thing, and they might hit each other. One of the men leveled a handgun at his head and asked, in English, "Where were you? Do you work for the CIA?"

"No, no," Kupke said. "I was over by the burn machine."

"No, you weren't. Tell us who you work for. If you don't tell us right, I'm going to shoot you."

He told them the truth. "I work for the State Department," he said.

The man pulled the trigger and the hammer snapped on an empty chamber. Kupke's legs gave way. He was pulled back to his feet.

"Open the safe," the English-speaker demanded.

"I don't know the combination."

The Iranian spun the chamber of the revolver and pressed the muzzle to his captive's left temple. Kupke's eyes were rolled so far to the left he was afraid they would lock in that position as he strained to see if there were rounds in the chamber. The trigger was pulled and the hammer snapped. The blow to the head had dazed him, so the sound reached him in a slow-motion haze. He was not consciously afraid. He was more worried about being put back into the circle and being kicked and beaten again. But what happened next did scare him, knock on the head and all.

Kupke was thrown to the floor and one of the older Iranians, a short fat man, sat on his stomach. Others grabbed his feet and pinned his arms. Kupke could smell the man sitting on him as he leaned close with a knife.

"I'm going to cut your eyes out," he said. "I'm going to ask you some questions." He tapped the flat of the blade against Kupke's left eye. "I want you to open these safes, and if you don't open them I'm going to cut out this eye first. Then, I'm going to cut out this eye," he said, tapping Kupke's right eye.

"You've got to believe me," said Kupke, pleading now. "I work here in the coms center. I send and receive messages for the embassy! If I knew the combination to the safe, I would open it right now. I don't want my eyes cut out!"

The man got up and led Kupke into the hallway where Jones was standing blindfolded against the wall, looking disheveled, with his hands tied behind his back.

"Charles," Kupke blurted. "If you know how to open the safe, open it."

Jones knew the combinations. The Iranians grabbed him by the necktie and choked him, but he refused to help. He was terrified but something in him balked at the threats, and he was convinced beyond reason that this wasn't real, that it would all be over soon and things would be back to normal. He was more concerned about protecting his jewelry, which he kept in a drawer in one of the vault's safes, figuring it was the safest place on the compound. When they had begun emptying the safes earlier, Jones decided to put on all his valuables—he had heard that in the February embassy invasion none of the Iranians had patted down the embassy personnel—so he had put it all on, three chains, seven rings, three watches. Before Ahern opened the vault door, he had reached under his collar and removed one of the chains, which held a golden Star of David, a gift from the years he had spent assigned to Israel. Figuring it was a symbol that might provoke his captors, he had hidden it under one of the counters.

Mostly, Jones was angry about getting roughed up. When they had first taken him, he had been blindfolded and led out into the corridor.

"Hey, who's next to me?" asked the man next to him, who was Ahern.

"It's me, Charles," said Jones, at which point an Iranian had slammed his head against the wall. The man had snatched a chain off Jones's neck, and then knocked him to the floor and kicked him. In the process he had stepped on his hand, which hurt.

Now, as he was being choked by his necktie, Jones was angry and determined to be unhelpful.

"What's wrong with you?" Kupke pleaded. "Man, they're bouncing me off the walls in the other room, Charles."

Jones was pushed to the ground, beaten and kicked again.

Englemann was ordered to open the safes, which he did not know how to do. Instead he led some of his captors out of the vault and down the hall to his own office. He had already emptied his safes of anything sensitive and fed his files into the disintegrator, so in a great show of helpfulness he spun the combination locks and opened them. Inside were unimportant files and a pile of picture books. They seemed pleased.

Hermening was pulled to his feet and led back into the vault. One of the Iranians now pressed the barrel of a pistol hard into his temple, right beside his eye.

"Open the safe!" he demanded.

"I don't know the combination," Hermening protested. He was shaking.

"Open the safe!" the man shouted again.

"I don't know the combination. I don't even work in this office."

"Sure," the Iranian said. "Then what were you doing in here?"

Hermening had never been so scared. He didn't know the combination, and he was afraid he wasn't going to be able to convince the man with the gun that he was telling the truth.

"If I did know it, what good is it going to do for you to shoot me?" he said. "Then you'll never get the combination."

Eventually he was led back out to the hall and a gas mask bag was pulled over his head. He heard someone being beaten in the room behind him.

Golacinski was on the floor with them, blindfolded again, his head still ringing, when he saw out of the bottom of the blindfold that one of the Iranians was unscrewing a wall socket.

"We're going to burn you," he said. They were still trying to force someone to open the safes for them.

Golacinski spoke up to his colleagues in a loud voice, "If any of you can open the safes, open the damn safes!"

Everyone still refused. Golacinski was taken into the vault and ordered to open them.

"None of us can," he said. "All of the combinations were written down and they have been destroyed. They burned them all."

In the midst of all this conflict over the safes, a group of young Iranians showed up with food—bread and eggs and pickles. It was strange; one minute Hermening had a gun pressed to his head and in the next an Iranian was offering him an egg salad sandwich. How was he supposed to feel like eating?

He refused the food and was taken to one of the offices down the hall. The door was shut behind him. When the bag was taken off his head he faced several protesters seated in the office chairs and on the desk. The office had been ransacked, the drawers pulled out, pictures were crooked on the walls. Framed photos of President Carter and Secretary of State Vance had been thrown to the floor and their glass covers smashed. He thought it was his turn to be beaten and his tough marine mask crumbled. He was instead a frightened nineteen-year-old, and he started to cry.

"I don't know the combinations!" he pleaded. "I'm just a security guard!"

One of his captors was clearly in charge. He told Hermening in English that unless he was more helpful, the others were going to be "turned loose" on him. The marine fought to free his hands so that he could fend off the blows, but apparently he had managed to convince his questioner that he knew nothing. He was not assaulted. Instead, he was led downstairs.

"We want to see where you work," the Iranian told him.

On the foyer floor downstairs he saw the American flag, scuffed and dirty. One of the protesters was sitting in a chair at the front entrance guard post wearing a marine helmet. Scattered around were the half-burned newspaper torches the protesters had used to battle the tear gas. He was taken into Gunnery Sergeant Mike Moeller's office, where earlier he had been working on the meal accounting. Hermening showed them the money box and the papers he had been working on and explained what he had been doing. Then they took him to the guard post's electric switchboard, which controlled locks for various portions of the building. They had been unable to open a door that led to the east-side hallway on the first floor. They told him to push the right buttons to release the locks. Hermening reached under the switchbox, where they could not see his hands, and yanked out the wires that connected the switches to the electric locks. Then he pushed buttons at random. Of course, nothing happened.

He looked up with a confused expression. "It's always worked before," he said.

11

GAPTOOTH

Kupke's pockets were emptied of cash and jewelry and he was taken down the hall to Laingen's office, where he had the distinction of being the first American hostage to meet Hussein Sheikh-ol-eslam, a skinny young man with a dreamy, distracted manner, a thick unruly mop of curly black hair, and a full black beard, a radical filled with the absolute certainty of divine purpose, whose occasional sweetness itself was in service of a brutal righteousness. He was missing his left front tooth, and the hostages, who would come to know him well, called him "Gaptooth," or "Snaggle-tooth." Because he spoke perfect English, he would become for them the most visible member of the students' leadership. In the early seventies he had studied at the University of California, Berkeley, a center of student radicalism in America during the anti–Vietnam War era. Sheikh-ol-eslam had digested the fervent rhetoric of those activist years, the rants against the "tyrannical," "racist," "imperialist" American establishment, and now, back in Iran, where there had been a real tyrant to oppose, he had taken part in something the old fire-breathers at Berkeley had only dreamed about—an actual revolution. And here, at his mercy, were the very agents of American imperialism denounced in that hyperbolic campus rhetoric. He would make the most of it.

Outside the tall windows it was growing dark; Kupke figured it was about five o'clock.

"Who do you work for?" Sheikh-ol-eslam asked.

"I work for the State Department," Kupke told him.

"Why didn't you surrender with everyone else?"

"I was destroying documents."

"Why were you destroying documents? What were you hiding?"

"Nothing. Those documents were the property of the United States," Kupke told him. "It's our job to destroy them before letting them fall into your hands."

The questioning went on. Clearly, the circumstances of his capture, hiding out, and destroying documents made Kupke and the others in the vault particularly suspicious. Sheikh-ol-eslam asked where he had been hiding when the others were taken from the vault. Kupke, afraid that the students would find the weapons on the roof, said that he had crouched behind the incinerator. It occurred to him that there was information in the vault that might reinforce the idea he was a spy. When he had been working in the Sinai outpost, he had obtained two sets of passports, one for passage into Arab countries and the other for traveling to Israel—Arab nations would not let anyone enter whose passport had been stamped in Israel.

"You know, eventually you're going to find a lot of IDs in one of those safes, both Arab and Israeli," Kupke said. "And that doesn't mean I'm a spy. It just means I was working and passing through the Sinai Desert on both sides."

Sheikh-ol-eslam listened and nodded with evident disbelief.

With men grabbing both his arms, CIA station chief Tom Ahern was led down the littered second-floor corridor to his office. *How did they already know which one was his?* Ahern figured somebody in the first hours must have started helping these thugs. He was alarmed but not terribly surprised. He remembered a conversation he had shortly before leaving on this assignment, with an agency friend who had just returned from Tehran. He had asked how much he might count on the staff there to protect his identity.

"If they bring everybody in the embassy staff out and they line them up against the wall and they say, 'Now, we want to know who the CIA people are,'" Ahern had asked, "are my embassy colleagues going to protect me?"

His friend had laughed.

Ahern was pushed into a chair, his blindfold was removed, and the first thing he noticed was a file folder on his desk that he had overlooked. He was the one who all morning had been most concerned about destroying sensitive material and, indeed, he thought he had rounded up everything of his own, but there, sitting on his desk, was an informal report he had written the day before to "Edward J. Ganin" (a code name for CIA director Stansfield Turner) under his own cover name, "Donald C. Paquin," and with his title "Station Chief, Tehran." It was a routine summary for headquarters of everything he and his agents had been doing, and his assessment of what was likely to happen in Iran, nothing very dramatic or important (and, as time would show, mostly wrong) but under the circumstances a very damaging document.

In it, he described the four months he had been in Iran as a period of "elbowing and maneuvering for position" among the country's various political factions, and predicted "the gradual erosion of Khomeini's personal authority." This would lead, he had written, to a period of disorderly—sometimes violent—competition, with no single contender possessing enough guns or popularity to prevail. "Things could be very different if the military chooses sides," he had written, "but they are still thoroughly intimidated. Discipline is poor, professional élan practically nonexistent, and no prospective leaders have yet emerged who look as if they can restore institutional pride."

It went on:

> You asked me to comment at some point about our prospects for influencing the course of events. Only marginally, I would say, until the military recovers, and that is a process we can do almost nothing to affect. What we can do, and I am now working on, is to identify and prepare to support the potential leaders of a coalition of westernized political liberals, moderate religious figures, and (when they begin to emerge) western oriented military leaders. The most likely catalyst for such a coalition is Ayatollah [Kazem] Shariatmadari; I have compartmented contacts with several of his supporters.
>
> Prospects are not bright for resuming operation of the TACKS-MAN sites in a role which will provide us telemetry on Soviet missile testing. The reason is that this would require a degree of American participation which the Iranians are not likely to find politically acceptable. Accordingly, we are proceeding with an operation designed to provide clandestine collection of telemetry; this is proceeding well, and with some luck could be functioning fairly early in 1980.

Ahern had concluded the cable by requesting an additional case officer, and by acknowledging the help he had received weeks earlier in the form of Bill Daugherty, whom he had *named* in the cable!

He tried not to stare at the folder but was stunned at his oversight. There was, in summary, the current feeble efforts of the CIA to sort out what was going on in Iran. Given in particular that the letter named

Ayatollah Shariatmadari, and discussed the deeply clandestine effort to replace the Tacksman telemetry collection effort, it was an egregious lapse. The paragraph about potential for "influencing the course of events" would confirm the Iranians worst suspicions about American intentions in their country, particularly in light of the 1953 coup. That effort had succeeded with the help of Western military leaders, too. It was a shock, an embarrassment, and sure to be trouble.

For the moment, his captors paid no attention to the folder on his desk. They wanted Ahern to open the office safe. He refused. There wasn't much in it, only what little was left of his files, some correspondence related to the earlier regime, and some chemicals used in preparing or reading invisible ink. Ahern wasn't eager to share it with them, and if help was going to be arriving soon—as he and the other captives all assumed—then there was much to be gained by delay. He also didn't want to acknowledge that it was *his* safe.

Then one of the older captors produced a .38 caliber handgun and pointed it at his face. He told Ahern to open it or be shot.

The veteran CIA officer was unconvinced. *He's not going to shoot me, maybe later, but not now.* Ahern knew that it was always a mistake to open an interrogation with your heaviest threat. If these people wanted the combination to his safe, then shooting him would be self-defeating.

"It's not my safe," Ahern lied.

The man with the gun grumbled at him threateningly, but gave up and walked away.

12

GO AND KICK THEM OUT

By midafternoon nearly all of the Americans seized on the compound had been herded into the ambassador's residence or into the four small cottages behind the chancery. Most were blindfolded and had their hands tied. Their captors were giddy with success but seemed not to know what to do next. The five American women seized during the takeover were taken to a separate room, where they were tied to chairs and blindfolded. They were asked to state their name, section, and title.

"Terri Tedford, administrative section, secretary," said the slight, brown-haired woman in the first chair.

"Joan Walsh, political section, secretary," said the second, and so on, around the room, until they came to Ann Swift.

"Ann Swift, first secretary, political section," she said. Swift spoke some Farsi, and when she heard her job title being translated as "typist," her ego bristled and she immediately corrected them, a reflex she would live to regret.

"I'm not a typist," she corrected. "I'm the first secretary," and went on to explain that she was, in effect, the highest-ranking embassy official they had in captivity.

A small group came for Limbert in the ambassador's residence. He asked where they were taking him.

"We want you to come with us to the vault," one said.

"Oh, of course, I'd be pleased," Limbert said. "Nothing would make me happier. It would be an honor."

Relaxed now after the ordeal on the staircase, he fell back on the elaborate formal courtesies of Farsi. So long as they spoke to him nicely, as this student had, then he would respond in kind. He was, after all, a diplomat. And under the circumstances it didn't hurt to remind them of their culture's traditional politeness.

They escorted him across the darkening compound to the chancery, showed him the basement window where they had broken in, and then led him to the top floor. The coms vault at the west end looked like it had been ransacked. He saw Ahern, Jones, Barnes, and the others who had evidently locked themselves inside for hours sitting outside it on the corridor floor against the wall with their hands tied. Limbert was led into the vault.

"What is the combination to this safe?" they asked.

"I don't know," Limbert said. "I don't work here."

"What is in these safes?" they asked.

"I don't know," he said, truthfully.

"What are they in here for?"

"I presume for safekeeping," he said. "I am not even allowed to enter here."

Then they showed him his wallet. He had left it in the vault early that afternoon before stepping out to talk to the students on the steps. Ordinarily he was not allowed in the vault, but today it had seemed prudent to leave his wallet there.

"If you don't give us the combination, we'll shoot everybody here," his questioner said.

It seemed unlikely. In the few hours he had spent with this crowd so far he had judged them to be amateurish and, in their own way, well intentioned.

"That's an empty threat," Limbert said. "I can't give the combinations to you because I don't know them."

Taken back to the residence, Limbert passed Barry Rosen in the hall and said, "Barry, here it goes again," referring to the February takeover, in which Rosen had been briefly held captive. "You should have known better than to hang around."

Rosen, the embassy's press attaché, was a cipher to his captors. He was short, dark-skinned, and bearded, and he spoke such fluent Farsi that they were reluctant to believe he was an American.

"I'm an American and proud of it," he told them, still cocky and still convinced that these renegades would be chased off the embassy in short order.

He was taken to the bedroom of the Pakistani chef who lived and worked at the ambassador's residence, where he was briefly questioned by a young woman who wore a long brown *jilbab,* or robe, and *khimar,* or head scarf, which covered most of her face. She had beautiful eyes, Rosen thought, but nothing else about her was appealing. She seemed to regard him as the personification of evil. Here before her was the architect of everything wrong in Iran in modern history, and she nearly spat out the words she spoke.

"What is your job?" she asked.

Rosen told her the truth.

"What is the true function of a 'press attaché,'" she asked, implying that the job description was a cover. "Who are the Iranian 'journalists' you had contact with?"

He told her that he would be happy to discuss his job with her at some other time.

"This isn't the time or place," he said. "This is the territory of the United States, which you have invaded."

She responded angrily. This was *their* country, not his. The so-called embassy was actually a spy den, and now she and the other students had taken it back. He and his colleagues were the invaders, planning their "conspiracies and corruptions."

Rosen had noticed that Yusef, the chef, had a large bottle of scotch on a nearby shelf, so instead of engaging in pointless argument with the woman he reached out to the bottle and suggested that they both have a drink. Her eyes widened in horror. In the new Iran to offer alcohol to a pious daughter of the faith was unforgivably rude, an insult to the purity of Muslim womanhood. She threw up her arms in disgust and exited the room, slamming the door behind her in a dismissive swish of fabric.

Ibrahim Yazdi, the foreign minister, had left Laingen, Tomseth, and Howland at midafternoon for the hour-and-a-half drive to Qom to meet with Khomeini. Before leaving, Yazdi asked Laingen, "Where do you and your colleagues propose to go?"

The chargé, still hot, told Yazdi that it was up to the provisional government.

"You have an obligation to protect us," Laingen told him. There were anti-American mobs on the streets all over Tehran; indeed, the chargé had learned that an armed gang had already been asking for him and the other two Americans at the front gates of the Foreign Ministry.

Yazdi said he didn't believe the situation was that bad but made arrangements for the three to spend the night in the Foreign Ministry building. He was exhausted. His plane from Algiers had flown through the night and arrived only that morning, and he had not slept for two days. He snoozed in the car on the drive east to the holy city.

Khomeini normally rested in the afternoon and received guests early in the evening. When Yazdi was shown into the imam's receiving room he sat on a floor cushion alongside the white-bearded cleric and told him what had happened at the U.S. embassy. It was his impression that Khomeini was hearing the news for the first time.

"Who are they?" he asked. "Why have they done this?"

Yazdi explained that the hostage takers appeared to be university students, and that they were demanding the immediate return of the shah and his assets.

"Go and kick them out," Khomeini said.

Yazdi did nothing with those instructions at first. There didn't seem to be any reason for haste. The takeover was accomplished. With the imam's permission it would be a simple matter to clear out the students and give the compound back to the American mission, and it might be best to let things cool off for a few hours before starting. He briefed Khomeini on the now controversial meeting he and Bazargan had held with Brzezinski in the prime minister's hotel room in Algiers. Then he got back in a car for the drive to Tehran and figured he would relay the imam's instructions about the embassy to Bazargan when he returned.

So the weary foreign minister was startled that evening in Tehran, after he had been driven back from Qom, when he heard on the radio the imam's first public statement endorsing the takeover and the goals of the students. It wasn't halfhearted either. In a complete reversal of the sentiments he had expressed earlier, Khomeini warmly supported the move and praised the students. Yazdi was not surprised. He had come to know Khomeini, and despite the ayatollah's fierce visage, he was a maddeningly vacillating man. In political matters, he tended to side with whomever last had his ear, and because he often regarded the affairs of state as trivial compared to his spiritual concerns, he was usually reluctant to make unpopular decisions. The jubilant scene outside the embassy was being shown on television throughout the country. Yazdi was impressed by the way this stunt had been orchestrated. Whoever was responsible, he thought, had wisely avoided informing the imam in advance, knowing that Khomeini would be less likely to oppose a popular fait accompli than a half-baked idea. The planners had done a great job of getting out the crowd, too. Yazdi had reports of food being served, street performances, and people being delivered by the busload from all over the region. Some of it might have been spontaneous, and the celebratory mood was definitely real, but some serious planning had gone into it.

In between the imam's meeting with Yazdi and the radio broadcast, several things had happened in Qom. Ahmad Khomeini, the imam's son, had received a phone call from his friend the popular young Tehran cleric Mohammad Asqar Mousavi Khoeniha, the students' "spiritual leader." He had assured the younger Khomeini that the *geroghan-girha,* the hostage takers, were devout Muslims, not the leftist hooligans who had seized the embassy in February. They had acted, Khoeniha said, in response to the imam's call for students to "attack" America. Ahmad Khomeini agreed to fly by helicopter to the U.S. embassy and see for himself what was going on.

Arriving on the scene, the younger Khomeini had literally been carried away by the rapture of the mob dancing in the streets. He was lifted bodily over the embassy walls, his presence alone interpreted as the imam's imprimatur. The young cleric briefly lost his black turban and a slipper in the excitement. After touring the embassy and viewing the captive Americans he had returned to Qom with a glowing report on the students and the suspicious American spy documents and equipment they had seized. When it was clear that what had happened was enormously popular, and that the action had the support of influential clerics like Khoeniha, the imam understood that what to Yazdi was a nuisance was in fact an opportunity.

As he prepared finally for bed, Yazdi knew there was now nothing he or the provisional government could do. The matter was out of their hands.

13

WHEAT MOLD

Before he was blindfolded again, John Limbert watched from a chair at the residence as the twilight faded, sitting alongside the Filipino cashier, whom the students had not yet decided whether to consider an American spy or an oppressed Third World national. Limbert had given his name and job title when asked and had refused a cigarette. He had learned that these protesters called themselves "Muslim Students Following the Imam's Line," and understood that they were religious and more aligned with the mullahs than the leftists, who predominated on the college campuses. Most of those he had talked to so far were more curious than hostile. Some were from rural areas, small towns, and they reminded him of the students he had taught in Shiraz. He saw that they were in over their heads but didn't know it yet. They had been brought up with a very narrow idea of the world. Most of them probably had no idea where America was on a map, much less any understanding of U.S.–Iran relations. For most, this was probably their first encounter with Americans and, given the ridiculous propaganda in the previous year, they were no doubt surprised to find that the embassy personnel didn't have horns. Limbert couldn't help himself; he liked them.

As soon as he figured out who they were the events of the day came into better focus. It wasn't clear if they were acting with the approval of the imam, as their name implied. Limbert suspected not. The atmosphere in the crowded residence was strange. Some of the initial tension evaporated for the Americans when it was evident that they were not going to be harmed, at least not immediately. Captors and prisoners were talking freely to each other, and at one point a student brought a radio into the room, and everyone sat together listening eagerly to hear how the day's event was reported. They listened to Radio Tehran and the BBC international report, and he could see that the students seemed a little disappointed when the embassy takeover was treated in the London report as a relatively minor story. The students considered their "victory" nothing short of miraculous. They had stormed the American fortress and overrun it without a casualty! In one sense it was too good to be true, and in another . . . what were they supposed to do now?

He heard the guards whispering excitedly among themselves about the visit of Ahmad Khomeini, and then, passing the word from guard to guard, they removed the blindfolds from Limbert and the other hostages in the room. They apparently did not want the imam's son to see that they had blindfolded the hostages. When Limbert's came off he saw that seated alongside him was Charles Jones, who kept trying to tell his captors that he had high blood pressure and needed his medicine. Jones asked Limbert to explain in Farsi. The two of them started nagging the guards, in English and in Farsi, pleading for the medication, which worked, although it took a few tries. The guards kept coming back with the wrong medicine, and each time Limbert complained to them about the seriousness of Jones's condition. Were they trying to kill him?

Limbert sat up late in a downstairs bedroom talking earnestly with his young captors. They said they were staging the demonstration in order to force the United States to return the shah in order to stand trial for his crimes.

"I don't think you have much of a chance," said Limbert.

They tried to engage him further in a political discussion but Limbert avoided it. The little training he had been given about being taken captive warned against getting drawn into political discussions. So he kept changing the subject, asking questions. They were shocked at how well he spoke Farsi, and how much he knew about their country, its history and literature—more than they themselves did.

Throughout the residence, Americans were bound to chairs. Joe Hall, the warrant officer who was convinced his capture meant he would be sent home early, was in the basement TV room, which had a door to a storage area stocked with sodas, canned goods, and candy. He watched as a procession of the young Iranians raided the stash. One came out grinning, and with hands that seemed grubby to Hall he popped a piece of candy into the captive American's mouth.

The same young Iranian who had earlier posed with a knife pressed against the side of marine guard Rocky Sickmann's head now offered him candy.

"No, I don't want your fucking candy," said Sickmann.

"I'll take it," said vice consul Richard Queen. "I'm hungry."

"The shah didn't feed prisoners," said one of the Iranians, who nevertheless placed a date in Queen's mouth and then held up a small plastic bowl for him to spit out the pit.

As the hours dragged on, Hall's hands, which were tied behind his back, began to hurt, and he asked if the cloth could be loosened.

"They're cutting off my circulation," he said.

A young Iranian bent over and removed them, and for a while Hall sat with his hands in his lap. Then an older student saw him untied and angrily instructed the others to retie him. This time his hands were bound in front, which was a little more comfortable.

In the room with him was an angry little guard with a big nose whom Hall dubbed "Rat Face."

"You are See-ah [CIA]," he sneered at the bound American.

"I am not CIA."

"Yes, you are all spies here."

"Yeah, you're right," said Hall facetiously. "I'm See-ah."

Rat Face brightened at this, accepting it as an admission.

"What was your job?" he asked.

Hall thought for a moment, and then said, again facetiously, "I was in charge of wheat mold."

"What is wheat mold?"

"You know the wheat that grows and that you use to make bread?" Hall explained, warming to the joke. "Well, mold is something that happens to the wheat that makes it no good. I did all that. I was the CIA agent in charge of wheat mold."

The young Iranian absorbed this intently—indeed, the CIA plot to destroy Iranian crops would become part of the list of "revelations" later claimed by the hostage takers.

"How long is this stuff going to go on anyway?" Hall asked. "You guys aren't going to be able to carry this off very long."

"Maybe one year," said Rat Face.

He then bent over and removed one of Hall's shoes. He pulled the TV cord from the wall, doubled it over, and, grabbing Hall's foot by the toes and pulling it up, slapped the cord across the bottom of his foot.

"This is the way the shah's army tortured innocent Iranians," he said, and he slapped the cord across Hall's foot again.

He didn't hit Hall hard enough for it to hurt. When he dropped his foot, Hall slid it back into his shoe.

Later, he was taken upstairs, to one of the residence's larger rooms, where the Iranians were intrigued by decorations left over from a Halloween party that had been organized the week before by Hall's subordinate, Joe Subic. One of them fingered a hanging cartoon skeleton and asked, "What's this?"

"It's part of a holiday celebration, a holiday for children," Hall said.

"You do this sort of stuff for children?" the Iranian asked, surveying the images of witches, goblins, and spooky pumpkin heads.

"It's an old custom," Hall started to explain but then realized how peculiar the holiday actually was. "We give candy to children."

Hall saw Subic in that upstairs room, and true to form the eager young sergeant was volunteering to be helpful. He had a yellow legal pad and was pointing out all the captives and giving their names, job titles, and descriptions. He seemed to be enjoying himself. They would stop at a blindfolded prisoner, and Subic would say, "This is Greg Persinger. He's a marine sergeant," and then they would move on to the next person. Before Sharer, he said, "This is Commander Don Sharer, he's an F-14 expert, he works for the United States Navy, and he was in Vietnam." Sharer had earlier given his name as "Mickey Mouse." Many of the top embassy officials had been trying to keep their status and responsibilities obscure. "It would probably be best to just drop 'sir' from your vocabulary for the time being," consular officer Don Cooke had advised the marines bound to chairs near him. Whatever Subic's instincts were, they didn't run along these lines. Before Colonel Scott, Subic said, "This is Colonel Chuck Scott, the military liaison officer. He's been in Iran many times before. He was an attaché here in the sixties and he speaks fluent Farsi." Scott would like to have punched the young sergeant in the face, both for being so helpful to their captors and for calling him "Chuck," a level of familiarity that ignored their difference in rank and actual relationship. Some of those identified asked Subic, "Why are you doing this?" or told him angrily, "Keep your mouth shut," or "Leave it alone, Joe." It didn't seem to bother or deter him at all. Hall had found Subic a difficult employee ever since he had arrived in Tehran. The chubby soldier with glasses and dirty-blond hair was so eager to take on responsibility and to get involved with work others were doing in the embassy that he tended to neglect his own duties. Subic was a well-meaning busybody, who seemed compelled to be at the center of attention, and now he was doing it here, with all of his colleagues tied to chairs.

"Joe, sit down and mind your own business," Hall told him.

"Shut up!" one of the guards shouted at him. "No speak!" The way the guards pronounced "speak" added a vowel to the front end, so it came out as "*Eh*-speak," a phrase the hostages would hear again and again in the coming months.

Subic kept talking. Hall overheard the sergeant say, "Well, I can take you and show you."

Marines Sickmann and Persinger were bound next to each other. They were approached by an English-speaking Iranian who had a cameraman with him. He asked them their names and what their jobs were.

"We're pizza runners," said Sickmann.

"We work for the laundry department," said Persinger. "We clean laundry, and this guy"—nodding toward Sickmann—"he gets pizzas for all the marines. In fact, I'd like a pizza right now."

They speculated on how long they would be held. Some felt it might be until Christmas. Sickmann, who had heard that his captors were students, assumed that like American college students they would all be finishing their school year next May, so he predicted it might last until then.

Dinner was served in shifts in the residence kitchen. Young women in *jilbabs* threw frozen steaks into frying pans, cooked them until the outsides were brown, and served them—inside, the meat was still frozen. Richard Queen was not allowed to use a knife, so he picked up the slab of meat and tried to gnaw off a corner.

"Would you like a beer?" a young man asked him.

"Yes, I would," said Queen.

The young man left and never returned.

After the moment captured in the much-reprinted photo of Bill Belk, he had been marched across the compound to one of the yellow cottages.

"We are going to teach you," his captor told him.

Belk wondered what that meant.

"We will teach you about God," the young man said. "We will teach the CIA not to interfere with our country."

Uncomfortable with his hands tied behind his back with nylon rope, Belk fidgeted for about three hours, listening to the din outside. He kept asking his guards if they would give him one of the cigarettes in his shirt pocket.

"Don't speak!" the guard said.

He persisted, and finally one of them removed a cigarette, put it between his lips, and lit it. Belk almost choked trying to smoke it. He had no way of taking it from his mouth. He did the best he could, but after a few puffs he spit it out. At one point, early in the evening, somebody fed him a spoonful of ice cream. Later he was escorted to the toilet, where his hands were unbound and, still blindfolded, he did his best to hit the bowl. When he finished his hands were retied and he was returned to the chair.

Belk was miserable, hungry, and increasingly worried about what would happen next. The nylon rope cut into his wrists. He finally managed to fall asleep in the chair.

Charles Jones finished the day in Bruce Laingen's upstairs bedroom with some of the marines. He flopped on Laingen's bed and fell asleep, snoring contentedly. Hermening watched him with admiration. *How could he just fall asleep?* Now and then a big, bearded Iranian would step into the room. In one hand he carried a club, which he tapped menacingly against his other hand and glared down at his American prisoners.

When Kupke's questioning ended, he was taken to the ambassador's residence and deposited on the floor in an upstairs bedroom, blindfolded and tied hand and foot. He turned on his side and tried to get comfortable on the carpet, but he was bruised and sore. His head was pounding with pain and it felt like his jaw was broken; he could not completely close his mouth.

In the middle of the night he was awakened by an Iranian.

"Can I get you anything?" he was asked.

Kupke asked for some water and was given some.

"I would give anything for some aspirin," he said. His guard fetched him two tablets, then left. Kupke had forgotten to ask for more water, so he put them in his mouth and chewed them.

Queen and Limbert got beds of their own. After his long, harrowing day, Al Golacinski slept fitfully on the floor under his chair.

At the Foreign Ministry, Bruce Laingen, the chargé, dozed on a couch in the huge formal dining room.

Marine Kevin Hermening woke up at about three in the morning in the bed alongside two fellow hostages. He lifted his head and looked around and was surprised to see about twenty of the students in the room in various postures of sleep, some of them in chairs, others sprawled on the floor. It was like a big sleepover.

Downstairs, Joe Hall woke up at five. It took him a second or two to focus. Around him were guards and beneath the blanket one of his hands was still bound with cloth.

My God, he thought. *It wasn't just a nightmare!*

14

OKAY, GO AHEAD
AND SHOOT

There was to be little sleep for Bill Daugherty, who was taken early in the evening from the ambassador's residence by a student with a .38 caliber pistol, who called out his name and told him that he was wanted for questioning. The novice CIA officer was escorted across the embassy grounds back to the chancery, up the steep staircase of the back entrance, and then up the central stairway to the second floor. He was taken into his own office, still bound and blindfolded, and leaned gently against the wall. It was well after midnight but crowds were still celebrating outside. He was exhausted and could still taste tear gas deep in his nose and throat.

He had more reason than most of the newly taken hostages to fear questioning. Daugherty had been assigned to Tehran only six months after joining the agency. He did not speak Farsi, and had been in Iran for only fifty-three days, barely long enough to figure out what his job was and how to get it done. Each of the spy agency's employees at the embassy had a cover, a regular State Department job, but their identity was an open secret in-house. Everybody knew who worked in the suite of offices on the west end of the second floor. It included a small reception area manned by the agency's secretary and the offices of Tom Ahern; Ahern's senior field officer (who had left on home leave only a few weeks earlier); Malcolm Kalp, the newly arrived field officer; and Daugherty. There was a large vault in Daugherty's office, which was ordinarily closed and locked. He figured there were only three obvious ways his role could become known to his captors: they would have to discover some written record of it in the embassy files, one of his colleagues would have to tell them, or he would have to break down and tell them himself. The only one of the three he could hope to control was the last.

The chancery had been ransacked. Already the Iranian intelligence agents at the core of the takeover, led by Hashemi, had collected all the intact documents they could find, boxed them up, and carted them off the compound for scrutiny. They planned to stay for only a day or two, so it was important to get this done quickly. They had been disappointed to discover the disintegrator in the coms vault. What unrecoverable mysteries did it contain? Had the Americans managed to destroy all the evidence of their counterrevolutionary plots? There was no hope of restoring the blue powder left by the disintegrator, but perhaps there was a way to reassemble the piles of paper that had been fed through the shredder. Surely anything the Americans had taken such pains to destroy must contain valuable information.

Daugherty tried to prepare himself for what was coming. He was new to the spy agency and to Tehran, but he wasn't innocent. He knew most of the embassy's secrets, the small string of Iranian spies on the agency's payroll, the secret efforts to independently replace the Tacksman sites. He knew procedures, codes, and methods . . . a lot that his captors would like to find out. How should he handle himself? He was worried, but he was also determined not to act disgracefully. At the same time, there was no point in trying to play the hero. He was supposed to be a diplomat, that was his cover story, so he would act like one. The truth is he was so green that he could as easily assume the identity of a foreign officer as any other. He would engage his questioners, attempt to challenge them for this unwarranted outrage. It would not be an act.

It occurred to him that his captors must believe him to be someone more important than he was. His office was large and well furnished, and it was the only one in the suite with a walk-in safe. Sure enough, when the questions began, he was accused of being the "real power" in the embassy.

Daugherty was blindfolded so he couldn't see his questioner, but the voice was male and soft, and the English was very good, only lightly accented and with an educated vocabulary. The CIA officer would later write out a reconstruction of the session.

"Is this your office?" he was asked.

"Well, not really."

"What do you mean, 'Not really'?"

"Well, I'm here temporarily because I'm a new arrival and my office —you can go see—it's down the hall. It's the room that serves as the library, but they haven't gotten around to moving the books out yet."

"Okay," said his questioner. "Who sits here outside this office?"

"The secretary who works for the guy in the other office [Ahern's suite]."

"Who's the guy in the other office?"

"He's the drug enforcement representative." This was Ahern's official cover.

"What's his name?"

"I'm not sure. Like I said, I'm new here, and I haven't gotten to know everyone yet."

"What does he do?"

"He works with your police forces, I think, to try to do something about stopping drugs. I don't know. I don't really know him well."

His interrogator pressed on in a steady, unemotional way and followed up quickly, probing, testing. This was not an amateur. He never lost control of the dialogue, even though Daugherty was looking for a way to derail it.

"You mean they put you in this office with people you don't know?"

"Yeah, because my office isn't ready yet."

"Who's your secretary?"

"I don't have one."

"Do you write cables back to Washington?"

"Yes."

"Well, who does that for you?"

"The secretary across the hall who works in the political section, because I'm a political officer."

"What about this secretary out here?"

"No, she just sits outside this office. I'm just here temporarily."

The questioner was getting frustrated but he kept his cool. He didn't raise his voice, though he spoke a little faster. The questions came back more quickly. He doubled back over the same ground, asking the same questions several times, waiting for Daugherty's story to slip up. He was not buying the answers. He mentioned the possibility of a firing squad and how many Iranians were familiar with torture methods, having been practiced upon by SAVAK. He played with an apparently empty pistol as he spoke, spinning the cylinder, cocking the hammer, and then easing it back down. He would pull the trigger when he wanted to emphasize a point, which made a sound that concentrated Daugherty's mind.

He didn't believe he would be shot . . . at least not yet. If they were going to shoot people, it wouldn't make sense to do it right away, not when they were looking for information. Daugherty could see that the embassy invaders were trying to figure the place out, who was who, what their jobs were, what exactly they were doing here. He had already deduced that these "students" did not have official government approval and were unsure how this sit-in, if you could call it that, was going to play. If they were going to be chased out of the embassy, which Daugherty still believed was the most likely outcome, they wouldn't want to have American blood on their hands.

Still, his interrogator seemed to know that Daugherty wasn't telling the truth. He had already learned from someone that Daugherty was CIA. How could he be simply a junior foreign service officer when no one else had such a giant vault in his office, not even Bruce Laingen, who was supposedly in charge? His questioner pointed out that Daugherty's age disproved his claim of subordinate status—he was six or seven years older than most of the junior staff members. He wanted Daugherty to confess that he was running America's "spy operations" in Iran. And he wanted him to open the vault. There was a clicking noise coming from inside it that sounded like it might be someone tapping on an electric typewriter. The Iranians were convinced that someone was communicating with Washington from inside, and they were determined to open it and find out.

Daugherty forced himself to laugh at the suggestion that he was secretly in charge, but inwardly he was stunned by how rapidly they had homed in on him. Was it only a coincidence? Did they know he was CIA? If they knew, how did they know?

He kept talking.

"I *am* just a junior officer," he said. "I've only been here for less than two months. You can verify that. You guys have my wallet. Go look at my embassy ID card, it's got the date of issue in it, which was a couple of days after I arrived. They checked me in through the border control at the airport, go pull up my arrival card."

"Are you sure you didn't sneak in?"

"Go to the personnel section, look at my arrival date."

"We will."

"Go to the airport authorities and check there. You've got my passport."

"These documents can be faked. You can pay people off to get them."

"Talk to the Iranians who work here at the embassy," Daugherty suggested. "Ask them when I came."

"Well, who do you know in the embassy?"

"I hardly know anybody."

"Where have you been in Iran?"

"I've been to a couple of restaurants in town, and I've been, as your records will show, I've been with the chargé down at the Ministry of Defense a couple of times and to the Foreign Ministry. But otherwise I'm in the apartment building right behind the embassy. I haven't had time to find my way around. I'm just here, this is a new job for me, what do I know?"

Daugherty talked about how he had just finished his doctoral studies in California. It was all true . . . mostly. He said the man who normally had that office was in the United States—indeed, the senior field officer had left on home leave only weeks before—and that he was the only one he had ever seen open the vault. He had no idea himself.

He had been standing for a long time. At one point he said he had to use the toilet and, much to his surprise, the questions stopped and he was led down the hall to the bathroom. He used the toilet and then splashed water on his face and collected his thoughts.

When he returned the interrogator pressed harder about the vault. He never raised his voice but he wanted the vault opened.

Daugherty tried to fight back with indignation. The invasion and interrogation were against all rules of diplomatic behavior. He demanded to be returned to his colleagues and that they all be released. He knew it was ridiculous of him to be making demands, but he said anything that came into his head to change the subject.

The truth was, of course, that it *was* his office and he did know how to open the vault. There wasn't anything in it, so far as he knew, that merited a heroic defense. But unlike the State Department, the spy agency had a strict culture of secrecy. No documents were kept at the embassy beyond thirty days, and the rule specified that the amount of files should not exceed a pile that could be destroyed in thirty minutes. The most sensitive material was kept in the larger coms vault, where Ahern and the others had locked themselves. That morning, as soon as the embassy grounds were invaded, Daugherty had emptied the four safes in his own vault and personally passed all of it through a shredder. He had left the shredded paper in a big pile on the floor when he had closed the door on it earlier. He had thought about flipping a match into the pile but he decided against it, figuring this demonstration would probably be over in a few hours and he didn't want to damage the interior of the vault. How could a government allow a bunch of college kids to seize a foreign embassy, the embassy of a country that had been so important to it, a country that, to consider only the practical concerns, was holding more than six billion dollars of Iran's assets in military contracts? To grab the embassy made no sense. If the contracts were to be canceled, then the money would have to be returned. These were matters that required discussion, planning . . . the kind of things embassies did. When a country was unhappy with another nation's diplomatic mission, that country's authorities simply ordered diplomatic personnel to leave. It happened all the time. But to seize the embassy, these buildings and twenty-seven acres, at the risk of forfeiting billions . . . how would that figure? It was self-defeating beyond belief. If this was all going to be over in a few hours, Daugherty didn't want to be known as the guy who panicked and burned down an American embassy. So he hadn't thrown the match.

He knew there was no overwhelming reason to keep them out of the vault, except his reluctance to cooperate. But now his cover story depended on it. If they found out now that he could open it, they would know he had been lying to them. He kept insisting that he didn't know how.

The interrogator left. Daugherty was led into the agency secretary's office and his blindfold was removed. He was surrounded now by an angry group, about a dozen men, all of them a lot smaller than he, very young—they looked like college students—wearing the standard jeans and army jackets or worn sweaters, with long hair and beards or half beards. Several had automatic weapons, including Uzi machine pistols.

What looked like the eldest of the group, one with a .38 pistol, ordered him to open the vault.

"I just got here. I don't know how," said Daugherty.

This set them off. Now they were all shouting at him at once, waving weapons.

"Open the vault!" one of them screamed at him.

"I can't open it, I can't open it," Daugherty told them.

Voices were heard shouting down the hall. He smelled smoke and heard gunshots from somewhere on the grounds. Something was burning inside the building. The crowd noise outside seemed to have grown louder, even though it was now nearly two in the morning. It all notched up his sense of alarm.

One of the young men with an Uzi, a teenager, then pointed at the secretary's desk.

"Who sits here?" he asked.

"A secretary."

"Can *she* open it?"

"Like I said before, she's the other guy's secretary. I don't know. I've never seen her open it. I don't think she can open it. She never came in that office. I don't think she knows how to open it."

"Go get the secretary," the elder of the group told one of the others, in English. "Go bring her up here."

That did it for Daugherty. He had carried on the charade as long as he could. He did not want to subject the woman to this scene. Daugherty had a courtly manner with women, and the idea of putting the secretary—even if she was a CIA employee—in this position was not acceptable to him. She was not getting paid to take the same risks that he was taking. He was not going to let them bring that woman up here and subject her to their guns and threats. She was just a secretary, and tended to be fairly high strung.

"No, leave her be," he said. "I'll open it for you."

And he did. They would know he had been lying to them but he would simply have to deal with the consequences.

He got a big laugh out of the astonished looks on their faces when they swung open the unlocked door. It was empty, lined with open safes with drawers hanging out, and a pile of shredded paper on the floor. The clicking sound had been coming from the door's alarm system, which had been set improperly. They looked at him as if he were crazy and then pushed him across the room, shoving him hard in the back.

"Who was in the vault?" one of them demanded. "Who shredded the paper?"

Minutes later, deposited in the chair behind the secretary's desk, he watched a parade of Iranians file into his office for a look in the vault. They moved in groups, silently, shuffling through papers that were scattered across the floor, moving around him as though he wasn't there. Among them were three junior clerics in turbans, one in a powder blue robe, another in cherry red, and the other slate gray, all wearing Reebok athletic shoes. They stopped to stare at Daugherty, no doubt, he thought, looking for horns on his forehead. He glared back at them with contempt. When he was left alone, he saw a pack of matches on the secretary's desk and again considered setting fire to the drapes. He decided against it.

When the line of gapers ended, Daugherty's group of young tormentors lifted him and threw him against the wall alongside another safe. He had been told when he first arrived that no one knew the combination for that safe; it had been lost in one of the changeovers of personnel. The secretary had been using the safe as a plant stand.

"Open it!" the leader demanded. One of the younger men had his Uzi pointed at Daugherty's belly. He noticed that the gun's safety was off.

"I can't," he said.

"You said you couldn't open the vault and you did, so open the safe," the young man said.

"This one I really can't open."

"Open it or I will shoot you," he said.

"Okay, go ahead and shoot," Daugherty said.

They were stumped. It was not the answer they had expected. He saw them looking at one another, as if to say, *Okay, what do we do now?* The young man with the Uzi had a look on his face that Daugherty interpreted as a mental shrug.

"What about the secretary?" the leader suggested. It had worked before, and at the suggestion they all stared at him, waiting for him to capitulate again.

"Okay, bring her up," Daugherty said. "I don't care. She can't open it either."

At that they gave up. They didn't send for the secretary. Instead, Daugherty was blindfolded again and led back across the compound. He felt like sunrise must be close, but he could see out of the edges of his blindfold that it was still dark. He was taken to the residence dining room and placed in a wooden chair. At the center of the room was a long table, a beautiful piece of furniture made of highly polished maple, which one of the invaders had apparently marred deliberately with a long, nasty scratch down the center. Around the table were eight other hostages, including Ahern and Golacinski.

They were not kept blindfolded or tied, and one of the students guarding them offered cigarettes. Daugherty had not smoked in months. He had picked up the habit as a teenager and had all but given it up when he went to Vietnam, where he had resumed it, figuring tobacco couldn't be any more dangerous than the missions he was flying. He had since, after considerable effort, at last given it up. But somehow these circumstances seemed to demand a cigarette, and he smoked one after another for an hour or so until he and the others were ordered to get up off their chairs and onto the floor to sleep.

Daugherty curled up around the foot of his chair, and awoke with his head throbbing, sick to his stomach. He asked to be taken to the toilet and retched up what little he had in his stomach. His head was pounding, and the taste of the tobacco was in his mouth and throat. All their captors would say was that they would be released "when the shah is returned." That and "Don't speak." The mobs outside still sounded as if they numbered in the hundreds of thousands, and kept up a constant, bloodthirsty din. However this embassy takeover would play in the rest of the world, in this city it was clearly a hit. He fell asleep eventually, even though his butt hurt from sitting in the same position for so long. He woke up some hours later feeling slightly better but foolish. What if he was taken for interrogation again, or saw an opportunity to escape? Had he weakened himself by his own stupidity? As the world awoke to the second day of a crisis in Tehran, Daugherty sat on a chair feeling stiff, sore, and ill, one of sixty-three Americans at the eye of an international storm, furious with himself for smoking cigarettes.

15

AN ISLAND OF STABILITY

Across a continent and a wide ocean, at roughly the same time that Iranian students had gathered in the Tehran morning rain for their bold intrusion, a different and more professional assault was being launched on a dark runway in a remote corner of Fort Stewart, a sprawling preserve of Georgia forest immediately west of Savannah. A parked Boeing 727 and a fortified building nearby were loudly and violently raided by two squadrons of seasoned, handpicked American soldiers. The exercise featured "hostages" and "hijackers," played by volunteers from the FBI and military intelligence units. On both sides of the plane, from padded ladders that had been stealthily leaned against the outer frame, the raiders blew off aircraft doors from the outside, tossed flashbang grenades, and then invaded, while at the same time across the tarmac others burst through doors and windows of the building. In a sudden crescendo of noise and confusion, the hostage takers were confused and overwhelmed by agile men moving with practiced speed and expert violence. The takedowns were the final and most dramatic exercise in a days-long official demonstration by Delta Force, a new army special operations unit. Observing the exercises were top government and military officials, including Army Chief of Staff General Edward C. Meyer and emissaries from the equivalent special forces units in England, France, and West Germany. Delta Force hadn't just passed the test, it had wowed the panel. The American military officially had a new tool in its arsenal.

That success had crowned two years of hard work by Colonel Charlie Beckwith, the unit's founder, his operations officer Major Lewis H. "Bucky" Burruss, squadron commanders Logan Fitch and Pete Schoomaker, and their approximately eighty men. The colonel and his top officers sat up until after midnight at the motel in Hinesville with several visiting generals, reviewing the exercise, drinking, unwinding, and celebrating. These were men who worked hard and drank hard, and they shared a strong feeling of accomplishment. They were eager to put their rough talent to work in the real world. At about half past two in the morning the group went out together for an early breakfast, and then at last came back to the motel to sleep. Many of them had been up for several days.

For Beckwith this was the capstone of his military career. A gruff, take-charge man, he had been preaching the virtues of a small, secret, unorthodox team of operatives for more than fifteen years, a force that could be deployed quickly in small numbers for very specific, difficult, and often dangerous tasks. The idea was at first a nonstarter in the army, in part because it created a privileged corps outside the normal chain of command that would get all the most daring and interesting missions, the kinds of missions that made and advanced ambitious officers' careers. Beckwith's personality hadn't helped. He was a difficult man, proud, tough, and at times arrogant and capricious, traits aggravated when he drank, which was often. A chain-smoker, he had mastered the art of keeping a cigarette dangling from his lips with up to an inch and a half of ash hanging precariously. Trailing the colonel around was an obsequious adjutant, a captain who smoothed his path and flattered him constantly, much to the annoyance of the men who worked most closely with him, who didn't feel Beckwith's ego needed encouragement. He disdained the often necessary rigmarole of army life, and his personal arrogance showed itself in constant run-ins with regular army officers, those who ranked above him and below, whom he tended to consider idiots until proven otherwise. Beckwith believed he and his men were engaged in the nation's most serious and important work, and even though it was entirely secret, anyone who failed to immediately recognize their claims to priority was considered a boob, an incompetent, or worse. If an army officer in Germany with the job of getting the colonel's possessions shipped back to the States persisted in trying to locate him—after Beckwith had mysteriously disappeared—his efforts made him, to the colonel, not annoyingly efficient but a "numb nuts." And God help the MP at Fort Bragg who failed to recognize Beckwith—he rarely wore uniform or insignia—and refused to let him immediately pass; the colonel would threaten to bust the man's rank.

He had the bureaucratic finesse of a middle linebacker. He looked like one, too, a broad, thick, active man whose short hair had gone white but whose dramatic, expressive eyebrows had not. The colonel was impulsive, demanding, fearless, and legendarily tough—as an officer in Vietnam he had survived being shot in the gut with a .51 caliber round, large enough to poke a hole the size of a grapefruit in cinder block. He was also breathtakingly impolitic. A year before this final Delta evaluation, at a time when the concept of such a force was still controversial, the newly assembled teams were forced by skeptical brass to take a proficiency test that they easily passed. Instead of leaving well enough alone, the surly colonel had taken the occasion to lambaste the generals who had demanded the exercise, accusing them of trying to undermine him. He had only one method and one speed. He was the kind of officer who everybody knew was important, but who was destined to retire as a colonel. And despite his down-home, just-folks manner, he was a determined elitist. He considered himself to be the best, and wanted a force composed of men just like himself. This was neither a man nor a dream calculated to win allies, especially in an organization as tradition-bound and formally hierarchical as the U.S. Army.

But events had finally caught up to Beckwith's fixed idea. The rash of airplane hijackings, the successful Israeli hostage-rescue missions at Entebbe, Uganda, in 1976, and the successful takedown of a hijacked airliner in Somalia by German special forces in the following year had all combined to make the case for a hostage-rescue force. After the Somalia rescue, President Carter had written a note to the joint chiefs asking, "Do we have the same capability as the West Germans?"

It turned out the American military did not. Patterned after the British Special Air Service (SAS), considered the premier counterterrorism force in the world, Beckwith and his staff had handpicked skilled, experienced soldiers, many of them Vietnam veterans, and had put them through a grueling selection process. The men chosen had demonstrated not only superior physical, mental, and basic soldiering talent, but had passed psychological tests and rigorous interviews designed specifically to weed out the macho supersoldiers such an elite, secret force might be expected to attract, what would eventually be called "Rambo types." Field testing for the army's special forces typically involved assessing a candidate's endurance and ability to handle stress. Delta deliberately added elements of confusion and uncertainty designed to break down a candidate's self-confidence. He would be dropped off in a remote area with directions to proceed cross-country alone and on foot to a distant point on the map, carrying a heavy rucksack. Without a time frame, only "Get there quickly," he was left to work against the clock without knowing what standard he was expected to meet. On arrival, hours later, he was curtly given a new destination. This went on for as long as the selection staff wished. For the candidate, there was no finish line; he kept going until he was told to stop. He would be deliberately driven to physical exhaustion, a point that marathon runners recognize as the place where a body has used up all of its fuel and begins feeding on itself. Yet unlike the marathon runner, who begins the race knowing where the finish line is and what time he wants to beat, the Delta candidate just kept going. They were never given an indication they were doing well; in fact, often they were deliberately led to believe that they were failing, just to make continuing that much more difficult.

After Logan Fitch, a tall, taciturn Texan, had hiked from rendezvous point to rendezvous point for days, he was finally told, "Get on the truck," and driven back to the unit's camp. He was left there without a word of explanation.

"What do I do?" he asked.

"Just stay here until we come and get you."

He spent a long depressing day, certain that he had been dropped from selection when just the opposite was true.

Many hard men cracked under treatment like this. If the physical demands didn't defeat them, the uncertainty did. Some foundered because they couldn't cope with operating alone in the wild for days on end. Their judgment failed them. Many of those who failed did so because they chose to give up.

It resulted in a different kind of military force, one in some ways starkly at odds with tradition. Armies had always been about teamwork, formal recognition for achievement, and a rigidly enforced hierarchy. Delta attracted men who preferred working alone, who shunned attention, and who had little patience for the protocol and rituals that defined military life. It was made up of mature, independent soldiers who had been chosen in part for their ability to function outside the chain of command. The unit's "operators," as they were called, or "shooters" (they disliked the term "commando"), dressed in civilian clothes, had civilian haircuts, and unless they were involved in a mission or exercise kept their own hours. When one of Beckwith's superiors floated the idea of coming down to Fort Bragg to do early morning physical exercises with the men, an honor for any other army unit, Beckwith had backhanded the gesture. It would be inconvenient, he responded. His men did not exercise together, but individually or in pairs, whenever they wished.

No matter how unpopular Beckwith and his unit were, however, they had cleared the army's last official hurdle. The colonel had gone to sleep shortly before dawn that morning with a sense of triumph.

Two hours later he was on the interstate back to Fort Bragg to begin the planning of Delta's first mission.

Beckwith was northbound on Interstate 95 when Hamilton Jordan arrived in Washington. The White House chief of staff had spent Saturday on Maryland's eastern shore at the home of a presidential friend and with two top members of Carter's reelection committee, plotting moves for the coming election year. The night before, he had received news that Senator Edward M. Kennedy, from whom President Carter expected a tough challenge in the coming Democratic primaries, had performed badly in a prime-time interview to air on CBS that night, stumbling over questions about his embarrassing role in the accidental drowning of a young woman ten years earlier at Chappaquiddick Island in Massachusetts. Despite that scandal, the Massachusetts senator had been an unofficial crown prince for almost two decades after the assassinations of his famous brothers, and was expected to announce his long-awaited campaign for the White House. Jordan hadn't seen the interview yet, but if the reports were true, then it was the kind of TV moment that might destroy Kennedy before he got started. Carter's longtime campaign manager, Jordan had gone to bed that night delighted with the news and scheming about how to capitalize on it. The call from the White House situation room awakened him at about four, informing him of the troubling events in Tehran.

Iran was not even on the radar as an important issue. Ever since World War Two, the oil-rich nation had figured prominently in American foreign affairs as a significant oil supplier and a bulwark against Soviet ambitions in the Middle East. On New Year's Eve in 1977, Carter had toasted the shah of Iran at a state dinner in Tehran, calling him "an island of stability" in that region. He had also saluted the ruler's "wisdom," "judgment," "sensitivity," and "insight," words that stuck in the craw of human rights activists in and out of Iran, who knew the shah as a patronizing dictator who employed brutal methods to suppress dissent and political opposition. It had been an uncharacteristic moment in Carter's term, because during his campaign and in office he had made morality a controversial priority in his foreign policy.

In style and character, the Georgia peanut farmer's administration could not have been more different than the Pahlavi monarchy. Carter came from rural Georgia, and despite his background as a naval officer in the nuclear submarine command he sold himself as a man with humble roots. His election in 1976 was in part a national purging of the Watergate scandal. Public distrust of the nation's traditional governing, ruling class was at its height, and the humble peanut farmer who promised he would never tell a lie to the American people had looked like an attractive alternative. His political cabinet was made up primarily of men like Jordan and press secretary Jody Powell, fellow Georgians who had been with him through the years he had served as governor of that state. They were exemplars of the modern South, with unpretentious good ole boy manners, first-rate educations, and solid liberal ideals. Carter was the latest beneficiary of the American electorate's occasional need to scratch a populist itch, a citizen president, shunning the trappings of power, right down to refusing a limousine and walking from the inaugural stand to the White House on the day he assumed office, making a point of carrying his own luggage. The Machiavellian style of the Nixon-Kissinger years was out, and in was the simple decency of Carter's born-again Christian faith. The new president bent the long-standing priority of containing communism, which had for decades justified American support and alliance with all manner of tyranny, to accommodate a stronger emphasis on human rights. Most recently and notably, he had withdrawn vital American support for Nicaraguan dictator Anastasio Somoza and, after he was chased from power, backed millions in aid to the leftist Sandinistas. Carter's rhetoric and actions had stirred hope to many in Third World countries, including those in Iran who wanted to oust the shah and form a truly representative government. Carter had dashed those hopes with that effusive televised toast at the state dinner in Tehran. It had been a mere formality for the president, a perfunctory salute to a longtime American ally, but the words carried tremendous significance in Iran. To the percolating revolutionists, America had once again chosen sides against the people. It marked Carter as a hypocrite and an enemy.

As tyrants go, Mohammed Reza Pahlavi was fairly tame. He was a timid, vain, vacillating man with good intentions who had been raised to rule and who bought readily into the anachronistic notion of the divine right of kingship. But it wasn't Allah who had placed him on the throne; it was Kermit Roosevelt, the CIA's man in Tehran. Pahlavi's father had been elected Shah in 1925 four years after the military coup and ruled until Great Britain and the Soviet Union ousted him early in World War Two after he leaned openly toward Nazi Germany. The Allied powers occupied Iran during the war, commandeering the nation's vast oil supplies to fuel Stalin's fight against Hitler. The young Pahlavi was handed his father's throne because it was convenient to maintain the fiction of Iran's independence. Educated in Switzerland, the young king passed his time during those years as an unimaginably wealthy international playboy, and he probably never would have assumed real power were it not for the Western appetite for Iranian oil.

To his credit, the young shah had tried to mollify the outright plunder of his country's natural resources after the war by urging the United States and Great Britain to share the profits from selling Iranian oil with Iran. Still just a figurehead leader, he argued that letting his country keep half of the profits would underwrite domestic prosperity and undercut the gathering socialist and nationalist political movements. The idea was rejected out of hand by the powerful Anglo-Iran Oil Company, one of the richest private corporations in the world. Outraged Iranians rallied behind the odd but charismatic Mohammed Mossadeq, a dour, frail, but principled descendant of the family that had ruled Iran for almost two hundred years before the Pahlavi family seized power. Voted prime minister by the Majlis in 1951, Mossadeq immediately did what the shah would never have dared; he defied the great powers by enforcing nationalization of the oil industry. The move was hugely popular at home and so potentially world-altering—a Third World country asserting ownership of its own resources—that *Time* magazine named Mossadeq its "Man of the Year." In a speech before the United Nations, Mossadeq said, "The oil resources of Iran, like its soil, its rivers and mountains, are the property of the people of Iran." While self-evident, the concept proved much too bold. The financial interests of the Anglo-Iran Oil Company and America's concern that Mossadeq would drift further toward a centralized socialist system and into the Soviet sphere combined to inspire a coup d'état, which was ordered by President Dwight D. Eisenhower and (with perhaps fewer pangs of conscience) by Britain's most famous diehard colonialist, Prime Minister Winston Churchill.

The young Pahlavi was perfectly situated to legitimize this plot. Through nearly all of its history, reaching back to ancient Persia, the country had been ruled by kings called "shah." Pahlavi's father had assumed power after ousting the nearly two-hundred-year-old Qajar dynasty, but assumed the title "shah" only with the approval of Iran's Congress, the *Majlis*. In those years, Iran was gradually evolving into a representative democracy, and the ouster of the elder shah during the war had speeded that transition. Mossadeq's popularity made it appear as though the young shah would remain an honorary figure at best. Roosevelt preyed upon Pahlavi's vanity and royal presumption by offering him "full" power (Iran would remain, of course, America's client state). The shah's support would give an authentic Iranian imprimatur to what was in truth a foreign-backed coup, enabling America to claim it was "rescuing" the government, not overturning it. A more honorable, selfless man would have said no.

Pahlavi said yes. Roosevelt shuttled back and forth to meetings with the shah in 1953, hidden in the backseat of a car under blankets, plotting to dismantle Iran's elected government and hand full power to him. By then, Mossadeq had been weakened politically by the financial fallout from nationalization; Iran lacked the know-how and resources to profitably operate its oil pumping and refining plants. Its customers found new suppliers, and economic stagnation set in. The affluent upper class that had profited under the old oil arrangements, including military leaders, had grown increasingly impatient with this radical nationalist experiment. Mossadeq turned in vain to the Eisenhower administration for help in brokering a deal with the British that would restart its oil industry under Iranian supervision. Instead, Washington decided to shove the vulnerable old man offstage.

Roosevelt orchestrated street demonstrations and a campaign of false stories in the Iranian press against Mossadeq, and systematically bought off military leaders, who arrested the prime minister on trumped-up charges of treason (he was convicted and after a three-year term in prison remained under house arrest until his death in 1967). During the days of the actual coup, the shah fled to Rome with his wife until it was safe to return—"to avoid bloodshed," he said, most conspicuously his own—and then assumed the throne offered on a platter by his American friends, adorning himself

"Light of the Aryans" and with pomp befitting a position known histori-cally as the "Peacock Throne." The new regime was offered a far better deal on oil revenues, and the shah promised nothing less than the com-plete modernization of his country in his lifetime, to make it the finan-cial and cultural equal of Europe. The United States subsidized this Pahlavian fantasy, cynically betraying its democratic principles in the name of containing communism and facilitating the uninterrupted flow of oil. And to some extent it worked, most of all for the United States. The shah's Iran helped keep the Soviet Bear from Middle East oil supplies and pro-vided a strong guarantee of Western access. Roosevelt's successful plot became the textbook CIA-engineered coup, and its fame spread well be-yond the secret walls of Langley, Virginia. An article by Richard and Gladys Harkness, in the 1954 *Saturday Evening Post* (widely reprinted in Iran), laid out the whole scheme as a clever American triumph against the creeping Red Menace. It made Roosevelt a legend in the world of clan-destine operations. Nearly a quarter of a century later Carter would be toasting the elaborately bedecked, gray-haired shah's "stability."

Eventually the shah did wrest billions in oil profits for his nation and presided over several decades of relative prosperity, empowering women and moving his country away from literal adherence to the Koran. His rule became increasingly strict and self-assured as he became more and more self-deceived, believing that God Almighty was behind the squalid machi-nations that had placed him in power, and that his state decisions, being divinely inspired, were infallible. "My visions were miracles that saved the country," he boasted to Italian journalist Oriana Fallaci in a series of in-terviews two decades after the coup. With American help he had blossomed into an openly arrogant monarch, proud of his unflinching willingness to shoot dissidents, convinced of the inherent inferiority of Western-style democracy. He presided over a military large and modern enough to rival Israel's but wasted billions on ill-conceived economic schemes. Despite his "expert" personal reconstruction of Iran's economy and culture, the majority of his people stayed poor, and remained devout. Land reforms improved agricultural production, but not fast enough for Iran's mush-rooming urban population, and by the mid-1970s more than 40 percent of its people were undernourished. Oil wealth fed urban enclaves of educated, Westernized, well-connected citizens, loyal to the regime, but the dispar-ity between this small affluent class and the majority of Iranians was vast and growing. By the twentieth year of his reign, the shah was deeply unpopular, reviled by Iran's educated class as a tyrant and American puppet and by the multitudes of poor and uneducated for his efforts to dismantle their religious traditions. As discontent grew, the usual cycle of repression and rebellion set in. The shah relied more and more on SAVAK, his secret police, to root out and smash rebellion, which spread discontent and turned it into hatred. Dissident mullahs such as the Ayatollah Khomeini, too popular to imprison or kill, were exiled.

Carter's natural inclination was to knock the shah down a peg by insisting on democratic reforms in Iran, but the country's geopolitical importance and the uncertain prospect of what might come after the monarchy counseled a warm outward acceptance of the status quo. In private, the shah was pushed to make his country more tolerant and liberal, and he responded with democratic gestures that had the unintended effect of uncapping decades of suppressed anger. As Iranians tasted new freedom to express themselves, the volume of protest grew and the population was further emboldened. Long-simmering economic problems came to a boil. There were crippling strikes and a mounting series of humiliating and threatening street demonstrations that the shah dared not ruthlessly suppress. No one opposition faction had the power to remove him, but together they were unstoppable. By 1978 the Peacock Throne was teetering. Not that American intelligence and military assessments realized it; it was uniformly predicted that the shah would weather the storm.

What the Western intelligence reports missed was the awakening giant of traditional Islam, a grassroots rebellion against the values of the secular, modern world. The rise of Khomeini and the mullahocracy took everyone by surprise. The turbaned classes were overlooked because they were considered vestiges, representatives of a fading ancient world. But away from the affluent, Westernized neighborhoods where American diplomats and visiting military officers lived and visited, the mullahs had been building a national network of mosques, which waited patiently for the moment Islam would rise up and smite the infidels and their puppet king. The true believers found unlikely allies among the more worldly socialists and nationalists of the middle and upper classes. Support for change grew openly on college campuses, and even among the vast military bureaucracy that maintained the shah's war machine. In this, Iran's secular rebels underestimated the mullahs. They saw in the mosque network a useful method of rallying huge public displays and giving their movement muscle, but assumed the ayatollahs would retire to Qom after the revolution and tend to strictly spiritual matters. United in their hatred of the shah, they accomplished the revolution that one State Department official had called "unthinkable." Sick with cancer, the shah, along with his family, had flown out of Iran in February 1979, never to return.

Nine months later, the crisis seemed to have passed. In Washington, the collapse of the Peacock Throne had been a shock and a blow, but from all appearances the mullahs and other factions involved were feuding too badly to agree on what to do next. And despite the steady stream of anti-American rhetoric from Khomeini and lesser Iranian leaders, there were signs that the practical value of a working relationship with the United States was beginning to offset ideological objections. In the previous month, the country had accepted Bruce Laingen's appointment as chargé d'affaires, resumed importation of spare parts for its American-built jets, and unofficially initiated closer ties—Prime Minister Bazargan's unscheduled meeting with Brzezinski in Algiers. Carter knew that allowing the shah into America would set back these gains, but despite an immediate outpouring of anger none of the dire predictions had come to pass. By this first week of November, the shah was recovering from surgery in a New York hospital and Iran had become just one of many troubling situations around the world, one that seemed to require observation more than management.

More pressing for Carter and his inner circle was the coming election. Going into that contest, the administration's foreign policy record was counted a strength. Chief among Carter's successes had been the hard-won Camp David accords, which had ended years of hostility between Egypt and Israel and placed on more hopeful footing the seemingly implacable Arab-Israeli conflict. There was also the historic new nuclear arms pact with the Soviet Union (the Strategic Arms Limitation Agreement). At its essence, the Cold War was an ideological clash stalled on the doorstep of an annihilating nuclear exchange, and for decades most experts feared the most likely trigger would be war in the Middle East. With its vital oil resources, both the communist and capitalist worlds had a huge stake in the region's local disputes, so any time there was war in that part of the world there was the overarching fear that it could escalate and engulf the planet. Carter's efforts had made that prospect less likely.

The frightening potenial for an all-out nuclear war, however, is what first occurred to Jordan when he heard the news of the embassy takeover. If it meant the United States would be going to war against Iran, how would Moscow react? Where would that lead? The possibilities were scary, but upon reflection the episode, while an outrage, appeared less portentous. When the embassy had been overrun in February, it had taken only a few hours for the country's provisional government to chase off the invaders; it had behaved very responsibly. There was every reason to think this would happen again. Ties between the United States and the interim authority had marginally improved, and Iran's best interests, always the most reliable guide to a nation's actions, dictated a swift and peaceful resolution. Jordan decided against calling the president. As he drove into Washington a few hours later he was disappointed to find that the talk on the radio was all about Tehran instead of about the pending Kennedy interview.

National Security Adviser Zbigniew Brzezinski presented a measured assessment of the crisis at a meeting with the president and vice president later that morning, and chaired the first session of a newly constituted Special Coordinating Committee, formed to deal with the situation in Tehran. There he heard CIA director Stansfield Turner explain that the spy agency was not even sure which faction in Iran's roiling political pot was responsible. Turner, an admiral who had been a classmate of the president's at Annapolis, was embarrassed by his agency's lack of sources and access in Iran; the most reliable information was coming from news reports, as there was a significant international news presence in Tehran, including several American newspaper reporters and the BBC. Yet no one seemed to know who was behind the attack. Because they didn't know for sure what was going on, all agreed that caution in public statements would be wise—an angry or belligerent response might alienate a potential ally. The committee decided to send two special emissaries to Tehran immediately to explore a resolution and resolved to ask two prominent Americans who might be viewed favorably by the revolutionary powers there: former U.S. attorney general Ramsey Clark and William Miller, staff director for the Senate Select Committee on Intelligence. A frequent critic of American foreign policy, Clark had befriended many anti-shah Iranians living in the United States prior to the revolution and in the previous year had marched with anti-shah protesters, and Miller some years earlier had protested America's relationship with Iran's monarch by resigning as political section chief in Tehran, the same position now held by Vic Tomseth. After deciding on emissaries, Brzezinski's committee took up other options. What impact might it have on international oil supplies? Iran was responsible for only about 4 percent of the oil imported to the United States, a percentage that could be readily made up from other sources, so there wasn't much concern that the incident would return the nation to gas lines and rationing. What countersteps might the government take against Iranian diplomats and the thousands of Iranians living in the United States? What punitive measures might be taken? How feasible was a rescue attempt?

To address this last question, a special group consisting of Turner and joint chiefs chairman General David Jones met with Brzezinski afterward in his office. They agreed to set up a planning group immediately to figure out what, if anything, the military could do. The wiry, Polish-born intellectual was more cold-blooded about foreign affairs and American power than the president and most of his advisers. Carter had apprenticed himself to the former Harvard professor a decade earlier when he first began considering a run for the White House, in recognition of his shortcomings in this area, and had called himself Brzezinski's "eager student." He had installed his tutor at his right shoulder in the White House, where Brzezinski was the voice of experience and hard-edged realism in an often idealistic inner circle. The national security adviser was the son of Polish diplomat Tadeusz Brzezinski, and living abroad with his family as a boy he had watched the Nazis come to power in Germany in the 1930s and, later, lived in Moscow during the years when Stalin was at the height of his murderous rule. His home country had been conquered twice in the ensuing world conflict and was still a Soviet satellite. Educated in Canada and at Harvard, Brzezinski knew foreign policy as a "game for grown-ups," as he put it, and knew that sometimes the imperatives of state, driven as they were by the vital interests of millions, could not be swayed by concern for the well-being of individuals trapped in the wrong place at the wrong time. He was something of an anomaly in Carter's inner circle, but was placed there for precisely that reason. Even though he wanted various military options explored, Brzezinski was initially confident that this outrage in Tehran would swiftly be put right by the Iranian authorities.

Across town, on the seventh floor of the State Department building, Iran Desk chief Henry Precht held a less sanguine view, especially when word reached Washington that Khomeini had endorsed the action. He suspected this meant they were in for a long standoff. The Iranian "promise" that the White House was leaning on so heavily had been tentative at best. Precht had been in the room in Tehran when it was given, after he had personally informed the provisional leadership of Carter's decision to admit the shah.

It was at that meeting that Ibrahim Yazdi had predicted trouble. He had said, "We'll do our best . . . we'll do what we can."

It was hardly an ironclad assurance. Now, with Khomeini backing the students, Precht knew Bazargan's government would be powerless.

He had heard about the embassy takeover in his car, driving home from upstate New York on Sunday with his wife after a day visit with their son at Colgate University. He had gone straight into the office, where he had helped set up the crisis room, right around the corner from the office of Secretary of State Cyrus Vance. It was equipped with a long table and lines of telephones and telex machines.

Precht was asked to draft a letter from President Carter to Khomeini, something that could be hand-delivered by Clark and Miller. The standing instructions for such letters was that they be written with the expectation that they would be leaked, that they would soon appear on the front page of the *New York Times,* which meant, Precht knew, that the White House would want to sound tough. The mood in the country was angry. But from what he knew about Iran he doubted tough talk would help. In Shia Iran, the threat to spill blood only played into the country's fetish for martyrdom. Khomeini would almost certainly call America's bluff, and Carter would then be compelled to act. Precht counted many friends among those now tied to chairs in Tehran, and he knew that any American military action would likely mean death for some or all of them. He had talked some of those Americans into taking postings in Tehran, including one junior consulate officer who had told him during his last visit there that things were "crazy" and that they all ought to come home. Precht had reassured him, as well as plenty of the others. Now he felt personally responsible for their safety. His draft of the letter to Khomeini struck a conciliatory tone, one that acknowledged the legitimacy of some of Iran's grievances and that was less concerned with expressing American indignation than with persuasion. He wanted to convince the imam, not confront him.

The letter would get a stern reworking by Brzezinski, but remained a remarkably restrained document. It contained neither threats nor concessions. America wished to reopen a dialogue with Iran and to restore friendly ties. The shah would stay in the United States until his treatment was finished but there were assurances that the stay would be temporary, and to offset suspicion that he had been admitted for reasons other than medical, Iranian authorities were offered access to the doctors treating him. The independence and territorial integrity of Iran were acknowledged, and the mutually beneficial possibility of reestablishing a military supply relationship was mentioned, but in the final draft there was no hint of Precht's "legitimate grievances." It read, in part:

> In the name of the American people, I ask that you release unharmed all Americans presently detained in Iran and those held with them and allow them to leave your country safely and without delay. I ask you to recognize the compelling humanitarian reasons, firmly based in international law, for doing so.
>
> I have asked both men to meet with you and to hear from you your perspective on events in Iran and the problems which have arisen between our two countries. The people of the United States desire to have relations with Iran based upon equality, mutual respect and friendship.

Clark and Miller were invited to the White House, and indirect contacts with Ayatollah Mohammed Behesti, head of the Revolutionary Council, indicated that if these two men came as Carter's personal emissaries—unlike the formal American mission in Tehran—they would be politely received.

This mission was supposed to remain top secret, but Richard Valeriani, who covered the State Department for NBC, found out. A veteran on the beat who had traveled the world with Henry Kissinger, Valeriani had gotten to know people in the State Department office who handled the logistics of official travel. On the hunch that the White House would be sending an emissary to Iran, he called up the office and pretended to know there was a mission afoot.

"Do you know yet who is going?" he asked his friend.

"Ramsey Clark," the source said, "and some other guy." As Valeriani scribbled, the man turned away from the phone and yelled across his office, "Who's going to Tehran with Clark?" Then he came back on the line. "Bill Miller," he said.

Valeriani took the scoop to Hodding Carter, the State Department spokesman, for confirmation.

"You can't use that story," Carter told him.

Valeriani had already alerted his bosses in New York, who were excited to have it first. Valeriani said he didn't think he could stop them, so the White House intervened with top executives to hold the story.

"We don't have formal permission yet for them to land in Tehran," explained Carter. "If you run the story tonight, it will make it look like we are putting pressure on them. It could kill the mission."

NBC agreed to sit on the story, but not for long.

16

TWO MINUTES OF HATE

Monday morning brought sunshine to Tehran. It slanted in through the tall windows of the ambassador's residence, which was now crowded with Iranian guards and blindfolded Americans tied to chairs or beds or scattered on floors everywhere. In fewer than twenty-four hours the carefully planned demonstration had stirred an international storm. Protests would come from most of the world's nations, but there was also approval. The embassy seizure had tapped a well of Muslim resentment that stretched well beyond the borders of Iran. In practical terms it was nothing more than a cheap shot—the embassy had been defenseless—but symbolically it was a major blow.

The students who had spent a cramped night with their hostages didn't understand this yet, but they could feel it. Overnight, with Khomeini's endorsement, they had become national heroes. It was as if they had captured a dragon. The jubilant throngs ferociously cheered as the embassy's new occupiers carried out trash in American flags or led an American out a door bound and blindfolded. Their glee rattled the walls and vibrated the floors. The crowd also acted as a human shield, protecting its new young champions from an anticipated American counterattack. The imam's decision to endorse the takeover had dramatically undercut the provisional government and strengthened the hand of religious radicals.

Inside the residence and at various other places where hostages were being held on the compound, the almost giddy mood of the first night had evaporated. After a traumatic day and night, the new morning brought a sense of heightened risk and darker consequences.

"No speak! No speak!" the guards kept shouting.

They seemed fearful, as though expecting an attack. Some of the hostages' chairs had been moved directly in front of windows, apparently to inhibit anyone trying to shoot their way in. Nearly all of the students were now armed, many with weapons they recovered from the embassy, and which they were unsure how to use or even hold safely. Some of the young men strutted triumphantly, cocking and recocking their new toys. The military men among the American captives cringed. They figured it was only a matter of time before there was an accident.

Joe Hall noticed that one guard across the dining room was casually cradling a shotgun that was pointed right at him. The guard even had his finger resting on the trigger as he chatted animatedly with one of his comrades. Hall finally got the attention of another guard, closer to him, and asked, "Could you ask that guy to point that thing somewhere else?"

The request was relayed to the guard with the shotgun, who immediately pointed it at the ceiling and gave Hall a sheepish smile.

In a sense, the enthusiastic endorsement of their action had called the students' bluff. The overwhelming acceptance of their act trapped them in it; rooted them in the spotlight. It was both exciting and frightening. The tension was evident in the way guards were now shouting at the hostages and treating them much more roughly. It alarmed Ibrahim Asgharzadeh, the tall young man with a neatly trimmed beard who had come up with the idea of seizing the embassy. He sensed that control of the event had already slipped out of his and the other students' hands, that powerful men had moved into position behind them. In their planning sessions, he and the other students had imagined something nonviolent and symbolic; they would treat the American captives gently and with respect while at the same time dramatizing to the whole world the offended sovereignty and dignity of Iran. Instead, some of the captives had been paraded blindfolded before threatening, jeering crowds. Some had been threatened with guns and roughed up. While he and the other original planners remained ostensibly in charge, the others they recruited, men like Mohammad Hashemi and his crew, the men with guns, seemed to be pursuing their own agenda. The demonstration had become something else, but they were not free to leave. History had them in its grip, protesters and hostages alike.

But most of the hostage takers basked in their sudden enormous popularity, at least for the first few days. They held press conferences at the embassy to display the piles of shredded documents, the smashed communications equipment in the vault, and the invisible ink kit they had found in Ahern's office. They were particularly thrilled with the Bubble. It all seemed to make a compelling case for the students' claim that the embassy had been engaged not in diplomacy but in espionage. Individual students took turns mounting the walls of the chancery to harangue the adoring multitudes and lead them in prayers. The various student committees scrambled to organize food preparation and living arrangements for the hostages, who it seemed they were going to be watching for longer than expected.

For the hostages, the anger many had felt in the first hours was largely overtaken by fear. They sat bound, blindfolded, and helpless, at the mercy of these young Iranians who seemed ill-organized, arrogant, and capable of anything. If they didn't turn their captives over to the bloodthirsty mob, they might lead them all out and shoot them—some hostages had been threatened with both possibilities. Then there was the prospect of being killed in the crossfire of an American rescue attempt.

John Limbert was discovering degrees of terror. The political officer with the shaggy hair and dark-rimmed glasses had come down from the intense fear he had felt on the chancery steps the day before, when he had tried vainly to negotiate. The night before, he had relaxed and even felt a certain professorial rapport with some of his captors. But this morning dawned with dark flutters of foreboding. He kept hearing the sound of helicopters overhead. Could they be American? Would President Carter attempt a rescue? The thought at once excited and terrified him, but then he thought, no, it wasn't possible. It's the sort of thing that happens only in the movies. Where would American helicopters come from? Tehran was too far from any air base where Americans would be able to launch such an assault.

Every new sound had an ominous implication. Just behind him he heard crumpling paper, and because he knew the custom was to pin a list of the condemned's crimes to his shirt before execution, he worried that such lists were being prepared.

Playing outside over a loudspeaker were the moody, ominous notes and brooding drums of Henry Purcell's "Music for the Funeral of Queen Mary," well known from the haunting electronic version in the movie *A Clockwork Orange*. The music formed a surreal backdrop to the viciously joyful chanting beyond the walls. The whole scene reminded Limbert of the "two minutes of hate" in George Orwell's novel *1984*, in which everyone stops for a brief period each day to publicly vent hatred for the country's enemy, the source of all fear and evil. These "two minutes," however, kept on hour after hour, and Limbert and his colleagues were the enemy.

Limbert tried to reason through his fear. There was nothing he could do. Either he would survive this or not. They would probably all be shot. That was the worst thing that could happen. Everyone dies. Perhaps this was his time. He decided that he had lived a good thirty-six years. He thought of his wife, Parvaneh, who was in Saudi Arabia with his children. They were no doubt worried about him. The prospect of their grief over his death pained him. Combined with the chanting and the soaring funereal music of Purcell, these thoughts were chilling. Then he had a different thought. He still had plane tickets to Saudi Arabia. He was scheduled to fly there on Friday for a visit. This thing would probably be over by then, and what a story he would have to tell! *God, I hope I'm out by then. I hope I make that flight.* Maybe the crumpling paper sounds he heard were just someone reading a newspaper. If they were going to be shot, that would be better than to be turned over to that crowd. They would surely be lynched or torn limb from limb. Such thoughts made him shake. He tried to stop worrying about it, since there was nothing he could do to influence matters. He worked at accepting whatever came, but as he waited his mind turned these thoughts over and over.

It seemed bitterly ironic that he, John Limbert, of all people, had come to such a spot. He *loved* Iran, arguably more than any other American. He had first visited in 1962 when his father was working for the U.S. Agency for International Development. A college student, he had felt instantly at home. Everything about the place had fascinated him, its people, its history, its culture, its language. Limbert was a language sponge, and Farsi he found deeply melodic and beautiful. When he graduated from college he joined the Peace Corps and returned. He taught for two years in Kurdistan, where he had met and married Parvaneh. He had come back to the States to get a Ph.D. in history at Harvard, and then the two returned to Shiraz, where Limbert finished his thesis and took a job teaching at the university. He had left that to join the foreign service, and, given his background, he was immediately asked if he would like to be assigned to Tehran. He declined, in part because he wanted to try something new, but also because he disapproved of the relationship between the United States and the shah. He did not want to be party to that policy.

Only after the shah's flight had he agreed to return, and when he did in August he had found the revolution's potential to be thrilling. In former years, political discussion in Iran had always been fearful and muted. When people spoke about issues and current events they did so in hushed tones and in language laden with double meanings. Now politics was a loud public obsession. There were at least a hundred different newspapers, each barking a different line, and the TV, radio, and coffeehouses were filled with discussion and argument. The country was remaking itself, riding a burst of emotion and creative power that had been suppressed for a generation. Everything about the country was up for grabs. A new Iran was struggling to take shape, and Limbert was delighted to help design America's new role in it.

At some point that first morning he was able to get a glimpse in the direction of the paper noise behind him and saw to his relief that one of his captors was reading a newspaper. Then the hostages were untied late in the afternoon, two at a time, and taken to the kitchen, where they were fed.

Limbert thought, *They probably wouldn't be feeding us if they were going to shoot us,* and that was a turning point. Gradually, he was able to untie the knot in his stomach. Late on the evening of the second day, a group of his captors approached him with a Super 8 movie camera and a small cassette tape recorder. One by one, they were questioning the men tied to chairs.

"What is your name?" Limbert was asked in English.

He told them.

"What do you do?"

"I am the second secretary."

That was all he said. The others in the room responded in the same way, offering only their name and job title.

As the night wore on, he and the others nagged at the guards to let them out of the chairs so that they could sleep, and eventually this was allowed. A long rope was used to tie their feet together; Limbert was bound this way to Charlie Jones. They stretched out on their backs on the floor, and for the first time in two days the second secretary dropped off into a heavy sleep.

*   *   *

Through that long second day there were still nine Americans attached to the embassy who were at large in Tehran. Kathryn Koob had waited out the beginning of the hostage crisis across the city at her Iran-America Society campus. After losing touch with the men in the embassy vault, she and her assistant Bill Royer and their staff had stayed on the phone with Washington all day and into the night, relaying whatever information they could find.

Koob was an officer in the International Communications Agency (ICA), a branch of the American foreign service (soon to be called the U.S. Information Agency) that dealt with cultural affairs. She was a big, wide, soft woman of prodigious energy and idealism, who brought a missionary zeal to her work. As she saw it, politics dealt with the things that kept people apart, but culture—theater, painting, literature—dealt with the things that tied all people together. She was an idealist but not a cockeyed one. She knew her effort to forge creative ties with this hate-filled new order would be fraught with difficulty. At her apartment she had a bag packed at all times in case there was an emergency evacuation, and she had sat in on the regular security briefing at the embassy where the practical risks had been evaluated. She and Bill Royer, who had arrived six weeks earlier, had been issued two-way radios to monitor the frequency used by the marine guards. In the event of an emergency they had been instructed not to call the embassy; it would only add to the confusion. So as their colleagues were taken hostage, Koob and Royer had stayed by the phones in Koob's office.

Close to midnight Mark and Cora Lijek, Bob Anders, and Kathy and Joe Stafford arrived. They had been among those who just walked away from the consulate and, unlike some of their less fortunate colleagues, had made it back to their apartments. They manned the society's little phone bank through the night while Koob and Royer got some sleep, curling up on couches. In the morning of the second day, the others left to link up with Lee Schatz, the agricultural attaché who had watched the takeover from his office in a high-rise across the street from the embassy and who was now being sheltered at the Swedish mission.

Suspecting that it was only a matter of time before her own complex would be overrun, Koob had some of the society's most important papers —those defining its status as an Iranian organization—removed to the home of one of her board members, and even arranged to have several rugs she had borrowed from a local merchant returned. She and Royer were both on the phone to Washington when a staff member interrupted at about one-thirty in the afternoon to say, "They're here."

They both knew immediately who "they" were.

Koob and Royer set down the phones, walked quickly down a back staircase, and left the building through a door to the parking lot. A secretary was waiting in a car, and she pulled out of the lot and into the busy street in front of the campus. As part of her preparations for this, Koob had phoned the West German Goethe Institute and had been assured of safe haven there by its director. The institute was only three blocks away, and she and Royer were received warmly. They sipped tea and discussed their next move when a secretary from the society called to say that the "students" who had come for her had left. So Koob and Royer went back to their own complex and once again successfully dialed up the connection to Washington.

She kept the line open until the students arrived again late that afternoon. Koob and Royer tried to sneak out the back door again with Lillian Johnson, one of the embassy secretaries who had been stranded at the airport the day before waiting for a flight home, but this time the students had surrounded the building.

Koob and Johnson hid in a basement lavatory, crouched silently in a toilet stall, but were eventually found. As the three were being driven through slow-moving traffic across Tehran toward the embassy, Koob contemplated jumping from the car with her colleagues and making a run for it, but she decided against it. Where would they go? In the present climate, if Iranians on the street saw Americans being pursued they might attack. The students in the front seat were talking softly to each other and she strained to listen. They were speaking in Arabic. They must have known she understood some Farsi.

As they approached the embassy neighborhood, Koob could hear the roar of the demonstrators outside. It was an ugly, hateful sound, "*Magbar Cartar! Magbar Ahmrika!*" Their car was enveloped by the mob as they approached the gates to the motor pool. Revolutionary Guards pushed the crowds back, but people leaned toward the car waving their fists, their faces twisted with hatred. One of the Iranians in the front seat triumphantly held up Royer's radio and briefcase to the guards at the gate, as if to say, *Look, we caught another American spy red-handed!*

They were let out of the car near the motor pool gate and advised to keep their heads down as they ran the short distance into the compound. Once inside they were instructed to sit on a small plot of tall grass behind the chancery. It had been raining the day before but the ground and grass were already dry, even dusty. A short while later they were led to the second of the three staff cottages by a female guard in a chador, the full-length black drape worn over the head. Inside, passing the living room, Koob caught a glimpse of some of the embassy men tied to chairs. Royer found it strange that none of the Americans he saw, all of whom looked him up and down as they entered, uttered a word of greeting. Koob was searched, first hesitantly by a young woman clearly embarrassed to have her hands on her, and then a second time, more aggressively, by the same young woman after she had been instructed to do a more thorough job. This time she told Koob to remove her dress and then carefully patted down the American woman's ample girth front and back and ran her fingers through Koob's thin brown hair. Dressed again, she was reunited with Royer.

The guards demanded that they turn over their jewelry. Koob handed over her rings.

"One of our experts will examine these," a guard told her.

"For what?" she asked and was amused to be informed that they were checking for communications or homing devices. If it hadn't been so serious, Koob was inclined to laugh.

In another room, Royer was asked to hand over his wallet and watch, which was examined carefully—for what, he wasn't sure—and handed back to him. His briefcase was opened gingerly, as if it might hold some kind of explosive device. As a veteran ICA officer, Royer was used to people in foreign countries assuming he was a spy—his was only another obscure American foreign operation with its own set of initials, wink, wink—even though his primary responsibility had always been to teach English. Any suspicions these young Iranians had about the initials ICA were overwhelmingly reinforced by the bulky two-way radio he had been carrying. There was nothing he could say that would explain that satisfactorily to this bunch. He could only look on and patiently deny that he was a spy. Inside the case was a set of prized gold Cross pens. The students examined these with care, unscrewing the tops and taking out the ink cartridges, shaking them and holding the parts up to their ears. It was all Royer could do to keep from chuckling. He was told to remove his shoes, and the heels and linings of these were checked. His possessions were then placed in plastic sandwich bags and he was promised he would get them back.

He was put in a bedroom with Koob, who hadn't slept more than a few hours the night before. She was overcome with fatigue but was too anxious to fall asleep. There was a steady procession of students in and out of their room, male and female. The embassy compound had become an exhibit, with all of these Americans on display. Groups of young Iranians, obviously excited and fascinated, would enter the room and gape at them for a few minutes, then move off to look at the next group of "spies" on display.

Koob finally fell asleep late in the night. Blankets had been hung from the windows to block out glare from the spotlights outside. She wrapped her green wool cape around her and on the other bed Royer slept in his tweed sport coat. She had finally dozed off when she was awakened by a voice.

"Hahnum," said a male guard, using the polite honorarium for a woman. "You mustn't do that."

"Do what?" she asked.

"Signal your partner with your eyes."

Koob blinked with astonishment and asked him to explain.

"Your eyes," he said. "You mustn't use them to signal your partner. That is foolish and dangerous."

When the guards learned the next morning that Koob and Royer were not husband and wife, they were appalled to have left them together in the same room and immediately separated them.

There were now sixty-six hostages.

17

OBVIOUSLY, WE DON'T WANT TO DO THIS

Two days after the embassy takeover, General David Jones, chairman of the joint chiefs, and the rest of the Pentagon brass met in the "Tank," the top-secret briefing room in the massive building's inner rim, to hear what kind of emergency plan their staff had prepared for rescuing the hostages. A twelve-man team had been working around the clock for two days, sketching out a reckless thrust that, if necessary, could be attempted immediately.

From first word of the hostage taking, President Carter's fear was that the students would begin executing the captives. What could the United States do? There were plenty of punitive options. Iran's oil refineries and ports could be leveled, for one thing, and under such circumstances most Americans might applaud. That had been the underlying logic of the nuclear age: our enemies dared not attack because they would be annihilated. But the logic of deterrence seemed not to apply to rogue hostage takers in a country that celebrated martyrdom. If the threat of retaliation wasn't enough, could the hostages be rescued? It would demand something a lot more difficult than air strikes, naval blockade, or bombardment. What was needed was a fast, pinpoint strike, one that relied on a few well-trained men who could descend on the embassy in a sudden, furious thrust. This, of course, was why Colonel Charlie Beckwith's new counterterrorism force had been created.

When the Delta Force commander had arrived at Fort Bragg on the first day of the takeover, he had told his men, "This is going to be a hard nut to crack." He had hoped for something a bit simpler their first time out.

He had immediately sent his operations officer, Major Bucky Burruss, and a legendary special operations veteran, Dick Meadows, who was serving as a civilian adviser for Delta, to join the small planning cell that was setting up shop in the J3 Special Operations Division, behind a door labeled 2C840, which opened to an L-shaped suite of offices that even in the inner rim of the Pentagon was secured with coded locks. Led by Major General James B. Vaught, a lean, flinty-looking man with a deeply lined face who was both a scholar and a decorated battle veteran, the entire operation was going to be run "off line," which meant it would have no visible budget and would be unknown even at the highest levels of Pentagon bureaucracy. Even the mission's code name, Rice Bowl, was deceptive; it was meant to suggest an operation in Asia. General Vaught had received his orders in London to report back to Washington "ASAP, on the next direct flight," which had happened to be an Air France Concorde. It got him to the Pentagon fast, but the general had charged the trip to his personal credit card, and it would be months before the army could be persuaded to reimburse him. To help maintain secrecy, Vaught spent much of his day working his regular job in the Pentagon heading an army counterterrorism command, and would drop down to the planning suite at odd hours of the day and night. Both Burruss and Meadows were decorated combat veterans. Burruss, whose Virginia drawl and fun-loving manner belied a serious and careful mind, had led a "Mike Force" battalion, a daring mobile strike unit made up primarily of Montagnard soldiers that operated in some of the most dangerous fields during the war in Vietnam. The smoother of the two was Meadows, who had fought in the Korean War as the army's youngest master sergeant and had received a battlefield commission in Vietnam running a special forces unit that captured more North Vietnamese troops than any other. Dark-haired, impeccably groomed, with a quiet, unflappable, and unassuming manner, he seemed more like a business executive than an elite soldier. Both men were prototypes of the soldiers who made up Delta Force, in that their manner and appearance were deceptive. They didn't look or act like soldiers. In fact, they were two of the best the army had, not just smart but possessed of battle-tested cunning and courage. They were tough, poised, irreverent to the edge of cynical, and impatient with military bureaucracy. They had been told to design a mission that would leave for Tehran directly from American soil without intermediary stops.

The Tank is a small conference room with a table large enough for the four service chiefs and the chairman, and with a few chairs on the side for staff members. Burruss presented what they had. The sandy-haired, ruddy veteran was nervous. There was no higher-ranking audience in the American military.

"Obviously, we don't want to do this," he began, and explained that with more time a better plan could be devised. Tehran was remarkably isolated from an American military point of view. The nearest friendly country was Turkey, but given how important it was to surprise the hostage takers, asking for help there posed an impossible security risk. Asking any nation other than a close ally for help invited leaks. Just to position forces in Turkey would arouse suspicion—the Soviets kept a vigilant watch on American troop deployments from satellites and high-flying aircraft, especially in that part of the world. There was already a fleet of warships in the Persian Gulf, five hundred miles away. The United States did not have helicopters that could fly those kind of distances without refueling, and choppers that refueled in air were not yet available. Launching a mission without help in the region seemed impossible, but asking for help would likely betray the mission. Burruss said that Delta Force could assault the compound and free the hostages, but getting there and back was a different order of problem.

What they had come up with in two days was a plan so reckless it was just shy of ludicrous. It proposed parachuting soldiers at low level into an area east of Tehran where there was a road that was usually busy with trucks. They would then hijack the vehicles needed to drive their force into central Tehran, raid the embassy compound, load the hostages on the trucks, and then drive and fight their way to the Turkish border four hundred miles away. One variation of this plan, provided the Turkish government would cooperate, would be to fly helicopters in from that country and pick up the rescue force and freed hostages. Another variation called for driving the hostages out of the city either to an airport seized by a second team of soldiers or to a makeshift airstrip in the desert, where everyone could board planes and be flown out of Iran.

"As I said, we don't want to do this," reiterated Burruss, noting his audience's disbelieving looks. The action would be accompanied by both punitive and diversionary air strikes and raids throughout Iran. One recommended target was the Abadan oil refinery; crippling key components there could effectively disable fuel oil production in Iran for months. Since it was the beginning of winter, there was little doubt such a loss would be felt throughout the country. The cell had already begun to identify and recruit Farsi-speaking soldiers or translators to take part in the action.

Burruss and Meadows explained how their men would choose an hour soon after midnight to storm the compound over or through the back walls, with the aid of a high-flying AC-130 gunship, which could lay down curtains of intense fire with great precision on the streets around the embassy. The raiding parties would be wearing night-vision devices, which would give them a major advantage as they took down the various buildings in the compound and rounded up the hostages. They had only a vague notion of where in the compound the diplomats were being held, most of it gathered from close satellite surveillance and TV reports; the CIA at that point had nothing to offer.

As the joint chiefs questioned and discussed the option, General Robert Barrow, the Marine Corps commandant, said he was uncomfortable with the whole plan, which prompted General E. C. Meyer, the army chief of staff, a hard-bitten character who was sitting with his feet up on the table, to quip: "These are soldiers, not marines."

Accepting or rejecting this emergency plan was not an issue, it was the *only* plan, and if American diplomats were being publicly executed in Tehran the United States would have to try something. The principals left this meeting praying that wouldn't happen. What the crash exercise had done was identify the biggest hurdle to such an operation: getting Delta Force in and getting them and the hostages out.

At this point, even the soldiers planning a rescue mission doubted it would ever be undertaken, and not only because it was so difficult and unlikely to succeed. As frustrating as the embassy takeover was to Americans, it was clearly a provocation that called for a measured response. It seemed likely that the seizure had taken Iranian authorities by surprise as much as it had Americans, and it made sense to allow time for the confusion of powers in that country to sort out its response. At a meeting of the National Security Council in the White House that morning, Carter had approved the idea of sending Ramsey Clark and William Miller to Tehran with their carefully composed letter, but on his way out of the room the president vented his impatience.

"By the way, I'm tired of seeing those bastards holding our people referred to as 'students,'" he said. "They should be referred to as 'terrorists,' or 'captors,' or something that accurately describes what they are."

"Yes, sir," said Jody Powell, his press secretary. After the president left the room, Powell mused, "How about 'Islamic thugs'?"

Any hope of the higher powers in Iran backing away from the embassy takeover dimmed further when Khomeini gave another speech in praise of the students.

"When we face plots, our young people cannot wait around," he said. "Our young people must foil these plots. . . . We are facing underground treason, treason devised in these very embassies, mainly by the Great Satan, America. . . . They must be put in their place and return this criminal to us as soon as possible. If they do not, we shall do what is necessary."

Predictably, public endorsements had quickly followed up and down the emerging Tehran establishment, from Ayatollah Mohammed Behesti to Ayatollah Husayn-ali Montazari, the spiritual leader of Tehran. Close behind came news that Prime Minister Bazargan and his entire cabinet had resigned. Given their precarious status since news of the meeting with Brzezinski in Algiers, they were in no position to buck the tide. They lacked the power to evict the students anyway. Khomeini had made efforts to talk Bazargan into staying on—the beleaguered prime minister had tried to resign three times earlier that year as it had become increasingly apparent that the new Iran would be ruled directly from Qom—but had been induced to stay. Not this time. He told Ahmad Khomeini, the imam's son, "My existence as prime minister has become useless in this country."

In less than forty-eight hours, a group of students from the big universities in Tehran had engineered a mini–coup d'état. The takeover of the U.S. embassy had ignited a great storm of anti-Americanism and anti-secularism, which swept aside any prospect of a conventional, Western-style nation. Religious conservatives were going to shape Iran's future, not the secular nationalists, socialists, and communists who had dominated the movement's educated class. The young leftist cleric who had "advised" the students, Mousavi Khoeniha, had foreseen the possibility of this happening but had never guessed that it might work so well, and so fast.

Ibrahim Yazdi left his office at the Foreign Ministry that day feeling defeated and angry. He was angry at the United States for historically bad policies in his country, and for the colossally insensitive and unnecessary blunder of allowing the shah to travel to New York; why couldn't the doctors have gone to see him? Yazdi didn't know what was going to happen, but even beyond the danger of provoking the United States he was convinced that taking diplomats hostage was going to do lasting damage to his country. Since when was national policy set by secret societies on college campuses?

He was not that angry with Khomeini. Despite having been personally accused of treason by the more rabble-rousing elements of the religious camp for meeting with Brzezinski, Yazdi was comfortably ensconced in Khomeini's good graces; he had served him tirelessly during his years in the United States and in Paris during the year before his triumphal return to Iran. The imam urged Yazdi to take a position with the now ruling Revolutionary Council (as Bazargan did), but the departing foreign minister declined. He didn't trust the mullahs; behind closed doors they said one thing and publicly they did another. Instead, he accepted an appointment as Khomeini's special emissary to resolve political disputes in outlying provinces. He knew that the old man was well intentioned, but he was also largely ignorant of the outside world and vulnerable to manipulation. When he had the imam's ear, as he had briefly the previous day, Yazdi could convince him that holding diplomats hostage was not something that a responsible government did, that the world of diplomacy was vitally important for all countries; at its best it preserved options in a time of crisis, it prevented misunderstandings, and when circumstances seemed hopeless it sometimes provided a peaceful way out. Violating the protocols of statesmanship so blatantly would withdraw Iran from the community of nations and would deprive it of this essential tool for interacting with the rest of the world. Such arguments appealed to Khomeini's humility and wisdom, asking him to look past the passions of the moment toward Iran's long-term interests. But he knew the ambitious mullahs around Khomeini had their powerful ways of appealing to him, too. They would argue that severing ties with the Western world was critical for ensuring the success of the revolution and in creating a pure Islamist state. They fed him the stories about American plots, some of which Yazdi himself believed were true. There were those in Khomeini's religious inner circle in Qom who were sincere, but others were like power-hungry courtiers anywhere. They were opportunists, and in this embassy seizure they saw their chance. Yazdi counted Ahmad, the imam's son and heir apparent, as one of those. There was no mistaking who had the imam's ear last.

In his speech that day, Khomeini called the takeover "a second revolution, more glorious than the first."

In Washington all this removed the best hope for an early resolution. At a second meeting of the National Security Council that afternoon, General Jones presented the rescue option he had heard from Burruss that morning with his own pessimistic assessment of its chances. Ramsey Clark and William Miller flew from Washington to Greece, and then to Turkey, awaiting permission to enter Iran and deliver the letter crafted so carefully by Precht and White House officials. Their mission stalled there, as they waited for confirmation that they would be welcomed in Tehran. NBC's Richard Valeriani, who had been sitting on the story, finally aired it on the *Today* show after the State Department relented. The network had cameras pointed at the stalled plane in Turkey, where it sat and sat. Finally official word came from Tehran that the emissaries would not be allowed into the country. To make matters worse, the students issued a statement promising to execute the hostages if America made an effort to free them. Carter was hamstrung. He lacked a viable military option and there seemed to be no one in Iran willing to negotiate.

As Hamilton Jordan left the White House that evening, November 6, he noticed a big crowd outside the Iranian embassy on Massachusetts Avenue.

"Let our people go!" they chanted, as passing cars honked in approval.

Jordan was struck by the contrast: the powers in Iran applauding the seizure of America's embassy, while in D.C. police had carefully roped off an area around the Iranian embassy and were busily protecting it from angry Americans.

18

YES, AND THIS IS FOR YOU

The hostages at the embassy had no idea what effect their kidnapping was having around the world. They lived in enforced silence, cut off from anything outside the four walls of whatever room held them. With mobs howling outside for their blood, it was hard to think past their immediate predicament.

Bill Belk spent most of his first week in captivity tied to a chair in one of the cottages. A picture of him snapped on the day of the takeover, a tall man with longish hair and long sideburns, blindfolded, bound, and proudly erect, standing a good foot taller than his captors with his head held high, had been reprinted in newspapers and magazines all over the world. Unbeknownst to Belk, his image had come to symbolize the crisis.

He was a well-traveled member of the foreign service, an adventurer who often volunteered for difficult assignments around the world. He had discovered that the danger in these places was often overstated, that prices were generally low and the food was good. He had known little about Iran before taking the post in Tehran. He knew there had been a revolution only weeks before he had arrived, but he neither knew nor cared much about how or why it had happened. His job was to operate the new communications equipment called TERP, which had simplified a lot of the old teletype rigmarole by projecting a video image of the received message before it was printed out. It eliminated the need to retype the coded material because an optical character reader translated the messages and gave the communicator a chance to make small corrections on the video screen before printing it out. The flow of messages in and out was brisk, and keeping track of it was a full-time job. His was a narrow but necessary skill, and with it Belk had seen the world. Of all the places he had been in his career, mostly in Asia and Africa, he thought Iran was the prettiest, with its beautiful snowcapped mountains and endless deserts. Tehran was inexpensive and had good restaurants and shops. People would stop him on the street, grabbing his hand to admire his diamond rings and watch. Belk collected beautiful things, and he enjoyed shopping for exotic treasures. In Iran he had particularly admired the delicate workmanship on picture frames fashioned out of camel hair, copper, and wood.

Being tied to a chair for three days was mighty uncomfortable, but even worse, thought Belk, were the windy lectures of a pious guard named Seyyed. Filled with the arrogance of youth and flush with triumph, he held forth endlessly in passable English to his captive audience on the theocratic and philosophical underpinnings of the revolution. It held little interest for Belk, who was tired, hungry, stiff, and sore, and who was disinclined to deal in deep abstraction under the best of circumstances. To him, all this heated reasoning was Seyyed's way of convincing himself that it was right to hold diplomats hostage.

The nylon rope that dug sharply into Belk's wrists was finally replaced by a strip of white cloth, which was a tremendous relief. The cloth was more a token than actual restraint, because it would have been easy to slip his hands out. On the fourth day he was placed in a room with Don Hohman, a lean, red-haired army medic who had been deployed to Tehran for six months because the State Department had been unable to find a civilian nurse who would take the job. He was the embassy's official doc. Hohman was less stoic than most about the treatment they were receiving, and he amused Belk by his sturdy defiance—Belk saw him as a typical red-haired hothead. He complained to the guards constantly and about everything. He refused the mashed peas and rice they offered at mealtime—"I don't want your goddamn food"—and even water—"I don't want your goddamn water." He constantly interrupted Seyyed with such determined insults that Belk was certain the medic was going to be taken out and shot.

After several days together, Belk felt the sting of an insect bite and, shortly afterward, the symptoms of an allergic reaction. His breathing began to grow labored.

Hohman knew exactly what was happening. Belk's windpipe was swelling up, choking him from the inside. He screamed at the bewildered guards that his colleague needed a shot of adrenaline immediately or he was going to die. Two of the Iranians were medical students, and they could see that Hohman was right. Belk's skin was flushed and forming hives, and his breathing was so strained he looked ready to pass out. They untied Hohman and he took off running for his medical office. The guards ran after, trying to maintain the pretense of escorting him. There was a real danger of Hohman being shot as an escapee; that's what he looked like, racing across the compound with armed guards in hot pursuit, and when he got to the chancery a startled guard there hit him with the butt of his weapon. He then pointed it at the two Iranian guards who came running up behind the stunned medic.

The medical students explained the emergency while Hohman swore and fumed, and finally he was allowed to run to his office, where he grabbed a bottle of epinephrine, Benadryl, a bottle of oxygen, and a cardioverter, a device for administering an electrical shock to the heart in case things got really bad. He ran back to the cottage, found Belk unconscious, and injected him with epinephrine. That quickly restored his normal breathing and Belk woke up.

His eyes were swollen shut and he was covered with hives. The guards asked him if he wanted to go to a hospital and Belk said no. He had heard of a hostage taking in Africa where a woman was taken to the hospital and never seen again.

"I'll stay here with my friends," he said. Hohman gave him some Benadryl for the hives. The guards brought a mattress in so that Belk could lie down instead of sitting in the chair, and they allowed Hohman to sit beside him. The medic sat up all night monitoring Belk's pulse and breathing. Hohman had impressed the guards with his competence and quick action and he would be accorded a measure of respect for the remainder of his captivity. Belk felt better in a few days and remained deeply grateful to the young red-haired sergeant who had risked being shot as an escapee in order to save his life.

As the students scrambled to organize themselves for a longer siege, one decision made quickly was to take a small group of hostages away from the embassy, to be held as insurance against a rescue attempt.

One of those chosen to go was Dick Morefield, the balding consul general, who was awakened in the middle of the night.

"Are you Mr. Morefield?" the guard asked.

He was handcuffed and a blanket was draped over his head, then he was led out of the ambassador's house. He assumed the worst. Since he was one of the highest-ranking members of the embassy staff, he assumed he was being taken out somewhere to be executed.

From the backseat of a car he watched as men in military fatigues led other hostages out of the building. They were all driven someplace else in Tehran and led down to a basement, where they were placed on a bench. A bright light was shone down. Morefield's hands were cuffed to the men on either side of him.

Then they were all told to lie prone on the cold concrete floor. Out of the bottom of Morefield's blindfold he could see a drain on the floor. He heard the guards preparing their weapons.

For him the moment was surreal. Three years earlier, in March 1976, his nineteen-year-old son and namesake had been murdered in a holdup at a Roy Rogers restaurant in Fairfax County, Virginia. It was one of the most sensational and cruel murders in the D.C. area in many years. Young Morefield had been one of four workers who were forced to lay prone on the concrete floor of the restaurant's walk-in refrigerator. The robbers then methodically shot each three times in the back of the head. It had been an agonizing loss that had left Morefield and his wife and daughter shattered. The pain had created a rift in his marriage, and he had accepted the Iran assignment (after initially turning it down) in part because he felt the need to escape for a while. And here he had managed to place himself in precisely the same predicament as his dead son, facedown on the concrete with a gun over his head. He felt himself entering into his son's terrified last moments.

The muzzle of the rifle was pressed against the back of his head and he heard the click of the firing mechanism . . . then nothing. The chamber was empty.

When he was pulled back to his feet he was spent. The shock had been cathartic. He no longer felt as frightened and he knew two things. First, these people meant business and he was unlikely to be freed any time soon; and second, nothing they could do to him from then on could be worse. He was a man acquainted with the random unfairness and cruelty of life and had arrived at a hard-bitten acceptance of it. He calculated his odds of getting out of this alive at about 10 percent, but for him, dead or alive, the worst was over. His fear for himself and his anger at this situation were real, but paled in comparison to the helpless rage he had been carrying around with him for more than three years. If they killed him . . . well, he had seen his wife and daughter battle through the tragic and senseless loss of his son, so he knew they could cope with his loss if it came to that.

Bob Ode, the eldest of the hostages, seemed to feel the injustice of captivity more deeply than his colleagues. He had signed on for just a short tour in the Tehran consulate, and as the days dragged on, without a rescue or sign of release, his outrage grew. He had struggled briefly with the guards on the first day when they'd confiscated his jewelry, concerned particularly about losing his precious rings, one given to him by his parents on his long-ago twenty-first birthday and his wedding ring—he had met and married his wife, Rita, a fellow foreign service officer, twenty-two years earlier. He clenched his hands into fists and resisted as the guards tried to pry his fingers open.

"Leave him alone," protested marine guard Rocky Sickmann. "He's just an old guy."

At sixty-four, Ode still bristled when he was called "old," but he was grateful for the marine's sentiment.

"You're a bunch of goddamn thieves," he told the guards, who eventually got his hands open and removed the rings, assuring him that he would get them back.

"Look," said one, holding up a big yellow envelope with "Odie" written on it.

"You don't even have my name spelled correctly. How in the hell are you ever going to get these things back to me?"

They took the rings.

"Goddamn thieves," said Ode.

Ode was tall and thin, with a face that looked like it belonged in a Norman Rockwell painting, long and narrow with a high forehead and a chin that got lost somewhere between his lower lip and his collarbone. He wore big glasses that accentuated the narrowness of his face and magnified his eyes, which gave him, with his big nose, the slightly comical appearance of someone peering into a fish-eye lens. Four years earlier he had been forced out of the State Department because of its mandatory retirement age of sixty. The postwork lifestyle hadn't suited him, or his family budget. He had gotten himself a real estate license and was making a decent living at that, but he had always been a world traveler, a kind of professional tourist, and selling homes in the Virginia suburbs didn't excite him. So when the department began offering retirees a chance to take temporary postings around the world, filling in for full-time officers who needed a break, Ode had embarked on a series of foreign adventures. He had gone to Guyana to help out after the messianic preacher Jim Jones and his followers committed mass suicide, and had taken a three-month posting to Jamaica. In Tehran he was filling in for a consular officer who was taking a three-month medical leave. Ode had not even agreed to the full three months. He had stipulated that he would take the job only if he could be home in time for Christmas, so the department had enlisted him for only forty-five days, thirty of which were gone. He had spent his free time in Tehran taking long walks around the city and snapping pictures.

He lost his defiant, seen-it-all attitude only once in the first weeks, when his captors demanded that he tell them where he had been living. He had been using the apartment of the vice consul on leave, and he realized he didn't know the address. He knew how to walk to the apartment, however, so he drew them a map.

A navy veteran of World War Two, he was so certain in the beginning that President Carter would attempt a rescue that he refused to remove his shoes. They were new ones, Hush Puppy loafers, and were still a little stiff and hard to pull on without a shoehorn. He had taken them off the first night, and it had been such a struggle to get them back on that he kept them on, for fear of being shoeless when the time came to run. He could see how disorganized and amateurish his captors were and figured they would be a pushover for any military unit with the smallest level of discipline and training. Surely somewhere in the multibillion-dollar American military arsenal was a commando unit similar to the Israelis who had made the rescue at Entebbe. He tried to picture in his mind how the attack would happen, how the American force would enter the building, how they would take them out. He was good to go.

He had no patience whatsoever for the idealism or rhetoric of his tormentors, and more than most of the hostages, perhaps with the license of old age, Ode flaunted his contempt. On the night of the second day the students had brought a camera crew through the residence and had awakened him with its bright lights. He rolled over and elevated a long, bony middle finger.

"This is for television!" one of the crew gasped.

Said Ode, lifting the finger still higher, "Yes, and this is for you."

In the first week of his confinement, Limbert was roughly awakened.

"Come on," the guard said. "Get up."

His first thought was they were being released. A blanket was thrown over his head and he was led downstairs and placed in the back of an open truck with several other hostages. As they drove off, he reluctantly concluded that they were not bound for freedom. They stopped just a short distance away, still inside the compound, and were led into a large waiting room at the consulate. It was the room where visa applicants were lined up as they waited to submit their applications, windowless, with parallel rows of railings to control the flow of the lines, brightly lit by fluorescent ceiling strips. Limbert and the others were assigned blankets that were spread out on the hard floor. He counted nineteen other hostages, about one-third of the staff. Two armed guards roamed among them rapping long sticks against the railings, enforcing the rules against speaking or standing, and a third guard with a machine gun stood at one end of the room. They would spend the next two weeks there.

They communicated with gestures and facial expressions. Limbert was pleased to see that no one seemed unduly intimidated or upset. There were occasional chances to whisper to the person on the next blanket over, and a rumor made its way around the room that they were to be visited by some international figure, which made sense, because they continued to count the passing days with disbelief. Surely there would be a resolution soon. Occasionally the students would pass around copies of a document they had found in the seized files that they considered particularly damning. The only time Limbert got to stir from his blanket was when he had to use the toilet. He would stand, wait to be blindfolded, and then was led to the bathroom. The students distributed some magazines and books— Limbert got a copy of *Apartment Life,* which dealt with home decoration

—and brought in fast food, mostly hamburgers, but once from the local Kentucky Fried Chicken outlet, which, despite the Iranians' loathing for all things American, apparently was still thriving.

The first group of students who had taken them hostage was largely replaced. The new guards were about the same age as the first crowd but seemed all business. They rarely spoke to Limbert; he could see that any of them who began to converse with him was glared at by the others, so clearly they were under instructions not to interact with the American devils.

Limbert found a small way to break through that reserve at mealtime. He exploited *ta'arof,* the elaborate ritual protocol of Iran. When he was served food he would offer some to the student who delivered it.

"Please, before I take a bite, go ahead and have some of my food."

"No, thank you," the server would respond.

"But you must," Limbert would insist.

"No, please, excuse me, but I wouldn't dream of it," the server would say, following the standard rules of this game.

The guards were disarmed by his fluency with their language and customs. As Limbert saw it, such moments forced them to set aside their stern demeanor and act more human.

Some of the military officers were annoyed by this behavior, which they interpreted as inappropriate cozying up to the enemy. It particularly bothered Colonel Leland Holland, an assistant defense attaché. When he overheard one of the young naval officers addressing a guard with what he regarded as excessive politeness, he took advantage of the first opportunity to whisper to his colleague, "Tell these motherfuckers to shove it. Don't be so goddamn nice to them."

After a few days on the hard consulate floor, the hostages were given mattresses, which were a terrific comfort, and which had the effect of more clearly defining each man's space, which some found vaguely reassuring. The fear of execution was still strong. Richard Queen requested a pencil and piece of paper and wrote out a will to his parents, telling them, "I don't expect to ever be seeing you again, . . . I love you more than I can say. Thank you for being my parents."

Occasionally the higher-ranking students would come through trying to confirm the name and job of each captive. Limbert noticed that his colleagues were being taken off one by one, and would return hours, or sometimes days, later. He assumed they were being interrogated.

*   *   *

Bruce Laingen, the embassy's indignant but ever hopeful chargé d'affaires, along with Tomseth and the embassy's second-ranking security officer, Mike Howland, were undergoing captivity of a different sort. Still stranded at the Foreign Ministry, they were in the curious position of being both inside and outside the ordeal.

They had watched the provisional government collapse, which reduced them to being vagabond emissaries to a government that did not exist. In the first days they had been treated like diplomats, important men. They had received visitors from other embassies during the day in the ministry's diplomatic reception room—struggling to keep themselves presentable in clothing they had worn day and night—and talked to Washington regularly by phone. Tomseth spoke fluent Farsi, so he translated the reports on television, radio, and in Tehran's newspapers. They followed with hope and then disappointment the aborted mission of Clark and Miller. An effort at mediation by the Palestine Liberation Organization was reportedly under way, but, so far, had yielded no results.

They were not officially hostages. They had not been directly forbidden to leave for a friendly embassy, but even if they were not stopped on their way out, the practical problems were considerable. Any embassy that accepted them would itself become a target for these fanatics. How could they impose on their friends like that? And how could they just walk out on their colleagues? Staying on had its own logic. Laingen not only believed but expected that the outrage would be set right. After the failure of the Clark/Miller mission, there seemed to be no way for Washington to establish a dialogue with Iran. The crisis then worsened with a round of spiteful gestures. Carter froze six billion dollars of Iranian assets and suspended oil imports from Iran, and the imam responded by banning exports to America, which said, in effect, *You can't refuse to buy our oil because we refuse to sell it to you.* The crisis was at a complete impasse. But so long as he stayed under the foreign minister's feet, a constant reminder of the ongoing insult to his country and to their shared profession of diplomacy, Laingen felt there was always a chance that such a dialogue might begin with him.

They slept on sofas in the ministry's long and narrow formal dining room and spent most of their time during the day in the reception area's central salon, a larger room forty feet wide and seventy feet long. The wood floors were creaky, the ceilings high and hung with beautiful crystal chandeliers. It was a sunny, airy space. Large windows faced north toward the snowcapped mountains, but most days the city's heavy smog completely cloaked the view. The ornate rugs were thin and faded with age and traffic. Unlike their colleagues, they were not bound, blindfolded, harangued, and interrogated, and they had access to the local news. Laingen, an avid tennis player, was used to being outdoors and exercising, and as the ordeal crept along through the first week, and then into another, he could not recall a time when he had been so long indoors. A kindly official in the protocol section had brought them clean socks and underwear, so they could alternate, washing the dirty underclothes in the morning and hanging them on the legs of the table leaves that were set upside down on the dining table. They could still communicate with Washington via telex, but because it was an open line they could not have candid exchanges.

Laingen was bewildered. He was a true believer in the diplomatic calling, in the power of polite dialogue between nations. Iran was clearly hurting itself more than the United States by this assault on that tradition. It was, in his eyes, blindly self-destructive and utterly unwarranted. His entire professional frame of reference had been upended. He began a diary on the eighth of November, and in its first entry asked:

> Why? To what end? What purpose is served? We have tried by every available means over the past months to demonstrate, by word and deed, that we accept the Iranian revolution, indeed, that we wish it well—that a society strongly motivated by religion is a society we, as a religious nation, can identify with. Far from wishing to see this nation, this government, stumble, we wish it well and hope it can strengthen Iran's integrity and independence.

Laingen's sympathetic spin on the revolution was of no use now. Perhaps the hardest part of his predicament was being rendered irrelevant. Trapped in the grand halls of Iran's Foreign Ministry, he and Tomseth had ringside seats to the unfolding drama, but Laingen felt increasingly cut off from the powers in that country and his own. Watching the unanimous chorus of hatred directed at Americans from all directions, he saw early on that the embassy takeover, if it had in fact been conducted by idealistic students (and he doubted this), had evolved very quickly into something else. Less than a week into his velvet confinement, he wrote:

We feel compelled and obliged to watch the TV news, even though the constant barrage of anti-American propaganda becomes hard to take after a while. What is it doing to public opinion out there? What's behind it? What is its purpose? Clearly it is the product of something more by now than an "unanticipated" attack by a crowd of students. Others have clearly seized upon it and are carrying this to ends not then planned or seen. Or is our assessment of this place again flawed, as it has been so often in the past?

His new irrelevance was brought bitterly home on the twelfth, when the newly appointed foreign minister, Abolhassan Bani-Sadr, meeting with his staff for the first time, needed the reception room that had become home to the stranded Americans. Laingen, Tomseth, and Howland were removed to the big dining room, and while Bani-Sadr presided over his formal introduction in the next room, the three waited alone in grand emptiness next door, their shabby presence mocking the grandeur of their surroundings and the ritual in the next room. They sat at one end of a table built to accommodate forty. One played solitaire, one read a book, and the third took a long walk around the room, again and again, making circles.

19

GEORGE LAMBRAKIS

Having accomplished more than they could have hoped, the students were at a loss. They owned the American mission, the embassy, the grounds, sixty-six Americans, and many thousands of pages of confidential files, but what were they going to do with it? They were convinced they knew in a general way exactly what had been going on in the embassy. The intelligence scandals of the 1970s in America had provided plenty of examples of CIA handiwork against revolutionary leaders—the clumsy attempts to assassinate the Cuban leader Fidel Castro, the successful hunting and killing of Ernesto "Che" Guevara, the plot to kill the Congo's Patrice Lumumba, the overthrow and murder of leftist Chilean president Salvador Allende, to name just a few. They had the example of Mossadeq in their own modern history. But whatever the current plot was, it wasn't immediately clear. Neither the students nor the clerics advising them had any practical understanding of how espionage or even how such a large embassy worked, or what all these people now in custody had been doing inside its high brick walls.

Before storming the compound, if the students had an idea about espionage it had been shaped more by Ian Fleming than by reality. This explained their suspicion of American watches, shoes, radios, and communications equipment. But apart from the apparatus of institutional secrecy, what they had found was for the most part opaquely pedestrian, an office building and its people. In their eyes, every American inside the compound was implicated in sinister doings, as either a spy or an employee in the service of the nefarious spy enterprise. Their task would now be to unravel the mystery.

Who had they actually taken hostage? At the Foreign Ministry were the embassy's two highest-ranking officials, Laingen and Tomseth. Among those at the embassy were the heads of the mission's eight sections: politics (headed by Tomseth), economics (Morehead "Mike" Kennedy), security (Golacinski), administration (Bert Moore), the consulate (Dick Morefield), the ICA (John Graves), the defense attaché (Colonel Tom Schaefer), and the military liaison group (Colonel Chuck Scott). Each section employed military or foreign service officers, and each had a support staff—clerks, secretaries, and several had communications specialists. The marines were under Golacinski. Koob and Royer, who had worked across town at the Iran-America Society, reported to Graves, as did the press attaché, Barry Rosen. Reporting to Laingen but operating with greater independence was the small CIA contingent, station chief Tom Ahern and his two subordinates, Daugherty and Kalp, who reported directly to Langley and had their own secure communications equipment. All had perfectly ordinary "cover" jobs at the embassy, so at first the students had no idea which of their captives they were. Thus the captors assumed everyone was a spy.

In the beginning, the students lacked this overview of the embassy bureaucracy. They had an overheated, sensational idea of what an embassy did that did not account for the more mundane tasks that formed the bulk of its activity. In that sense, their prize would prove to be something of a disappointment. They hadn't imagined someone like, say, Bill Keough, the towering middle-aged former principal of the American school in Tehran, an institution that at one point had taught more than four thousand students, the sons and daughters of the then extensive U.S. government presence in Iran. To his captors, Keough was just a very large middle-aged white American of some importance, which meant he was probably a top spy. In fact, he was a lifelong educator who had spent most of his career teaching or managing schools in rural Vermont. He had been lured to the school in Iran by his love of classical history and literature— he had read of ancient travels in Persia and wanted to see the place himself. When his school had been depopulated and then closed after the revolution, Keough had transferred all the books and student records from the old building to the embassy grounds for safekeeping. He had since accepted a position as principal of the International School in Islamabad, Pakistan, and had briefly returned to Tehran to recover the most current of those old records—those for boys and girls still in school or applying to universities who needed their transcripts. He had been scheduled to fly back to Islamabad on November 5. When the students came over the walls he had been packing suitcases with the most critical of the old student files, and his biggest worry in the first days was that those files might be lost.

There had been some real spying going on at the embassy, but most of it had little to do with Iran itself. Major Neil Robinson, who worked for the defense attaché, was employed by the Defense Intelligence Agency and was trying to make sure that the sophisticated U.S. surveillance equipment used to monitor Soviet missile testing did not fall into the wrong hands. Navy Commander Donald Sharer had been working to make sure that some of the systems the American air force had installed on Iranian F-14s did not fall into Soviet hands. The plane itself was state-of-the-art, and it had the AWG-9 weapons system (Airborne Warning Group-9), which was capable of radar-tracking twenty-four targets simultaneously and firing upon six of them at the same time at a range of well over one hundred miles. It was classified. There were similar but less pressing issues surrounding Iran's fleet of F4s, F5s, C-130 transports, and the surface-to-air anti-aircraft I-Hawk weapons system. Sharer had managed to find and destroy an I-Hawk manual inadvertently left behind in Iran that contained secret electronic countermeasures, which had not been shared with the Iranian army. He had volunteered to help clean out old American offices and, discovering the manual in a safe, had tossed it on a pile of trash, which had been taken out and burned. He regarded it as the most significant thing he had accomplished in his brief stay in Iran.

These kinds of things were not, of course, what the Iranian students had in mind when they set about unearthing American plots. Certain that they had seized a gold mine of proof about America's clandestine efforts, the students set about trying to solve the mystery for themselves. They would dissect this beast and lay its slimy entrails in the sun. It was not an objective study but one driven by prior conviction. They set about unearthing facts and confessions to substantiate their beliefs. Part of this effort involved cataloging all the "Spy Den" documents, including a project to painstakingly reassemble shredded files, but the other big part would be the methodical interrogation of nearly all the Americans in custody.

Colonel Chuck Scott was told to strip to his shorts, and as he sat and watched they tore apart his clothing inspecting pockets, linings, everything, looking for secret communications devices. He then endured an abusive session during which he was accused of being someone else, in particular, someone named George Lambrakis, a former embassy political officer who they were convinced had been CIA. Scott, a short, solid man with a square face and big glasses, resembled Lambrakis and had met him but could not convince his questioners that they were not the same person.

"You were born in Greece and you have worked many years for the CIA and the shah's SAVAK to oppress, torture, imprison, and kill innocent Iranian people," said his interrogator. "We have proof of this from files in the embassy and from some of your friends who have already given us information. We do not want to have to hurt you, or to kill you, but that is up to you."

Scott found the accusation insulting. He regarded his position as chief of the military liaison group to be more significant than any post Lambrakis had held; why wasn't his real identity interesting or significant enough?

Vice consul Richard Queen spent long hours explaining to his interrogators AVLOS, the new computer system in the consulate, the one he had been working on the day of the takeover. A precise man, he described in detail how it provided a database of visa applicants that could be readily accessed by American consulates around the world. He was telling the truth, but it was clear to him that his questioners didn't believe him. Nothing about his work or his life was remotely secret; he was a relatively low-level functionary at the embassy, a beginner in the foreign service profession. But no matter what he told them, the truth wasn't cutting it. There were no innocent explanations. Everyone was guilty; everyone was a spy. He could see his captors working hard to see through all the imagined lies in order to grasp the true devious machinery of the place. If it weren't so sad it would have been funny.

"How much money do you earn?" he was asked.

"About eleven hundred a month," he said.

"Don Cooke said you make thirteen hundred a month."

Cooke, another vice consul, handled payroll, so Queen wondered if he had been given a raise without being informed.

Kathryn Koob walked her questioners patiently through her foreign service career, from the eight-hour foreign service exam she took in Denver in 1969 to her first posting in Abidjan, then on to Bucharest and then Zambia. She explained how she was drawn more to the job than to the place. A foreign service officer she had met early in her career had advised her, "If you have a miserable job in a wonderful place, you will be miserable, but take a wonderful job in a miserable place and you will be happy." Iran was a "miserable place," she explained, only in the sense that there was so much anger and mistrust of Americans. Koob's life was devoted to knocking down barriers and grew right out of the prairie Lutheranism that she had absorbed growing up on a farm in Iowa. Her tradition informed her that all conflict was rooted in misunderstanding, and her passion was to crush misunderstanding with art. Koob laid it all out, from Iran backward, providing places and dates of arrivals and departures.

"You made that up," her questioner said when she was done, pointing out how deftly she had produced places and dates off the top of her head. In fact, she had recently been asked by the ICA to write out a history of her employment, so the details were fresh in her mind.

A copy of that cable was in her files.

"You will find it in my office," she told them.

Al Golacinski was questioned about his watch, which was a modern style with a blank face that lit up with a digital display of the time when a button was pressed on its side.

"Is this a radio?" he was asked.

"No, it's a watch."

"Well, if we find out it's a radio you're in big trouble."

"It's not a radio."

One interrogator later threatened to put the security chief's feet in a pan of boiling oil, an ultimatum Golacinski found too grotesque to actually believe. The line they had used on the day of the takeover, "You will see what we will do," had been far better. It had left the terror to his own imagination. If you were going to scare a man with a pan of boiling oil, you would show him the red-hot pan and start taking off his shoes. The State Department security man felt professional disdain; he saw his questioners as amateurs playing at some cinematic notion of torture and interrogation.

John Limbert was questioned by a young man wearing a bag on his head, one of the embassy's "burn bags." He had cut holes in it for his eyes. It was all Limbert could do not to laugh. It seemed to him that they had things backward—he was the one being interrogated, shouldn't *he* have the bag on his head?

"I am sorry to have to talk to you in this way," the young man said.

"It's all right," Limbert told him. "Don't worry about it."

"What was your role in the coup of 1953?"

"I don't know anything about it," Limbert said. "I was ten years old at the time."

Those interrogated were struck by how determined their captors were to believe any scrap of information that buttressed their theory, and by how dismissive they were of anything that contradicted it. Joe Hall, the army warrant officer, found himself being questioned about the "wheat mold" plot he himself had made up as a joke on the night of the takeover.

Many of these sessions were conducted by Hussein Sheikh-ol-eslam, the gap-toothed former Berkeley student. In the second interrogation of Golacinski, Sheikh-ol-eslam presented the embassy security officer with evidence of his "secret counterrevolutionary activity." In a search of his office and home they had found grenades and other weapons and a number of other suspicious items, including counterfeit twenty-dollar bills. They had also learned some things about him from Joe Subic, the unusually cooperative army sergeant whom the hostage takers had dubbed "Brother Subic." The helpful sergeant had told them about a project Golacinski had undertaken with the U.S. Secret Service. He didn't know much about it, just that Golacinski had been working on the project, and that it involved fake twenty-dollar bills. In fact, it was an investigation into an Iranian counterfeiting ring. Golacinski had a big file on the case that contained a stack of counterfeit notes; he had been excited by the opportunity to work on the case. His interrogators, however, surmised from the suspicious title "Secret Service" and the counterfeit bills a vague plot to somehow undermine the Iranian economy by flooding the country with fake American currency. It wasn't clear exactly how this was supposed to have worked, which is one of the things Sheikh-ol-eslam wanted Golacinski to explain. The files revealed that Golacinski had helped question some of the suspected Iranians, so to the other allegations against him was added the label "torturer."

"Where are the rest of your weapons?" Sheikh-ol-eslam asked him.

"I don't have any more weapons."

"Why were you torturing Iranians?"

"I don't know what you're talking about. I have never tortured anyone."

He told Sheikh-ol-eslam about guard shifts and talks with the local police about problems at the gates, and whenever he got the chance he asked a question. Sheikh-ol-eslam, in particular, could not resist the chance to hold forth on his theories. He explained to the security chief how in the United States oppressed minorities and politically enlightened Americans were rallying behind Khomeini and assured him that the revolution in Iran was just the beginning. Eventually the whole world would embrace the perfection of Islamic heaven on earth. "The American people will revolute!" he said.

Golacinski listened happily. So long as Gaptooth was holding forth, he didn't have to say anything, which suited him fine.

Air Force Lieutenant Colonel Dave Roeder was privy to national secrets in his defense attaché job; he held one of the most important and sensitive positions at the embassy so as he awaited his interrogation, he plotted an opening gambit.

Seated on a chair in a room he thought was the chancery basement, blindfolded, he heard male voices speaking in Farsi and was then addressed by a woman who spoke flawless, American-accented English.

"Who are you?" was the question. The voice belonged to Nilufar Ebtekar.

She was a round-faced young woman with doe eyes and a pretty smile who was among several fluent English-speakers recruited by the students after the takeover. She had spent part of her childhood in Philadelphia while her father had worked on his Ph.D. at the University of Pennsylvania, and she had fully absorbed the language. In fact, when she had returned to Iran as a young girl, her English had been better than her Farsi. At Amir Kabir University, she was formally a second-year chemical engineering student, but she had long since grown more interested in the turbulent postrevolutionary politics playing out on campus. She had been raised in a Western-style home but had embraced the distinctively political Islam taught by Ali Shariati and others, who subscribed to the traditional leftist belief that capitalism was, at its core, the systematic exploitation of the weak. In the years prior to the revolution, she had come to see the popularity of American culture and consumerism among her peers as evidence of a Western plot to undermine Iranian culture and traditional morality and to further the imperialist designs of the United States. She had embraced *hijab* as symbols of her liberation from this plot and wore a black chador that covered everything except her face. Ebtekar was one of many smart young Iranian women swept off their feet by the revolution, who despite their education and ambition voluntarily adopted the submissive role accorded women by the Koran. She regarded submission as liberation. It offered freedom from capitalism's soulless marketing of female sexuality. Unlike the women of an earlier generation, who covered themselves out of modesty, Ebtekar covered herself out of pride. Her black robes and veils announced her Islamist beliefs. She had actually met Shariati once, in 1977, before he had fled Iran for London, where he had died weeks later. Along with many students who for years had circulated his banned writings and lectures hand to hand on Iran's campuses, Ebtekar was inspired by his vision of Islam as a divine third force, a deeply rooted traditional alternative to the demons of capitalism and communism that were at that time vying to control the world.

She knew Mohammad Hashemi and several of the other leaders of the protest, and three days after the takeover she was approached on campus and asked to help out with interpretation and "public relations."

The next morning Ebtekar had presented herself at the front gate and was immediately introduced to the "Central Committee." Despite some hostility from male students who disliked the idea of a female spokesman, she would soon become the public face of the hostage takers. She was thrilled in every way by the action, which she saw as a great victory of righteousness over evil, an historic and world-altering event that she was privileged to join. Thrust before the cameras to answer questions from the press, local and international, she became famous overnight in Iran and infamous in the United States. The day after she started, she was visited at the front gate by a starstruck delegation from a shoe factory where she had taught for several months as a volunteer in a literacy program. Her former students were delighted that their teacher had become one of the "conquerors of the embassy." They carried a banner that read, "All Our Sufferings Are from America." Ebtekar was moved; the encounter

convinced her that she and the other students were the true representatives of the people.

Inside the compound she worked as an interpreter.

"I am Lieutenant Colonel Dave Roeder," was the answer to the question she had posed to the former fighter pilot. "I'm the assistant air force
attaché of the United States."

"No, you're not," she said.

The interrogator spoke in Farsi again, and Ebtekar said, "We have
found evidence in your embassy here that you are a member of the CIA."

Roeder said nothing.

In fact, they said they had found a copy of a recent memo from CIA
station chief Ahern to Laingen asking what classified operations Roeder
had been briefed about prior to his arrival. This they said, confirmed that
he was secretly "See-ah." Roeder ignored them. It was the approach he
had decided on. In the first session he would tell them his name and
rank . . . period. They could do whatever they wanted with him, it was
all he was going to say. So he sat silently, which he found easier to do
blindfolded. He was asked a few more questions but he continued to
pretend he hadn't heard. Years before, in his survival school training class,
Roeder had gotten the instructors angry using this tactic. They told him
that the only reason he had the nerve to pull the silent act was because
he knew he was taking part in a training exercise, but in a true war
experience, where the fear was real and the threat of punishment, torture, and execution was real, nobody had the guts to play that game for
long. By holding his tongue, Roeder had decided to prove an old point
to himself.

He heard chairs move and then people leaving the room. He sat alone
for about ten minutes but sensed the whole time that someone was standing right behind him. Then his questioners returned and his blindfold was
removed. His questioner was a young man with a beard, and beside him
sat Ebtekar.

She translated a series of questions and Roeder pretended he didn't
hear her. He found her manner particularly grating. Because her English
sounded like the girl next door in America, there was something that
seemed traitorous about her, even though Ebtekar was Iranian through and
through. She had the smug self-righteousness of her cause; that was what

truly burned Roeder and would so annoy the other Americans who dealt with her in the coming months. Her familiarity with America added profound emphasis to her rejection of it.

Ebtekar translated a few more questions and Roeder continued to stare off into space. They left him again, tying the blindfold back on. He sat alone for a long time, until he could see under his blindfold what looked to be the first glimmer of morning light from a basement window. When his questioners returned, the interrogator was angry.

"You had better start talking to him," advised Ebtekar, "because I can't protect you anymore."

Roeder was amused by the idea of this woman "protecting" him. He said nothing. Then Ebtekar said something to the man in Farsi and he heard her get up and leave the room.

The air force officer tensed for whatever was going to happen next. He was hit in the head from behind by something that felt like wet cardboard. It didn't hurt, but it surprised him and dazed him a little. Once again he heard Ebtekar enter the room and speak to the man in Farsi, and then leave.

This time he heard or sensed something coming, because he ducked and the blow missed him. His chair was violently upended, leaving him on his back, still tied to it, his feet sticking up in the air. He was being kicked, but the arms of the chair prevented his attacker from landing a solid blow. Then it stopped. He lay there a long time on his back, blindfolded, until about an hour later someone came in, untied him, and led him back upstairs.

If they had a hard time believing in the innocent intentions of Queen, Koob, Golacinski, and others, there was no way the students were ready to accept that Michael Metrinko was just a diplomat. Multilingual, well connected, widely traveled and hyperkinetic, he was made to order for spying.

He possessed a stubborn streak that at times made him oblivious to danger. He had spent the first few days of the takeover tied to a chair, irate about missing his dinner engagement and standing up his friends. He didn't have time for this nonsense. What did they think they were

going to accomplish by this stunt? One of the students offered him a cigarette and Metrinko had reflexively said no. He was dying for a smoke
. . . but, no. It was a standard politeness; if you were going to light a cigarette, first you offered one to anyone else in the room. But under these
circumstances the gesture was jarring. Accepting anything from these
bastards, no matter how small, was acquiescence; it would imply that
there was something normal or acceptable about the situation, which
there was not. Metrinko resolved right then that, no matter how long this
took, he would take nothing from them. He would deny them even the
smallest satisfaction.

"This is ridiculous," Metrinko told one of the students who spoke
English. "The American government has accepted your revolution. We were
trying to come to terms with it. We're trying to find mutual interests, something to build on. What you've done is counterproductive."

The Iranian shrugged off Metrinko's argument. He made it clear that
he didn't believe a word of it, that he regarded everything this American
spy said as a lie.

Metrinko didn't speak to him in Farsi because he felt he would lose
an important advantage if they knew he was fluent in the language. They
were all conversing around him freely in their own language, assuming
that he couldn't understand. Having that secret had saved his life and that
of eight other Westerners ten months earlier in Tabriz.

He had been there in the weeks after the shah fled, camped out at
the empty American consulate. Iran was in its ecstasy of fulfillment and
expectation. The executions had not yet begun. Metrinko was the only
American in any official capacity to stay on in the northwestern city. When
the facility was evacuated, he had offered to remain in part to keep watch
on things, and in part because he felt responsible for four young Americans who had been locked up in a car-smuggling operation several months
earlier. The consulate was a fifteen-acre walled estate with beautiful gardens, tennis courts, and a swimming pool. He had opened up the grounds
to local Iranians the previous summer. Now whatever goodwill that gesture earned was forgotten in a tidal wave of anti-Americanism. Demonstrators gathered to stone and jeer the compound and to taunt its Iranian
guards, who like most of the police and army (as opposed to the air force)
had stayed loyal to the shah. They felt angry and betrayed by his depar-

ture. There had been a few testy moments at the gates. Once, when his army guards had responded to taunting demonstrators by leveling their guns, Metrinko had stepped between them and talked the guards into backing down. He felt relieved and even vindicated in those days, being the one American in Tabriz who had judged the situation safe enough to stay. At that point, no matter what was happening outside his walls, the maid and the cook were still showing up for work, the guards were still keeping watch, and he was enjoying himself, watching TV at night, drinking, smoking cigarettes, and playing cards. He was excited to be there, by the buzz of possibility in the air.

He was also glad that the shah was gone. The whole story of American involvement in Iran twenty-five years earlier was a disgrace. As a freedom-loving American, he was embarrassed by his country's abandonment of its basic principles and by its support of the shah's often heavy-handed regime. Back when he was a Peace Corps volunteer, he had seen some of his students hauled off to jail by the police just for speaking critically of government policy. He was in Tabriz because of his enthusiasm and fascination with the unfolding changes. He was looking forward to rebuilding relations between America and Iran on sounder footing. Metrinko wished the revolution well. He understood what most Iranians wanted from it. On the first of February he had watched on TV as Khomeini returned to Tehran, a day of intense national celebration. He and the guards heard the cheers and blasts and blaring car horns outside their walls. It wasn't a bad thing, he thought. Public enthusiasm had elevated Khomeini to the status of a king, or a god, which made him dangerous, but most indications were that he would retire to Qom and continue leading a nice, quiet, religious life. The more secular revolutionaries who had surrounded him in Paris, men like Bazargan, Yazdi, and Abolhassan Bani-Sadr, had advocated free elections and an Islamic-flavored but essentially democratic state. There was reason to hope for a return to stability and a whole new and better Iran. America would have a lot of repair work to do, but there were deep connections between the two countries—financial, military, and geopolitical—that would be foolish to discard.

Those weeks before Khomeini's return were like living in the calm before a pending eruption. The headless regime's army and police were still in place, people were still going to work every day, things appeared normal but you could feel the pressure building. When Khomeini's plane landed all hell had broken loose. Revolutionary forces rose up everywhere to tear down all remnants of the shah's power. In the days before it happened, Metrinko got a tip from some Iranian friends allied with the revolt that the prison in Tabriz was going to be liberated, so he had visited the young Americans locked up there and advised them to come directly to the consulate when they were freed. He gave them small maps to show them the way and promised not to leave without them. He liked them. They were victims, nice, adventurous kids who had been given two hundred dollars each to drive cars to Tehran during their school break. They had delivered the cars as promised, but had been arrested when they tried to take the train west out of Iran with their money back to Europe. Their passports indicated they had entered the country with cars, and now they were leaving without cars, and without having paid the customs fee. So they went to jail, charged with smuggling. They had been there through Iran's eruption. Now they were an afterthought, accused of a minor crime by a regime that no longer existed. As predicted, the prison was stormed and all of its inmates freed. The four arrived on foot, elated, still wearing their inmate pajamas and slippers, enormously relieved to be free but now imprisoned with Metrinko in the consulate with the country coming apart all around them. They were joined by four fellow escapees, two Germans, an Austrian, and an Australian.

Tabriz was in chaos. Anger, revenge, religious fervor, and revolutionary zeal combined to unleash a nationwide spasm of bloodletting, a season of murder. Many associated with the former regime were hunted down and killed, policemen, bureaucrats, local and national leaders, civilian and military. In some cities the entire police force was executed. Nobody was even keeping track. The raid on the prison had been followed by an attack on the main military base and a general collapse of authority. The armory had been looted and the streets were full of excited amateur gunmen with a seemingly limitless supply of ammunition. It seemed as if everybody was fighting everybody. Metrinko heard by radio that the American embassy in Tehran was in danger of being overrun. Telephone service was up and down, but mostly down. Much of the fury at large was anti-American, but for a time it seemed to bypass the consulate, which looked empty. His guards and staff had melted away. Metrinko and his eight charges huddled down. It was too dangerous to go outdoors, even inside the compound. Next door, a SAVAK crew was cornered and fighting for its life. Once they counted more than seventy rounds fired in a minute. Metrinko had been able to arrange with the besieged staff in Tehran to have a team of Americans waiting for him and the students across the border in Turkey, but with the violence in the streets there was no safe way to move. They were stuck and for a time, it appeared, forgotten. Metrinko had put his charges to work helping him to destroy every letter, file, memo, note, and report in his office.

On Valentine's Day, the embassy in Tehran was invaded. In Tabriz, Metrinko was in his office when he saw a group of armed men in Iranian air force uniforms come over the compound's back wall. They opened fire on the consulate, shooting out the windows. He dropped to the floor be-behind the desk and made a quick phone call—the phone was working!—to an Iranian friend, Ali, who was part of an activist group allied with the revolution. The man's mother-in-law picked up the phone. Metrinko told her who he was and what was happening before the armed invaders burst in, grabbed him, and tied his hands.

Metrinko and his charges were marched to one of the kangaroo courts that were in full swing throughout the city. This one was a former government building, the Youth Palace, which had been commandeered. There were several bodies dangling from a tree in the front yard. They were placed in a holding room with others awaiting their turn before the kangaroo court—Metrinko would later see some of those he waited with hanging with the others out front.

They were rescued by his friend Ali, who had gone immediately to the Youth Palace when he got the message from his mother-in-law, but he'd arrived there before Metrinko and the others had. No one at the palace knew what he was talking about. Ali had then set out on a dangerous search, braving heavy gunfire on the streets, going from one place to another until he finally ended up where he had started, and found his friend Metrinko and the eight others. Ali's revolutionary credentials and bravado, combined with many shouted threats, succeeded in getting Metrinko released, but then the American consul refused to leave without his eight young companions. Finally, the self-appointed enforcers relented, and all nine of them were allowed to go. Ali took them all to his family home for dinner and then delivered them back to the consulate, where he left them under the protection of a group of revolutionary soldiers.

Still the saga continued. No sooner had Ali left than the soldiers guarding them turned on them, ordering the nine to sit on chairs in the living room, pointing guns at them. The guards spoke to each other in Turkish. They had heard Metrinko speaking with his friend in Farsi and never dreamed he was also fluent in Turkish. So the soldiers spoke freely over the course of the day, as higher-level revolutionary figures came and went from the consulate. The men were bored with the detail and began planning among themselves to shoot Metrinko and the students in the yard that night and claim the group had tried to escape. Metrinko didn't bother to tell the students what he had learned; he figured they were better off not knowing. But when a higher-ranking official stopped by to check in on them that afternoon, Metrinko told him that he had some communications gear in a back bedroom he wanted to show him. When they retreated there, Metrinko hurriedly explained the guards' plan.

"I can't do anything about them now," said the official. "They aren't my men. Hold on, and I'll try to get some help."

Some time later the official returned with a new group of soldiers to replace the guards who had planned to kill them.

Over the next two days, whatever semblance of leadership that existed in Tabriz decided that it would be best to ship Metrinko and the others to Tehran, where, for the time being, a deal had been worked out to protect the U.S. embassy. Metrinko outfitted his charges with his wardrobe; he was five-ten and wide and the students were much taller and thinner. Ill-fitting clothes and all, they had made their comical arrival just as the bulk of the American mission was being evacuated. Buses were taking wives and children and unessential personnel to the airport in convoys. The American students all returned home safely. Metrinko had no intention of going home. Things were getting interesting. That was when he had agreed to stay on in Tehran as a political officer.

He had reason to remember all this in November as he sat listening to the guards laughing and joking freely with one another. But Metrinko's fly-on-the-wall status was short-lived. A student shouted a question in Farsi at one of the other hostages, and the man, rattled and at a loss, said, "Ask Metrinko, he speaks Farsi."

So that was that. In the chummy atmosphere that prevailed for the rest of that evening, Metrinko had sat with a young Iranian science student and translated an article from *Time* magazine for him. He had been a teacher in his years with the Peace Corps, and the role came naturally. Then he was escorted into another room and allowed to watch a TV program. He had tea and chatted amiably with several of the students. He found them quite intelligent and politically astute. They told him that they had cased the embassy by coming in to apply for visas, mapping out where all the buildings and offices were. They were very proud of themselves.

"It had to be done," one of them told him. "We had to do something to show people that Americans would not be allowed to regain control of Iran."

Metrinko told them the truth about himself, and they didn't believe him. They demanded that he open his safe for them and he complied. Inside were a few papers, nothing important. He did not keep many files in his office. The most damaging thing, what he worried about, was his personal directory, full of names, addresses, and phone numbers, which he kept at his apartment. He figured it was only a matter of time before they found that. Any of his many friends listed there could be subjected to the dictates of this inquisition. In this first interrogation session he was relieved right away to see that the papers in his safe contained nothing even remotely compromising.

His questioners were persistent but not abusive. The daily sessions continued over weeks. Eventually they stopped blindfolding him, which he saw as a bad sign; it suggested that they were not afraid of his knowing who they were. Over time, they grew more irritated and hostile. He was not telling them what they wanted to hear. They told him that they knew he was lying and tried to coerce him by keeping him awake all night, but then they would leave him alone for hours during the day. Metrinko had a fortunate facility for dozing. He had always been able to put his head back and nod off. It was a talent that had gotten him in trouble in meetings from time to time, but now it served him well. Whenever he was left alone, even briefly, he would nap. It was enough to foil their amateur efforts at sleep deprivation. Metrinko had not been trained in methods of resisting interrogation, but he found he could manage quite well. The sessions were a welcome break from staring at the walls. He was able to figure some things out from the questions they asked. For instance, he was heartened by the realization that his captors had no access to Laingen or Tomseth, who had left for the Foreign Ministry before the takeover. They were asking him questions that both men could and would have answered readily, but which Metrinko could not. That meant the chargé and his assistant had either gotten away or were being protected by the provisional government (he did not know that it had resigned).

Like Koob, Metrinko went through his entire history in the foreign service with them, from high school in Scranton to Georgetown, to his work in Turkey for the Peace Corps. He talked their ears off. He gladly told them about the two years he had spent teaching English at a literacy training center outside Tehran, how he had joined the foreign service five years earlier, and then had spent two more years in Turkey, as a staff aide, before moving to Damascus. He had been in Tabriz since 1977 and had come to Tehran only after bozos like them had closed the consulate there. Of the things he could be open about he spoke freely. He was especially glad to tell them about the lovely dinners and drinks, cocktails and wine—especially the cocktails and wine—he had shared with the families of prominent religious leaders. Still angry at the Taleghani brothers for what he thought had been a setup, making sure he was at the embassy to be taken along with the others, Metrinko talked freely about the late ayatollah, about how strongly it appeared that he had been set up and murdered by their pious religious bosses. What his captors saw as divinely inspired leadership, Metrinko saw as simply another ugly political faction using treachery and violence to prevail. He tried very hard to avoid mentioning the names of his friends. He would talk only about those he knew had already fled the country. After a session he would sit alone and go back over every question and answer, examining his performance and analyzing the questions they had asked to figure out what was going on. In a sense, he was still doing his job.

In the beginning, Metrinko was kept with a large group of his colleagues on the floor of the consulate waiting room, but in mid-November he was isolated in a chancery basement room. It was a very small, windowless storeroom that was about ten feet long and narrow enough so that when he held his arms outstretched he could touch both walls. When he held his hands over his head they touched the ceiling. The air was stale and there was a fluorescent light overhead that was left on continuously. He was given an air mattress that pretty much covered the floor space.

This is where he would spend the next five months.

20

"R" DESIGNATION

Despite their clumsy and sometimes comical methods, the students did make some headway toward sorting out the embassy and learned things that would have dire, even fatal, consequences for some Iranians who had cooperated with the American mission. They suspected from the start that Bill Daugherty, the former marine flier, was a spy, and believed wrongly that he was the station chief. He was the one whose office on the east wing of the chancery's top floor had the biggest safe, and under duress on the first night he had relented and opened it. They knew from preliminary interviews with several hostages that that part of the chancery was CIA.

Daugherty was treated like any other hostage in the first days, shuffled from room to room in the staff cottages, where a marine showed him how to slip a piece of wire into the lock of his handcuffs and pop them open at will, a great relief. He wore the cuffs whenever the guards were present, but when he could, such as at night with his hands under a blanket, he would slip them off. On the evening of November 22, he was taken from a cottage and placed alone in the office of Tom Ahern, his boss. Everything had been removed from the room but a desk, a chair, and a foam-rubber pallet on the floor. Its windows overlooked the front of the chancery and Takht-e-Jamshid Avenue, which seemed permanently jammed with demonstrators. Their angry din echoed in the empty space beneath the room's high ceiling, rattling Daugherty, who fantasized about easing down over the city in his old F-4 and painting the crowded avenue with a long string of napalm.

After a few days alone in this space, Daugherty was taken for six interrogations over the next two weeks. He was prepared for them, and had given a lot of thought about how to handle himself. Years earlier he had taken a training program for marine aviators who might find themselves in a North Vietnamese prison camp and had been through exercises designed to help resist hostile interrogation—he had even been locked for several hours in a small metal box. He had already decided that his circumstances in Iran did not require him to adhere to the military code of "name, rank, and serial number." Since he was in Iran ostensibly as a foreign service officer, not a spy, he was determined to act like a State Department employee, that is, he would talk at length and try to engage his captors in dialogue. He had two personal guidelines. He would do his best not to reveal secrets or to say or do anything that might make life harder for his fellow captives.

For each of the sessions he was taken to the top floor of the chancery. The last three sessions were in the bubble. Each time his interrogator was Hussein Sheikh-ol-eslam, the former Berkeley student with the missing front tooth. The work seemed to be wearing Sheikh-ol-eslam down; he looked exhausted, with big bags under his eyes. With him were two others, a large Kurdish man and a high-strung young man who spoke little but who had also spent some time in the United States.

Sheikh-ol-eslam asked most of the questions. For the first two nights, blindfolded and handcuffed in his chair, Daugherty was harangued. He was shown grotesque photographs of dead men stretched on slabs at the morgue, their bodies mutilated. There were books filled with such pictures, all purported victims of SAVAK and, by proxy, the CIA. It seemed very important to Sheikh-ol-eslam and the others that Daugherty understand that their revolution, the widespread arrests and executions that followed, and this seizure of the U.S. embassy were morally justified. So Daugherty deliberately challenged them on it, to waste time. He argued with them and asked questions that he knew would set them off. He stuck to his story of being a foreign service officer. The three did their best to maintain the atmospherics of an interrogation session—each claimed to have been interrogated by SAVAK—but they were not especially good at it. Their problem was not getting their subject to talk but to get him to stop talking. Daugherty led them into long conversations about American life and values, taking advantage of any opportunity to turn the discussion back to the familiar safe ground of home.

"We're not interested in what you did in the United States!" Sheikh-ol-eslam would complain. "We are only interested in what you have been doing here in Iran."

Daugherty frequently asked to use the toilet and would be given a break. He would splash water on his face, do deep breathing exercises, and collect his thoughts. There were further breaks for tea, during which the conversation would proceed informally. Eventually his questioners dispensed with the blindfold. Daugherty felt that he had the process so well in hand he began looking forward to the sessions. It was better than sitting alone in his room and listening to the mob outside.

In the third interrogation the tone changed. Sheikh-ol-eslam seemed to have very specific information about him, things he had either just learned or been deliberately holding back during the first two sessions. He asked where Daugherty had been on certain nights, who he had been with, what they had been doing. Not long before the takeover, the CIA officer had accompanied a group from several other embassies on an overnight pleasure trip to Isfahan. These were the dates Sheikh-ol-eslam harped on. Isfahan was regarded as a center for American spying because it had been a helicopter air base for the shah's army and air force and had employed a fairly large number of American military technicians. Sheikh-ol-eslam and the others scoffed at Daugherty's story that this had been an informal sightseeing trip. He wanted to know everything Daugherty had done in Isfahan.

The American was happy to oblige. It had been a pleasure trip. He told them of his visit to the city's beautiful mosque and its bazaar. He described each of his companions, their conversations in transit, where they dined, and what they ate. It grew tedious, so Daugherty decided to have some fun. He had spent much of his time with a woman from the Austrian embassy, just a friend, but as Sheikh-ol-eslam pressed for more and more detail, Daugherty began to spice up the story by fabricating a romantic relationship—to liven things up and to bruise his questioners' delicate Islamic sensibilities. He had himself tearing off the woman's clothes in a hotel room when his questioners shouted, "Shut up! Shut up!"

Daugherty got another bathroom break, and then the four men sat together around the table in the bubble sipping tea and chatting as though the previous unpleasantness hadn't happened. Then Sheikh-ol-eslam stood.

"You are telling us that you are not CIA?" he asked.

"That's what I'm telling you," said Daugherty, feeling cocksure.

Sheikh-ol-eslam picked up a slip of paper, walked around the desk, and handed it to Daugherty.

"Read this," he said.

Daugherty read with mounting shock and disappointment. It was a cable, something that had apparently come from Bruce Laingen's safe, written some weeks before he and Kalp had arrived in Tehran. It began:

1. S.[secret]—Entire text.
2. I concur in assignments Malcolm Kalp and William Daugherty as described Reftels [in reference to prior telecoms].
3. With opportunity available to us in the sense that we are starting from a clean slate in SRF [Special Reporting Facilities, a euphemism for the CIA] coverage at this mission, but with regard also for the great sensitivity locally to any hint of CIA activity, it is of the highest importance that cover be the best we can come up with. Hence there is no question as to the need for second and third secretary titles for these two officers. We must have it.
4. I believe cover arrangements in terms of assignments within embassy are appropriate to present overall staffing pattern. We should however hold to the present total of four SRF officer assignments for the foreseeable future, keeping supporting staff as sparse as possible as well, until we see how things go here.
5. We are making effort to limit knowledge within emb of all SRF assignments; that effort applies particularly to Daugherty, pursuant to new program of which he is a product and about which I have been informed.
6. I suppose I need not remind the Department that the old and apparently insoluble problem of R designation ["R" stood for "reserve" foreign service officer, the traditional way of designating CIA officers with a State Department cover] will inevitably complicate and to some degree weaken our cover efforts locally, no matter how much we work at it.

                                                            LAINGEN

Daugherty's mouth went dry. There was no doubt the cable was authentic; he had seen a copy of it in Washington before he left. Laingen was giving his nod to bringing him and Kalp on as CIA officers in the embassy and worrying about their cover status. Daugherty had no idea why such a thing had been put to paper and was flabbergasted, since it had been, that no one had destroyed it months ago! There was no reason to keep it. For God's sake, it *concerned* the extreme importance of protecting their spy status even *within the embassy!* He sat there in disbelief with the cable in his hands and read it again, and then looked up. Sheikh-ol-eslam was sporting a wide, gap-toothed grin. The others clearly shared his delight. They had him red-handed. The language in the cable was only slightly obscure—they wouldn't know what "Reftels" were or "SRF," but the thrust of it could not have been more clear.

"Well?" said Sheikh-ol-eslam.

"Okay, I'm CIA, so what?" Daugherty said, handing the cable back to him. He couldn't think of anything else to say.

Now it was their turn to be shocked. The last thing they expected, even after showing Daugherty the document, was for him to admit it. At that time and place such an admission almost certainly meant death. Daugherty's flat acknowledgment left them momentarily speechless. They looked at one another, and then back at Daugherty, who smiled at them.

Then they erupted. All three of them shouted at him at once, venting their anger about the United States, the shah, SAVAK, all the primary sources of evil in their world. Here sat the personification of all they feared and despised. He would be the first one of the hostages executed, promised Sheikh-ol-eslam. No need for a trial. He admitted it!

"You've lied to us all along," said Sheikh-ol-eslam. "You've wasted our time. You really are CIA. You're an enemy of our country."

Then Daugherty lost *his* temper and began shouting back at them, cursing them, calling them lousy Muslims and idiots. The four men sat in the strange little plastic room bellowing at one another.

"You guys don't know *jack shit* about the world," said Daugherty. "This is going to be terrible for your country in the long run."

He felt hopelessly trapped in the web of their vicious mythmaking. The idea that his job with the CIA, in reality fairly minor and posing no threat whatsoever to the emerging government of Iran, made him the devil incarnate in their breathless cockeyed worldview, and that their ignorance might well cost him his life, made him suddenly both furious and fearless. Out spilled weeks of outrage. He had watched and listened as this unwashed, arrogant young rabble had insulted and humiliated his country and his colleagues. He was madder than he had ever been in his life and with nothing to lose he unloaded on them, resurrecting an awful extravagance of obscenity collected in military school and eight years as a marine, insulting their intelligence, their cause, their leaders, their parents, their sisters . . . and their culture.

"You think you're civilized because you had civilization here three thousand years ago! Well, there's no fucking trace of it anymore. You guys are nothing but animals!"

They were too busy with their own insults and accusations to even hear. All this anger roiled and then, as abruptly as it had begun, it subsided. Daugherty leaned back in his chair, exhausted. They had more tea.

Sheikh-ol-eslam, weary but determined, resumed questioning.

"Okay, look, we've got to get into this now," he said. "We know you're CIA, so let's just start at the beginning. We want to know where you were trained and who trained you and who you work with in Washington."

"Wait a minute," Daugherty said. "All along you've been telling me that you didn't care what I had done in the United States, all you cared about was what I've done in Iran. And here you accuse me of hurting your country, of harming your people. I'm not going to tell you what I've done in the United States. You only care about what I've done in Iran and that's all I'm going to talk about."

Sheikh-ol-eslam sat back and thought this over for a moment.

"Okay," he said finally.

And they never again asked him questions about his recruitment or training. Daugherty couldn't believe it. It was too good to be true. It eliminated a large category of concern. Everyone he had worked and trained with in the States maintained a cover, and those who had prepared him for Iran had been in and out of the country themselves in undercover roles for years. Each had contacts and cover stories he felt obliged to protect. He knew at least twenty of them. If that all remained off-limits (and it did), what a relief!

"Look, I may be a CIA officer instead of state, but I still only got here on the twelfth of September," he said. "I still was only here for seven or eight weeks, or whatever it was. I still don't even know the city."

Sheikh-ol-eslam wasn't buying that.

"You must know all the spies," he said summarily.

"I'm a new guy," Daugherty explained. "I've never done this before. No boss, no espionage boss is going to immediately give spies to an officer so newly arrived in a country he has never visited, where he knows virtually nothing of the circumstances, customs, culture, or language. The first thing you have to do is learn the city. I could barely find my way from here to my apartment behind the building!"

Their own prized captured document confirmed that he had not been in the country for long.

And the part about finding his way around the city was true, too. Ahern had given him the first two weeks just to explore. After that he had concentrated on doing his State Department cover job during the day and had started feeling his way into agency work at night. For about five weeks he had met with some of the contacts the agency had wanted him to explore. The CIA had not been actively spying in Iran for years. That was part of the problem. It was why no one had adequately foreseen the collapse of the shah's regime. The agency had more or less ceded all intelligence work inside the country to SAVAK, since the shah's enemies tended also to be enemies of the United States. For years, little intelligence was collected from Iran that did not originate with the shah's own regime, who of course downplayed civil unrest and political opposition. Now, with Iran suddenly under new masters and the situation in constant, confusing flux, the agency was starting from scratch—note the reference to a "clean slate" in Laingen's cable—and it was desperate for anyone who could help explain what was going on, anyone close or potentially close to those in power. The agency was pathetically far from being able to influence events, despite the overblown fears of most Iranians, who saw the CIA as omnipresent and omnipotent. The members of the recently resigned provisional government were now being accused of working secretly for the CIA, and the satanic agency was accused of orchestrating everything from natural disasters to civil disturbances to running a troublesome insurgency in Kurdistan. The feverish effort under way to patch together and decipher all of the embassy's files would in the coming months "confirm" such links and send many to prison or execution.

In fact, the agency had never been so lacking in power and influence. Ahern was running an operation that consisted of himself, his secretary, Daugherty, Kalp, and three communicators—Jerry Miele, Cort Barnes, and Phil Ward, who handled communications in the embassy vault. No one working for the agency in Tehran even spoke Farsi!

Still, in his roughly five weeks on the job, Daugherty had met with a number of Iranians the agency was eager to recruit, and had even had some luck with two of them. He hoped those contacts had had the good sense to leave the country.

"You were at Berkeley," he told Sheikh-ol-eslam. "You were in San Francisco. Did you come to know American customs and the layout of the city of San Francisco in the first week you were there? No? Well, then how should I know the customs and the city of Tehran the first week I'm here?"

His interrogators were flabbergasted and disbelieving. Why would the CIA send an officer to their country who knew nothing of Iran and who didn't even speak the language?

"There were many Iran specialists in our government who could have come here, but they all turned down the assignment," Daugherty said.

"Why wouldn't they come?" asked the younger man, who seemed to take it as an insult.

"Because they were afraid."

"What could they be afraid of?"

"They are afraid of *this*," said Daugherty, lifting his bound hands.

He told them they could learn more about the CIA by reading the various books that had been published about it than by interrogating him.

But Sheikh-ol-eslam seemed to have even more information about Daugherty. In the fifth interrogation they asked him about specific nights in the previous months. Where had he been on this night? With whom had he spoken? What Iranians did he know? This was homing in on one of the few areas of local information that Daugherty felt most obliged to conceal.

So far he had been a bust as a spymaster. He had been given two Iranian agents to contact when he arrived, and one, a woman who worked in the foreign affairs ministry, did not even regard herself as a spy and didn't appear to have access to any interesting information. The other was a military officer with access to Khomeini's inner circle and potentially a valuable source. The agency was depositing money in a Swiss bank account for this contact, a lieutenant colonel or colonel. Daugherty wasn't even sure of the man's rank. The military had not yet been completely purged, and there were still some very-high-ranking officers who were pro-American. Daugherty had arranged several message drops for him, parking his car in a business district in northern Tehran and leaving the window slightly open. When he returned there would be a letter on the seat, which, when opened, looked like a simple missive, a letter written to a sister or daughter. But written in invisible ink on the same sheet was a message to the embassy. He had met with the man twice at night. They had driven around Tehran talking, occasionally parking in isolated areas so he could take notes. Daugherty had never been able to arrange a real sit-down, where he could sit and interview him and takes notes at length, develop the kind of information he could use to really steer the spy, and though he had hopes for this contact so far he had learned little of consequence from the letters or meetings.

Other than those two, Daugherty had been expected to cultivate sources on his own, through people he met in his "official" job as a political officer, the same job held by Limbert and Metrinko. He had attended high-level meetings at the Ministry of Defense and the Foreign Ministry, looking for people with whom he could develop a rapport, maybe invite to play tennis or for a meal. The idea was to nurture a personal relationship, one that might evolve into a more serious professional one. He had reached out to one Iranian official who had met in the past with one of his predecessors. When he finally got the man on the phone, the man swore at him in Farsi and hung up. At this point most people in Tehran assumed their phones were tapped, and any connection with Americans was considered dangerous—thousands had been executed by the revolutionary regime. Taking a call from the U.S. embassy could mean serious trouble. Another potential contact, an army colonel, agreed to meet Daugherty for dinner after he learned they had mutual friends. At the restaurant the colonel was arrogant and condescending. He had apparently expected someone a lot older, somebody more befitting his own rank, and he made it pretty clear to Daugherty that he didn't want him wasting any more of his time.

His one other attempt to recruit a spy had not so much fallen flat as left him feeling confused. He had invited to dinner a man who was working in Prime Minister Bazargan's office. The man seemed well disposed toward the United States, and after that first meal he invited Daugherty to dinner at his house.

This source seemed so promising, and Daugherty was so eager, that he had actually made a pitch for the man to work for him. He explained that it was very important for the American government to know what the Iranian government was doing in order to improve relations. So such information would benefit both countries. His effort to spin the job as a patriotic act was unnecessary.

"The Soviets made me the same offer last week," the man said.

Daugherty didn't know what to say. No one had ever mentioned this scenario in training. They had told him how to deal with a "yes," a "no," and even a "maybe." They had talked about the possibility of the offer being met with a hug and a "What took you so long to ask me?" or even by a punch in the nose. But no one had coached him on what to do with a potential source trying to start a bidding war for his services.

"You didn't take them up on it, did you?" was the best he could think of to say.

He laughed and they dropped the matter. They had agreed to meet for dinner again. That had been ten days before the embassy was taken.

Of all these contacts, the one Sheikh-ol-eslam seemed to have the most information about was the woman at the Foreign Ministry. Her name was Victoria Bassiri, and she had a job overseeing the progress of Iranian students who were receiving government money to study overseas. It was not an especially sensitive position, but there was a chance she would eventually be promoted and the agency was desperate, so she had been considered a source worth cultivating. Bassiri had recently returned to Iran from India, where she had been recruited by another CIA officer, the idea being that she might be able to provide useful information once she returned to her job in Tehran. Daugherty had followed up on the contact and met with Bassiri four times at her home. She was a pleasant, middle-aged married woman with children who, like many middle- and upper-class Iranians, had little affection for the emerging theocracy. He had the impression that she had been marginalized in the Foreign Ministry because of her gender, which had made her angry but which also had removed her from the ministry's inner circle. Over dinner with Bassiri and her husband, a poet, Daugherty discussed the chaotic circumstances of Tehran and listened to talk about office politics in the ministry. It was clear after their second meeting that she had little information that was useful, but Daugherty offered to pay her $300 a month for her continued assistance. His impression was that she did not see herself as a spy; she preferred to see it as more of a consultancy, a high-level social and diplomatic connection. The money was always presented to her as a gift, not a fee. Inflation was a problem for most Iranians, and every little bit extra helped. Daugherty did not regard her as a committed clandestine asset, and he had the impression that if he ever asked her to do something that was unmistakably spying she would have refused. Still, she would have to have been foolishly naive not to know that she was playing a dangerous game, especially after the embassy was seized. Daugherty assumed she would have been smart enough to flee.

It was clear from the questions that Sheikh-ol-eslam was asking that he knew a lot about Bassiri. He knew the dates the two had met. He showed Daugherty patched-together documents, reports he had written about his meetings with Bassiri, and though she was not named in them, the description of her and her job was specific enough to readily identify her. Concluding that the woman's cover was already blown, Daugherty decided to admit his relationship with her in hopes of bringing out how insignificant it had been.

"Your story must jibe with hers precisely or she is going to be in real trouble," Sheikh-ol-eslam said.

"I want to help her because she's a very nice lady," Daugherty said. "And, I've got to tell you, she didn't give me any secrets."

"I don't care what she told you," Sheikh-ol-eslam said. "Tell me the nights and times you met."

Daugherty explained that they had met at her home. The times varied, anywhere from seven to nine in the evenings, mid-week. Sheikh-ol-eslam wanted exact dates and times, and they tried to work that out. The Iranian scribbled notes furiously as Daugherty spoke. This went on for ten minutes, twenty minutes.

"Then, after the second meeting, we skipped a week," said Daugherty. He stopped. "No, maybe it was after the first meeting that we skipped the week."

Sheikh-ol-eslam erased and rewrote.

"No, wait a minute. What time did I say we had that second meeting?"

Sheikh-ol-eslam consulted his notes. "Seven-thirty," he said.

"I think the third meeting was at seven-thirty and the second meeting was at nine."

More erasing and rewriting.

"No, now you've got me confused," Daugherty said. "The first meeting was at nine and the second meeting was at seven-thirty."

By now the annoyed Sheikh-ol-eslam realized that Daugherty was playing with him. He balled up his notepaper, threw it across the room, and said, "Get him out of here!"

He was taken to the toilet and then brought back for more tea. When he returned he resumed "sorting out" all the dates and times, confirming some of the information they had pieced together in the shredded files but sowing more confusion in the process. That was his goal. He hoped that Bassiri was long gone, and figured if she wasn't, then whatever happened to her was her own fault.

His interrogation continued off and on for two more days, but after the session concerning Bassiri it seemed Sheikh-ol-eslam was running out of questions. Daugherty was immensely relieved not to have been asked about his contacts with the military officer, the one serious agent he had. He assumed that his reports of those meetings and letters had been burned in the incinerator. As Sheikh-ol-eslam fished for a new direction, Daugherty seized every opportunity to ask questions, to engage him and the others in political debate, or to provoke them, and they were undisciplined enough to fall for it again and again. He made no headway in these discussions, of course. His younger captors had virtually no knowledge of history or experience in the larger world—Sheikh-ol-eslam was the exception—but they were completely and serenely convinced that they were right about everything. They believed, simply, that the United States government was controlled by a rich Jewish cabal that acted, in Iran, in Vietnam, in the Middle East, strictly out of corrupt self-interest and often for the sheer pleasure of torturing and killing Muslims and other "inferior" races. America was responsible for plagues, famine, war, and even natural disasters such as earthquakes and hurricanes, which were manipulated by its evil scientists. Whatever examples of American contributions to the world—the Salk vaccine, the Peace Corps, billions in disaster assistance, etc.—were dismissed as ploys or sinister plots to further subjugate the planet. America had been Iran's enemy for four hundred years! one of his captors lectured and then waved a hand dismissively when Daugherty told him that the United States had been founded only two hundred years ago. It was so because Khomeini had said it was so.

Their pomposity encouraged Daugherty's wit. He especially enjoyed baiting the big Kurd, whose pride was easily wounded. When he mentioned, in passing, that he had once ridden an ass from Qom to Isfahan, Daugherty quipped, "How did people know who was riding and who was being ridden?" The Kurd leapt at him and began swinging, but Sheikh-ol-eslam pulled him off. When Daugherty learned that the younger questioner, a pious Muslim, had spent some time in Pensacola, Florida, an area known for its wide beaches and college spring break, Daugherty teased him about how much he must have enjoyed getting drunk and ogling the coeds in their bikinis.

The young man flew into such a rage that Sheikh-ol-eslam told him to leave the room. At one point his interrogators grew so frustrated that they beat him. His wrists were bound so tightly that the skin of his hands turned white and became extremely sensitive. Sheikh-ol-eslam ordered Daugherty to place them palms up on the desk and produced a length of heavy rubber hose. Demanding an answer once more, and dissatisfied with the response, he had the Kurd rap Daugherty's tender palms with the hose.

It was the worst pain Daugherty had ever felt, a blinding shot that kept hurting well after the initial blow. He would have told them anything they wanted to know, but he genuinely did not know the answer to the question he was being asked.

"Believe me, if I knew I'd tell you!" he pleaded.

The students realized soon enough, of course, that their prize catch was Tom Ahern, the CIA station chief, who watched from an upstairs room at the ambassador's residence as one after another of his colleagues was taken away. He assumed that they were being taken off for interrogation, and that they were saving him for last. Given his role in Tehran, he was clearly the person in the most jeopardy, and he knew his wife and daughter at home in Virginia would be terrified for him. The pattern seemed to confirm that they knew who he was. And as the number of colleagues around him dwindled, he grew more resigned. From time to time his guards would bring him graphic photographs of freshly severed human body parts, claiming it had been the handiwork of SAVAK. How could he willingly associate himself with an organization like that? Their tone was one more of reproach than accusation. He denied that he worked for the CIA, and denied that the agency had anything to do with such things. The language barrier constrained any serious dialogue.

When his turn came for interrogation he was walked across the compound to the chancery and taken up to the bubble, where he was placed in a chair before a table. Across from him was an unkempt synod of inquisitors, five students who were apparently the ringleaders of this fiasco. In the relatively soft light inside the bubble they were arrayed like the apostles in Leonardo's *Last Supper*, which is the image that popped into Ahern's head. They began questioning him as though they didn't know who he was. The lead questioner was Sheikh-ol-eslam, whose thick black beard and missing tooth made him look to Ahern like a mad prophet.

"What was your job?" Sheikh-ol-eslam asked.

Ahern stuck with his cover story. He was the embassy's antinarcotics officer.

"What have you been doing?"

He went through the meetings he had held with Iranian police and government representatives in his "official" capacity. Ahern had always considered the cover story half-assed, but once he got into it he was moderately impressed at how flexible it could be. Sheikh-ol-eslam and the others asked a lot of questions, which he easily answered, and as he warmed to the exchange he grew more confident. Still, in the back of his mind he remained convinced that they knew perfectly well what his real job was, so the whole exercise had the feel of play-acting. It went on for about an hour.

He was then escorted back to his old office, where there was now a mattress on the floor, and brought back for a second round the next day. The same cast of characters was arrayed behind the desk.

Sheikh-ol-eslam began by telling him, "We know who you are. You are the CIA station chief."

Ahern denied it. He was determined to tell them nothing, even if his denials angered them. It wasn't only his own skin he was worried about, but that of his other officers, his agents and contacts. Like Daugherty, he figured any of his Iranian agents would have fled the country fast as soon as the embassy was seized, but he owed it to them to buy as much time as possible. Part of his stubbornness was simple pride. He was being tested, and he was determined to live up to his own high standards. He had no heroic illusions; he knew eventually they could force him to talk, but he was going to hold on as long as he could. They showed him documents they had found in Laingen's safe that identified him as the CIA station chief, along with the one that mentioned the covert roles of Daugherty and Kalp. The exchanges grew more hostile. They had connected the name "Donald C. Paquin" to him. He denied it, clinging to his cover story, until his questioners were fed up with him. They produced the rubber hose, told him to place his hands palms up on the table, and smacked them hard.

It hurt, a blinding flash of pain every time they struck, but Ahern refused to alter his story. The pain was bad, especially after his hands became bruised and swollen, but it wasn't, he decided, intolerable. He noticed that, once the beating began, one or two of his questioners disappeared and didn't come back.

After two sessions using the rubber hose on his hands without effect, Sheikh-ol-eslam and the other interrogators ordered him to remove his shoes and socks and lie flat on the floor. He did so. Ahern knew that beating on the soles of the feet was particularly painful and wondered how much of it he could endure. He decided he had to accept at least one blow, to see if he could take it. Once he had felt the blow to the hands, for whatever reason he had quickly concluded that it was a pain he could endure. But as he lay prone waiting for the first blow to the soles of his feet, it never came. He heard his interrogators whispering urgently to one another, and then he was hauled back into the chair.

"Put your socks back on," he was told.

PART TWO
DEN OF SPIES

Mohammad Reza Shah Pahlavi and
President Carter during a state visit.
(© Owen Franken/CORBIS)

"Imam" Ayatollah Ruhollah
Khomeini. *(Courtesy: AP)*

Ibrahim Yazdi, foreign minister of Iran's
Provisional Goverment. *(Courtesy: AP)*

Abolhassan Bani-Sadr, President of
Iran (1980–81). *(Courtesy: AP)*

1

WE DON'T HAVE THE
SHADOW OR SUPERMAN

Several weeks into the hostage crisis, American television networks broadcast film of hostage Jerry Miele (he was not identified by name) being led blindfolded to the front gate of the embassy, where the bloodthirsty crowd vented its rage from behind the tall iron gate. Miele was then paraded around to another location for more of the same. It was the first glimpse of a hostage since the day the embassy had been taken, and it galled millions of Miele's countrymen who saw it. The film clip accompanied the first reports that some of the hostages were being mistreated—beaten and interrogated—and it fed a mounting national rage.

In a report from the State Department, CBS reporter Marvin Kalb described the mood at Foggy Bottom, but he might as well have been talking about the entire country: "There is a very deep, deep frustration," he said, "a feeling that the United States is helpless to determine the outcome . . . that we have tried everything and most of our efforts have not borne fruit." The United States of America was stymied. Kalb quoted an unnamed State Department official, who said, "We don't have the Shadow or Superman in our employ."

Walter Cronkite, the veteran, influential CBS anchor, delivered daily reports on the crisis with thinly disguised contempt, noting the "stark, depressing reality" of the standoff and itemizing each day's new insult and outrage. More than any foreign policy episode in American history, the Iran hostage crisis would be shaped by television. In any age, the capture of several score Americans in an obscure world capital would have been a big story, but one that in time would have faded. Prior to the television era, those directly interested in the story would have followed it in newspapers and magazines, of course, but for the masses of Americans concern over the captives' fate would have diminished and eventually dropped off the front pages.

But this was a story made for television, particularly at a time when satellites had enabled instant reporting of events from almost anywhere in the world. It was a suspenseful, unfolding story, a real-life cliff-hanger, and it tapped an insatiable appetite for political intrigue, scandal, military analysis, drama, and pathos. It was a huge story for newspapers and magazines, too, but the tube was in just about every living room in America. The story grabbed the nation by the neck and held on. The United States was being publicly humiliated, goaded, maligned, and insulted on an international stage. The students themselves were media savvy, and with regular press conferences and dramatic pronouncements made sure the story didn't fade. Reporters from American newspapers and the big three TV networks were allowed to set up in Tehran and file daily reports—ABC's were delivered nightly by future anchorman Peter Jennings. The constant torrent of demeaning images and disturbing rhetoric from this obscure and exotic land was both frightening and fascinating. Why did they call Americans devils? Why did they assume all the diplomats and marines they held were spies? Some of the questions they raised seemed plausible. By 1979 most Americans knew that their country was not above undermining the internal affairs of small foreign countries. Were these accusations true? Did the hostages deserve what was happening to them?

On a national level, the Carter administration appeared to have badly blundered by admitting the shah. Why had the embassy not been closed first? Weren't the consequences entirely predictable? Every night a wide range of experts was invited to interpret each mystifying new twist of the drama. Why couldn't the United States respond militarily? How could we let these Iranian hotheads get away with this? The story had another thing going for it. Each of the sixty-six Americans in captivity had hometowns, families, relatives, friends, and coworkers. Every local news outlet in the country had a local angle. Hundreds of city TV stations were used to just taking the network feed for breaking national and international stories, just as its newspapers tapped wire services, but with this one they could break their own stories and view the crisis through their own fresh and emotionally powerful lens. Over the first weeks, local reporters scrambled to learn the names of the hostages—with some diplomats still hiding in Tehran, the government refused to release a complete list of names—but gradually the identities of all of the Americans were revealed. Reporters and cameras descended on quiet neighborhoods in just about every state. The hostages' families found themselves at the center of a media storm. Every word they uttered, every tear they shed, was suddenly news. Stations in local markets vied for access to them. Dorothea Morefield, the poised, articulate wife of consul general Dick Morefield, who had undergone the terrifying mock execution, became a regular on San Diego television. "My heart aches," she told a reporter there, watching new film of the hostages on the day of capture. The mother of marine Billy Gallegos wept for cameras in Colorado, one of many hostage family members who broke down for local newsmen. State Department communicator Bill Belk's wife told the camera, "There are no words to explain how I feel."

The crisis was a ratings dream, a conundrum, a scandal, and a tearjerker, with no clear resolution in sight. Every day brought new provocative twists. Some Iranian students on college campuses in the United States defended the embassy takeover and were confronted by crowds of angry American students. There were isolated acts of retaliation against Iranians living in the United States, fear of oil shortages, signs of military maneuvers, and countless gestures of citizen support for the captives. Cable television and the advent of the twenty-four-hour news cycle were still a few years away, but the decade-long ratings success of the CBS weekly news show *60 Minutes* had awakened the networks to the commercial success of news programming, and here was a story that stretched the potential of the medium from an exotic foreign capital to their own neighborhoods. America was riveted.

The networks extended their newscasts and packaged hourlong specials in prime time to update and analyze the story, but despite all the hours of television time devoted to the crisis very little effort was made to understand why there were mobs of fist-waving Iranians massed outside the Tehran embassy, or why the students had been motivated to take Americans hostage. The students were referred to as "militants" or extremists, and their action was seen as a wild, inexplicable act of fanaticism. There was little or no explanation of the role played by the United States in overthrowing Iran's government more than a quarter century earlier, or any of the other reasons for Iranian anger or suspicion. Iranian rage was presented as something incomprehensible, something mad. Americans were no longer surprised by Third World hostility; the sentiment "Yankee Go Home" seemed to require no explanation. By the end of the 1970s America had come down hard from its post–World War Two fantasy of invincibility; it had weathered the tragedy and humiliation of Vietnam, the Watergate scandal and concurrent revelations of CIA and FBI excesses, the long lines at gas stations that resulted from the OPEC embargo. While still ostensibly the leader of the "free world," the nation suddenly seemed powerless, corrupt, inept, and despised. Many of the bad things people said about us had turned out to be true. A seized embassy and scores of American officials held hostage was just further confirmation of a depressing new reality. The images on television reinforced a decade of American disappointment.

For the Carter administration, this confluence of story and medium was pure disaster. Already Jimmy Carter had demonstrated a gift for making Americans feel bad. His effort to introduce morality and concern for human rights in foreign policy was seen by more bellicose citizens as a strategy of compromise and retreat. In the most ill-considered idea in the history of public relations, Carter had devised the "misery index" to gauge the national mood, as inflation and rising oil prices battered household income. His decision to give back the Panama Canal, while entirely defensible, was seen as yet another retreat, as was his prudent call for Americans to conserve fuel, which he called "a real challenge to our country, a test." He was right, even prescient, but it was stern medicine, delivered by a homely, preternaturally sad-looking man in a somber, earnest monotone. In his bad-news mode, the very folds of the president's face and the hang of his heavy lips seemed a mask of disappointment. The leader of the free world looked whipped. And now this. The hostage crisis seemed designed to complete the unfair image of Carter as a weak, apologetic leader. A rabble of college students seizes an American embassy, holds his countrymen hostage, sends daily taunts, insults, and accusations across the ocean, and the president of the United States does . . . nothing. At least it seemed that way. On just a moment's reflection, though, it was easy to see that anyone in his position would have been hamstrung, but no one else was in Carter's position, and the longer it lasted the more he seemed somehow to *deserve* it.

Everyone wanted Carter to do something, but there were few good ideas about what it should be. Public sentiment ran in favor of striking back at Iran, but ran just as strongly in favor of taking no action that might harm the hostages.

In a speech before Congress, Representative George Hansen, a Republican from Idaho, called for Carter to be impeached "if he doesn't do something," and referred contemptuously to the administration's "weak-kneed nonpolicy." He offered no suggestions.

Senator Frank Church, a Democrat from the same state, whose committee hearings had famously exposed CIA excesses just a few years before and prompted severe restrictions on intelligence-gathering methods, now complained about the dearth of intelligence. "It's extremely frustrating and difficult to find the [Iranian] government or determine who speaks with authority."

"Carter should get off his duff," said one man stopped on the street in Dallas for a TV interview, expressing a widespread feeling.

"What do you think he can do?" the reporter asked.

"I don't know," said the man.

A woman stopped on the same sidewalk said, "Force should be used."

"But what if responding militarily would mean that the hostages would be harmed?" she was asked.

"No, then we shouldn't use force," she said. "I don't want them to be harmed."

Americans had long enjoyed the luxury of neither knowing nor caring about the grievances of small foreign nations. Suddenly, the Third World had found a way to compel their attention. Where was Iran? Who were these "militant" students? What was an ayatollah? Why did they hate us so much?

ABC aired a long interview with Italian journalist Oriana Fallaci, chain-smoking and looking gloriously bored, whose insights were close to the mark.

"I believe the crowd is in control of Khomeini," she said. "When I saw that Ahmad was going to the embassy, I was very surprised. . . . He is a little more open than his father. I was surprised." Americans who called for a punitive military strike against Iran were, she said, "as irresponsible as the Iranian crowd."

"What should the United States do?" she was asked.

"Don't send the marines," she said.

2

FORGIVE ME, OH IMAM

On a chilly Thanksgiving morning in Tehran, Marine Sergeant William Quarles was taken to breakfast, as usual, and when he was finished the guards didn't rebind his hands. That was a first.

"Hey, aren't you going to cuff me?" asked the big marine, holding up his hands.

His guard made a gesture as if to say, *Don't worry about it.*

From the first day Quarles, an African-American, had been treated slightly differently by his captors. He had been kept bound and confined to a mattress in one of the cottages, like everyone else, but his captors always made a point of acknowledging his blackness and conveying a sense of solidarity with his presumed second-class status. If he wanted more food they would always bring him extra portions. If he asked for a cigarette, someone would run out and bring him a full pack. Once, when a glass of water was placed on the table between him and one of the white hostages and the white hostage took it and drank from it, the guards confiscated the glass and lectured the offending white hostage about American oppression of black people. Quarles was startled, because he had assumed, as undoubtedly the white hostage had, that another glass was on its way. Instead, Quarles was presented with a full glass of ice water and the white hostage was denied anything more to drink.

From the beginning, a few of the student leaders visited him to explain at great length the reasons for their actions. They talked to him about their kinship with what they wrongly supposed to be millions of black American Muslims, and the special place for black people in Islam. They showed him albums of charred and tortured bodies and explained the horrors of life under the shah. One of the older ones, a round, bearded man, told Quarles of the torture and execution of his father and other family members under the shah and broke down crying.

Again and again they stressed that they identified with him as a member of the "oppressed" races of the world. They brought him documents they had seized during the takeover and explained that the memoranda, which Quarles didn't read and couldn't follow, proved that America had been interfering with Iranian society and was working to undermine their revolution. Quarles had little interest in the fine points of Islam, history, or international politics. He wanted to avoid being shot and, if at all possible, to go home. He knew that his captors were trying to indoctrinate him and, for the most part, he let what they told him travel in one ear and out the other. But some of the more moving things, some of the photos and heartfelt testimony of a few guards, touched him. He was inclined to believe that his country *was* responsible for much of the suffering in Iran, and found it easy to believe that the United States was working to undermine their revolution in hopes of maintaining control over the country's oil. But when the captors circulated a petition asking for the shah's return, the young marine had refused to sign it.

After breakfast on Thanksgiving morning the uncuffed Quarles was led into a room in the motor pool building. In an adjacent room he saw fellow marine Sergeant Ladel Maples, who was also untied. Quarles considered trying to bolt. The men guarding him were much smaller than him. But he thought better of it. Even if he got free of the compound, where would he go? His skin color meant there was no chance he could blend into a Tehran crowd.

Then, one after another, a procession of his captors came in the room to lecture him again in English about the rightness of their action, the sins of America—beginning with slavery and genocide against the American Indian—and the glory of Islam and Khomeini. Quarles began to suspect that he was going home. The lectures struck him as preparation; they were prepping him for the press attention he would get on his release. Later that evening he and Maples, also an African-American, were put together in the same room.

"Goddamn, man, you think we're getting out of here?" Quarles asked.

"I don't know," said Maples. "We just might get out of here. I don't know what the hell is going on."

"You think anybody else is getting out?"

"I hope so."

The lectures continued. They were served hamburgers, potato chips, and pickles for supper. Clearly, their captors were trying to make a good impression. When they were led outside, Quarles felt blinded by the television lights. He had trouble walking. He had been sitting for so many days that it was hard for him to keep his balance. He and Maples and an embassy secretary, Kathy Gross, were led into a large room next to the commissary before hundreds of reporters, American and Iranian. Quarles felt frightened. He needed help putting on a slight green jacket, and he was shaking; he didn't know if it was from the cold outside or from fear.

"Nobody is going to hurt you," one of the guards told him. "These are just some people who want to see you."

Quarles realized that he was part of a publicity stunt. He didn't know what was going on, but he knew that the lectures he had been getting were to prepare him for this attention. He sat on a stage with the two others before a giant poster of Khomeini and some writing that he didn't understand. The reporters had all been assigned numbers, and one of the Iranian students called off the numbers and allowed some of them to ask questions. In response to one, Quarles said:

"In the past, I had heard something about U.S. imperialism, but as an American marine I had always dismissed them out of hand. But after having heard the other side of the story I now believe these people might have some legitimate complaints. . . . I learned a lot from what I read and saw, and was very saddened by some of the things going on under the shah. I think the American people have to turn around and look at—and there are always two sides—and I saw the other side of the story. The other side of American imperialism."

What he really wanted to say was, *Hey, get me the hell out of here, I'm tired of this shit.* But he felt obliged to get across the points that had been hammered into him for weeks. He knew if he played along he might get to go home.

Quarles told the reporters that he had been kept in the living room of one of the staff cottages for most of the time. As for the embassy being a "den of spies," he said, "The Iranian people felt that it was not an embassy." He said that he had no knowledge of any American spying, then added, obligingly, "Under their ideology, I'm sure they're right."

"Why didn't you sign the petition?" a reporter asked.

"I didn't want to put my signature on something that might be derogatory to my government," he said.

The event seemed to last forever. Quarles felt like he was in a state of shock. He couldn't wait to be taken out of the room. When he was, he was led into a small room to face an Iranian camera and a beautiful Iranian TV reporter.

"Do you have any regrets?" she asked.

Quarles said something about being glad to be going home, although he wasn't sure yet that was happening.

As he was being led out of the room, still frightened and bewildered, one of the students whom he had come to know, a small man who had always treated him gently and as a friend, told him, "You know, you are going to be a very big man when you go back to America."

"Oh yeah?"

"Yeah, you will be. Very, very famous."

He and Maples and Gross were taken out to a Range Rover and driven to the airport. Quarles's small Iranian friend hugged him.

"Come back to see me," he said.

Behind Quarles in the van was a guard with an Uzi. Quarles didn't trust the gun; he knew it had a hair trigger, and as their car darted erratically through traffic he and Maples worried that it would go off. He felt more frightened than at any point that day. His stomach felt fluttery and he was glad when they arrived at the airport that he was given a chance to sit alone for a few moments and collect himself.

As they were being led to the plane, an Iranian baggage handler went berserk. The man had to be restrained from coming after Quarles and the others.

"What's the matter with him?" Quarles asked.

"The shah killed his family," a guard said. "He's very upset with Americans."

It seemed to Quarles that every Iranian he met had lost someone to the shah. The image of the berserk baggage handler stayed with him a long time.

Quarles, Maples, and Gross were the first of thirteen black and female hostages Khomeini had ordered released as a gesture to oppressed

African-Americans and as a demonstration of the "special status" accorded women under Islamic rule. The students had high hopes for this gesture. They had long believed that black Americans would identify with their struggle and take to the streets all over the United States in support; they felt sure this release would help spur such demonstrations. Ironically, among the blacks released was Air Force Captain Neil Robinson, one of the most important intelligence officers at the embassy. There was racism in the Iranian assumption that blacks and women would have held only menial jobs. Charles Jones, the only African-American hostage who was not released, had forfeited his status as an unimportant black man by having been caught inside the communications vault on the day of the takeover. There were only two women left behind: Ann Swift, who had announced her own importance, and Kathryn Koob, whose directorship of the Iran-America Society had marked her for certain as a spy.

Joan Walsh, the political section secretary, was among the ten released the next day. She was allowed to shower for the first time in two weeks and was given a clean pullover shirt and slacks. She and the others were seated in a row beneath a large, hand-lettered sign condemning the United States for sheltering the shah. It read, "America is supporting this nasty criminal under the pretext of sickness." The hostages sat before a long, low row of tables set with microphones. Orchestrating was the wiry, bushy-haired Hussein Sheikh-ol-eslam, who instructed the gathered members of the press that while they were not allowed to ask any questions of an individual hostage; they could ask general questions. The microphone would be passed down the line, he said, and each question would be answered by the hostages in turn.

"And I will tell you the name of the hostage as the microphone gets passed along," he said.

"Can they also tell us their name and hometown?" one of the reporters shouted. Walsh flushed with pleasure to hear an American voice. She felt more comfortable.

Walsh was led back with the other women to one of the cottages after the press conference, and the Iranian women there were suddenly bubbling with excitement and friendly, as though they were supervising a sleepover. Walsh did her best to stare right through them. She wasn't inclined to forgive and forget.

They were put in vans and driven through the hostile mob at the gates. Cameras recorded them smiling and waving as they drove away from the embassy and to freedom.

The release of the thirteen black and female hostages was accompanied by a kind of media blitz within Iran. The same day that Quarles, Maples, and Gross were flown out, the imam himself granted interviews to all three major American TV networks. Robert MacNeil, of the PBS news program *The MacNeil/Lehrer Report,* flew to Tehran but returned home when he was informed that the three commercial networks would get to interview Khomeini first.

Mike Wallace of the CBS show *60 Minutes* got to go first and spent an hour questioning Iran's supreme leader. Sixty-five million American viewers saw the grim, white-bearded ayatollah easily parry the reporter's extremely respectful questions—"He [Anwar Sadat] called you, forgive me, imam—his words, not mine—a 'lunatic.'" The imam didn't flinch. The hostages would be released when the shah was returned. The hostages were spies. They had been caught red-handed.

"As long as Mr. Carter does not respect international laws, these spies cannot be returned," he said. Khomeini said that releasing the hostages after the shah's return would be a kind gesture on his part, not a quid pro quo. "In reality, these spies should be tried."

"Is Iran at war with the United States?" Wallace asked.

"What do you mean by war?" Khomeini answered. "If you mean our armies going against the United States armies, no. There is no such war. If you mean, it is a battle of nerves, it is Carter's doing. We are against war. We are Muslims. We desire peace for all."

Taking a stab at unofficial diplomacy, Wallace tried to extend the interview with a question that had not been submitted in advance.

"As one human being to another," he asked. "Is there no room for compromise?"

The interpreter balked, but the correspondent prevailed on him to put the question to the imam. Khomeini refused to answer it.

The interview was watched at the White House with great interest. No matter how fruitless, the TV network had gotten a lot further in establishing a dialogue with Iran than had the administration. Jody Powell found Wallace's deference to the ayatollah appalling. The press had become openly contemptuous in Washington; reporters were beating up the Carter administration daily and pitilessly for its handling of the crisis, yet the chief kidnapper was questioned with what sounded like obeisance: "Forgive me, Oh Imam, his words not mine" became a frustrated laugh line in the White House.

The release of the thirteen was accompanied by a chilling threat. Khomeini announced that the remaining Americans were going to be placed on trial "soon" as spies. It was precisely the scenario Carter most feared. He publicly ordered the aircraft carrier *Kitty Hawk* to sail from waters near the Philippines to the Indian Ocean, off the coast of Iran. At a press conference in the East Room of the White House, an especially dour president said Iran had created an "unprecedented" situation. "For a government to applaud mob violence and terrorism, . . . to participate in the taking of hostages, ridicules the common ethical and religious heritage of humanity," he said, and added that the United States would employ "every means available" to deal with it.

ABC reporter Sam Donaldson asked the president whether the United States would be willing to let such an outrage continue "indefinitely."

"It would not be advisable for me to set a deadline," said Carter, who added, "any excessive threat . . . might cause the deaths of the hostages, which we are determined to avoid."

3

ONLY WHORES GO WITHOUT UNDERWEAR

As winter settled over Tehran, a season of short days, rain, and occasional snow, the trappings of imprisonment began to feel more permanent. The students who had planned the takeover of the embassy receded from daily view, replaced by a rougher breed of guards, many from the ranks of Revolutionary Guards, who hadn't been students since attending the shah's secondary schools. Most of the male hostages were moved to a large rectangular room in the basement of the warehouse. It had once been used to house electronic equipment that analyzed data from the Tacksman sites but had been emptied months before. There was a row of pillars in the middle of the space, and because it was windowless and damp, perfect conditions for growing fungi, it was christened the Mushroom Inn. Its white acoustical ceiling tile was high, almost fifteen feet up, and the space was starkly lit day and night by recessed fluorescent bulbs. Diesel engines were used to generate power for electricity and the sickly sweet fumes hung perpetually in the air. Hostages were assigned places on the floor, and each had a thin foam mattress. In time the guards used empty bookshelves to divide the space into separate cubicles so that, unless he stood, a prisoner could see only the man directly opposite him.

There was some comfort in being surrounded by the others. Golacinski had Vice Consul Don Cooke to one side and marine Greg Persinger to the other. Directly across from him was the assistant defense attaché, Lieutenant Colonel Dave Roeder. In a side room the guards rolled in a TV set and played some tapes of American shows, escorting small groups of hostages in on an irregular schedule. Golacinski's group watched an episode of *The Carol Burnett Show,* and then an old baseball game. When the "Star-Spangled Banner" was played before the game he felt a powerful pride welling up and noticed that the others in the room were smiling and winking at each other. Because Golacinski was familiar to so many of his captors due to his role on the first day, he was one of the few to whom they would speak. One, a medical student, told him that President Carter was sending Ramsey Clark, the former attorney general, as an emissary to Tehran to negotiate for their release. Golacinski asked if he could tell the others. He was taken to a corner of the room and told that he could say that Clark was coming, but nothing else.

Golacinski stood and got everyone's attention. He announced in a loud voice that Clark was coming to start discussions, which created a stir. "Are there any questions?" he said, and when he was promptly pulled from the chair the big room echoed with laughter.

Light moments like this were rare. All of the Americans had been threatened repeatedly with execution, and they took it seriously. Golacinski and Roeder had been handcuffed together one night and, with blankets thrown over their heads, taken upstairs and outside, where they were told to stand against the wall.

"Nothing will happen to you," the guard told him reassuringly, and then added, less so, "It will be quick."

The guard didn't speak English well, so he probably meant that they would not be left standing there long, but the expression had chilling implications. Golacinski doubted that they would be shot, and the longer he stood there he doubted it more. It turned out that they were just being moved to a new spot.

Richard Queen, the gangly vice consul, felt himself slipping into depression. He knew the symptoms. Long hours of sleep, a general listlessness, a chronic sense of despair and hopelessness. Tehran was his first assignment as a foreign service officer. He had grown up in suburban New York and distinguished himself as a middle-distance runner on his high school track team, fast enough to be among the better runners in the state, but not fast enough to compete beyond that level. Running suited Queen because it was a solitary pursuit, and he was in all things a solitary, precise man with extraordinary patience for detail work. He loved, for instance, a Civil War board game that came with a set of instructions that totaled more than three hundred pages, and which took months to play. His interest in war and history prompted him to apply to West Point, where he had been accepted, only to be turned away because of poor eyesight, a disappointment that had led to what he considered the happiest four years of his life at Hamilton College in Clinton, New York, where he had ma-jored in history. He had gone on to earn a master's degree at the Univer-sity of Michigan and had been proceeding halfheartedly toward a Ph.D. when he had taken the foreign service exam and done surprisingly well. Making history, traveling to exotic places on a government payroll, sounded a lot more interesting and secure than teaching it at a commu-nity college somewhere, so when the job was offered Queen grabbed it. He liked Tehran, despite the hardships. The work itself didn't appeal to him, but he enjoyed the informal, fraternal atmosphere, which he imag-ined was like soldiering together in a besieged fort. He also liked going to work in blue jeans.

Even before he was taken hostage, Queen had come to dislike Irani-ans. He fought against it, because he knew such a feeling was unfair, but in his visa work he had spent long parts of every workday interviewing ap-plicants, who one after another lied to him. It was a desperate time for many Iranians trying to escape the ongoing political tumult and violence. His job was to avoid giving visas to those who were looking only for an excuse to get to the United States, who had no intention of coming back. So-called students would bring school records with them that were obviously forged —Queen would hold the paper up to the light and see through the smudges and erasures. He had begun to believe that cheating the American consu-late was a national pastime. It seemed every Iranian he met, on or off the job, wanted him to help them get a visa, if not for themselves then for a family member or friend.

Once, returning from a small party in north Tehran, he and fellow vice consul Mark Lijek had been stopped at a roadblock manned by a motley crew of Revolutionary Guards. The diplomatic license plates on their car prompted questions, and their American citizenship earned them a trip to the guards' local headquarters. Queen had been drinking enough that it showed, and the session there began with a pious official berating them for violating the "Islamic purity" of the nation. One of the guards in the room had sat spinning an automatic pistol around his fin-ger. They were lectured about America's sins and asked what their jobs were at the embassy. When Lijek said that they worked at the consulate, the tone of the session abruptly and dramatically changed.

"Can you help us get a visa?" the official asked, and out came a fa-miliar tale of woe.

They heard the same sob stories often, as if there were stories circulating on the black market that were guaranteed to unlock the stone heart of American officials. He got so tired of hearing them that he found himself rewarding the occasional applicant who appeared honest. One young woman told him that she needed a visa because she wanted to attend high school in the United States.

"We don't give visas for high school," he told her.

"Oh."

She appeared ready to leave it at that, which was so refreshing that Queen had pressed on.

"Why do you want to go to high school in America?"

"I'd like to go because my parents are arranging a marriage for me and I don't want to get married."

Queen was startled by her candor. This sounded like an honest reason. It wasn't up to the usual standards for granting a visa but Queen was impressed.

"What happens if you don't get the visa?"

"Then, I don't get the visa," the woman said simply, shrugging. Here was someone looking for a way out of a difficult spot.

"Okay," he had told her. "You're honest. You get the visa."

As a captive now, he passed most of his time in slumber so heavy he felt drugged. Even when he was awake he spaced out. He worked at remembering and imagining the pretty girls he had known in college, some of whom he had admired urgently from a distance but never approached, and he kicked himself for his lack of gumption. This stint in Tehran had enriched his appreciation for girls, particularly American girls, with their laughter and their gorgeous long legs in tight Levi's and clean sneakers and beautiful white teeth. Why hadn't he approached one of them when he had the chance? They surely wouldn't find him appealing now. He was unshaven, his hair hung down over his ears, and he reeked. He had not been allowed to shower or change his clothes in weeks. His underclothes were filthy. When he was finally allowed to take a shower, he washed out his clothing and was given a clean pair of underpants, only they were in a boy's size. His complaints were shrugged off. Feeling humiliated, he stretched the underpants and squeezed himself uncomfortably into them. Better discomfort than disease. He became obsessive about cleanliness, policing the space around his mattress for every mote of dust or crumb of food. It gave him something to do that had a marginal claim of importance.

The two remaining female hostages, Kathryn Koob and Ann Swift, were kept apart from the men and watched over for the most part by female guards.

Like Queen, Koob's response to solitude and boredom was to turn inward, but for her the experience was spiritual, and exhilarating. On the second night of her captivity she experienced something that, the more she thought about it (and she had plenty of time to think), seemed to be a miracle. She had been sleeping on a bed in one of the staff cottages under a cape her grandmother had made for her years before when she was awakened by someone sitting down next to her on the bed. There was no sound, and no one touched her, which was the way her older sisters would sometimes gently awaken her at home when she was a child. One or the other would sit on the bed beside her and, instead of poking or shaking her or even speaking to her, would wait patiently for her to stir. As Koob surfaced from sleep, she realized that this "sister" was surely one of her Iranian guards. She opened her eyes—*What does she want now?*—and there was no one there.

In that moment she no longer felt alone. She believed she had been visited by an angel, her guardian angel, and was reminded of the constant presence of God, and after that she increasingly found solace in prayer. She had been raised on a farm with her five sisters in the Lutheran tradition her German great-grandparents had brought with them to Iowa. As a girl she had worked at a local Lutheran church to earn a scholarship to little Wartburg College, the Lutheran school. Her original ambition had been to become a high school drama teacher, and she taught speech and drama until she earned a master's degree from the University of Denver in 1968, where she first learned about the foreign service. It had appealed to a part of her that had no obvious antecedent; the wanderlust seemed hers alone. Years of travel had pulled her away from her family, her religion, her roots. Now, ironically, alone in captivity, alone with her thoughts day and night, she felt herself more than ever before surrounded with love and family. Emotionally, she had rediscovered home.

It gave her a sense of calm and of purpose. She set about disarming her guards' hostility with submission and kindness, as a novitiate in a nunnery might submit joyfully to religious discipline. When they insisted on binding her hands with a strip of cloth during the night, removing it in the morning, she took the cloth strip and neatly folded it like a bandage and tied it with a few unraveled threads. When the guard came looking for the cloth strip to tie her the following evening, she handed him the tidy bundle and he held it in his palm with wonder. He laughed and took it off to show the others, and didn't come back. In the first few weeks she got to know the young women who guarded her in shifts. They loved to talk and to practice their English. They were all romantic and excited and completely transported by their cause, by the rightness and importance of it. One of the girls—they were all in their late teens—was happily expecting to be killed.

"Obviously, the United States will send its military people in and we shall all die, and I shall be a martyr," she said.

"No, no," Koob protested. She said the United States would not want any of them to die, hostages or students.

The Iranian girls were surprised that Koob had never married. They asked her question after question about things that she regarded as strictly personal, and Koob did her best to give them answers. She was moved in the second week to the living room of the ambassador's residence, the same room where they had gathered for a Halloween party weeks ago. Jack-o'-lanterns leered down at her from the walls. She felt dumpy and ragged. She had been living in the same green wool dress for weeks. It was limp and shapeless. Her stockings had runs in them and, with a needle and various colors of thread given her by the guards, she stitched them back together. She had not been allowed to bathe, and when her captors agreed to take her underwear and launder it, they didn't bring it back. She waited for a day or two and then complained.

"They are being washed," said the imperious young woman who had taken charge of guarding them. Koob called her "Queenie."

"Can you find me some in the commissary?"

"*Miad*," said Queenie, a word meaning "it is coming," used much like the Spanish word "*mañana*."

"You said that two days ago. In my country, only whores go without underwear. I would like some panties and a bra. I am as embarrassed to go around without underclothing as you are to go out in public without your chador."

She got clean underwear that day.

Eventually, Koob and Swift roomed together in the residence's library, a small room painted yellow with pale blue drapes. It had been vandalized by the invaders, furniture had been heaped in the corners, much of it broken, and the walls were spray-painted with the usual revolutionary slogans. The room filled up at night with the female guards. They stretched out, twenty or thirty of them, and slept between their shifts. If a male guard came to the door before all the women had had a chance to throw chadors over their blue jeans and shirts the girls would scream in mock horror. They were clearly having fun.

One day, when Swift was taken off to the bathroom, Queenie questioned Koob about their professional relationship.

"What do you report to Miss Swift?" she asked.

"I don't report to Miss Swift. I report to Mr. Graves, my supervisor," she said.

"Miss Swift said you report to her. What kind of things do you tell her about?"

"I don't report to her."

"She says you do. Are you calling her a liar?"

Koob said she didn't understand why Swift would have said such a thing, if in fact she had. Swift had held a higher-ranking position at the embassy, so in that sense she "reported" to her, but not literally. Their exchange ended when Swift returned.

On Thanksgiving night Swift was taken away.

4

WORLD-DEVOURING GHOULS

Perhaps because he seemed so listless and beaten, Richard Queen was the first hostage asked to sign the petition the students had drafted demanding the return of the shah. The young vice consul actually thought Iran had a good case for demanding the former monarch's return, but at first he refused to sign.

"I thought your country was a free country," the student with the petition asked. "If you agree, why don't you sign it?"

"I don't *want* to," said Queen.

When he was shown the same document the next day with thirty hostage signatures at the bottom, he relented.

"It doesn't make any difference anyway," he said.

He signed his name so illegibly that they demanded he print it alongside the signature, and he managed to do that so imprecisely that later reprints of the document would identify him as "Richard Owen."

Thirty-three hostages signed the petition, more than half of those in captivity. Most saw it as meaningless, clearly a document signed under duress, and that under the circumstances no one would take it seriously at home. But the petition caused a sensation in the United States. Written in awkward English ostensibly in the voice of the hostages, it called for the shah to be returned immediately.

"In this way, we will be free," it said.

It had been carried out of Iran by the Swiss ambassador. The White House dismissed it summarily. State Department spokesman Hodding Carter said that it could hardly be accepted as a freely expressed appeal under the circumstances.

"If such a document does exist and if it's authentic, it's understood that statements made under duress have absolutely no validity and their only impact is to reflect adversely on the captors," said Jody Powell.

"Everyone ought to understand that such statements or petitions will have absolutely no bearing upon the actions of the United States. They simply do not exist."

Public opinion in America was at a boil. Television coverage was unrelenting. The three networks focused on the crisis as though nothing else of importance was happening in the world. It wasn't simply several score American citizens held hostage, it was "America" held hostage, as if every part of the government had been paralyzed. And journalists continued to receive more access to Iranian leaders and the captors than anyone in officialdom.

A reporter from the University of Dayton's radio station, WHIO, scored a minor coup by phoning the occupied embassy and, through an Iranian student translator, spoke for nearly an hour with the Iranian occupier who picked up the phone. The voice on the phone in Tehran identified himself only as "Mr. X."

"Will you release the hostages once you have made your point?" the reporter asked.

"We cannot at this time, but we will have a statement later," stated Mr. X, who said the students would not negotiate with the United States government.

The reporter suggested that they release one hostage as a show of good faith.

"We'll think it over," said Mr. X.

Most Americans wanted to strike back, and there was no shortage of ideas, everything from severe economic sanctions to nuclear weapons. Senator Barry Goldwater, the former Republican presidential nominee well known for his hard-nosed approach to foreign crises, proposed that the U.S. Air Force destroy Iran's oil industry, "and let them sit there and starve to death." A message hung on the front of the Chronicle building in San Francisco read, "Expel all Iranian students." Those Iranians who dared rally in the United States in support of the embassy takeover were challenged by large, unruly crowds. After a number of violent incidents around the country, shows of revolutionary solidarity by Iranian students in America came to a halt. One group in Washington obtained a permit for a march, but when the day came for the march no one showed up. An Iran Air flight to New York had to be diverted to Montreal when union workers at JFK International refused to service the plane. Long-shoremen were refusing to load or unload any ships flying the Iranian flag.

Protesters burned the Iranian flag before that country's consulate in Houston. In Riverside, California, an Iranian student was found shot to death, "execution style," according to the police. At St. Louis University, a man with a shotgun was disarmed after he walked into an administration building demanding to know the names of Iranian students attending the school.

A small portion of the anger was directed at the White House. Some blamed Carter for creating the circumstances that led to the takeover, others for failing to take immediate military action. Conservatives saw America's restraint as a sign of weakness—"Keep the Shah and send them Carter" read a placard carried by a protester in Texas.

National Security Adviser Zbigniew Brzezinski advocated a series of steps that would gradually tighten a noose around Iran, only to encounter resistance from within the administration at every turn. He proposed an immediate naval blockade on Iran, shutting down all of its imports and exports, a move that would have had the added benefit of pressuring European allies who relied on Iranian oil. It was opposed by the State Department, which felt it would do more to harm American alliances than to end the crisis. The president did act. Over the concerns of the Justice Department, Carter ordered most Iranian diplomats to leave, began deportation proceedings against all Iranians in the United States illegally, and banned oil purchases from Iran. He also froze the billions in Iranian assets in American banks.

Rescuing the hostages, furnishing the episode with a Hollywood ending, appeared to be nothing more than a fantasy. The isolation of Tehran, the location of the embassy compound in the heart of a city on fire with anti-Americanism, the easy opportunity for retaliation against the hundreds of American citizens living there—reporters, expatriates, spouses of Iranians, businessmen—all made it a very unattractive option. At the highest levels of government, Secretary of State Vance and his deputy Warren Christopher were dead set against any military effort to rescue their colleagues, and at that point in mid-November even the men secretly planning hard to create that option regarded it as foolhardy. Colonel Beckwith himself set the probability of success at "zero."

The cover story of *Time* magazine on November 19 weighed the possibility of a rescue mission by interviewing "two dozen experts in and out of government," and the consensus was that such an effort would be self-defeating and probably suicidal. Said Elmo Zumwalt Jr., the former chief of naval operations, "I think it's pretty much out of the question. . . . Surprise is so difficult to achieve because U.S. planes would be detected as they neared Iran." Zumwalt said approvingly that the Carter administration "has never seriously considered the military option."

Inside the White House, there were two schools of thought about how to deal with the crisis. They were represented by Vance and Brzezinski, who were increasingly at odds. Vance was a patrician lawyer and a gentleman who placed a great deal more faith than the national security adviser in the rationality and decency of his fellow man. His formative experience in public life had been the Vietnam War, which he had originally endorsed as President John F. Kennedy's secretary of the army, but which he turned against late in his tenure as President Lyndon B. Johnson's deputy defense secretary. He had been a member of the American delegation to the Paris peace talks in 1968. Experience had made him a strong believer in negotiation, and that, along with his direct responsibility for the State Department employees held in Tehran, led him to place paramount importance on their safe return. Brzezinski thought more in terms of vital national interests and the importance of America's world stature. If the United States and its diplomats could be attacked and hog-tied with impunity by a rabble of Iranian amateurs, then could American officials be considered safe anywhere in the world? For his part, the secretary of state cited the restraint with which President Harry Truman had handled a hostage-taking incident in 1949, when Chinese officials arrested Angus Ward, the U.S. consul general; Ward was eventually released and deported. Vance was meeting regularly with the families of the hostages and had taken Carter to one of the sessions five days after the takeover.

The first big session was held at the State Department in late November. The families, who traveled at government expense, were escorted into the building through the grand marble lobby beneath its colorful forest of flags. For those with little experience in official

Washington—spouses of the marines and lower-level embassy staff personnel—it was exciting and intimidating, and they were grateful that the country's most important officials were taking the time to brief and reassure them. But to the more experienced family members of foreign service officers, the hidden agenda of the meetings was clear. Barbara Rosen, a tough-minded Italian Catholic woman who taught school in the Bronx, had known from the first solicitous calls from Washington after the takeover that the unspoken message was not to break ranks and criticize the president or the administration.

That was not the sentiment for most in the room. All of the family members were under siege by local and national press; whatever they said was printed and broadcast across the country. Rita Ode and her captive husband Bob were retirees; he had taken the Tehran assignment as a temporary fill-in position, with the promise that he would be home for Christmas. They were building a retirement home in Arizona. When would he be home now? Dorothea Morefield, whose husband Richard was the embassy consul, believed strongly that the embassy should have been evacuated and closed before allowing the shah to enter the United States. Now she was at home in San Diego with four children, wondering if they would ever see their father again. Barbara Rosen considered Carter's response to the takeover to be flabby and indecisive; she felt strongly that the United States should have immediately cut off all ties with Iran, and refused to deal with them until her husband Barry and the others had been returned. But these were not the sentiments the department wanted aired. Except for the parents of the young marines, the wives and families of the military and CIA hostages seemed to be more at peace with the predicament; an element of risk was assumed in their work. Many of them were ready to accept the need for the United States to act militarily, and some were disappointed that Carter had not done so already. But many of the spouses and families of the foreign service officers, and those of the two stray civilians trapped at the embassy, California businessman Jerry Plotkin and school headmaster Bill Keough, were indignant. They and their husbands had not signed on for something like this. Why had Carter not closed the embassy and evacuated American personnel before permitting the shah to come to the United States? This response should have been foreseen.

Penne Laingen, the chargé's wife, was asked to write a letter welcoming everyone. It had been copied and placed on all the chairs in the auditorium. Mindful of the anger felt by many, she urged that such feelings be set aside. Dwelling on the administration's mistakes was unhelpful, she explained. What was needed was to rally behind the president. As she took her seat, she noticed that the young women next to her, daughters of Bill Keough, had drawn dark lines through much of what she had written. One of them stood, held up the letter, and made a show of tearing it into small pieces. Laingen would later hear herself denounced by some family members as "a State Department stooge."

Despite an official desire to keep the session private, some of the family members carried tape recorders and would deliver recordings of the session to reporters waiting outside. Journalist Robert Shaplen of *The New Yorker* was in the audience taking notes and would file a detailed report of it in the magazine.

Vance opened the session, promising the families that the government was doing everything in its power to bring their loved ones home safely. He urged them all to keep writing letters to the captives, although it was doubtful any would be delivered. More reassurance came from Under Secretary of State David Dunlop Newsom, who pledged to hold meetings of the families whenever they felt the need.

"I want to know if they're being brainwashed. Are their feelings being deformed?" asked one wife.

More challenging questions followed. Even Vance's request for them to write letters was challenged.

"I don't want them to get hold of my handwriting," said one woman. Captain Neil Robinson, one of the hostages just released, was present at the meeting, and he said he had been reluctant to write his wife from Tehran because he didn't want the Iranians to know where she lived.

A heated discussion sprang up over the point Penne Laingen had wanted to avoid, namely, Why had the shah been allowed into the country when it was known that doing so would place the embassy at risk?

Newsom talked about the assurances they had received from the provisional government, and about America's long "friendship" with the shah. "It was a difficult decision to make," he said. Those in the crowd were not in a forgiving mood. Many had received reassurances about the assignment that had proved hollow, and their loved ones were paying the price. Why hadn't they at least warned the embassy staffers beforehand, given them a chance to come home before the storm hit?

Penne Laingen spoke up.

"It was poor judgment, a monumental mistake, but we have done nothing wrong morally or legally," she said.

"I felt betrayed by the United States government," said Captain Robinson. "What happened should have been anticipated. Attacking Carter, though, will just make it more difficult now."

Penne Laingen told the crowd that she had been fortunate enough to speak regularly with her husband on the phone at the Foreign Ministry in Tehran and that he had urged everyone to be patient and to support the efforts of the State Department. A recent cable from the chargé was read aloud.

> We cannot and do not presume to know these men and women as well as you who are members of their families. But we do know them as able, dedicated, and loyal Americans, whose resilience and character, and, yes, their sense of humor will see them through this crisis.... To now describe these representatives of the United States as spies and agents of espionage is a travesty of the facts and an insult to human intelligence, both American and Iranian.

Many of the families weren't buying it. Some were panicky.

"People are getting angrier," said one.

"We're heading for another Vietnam War," said another, fearful of the use of military force.

One of the women asked if paying a ransom had been considered. Newsom said that was not under consideration. "The last thing to do is pass money around," he said.

Shaplen wrote: "The meeting broke up shortly after a discussion of the press, which some of the wives condemned for overpublicizing the militant captors and further arousing passions in America. 'We're very conscious of the level of hysteria,' Newsom said, in conclusion. 'For that reason, we're trying to step up visits to the hostages, to make them feel more secure and quiet things down here.'"

In the earlier session with just a few of the families that Carter had attended, the president had pledged not to "take any military action that would cause bloodshed or arouse the unstable captors of our hostages to attack them or punish them." Those present had been heartened by the words "our hostages."

At that meeting, Rosen had taken advantage of a brief moment with the president to hand him snapshots of her two daughters, and told him, "If you consider using guns, I hope you will think of the chance Barry will have." Carter put the photos in his pocket.

For his part, Brzezinski avoided those meetings. He did not want the emotions to interfere with his judgment, or, perhaps more to the point, to interfere with his ability to advocate placing the national interest above the lives of the hostages. Vance urged the president to get the shah out of the country, something the dethroned monarch had graciously volunteered to do already. Brzezinski counseled that such a move amounted to pure capitulation.

At a foreign policy breakfast with the president on November 9, the national security adviser had warned against allowing the crisis to "settle into a state of normalcy."

"If you do, it could paralyze your presidency," he had said. "I hope we never have to choose between the hostages and our nation's honor in the world but, Mr. President, you must be prepared for that. If they're still in captivity at Thanksgiving, what will that say about your presidency and America's image in the world?"

Vance continued to urge patience. He mentioned President Johnson's calm handling of the *Pueblo* incident.

"But that went on for a year!" said Brzezinski.

"And Johnson wasn't in the middle of a reelection campaign," said Jordan.

Brzezinski's position gained strength when the U.S. embassy in Islamabad was overrun by a mob and burned on November 21, killing two Americans and two Pakistani employees. A few weeks later, a mob in Tripoli attacked the U.S. embassy there and burned part of it, along with the cars parked outside. The fourteen Americans at that mission escaped unharmed. Vance told TV reporters that he did not see a pattern in these events, but he was probably the only one who didn't.

Carter was determined not to let his hopes for reelection dictate his handling of the matter, and no matter how it played politically he trod a careful line between his two advisers. The fact that it was virtually impossible to rescue the hostages made the decision easier. He had little choice but to pursue a negotiated solution, and to find ways to put more pressure on Iran, but every move seemed simply to worsen matters. There was apparently no way to even initiate dialogue. The crisis was at a complete impasse.

Carter's anger was kept under tight rein in public, but it showed in private. He ordered the military to draw up detailed plans for air strikes against Iran if and when the hostages were released.

"I want to punish them," he said. "Really hit them. They must know that they can't fool around with us."

Such strikes in advance of getting the hostages home safely might mollify public opinion but would only worsen matters. Brzezinski played out the scenario in his head: Iran would certainly retaliate by giving the hostages show trials and executing some of them. Apart from the appalling personal tragedy that would entail, it would compel an even more aggressive American response, which might bring the Soviets in on the side of the Iranians and lead to an uncontrollable conflict. No matter how much America cared about the hostages, their fate was not worth the risk of an all-out nuclear exchange. Such thoughts sketched out the recklessness of Iran's behavior.

The dilemma centered on one of the most basic and Gordian questions of democratic society: Which was more important, the individual or the state? Should Carter's priority be the larger national interest, or should national interest take a backseat to the fate of several score American citizens? These were, most of them, volunteers who had sought out hazardous postings. Brzezinski and Vance ably represented both sides of this question, but Carter was, above all else, a pragmatist. When possible, pragmatists avoid confronting the hardest questions. For a nation like revolutionary Iran, which saw itself as divinely inspired, the question was easy. The will of the state was the will of Allah. Millions might be blithely sacrificed in His name. But for America there could never be a clear answer. The preeminence of the individual was a bedrock principle of the state, yet all but the most fanatical libertarians knew of instances, say, in times of war or natural catastrophe, when the government was compelled to disregard it. Carter did not yet face war or catastrophe. He told his staff that so far as he was concerned the interests of the state and the well-being of the American hostages in Iran were one and the same, so there was no dilemma. The only sensible option was to wait and see if somebody in Tehran was willing to talk.

Waiting might have big political costs for Carter. The image of a timid, hog-tied president was too tempting for his political enemies to resist. Kennedy flailed around rhetorically, probing for a way to capitalize on Carter's predicament. He held a press conference to denounce the shah's regime, exaggerating its sins, criticizing Carter for allowing him into the United States, and calling for an "open debate" over America's role in propping up and sustaining his regime.

"The shah ran one of the most violent regimes in the history of mankind," Kennedy said. "How do we justify the United States on one hand accepting that individual [the shah] because he would like to come here and stay here with his umpteen billions of dollars that he has stolen from Iran, and at the same time say to Hispanics who are here illegally that they have to wait nine years to bring their children into this country." Kennedy said the administration should have known that admitting the shah would lead to a confrontation with the revolutionary leaders of Iran.

His comments were front-page news in Tehran and were warmly received, but they proved a bad miscalculation of the American mood. Iranian applause was political poison at home, where it smelled like capitulation, and Kennedy was criticized from every quarter. Stung, he promptly withdrew his proposals and said that a long conversation with Secretary of State Vance had convinced him that they were premature.

Henry Kissinger, whose advocacy on behalf of the shah had helped precipitate the crisis, surfaced on *The Dick Cavett Show* to urge that the shah be encouraged to stay in America as long as he wished. He advised his fellow Americans to "keep cool."

"This is a situation where we are all obliged to support the people handling it," he said, in a somewhat tepid endorsement of Carter, and then, dodging his own role in the affair, "There is no point in second-guessing it." He finished with a subtle stab at the White House, hinting at presidential timidity. "When this is over we should find out what it is that makes foreign leaders think they can deal with the United States in this manner."

Journalist Stephen S. Rosenfeld wrote in the *Washington Post* that the real error made by the Carter White House was not in admitting the shah but in pursuing "a constructive link with the new Iran" instead of cutting ties.

He wrote: "The administration's real vulnerability, I think, lies in its expectation—hardheaded in pursuit of oil, softheaded in its pursuit of Third World favor—that things were settling down in Iran, that the moderates were prevailing; that the extremists could be trimmed to size; that the United States could gain more from betting on the future (by providing its presence, arms, grain, heating fuel, schooling, etc.) than from cutting itself out of the game. . . . I sense a new rage, a disgust, building in this country against the president. He will pay."

Even though the polls did not yet bear out Rosenfeld's prediction, Carter knew that unless something happened they would. In a staff meeting at Camp David near the end of November, he reviewed all of the military options at his disposal and settled upon a broad strategy of ratcheting up pressure on Iran. First he would condemn, then threaten, then break relations, then mine three harbors, then bomb Abadan, and, if all this failed, put up a total blockade.

The president, at Brzezinski's urging, also authorized a private message to be conveyed through an intermediary to Iran's foreign minister, making a point of saying that the contents would not be made public so that there would be less danger of it being perceived as an empty threat: If *one* hostage was killed or seriously harmed, the United States would respond as though all the hostages had been, and the response would be swift and harsh.

On the last day of November, a Friday, Bruce Laingen watched as the day unfolded outside the tall third-floor windows of the Iranian Foreign Ministry's formal reception suite. Thanksgiving had come and gone and there was no change in the crisis. Initially, he, Tomseth, and Howland had stayed on at the Foreign Ministry out of solidarity with their colleagues, but their voluntary stay had evolved into something that, for all practical purposes, was imprisonment. Partly out of a sense of duty, partly out of loyalty to their captive colleagues, and partly out of respect for the other foreign missions in Tehran, the three were stuck, suspended in a bubble of increasingly awkward protocol.

It was a holiday in Iran, Ashura, a celebration of the martyrdom of Imam Hussein. The ministry building was empty except for the "security guards," who over the previous three weeks had begun to seem less like protectors and more like jailers. On this day Laingen noted that they seemed more nervous, with huge street demonstrations planned throughout the city. If a mob decided to storm the ministry and seize the despised American "spies," there was no way it could have been held off by such a small force.

Laingen watched as clumps of demonstrators moved in the streets below toward Tehran University for the Friday prayer meeting, center for the day's celebrations. Many carried homemade placards and posters. The whole nation was in the grip of Islamist fervor, a kind of mass hysteria. Abolhassan Bani-Sadr had lasted only a few weeks as foreign minister, ousted apparently by mullahs who felt he was insufficiently pious to represent the nation overseas, and when Laingen heard a helicopter approach and land in the ministry's garden, he recognized the figure stepping out as Sadegh Ghotbzadeh, the replacement, back from an overnight visit to Qom, the real seat of power now in Iran.

Ghotbzadeh seemed an unlikely choice, a suave, dapper, clean-shaven man who did not wear religion on his sleeve. He was a thickset, swarthy man with small, deep-set eyes and a great broad nose, whose face seemed bottom heavy, with a wide mouth and the chin and jaw of a cartoon boxer. Ghotbzadeh was a smart, ambitious nationalist who had earned a degree of flexibility in an increasingly rigid Iran by dint of the friendship and alliance he had formed with Khomeini in Paris. Still, today was a day that demanded a show of reverence. He stepped right into a waiting Mercedes, no doubt hurrying to the Friday prayers, a great public show of faith held weekly on the grounds of Tehran University. It was now mandatory for all high officials.

The prayer meeting was on the radio. Laingen had been to them often enough—most recently with Henry Precht—so he could picture the whole scene, which he recorded in his diary, something reminiscent of old Nazi newsreels or the images in George Orwell's *1984*, only with an Islamic cast:

> The high-pitched voice of the Friday (Jomeh) preacher, the Aya-tollah [Husayn-ali] Montazari, lecturing, cajoling, beseeching the crowds that by now jam every square foot of the university grounds

and spread out in adjoining streets in all directions. The radio speaks of a million, possibly two, citizens of Tehran listening, remarkably attentive and orderly. The women are carefully segregated, the children surely restless, yet there is little evidence of this to our ears. The preacher, bearded and turbaned, stands with a bayonet and rifle in one hand, gesticulating with the other, without notes. His rostrum is a stage erected at one end of the main plaza of the university grounds. White cloth banners, emblazoned with black revolutionary and religious slogans, completely cover the outline of this elevated stand. The backdrop is a vast drawing on cloth of the face of Ayatollah Khomeini, gazing unsmiling and stern at the crowds below. At the very mention of the name Khomeini, the vast throng erupts in sound with thundering repeats of his name and then subsides into respectful attention.

After Montazari's performance, a representative of the now celebrated Muslim Students Following the Imam's Line, heroic conquerors of the American fortress at the heart of the capital, urged the millions to march on the "den of spies." Hateful rhetoric about the United States was developing a florid lexicon. Americans were "world-devouring ghouls," who "skinned alive the meek ones" and "stripped nations of their resources."

"Carter is vanquished!" came a shout from the crowd.

"Khomeini is victorious!" came another.

Symbols had replaced reality. It was as though taking hostage sixty-six unguarded Americans amounted to a great military victory.

Laingen wrote:

> Through it all we are reminded of our colleagues inside the embassy compound ... Daily they are beset by the rolling pressing sound of thousands of voices from the streets around them, calling for death to America, Carter, and imperialism. We are sick at heart, always fearful that mass hysteria of this kind could erupt into violence ... We are saddened and depressed by this deliberate fostering of hate and venom and bitterness. We dread the thought of trying to sleep—sleep is almost impossible to achieve because of the pain and worry about where this tragedy will end.

To conclude the day's festivities, Khomeini had called on everyone in Tehran to go to their rooftops and shout, *"Allahuakbar!"* for fifteen minutes. Outside the embassy walls the cries rose all over the teeming city, especially from the seemingly endless expanse of low gray and brown structures of the crowded slums to the south. Over and over and over again:

"Allahuakbar!"
"Allahuakbar!"
"Allahuakbar!"

5

DAVY CROCKETT DIDN'T HAVE TO FIGHT HIS WAY IN

Immediately after wowing the brass at Fort Stewart in early November, and then staying up almost all night with Beckwith to celebrate, Major Logan Fitch had taken his newly certified Delta Force squadron for a week of skiing in Breckenridge, Colorado. He called it "winter warfare training" but the trip was primarily a reward, a chance to blow off steam. They all had been working for two years without a break. Fitch was an expert skier himself, and he hired some local instructors to assist him. They spent their days on the sunny slopes and their nights in the resort's bars and restaurants. But before the week was up, Fitch was summoned back east. He was flown back alone to the CIA "Farm" in southern Virginia.

There he met with Beckwith and the rest of the unit's commanders, and within two days, joined by his squadron and the one under Schoomaker's command, he began training to rescue the American hostages in Iran. None of the men had been given a chance to go home on a quick stopover at Fort Bragg to gather up their gear, and none was allowed to contact family members to explain where they were and what they were doing. Fitch's men had left for what they thought would be a week in the high Rockies and instead had disappeared into the sprawling acres of the Farm, a "secure, undisclosed location." It would be Christmas before they would have permission to visit home.

Less than a month after it had gone to work inside the secret suite on the inner rim of the Pentagon, the small group of unorthodox military planners had made substantial progress. Delta had the luxury of not worrying about how they were going to get to Tehran and back, so they concentrated on what they called "action at the objective," how to most effectively take down the embassy compound and free the hostages. The release of thirteen hostages had provided a bonanza of detailed information. Debriefing the released blacks and women, they learned a lot about who was guarding the Americans, what kind of weapons they had, where they were positioned inside and outside the embassy gates, and what kind of reaction they might expect when they stormed the compound. The fact that the guards appeared to all be untrained amateurs was good news. They learned roughly where the hostages were being held, in which buildings, and in what parts of those buildings, at least as of mid-November. The fact that the captors had created more or less permanent holding areas for large groups of hostages, such as the Mushroom Inn and the chancery basement, was more good news. Still, pinpointing and keeping track of where the captive Americans were being held would be a consistent problem.

At the Farm, an elaborate eight-by-eight-foot model of the compound was built, with the buildings reproduced in exact detail. There were two separate take-apart models of the chancery and warehouse. The roofs could be lifted off and upper floors removed so that the men could memorize the layout of each floor. The models, along with blueprints of the buildings and up-to-date satellite surveillance, allowed them to know the compound better than they knew their own homes. The drawings revealed the location of circuit breakers, where they could cut the electricity and black out the entire compound during their assault. From television they learned about how the compound and each building inside it was guarded on the outside. To practice storming the compound they used engineering tape to lay out a silhouette on the grass of the main buildings and outer walls, and then they timed themselves storming in from various directions, looking for the fastest way in and out. The tape would be taken up whenever Soviet surveillance satellites were known to be passing overhead. They spent hours and hours on scenario training, practicing moving into rooms and hallways and confronting guards, all the while fine-tuning their force structure. They did a lot of weapons training. Of great help was Captain Robinson, the intelligence officer unknowingly released by the Iranians simply because he was black. Robinson was able to answer a myriad of small practical questions. Do certain doors open out or in? What material is it made of? How thick? How thick were the walls in various places and how were they constructed? How thick was the brick wall around the compound? In the warehouse, the only access to the Mushroom Inn on the blue-prints was a narrow staircase that led down to a long hallway. This meant the raiding force would have to move to the bottom of the stairs and then race down a perilous length before bursting into the rooms where hostages were being held, allowing the guards potentially disastrous seconds to grasp what was happening and react, possibly by shooting hostages. From one of the freed hostages, Delta's planners learned that the wall at the bottom of the steps that separated the holding rooms from the hallway was flimsy and could easily be knocked down. So the raiding force could break directly into the rooms, saving precious seconds and adding the shock and confusion Delta needed to create in the attempt.

They planned to enter the compound stealthily, coming over the back walls and using weapons equipped with silencers to shoot guards who got in their way, but on the way out they planned to blow a hole in the wall big enough to walk all of the hostages out. So they built brick walls of identical thickness and practiced blowing holes in them.

It was an intricate maneuver that would require careful choreography; when Schoomaker likened the raid to a ballet one day he heard guffaws, but that's what it was. One of the men promptly produced a cartoon showing a fully outfitted Delta operator wearing a tutu and dancing on tiptoe. The men were broken into three teams—Red, White, and Blue—one to deal with matters outside the embassy walls, and two to conduct the takedowns inside. The Blue element, the smallest, was led by Major Jerry Boykin, and its primary responsibility was to cover the gates to the compound once the raid had begun and to storm, take, and hold the soccer stadium across the street to the compound's north. Inside the walls, the hostage takers had placed obstacles on rooftops, tennis courts, and any flat places where helicopters might land. Because of this the plan called for the hostages and rescue force to rally inside the soccer stadium, where the choppers would land, load, and leave. Boykin's force employed sniper teams with machine guns to prevent any Iranian force from entering the compound or stadium. Fitch's White team had the biggest job, assaulting the ninety-room chancery, which had been "hardened," outfitted with barred windows, sandbags, and heavy doors prior to the takeover. If the hostage takers utilized the defensive measures, the main building was going to be a damn hard target. Schoomaker's Red team was going to assault the warehouse that contained the Mushroom Inn. There were also two command elements, a primary one led by Beckwith himself and a backup led by Burruss.

They were constantly fine-tuning the ballet. They had chosen to go over the walls to begin the raid by ascending ladders from the outside and then jumping down six feet to the tennis courts. One day, Intelligence Sergeant Gary Moston made a surprising discovery poring over satellite photos. Examining the shadows around the tennis courts, he noticed that they were sunken; they were twelve feet from the top of the wall, not six! So the assault force would have jumped in the dark expecting to drop only six feet, and instead would have fallen twice that far. Burruss could picture his men in a helpless pile with broken ankles and legs, and with more men raining down on top of them. They chose a different spot for the ladders.

If things went wrong and the helicopters couldn't make it in, they practiced alternate scenarios to evade capture and escape by driving trucks into either Turkey or Afghanistan, three hundred to four hundred miles distant. Delta built portable facades that could be placed inside a vehicle so that if its back doors were opened it would look like it was loaded with canned goods or boxes—the hostages and rescuers would be hidden behind. The unit practiced dealing with customs questions and learned some key phrases in Turkish and Afghan. The military combed its ranks to select volunteers who spoke fluent Farsi to join the force as truck drivers.

By the end of November, Delta was basically ready to storm the compound, but the problem of delivering them and getting them out remained. It was determined that the only helicopters large enough for the job, with enough range and with folding tail booms that would enable them to be stored secretly belowdecks on an aircraft carrier, were navy RH-53D Sea Stallions, which were used primarily for minesweeping operations. The choppers would have to be hidden below decks because the Soviets flew regular reconnaissance over the American fleet, and they would surely notice eight additional choppers. The model could also be outfitted with additional external fuel tanks. The Sea Stallions had good range, but nowhere near enough to fly from the Persian Gulf or neighboring countries to Tehran and back without refueling several times, and the military lacked the capability of refueling them in the air. So they needed to establish a remote refueling point somewhere in the desert south of Tehran. In the

Pentagon suite, one group set about finding a suitable desert location, while another worked on plans for delivering the fuel.

An early scheme was to package the aviation fuel in rubber bladders big enough to hold five hundred gallons each and drop them from aircraft to the refueling spot. Parachutes would slow the multiton blivits' descent, and the forces aboard the choppers would then roll them into position to transfer the fuel with manually operated pumps. This would avoid the necessity of landing large fixed-wing aircraft in the desert, a risky maneuver.

It proved easier said than done. At a complete dry run of the mission staged in the Arizona desert outside Yuma at the end of November, Burruss was standing with General Phillip C. Gast, Fitch, and Boykin when a practice blivit-drop was attempted. It was a clear desert night with a full moon and they could clearly see growing black blobs against the dark blue sky as they descended. Major Schoomaker was looking up with night-vision goggles, expecting to see a neat row of pallets come flying out of the plane at intervals, then blossom with parachutes, and instead saw what looked like an airplane vomiting something off its back ramp. It was immediately apparent that some of the blobs were falling much too fast, plummeting actually. Something about their squishy bulk had played havoc with the rigging and their parachutes had failed to open. They streamered in, great black hurtling, truck-sized watermelons that hit the desert floor with a gigantic cracking *sploosh!* The air was suddenly pungent with the odor of splattered aviation fuel. More followed.

"Jesus Christ, I hope none of them is coming my way," said Fitch.

Cigarettes were hastily extinguished.

It was *sploosh!* after *sploosh!* as the blivits crashed in. Three of the ten blivits landed safely, but moving them across the uneven desert ground proved more difficult than imagined. Eventually the riggers would lick the problem of landing the blivits softly, but the time it took to move them and pump fuel from them, along with the unforgettable experience of hearing them crack into the desert floor, permanently soured the mission planners on the method. So it was back to the drawing boards.

The dry run had disclosed other serious problems. The navy chopper pilots were especially unimpressive. They were accustomed to flying relatively low-stress minesweeping runs over water. This mission would call for something much harder. The choppers were going to be loaded

right up to their maximum carrying capacity—Delta had carefully calculated how much ammunition and water each man could carry in order to
make sure they stayed just under the limit—which made them difficult to
maneuver in the best of circumstances. The pilots would be flying in blacked-
out conditions wearing night-vision goggles, which were a technological
miracle but which sharply reduced range of vision and could be worn for
only thirty minutes at a time before causing severe eye strain. The pilots
had to take turns wearing them on a long flight. Entering Iran stealthily called
for maneuvering in darkness through mountain ranges flying low enough
to avoid radar, which was often hair-raising. Landing and taking off in the
desert stirred up dust storms that often meant flying blind. After the first
dry run, one of the pilots begged off the mission. Beckwith wanted him court-
martialled, calling him a "quitter" and worse, and though the pilot was not
punished, he was forced to remain in isolation, for fear of leaking information. Eventually the entire navy squadron was replaced by marine pilots who
lacked experience with the Sea Stallions but who had more experience flying missions over land, and in combat. This did not completely placate
Beckwith and his squadrons, who had worked with veteran air force special-
ops pilots whom they trusted and greatly respected. But this was a "joint op,"
and the air force already had its piece of the mission, flying the fixed-wing
aircraft. Beckwith suspected, rightly, that the marines were given the choppers to fly to satisfy their need for a role. The marines believed their pilots
were at least as good as the air force's, if not better, but there was no convincing "Charging Charlie." As far as he was concerned, he was getting sec-
ond-string pilots because the brass was less interested in success than in
keeping things collegial in the Pentagon dining halls. This suspicion, that
Pentagon politics was being given a higher priority than excellence, would
continue to influence morale. Delta believed the men recruited to deliver
them and fly them out were not in their league.

The biggest problem remained intelligence, specifically what in tactical parlance was called EEI (Essential Elements of Information). There
was no CIA presence in Iran—the three agency officers were being held
hostage. In a message to General Vaught after the Yuma exercise, Beckwith
produced an alphabetized list of concerns.

My most critical EEIs remain unanswered. These are the vital questions which must be answered to reduce the current risk and accom-

plish our rescue mission: A. Are all the hostages actually in the embassy compound during the hours of darkness? B. Where and in what strength are check points along major routes in Tehran which lead to the embassy compound? C. What assistance and support can be provided to Delta by in-place assets? D. Who will drive the trucks if and when [they are obtained]? E. Are there any safe houses in the vicinity of the compound Delta could use prior to the actual rescue? F. What is the night time MO [modus operandi] of roving patrols and sentry posts in and around the compound? G. What is the strength of the enemy inside the compound during the hours of darkness? Can the enemy reinforce the compound? If so, in what strength?

As problems were identified, the number of mission planners at the Pentagon kept growing. They were crammed into a relatively small space, along with tables, chairs, filing cabinets, maps, and displays. Room 2C840 was off the chairman's corridor, a ceremonial stretch of hallway lined with portraits of the lengthening line of men who had served as chairman of the joint chiefs. There was a cipher lock on the door to enter the outer office, and a second steel door inside with another cipher lock that led to the inner sanctum. It was a classic boiler-room environment, windowless, crowded, and noisy with conversation and ringing phones. The space was so cramped that it resembled the inside of a submarine, with exposed wires and pipes in the ceiling and wall-to-wall desks, safes, files, maps, and people. The air-conditioning didn't work well, and about half of those in the room smoked. Briefings were held every morning and every afternoon for the chairman of the joint chiefs and the secretary of defense, Harold Brown, and in the afternoons Brzezinski usually sat in. Sometimes Hamilton Jordan stopped by. Brzezinski dominated the meetings, going on often at sometimes infuriating length about theoretical things that the nuts-and-bolts men in the room found irrelevant. The chairman, General Jones, was so soft-spoken and deferential that even when he spoke the men in the room sometimes couldn't make out what he was saying. Brown would fiddle with his glasses and sometimes look at Jones imploringly, as if to say, *Tell me what to do here.* The goal was always to reach a point where Jones and Brown felt comfortable that the mission had a reasonable chance of success, and day after day it was clear that they were still a long way from that goal.

The mission posed problems that seemed insoluble, but giving up was not an option. Early on, one of the officers involved tried to capture the improbability of the exercise with a list of "requirements" and "conditions," all of them true.

Requirements
1. Fly 15,000 miles around the world—850 miles of it in Iran.
2. Enter into Tehran undetected.
3. Breach the embassy and rescue the hostages.
4. Return the hostages without harm.
5. Don't hurt any civilians, Iranian or otherwise.
6. Rescue the three Americans at the Foreign Ministry simultaneously.
7. Do not permit the Iranian forces to be aware of or react to our presence.

Conditions
1. No country will help you.
2. You must invent the force to do the job. It does not now exist.
3. The operation could go in ten days and you must always be ready to execute in ten days.
4. The entire training program must be kept secret—not only from the public but from most of the services themselves.
5. There will be no money directly provided for the program.
6. Most service points of contact cannot be directly approached.
7. The entire operation must take place in darkness.

Beckwith did away with the fifth of the "requirements." At one of the early briefing sessions, as he outlined the plan for assaulting one embassy gate, a high-ranking navy officer asked, "What about the guard?"

Beckwith was startled by the question and leaned his imposing mass across the table in the questioner's direction, looking him squarely in the eyes.

"He will be taken out," he said.

"You mean killed?" asked the officer, who seemed shocked.

Beckwith growled at him, "I'll shoot him right between the eyes and then do it again just to make sure."

The failure of the blivits meant that they would have to land large fixed-wing aircraft in the desert, which meant finding a location with hard enough soil and flat enough ground to serve as a makeshift runway. Some thought was given to simply seizing an airport outside Tehran, but that would have blown the surprise critical for Delta's success.

By the end of the month a mission was taking shape. Sea Stallion helicopters would fly off the aircraft carrier *Kitty Hawk* in the Arabian Sea. They would cross over into Iranian airspace at locations known to be uncovered by that country's radar intercept system—Americans had designed it and built it, so they knew its weaknesses. Six choppers would fly to Desert One, an as yet unidentified rallying point in the desert. At the same time, six MC-130 transports equipped with sophisticated navigation and electronic countermeasure devices would fly from Wadi Kena, an airstrip in a remote corner of Egypt that had been built by the Russians a decade before. They would use the same secure flight path and land on a rudimentary strip that would have to be prepared by a clandestine mission in advance. The transports would carry Delta Force and the fuel bladders that had failed the drop test.

At Desert One, the spent choppers would be refueled from the bladders and boarded by Delta. The transports would take off and fly back out of Iran to prepare for return flights the following night, and the choppers would fly to secure locations outside of Tehran where they and the Delta assault force would be parked and hidden throughout the next day. Securing these hide sites was only one part of a mission that would be completed by Delta Force and CIA agents who would sneak into the country days before the rescue attempt.

On the second night, Delta would be driven to the embassy compound on trucks and carry out their assault. At the same time, a ranger company would take a little-used airport outside the city. A separate army special-forces unit would raid Iran's Foreign Ministry to free Laingen, Tomseth, and Howland. Overhead, two fixed-wing, four-engtine AC-130 Spectre gunships would provide heavy firepower over the embassy to suppress crowds or any military force that scrambled to counter the raid. Once the raiding force and freed hostages had crossed the street to the soccer stadium, the choppers hidden through the long day before would fly in and carry them out to the seized airport. Big C-141 transport jets, one configured to provide emergency medical care, would land at the occupied airport, load up Delta, the rangers, and the hostages, and fly out of Iran with a fighter escort. The choppers would be destroyed and left behind.

It was as inelegant as a Rube Goldberg contraption, with parts borrowed from everywhere. Everyone, including Delta, was going to be attempting something they had never done. Any operation this complex, with this many difficult and critical pieces, was a sitting duck for Murphy's Law. Success was a long shot at best. None of the senior commanders at the Pentagon believed it would be successful. Those preparing for it did so with a sense of fatalism that waxed both grim and cheerful.

"The only difference between this and the Alamo is that Davy Crockett didn't have to fight his way in," quipped Captain Wade Ishimoto, Delta's assistant intelligence officer.

Not the least of the problems faced by the rescue force was maintaining secrecy. The planning effort at the Pentagon alone now numbered more than forty-five. Because the rescue force had no budget, it simply took what it needed. During the dress rehearsal in Yuma, local commanders complained about planes and helicopters gobbling up aviation fuel without accounting for it. They were silenced by a call from the Pentagon. It was a challenge to assemble all the night-vision goggles needed by the operators and mission pilots. The amazing goggles, which illuminated the darkest night in monochromatic shades of green, were new, expensive, and rare, and the units who had them were loathe to part with them. They had to be commandeered without explanation. To cover the absence of Delta Force, which was spending most of its time at its "undisclosed location" in Virginia, a skeletal undeployed staff at its Fort Bragg "Stockade" worked overtime to maintain the appearance of normalcy, answering phones, driving out to the firing range and shooting off enough rounds to make it sound like the unit was doing its usual practice sessions, moving vehicles around to maintain the appearance of normal workday comings and goings. The staff did its best to handle the volume of phone calls, but one persistent general insisted on speaking to Beckwith himself. The colonel ignored him until the general became abusive to the staff, at which point Beckwith asked General Vaught to get rid of the caller.

By the end of the month six Sea Stallion helicopters had been moved on one pretext or another to the *Kitty Hawk,* where they were now stashed safely belowdecks. Not even the carrier's commander was fully aware of their purpose. An alert reporter for a local newspaper had noticed the choppers being loaded on a giant C-5 Galaxy transport to be ferried to the carrier and speculated in print—with pictures!—that they might be on their way to a staging area for a rescue mission in Tehran. Fortunately, no one else picked up on the story.

The assault force rehearsed its violent ballet over and over again. There was so much about the mission that Beckwith couldn't control that he was determined to get his piece of it perfect. At Camp Smokey, life settled into a routine. The men studied in the daytime and rehearsed at night. When they weren't working they had permission to shoot deer, so they practiced with their expensive sniper rifles and their cook prepared venison dinners. Late at night many of them drank. For men who liked this kind of life, it was pleasant and without stress. Despite the seriousness of the planning and training, few believed they would ever be deployed.

Fitch was convinced of it. He put his heart into the work—the tactics they were perfecting had lots of potential applications, so none of the effort was wasted—but he believed that the chance something this risky would be attempted by this president was about nil. He didn't believe Carter had the balls.

6

THE CORRUPT
OF THE EARTH

In early December, John Limbert was placed in a van and driven off the embassy grounds. Initially, he was elated; he was wired that way; his first instinct was always hope. Maybe they were being released! He knew he would make quite a picture on the evening news. He had lost weight and was unshaven and haggard. On the morning of the takeover he had wanted to get a haircut, now his thick dark hair was so long he doubted his wife, Parveneh, and their two children would recognize him. But it was soon clear that he wasn't going home.

Instead he was led into a large private home with marble floors and a grand foyer with a high ceiling from which hung an enormous, gaudy chandelier. At the center of the house was a wide, curved staircase, which led up to a carpeted landing with hallways leading off in several directions. It was luxury abandoned in haste. Limbert and his two new roommates, State Department communicator Rick Kupke and the ICA chief John Graves, found expensive clothes still hanging in the closet. It must have been the home of someone important in the royal regime. The windows in their upstairs room had been sealed shut and blackened. They soon perceived that other hostages were there too. Dave Roeder and Bob Ode were down the hall.

Limbert took this move as bad news. It suggested a higher level of coordination and resolve and felt like a long step away from freedom. They were watched over by a guard they dubbed "Two Shirts," because his wardrobe alternated invariably between a pink one and a green one. Two Shirts had no sympathy for his captives' physical discomfort. He accused them constantly of surreptitiously communicating and ordered all three of them to face different walls. This meant Kupke and Graves had to lie in bed for the guard's entire eight-hour shift, in the same position, staring at the tan walls. Limbert, who conversed with most of the guards at length, had such contempt for Two Shirts' inflexibility that he would turn his back to him every time he came in the room. The other guards sometimes took pity on them. Kupke and Graves were allowed to sit up and place their feet on the floor, and once or twice they were allowed to stand and walk around the room, but not often.

Limbert spoke to the guards in Farsi, while Graves, a tall man with a full graying beard and a mustache he waxed and drew out to points at each end, seemed calm and aloof, puffing away obsessively on his pipe. Kupke retreated into hours of reverie, imagining himself as the star in football games he had watched as a boy from the stands, or taking long walks down Main Street in his hometown of Rensselaer, Indiana, stopping to chat with people in every store. Passing the hours on his mattress on the floor, Limbert finally let go of his expectation of early release, reconciled himself to open-ended confinement and uncertainty, and began the routines that would see him through the ordeal.

The goal was to structure this ocean of time and use it productively. He had read that keeping fit and clean were two simple things that passed time and fostered health in confinement, so he commenced doing sit-ups and leg lifts. He avoided working up a heavy sweat, because he was allowed to shower only once every few weeks and he didn't want to smell worse than he already did. Meals came regularly, and the food was edible, but he was still dropping weight. His pants swam on him.

Day and night he read. Because he knew Farsi he had more options than the other hostages, and he made a point of asking the guards for books about their revolution. They were eager to oblige. They brought him first the writings and speeches of Ali Shariati, the intellectual father of the revolution, and then other books by revolutionary leaders. Limbert's erudition and fluency intrigued his guards, and he made an effort to engage them in conversation whenever they came to the room. Kupke and Graves listened silently to long conversations they couldn't understand. Limbert knew that hostages who made a connection with their captors had a better chance of surviving, so while steering away from political topics he asked the guards an endless stream of questions about themselves. Most of them were young, naive, and far too polite to tell him simply to shut up. When he asked a question about their religion, such as, "Explain martyrdom to me," they would typically oblige with a lengthy and spirited answer, seeing an opportunity to enlighten the infidel spy. Limbert would listen patiently and ask still more questions. He had nothing but time. Drawing his captors out relieved his boredom, helped satisfy his curiosity about them, and had an element of self-preservation. He was determined to see his guards as individuals, and for them to see him as one, too, as someone with feelings and ideas rather than just another Yankee imperialist. It was a survival tactic. If he fell ill and needed help, it would be a lot easier to ignore someone you didn't know or like. After a month, all of the hostages were devising their own strategies to cope, and his was conversation. If there was a rescue attempt, then the guard in the room with him might have thirty seconds to decide whether to shoot him. If he hesitated, even for only a few seconds, it might spare his life. So Limbert chatted with them and drew them out as though his life depended on it.

It wasn't always easy or pleasant. Most were shockingly ill-informed and uneducated, and if they were abusive or arrogant it was easy to dislike them. Others he felt sorry for. He believed they were being manipulated for reasons they couldn't begin to understand. He recognized certain types of young Iranians from his years of teaching in Shiraz. They were confused kids living in a bizarre society that for reasons of religion or tradition closed off most of the usual avenues of growth and self-improvement. It produced young people who were restless and ignorant, ripe for a demagogue, and in Khomeini they had found their man.

There was one young guard, a teenager, who spoke with such a pronounced Turkish accent that Limbert could tell he was from a provincial town in the Azerbaijan region. Clearly the most thrilling, important thing this young man had ever been asked to do was guard these American devils, and his excitement and anxiety were both evident. Limbert asked him at one point, "What part of Azerbaijan are you from?" The young man was shocked that his captive knew this about him. Afraid that he would be chastised for giving information to a hostage, but too polite to refuse an answer, he wrote down the name of his village on a piece of paper and handed it over. Limbert counted such small interactions as victories.

The captive diplomat had first visited Iran in 1962 as a young man stirred by the rhetoric of President Kennedy. A recent Harvard graduate, he had wanted to help less fortunate people and he wanted to travel, explore, and learn. Some of the guards told him that the only other Americans they had met were Peace Corps volunteers like himself, teaching in secondary schools in small towns. Several even said how much they had respected these teachers. It made Limbert want to laugh. These were, in effect, *his* students. This wasn't how things were supposed to have turned out. But, then, he had never seen things accurately through Iranian eyes. How unprepared he had been to teach children in a culture and language entirely foreign to him! But if it had been difficult for him, then what must it have been like for his students? How patient they had been with him! If Kennedy had expected the Peace Corps experience would build political and cultural bridges to the Third World, he had underestimated the complexity of such a task. A bridge requires firm foundations on both sides of a divide. The Iranians he met and worked with had no desire to build a bridge to the United States. They were perfectly capable of liking and admiring him and the other volunteers personally, but they were distrustful and increasingly angry with the American government, its values, and its policies. He remembered listening to the radio in the summer of 1965 as President Johnson announced his decision to send more troops to Vietnam and then to bomb Hanoi. Many of his Iranian friends had been angry about that then, but it had never interfered with their warm feelings toward him. He was an American, yes, but he was first and foremost *himself*, a caring, decent young man, someone in love with all things Persian, a human being trying to do the right thing with his life. The personal and the political ran on separate tracks. It took something like a revolution to push these two tracks together, to make Iranians take out their anger with the U.S. government on individual Americans—which is what had so dramatically happened here. Afire with their new political power and visions of remaking the world, all their stored antipathy and resentment had demonized him. It was shocking, and yet when he had reflected on it more he concluded that it was something he should have seen coming a long time ago.

Things had taken a turn for the worse when he was in Shiraz finishing work on his Ph.D. in the late sixties. At first he recognized the usual undercurrent of anti-Americanism in his students and colleagues, but still it rarely surfaced, and it didn't color their appreciation of him. By that time Limbert was fluent in Farsi. He was, in effect, the ideal Peace Corps graduate, an American who had fully blended with his host country. He had met and married Parvaneh; they were at that point as much Iranian as American. He considered Shiraz as much his home as any place in America. The college where he taught had a contract with the University of Pennsylvania and was becoming an international English-language university, with faculty from all over the world. It was as cosmopolitan as the student body was provincial. Most of Limbert's students came from small towns and cities that were religious and very conservative, and the values he confronted on campus and in the classroom clashed sharply with his own. Some of the students, a few, threw off their past and embraced the newer Western world, but other students—looking back now he realized it was most of them—rejected the secular, tolerant, gender-equal ways of their professors. One of his pupils, a good student, was killed when a bomb he was making with some of his friends in the dormitory had blown up prematurely.

There was another incident that came to mind, and which now assumed more meaning. An American teacher had founded a modern dance troupe at the university. Male and female dancers in tights performed together in shows that were commonplace in the West. The troupe had performed for the queen when she was in Shiraz for an arts festival—the shah and his wife vigorously encouraged things modern and Western. After the royal performance, arrangements were made for the dance show to be performed for the student body. The same routines that elicited enthusiastic applause in the earlier show provoked a riot. The troupe was unable to finish. To most of the students, undraped female forms cavorting on stage with undraped males was an outrage. It was alien and unwelcome and they didn't like it one bit. Limbert remembered the distress, confusion, and disbelief of the American woman who had started the troupe. She could not fathom how something as benign and beautiful as a dance could provoke such violent rejection.

These were the kinds of things entirely missed by American policy makers, who dealt only with the shah and assumed that anyone who disagreed with him was backward and would remain powerless, not worth their attention or concern. America tallied up the number of machine guns in the shah's arsenal and felt comfortable but failed to consider that a machine gun is useless if the man behind it refuses to shoot. The undercurrent wasn't visible to those who visited Iran for a few days or weeks.

You saw it only when you immersed yourself in the country, as Limbert had, and even he had misjudged it.

There had been things about the shah he disliked, but he accepted the monarchy because historically Iran (or Persia) had been ruled by kings. He disdained the royal security policies, and he knew there was corruption at the highest levels of the regime, but like most of his Iranian family and friends he considered these things simply a fact of life in the Third World, something that required the slow progress of modernization to change. As the revolution demonstrated, however, sometimes change can come fast, and in an unexpected direction.

He still didn't understand how it happened. Historians say that revolutions come in a country not when things are at their worst but when they begin to improve, when an entire generation has been well fed, sheltered, and educated so that it feels its strength in a way previous generations, ignorant, ill fed, and unhealthy, did not. Some blamed the revolution on Carter's liberal policies; his insistence on human rights reforms in Iran had weakened the shah enough to make him vulnerable. Others blamed the administration's hard-line policies, epitomized by Brzezinski, who had encouraged the shah to crack down more violently against protesters once the upheaval began, which proved to be too little too late, and which had only fueled the flames. Some blamed the shah for being timid and vacillating. Limbert knew that none of these explanations was sufficient. Iran had been long spoiling for change. There had been two major currents of opposition, the nationalists, who owed their loyalty historically to Mossadeq and who were divided between those who wanted a Western-style democracy and those who wanted to establish a Marxist-style state; and the Islamists, a new totalitarian strain rooted firmly in centuries of tradition, who wanted to return Iran to some dimly remembered utopian past where clerics ruled like philosopher kings. The shah had played these two currents off each other skillfully for years. The nationalists viewed an Islamist state in the same way the Western powers did, as a hopeless anachronism, a giant step backward in time. The shah was able to say to them, *Look, you may not like me but I am your bulwark against these primitives who would undo all of the technological and social progress that we have made.* The Islamists viewed the nationalists as infidels, heretics, and sellouts. But for some reason that Limbert didn't fully understand, the two currents had abruptly joined in 1978. The mullahs had their own sophisticated mosque-based organization, but suddenly they had the support of otherwise secular civil servants and white-collar workers, who could shut down overnight government offices, banks, and even the military; one of the turning points of the revolution had been the support of thousands of mid-level military officers and technicians, who had short-circuited the shah's response to the threat.

The postrevolutionary struggle was between the victors: the nationalists and the Islamists. They had united to throw out the shah but were now locked in a struggle to shape the new Iran. Limbert saw that he and his colleagues had become pawns in this struggle; they were being used by the fundamentalist mullahs to finish off their former nationalist allies and even moderate clerics who opposed a totalitarian theocracy. The simple black-and-white logic of religious rhetoric spoke powerfully to the young who, like Limbert's own students a decade earlier, came from small-town, traditional backgrounds. Anti-Americanism was the right tool in this fight, because nationalists like Bazargan, although personally religious, shared Western democratic values. The goal of this new phase of the revolution was to bury the passion for freedom and democracy under fears of an American-led countercoup. America was the Great Satan, and Iran-loving, former Peace Corps volunteer Limbert one of its lesser devils. He had come to Iran almost twenty years ago to change the world. Well, it had changed all right.

He did not know exactly what was happening in the larger world, or what efforts the United States might be making to win their freedom, but he understood that President Carter had few options. At first he had thought that Khomeini, as the ruler of a state, could not allow a diplomatic mission to be arrested and held hostage. Now it was clear he had either overestimated or underestimated him. The part Limbert did not know was how this embassy stunt was affecting the local political situation. His perception was, in a way, stuck back in the heady first few days and weeks. But as the weeks wore on the stated purpose of the takeover—demanding the return of the shah—had receded, and an underlying purpose was becoming more clear.

Taking the embassy had toppled the provisional government, and as the country voted to endorse the language of a new properly Islamic constitution, the students and their extremist political allies were using documents and testimony wrung from the embassy staff selectively as propaganda. Most of the papers seized at the embassy were historical and did show the close relationship between the U.S. embassy and the shah's regime, but many of the most recent filings were biographical. In their effort to make sense of postrevolutionary Iran, the staff collected information about many newly prominent Iranians, most of it gleaned from newspapers or other innocuous sources. Many of the files included little more than a name, age, job description, and contact information. But for some time it had been the policy to routinely classify even the most cursory file as "Limited Official Use," if for no other reason than to help keep the collection together by restricting its distribution. In the climate of runaway suspicion that caused the embassy seizure, that designation of secrecy was enough to label any Iranian in the file as a collaborator or spy. As the weeks went on, the students and their clerical advisers would begin to produce some of these documents to discredit politicians and even religious figures they opposed. Any hint of a "secret" association with the Great Satan was enough to destroy a career, at the very least. It could also lead to prison and execution.

Limbert hadn't known either Kupke or Graves, and because they were not allowed to speak he didn't get to know much about them in the three weeks they would spend together. Day after day he did his small exercise routines, read, ate his meals, slept, and talked with his guards. He and his roommates could hear birds outside and the voices of children playing in nearby yards. They were able to convince some of the guards to leave one window open a crack to get some fresh air. For some reason, Graves was kept supplied with tobacco, and the smoke from his pipe hung in the air day and night. Through the walls they sometimes heard other American voices, but usually only a few words. The only break in the routine came when they had to use the toilet. A guard would blindfold Limbert and lead him down a flight of steps—he counted thirteen, and remembered it, in case he would ever have to go down them himself in the dark and in a hurry. In the bathroom was a shower, an unbelievable luxury, which he was allowed to use twice during his stay there. He thought a lot about escaping, but even though his mastery of Farsi would have given him an edge over most of his colleagues, it was winter and he had no shoes, no warm clothes. If he managed to slip out of the house, where would he go? Who would help him? Like most of the hostages, Limbert had concluded that the United States was not going to make a rescue attempt. If they had the capability or will to do that, it would have already happened.

It was in this room that Limbert pieced together from bits of radio reports that drifted in from down the hall that thirteen of their colleagues had been released.

THE LARGEST THEFTS AND EXPLOITATIONS IN HISTORY

It would be hard to tell which came first, the unrelenting press attention or the public obsession. The story of sixty-six Americans held hostage by a distant, forbidding theocracy provoked indignation but also piqued the country's imagination. Scott Miller, the station manager of KOBL in Oberlin, Ohio, had himself locked in a recording studio with only a sleeping bag. He spent part of every day tied to a chair, telling listeners he wanted to share the experience of the hostages.

At the National Cathedral in Washington, bells tolled each day at noon, once for each day of the lengthening captivity. In Lawrence, Massachusetts, all of the churches around its city hall sounded their bells fifty times each day at noon to remember the American captives. In Columbus, Ohio, protesters marched to express their anger at Iran, chanting, "Nagasaki, Hiroshima, why not Iran!" A popular country tune of the radio, "Message to Khomeini," predicted that Iran would be turned into "an oil slick." A man from Flushing, New York, climbed to a dangerous perch atop a West Hollywood billboard to protest American inaction, and ten thousand cabdrivers in Manhattan drove for a day with their lights on to express their solidarity with their captive countrymen and -women.

It was not hard to see where all this anger was heading. Carter's public support was still high but voices of criticism and blame were already being heard. A former CIA director, Defense Secretary James R. Schlesinger, criticized the president for not immediately setting a deadline for the hostages' release, although he was vague about what consequences there ought to be for failing to meet the deadline. Ronald Reagan, likely to be one of the leading Republican challengers in the 1980 election, had already blamed Carter's "weakness and vacillation" for causing the crisis in the first place, and dropped larger and larger hints that if he were in power America would not be pushed around by a "demented dictator" and his "rabble." In his own party, Carter was cruising high in the polls ever since Senator Kennedy had shot himself in the foot with his conciliatory remarks, and although the Massachusetts senator was in the race to stay he would never recover.

Carter was considering tough options. In an exchange of memos with Brzezinski on December 21, the president directed that the National Security Council "list everything that Khomeini would not want to see occur and which would not invite condemnation of the U.S. by other nations."

By now the families of many hostage members were becoming regulars on nightly news programs around the country, and so far there was not a negative word to be heard from them about the administration's actions. They knew nothing of a possible rescue mission, and most were reassured by the president's promise to take no action that might jeopardize their loved ones. Penne Laingen, the chargé's wife, was seen as an unofficial spokesman for the families, and her comments on TV were uniformly supportive and upbeat—she might as well have been working for State Department public relations. Dottie Morefield and her family were so conspicuous in San Diego that they were invited by the owners of the city's pro football team to be special guests at a *Monday Night Football* game between the Chargers and the Miami Dolphins.

Mindful of the promise to those families, and his department's responsibility to its employees, Vance continued to argue against applying any pressure on Iran. He consistently counseled patience, pointing out that Iran was a nation in turmoil, its future course still uncertain, and new opportunities arose nearly every day to reopen diplomatic channels.

"Cy, you always have another diplomatic channel," said Brzezinski.

On the tenth of December, NBC-TV aired an eighteen-minute interview with marine hostage Billy Gallegos, the first with a hostage broadcast in the United States. Clean-shaven and wide-eyed, he looked like a frightened, big-eyed boy.

Before this, the only other hostage voice heard was that of Jerry Plotkin, the middle-aged Californian who had come to set up a personnel agency—matching American workers to jobs in Iran—and had made the mistake of stopping by the embassy on the morning of the takeover. He had been allowed to speak on the phone for seven minutes to a Los Angeles radio station in late November, delivering remarks that had obviously been written for him, right down to the standard Islamic preface, "In the name of God." He had also called for the return of the shah, and went on to woodenly read, "Let the world know no tyrant or dictator can ever find safe harbor in the United States. I am well both mentally and physically. We have been treated humanely. The students treat us kindly and with respect. The quality of the food is adequate and we are given three meals a day. The hostages' living area is clean and each of the hostages has a mattress, blanket, armchair, and table."

So far, the students seemed to see the American press as an ally. It made for a strange situation. The United States was, in effect, in a stalemated state of war with Iran, but while fifty-three of their countrymen were being held prisoner, dozens of American journalists moved freely in Tehran, scrambling to get access to the compound and the captives. ABC's Peter Jennings was among them, wandering the streets to solicit the opinions of random Iranians and doing feature stories about postrevolutionary life. The other networks had their own regular correspondents on the scene, as did most major American newspapers, and it was clear from some of the footage shown on TV that they had established a rapport with the dapper foreign minister, Sadegh Ghotbzadeh, who made himself available daily. Yet the United States government, by all appearances, was unable even to start a dialogue with the country's rulers. Many of the TV correspondents would set up for their nightly broadcasts immediately outside the embassy gates, surrounded by Iranians chanting "Death to America!" and "Death to Carter." Rarely was this rhetorical hostility directed at the American journalists personally. Thomas Fenton, a CBS correspondent, was confronted once outside the embassy by an Iranian who shouted at him accusingly, "CIA!"

"No, CBS!" Fenton retorted, which got a laugh.

No one had succeeded in getting access to the hostages, so when the major TV networks were approached with an offer to participate in the Gallegos interview, their executives were eager. But the students demanded that all questions be submitted in advance, that the interview be aired in prime time in its entirety with no editing, and that the students be allowed to ask questions and make statements on the film. None of the networks accepted the initial terms, but the big three, ABC, CBS, and NBC, were eager to bargain. Eventually NBC came to terms. They would be allowed to question the hostage with their own correspondents, Fred

Francis and George Lewis, and they did not have to clear their questions in advance. A student would be allowed to make an opening and closing statement. Nilufar Ebtekar was chosen by the council, because of her fluent English and because the council liked the idea of having their arguments presented by a woman. At first, Ebtekar was reluctant to appear on camera, but she agreed when it was decided to identify her only as "Mary."

She and the other hostage takers had been mystified by the lack of American support for their action, particularly the lack of sympathy from American blacks and other "oppressed minorities," and had concluded that their problem was media censorship in the United States. The American government was blocking and distorting their message. One effort to break through this supposed censorship was a half-page ad in the *New York Times* (the *Washington Post* refused to run it) calling on Americans to "Rise Up Against Oppression," referring to the hostages as "spies" and placing Carter in "the vanguard of the world's oppressors." The Gallegos interview was part of this publicity campaign. The students demanded that Ebtekar's remarks be presented unedited and in their entirety. In fact, the justifications and complaints of Iranian hostage takers had become tiresomely familiar to Americans, but when NBC proposed trimming her harangue by about two minutes the students held fast. Ebtekar interpreted the request to edit her speech as proof that there existed a secret U.S. government rule prohibiting, as she would put it, the broadcast of any "anti-government declaration lasting longer than five minutes."

Her chubby frame draped in dark robes and her head wrapped in a powder blue scarf, Ebtekar lectured the American people in her perfect American English about the evils of their government and accused the shah of "the largest thefts and exploitations of history."

Gallegos sat in the chancery library beneath a portrait of Khomeini. He had agreed in advance not to describe where he was being kept on the embassy grounds or to describe the security procedures. The young marine was one the students' favorites. He was chosen for the interview by their governing council because of his "honesty and simplicity," which suggested he was not likely to be unpredictable, because his behavior had been docile, and because his background was "Latin." In the interview the young marine spoke of his impatience and argued for handing over the shah.

"I think he'd get a fair trial and if he is guilty he is guilty," Gallegos said. "If he is innocent, he is innocent. Nothing has been done for our release and it's been over a month now. I think the shah should be returned and that is not only my feeling, that's the feeling of all of the hostages. . . . I am in good shape but my mental condition is as good as expected in a situation like this, kind of on my nerves. . . . Before this I knew nothing of any spies, but it seems like the students have uncovered quite a few documents indicating people as being spies in Iran."

To Gallegos's parents, who were watching before cameras in the studio of a network affiliate in Denver, he appeared thin and pale, with telling dark rings under his eyes, but otherwise healthy and unharmed. The cocky young man who had volunteered for the most dangerous postings, and whose eagerness for confrontation with America's enemies was sometimes a concern to his fellow marines, had softened his outlook considerably in captivity. He said that he and the other hostages had not been mistreated by their captors, nor brainwashed, and were surprised by their country's refusal to hand over the shah. He said they resented being held captive to protect a dictator who deserved to be put on trial and punished, and managed to imply that even his own role as an embassy guard might have had a clandestine side.

"I'd give my life for any American," he said. "I can't see it now. In some ways, I don't see this as a good cause. . . . The students have been really good to us. It's hard to believe, I know, but we haven't been asked any questions about what really our job was."

Yet the young marine was still loyal to his country.

"We're relying on his [Carter's] decision, no matter what," he said. "I'm leaving it up to my country and my people. I have great faith in them."

When Gallegos had answered the last question, one of the interviewers turned to Ebtekar and asked if he might direct a question to her.

"No you may not," she said. Ebtekar regarded the question as a violation of the agreement.

The program aired in full, but the students still felt betrayed when NBC intercut images of Gallegos's parents watching.

Carter was furious with the network for airing the interview. The flood of reporting from Iran during the crisis had been both aggravating and helpful; the nightly reports were being scrutinized carefully in the Pentagon for scraps of information about how the gates were guarded, what kinds of weapons the students carried, etc., but apart from this practical value, the constant network focus on the crisis played into the hands of the hostage takers. The more attention they got, the more convinced they were of their own importance, and the more pressure was put on the White House to react, either to give in to this infuriating extortion or to lash out at Iran in a way that would almost certainly make the situation worse for the hostages, if not kill them. There was no danger of "Mary's" lecture finding sympathetic American ears. A small woman dressed like a nun hectoring the American people in their own living rooms about the sins of their government made for a unique national TV event that no doubt swelled the ranks of those who preferred to nuke Tehran and be done with it. What Carter needed most was for this story to fade off the front pages, so that the students could be isolated as a troublemaking fringe and sensible people in Iran would again dare to assert control.

House Speaker Thomas P. "Tip" O'Neill condemned the network for airing Iranian "propaganda." Ford Rowan, NBC's Pentagon correspondent, no doubt getting an earful from his military sources, resigned in protest.

Psychologists were enlisted by the networks to explore the concept of brainwashing, and military and intelligence analysts pored over Gallegos's remarks for clues about where and how the hostages were being guarded. They were especially intrigued by one of the marine's brief comments in passing. Near the end of the interview, Gallegos had been asked about which Americans he had been housed with.

"I was with a couple of political officers before we were up here in some of the houses," he said. They understood that by "houses," he meant the staff cottages on the embassy grounds. "I was with them and, after that, we were moved down to this other place, the mushroom . . ."

Mushroom? What had he meant by that?

Delta knew. They had learned of the nickname from the released hostages. It reminded the analysts of the old soldier's lament, "I must be a mushroom because they keep me in the dark and feed me horseshit."

Given the bewildering variety of news reports, it was impossible to sort out fact from fiction or, as intelligence analysts put it, information from noise. Every day there was a break in the saga from somewhere in the world, sometimes hopeful and sometimes alarming. The hostages were going to be released, or the hostages were going to be put on trial; the hostages were going to be tried by the students themselves and then executed, or the hostages were going to appear before a revolutionary tribunal and then be released. Some of the hostages were going to be released for Christmas, then none of the hostages would be. Iran's terms for releasing them varied, depending on who was speaking. Iran was an enigma because no one appeared to be in charge. Everyone said Khomeini was, but the old prophet stayed aloof from the day-to-day workings of the state. He kept to his spiritual regimen in Qom and spoke only at intervals and rarely about specifics. Those known to be close to him, clerical figures and politicians who advised him and interpreted his words, were singing different songs, some of them confrontational and some of them conciliatory. The tune seemed to change daily. In a speech days before Christmas, Khomeini said the American captives convicted of spying "might not" be executed.

Feeding the confusion was the competitive scramble for scoops by every news agency in the world. There was no shortage of people to interview. One of the favorites was Abolhassan Bani-Sadr, the most unlikely of Iranian public officials in the postrevolutionary period, a Chaplinesque little man with a peculiar pompadour, thick-rimmed glasses, and a carefully trimmed little mustache. He had been dumped as foreign minister by the Revolutionary Council but had not gone away. Khomeini had promptly named him economic minister, and as the weeks of the crisis wore on Bani-Sadr grew more and more openly critical of the embassy takeover. Originally he had spoken in favor of it, but by early December he had changed his mind. He told a French reporter that he opposed trying the hostages because such a step would violate international agreements that protected diplomats, as though taking them hostage itself wasn't violation enough. Days later he told a Beirut correspondent that Iran ought to drop its demand for return of the shah, that the tactic had failed, and then a few days later he called for the hostages' release. Ibrahim Yazdi, his predecessor as foreign minister, who had resigned the position after the embassy was overrun, now spoke out in favor of putting the Americans on trial, saying that such a step would provide a "strong motivating force" for the Iranian masses to rebuild their society. Ghotbzadeh, Bani-Sadr's successor as foreign minister, set off a storm of confusion by suggesting that one step toward resolving the crisis would be to create an international grand jury to investigate U.S.–Iran relations. The proffer was promptly rejected by a spokesman for the students, who in typically colorful language suggested that Ghotbzadeh was a traitor—"On occasion he has spoken irresponsibly and led the enemy to his filthy and satanic whims." This provoked the Ayatollah Mohammed Behesti, chairman of the Revolutionary Council, to defend Ghotbzadeh, pointing out that the foreign minister spoke not only for himself but for the council and thus for the imam himself. Dustups like these raised all sorts of questions in the White House. Who was really in charge? Who could be taken seriously? With whom should they be negotiating, the students? The Foreign Ministry? The Revolutionary Council? Khomeini?

Sadeq Khalkali, the revolution's bloodiest ayatollah, most notorious as a "hanging judge," told one interviewer that none of the American hostages would be executed, and then told another, weeks later, that only those convicted of spying would be sentenced to death. Then, later in December, he called for the hostages' release.

"Every embassy has spies in it," he said. "We cannot execute any spies according to Islamic laws. They will only be executed if they were directly responsible for ordering a murder. Even if we try the hostages, we do not want to condemn them. We want to condemn Carter and the American government."

When the shah attempted to defuse the crisis in mid-December by leaving New York for Panama—an arrangement worked out by Washington with the obliging dictator Omar Torrijos—Khalkali announced that Iranian hit squads would assassinate the shah there, setting off weeks of anxiety throughout Central America, as nations scrambled to locate the assassins. Khomeini quickly pronounced the shah's move to Panama meaningless, portraying it as nothing but a public relations maneuver and calling the small nation an "American puppet." He wasn't far from right. Hamilton Jordan had worked out the move, assuring the shah and the princess that their children could stay in the United States and continue their education, and even arranging for a mobile medical team to deliver to his new tropical home the same care the shah enjoyed in New York. Jordan also promised to help find Pahlavi a more permanent home, but soon learned how much of a pariah the former Iranian ruler had become. Only Panama and Egypt were willing.

As the stalemate dragged through its second month with no sign of solution, rumor became news. The Libyan dictator, Moammar Qaddafi, told

Oriana Fallaci, "I have bad news. There is movement in the American military in Europe. The Americans are preparing parachutists and arming with armored vehicles, missiles, gas, neutron bombs, and other materiel." He predicted the coming of World War Three. On December 11, both UPI and ABC-TV falsely reported that President Carter had set a ten-day deadline for the release of the hostages, which seemed to coincide with a statement from Tehran by Ghotbzadeh, who had called for an international tribunal to consider Iran's grievances against the United States in ten days. It was implied that if the hostages were not released by that deadline America would launch some sort of punitive strike. An article in *Pravda*, the Soviet Union's mouthpiece newspaper, reprinted under bold headlines in Tehran's newspapers, suggested that the United States was preparing to use nuclear weapons against Iran. The article was signed "Alexei Petrov," a well-known pseudonym for the highest-ranking officials in the communist state. A Kuwaiti newspaper had its own scoop from Tehran. The hostages were all going to be released before Christmas as a gesture of Islamist goodwill, and that in return Carter was going to make a televised address praising Islam and Iran and condemning the shah. Another Kuwaiti newspaper reported that the United States was planning to attack Iran on Christmas Eve.

The confusion mirrored events in Iran, where Khomeini's efforts to consolidate power were being severely challenged. The nation voted in early December to approve a new Islamic constitution that handed Khomeini supreme power for life, but there were reports that large numbers of Iranians had refused to vote in protest. The persecuted secular leftists who had allied with the mullahs to overthrow the shah were now openly warring with the emerging religious regime. The hostages heard nightly gun battles in the streets. There were organized uprisings in the ethnic regions of Baluchistan, Kurdistan, and Azerbaijan, where rebel forces briefly took control of the city of Tabriz until driven out by Revolutionary Guards. The rebelling Kurds rejected a proposal by the Revolutionary Council for "self-administration," demanding full autonomy. Many of those battling Khomeini loyalists were followers of Ayatollah Kazem Shariatmadari, one of the premier clerics in Iran, who had publicly condemned the hostage taking. Purges in the Foreign Ministry resulted in the sacking of forty-five of its diplomats, all but three of them ambassadors, from Iranian missions around the world.

Iran was not just confusing, it was confused. The only common article of faith in the country was hatred and suspicion of the United States, which was just as strong among the Shariatmadari enthusiasts as their Khomeiniite rivals. The imam blamed all the upheaval on Carter who, he said, was fomenting unrest in order to distract the world from his own crimes. On December 19, the English-language newspaper *Kayhan* printed as its "Thought for Today" the following: "U.S. is hatching a plot against the Islamic Revolution every day. Don't forget that U.S. is your worst enemy. Don't forget to chant, 'Death to U.S.' along with 'Death to Saddam.'"

Hatred was a useful emotional rallying point, but the country had not yet figured out how to govern itself. No formal government was in place. There were sharp divisions on the Revolutionary Council about how to respond once the shah left the United States. They debated the question for four hours without reaching an agreement. One option considered was simply to release the hostages, since the departure of the shah from America would render moot the demand for Carter to return him. This was rejected as too humiliating. Another alternative was to immediately put the embassy "spies"on trial, to punish America for not complying with the students' demand. But this was a step that would invite further international outrage and a likely military attack by America. Increasingly, the imam seemed to be taking his cue not from the circle of mature leaders who had come to power with him but from the young hostage takers, whose popularity with the masses gave their statements political weight.

At the White House Brzezinski and Vance continued to spar. The secretary of state was resolutely in favor of restraint and the pursuit of peaceful means, while Brzezinski leaned toward the old Cold War approach, exploring the feasibility of toppling the Islamist regime and urging the State Department in a December 4 memo to feel out foreign leaders to see which "alternative leaders and rival groups within and outside Iran" they might be willing to support as alternatives to Khomeini. President Carter stuck with a middle line. Public opinion polls so far showed strong support for his handling of the crisis, the typical surge of solidarity following a threat to the nation, but the president knew the boost would not last. Early in December he had held an interagency meeting to discuss ways that the United States might bring economic and/or military pressure on Iran, but there were few new ideas. Economic sanctions depended on worldwide cooperation, which was hard to make happen even after both the UN Security Council and the International Court of Justice at The Hague officially called for the hostages' immediate unconditional release. Both the resolution and the order were shrugged off by the student captors and Iran's revolutionary leaders. Carter's call for a review of every visa held by an Iranian in the United States—there were about 50,000 of them—was quickly challenged in court and halted, at least temporarily, by a federal judge. Every move the president made just seemed to underscore his impotence.

In a series of speeches in mid-December, Khomeini mocked the president.

"The Americans don't simply want to free these spies, all this crisis is to help Carter get reelected ... Carter doesn't understand more than this. He doesn't attach any importance to human beings ... he has suffered a political defeat in the eyes of the world. This 'humanitarian' thinks he can mobilize the whole world into starving us. Unfortunately for Mr. Carter, his secretary of state went round but nobody took any notice of him. They all turned him down. This 'humanitarian' intends to expel fifty thousand of our young people for one reason or another. . . . Recently we heard that a judge had pronounced this to be against the law."

Despite his promise to the hostages' families, Carter was inching reluctantly toward military action.

The president was briefed daily on the progress of planning for the rescue mission. Despite the fact that at least a dozen of the hostages, maybe more, had been moved off the embassy compound, a fact well known enough in Iran for there to be crowds around some of the north Tehran residences where they were being held, the complex assault plan remained focused on the embassy. A ten-man squad was going to hit the Foreign Ministry to free Laingen, Tomseth, and Howland, but the other, scattered hostages were off the radar.

Delta Commander Beckwith kept adding men to his assault force; the original sixty men became seventy-five. As the number grew, so did the need for helicopters. Two more Sea Stallions were added to the mission plan and began making their way to the *Kitty Hawk* in the Persian

Gulf. Intelligence analysts had located an airstrip, a thirty-minute helicopter flight from Tehran, that the rangers would seize for the final
evacuation of the hostages and rescue force. It was an unoccupied as-
phalt strip at Manzariyeh that had been part of a bombing range and that
was apparently manned now by just a small unit of Iranian army engi-
neers. A company of rangers would seize the strip at the same time Delta
was hitting the embassy. It was determined that the runway was long
enough and flat enough to receive the C-141s that would carry everyone out.

Reliable intelligence remained the biggest challenge. In mid-
December the CIA managed to place an agent in Tehran. It had called out
of retirement an elderly World War Two–era spy of eastern European
origin called "Bob," a tall, thickset man in his sixties with leathery skin who
had been living in South America. He spoke a variety of languages from
that region, but not Farsi. He agreed to enter Iran as a businessman, along
with two friendly Iranians, one who was sick with cancer and thus fatalis-
tic about the risks and the other a young Iranian-American air force crewman code-named "Fred," who had family there. They scouted out the
possibilities for obtaining a warehouse and trucks—the warehouse to hide
Delta Force through the long day preceding the assault, and the trucks to
deliver the force from the hiding place to the embassy. Bob landed on a
commercial flight at Mehrabad Airport and breezed through customs; Delta
Force noted with surprise the ease of entry.

Beckwith's concern for secrecy closed one potentially rich avenue
of information. A West German special forces unit offered to let Delta place
several of its men with a TV crew that was being sent to Tehran, ostensibly to report for one of that country's television networks. The students
often allowed TV crews other than American, particularly German ones,
fuller access to the embassy. But Beckwith did not want the military of any
foreign country involved, even a friendly one.

To solve the fuel blivit problem, it was decided that two C-130s carrying the rubber bladders inside would have to land at the first night-
chopper refueling point, which meant they needed to find a patch of desert
large enough, flat enough, and solid enough to support the large aircraft.
The only way to make sure about the firmness of the ground—loose sand
would bog down the big planes—would be to send someone into Iran to

inspect the location, so plans were put in motion to send a small, daring reconnaissance group to the Iranian desert.

The president canceled his annual trip home to Georgia for the Christmas holidays in order to remain in the White House and deal with the crisis. He ordered that the lights on the White House Christmas tree be left dark.

8

THE CURE IS AN AIRLINE
TICKET OUT OF HERE

On the embassy grounds, in the basement of the warehouse across a narrow hall from the Mushroom Inn, vice consul Richard Queen shared a room with warrant officer Joe Hall. The fluorescent overhead lights hummed day and night, casting enough light to be annoying when they wanted darkness but not enough to comfortably read. Nothing could be heard through the warehouse walls, and it was constantly cold and clammy.

As Christmas approached, they were let outdoors to walk in small circles in the walled courtyard of the ambassador's residence. Hall was so moved by the fresh cold air, by the direct sunlight, the newly fallen snow, the crows circling in the blue sky overhead, that he wept, but when Queen was offered the same chance he declined. Hall was amazed that anyone would refuse an opportunity to go outside, but his roommate said that for some reason he had begun to feel woozy.

Queen experienced wide mood swings in captivity. He understood some Farsi, and he spent a lot of time eavesdropping on the guards, but he understood only about half of what was spoken and in his anxiety he tended to draw dramatic conclusions, good and bad. Once he thought he had heard two guards discussing plans to shoot all the hostages. He didn't share the information with Hall, sparing his roommate the fright, but the prospect tormented him night and day. When the guards took away their shoes and replaced them with Iranian-made plastic sandals—with images of elephants embossed on the soles—Queen threw a fit. Hall didn't understand why his roommate was so upset, but Queen had this image of being lined up in front of a firing squad wearing goofy plastic slippers. The day he had feared passed without incident.

When he thought he'd heard good news, Queen did share it. One day he was convinced that the guards had been discussing the purchase of plane tickets to fly the hostages home. He was sure he'd heard the airlines Alitalia and Lufthansa mentioned. He told Hall and their excitement grew.

As the day approached, Queen was counting down the hours. He woke up on the appointed morning filled with joy. As he returned from his morning wash, he whispered happily to a hostage passing him in the hall, "We're going home!"

When he got back to the room he asked a guard, "When are they going to take us out?"

"Take you out?" said the guard. "What do you mean?"

"When are we going to be released?"

"You aren't," the guard said.

Queen was crushed. He spent the better part of that day motionless on his mattress, his face turned to the wall. He cursed himself for letting his hopes get so high and concluded that the guards were doing it to him on purpose. They knew he spoke some Farsi, but not a lot, and was convinced they were toying with him.

While some of the guards were petty and even cruel, others were kind, in particular a tall, slender guard with a long hook nose, mustache, and sideburns named Akbar. He dropped by and asked Queen and Hall if they would like anything from their apartments. They both made lists. Queen wrote down blue jeans, changes of underwear, his beloved, well-traveled "War Between the States" board game, a *Lord of the Rings* game, pipes, and tobacco. Hall made up his own list. Weeks later Akbar brought Queen two pairs of jeans, two shirts, a blue sweater, and much-appreciated clean well-fitting underpants—the long-suffering vice consul had been wearing the undersized drawers for weeks. There was nothing for Hall. As he had surmised weeks before, his apartment had been ransacked and all his possessions had vanished. Queen sorted his bounty and shrugged apologetically at his roommate.

The young vice consul wrote a letter to his parents and his brother Alex: "This past week I was hoping, praying, pleading to God so hard that I would be able to return home to you in time for Christmas, but I guess to no avail."

Queen didn't mention something troubling that had occurred shortly before Christmas. In the shower one day he noticed that his left arm and hand felt numb, a peculiar sensation he had never felt before. He thought it was probably because he had slept on that side and had curled his arm under his body in an awkward way. When it didn't go away he mentioned it to Hall.

"You ever have numbness in your hand?" he asked.

"You mean like pins and needles? Like when your circulation is cut off?" said Hall.

"No, more like what you'd feel if you plunged your hand in snow and kept it there for a very long time."

Hall thought he should ask to have it checked out.

Queen decided to wait. Maybe it would go away. He didn't connect it with his occasional bouts of wooziness and took neither symptom very seriously. He had no reason to suspect his body would betray him in an important way. He didn't look it, but Queen was an exceptional athlete. In high school his tall, lean frame had breezed through subminute quarter miles like clockwork. Ailments and injuries had always gone away quickly. But this felt truly odd, unlike anything he had experienced, and over time it didn't diminish; it worsened. Finally he told a guard about it and they sent a young pharmacy student to look at him. The druggist-in-training diagnosed the numbness as a reaction to a draft coming from a vent over Queen's space. He arranged to have his mattress moved to a warmer spot and for him to be left unbound—the guards were still using torn bedsheets to tie his hands day and night. When none of the changes helped, Queen was visited by a middle-aged Iranian doctor who claimed to have been trained in the United States. Queen found him unimpressive.

"It's nothing, it's nothing," the doctor said after a cursory examination. He diagnosed a "twisted spine" and predicted that the symptoms would soon vanish. On his way out he asked Hall how he was doing.

"I'm sick, too," Hall said. "Homesick. The cure is an airline ticket out of here."

The Mushroom Inn had settled into a dull routine broken only by changes of guard shifts and trips to the bathroom. The shelves that divided each hostage's cubicle were remnants of the library at the old Iranian-American high school, where in happier days the offspring of embassy workers attended classes, and the books to that library, hundreds of them, were also stored in the basement in boxes. When Queen asked, he was given permission to unpack them and operate a lending library. He brought to the task his delight for careful detail, sorting the hundreds of books by subject matter. There was even a catchall stack of books Queen believed no one would find interesting. Within each subject category he broke them down further into fiction and nonfiction. The fiction was sorted by author, the history chronologically. He arranged the books in vertical piles of fifteen on the floor, with a sign atop each indicating what subject it was.

Overseeing this effort was Hamid, a slight man in a green army jacket with a fair, angular face, reddish brown hair, and a sparse beard, who because of his propensity to cheerfully mislead his captives was dubbed "Hamid the Liar." His hair and skin color were untypical for an Iranian, which he seemed to compensate for with an overabundance of zeal. Intensely suspicious, he had been the one on the second night of the takeover to warn Kathryn Koob against sending messages with her eyes. He was both ignorant and arrogant, traits which for the hostages seemed to sum up the revolution. When Hamid the Liar played checkers, he jumped over his own pieces on the board as if they weren't there, a clear violation of universal rules, and when his opponent complained he would cheerfully explain, "In Iran we always play this way. These are my men and if I choose to jump over them it is up to me!"

Hamid had earned his nickname by routinely lying about the mail, telling the hostages that none came when everyone knew (from the other guards) that mail from the United States arrived daily in sacks. When he did hand out letters, he played favorites, rewarding some hostages and punishing others. He was, of course, ready to believe any theory of American malevolence, no matter how wild. When one letter arrived making the case that World War Two had resulted because Adolf Hitler was determined to prevent America from seizing the oil supplies of Peru, Hamid was so impressed that he photocopied it and passed it around. In his role as library supervisor, Hamid permitted books to be borrowed only after he had checked personally to make sure they weren't

"CIA"—even though his English was rudimentary at best. Returned books had to be given first to him, so he could check to make sure no secret messages had been written or inserted in them. In his fractured English, he wrote out rules:

ATTENTION: LIBRARY PROCEDURES
  1. You may never to take more than 20-twenty-20 of books from the month.
  2. You may never to write in the twenty books your messages.
  3. To stack you found them return your books—20.
  4. A student good in English will check for messages you should not write, if he finds this library will be destroyed.

Given the borrowing limit, fat books were especially prized. Don Sharer read *War and Peace* and *Moby-Dick*. Barry Rosen began a steady diet of prison literature, beginning with Aleksandr Solzhenitsyn's *Gulag Archipelago*, MacKinlay Kantor's *Andersonville*, Billy Hayes's *Midnight Express*, the autobiography of French prison-escape artist Henri Charrière, *Papillon*, and James Clavell's *King Rat*. He took comfort in the knowledge that he was not the first innocent man imprisoned, and that he and the other Americans were comparatively well treated. Marine Greg Persinger tackled one of the volumes of the *Encyclopedia Britannica*, working his way through alphabetically.

Many of the bored, confined Americans began improvising exercise routines in their cramped spaces, though some had not worked out in years. Bill Royer, the assistant director of the now defunct Iran-America Society, was attempting a yoga move, lying flat on his back, raising his feet and reaching up to touch his toes, when he felt a sudden stab of pain in his chest. He thought he was having a heart attack at first, but the pain was in the wrong place, and very localized. After complaining to the guards a medical student gave him a cursory exam and reassured him that his heart was normal. It took weeks for the sharp pain to subside. He learned much later that he had broken his rib.

Enforced silence was defeated by a tap code, a system where letters of the alphabet were arrayed on a grid and words were spelled out painstakingly by tapping out numbers indicating each letter's horizontal and vertical position. A diagram of the tap code was drawn on the inside of a chewing gum wrapper, which was balled up and then tossed from space to space. Sadly, there wasn't much news to share. A hostage got one that, after much decoding effort, asked, "When do you think we'll get out of here?"

Some of the hostages just ignored the petty procedures. When big Bill Keough needed to use the toilet, he would stand up, announce "Toilet," and start in that direction. The guards would scurry behind him, more like his entourage than his captors. Traffic to the bathroom was constant, given that it was the only time the captives got to stand, walk, and leave their space. The guards must have been impressed by American dental hygiene; everyone brushed at least three times a day.

They were beginning to look ragged. Clean State Department and military faces sprouted stubble and then full beards; well-trimmed hair grew shaggy and then long. Beneath the oppressive boredom was constant tension, which sometimes boiled up. Colonel Chuck Scott, who had endured a difficult interrogation before his captors decided he was not the supposed CIA agent George Lambrakis, blew up after being served a supper of what had been billed as "chicken soup." It consisted of a cup of lukewarm water with a partly dissolved bouillon cube floating in it. He threw his cup across the room and loudly complained and was immediately surrounded by guards with automatic weapons. Scott began venting a stream of angry Farsi—"You people treat us worse than dogs!"—when Golacinski looked across at the recently returned Dave Roeder and, without a word, they stepped between the angry colonel and the guards. Golacinski tried to calm Scott down. When guards demanded that Roeder and Golacinski go back to their places, they refused.

"As long as you're pointing that weapon at me, I'm not going to move," said Roeder. "I'm not going anywhere. Point your gun down and I'll go, but I'm not moving until you do."

The guards backed down. They lowered their weapons and Roeder and Golacinski returned to their cubicles. By that time Scott had calmed down, but he continued berating the guards.

One of them said, "Many people in Iran are eating less than you. This is not a hotel. You cannot order anything you want. You are a hostage, you have no rights. If you do not shut up and stop complaining, you will be in much trouble."

The guard then vented his own anger at the Americans, claiming that all they did was eat, sleep, and make love. The standoff ended with Scott and the guard glaring at each other silently from across the room.

9

ESCAPE

Bill Belk had been moved away from the medic Don Hohman only after the guards were convinced he wasn't going to stop breathing again. He was shuffled around from week to week and wound up in a small upstairs room in the ambassador's house with Malcolm Kalp, the CIA officer. So far the highlight of Belk's captivity, apart from nearly dying of an allergic reaction to an insect bite, was the day he had inadvertently received two cans of beer with his lunch. The guards always put two cans of soda on the table in his cubicle in the Mushroom Inn, where he had stayed for several weeks. Apparently they didn't realize the difference in the cans of soda and beer. He said not a word and calmly savored his first alcoholic beverages since the takeover.

Mostly Belk felt bored, and stiff. Some days the only time he stood up was to go to the bathroom or to go eat. For the first month, every time he heard a helicopter his heart leapt. *Is this it? Are they coming for us?* By mid-December he was convinced no one was coming.

He and Kalp had mattresses on opposite sides of the room and were not allowed to speak. A guard sat outside the door. Passing notes back and forth, they began to plan an escape. Kalp said he wanted to go, but he didn't want to hurt anybody doing it. Belk argued with him in the notes.

"That's no way to feel!" he wrote.

Belk said that if they tried to go, it would have to be all-out, "us or them." If he had to hurt or even kill somebody, he was ready to do it. The more he thought about it, the more determined he became. He was going to try and, if necessary, he told Kalp, he was going to go alone. If Kalp was going to shrink at jumping a guard, he didn't want to have him along.

One of the guards always fell asleep soon after his shift started. Two days before Christmas, Belk waited until he nodded off, bundled his blanket on the mattress to make it look somewhat like he was wrapped in it, and walked out the door. He tiptoed down a back stairway toward the kitchen but he heard voices, and peering through the crack of the door he saw that it was full of Iranians. So he walked back up the stairs. From a window in the hallway he could look out over the back of the residence. The first-floor roof extended from the wall out toward a patio and swimming pool. Weeks earlier he had pried off a small blade from a Gillette shaver and hidden it in his shoe. Now he took off the shoe and retrieved it, using it to cut a neat hole in the window screen. He crawled out onto the first-floor roof.

Immediately he was struck by two things he hadn't considered. It was bitterly cold and the compound was brightly illuminated by spotlights from front to back. It wasn't usually like that at night, but for some reason, on this night, every damn light was ablaze. He could see armed Iranians walking all over the compound. His heart sank and he considered crawling back inside. He sat there, on the roof over the crowded kitchen, watching his breath trail off in gusts of steam, pulling his sweater tighter around him, expecting alarms to sound and people to shoot at him, but nothing happened. None of the Iranians looked up. So far so good. He decided to push his luck. He scouted around the edge of the roof and found a place where he could lower himself into the back patio by stepping down on an air-conditioning unit that protruded from a window. There were some large gas bottles on the ground beneath that fed the kitchen stoves and he dropped among them and squatted out of sight. The bottles were warm, so it was comfortable. He stayed there for about an hour.

The patio was enclosed by high walls. If he tried to climb over he would immediately be spotted. The gate was padlocked and the only other one had a guard posted alongside. He figured that gate was his only way out. He waited until a group of about six students emerged from the kitchen and proceeded through the gate, laughing and talking, absorbed in their conversation, and with his heart pounding Belk stood up and fell in behind them, drawing his sweater up over his head like he was pulling it on and adjusting it as he passed the guard. He stepped out of the gate and turned immediately to his right and kept walking.

He followed a fence that ran from the back of the ambassador's house over toward the warehouse. There was a break in the fence ahead that opened into the spacious pine woods in front of the residence, and he was making for them when he heard over his shoulder, "East!," which meant, "Stop!"

It was a female voice, one of the guards. He turned and saw her standing right over him on a small platform, pointing a rifle. She repeated excitedly, "East! East!"

He grabbed her and her weapon, twisting the barrel up and reaching for the switch that released its ammo magazine. The guard got off one shot into the sky before Belk managed to eject it. He knew she still had one more round in the chamber. She fired that one into the air, too, and Belk ran.

He headed back toward the residence, then heard another shot. Someone else was now shooting! He sprinted across the compound toward the tennis courts and a point on the back wall where there were steps leading up, a place where he could climb up and look over the top. He heard another shot snap, the round passing close as he bounded up the steps. He planned to pull himself up and over the wall, but when he peered over it he saw two policemen in the alley who had obviously been alerted by the shots inside. He stopped himself so abruptly that he lost his balance and fell off the stairs and twisted his right knee when he hit the hard ground. When he stood the knee buckled. He couldn't run. Right beside the stairs was a metal container, about the size of a big ice cooler. It didn't look large enough for a man to hide inside but Belk had no choice. He raised the lid and wiggled his six-foot frame inside.

It was filled with ice-cold water. The lid to the container didn't close tightly, so he could see out across the compound, where guards were now running toward him from all directions. When they got close, they split up and fanned out to search back across the compound without bothering to look inside the cooler. Belk sat there in the freezing water trying not to breathe. He tried to raise himself to climb out once the guards had left that spot, but now his knee hurt even worse and he was also frightened. He thought if he raised the lid and tried to climb out he would be shot. So he stayed.

Soon a group of twelve guards reconvened at the stairs carrying flashlights and began conferring in rapid-fire Farsi. Belk could have reached out and touched them, they were that close. If they would just move again, Belk thought, maybe he could summon the strength to climb out and over the wall. The icy water had numbed him so he no longer felt any pain in his knee. He would head for Bert Moore's house at the end of the alley immediately outside the compound. Maybe he could hide there through the day, and then hijack a car and drive toward Turkey. Or maybe he would try for the British or Canadian embassies. He stayed still for several long minutes until one of the guards looked down and noticed something.

"Oh!" he said, and jumped backward. Immediately all the guards pointed their weapons at the cooler. Belk slowly opened the lid and tried to stand. He was grabbed under both arms and hauled out. One of the guards slapped him and then pulled the wet sweater up over his head, pinning his arms. Then he clapped his arm around Belk's head in a wrestling hold. The others slapped and kicked at the captive and hit him with their guns. He couldn't stand because of the knee, so he was dragged to a car, thrown in the backseat, and driven to the chancery, where he was hauled into a first-floor room, what had been Bert Moore's office. They threw blankets over him, handcuffed him, and began to berate him and to question him.

"There is no escape!" one of them told him. "Allah is against you!"

"You are CIA and you were taking a message for Malcolm Kalp," his questioner said. "Who were you going to see?"

"No way," said Belk. "I was just going home for Christmas."

"What is your code name?"

His questioner reached down and tightened his handcuffs and then leaned on them, digging the steel into his wrists.

"It hurts!" Belk protested.

"It doesn't matter," the interrogator said.

Belk was left alone for the remainder of that evening. The cuffs were so tight his hands swelled and ached. In the room next door he heard Joe Subic and Kevin Hermening talking. It sounded like they were planning some sort of Christmas party and talking about getting out their Christmas cards! One of them was working a typewriter. It seemed weirdly incongruous to Belk, who was wet, cold, frightened, and in pain.

The next day six students came in and questioned him again, asking him about Kalp and where he had planned to go. When Belk told them the truth, that he had left by himself and didn't know where he was going to go, they kicked his injured leg and hit him several times over the head.

"People that try to escape get shot," one of them said.

One put a .45 caliber pistol to his head and pulled the trigger. Belk heard the hammer snap and at that point didn't care. He begged them to remove the handcuffs. His hands had turned a faint blue and the pain was intense.

Finally, one of them loosed the cuffs. He was taken to another room in the basement and tied with nylon ropes hand and foot to a straight-backed wooden chair. He was untied only to eat and use the toilet. This is how he spent the Christmas holidays.

The approach of Christmas was a very emotional time for Kathryn Koob, who felt both joyful and sad. Like the rest of her colleagues, she stood accused of being a spy and had been told to expect a trial and what seemed like a strong chance of execution. Since she had been moved from the ambassador's residence in early December to a small room on the top floor of the chancery, what had been the political section's library, she was much closer to the chanting multitudes outside the compound's front walls, and because she understood at least some Farsi it meant living with calls for American blood—her blood!—ringing in her ears day and night. In the crowd she could also hear vendors circulating drinks and snacks. It was bizarre, an ongoing festival of death and revenge. Her greatest fear, even greater than trial and the hanging judge, was that her captors would give her to this mob.

Ever since Ann Swift had disappeared after Thanksgiving, Koob had been held alone. She spent her days sitting in an armchair reading novels under the watchful eye of the punctilious female guard she had dubbed Queenie. Koob ate sparingly and savored what she was given at mealtimes, and she could feel the excess pounds she had accumulated over years falling off rapidly. She was still wearing the green wool dress she had on the day of her capture, although she also had a pair of slacks and a pullover shirt that the guards had brought from the embassy co-op. After weeks of such rigid confinement, she decided that she needed some sort of exercise regimen to supplement the ten minutes a day she was allowed to stand and do calisthenics. She worked out isometric routines she could do in the chair, stretching, lifting herself by pressing down with her hands, pushing her hands together, alternately flexing and relaxing sets of muscles. As she grew thinner she also grew stronger and despite the restrictions felt herself becoming more flexible. On the wall opposite her chair one of the students had spray-painted the words, "Down With the Carter," and some weeks later another had brought in an idealized portrait of Khomeini and tacked it over part of the slogan, so she now faced the imam's portrait under the words "Down With." Since none of her guards spoke English very well, nobody noticed the ironic juxtaposition, and she was silently amused by it. It symbolized for her the intellectual clumsiness of this whole terrifying exercise.

She, too, contemplated escape. There was a good chance that an Iranian family she knew who lived only a few blocks from the embassy would hide her if she could get there. A woman in Iran had a better chance of staying hidden than a man, because she could drape herself from head to toe in a chador and move around with relative freedom. Her Farsi was limited but serviceable. She tried to remember exactly how far it was from the ambassador's house to the wall. There were trees along the inside of it. With her newfound agility, she might be able to pull herself up to a low branch, which would give her the step up she would need to get over. All she had to do was wait for her guard to fall asleep, which happened often enough.

But she had never tried it. Partly because the attempt would have been risky and bold, Koob always found a reason, or was given one, to delay. Then one day a young woman named Sheroor, who was the kindest of her guards, allowed her to spend a few minutes on the front porch of the residence. It was the only time she had been allowed outside since the day of the takeover. Standing in the clean winter air, savoring blue skies and the sweet odor of the pine grove that filled that side of the compound, admiring the glimmer of moisture on the grass from a recent shower, Koob also scouted for an escape avenue. She was dismayed to see that the wall was much higher and farther from the house than she had remembered. None of the trees had branches low enough for her to reach, and the inside perimeter was busy with armed guards. There was no chance she could escape in the way she had imagined.

When the interrogation sessions ended after the first days, Koob concluded that the documents in her office at the Iran-America Society had confirmed her stories and quashed any remaining suspicions of her work in Tehran. But then she noticed Queenie surreptitiously taking notes after they spoke. Her chief guard would seize upon some comment or phrase and twist its meaning into something sinister. Chatting one day about the Iran-America Society, her efforts to revive the Cultural Center in Tehran, Koob mentioned that she had been interviewed from time to time by reporters about the organization's events or plans. Queenie seemed particularly interested in this.

"How did you relate to them?" she asked. As Koob described how she had tried to be helpful with the reporters, how she had welcomed the publicity and tried to encourage their interest and coverage, she noticed that her chief guard was scribbling furiously behind a stack of books. It dawned on her that Queenie had a completely different take on what she was talking about.

So she asked, "Hahnum, when you were just talking about reporters, you were talking about Iranian reporters who came to me to find out about American things, right?"

"No," said Queenie, and she explained that she had been talking about *American* reporters. Koob suddenly understood. Queenie had the idea that the "reporters" were actually spies, who reported the information they had gathered about Iran to her. Koob explained that this was not at all what was going on and Queenie dropped the subject. It consistently surprised Koob to glimpse such deep-rooted, unshakable suspicion.

She coped with her isolation and boredom by imagining her confinement as a religious retreat. The comforting miracle of her sister's presence that she believed she had experienced on her first night in captivity fired her religious convictions. She had often wondered about and admired Catholic women who entered convents or contemplative communities to live in self-imposed isolation, silence, and prayer. She began to emulate what she knew of such lives, creating for herself prayer schedules and disciplines. Her captivity was a chance to direct the ambition and energy she had poured into her career into spiritual pursuit. It was hard work. She found it difficult to sustain prayer; anything more than a simple request for strength or deliverance or blessings on her family and friends challenged her patience and creativity. So she created categories, morning, afternoon, and evening devotions, and assigned different objectives for each. In her morning devotions, she set aside Mondays to pray for church institutions, Tuesdays for human crises around the world, Wednesdays for her family, and so on. To sustain prayer for her family she sought divine favors for each member individually, one by one, beginning with her parents in Iowa and then moving around the United States to each of her siblings and kin. She designed a worship ceremony for herself and began to see her religion not just as a backdrop to her life but as a practice, something that demanded mindfulness and effort at every moment. When she was allowed to keep an armed forces hymnal she'd found on a shelf in the residence library, she memorized the songs and sang them to herself. Later she was given a Bible.

In the weeks before Christmas, Koob had felt all of these currents coming together, her fear, her sadness, and her joy in the new religious life she had built for herself. Surrounded by hatred, she was determined to turn herself into a beacon of Christian love. She talked to her guards about the way her family celebrated Christmas at home, the cookies, candies, the oyster stew they always ate early before setting out for evening services. Given a branch from an artificial tree, she placed it upright in a flag holder and turned it into a Christmas tree. She tore pink routing slips she'd found in a desk drawer into strips and fastened them together with tape to create a chain she wrapped around it. She folded sheets of white and brown paper into snowflake designs, and shaped one sheet into a small cross and placed it on top. Then she got more ambitious, creating a whole manger scene complete with Mary, Joseph, and the Christ child and even an angel to hover over the scene. Her guards were so intrigued by her labors that they began imitating her, fashioning their own paper ornaments and hanging them on her "tree."

10

CAPTIVITY PAGEANT

On Christmas morning, marine Kevin Hermening was given a clean turtleneck sweater and he, Joe Subic, embassy administration officer Steve Lauterbach, and Jerry Plotkin were taken to an office at the motor pool where TV cameras were waiting.

Their captors wanted them to make a statement on camera as part of the Christmas party they would hold later that day. Over in the Mushroom Inn, unbeknownst to Hermening, his fellow marines had refused. He had been separated from the others several days earlier after threatening a guard and tearing the startled Iranian's schoolbook in half. Locked in a basement room for nine hours, blindfolded, cuffed, and tied to a chair, the nineteen-year-old marine, the youngest of the hostages, had broke down and sobbed until he fell asleep.

He had been awakened by a voice speaking to him in perfect English.

"So, Mr. Hermening, I understand you're giving the guards a little bit of trouble?"

"No, sir," he said. The situation felt like being chewed out in boot camp, only he was more frightened this time.

"Well, do you think you want to talk about it a little bit?" his questioner asked.

"I sure would."

His blindfold was removed and before him, to his great surprise, had been Subic, the army sergeant, just a few years his senior. He didn't recognize him at first, because Subic had grown his hair long and had a full beard. He was wearing a winter coat and had sweaters on underneath.

"Joe, what are you doing?" Hermening asked.

Subic explained that the students had come to him complaining that Hermening had been causing trouble and asked him to help.

"I told them I would talk to you and try to resolve things," Subic said. He added that he might be able to help Hermening understand what was going on.

The young marine was shocked, not only by Subic's approaching him on behalf of their tormentors but because he was so bundled up. Warm clothing was scarce. Most hostages were wearing the same now ratty clothes they had been wearing on the day of the takeover, with a single change of underwear or socks if they were lucky.

Subic and the guards walked Hermening across the compound—it was the first time the marine had seen an American walking outside without being bound and blindfolded—to the first floor of the chancery. In this room Subic had snack foods, Fritos, peanut butter, peanuts, ketchup, salt and pepper, potato chips! He told Hermening that he had raided the commissary and gone on a spree, without explaining why he had been allowed to do such a thing. Then he said he was planning an escape, which would probably take place early in the new year if they were still captive—they were all waiting to see if they would be sent home over the Christmas holidays. In the meantime, Subic said that he was putting together, at the guards' behest, a Christmas party. He was their "consultant" for the party, he said, and had helped them decorate for it. Subic's room also had a desk and a telephone that he said he had used on occasion to call out to other embassies in Tehran. All of this apparently with the guards' permission!

Hermening helped with some of the Christmas decorations and wrote Christmas cards to his mother and other family members, coached by his student guards.

"Since we have been hostages, we have been shown many documents, pictures, and other information which has convinced us that the ex-shah did indeed commit many crimes in Tehran," Hermening wrote. "We believe that the students' demand for the ex-shah's extradition is justified and we urge all Americans to write to their senators and congressmen and ask them to do all they can to bring about the return of the ex-shah to Iran and obtain our release. The Iranian students are positive that the ex-shah will be returned to Iran and are willing to wait as long as it takes to accomplish this. They have only one demand with no negotiation possible . . . They will never back down or give in."

This letter was mailed to twenty American newspapers. When he was asked to make a statement on Christmas morning before the cameras with the others, Hermening said he would say something, but he didn't want to have to do anything "controversial."

He was excited about being on TV. Maybe his family would see him. This ordeal was making him famous, he was sure, and with that fame would come opportunity. At the motor pool he met Ebtekar and fell into easy conversation with her. Hermening told her that he was surprised a woman held a position of such importance. He said if she were so successful already, maybe someday she would be a big leader in Iran.

"If I ever get back to the United States, and get into politics, maybe I'll become a leader there," he said. He joked that the two of them, years from now, would be shaping world events. Ebtekar laughed gaily at the idea.

The four captives performed precisely as their captors wished. Each read a statement critical of the United States. Both Hermening and Lauterbach read the statements in a flat monotone; Lauterbach had not seen the statement beforehand. The foreign service officer, his hair long and his beard untrimmed, seemed particularly pained to be participating. Plotkin seemed more comfortable but Subic, who sat at the center and held the microphone, appeared to be relaxed and speaking in full earnest.

Some of the statements Hermening read had been prepared for him, and some of it was what he had written, about getting letters from home and receiving medical care when it was needed. The students had added lines about how the American government had sold fertilizer to Iran that killed all its crops. Hermening read on. The statement went on to summarize the American-led coup that unseated Mohammed Mossadeq in 1953, before he was born, and how the United States had placed the shah on the throne and that he and the other hostages were suffering because America refused to own up to its crimes and return the shah.

"It hurts us to have to say that, but that is what we believe to be the situation," he said. "We will always be Americans and still pray that they make the right decision as soon as possible."

Clean shaven and neatly groomed, his hair trimmed and parted down the middle, Hermening looked hale and fit, towering over the guards in the room, and despite his wooden performance he did not seem like a man being forced to do something against his will. Although he felt awkward about reading the statement even as the words came out, he figured, *Who is going to believe this?* Clearly it was being made under duress. So he didn't worry about it. Maybe his family would see him on TV!

Plotkin read with apparent feeling: "Why is the ex-shah given protection and sanctuary in the United States of America? He is an accused criminal and admitted his abuses of power on Iranian TV before he was dethroned. Why isn't he extradited like any other alleged criminal would be? The Imam Khomeini and their new government have promised a fair and open international trial with all nations and churches invited to see that justice is done."

Only glancing at the prepared statement, Subic offered the most dramatic personal testimony. He said that in his short time of traveling in Iran with Lauterbach before the embassy was taken, he had begun to see the evils of the American-supported shah. "We started to see more and more poor people, people without homes, food, education. I asked myself what had the shah done? My thinking started to turn around. My eyes and mind were starting to awake to the truth."

Subic then stepped around to the front of the table, holding the microphone in one hand and in the other displaying a "special" Christmas card that "the hostages" had made for Khomeini. Smiling, he read from the card: "A Christmas wish especially for you, Imam Khomeini. Merry Christmas. May Christmas bring you lasting joy and lovely memories. Merry Christmas, the American Hostages, 25 December 1979. Tehran, Iran." If he was aware of how he would appear to his fellow Americans, seething at this prolonged international extortion, Subic showed no sign of it. He seemed proud of himself, cheerful, sincere, and entirely at ease.

In what the students regarded as a "major concession," they allowed three American clergymen to visit and celebrate Christmas with the captives. All three were chosen, according to a spokesman for Iran's Revolutionary Council, because of "their militant history against imperialism." Most famous was the Reverend William Sloane Coffin, the celebrated senior minister of New York City's Riverside Church. Coffin was a large man with sloped shoulders and long curly dark hair that was retreating fast toward the crown of his head but which still fell thickly over his ears. He did not seem ministerial, with his up-from-the-streets New York accent, earthy humor, and background as an officer in the army and then the CIA, but he had seen the light, left the agency, and entered the ministry, achieving prominence as the chaplain of Yale University and for his civil rights work long before he became nationally known for his often eloquent opposition to the Vietnam War. Accompanying Coffin were the Reverend William Howard, a tall, urbane, dignified African-American minister who headed the National Council of Churches and was a noted civil rights and anti-apartheid activist, and Bishop Thomas Gumbleton, an activist Catholic leader from Detroit famous for his advocacy of liberal issues inside and outside the church. Coffin had defended the hostage takers in public statements in the United States, saying, "We scream about the hostages, but few Americans heard the screams of tortured Iranians."

Together with the Catholic cardinal of Algiers, they presided over a series of holiday services for hostages who were brought to them in small groups throughout Christmas Day. In session after session, wearing flowing maroon-colored robes, Coffin warned against the vice of "self-pity," and encouraged the captive Americans to sing along with him as he played the piano and led them in carols. The ceremonies were held in a back room of the warehouse, which Subic had helped decorate, along with the usual wall decorations of anti-American, prorevolutionary slogans. Cameras and lights recorded the event for Iranian TV as armed guards lined the walls looking on happily, convinced they were making the saintliest of gestures, allowing these infidels a Christian celebration. Khomeini, in response to President Carter's call for Americans to ring church bells in remembrance of the hostages, called for his countrymen to "ring the bells in support of God."

Many of the hostages were appalled by the event, at being made part of what they saw as a propaganda stunt, but Rick Kupke set aside his resentment when he spotted the treats laid out on the table—brownies, nuts, apples, and oranges. There was even a roasted turkey on a plate! Marine Paul Lewis was impressed enough with the goodies to go through the motions during his ceremony, but ignored Coffin's exhortation to hold hands with his fellow hostages and sing. Many of the marines refused to sing, and a good number of the hostages showed little emotion or enthusiasm. Coffin hugged each one at the end of the ceremonies, and when he came to Lewis the young marine whispered to him, "It's all bullshit." In a brief conversation with Bill Keough, Coffin remarked, jokingly, that he had often longed for an extended period of quiet where he could read and think and contemplate. Keough smiled grimly. It was the remark of a man who had never been taken hostage in a foreign country and threatened daily with trial and execution. At the ceremony he attended, Golacinski leaned over to Reverend Howard and whispered, "Don't believe what you are seeing. We're being treated like animals."

"So I gathered," said Howard.

The Baptist pastor managed to convey to each group that all of America was intensely concerned with their fate, not just their own families and friends. At each of the sessions, hostages were allowed to write a brief note on a card to their families, which for many would be the first communications since the takeover.

Forbidden to talk about politics or their own situation, Colonel Scott asked Howard, "What's the price of gasoline in America today?" Scott had thought long and hard about what question to ask if he got the chance, and decided that the current price of oil would help him gauge how events in Iran were playing around the world. Howard looked at the gallery of armed guards and asked them, "I don't suppose I should answer that question, do you?" Scott was annoyed. *Why couldn't he just have blurted out an answer? Why was he bending over so hard to be helpful to these bastards?*

Seeing Scott's anger, Howard tried to lighten the mood. He said he noticed in looking over the lists of hostages that Scott was from Georgia and began a story about the difficulties he had faced as a young African-American traveling in that state. This further angered Scott, who felt as though the preacher was blaming him for the racism he had encountered.

For some of the hostages, however, the ceremonies were rich with feeling. The songs, no matter how off-key, and the decorations, no matter how impoverished, brought back memories of family and of past Christmases and gave them a fleeting sense of connection with home.

Kathryn Koob fought to hold back tears during her ceremony. She was profoundly sad to be cut off from her world, and yet somehow as a prisoner, isolated from her family and any community of Christians, from familiar Christmas music, the swirl of shopping, cards, parties, and gift giving, the holiday if anything became more meaningful to her, so that as she stood, reunited for the first time in a month with Ann Swift before Bishop Gumbleton, she felt herself trembling so violently that it took all her strength not to break down before the cameras. She balled her hands into fists so tight that her nails cut into her skin.

Several days after the Christmas celebrations, a nearly hourlong film was released and portions played on the big three American TV networks and in Iran. The film had been offered the week before, but the networks balked at paying $21,250 and promising to air the film in full. After a few days, the students dropped the demands and handed over the film. Their propaganda show was meaningless if no one saw it.

On the third floor of the Foreign Ministry, where the three trapped Americans Laingen, Tomseth, and Howland were allowed to watch television, the chargé was shocked. He wrote angrily in his diary that evening, "I think tonight I have learned to hate."

> Far and away the bulk of the film was of these hostages [Subic, Hermening, Plotkin, and Lauterbach] reading a prepared statement, praising the revolutionary zeal of their captors, reciting the misdeeds of the embassy in supporting the Shah, citing documents discovered in the embassy to suggest "espionage," and calling on the US government to return the Shah to Iran. All this was done in what appeared to be a rehearsal reading, seriatim, by the hostages of their statement, the desk in front of them displaying "evidence" of one kind or another. Only one (Steve Lauterbach) of the four seemed in any way hesitant in what he was reading. The hostage who seemed to preside, Joe Subic, clearly was, or seemed to be, relishing his role. A young marine, Kevin Hermening, too, seemed relaxed and at ease. The fourth, the businessman Jerry Plotkin, read a separate statement, and he, too, seemed in control of himself.
>
> All of this culminated in young Subic displaying a Christmas card from which he read a special greeting to Imam Khomeini on behalf of the hostages. All of this is incredible. I have heard of brainwashing and mind control. I have read of such and recognize that in all hostage situations this is commonplace. But here is an example involving people I know and whom I respect . . . Eight weeks of confinement and harassment by sound from the crowds in the streets brought the hostages to the point of servitude to their captors' purposes. And all this in a setting of Christmas with the two priests sitting docilely, watching and listening to the entire charade.

If the students felt such images were going to affect public opinion in the United States, they were right. Americans were horrified. There was an outpouring of sympathy for the hostages. Bishop Gumbleton explained in press conferences at home that the four men had clearly been forced to make the statements. He told reporters that while the men were reading the statements, one of them [Hermening] had whispered to him, "This is just a put-up job. Don't pay any attention to what you hear."

Gumbleton said he had asked, "Aren't you afraid of what might happen if I report that when I return?"

"Just tell the truth, sir," the hostage told him. "That's all we care about."

Laingen didn't need the bishop of Detroit to tell him that. He knew what kind of stress his colleagues were under and felt guilty that his own circumstances were so much more comfortable. On Christmas Eve they had been delivered a gift basket from the Spanish ambassador, a wicker basket stuffed with various kinds of Iranian candy, and a visit by the British ambassador, who brought sturdier fare, a basket with a variety of meats and snacks and a bottle of "cough syrup," which contained a lovely red wine—all the more delicious with dinner that evening after such long deprivation. Coffin, Howard, and Gumbleton paid them a visit, and they talked with the clergymen for hours. Tomseth was impressed with Howard and Gumbleton, whom he found to be sincere and there purely for humanitarian reasons. He was suspicious of Coffin, who had the air of a grandstander about him. It seemed to the veteran diplomat that the famous leftist preacher was playing to his home audience. In one glib aside he had remarked, "This situation is much too serious to be left in the hands of professionals!"

The minister seemed not to appreciate that he had just insulted three foreign service professionals.

"You are being absolutely silly," Laingen told him.

When they left, Laingen hoped that their visitors, whatever their motives, had been appropriately shocked by the zealotry of the students and the new strange political contours of this land. Islamic fundamentalism posed a threat that transcended the traditional liberal-conservative polarity that had defined Western politics for generations. There was a natural tendency of liberals like Coffin, Howard, and Gumbleton to seek dramatic change and to see any revolutionary as ideological kin, but they needed to be careful in this case about who they were cozying up to. The world was a more complicated place than they imagined. A new form of totalitarianism was taking shape, a religious variation on an ugly twentieth-century theme.

In the end, Coffin, Howard, and Gumbleton would fly home with their own sketchy notions of what was going on in Iran, while Laingen and the others were left behind as its captives.

Vice consul Bob Ode stewed over the Christmas party for days afterward. In the brief chance he had to speak to Coffin—the minister knew he was the eldest of the hostages and had sought him out to ask how he was doing—Ode had said, "If you are under the impression that the students are being kind to us, then you are mistaken."

Ode's wedding ring had been returned, but he had not been given back a ring that his parents had given him when he'd turned twenty-one and that he had worn his entire adult life. The naked finger reminded him every day of the injustice. Several days after Christmas he asked for paper and a pen and wrote numerous appeals, each in neatly printed capital letters. He wrote to Coffin, politely thanking him for coming, and then spelled out his misgivings about the ceremony and the minister's apparent misplaced sympathies. He wrote another to the *Washington Post,* and others to President Carter and several other likely candidates for president in the coming year.

In one of his letters, Ode expressed thanks for the various cards that had been sent to him and others by strangers from around the United States, all of them promising to pray for their release. "I don't mean to be unappreciative," he said, "but what we need most is action—not prayers."

Despite its obvious propaganda value, John Limbert felt that the Christmas event had also been a genuinely kind gesture by at least some of the students. He found that comforting. It seemed unlikely that after such a public display of charity they would be marched out to be shot any time soon. Even more reassuring was the visit several days after the holiday by Ayatollah Montazari, a chubby, often jolly middle-aged cleric who was reputed to be the first in line to eventually succeed Khomeini. The students were very excited and nervous about the visit. Montazari arrived at the Mushroom Inn with a TV crew in tow and addressed all of the hostages in the basement prison in a calm, friendly way. He was known among the hostages as "Screaming Monty," because of thundering, feverish orations that drove the devout to great exertions of public prayer and denunciation. In person he was a short man with a face full of blackheads and sprouts of hair projecting from both ears. He reiterated the students' demand for the return of the shah, and spoke to the hostages of his own years of imprisonment under the old regime, assuring them that they, too, would survive and prosper. When America relented, he said, they all would be released.

Colonel Scott, though relieved to hear that they would eventually be released, found the speech depressing. The bottom line, as he saw it, was that the Iranian clergy were holding fast to the students' original demand that the "criminal shah" be returned for trial, which meant, as far as he was concerned, a very long stay.

When he finished speaking, Montazari walked around the crowded basement room and shook hands with each of the hostages.

When the cleric approached Limbert, the hostage took his hand and reminded him in Farsi, "We have met before."

"Yes, I remember," Montazari said, surprised. "You came with Mr. Precht to see me."

It was an important moment, Limbert thought, because he knew the students were accusing anyone who had met with Americans from the embassy of spying. Those in the ayatollah's entourage were visibly shocked. The meeting had taken place weeks before the takeover, and Limbert had accompanied Henry Precht as an interpreter. He had liked the cleric, who seemed less rigid than others he had met. He was impressed by the fact that Montazari seemed to harbor no grudge against the shah, this in a country where grudges seemed the guiding spirit of the day.

Montazari stopped into the room where Hall and Queen were being kept. Hall noted with displeasure that the great man's entourage was wearing muddy boots. The ayatollah spoke to Hall and Queen through a translator.

"How are you?" he asked.

Hall was never sure what to say or how to act in this situation. Should he curse at the cleric or behave politely? He wanted to conduct himself with dignity, as a professional and an adult, but under these circumstances how exactly was that to be done? He saw some of his colleagues take perverse pride in treating their captors with nothing but scorn and bile, while others had become sickeningly meek and submissive. Some, like Subic, were actually trying to be helpful. He saw himself as somewhere in the middle. So how should he respond? Both he and Queen told Montazari that they were fine, but in a way that made it clear that they were anything but.

"Oh well," said Montazari, "I stayed in one of the shah's prisons for two years and I came out alive, and so will you."

It was meant to be encouraging, but all Hall could think about when he left was, *two years?*

To butter them up for the ayatollah's visit, most of the hostages were given mail. Limbert got a letter from his sister and her family, but most of the others weren't so lucky; they were handed mail addressed to them from perfect strangers who had responded to the plight of their countrymen by writing in a show of support. The embassy was inundated with them. "Dear hostage," these letters typically began. It was a sweet gesture, and the TV networks at home enjoyed airing pictures of schoolchildren all over America leaning over their desks, pencils working away, sending love and good cheer to their captive countrymen. They arrived at the embassy in sacks piled on pallets, another picture the American TV cameras loved. The gesture created such a flood of mail, however, that real letters from the hostages' loved ones got lost. Golacinski was somewhat luckier; he received a letter from a young woman he had helped in Morocco, thanking him, but it had been written and mailed before the takeover. It was nice, but in the present circumstances, when he longed desperately to hear some news from home, he was crushed.

Michael Metrinko spent the holiday as he had spent all of his days since the first week of the takeover, locked in a windowless basement storage room by himself. He had been invited to the Christmas party but he wanted no part of a propaganda show. His guards brought him a gift from the ceremony, a plate of turkey and stuffing, cookies, and decorated marshmallows. Metrinko was hungry, and the food was tempting, but he was galled by how self-congratulatory his captors seemed, how generous and noble and proudly Islamic. He accepted the plate, and when they left him alone to eat it he sat staring at it for a long moment.

Then he knocked on the door and said he needed to go to the bathroom. When the door opened, holding the gift plate before him, Metrinko marched down the hall and dumped the contents into the toilet. He made sure the guards saw him do it.

They were furious with him. The gesture prompted a fit of screaming. He had insulted their hospitality and kind intentions. He was crazy! When they shoved him back in his room and slammed the door behind him, Metrinko felt a momentary pang about losing the meal. What a glorious pleasure he had denied himself! But the remorse was nothing next to the pleasure he took in delivering the insult. It had hit home and wounded them and that was something he could take pleasure in for far longer than the food.

Metrinko fed off his anger. It kept him going. Ever since he refused a cigarette on the day of the takeover, the pattern of his captivity was set. He would not accept any rationale for the way he and the others were being treated. It was wrong by every measure, by the standards of international diplomacy, by the cultural standards of Iran, and by common decency. Going cold turkey on his two-pack-a-day cigarette addiction helped, in a perverse way. It fed his irritability and rage. He worked up a whole philosophy of anger. His sense of outrage was his last connection to dignity. A man had to hang on to his capacity to protest, to express his anger, to move up a few steps into the faces of his oppressors. It made him feel better about himself. In time, it was the only thing that did.

As Ebtekar, the hostages' spokesman, would later put it, Metrinko "hated everyone and was hated in return." And what he got in return was continued isolation. Metrinko spent hour after hour, day after day, month after month, locked in his tiny storage room with the fluorescent light buzzing overhead through day and night, with no fresh air and no companionship. Boredom was no longer an occasional state of mind; it defined him. He often had books, but one could read for only so long. He fought to find something to do to pass the time and frequently lost. He spent hours sitting and staring at the walls, brooding, lost in fantasy.

Now and then, one of his captors would come into his cell just to talk. They were convinced, of course, that Metrinko was evil. He was a foreigner, an infidel, an American, and they were certain he was "See-ah." So the conversations were one-sided. They avoided listening to him in the way one would avoid listening to the devil himself. They were there to enlighten him about the evils of the United States and the shah, the terrors of SAVAK, and the virtues of their own revolution—to which Metrinko was in sympathy although they would never believe it. Since he had known many of the leaders of the revolution personally, and knew how many had used the tumult simply to enrich themselves and exact revenge on their enemies or rivals, his sympathy for the ideals of the revolution was laced with cynicism.

For a man who lived to collect information, analyze it, and report it to others, solitude was a particular torment. He began doing calisthenics to fill the time and to wear himself out enough to sleep. He lost all sense of day and night. He would sleep for an hour or so, wake up, prop the big air mattress against the wall, and run in place and do sit-ups for an hour or so—he was doing hundreds of sit-ups a day. His time was spent alternately sleeping, running in place, doing push-ups and sit-ups, reading, brooding, going to the toilet, and waiting for food. He seized on any opportunity to break the tedium. Given some colored pencils, he began drawing on the walls. Using his food bowl, a glass, or a dish, he would trace interlocking circles, forming elaborate patterns, and then carefully color them in. He began a mental project. At home in Olyphant, Pennsylvania, his family owned a huge building, a onetime inn, with more than fifty rooms. He loved the place, and decided to completely renovate and decorate it, room by room. He remembered every corner of it vividly from his childhood. He tore wings off the building, stripping it down in his imagination to its original structure, then rebuilt the wings from scratch. He picked out colors for the walls, furniture, and rugs, redesigned the kitchens . . .

Books were the only consistent diversion from his own thoughts, and he devoured them. He read Herman Wouk's *The Winds of War*, a massive nine-hundred-page volume, in two days, then opened the first page and began again. He read the Bible and reread the New Testament several times. He pored over the Psalms, committing certain favorites to memory. Poetry was a source of great pleasure, because he could read and reread it with increased enjoyment. In a pile of books he was shown, he found *The Book of Living Verse* and *A Little Treasure of American Poetry* and never returned them. He practically wore them out. He read Solzhenitsyn's *Gulag Archipelago* and found its myriad accounts of men coping with captivity very useful in dealing with his own. He was pleased to read, for instance, that in captivity Solzhenitsyn thought mostly about his stomach. A myth about imprisonment is that isolation and deprivation incline men to great spiritual and philosophical insights, that in solitude the mind settles into great thoughts. Metrinko obsessed about food. He would think about lunch for three hours before it came: What will they bring for lunch? How long until they do? Will it be hot or cold? Then he would savor the memory of the meal for two hours after it was eaten, at which point it was time to start thinking about dinner. He felt guilty about the smallness of his thoughts and was relieved to read that he was not alone. The food was not bad, lots of rice and bread, occasionally a stew, but Metrinko's weight plummeted. He dropped thirty pounds in the first month of captivity. His jeans drooped badly and his captors had taken away his belt. He bunched up the waist in front and fastened it with a paper clip.

He welcomed the interrogation sessions and drew them out for as long as he could. Anything was a welcome break from his solitude and boredom. Even the prospect of being put on trial and executed didn't disturb him. He found himself perversely looking forward to it. The trial would at least be interesting. Months of sitting alone had made him desperate for any kind of stimulation, even death.

When he lashed out at his interrogators or guards, he would be punished. Sometimes he was dragged out into the basement hall and beaten. Once, after a particularly vicious outburst in which he had insulted the Ayatollah Khomeini and refused to wear a blindfold, he was handcuffed for two weeks. It was misery. His wrists were clamped in metal at his front, and after a day or so they rubbed his skin raw. Any movement that disturbed the cuffs became painful. He couldn't sleep comfortably. There was no place to put his hands that felt natural, and when he changed position he was shocked awake by the pain. When he moved his bowels he could not wipe himself clean, so he developed a painful rash. It was hard to eat. His food would come in a bowl, and he had a spoon, but it was difficult to put the spoon to his mouth without spilling it back into the bowl.

He endured this for two weeks.

11

INVASION AND OPPORTUNITY

Charlie Beckwith decided to give his men a break for Christmas. Delta had been preparing for the rescue mission nonstop for more than a month, and the basic plan was in place, despite lingering problems with fuel delivery and hiding choppers and men outside Tehran on the second day of the mission. The Delta major from Texas, Logan Fitch, and his men had been completely out of touch with their families since they had been summoned home from their "training" on the ski slopes in Colorado.

Fitch's wife, Sandi, was nine months pregnant. She knew that the nature of her husband's work meant he would simply drop off the face of the earth from time to time, and accepted it, but under the circumstances he was enormously relieved to have permission to return to Fort Bragg. None of the men was allowed to discuss where they had been or what they were doing, but nearly everyone around them understood.

Two other things happened on Christmas Day that would have important consequences for the hostage crisis, one of them shockingly public and the other a well-kept secret.

The public event was the Soviet Union's invasion of Afghanistan, the nation that shared Iran's eastern border and that, with Iran, lived in the Russian shadow. Concerned about a growing Islamist fundamentalist movement in that country, about four thousand Russian troops had seized government buildings in Kabul and installed a new, Soviet-approved leadership. It was news enough to chase Iran off American front pages and posed an entirely new, threatening, and unexpected twist to the confusion in that part of the world. There had been fears of Iran's clerics cozying up to the Soviets in the previous weeks, but they would certainly respond with alarm to this assault on Islam and the implied threat of an expanded Russian presence along their border. With ethnic unrest in provinces along the Soviet border to its north, and with mounting military probes by the Soviet-backed regime of Saddam Hussein to their west, Iran's world of trouble had just grown darker.

As had America's. The Soviet invasion altered the strategic map. Iran and the United States were no longer officially on speaking terms, but where the Soviet Union was concerned they had shared interests. Resistance to the Soviet putsch would come from the region's Islamic fundamentalists, which meant that there was not only less danger of Iran falling into the Soviet sphere, but incentive to form a tactical alliance with the West. The stakes were high. Brzezinski had long feared that Moscow would take advantage of Iran's confusion and lack of American backing to make a move on the Middle East, and Afghanistan looked as if it could be just a first step. In the White House, they war-gamed what the United States would do if the Soviet army pushed into Iran, bearing down on the valuable oil fields to the west. If it came to that, Iran's relationship with the United States would be irrelevant. The Soviets would have to be stopped. There was even discussion of employing tactical nuclear weapons to close potential gaps in the Zagros Mountains and bottle up a Soviet thrust.

The other significant event was the arrival of two men, Hector Villalon, a wealthy Argentinian expatriate and Cuban cigar distributor living in France, and Christian Bourget, a French lawyer and human rights activist, at the international airport in Panama City. They had flown there to deliver a formal request from Iran to Omar Torrijos, asking his government to extradite the shah and send him back to Tehran to face revolutionary justice. It was at best a perfunctory gesture. Torrijos was not about to send the shah back to Tehran, but that was the visitors' only announced purpose. What they told Marcel Saliman, a Torrijos assistant, was something else. They said they knew that there was no chance Panama would return the ailing shah, but the formalities might serve as a pretext to cover secret negotiations to free the American hostages. Iran was ready to talk.

Both men were friendly with Foreign Minister Ghotbzadeh, who, they explained, was officially hamstrung by the radicals who had seized the embassy. He and other moderates were being driven out of power by these young militants, who with their weekly press conference and "disclosures" were plucking them off one by one, exposing them as "traitors" and spies because they had met at one time or another with an American official. Ghotbzadeh wanted the sideshow to end. Sending the hostages home would disband the students and effectively end their reign of political terror.

Villalon and Bourget wanted to know if Torrijos could arrange a secret meeting with Hamilton Jordan. Why Jordan? They said that Ghotbzadeh did not trust the U.S. State Department, which he believed was controlled by Henry Kissinger and David Rockefeller, and knew that through Jordan they would have the president's ear.

In the second week of January, Hamilton Jordan, the president's chief of staff, was contacted by an old friend in Panama, who urged him to meet privately and soon with an aide to Panama's dictator Torrijos. He wouldn't say what it was about, but Jordan was intrigued enough to fly down to Homestead Air Force Base, twenty-five miles south of Miami, on a mystery mission. Negotiations to hand over control of the Panama Canal in 1977 had built close ties between the Torrijos regime and the Carter administration, and the dictator had recently done the administration a favor by agreeing to accept the shah.

In a nondescript brick office building Jordan was introduced to Marcel Saliman and to Villalon and Bourget. Since his initial meeting with the men, Saliman had flown to Tehran and seen Ghotbzadeh, confirming for himself that the link promised by the two French-speaking visitors was real. Despite all the public rhetoric to the contrary, Saliman now told Jordan, Iran was eager to begin quiet talks about the hostages. What the two unofficial emissaries from Paris had suggested was that Iran be permitted to file legal papers in Panama seeking the extradition of the shah. The request would go nowhere, Saliman promised, but the process would provide cover for the secret negotiations.

It was a slender thread, but the Carter administration had few other prospects. The new year had begun with bewilderment and disappointment. The president had turned his efforts in December to the United Nations, where the administration had mounted a full-court diplomatic press on Iran. Secretary-General Kurt Waldheim had agreed to personally intervene, and with the prospect of draconian economic sanctions in the balance it was hoped that Iran would bow to the weight of world opinion. Hopes were also high because the Soviet invasion of Afghanistan seemed to powerfully illustrate the threat posed by the great bear to the north, and now east. Soviet forces could easily push into Iran and grab the rich oil fields of the Persian Gulf; that had always been a big part of the logic in making the shah's army and air force effectively a regional branch of the U.S. military. Now, without American help, Iran's only ally was Allah.

These threats amounted to nothing in the febrile atmosphere of Tehran, however, where the alliance with Allah was considered very real and entirely sufficient. Instead of a breakthrough, the dignified Austrian diplomat, despite being wreathed in the prestige of the world body, had encountered nothing but suspicion and hostility. One Iranian observed the gaunt secretary-general "trembling like a leaf in the autumn wind" on an enforced tour of a graveyard to view the plots of those martyred in the revolution. He was escorted around Iran as a prop in the ongoing propaganda war. One morning on TV he was shown meeting "victims of SAVAK torture sessions," a room filled with the disabled and deformed, many of them victims not of the secret police but of accidents and birth defects. Death threats, angry denunciations, and riots chased Waldheim from Iran a day before his mission was supposed to conclude. He had met with the Revolutionary Council, but Khomeini refused to see him. Waldheim returned to New York shaken and empty-handed—"I'm glad to be back," he said, "especially alive"—even though from the White House's perspective he had all but groveled before the mullahs. That impression would be reinforced weeks later when administration officials received a tape recording of Waldheim's session with the council; in a memo to Carter, Hamilton Jordan would describe the secretary-general's presentation as "apologetic, defensive, and at points obsequious." The students, holding forth from their conference room at the so-called den of spies, called the secretary-general's visit "a vague and suspicious trip," and denounced him as "an American pawn."

"We are not afraid of economic sanctions," a student spokesman said. "They are not important for us or our people. We can stand it." His comments apparently reflected the public mood accurately. On January 5, an estimated one million Iranians marched in Tehran to demonstrate steadfast support for the students. The hostages would go nowhere until the United States handed over the shah.

It was a sentiment shared by at least some Americans. A group of ministers from the United States had visited Iran seeking a "spiritual resolution" of the crisis and returned home in January with words of encouragement for the captors. The Reverend John Walsh of Princeton, New Jersey, called for the shah to be returned to Iran immediately for a show trial and what would be certain execution.

"Let justice roll," he said.

Having thumbed their nose at the prospect of punitive sanctions, Iranian revolutionaries then had the pleasure of watching international willpower swoon. Waldheim himself argued to Carter that sanctions would only strengthen Iranian resolve. When Khomeini threatened to cut off oil exports to any nation that voted for sanctions, oil-dependent Japan quaked. The Soviet Union then twice vetoed the measure at the UN Security Council. Thus did the world organization dedicated to diplomacy acquiesce in the kidnapping of diplomats. When Carter proposed an economic boycott outside the auspices of the toothless UN, this, too, met with a cool reception. European nations found one reason after another to back away from holding Iran accountable. As far as the rest of the world was concerned, the captive American foreign mission was expendable.

The only bright spot came at mid-month, when Iran's Revolutionary Council decided to expel all American reporters from the country, accusing them of "biased reporting." As far as the White House was concerned, any easing of the media's fixation on the story was a relief.

So Jordan was more than ready to grasp at this straw from Panama. A burly Georgia lawyer with a round baby face and a youthful crop of dark hair, he had signed on years earlier as a driver in Carter's first, failed campaign for governor of Georgia. With a combination of native shrewdness and mutual loyalty, his role had risen with the candidate's political fortunes, becoming Carter's chief political strategist and managing his successful campaign for the White House. Unpretentious, informal, and blunt, his impatience for the niceties of wielding power in a tripartite government had made him few friends in the capital, where he was regarded by some as an arrogant amateur. But Jordan was a skillful behind-the-scenes horse trader, a man willing, despite his relatively provincial background, to throw himself into the most complicated matters, always with the complete trust of his boss.

Jordan told Saliman that even beginning an extradition process might spook the shah.

"If he gets scared and asks to come back to the States, we'd have to accept him," he complained. Jordan had worked hard to ease the ailing former monarch across the border.

"Don't worry," said Saliman, promising that the extradition process would be purely for show. "Besides, I don't even think the Iranians want him back."

He explained that the return of the shah to Iran, a year after his departure, would set off a big fight among Iranians over what to do with him. "They wouldn't know whether to torture him, shoot him, or hang him," he said.

Six days later, Jordan was in a London hotel room meeting again with Villalon, who explained how the embassy seizure had strengthened the hand of religious extremists in Iran against more moderate, democratic elements, who were eager to see it ended. Bourget arrived later that day from Tehran, and the two men—Villalon, a dandy with jet-black hair combed straight back on his head, and Bourget, who looked like a hippie lawyer, his head framed with bushy shoulder-length hair and a long thick beard—delivered their message for obtaining the release of the hostages: "Return the shah to Iran."

Jordan's hopes deflated.

"It is absolutely impossible!" he said, visibly irritated. Among those around Carter, Jordan had been the one most sanguine about this clandestine avenue. Now he felt duped.

The more they talked, however, Jordan realized that the demand had been offered only as a necessary opening gambit. Again, Villalon and Bourget explained that the remnants of Bazargan's crowd and the more secular men who had worked for Khomeini in Paris prior to the revolution were still in the fight. Though Abolhassan Bani-Sadr had been removed from the Foreign Ministry, he still held an important post and was a serious candidate for president, as was Ghotbzadeh, who had once been his boss in Paris. Under the new constitution, the president of Iran held considerably less power than the equivalent position in the United States, because the entire new government would remain subordinate to Khomeini, but the office was still important. Both Bani-Sadr and Ghotbzadeh, they said, privately deplored the taking of hostages but had to be careful about expressing that opinion publicly. The best they could do was applaud the takeover and suggest that the point had been made, as Bani-Sadr had already done. Ghotbzadeh was not prepared to go that far, but he was ambitious. An American concession of some kind might improve his standing prior to the vote, which could lead to a breakthrough. The moderates were, in any event, willing to talk. But before even considering a release of the hostages, they were demanding an international commission to study the crimes of the shah.

Here was where a strategic retreat by the White House might break the stalemate, they suggested. Carter had already said that he would not oppose such a commission, but only after the hostages were released. If he were to back off that position and allow the UN commission to visit Iran and meet with government officials, the student captors, and the hostages, there was a chance that the situation might improve.

The meeting ended with an agreement to continue talking. Bourget impressed Jordan with his access to Ghotbzadeh by picking up the phone in the hotel room and promptly getting the Iranian foreign minister on the line. The French lawyer tried to convince Ghotbzadeh to speak to Jordan, but the embattled Iranian declined. Talking directly to American officials had become a dangerous business in Iran.

PART THREE
WAITING

Nilufar Ebtekar with Kathryn Koob (left).
(Courtesy: Russ Kick, thememoryhole.org)

Demonstrators outside the U.S. embassy i
Tehran. *(Courtesy: AP)*

Christmas 1979. From left to right: Barry Rosen (back to camera), Hamid the
Liar, Rick Kupke, Hussein Sheikh-ol-eslam, Jerry Miele, Morehead Kennedy,
Joe Subic, John Graves. The Rev. William Sloane Coffin is at the piano.
(Courtesy: Russ Kick, thememoryhole.org)

1

THEY STARTED IT,
WE ENDED IT

After his questioners had backed off from beating the soles of his feet with a rubber hose, CIA station chief Tom Ahern was never again threatened with torture. His interrogators regularly promised him trial and execution but, for whatever reason, beating him was a line they would no longer cross. It surprised Ahern, because their revolution was hardly squeamish about such things. But it pleasantly surprised him to discover that his captors had limits . . . at least so far. He still did not expect to leave Tehran alive.

His chief interrogator, Hussein Sheikh-ol-eslam, seemed convinced that Ahern's goal had been nothing short of assassinating Khomeini, derailing their holy revolution, and installing another American puppet. They did not just suspect this, they *knew* it, and what they wanted from Ahern was the whole plot, in detail, along with the names of every traitorous coconspirator and spy.

It was not so much the fear of death that undid him. What finally broke Ahern's will was the fear of a *public* death, of a show trial and execution; this the singularly private man found particularly horrifying. It unnerved him. He had seen the grotesque images broadcast and printed in Tehran of the regime's enemies being shot, hung, or beheaded, particularly the Bahai, a religious minority. He knew the fear stemmed partially from what such images would do to his mother, his wife, and the rest of his family. But there was a deeper personal revulsion that he couldn't fully explain. It was the thing that worked at him most.

The fear and the pressure wore on Ahern until he schemed how to take his own life, which seemed the only way to escape a grim public spectacle. He played with the idea of electrocuting himself. He had found a paper clip and thought that if he put it into an electric outlet and dipped his other hand in a can of water on top of the radiator, that might do it. He never got to the point of trying it, but he rehearsed it and decided that if it appeared as though they were going to make good on their threats he would electrocute himself first. At one point he gave up eating and drinking for four days but was surprised to discover how hard it was to starve. He was a slender man, and naturally ascetic, so he ate very little anyway. After several days the hunger became uncomfortable, but he hadn't lost much strength or mental acuity. He decided that well before he died he would become terribly disabled, still at the mercy of his captors but severely damaged. The problem was that he wasn't suicidal, and couldn't make himself so, no matter how frightened and depressed he felt. No matter how bad things got, he would rather live and hope.

For some reason, the questions he dreaded most in these interrogations never came. The draft of his cable to CIA director Stansfield Turner, the one he had left on his desk on the day of the takeover, was enough all by itself to condemn him. The paragraph about waiting for the military situation to settle down before finding new allies, and the mention of Ayatollah Shariatmadari, who had emerged as such a rival to Khomeini, was especially damaging. He expected to have the document placed on the desk before him at any moment. In between sessions he would pace his cell working out ways to deny and evade what he had written, ways of limiting the damage it might do. He set detailed priorities of those things he would admit, under duress, those things he would admit only under severe duress, and those things he would try never to admit. Among the latter were names of agents and the secret project under way to purchase land in the mountains and get the clandestine Soviet missile observation project up and running. But his interrogators never brought these things up. They weren't interested in what he had actually been doing; they were interested only in what they *thought* he was doing.

At one point he was moved downstairs from his old chancery office to a small windowless closet either on the first floor or in the basement, he wasn't sure. It rattled him more than he imagined it would. It was a little like being placed in his own coffin. It was then, early in the new year, that he began to buckle.

Early on, Ahern had admitted who he was. He knew that alone probably meant he would eventually be killed, but he saw it as a first step down a long road. He would give in little by little, buying himself time. His identity and role were the most obvious bits of information they already had. That much was clear from the documents they kept bringing him from the State Department files, week after week, and, eventually, some of the restored ones that he and Daugherty had shredded. It was pointless to keep denying the obvious.

The students held a press conference to announce their outing of the embassy's CIA officers. They displayed Ahern's false Belgian passport and showed off the copy of Laingen's cable identifying Daugherty and Kalp by name. In the United States, these documents were displayed on TV along with the allegations without much comment. Network reporters noted that Ahern had been an Eagle Scout as a boy, and that he had attended Notre Dame University before joining the foreign service. Daugherty was shown in his marine uniform. The reports neither denied nor acknowledged that the men were spies and did not explain that it was standard practice for agency officers to work at American embassies under cover of the foreign service.

Despite a national obsession with the story, there was at this point little or no reporting in the United States, on TV or in print, about the revelations in the "spy den" documents. While they contained nothing like the conspiracy theories the students imagined, they were revealing. They confirmed the agency's presence in Iran, which was hardly surprising, and in many cases unveiled what it had been doing, or trying to do. One of the most significant revelations was the agency's relationship with Simon Farzami, a Jewish journalist known in the agency files as SDTRAMP. Farzami had been raised in Lebanon and Switzerland and first came to Iran after World War Two with his brother, David, to visit their stepfather's brother, Ebrahim Hakimi, who later became prime minister of Iran. Both brothers had been hired by PARS, the Iranian news agency, and over the years Farzami had worked for a variety of foreign newspapers and agencies, including the Associated Press and London's *Daily Telegraph*. David died young, but Simon had a long career in Tehran, becoming editor of the French-language newspaper *Journal de Teheran*. He was an avuncular, sophisticated, portly man who had excellent contacts in local power circles, having once served in the Ministry of Information, and played both sides during the Cold War. His connection with the CIA was long-standing, but at times he had been a kind of double agent, undertaking two trips to Israel at the behest of the Soviets to "gather information on Israeli policies," and to "establish contacts" with Israeli journalists and academics. He was paid 120,000 rials (about $1,700) for those trips, money that, according to one of the reassembled documents, he had been "allowed to keep" by the CIA—suggesting that the agency owned a certain priority of allegiance. Ahern had met with Farzami several times in his four months, a new station chief on unfamiliar terrain reaching out to a long-standing source for general guidance. It seemed to Ahern that the older gentleman enjoyed their orientation sessions. Farzami was not happy with his country's drift toward Islamic theocracy, and he appeared to be eager to offer whatever help he could. He deciphered for Ahern the byzantine Shiite subculture that had been thrust so unexpectedly into power, and he met with Barry Rosen, the embassy's press attaché, to discuss setting up an international newspaper in Switzerland that would present, according to one of the documents, "a true image" of Iran's revolution to the West.

Nevertheless, these relatively benign ties with the agency were enough to spell doom for Farzami unless he had fled. Ahern tried to buy him more time, telling Sheikh-ol-eslam that he couldn't remember SDTRAMP's last name, only his first. He said he couldn't remember the name of the newspaper where he worked. He was helped in this sort of stalling by Sheikh-ol-eslam's obsession with uncovering a plot to assassinate or unseat Khomeini. This is what the students were determined to find and were convinced existed. So the minor revelations in the documents were sometimes overlooked. In Farzami's case, however, it was not. Here was a person who had collaborated with the devil. He was arrested, charged with deliberately "mistranslating" government documents and with spying for the CIA. He would be executed by firing squad on December 16, 1980.

There were others. Under further questioning Ahern confirmed the identity of SDROTTER/4, a tribal leader from southwest Iran named Khosrow Qashqai, who had been encouraged and funded by the agency in his efforts to rouse local resistance to the emerging mullah-led regime; Rear Admiral Ahmad Mandani, a former governor of Khuzestan and more recently a losing candidate for president in the January elections; and

Amir Entezam, a diplomat who was involved with the effort to establish a Swiss-based Iranian newspaper. Qashqai would be captured in the summer of 1980 and publicly hanged in 1982. Mandani fled Iran and eventually settled in the United States. Entezam was arrested and jailed for life. The documents would reveal, and Ahern would confirm, earlier efforts made by the CIA to recruit Abolhassan Bani-Sadr, the current finance minister, who had been helpful to the agency in the past. Ahern's interrogation assumed a pattern. Instead of pushing him to tell them everything he knew, they would present him with documents and information that in most cases he would eventually confirm. He tried to confine himself to acknowledging only information they already had found on their own.

In time, Ahern rationalized his capitulation in another way. By helping them understand exactly what the "spy den" documents said, it might dispel some of their wilder fantasies about American spying in Iran. The contacts with Farzami and the others had been exploratory at best, and though there was no doubt that the United States was supporting Qashqai's efforts to oppose the new regime, and had hopes of doing more in the future, they did not reveal the plot the students were looking for.

Ahern's interrogations gradually ended. There would be days between sessions, then weeks. Finally, Ahern figured they were done with him, and his captivity became a struggle to fill time.

He was kept alone at all times. During the long months of interrogations he used every minute preparing for the next session, working out ways to delay, confuse, or avoid giving his captors information, but once the questioning stopped he was on his own with the four walls. He coped by finding activities that would bring him some lasting personal benefit, so that if he were ever released he could say that he had not wasted his time. He knew how to play the piano and was a lover of classical music, and when he asked his guards if he could have some of the sheet music he had kept in his apartment they shocked him by handing it over within days. He spent hours memorizing Schumann's *Carnaval* and piano works by Chopin, playing the music in his mind. He was given access to the library Richard Queen had set up in the chancery, and he chose mostly classics, plays by William Shakespeare, novels by Charles Dickens. He read Charlotte Brontë's *Jane Eyre* twice in French, and then, discovering two books of German grammar in the library, he set about teaching himself German, his wife's first language. It would be something he could surprise her with if he was ever released.

He did calisthenics and high-stepped around the room to simulate jogging, which he found had psychological benefits even greater than physical ones. It raised his spirits. If only to help break the monotony, he skipped the exercises every tenth day. He had always been a light eater, but now found himself voraciously hungry. The guards let him eat as much as he wanted, so Ahern would request three or four hamburgers at a sitting, or multiple servings of chicken. He had always been slender, and it seemed now that no matter how much he ate he did not gain weight. His face had always been slightly concave, and now there were caverns under his cheekbones and his eyes seemed to recede into deep sockets. His thin, straight brown hair grew down to his shoulders. He looked old, worn, harmless. He became emotionally numb.

Mornings were the worst times. He would be awakened early for breakfast, usually flat bread, butter, jam, and tea, and taken to the bathroom; then he would go back to sleep until about noon. After awaking again he would begin his routines—exercising, reading, "playing" music, "watching" a play. Sometimes he would read until three or four in the morning. Late at night was the best time. There were few interruptions from the guards. Ahern could drift off in his books or into his imagination until his eyes fell shut.

Ahern's colleague Bill Daugherty was making his own compromises, and dealing with the consequences. On the night of Valentine's Day, Sheikh-ol-eslam brought the CIA officer a standard State Department cable and asked him about the long lists of code at the top.

"It's just in-house stuff," said Daugherty. "It tracks where the cable originated, where it was sent, and how it was routed. It's all very simple."

Ahern had said the same thing but Sheikh-ol-eslam wasn't buying it. Daugherty grew impatient with him. He deliberately talked to him like a child. He said that if Sheikh-ol-eslam had ever had any experience with a large organization, he would know that such tracking policies were routine.

"You such a smart guy, why are you bothering me with things like this?" he said.

"You aren't being very helpful," the gap-toothed Iranian complained.

"No, I'm not," Daugherty admitted.

"You don't like doing this?"

"No, of course not."

He felt bad about any help he had given them, and when he asked about the fate of Victoria Bassiri, the Iranian woman whom he had met with the previous summer, Sheikh-ol-eslam told him curtly, "She was shot."

Shot? Daugherty was stunned. He pictured the woman laughing with him over dinner, doing her limited best to help him understand the shifting sands of local politics. She had been killed for that? Why hadn't she fled the country immediately when the embassy was taken? Maybe she had stayed because of her husband and children. Perhaps she believed her connection to the embassy had been so insignificant that it would never be noticed, or that he would have been able to protect her identity. If so, she had paid for those misjudgments with her life. Daugherty was appalled. She had done so little, nothing of consequence. He had tried hard to convince Sheikh-ol-eslam and the others that Bassiri was not a serious spy, hardly even worth their effort. She had never even been asked to gather sensitive information, assuming she would have been in a position to do so. He felt terrible about it but finally concluded that spies accepted such risks. How could she have been so foolish to stay?

After he had spelled out his real job, Daugherty was left alone for months. While the zealots did their best to spin conspiracy theories out of the mostly pedestrian cables and memos, the documents utterly exploded the myth of CIA omnipresence and omnipotence. They revealed that the agency's operation in Iran in November 1979 consisted of four Americans (one of the officers had been on home leave when the embassy was taken) who had been desperately knocking on doors and offering cash to anyone willing to help explain to them what was going on. Sheikh-ol-eslam found it incredible that the vaunted CIA had not one officer in his country that could speak Farsi. But the cables confirmed it. Their evil dragon had turned out to be a mouse. Daugherty sensed a palpable feeling of disappointment.

Always a solitary soul, he didn't mind spending his days and nights alone. When he was a child and his mother disciplined him by sending him to his room, she would complain that it fell short of real punishment because he seemed actually to enjoy it. As an adult he had always valued the time he spent living by himself. When he had gone back to school after returning from Vietnam he was older than most of his classmates and didn't have much in common with them, so he spent a lot of time alone, studying. In the chancery now there were plenty of books to choose from, and Daugherty was an avid reader. Books made all the difference. In his survival training he heard the story of Private Jacob DeShazer, who had survived the daring Doolittle raid over Tokyo early in World War Two and had been kept in solitary confinement by Japanese troops in China for forty months with absolutely nothing to do but stare at the walls. Daugherty felt that would have driven him crazy. But so long as he could escape into books he was okay.

He read voraciously. To his deep delight he found in the old high school library an edition of the two-volume classic Kelly and Harbison study *The American Constitution: Its Origins and Development,* which carried him off into his favorite field of study for as long as he cared to read. He used the back of these books to record a diary of his captivity, noting the passing days and, in a personal shorthand, any events that he wanted to remember. He also delved into novels and history books, including many that under normal circumstances he probably never would have read, such as the great novels of Charles Dickens and mysteries by Agatha Christie and Ruth Rendell. He plowed through thick volumes on British and American history and became particularly engrossed in a biography of Blanche of Castile, the wife of French King Louis VIII and the mother of Louis XI, Saint Louis. He resented being held captive, but he was grateful for the long stretches of time he was left alone. He believed that sharing a small space with one or two others would have been far more difficult.

Occasionally, Sheikh-ol-eslam would stop by to chat. Their conversations had become relaxed. He would ask if Daugherty was getting enough food, or sometimes simply ask how he was doing. He seemed to enjoy their exchanges.

One night between Christmas and New Year's, Sheikh-ol-eslam confessed that he was disappointed in the response their action had provoked in the United States.

"How can we convince the American people that what we've done is justified?" he asked.

On previous occasions, Sheikh-ol-eslam had told Daugherty of riots in the streets at home, stories he apparently believed. He had been at Berke-

ley in the late Vietnam War period when the campus produced some of
the most extreme leftist rhetoric, and had come home with the belief that
overthrowing the shah would be an important blow in the world revolution. So why weren't young Americans taking to the streets in solidarity?

"You're crazy," Daugherty said. "You want *me* to help you with your
propaganda to convince my countrymen that what you've done is right?"

The CIA officer's days fell into an almost comfortable routine, a
breakfast of bread, butter, jam or cheese, and tea. He would then lean his
sleeping pallet against a wall and spend several hours pacing back and forth.
Ten paces took him from one corner of the room to the other, and he would
walk until his feet were sore or he grew tired. The room was never cleaned,
so in time his exercise rubbed a smooth path through the layer of dust on
the floor. As he walked he developed elaborate fantasies to occupy his mind.
He designed houses, imagined them being built, landscaped the yards,
furnished the interiors, and chose colors for the walls and rugs. Then he
would imagine parties in them, inviting beautiful women. He thought a
lot about flying, dreaming up record-breaking challenges for himself, such
as breaking the speed record in a turbo-prop plane from Honolulu to
Dallas, deciding what kind of plane would be best and how to configure
the gas tanks and electronic instrumentation, calculating the speed and
fuel-consumption ratios, what altitudes to fly, how best to utilize the prevailing winds, and so on.

Applying the Kelly and Harbison volumes, he invented an imaginary
class in constitutional studies with eight students. He was the professor.
In his mind, lost completely in the fantasy, he would say, "Okay, today the
course is judicial politics and strategies and we're going to talk about building a consensus on the Supreme Court." Then he would lecture on a case
where initially the court had been divided, not only between conservatives and liberals but where there were opinions all over the map. Then
he would explain how the justices hammered out compromises and arrived
at an opinion. His imagination improved with exercise and soon he had
the sessions fleshed out in extraordinary detail. He had just finished graduate school the year before, so the setting was familiar to him. He gave the
students names and personalities, roughly based on students he had known
at Claremont. He had a class clown and a student who was very serious,
always taking notes, but who never spoke. Other students were frequent
questioners, and held differing political philosophies, and there would be

arguments and debates that he would moderate and steer. In those months he felt his mind was as sharp as it had ever been. Between the reading, thinking, and imaginary lecturing, he arrived at insights and ideas that had never before occurred to him.

This would occupy Daugherty until lunch, which tended to be American-style food that he assumed had been seized after thousands of American advisory troops had left Iran in the previous years. Some of it had been sitting around for too long. There was plenty of it, but much of it was unappetizing and he had begun to lose weight. He spent some time each afternoon picking the worms out of his powdered milk. He would repeat his morning routines after lunch, which kept him occupied until dinner. He considered how he might handle this crisis if he were president of the United States, drawing on his familiarity with military assets —what U.S. forces could and could not do. It galled him that he and the others were still in captivity as the weeks and months droned by. How could the American government let so many of its emissaries be abducted by these kids? How could Carter have allowed the shah in? And then he'd think of the anti-American graffiti he'd seen on the walls and the insults and he'd work up a slow boil over it. He thought the way to go would be to coerce Iran into backing down. As president, he would summon the Iranian military attaché, bring him into the Oval Office, and say, "General, in five hours I am going to launch all the B-52s and it's going to take them fourteen hours to fly to Iranian airspace. So that's nineteen hours. If within those nineteen hours our Americans, all of them, are not out of your country in good health, then the B-52s are going to destroy Qom, Isfahan, and Mashhad, or the oil refineries."

Then as president he would turn to his chief of staff and the chairman of the joint chiefs and order them to take the Iranian attaché to the tank in the Pentagon and let him monitor the B-52s' flight so that he could see them taking off and moving out over the ocean. Daugherty imagined the Iranian general watching the bombers reach Europe and then close in on Iranian airspace. He would know that it was not a bluff. Sometimes in Daugherty's mind the general would rush to a phone and convey the importance of immediately releasing the hostages, and other times he would have him sit and watch as the B-52s dropped their devastating loads on the country's cities. Daugherty would play through the scenarios in his mind.

The one thing he considered too far-fetched for serious consideration was a rescue attempt. He had heard, of course, about the Israeli raid at Entebbe, and figured if commandos stormed the building he would sit with his hands in the air. But Iran was a landlocked country, and the distance from Tehran to any nonhostile border was probably four hundred to five hundred miles. He knew there were no helicopters for a mission like that. Even if they had such choppers, in-flight refueling over enemy territory was generally considered too risky. Rescue was, he thought, practically impossible.

Sometimes in the afternoons he would nap. On the days when they let him take a shower he would step into the water fully clothed, soap up his shirt and pants, peel them off, wring them out, do the same with his underwear, and then wash himself. He had the yellow Brooks Brothers shirt he had been wearing on the day of the takeover and a pair of brown polyester pants, and the guards had brought him jeans, a sweatshirt, and several changes of underwear from his apartment. When he was finished showering he would don the dry set of clothes and carry the wet ones back to his room, where he would stretch them out to dry. After dinner he walked again. It helped tire him out enough to sleep.

Daugherty got along reasonably well with his guards. They tended to be very young men, in their teens or early twenties, and were educated far better in math and the sciences than in history or politics and had absorbed from their religious leaders strong opinions about people, places, and events about which they knew next to nothing. They had wild fantasies about the United States and the CIA. Most spoke little or no English, so even if he had wanted to converse with them he could not. There was little point anyway, he thought. Anything out of the mouth of an American was automatically suspect, and none of the guards he met showed the slightest propensity for critical thinking. Their minds traveled on fixed rails. To think for themselves or critically examine their own paths was nothing less than sinful, a temptation to stray from the One True Path. How do you converse with people like that? For a time, a guard was posted in the room with him twenty-four hours a day. Daugherty would do his best to make the poor young man's life miserable, offending his sense of modesty by wearing only boxer shorts, breaking wind, or coughing on him. Once, suffering a cold, he went out of his way to spread infection and was pleased to hear some days later that his guard had succumbed to the virus. Mostly, he minded his own business and tried to avoid trouble.

He wasn't always successful. The room where he spent the most time that winter was on the ground floor of the chancery's back side; its windows faced the embassy grounds. It had ceilings that were at least fifteen feet high and the windows were accordingly very tall. The bottom of his window was about four feet from the floor. On mild days he managed to open the window a few inches to let in some fresh air. At night he would sit beneath it enjoying the slight breeze and listening to the guards outside laughing, talking, and toying incessantly with the bolts on their rifles. Occasionally someone fired a shot, but given the way they handled their weapons Daugherty assumed that most often it was an accident.

One night, as he lay beneath the window reading, a breeze from the cracked window was bothering him so he shifted the curtain in an effort to block it. From outside, it looked as though he were sneaking a peek outside, which was strictly forbidden. As he resumed reading the door to his room flung open and five or six armed guards stomped in, expecting to catch him in the act.

"What's the problem?" he asked.

"You are looking out," said one of the guards in his tentative English.

Daugherty looked up at the window, three feet over his head.

"I am not. I'm reading." He laughed.

The men pulled him to his feet and approached him with handcuffs and a blindfold. He knew the drill. When a rule was broken he would be cuffed, blindfolded, and left to sit that way for hours. This time, innocent, Daugherty fought back. He pulled the lead guard over to the window and showed him how the breeze moved the curtain.

"I didn't do this," he shouted, trying to batter his way through the language barrier. "You just saw the wind blow the curtain."

He decided that if he was going to be punished this time, he would earn it. He squared off to resist them and just then a gust of wind moved the curtain. The lead guard, looking disgusted, waved the others away from Daugherty and they left the room. He was so pumped up with adrenaline from that encounter that he walked back and forth for hours trying to let off steam.

Once his imaginary games got him in trouble. He was given a pencil and paper by Sheikh-ol-eslam so that he could write a letter home, and after he finished the letter he played with the pencil, sketching out plans on large sheets of paper for an imaginary airport, the terminal, runways, the concourses, the tower, parking lots, garages, the firehouse, and maintenance hangars for three or four airlines. It was something to occupy his mind, and when he was finished he balled the papers up and later threw them in the trash can in the bathroom.

He didn't think about them again until a suspicious and angry delegation of guards showed up in his room. They accused him of drawing some kind of coded diagram. It took a moment for him to figure out what they were talking about, and when it occurred to him Daugherty laughed.

"Let's look at this logically," he said. "First of all, if I'm going to leave messages for the other guys, I'm not going to do it on paper this size and sort of halfway wad it up and stick it in a trash can in a bathroom that you guys use. Do you think I'm an idiot?"

The looks on their faces told him yes, because in their eyes this is precisely what he had done. He realized that part of the problem was that these young Iranians had never traveled, so they were not familiar with airports. His drawings made no sense to their eyes. Daugherty explained and answered their questions until they were satisfied. They gathered up the drawings and left the room. He heard no more about it.

When he was staying in this first-floor chancery room, Daugherty was visited by a representative of the Red Cross, a slender, clean-cut young man about his age, either Swiss or French, who seemed angry when he entered the room. Daugherty was surprised. Having been trained to expect the conditions American POWs experienced in North Vietnam, he had no severe complaints about his own treatment, but this Red Cross man was appalled. He asked how long Daugherty had been isolated.

"Since the first days of the takeover."

The man sat on the floor and took notes.

"Have you been abused physically?"

"Yes."

The man's disgust was evident, and the two or three guards listening to the interview frowned heavily. The students were keen to be seen as benevolent and this was clearly off message. But they didn't interfere with the interview. The Red Cross man thanked Daugherty before he left and expressed his anger over what he had heard.

Daugherty worried how his comments might affect people in the United States. He was worried they might conclude conditions in the embassy were worse than they really were, which would be hard on them. He wondered if he had done the right thing.

In mid-February, he was moved to the chancery basement. The room looked like it had once been part of a larger space, now halved by a flimsy-looking wall of acoustic tiles fitted to a wooden frame. The wall ran straight into a large air vent, about two feet by two feet, and he discovered that by standing with his ear to that corner he could hear what was going on in the next room. To his delight, he heard the voice of Colonel Tom Schaefer, the defense attaché, and soon the two men were whispering to each other, the first contact either man had had with another American in months.

"When are we getting out of here?" Daugherty asked.

"Let's make it interesting," said Schaefer, who proposed a twenty-five-dollar prize for whoever picked a date that came closest to their release. They jotted their predictions on pieces of paper and then passed the notes to each other through the vents. Daugherty picked the seventeenth of April. Schaefer picked the fifteenth of November. Already the air force colonel believed there was no hope for their release until after the American presidential election.

They had to be careful. Daugherty was convinced the guards outside his room were listening, hoping to catch the two violating the rules.

Every time Daugherty moved into a new space, the moment he was left alone he conducted a thorough search. In his new room he found an inch-long stub of pencil and a small piece of broken glass, about twice the size of a fingernail, with one very sharp edge. He put the glass shard to work on a corner of the tile wall behind his sleeping pallet and soon pried a tile loose. He poked around inside the wall and cut loose the tile to Schaefer's room.

"Check the loose tile in the corner," he whispered to Schaefer the next time they had a chance to speak.

After that, they limited talking directly to each other to urgent questions and left messages inside the wall. Daugherty used blank pages he tore from the backs of his books. In this way they carried on a running dialogue. Daugherty tended to stay up late into the night and sleep long into the day. After his evening meal and his long "walk," he got in the habit of sitting with his back against the wall with his legs drawn up to support a book. If anyone peeked in, it looked like he was reading. He would then write notes to Schaefer. When the lights went out, he pried loose the tile beside his pallet and slipped the note into the empty space between the walls. He would retrieve a return message from Schaefer when he woke up—the colonel was an early riser.

Neither man had much news to share, but the ability to communicate greatly buoyed their spirits. Daugherty wrote to Schaefer that when he was in Vietnam he noticed that military officers who became prisoners of war continued to receive promotions. "By the time we get out, maybe you'll be a general," he wrote. He made another wager, this one for twenty dollars, that they would be released before Easter, which the colonel accepted . . . and won. Daugherty asked where they would be taken when they were released, and Schaefer speculated that they would be flown to Wiesbaden, Germany. It was a nice thing to think about.

Sheikh-ol-eslam entered Daugherty's room one night wearing the same open-collared shirt, blue jeans, and sneakers he had worn throughout the interrogations. He announced that a video crew was coming in to take pictures and interview him. When he left, Daugherty whispered into the vent, "Did you hear that?"

"No," said Schaefer.

"They're going to videotape me for something."

"There's only one answer you give," said Schaefer.

"What."

"No comment."

When Sheikh-ol-eslam came back with the crew, lugging a big video camera, Daugherty noticed that they had placed and videotaped a hand-lettered sign on the outside of his door that read, "CIA Person." There were ten other Iranians who had come to either assist or watch—ever since Daugherty's admitted spy status, he had become an object of intense curiosity. Daugherty stayed on his sleeping pallet as they readied the equipment.

At last, Sheikh-ol-eslam asked, "How long have you been with the CIA?"

"No comment," Daugherty said.

"Were you a spy here?"

"No comment."

Sheikh-ol-eslam grew increasingly angry as each of his next ten questions met with the same response. He then turned to the camera and spoke at some length in agitated Farsi. Then he and the whole crew picked up the camera and left, slamming the door behind them.

He was in that same room, listening at the air vent, when Schaefer was questioned by Ebtekar. Schaefer had dubbed her "Miss Philadelphia." He endured repeated lectures from her about America's centuries of barbarity and exploitation, the genocide of native Americans, the enslavement of Africans, the slaughter of Vietnamese. Daugherty was listening in one night while Ebtekar lectured Schaefer about the inhuman, racist decision to drop atomic bombs on Hiroshima and Nagasaki.

"The Japanese started the war, and we ended it," Schaefer said.

"What do you mean, the Japanese started the war?" Ebtekar asked.

"The Japanese bombed Pearl Harbor, so we bombed Hiroshima."

"Pearl Harbor? Where's Pearl Harbor?"

"Hawaii."

Daugherty heard a moment of silence. Then Ebtekar asked, "The Japanese bombed Hawaii?"

"Yep," said Schaefer. "They started it, and we ended it."

Thus ended the interview.

2

WE KNOW WHAT ROUTE
THAT BUS TAKES

CIA officers Ahern, Daugherty, and Kalp were not the only ones still being questioned repeatedly months after the takeover. Most of the higher-ranking members of the mission were hauled back for repeated interrogation.

John Limbert was awakened in the middle of the night, blindfolded, and marched from the Mushroom Inn through the cold to the chancery. This time he was taken to a room in the basement, where he was placed in a chair. The blindfold was tied sloppily so out of the bottom he could see a man in a black ski mask and Sheikh-ol-eslam's reflection clearly in the glass. There were other Iranians in the room whom Limbert could not see but could hear. Their pens scratched furiously across paper whenever he spoke. Again, it seemed to Limbert that his captors had read a book about interrogation and had set the stage for this session carefully, trying to intimidate him, but their technique fell short. It was inauthentic. He did not consider himself to be a brave person, and he could readily imagine atmospherics alone that might terrify him, but this didn't. He, too, had some experience with the literature of captivity and interrogation, and he knew from his reading of Solzhenitsyn that the right way to survive was to play dumb.

Sheikh-ol-eslam started with the same questions Limbert had answered weeks before.

"Who have you met with?" and "What did you discuss?"

The embassy political officer gave the same answers. He wondered why they didn't just go through his Rolodex and ask him about each person listed, which would have made more sense. This way, asking him to remember names, gave him a chance to protect certain people. By marriage, he had extended family in Iran, but he never mentioned their names, although they were all listed in the Rolodex. When they asked him for an address, including his own, he made one up, knowing full well that the correct addresses were available to them. It all seemed ridiculously inept and he couldn't take it seriously.

"Tell me about your agents in Kurdistan," Sheikh-ol-eslam demanded.

Limbert smiled involuntarily.

"I can see you smiling at that," Sheikh-ol-eslam said.

Limbert couldn't help himself. It was like living in Wonderland. Limbert understood the reasoning behind the question about his "agents" in Kurdistan. There had been steady fighting in the northwestern part of Iran with Kurdish rebels. So of course Limbert, a high-ranking devil in the den of spies, would have "agents" there. When he smiled at the question, *that* became further evidence of its truth. It was groupthink, and it was unassailable.

"I don't know what you are talking about," he said.

"How do you communicate with your agents in Kurdistan?" Sheikh-ol-eslam asked.

"I don't."

"We know you communicate by radio."

"I don't know anything about radios."

"Then how do you communicate?"

"I don't know what you are talking about."

He asked Limbert when he had last seen one of the prominent Kurdish leaders, and the embassy political officer said he had never met the man.

"Look, I don't know anything about Kurdistan," Limbert told Sheikh-ol-eslam.

Sheikh-ol-eslam lectured Limbert in Farsi. They knew he had friends in Kurdistan and that he had visited there. These things were true and Limbert admitted them. But he had not been to Kurdistan in seven years, and certainly not since he had come to work at the embassy, and his friends had nothing to do with the disturbances there. But just the admission that he had friends there seemed the only part of what he said that Sheikh-ol-eslam heard. He had caught Limbert in a lie. If he had something to hide, he must be guilty.

"It's just not true," Limbert said.

"You know what we do with spies," Sheikh-ol-eslam said. "We can shoot spies."

"You can do anything you want to me."

The fear of being executed that had gripped him during the first two days had receded. It was there, but it had become background noise, a constant. Sheikh-ol-eslam's reminder was unnecessary and didn't alarm Limbert at all. If he felt anything, it was curiosity. He was so bored during the day that a session like this was a welcome break. The whole situation grew more and more irritating. What ate at him was not simply being held captive, his lack of freedom, his inability to see or communicate with his family, or even the uncertainty. All these things were, of course, deeply troubling, but on another level Limbert felt *professionally* disappointed—in *himself* and in his colleagues.

How could they all have been so blind? Just weeks before this had all begun, Limbert had shepherded around Henry Precht, director of Iranian Affairs for the State Department, on his last visit. They had gone to see Ayatollah Montazari, the leader of Friday prayers, and the ayatollah had asked who else they were planning to see. Precht named some of the people on his itinerary, all of them old-line nationalists, and Montazari had suggested that he add to his calendar the weekly prayer meeting at the University of Tehran. Limbert later warned that they would be wading into an unfriendly ocean of Muslims, but Precht liked the idea. So they went, accompanied by a representative of the Foreign Ministry, parking several blocks away from the university and walking in with the crowds. Limbert was content with a spot well outside the large tentlike enclosure where the prayer meeting was held, where they could see and hear at a relatively safe distance, but the Foreign Ministry man insisted they go all the way in. "My job is to get you two *into* the Friday prayers," he had said. They had some trouble getting past the armed guards at the front gate but were eventually let in after their minder somehow convinced the young guards that they were distinguished guests from the nation of Senegal! Never mind their white faces. Their escort warned them to avoid speaking English inside. When the meeting got revved up, the crowd began chanting slogans. Someone would step up to the microphone, scream something into it, and then everyone else would repeat it. Limbert and Precht felt compelled to shout along, so they found themselves chanting in Farsi the usual condemnations, including one that went, "Death to the Three Spreaders of Corruption, Sadat, Carter, and Begin!"

"Didn't that last one say something about Carter?" Precht whispered.

"Henry, just chant and don't ask questions," Limbert told him.

Their ministry escort was throwing himself into the work, red-faced with effort, rhetorically raining down the wrath of Allah on America and Israel and all their works, and when they were done he turned to them, the two official representatives of the Great Satan, and asked sweetly, "Would you care to join me for lunch?"

Moments like that had lulled Limbert, had lulled them all, into thinking that the hatred and malevolence was just rhetoric, that polite officialdom was somehow going to continue to control this whirlwind.

When he learned that the provisional government had resigned, Limbert had a better sense of the power shift taking place. Here he was, at the center of an international storm, someone who had trained his whole life to study and report on circumstances like these, arguably one of the Americans best suited for doing so, and he was utterly powerless to do a thing. He could question no one and write no reports. So in an interrogation session like this he at least had a chance to converse and to get some insight into what these captors of his were thinking, and what they were trying to accomplish.

Already he discerned an important shift in emphasis from the first few days of the takeover. At first many of those who took part did so as a kind of lark, a demonstration of youthful idealism, naiveté, and defiance. Their goals had seemed primarily rhetorical, to protest U.S. policies and to demand the return of the shah—a demand no one really expected America to honor. Those orchestrating it were acting out an arrogant youthful fantasy, nothing more. Now, listening to Sheikh-ol-eslam's detailed questions, he saw something new. The emphasis was now local, not global. They wanted information about Iranian officials that they could use against their political enemies. In the present atmosphere in Tehran, anyone could be smeared with suspicion of treason if it could be shown they had met with American "spies." Careers could be derailed, enemies brought down. Whoever was running this thing now had a very practical agenda, one that was local and ruthless.

In this context, Limbert also saw the logic in putting him and at least some of the others on trial. If they were going to make the charges against local officials stick, it would help to spell out conclusively the plots emanating from the den of spies. He knew he was not a spy, but he also knew he had to be very careful about what he said. He saw how wording in the documents was being twisted to support all kinds of things. *Anything* he said could get him shot or hung.

Sheikh-ol-eslam pressed him again to name those he had met with. He was fishing. When Limbert mentioned a name, one of hundreds, Sheikh-ol-eslam quickly asked, "Why did you meet with this person?"

"It was my job," said Limbert. He explained that his role at the embassy was to seek out Iranians, and listen and learn. "That's what a diplomat does."

Sheikh-ol-eslam mentioned that a train had been bombed recently in southern Iran.

"We think that the CIA did that, and you know who the people are who did it."

"Think what you want."

From time to time Sheikh-ol-eslam would leave the room and Limbert would sit blindfolded for ten or fifteen minutes. Then he would return with a new question. At the end, Sheikh-ol-eslam simply said, "That's it."

Lieutenant Colonel Dave Roeder, a pilot, was questioned—with Ebtekar translating—about the embassy's C-12. In the embassy files, they had evidently come upon a memo describing the first meeting Roeder had attended in Iran, one with the revolution's air force officials. During that encounter, Roeder had asked for permission to bring back the embassy's C-12, a small, two-prop aircraft that was used to ferry embassy officials to meetings around the country. It had been flown to Athens at the time of the shah's departure, and it had not been allowed back into Iran. Roeder had a personal interest in getting the plane back; it was his best chance of being able to fly regularly.

What he did not know was that there had been an international scandal recently in South Africa when the government there discovered that the U.S. embassy had been using its C-12 to take surveillance photographs around the country. To the Iranian students, Roeder's efforts to get the plane back proved he was a spy. Ebtekar explained the South African incident triumphantly.

"Did you have that same camera system on the C-12 you were using here?" he was asked.

"I have no idea what you are talking about," he said. He was lying. In fact, he knew well that C-12s were used for surveillance purposes at U.S. embassies around the world. He had used one himself when he was based in Panama.

"What kind of system is it?" he was asked.

Roeder just stared ahead, silent.

The interrogator stormed from the room and another entered, a small man in a silk jacket. He was well groomed and looked studious. He spoke calmly. He warned Roeder that the first interrogator was a violent man and that he was very angry.

"I'm really worried about what he might do to you," he said. He told Roeder that they wanted him to sign a statement admitting that the United States had used the C-12 to spy on Iran. Roeder knocked the paper and pen to the floor.

Ski Mask came back and began raging at him. Roeder was taken from the room and led to the building's cargo elevator shaft. It was freezing. Way up at the top of the shaft they had opened doors to the winter outside and snow gently descended. They chained him to one of the metal bumpers inside the shaft and took away his shoes.

He began to shiver and decided that the only way to stay warm was to move. He had, by now, plenty of practice at exercising in a small space, so he fell easily into his rhythm of jogging in place. Then he would stop and do push-ups against the wall. When his captors tried to prevent him from moving by dragging in a chair and chaining him to it, Roeder picked the chair up and continued jogging with it in his arms. When they found him doing this, his guards brought in a cinder block and chained him to that. Draped in chains, holding the chair in one hand, Roeder defiantly picked up the block and kept moving.

They left him there all night and throughout the next day. Then he was brought back for more questioning. He was taken this time to an embassy living room, placed in a comfortable, stuffed chair, and his blindfold was removed.

Sitting across from him behind a table was another young man with a two-week growth of black beard and Ebtekar, draped in her black robes, smiling politely. On the table was a delicate teapot and glasses, a box of biscuits, and a pack of Marlboro cigarettes.

Okay, here's the "good guy," he thought, *since the "bad guy" didn't produce.* And, sure enough, Ebtekar asked, "Would you like some tea?"

"No, thank you," Roeder said.

"How about a cigarette?"

"Yes, I would."

He lit the cigarette and took a deep drag. He hadn't had many in the weeks he had been captive.

The young man spoke and Ebtekar translated. "Why are you here?"

"I'm the assistant air force attaché. I'm a lieutenant colonel, my name is David Roeder."

"We have heard all that," Ebtekar said translating the questioner's response, "and we know that's not what you are."

Roeder clammed up again. He had told them the truth; if they were going to start playing games he wasn't going to play.

There was a long period of consultation between Ebtekar and the interrogator in Farsi, and then she said, "You've got to answer questions here. We know that you are not an air force lieutenant colonel."

What Roeder most felt was boredom, and he was genuinely curious about Ebtekar. Here was this young woman whose English was so fluent, and whose accent was so American, that she obviously had lived in the States at some point. She seemed bright and articulate. Why would she want to embrace this fundamentalist crap that denied her gender equal status with men? Why would she want to drape herself in dark robes?

"Why are you doing this?" he asked her.

She looked back at him startled.

"Look at your status as a woman in this society," Roeder said. "Why would you want this?"

Ebtekar was off like a shot. She launched into her rationale for traditionalism, how it was, in fact, liberating for women. She and her revolutionary sisters were actually much freer than women in the Western world, who remained enslaved by the twin satanic values of commercialism and sexual exploitation. "I believe in the fundamentals of Islam," she said. "And my faith requires women to do this."

Roeder argued with her, and she argued back, and the interrogation session came undone. Ebtekar warmed up readily to her standard jeremiad about the evils of America and Western society and the transcendental wisdom of Iranian Islam, Ali Shariati, the imam, the world's new Third Force. Roeder smoked and listened politely and relished the warmth. He felt sorry for her, and he felt pleased with himself for derailing his interrogation so easily. He thought, *What amateurs!*

Despite his crusty defiance, interrogators did finally manage to disturb Roeder. He was shown a picture of his wife, son, and daughter. It was a photograph he had kept on his office desk in a frame.

"Is this your wife and children?" he was asked.

"Yes. Where did you get that?"

The interrogator seemed to know a lot about his family. He knew that his son, Jimmy, was disabled. This shook up Roeder, although he tried not to show it. He had never considered that his family in Virginia would be at risk but, of course, there were many Iranians in the United States. His interrogator mentioned the stop where the school bus picked up his son every weekday.

"We know the route that bus takes," he said.

If he did not start cooperating, they were going to take his son off the bus.

"We will start sending pieces of him to your wife," he was told.

Roeder still refused to answer questions and was led back down to a cold basement room, but he was distressed. It was the lowest point so far in his captivity. His mind raced over the possibilities. Was his family under surveillance in Virginia? Was the U.S. government aware of this threat? Were they protecting his family? How seriously should he take it?

3

HAPPY NEW YEAR

After more than two months of captivity, the hostages and their guards were getting to know one another well and, in many cases, were getting along badly. One night Gary Lee heard an angry American voice say, "What the fuck makes you right and the whole world wrong?" It summed up perfectly the central complaint. Some of the hostages worked at tormenting their captors.

Marine guards Steve Kirtley and Jimmy Lopez, together in a room at the chancery, kept up a constant torrent of verbal abuse. Early on, Gunnery Sergeant Mike Moeller had begun substituting the word "Khomeini" for every foul word in the English language, and his fellow marines adopted it with relish. When they needed to use the toilet, they would tell the guard, "I need to take a Khomeini." They tried to remember every Polish joke they had ever heard and substituted for "Polack" the term "raghead," which they used for the Iranians in the mistaken assumption that they were Arabs. They would make sure to tell each other the jokes whenever a guard who spoke English was within earshot.

"You know how you can tell the shah was a raghead, Steve?"

"No, Jimmy, how?"

"Because he was too stupid to shoot enough of these other ragheads to stay in power."

When the guards passed around an item from the English-language *Tehran Times* detailing the abuse of Iranian students in the United States, the two marines made a big show of their delight.

"What's it about, Jimmy?" Kirtley asked.

"It's about all the great stuff Americans are doing back home," Lopez said. "They're siccing attack dogs on Iranians, running them over in cars, sheriffs in Texas are beating the shit out of them, stuff like that. It's great!"

When the two marines found a stack of the guards' plates and eating utensils piled in the bathroom they urinated on them. One night they wrapped a butter knife in a rag and took turns poking it at the exposed wires of their lamp. It shorted out the electricity in the chancery basement. They waited for the guards to replace the fuse and get the lights back on and then did it again. To the marines' amusement, the guards raced from room to room, convinced they were under attack. Kirtley cultivated a habit of farting loudly whenever he stood close to a guard. It would make them so angry that they would haul him out to another room and shout at him about his bad manners. He would return to his room grinning.

Finally they became so much trouble that they were separated.

Two of the other marines, Billy Gallegos and Rocky Sickmann, played similar games. Gallegos rigged a slingshot out of rubber bands, and he and Sickmann opened their window slightly one night after lights out and shot Geritol tablets at a guard standing outside next to the building's back wall. When the first pill pinged off a car nearby, the guard jumped. When the next pill hit, convinced he was under attack, he shot off his weapon. Soon there was a small crowd of guards, weapons up, shouting into their radios. Eventually the guards burst into the chancery and searched all the rooms, but the marines had long since closed their window, disassembled the slingshot, and crept back under the covers on their mattresses.

Once, when he was being questioned, Gallegos was asked if he had ever met with a SAVAK agent.

"Yes," he said, and pointed at the guard who happened to be posted outside his room.

"Him. He's one."

The panicked look on the guard's face had kept the marines laughing for days.

When the guards installed a camera in the bathroom, after catching on that their captives were leaving notes for each other there, the marines made a point of putting on lewd shows before it, offending their guards' Islamic sensibilities so badly that they gave up and took it down.

Bill Royer, the assistant director of the old Iran-America Society, noticed that antagonistic guards were generally weeded out. He had rubbed one of the guards wrong in the first days—Royer had smiled at the guard inappropriately, teasing him—and the young man had responded by elevating his middle finger. Royer had responded in kind. Two months later, the American found himself guarded by the same young man, who had not forgotten their exchange of ill will, and their mutual animosity resulted one night in the guard making a karate-style kick at the hostage's head. Later that evening one of the guard supervisors stepped into Royer's room.

"You seem to have some trouble with my friend," he said.

"Yes, and if he comes back I'm going to hit him," Royer said quietly.

"No, no, you can't do that," said the supervisor.

"If he comes back I am going to hit him," Royer repeated.

He never saw the guard again.

Once when Greg Persinger, a marine guard, was being led to the bathroom, ineptly blindfolded, he saw a guard playfully point his pistol at him as he approached. Persinger snatched the gun from his hand as he walked past, twirled it once or twice like a six-shooter, and handed it back.

"Don't ever point a weapon at me unless you're going to shoot me," he said and patted the guard dismissively on the head.

The guard was stunned. He didn't speak English, so he didn't know what Persinger had said. He looked around, hoping no one had seen. He wasn't about to report the infraction. How could he admit that the hostage had just snatched away his weapon? He settled back sheepishly in his chair.

As time wore on, there were many occasions when the marines, in particular, had opportunities to seize weapons from their amateurish guards. Sometimes they would allow the marines to play indoor soccer with them in the large open space that had once housed all the computer equipment for the Tacksman sites. It gave the young men a chance to vent some of their aggression and energy, an opportunity to actually run through space instead of jogging in place. The Iranians were more experienced ball handlers, but the marines saw to it that they collected plenty of bumps and bruises on their way to victory. Once, when they were shedding layers of clothes preparing to play, Persinger stooped to pick up some discarded jackets and move them to the side and was startled to find an Uzi in the pile. What could he do with it? Suppose he took it and pointed it at someone? Eventually he would either have to shoot somebody or surrender it. He was six-one, pale, with reddish blond hair; even if he made it off the compound, how far was he going to get? He scooped it up and put it down with the rest of the pile and then jogged out to play soccer.

Golacinski intimidated the guards because he was tall, muscular, and athletic. When he lost his temper, they shrank from him and raised their weapons. Once, when Don Cooke had laughed loudly after a guard dropped and broke a glass, he was seized angrily and was being led from the room when Golacinski intervened. He had been in the middle of a workout and had his shirt off and was feeling pumped up, so he jumped at the guard and pushed him away from Cooke.

"You're not taking him anywhere," he said. "If you take anybody, take all of us."

It was foolish. The guard was carrying a submachine gun and there were plenty more of them around the room. But in his shock at the sight of Golacinski towering over him, he backed away. The other guards came running with their weapons up.

Roeder and Don Sharer both stood up alongside Golacinski.

"You sit down!" the guards shouted at them.

"No," said Sharer. "You stop pointing those weapons at us and I'll sit down."

One of the guards broke the standoff.

"We just want to talk to him," he said of Cooke. "We'll bring him right back."

"If you don't, there's going to be trouble," Golacinski said.

They did bring Cooke right back, and that was the end of it, but it had made them more wary of Golacinski than ever. After that, for a time, whenever he exercised, they would position a guard directly in front of him. For a few days a guard sat before his space looking bored as Golacinski did his calisthenics. So he start hacking, coughing, sneezing, and deliberately spraying sweat and spittle, and the practice was promptly discontinued.

Kathryn Koob came to know well the young women who guarded her. Despite their traditional garb and enthusiasm for the revolution, they were not especially religious. Koob was a devout Lutheran who had grown up steeped in her faith, and felt she knew sincere piety when she saw it. The girls who fluttered around Koob were surprisingly Western and worldly. Underneath their manteaus they wore trendy jeans and silky colorful blouses. They colored their nails and wore jewelry and makeup. They were caught up in a tide of nationalist idealism that borrowed the rhetoric of the mosques for political purposes. The chadors they wore expressed solidarity and were the opposite of modest; they were worn not to deter but to attract attention. For many, the veil and chador were a rebuke to their mothers, part of a generation that had welcomed the Westernization of Iran under the shah. Koob, who was forty-one, had met many such women her age in Iran, women who loved Western fashion or who openly wore bright colors and uncovered their hair. At universities, middle-aged female professors once considered the vanguard of the new Iran were being fired for refusing to cover their hair, while for their students, some of them the young girls guarding Koob and Ann Swift, the future ran in the opposite direction, toward Islam and village tradition. Ironically, the old ways symbolized the new Iran. Donning the head scarf and chador was as much a rebellion for the new generation as shedding them had been for their mothers and older sisters. The girls who sometimes huddled in Koob's room would ask her why Catholic nuns in America had forsaken "their beautiful dresses." Among this crowd were some very serious, modest, religious young women, but very few. The most stern and dangerous of her female captors were the older ones, some of them true zealots. There was one who had instructed the newly armed young women on the first day of the takeover, "If they speak, shoot them."

One day a female guard came to her door with an old pair of her eyeglasses that Koob had kept in a drawer in her apartment. It upset Koob to be given such blatant evidence that they had broken into her home and rooted through her things.

"You asked for them," the woman said.

"I did not," said Koob. "I have my glasses. These are old ones for an emergency." She knew full well that they had searched her apartment as a follow-up to her interrogation, and because that had violated their own rules—the imam had instructed the students not to break into any more buildings—she knew this supposed request for glasses was a pretext. If she played along, it would validate what they had done.

So she refused to play along. It was one more unprovoked outrage and indignity and she lost her temper. She vented her spleen on the young guard, who endured it silently and then left to fetch one of her older, male supervisors. He spoke to her with false politeness that masked insufferable condescension.

"Hahnum, you must not act like this. You are making the sister most uncomfortable."

"You make me uncomfortable," Koob told him. "I am a diplomat. You kidnapped me, brought me here, and now you break into my house."

"You aren't a diplomat and you know it," he said.

"I *am* a diplomat and you know it. I've been accredited by several countries, including Iran, and you have broken all sorts of your own laws with this action. Now you've just broken another one, breaking into diplomatic property."

"You asked for your glasses," he said. "Besides, in some instances laws don't matter. There are special cases."

"'Special cases' if the laws don't suit you."

"We represent the people," he said. "Besides, you sent for your glasses."

"I most certainly did not. I have mine right here. These are old ones I keep for emergencies. You needed an excuse to break into my house and you used these," she said, shaking the old glasses at him.

"The sister said you wanted them," he said.

"Which sister? Bring her here."

"I've told you, you asked for them," he said.

"I didn't! If I wanted something from my house, it wouldn't be these. It would be a pair of shoes and a change of clothes. And books!"

The young man glared at her.

"I've told you *three times* that you asked for them."

And that was that. He had said it three times. He was the captor, she was the prisoner. Unspoken but clear was the assertion: *I am a man, you are a woman.* End of discussion. It was so because he said it was so.

Not all of the interactions were hostile. Some of the Iranian students were genuinely well meaning and tried to find ways to ease their captives' discomfort. Mahmoud, a small Turkish-Iranian guard with a boyish round face, announced that he had set up a barbershop in one of the rooms in the Mushroom Inn. Square-jawed Colonel Chuck Scott was one of the first to take advantage. A thoroughgoing army man, he was increasingly distressed with his shabby appearance; his hair was hanging in strings nearly to his shoulders and his beard had grown so long that the guards were teasing him that he was going to outdo the imam.

"I don't have any money," said Scott. "It was stolen by your friends."

"You can pay me when you are free again," said Mahmoud cheerfully.

When he was finished clipping Scott's hair and trimming back his beard, Mahmoud handed his customer a cracked piece of mirror to admire the transformation.

"Now, if your people decide to shoot us, at least my corpse will look better," said the colonel.

Mahmoud was distressed. He assured Scott that he and the others would not be shot, but then somewhat compromised that reassurance by adding, "If you are shot, it will not be our fault, it will be your government that should be blamed."

Richard Queen decided to keep his beard, but he trimmed it and then sat for Mahmoud's clippers. He emerged with a ridiculous bowl cut that made Queen look like Prince Valiant. To his chagrin, he was photographed not long afterward, and the pictures were published in *Time* and *Newsweek*. He felt not only abandoned, sick, and hopeless but silly. Mahmoud was disappointed that his clipwork had fallen short.

One day, when Bill Belk was standing at the broken window of his room in the chancery basement, looking up and watching snow fall, a young female guard with a G3 assault rifle stepped into his view. She smiled down to him.

"Hello, how are you?" she asked in English, as though they were meeting in a park. "It's snowing!"

"It's beautiful," Belk said. "I wish I could be out in it."

"Are you all right?"

"Yeah," said Belk, but he didn't sound convincing.

"Happy New Year," she said and then rolled a small snowball and pushed it to him through the hole in the glass.

Even Hamid the Liar had his softer moments. One night he delivered a cassette tape with a message from Cheri Hall to her husband, Joe. She had called one of the lines at the embassy that no one answered anymore and left a message on its answering machine in the hope that it would somehow find him, a desperate, loving gesture akin to throwing a bottle with a note into the ocean.

Hall, Queen, and Hamid stood around the recorder and listened to her voice. She started off strong, saying that she wanted him to know she was coping well and that she loved him dearly, and that everyone they knew was missing him and praying for him . . . and then she began crying. She choked up and found it hard to continue speaking. All of them, hostages and guard, started crying. Hamid let Hall listen to the tape several times.

* * *

Queen's mysterious condition was worsening. He was still bothered by bouts of wooziness and the strange numbness in his arm had spread.

One morning he was holding a plastic cup of tea in his left hand, waiting for it to cool, when, in the next moment, it was on the floor, hot liquid splashing everywhere.

"What the hell happened?" Hall asked, helping to sop up the spill.

Queen said he hadn't even felt the cup slip from his hand. The symptoms were strange. Why was only his left side affected? Increasingly his left arm felt not only numb but weak. It was growing limp and useless. He also had a terrible itch along the left side of his torso, so bad that at times he scratched himself until it bled. He didn't know why or how but it felt like parts of his body were dying.

He was visited again by the local doctor who had earlier diagnosed a "twisted spine." He had nothing new to offer and left Queen with a renewed supply of vitamins. Since he got so little exercise, and spent most of his days reclining or sitting, Queen couldn't easily dismiss the spine diagnosis. The vitamins did seem to help his mood, but they did nothing for his creeping illness, whatever it was.

4

THAT'S ILLEGAL!

On January 25, Hamilton Jordan hosted Ghotbzadeh's two unofficial emissaries in the White House. It was a happy day. News reports that morning said that Carter's chief Democratic rival, Senator Ted Kennedy, had severely depleted his campaign fund and there was reason to believe that a "major policy address" he had scheduled would include the announcement that he was dropping out of the race. That, coupled with the first real chance of finding a solution to the hostage crisis, gave the administration a glimpse of a break in what had been a long season of bad weather.

The first session with Villalon and Bourget in London had been disappointing, and CIA reports on the two men raised serious questions about whether they could be trusted, but Secretary of State Cyrus Vance, eager for any avenue to resolve the crisis diplomatically, had urged Jordan to pursue it further. He gave the two visitors a tour, and to bolster their own credentials the emissaries gave Jordan the tape recording of Waldheim's abject presentation to the Revolutionary Council—they said the tape was a gift from Ghotbzadeh.

Then the two secret emissaries delivered good news. They said that Iran's governing council had authorized Ghotbzadeh to begin negotiations over the hostages, an important step because it indicated that Iran's government, such as it was, appeared ready to assert its authority over the student hostage takers. It hardly guaranteed a solution, because if the council disapproved of whatever agreement they worked out, it could easily claim the foreign minister had acted on his own. Ghotbzadeh was sticking his neck out, and in postrevolutionary Iran there was no shortage of people willing to chop off his head.

That conversation led to discussions that went on for several days between Villalon and Bourget, and Jordan and Hal Saunders, an assistant secretary of state. The two emissaries outlined a road map to the hostages' release. The one thing Waldheim had brought home from Iran was a promise by the council to look kindly on the creation of a UN commission to study Iran's grievances against America. The United States would be encouraged to publicly oppose formation of this panel, because Carter's opposition would enhance the group's credibility in Iran, but the administration would have to promise to stop short of blocking its creation. After visiting Tehran, conducting its investigation, and presumably validating that nation's historical complaints, the commission would then have the moral authority in Iran to condemn the holding of hostages as "un-Islamic," and, Ghotbzadeh suggested, the imam would respond by letting the Americans go.

Jordan interrupted to complain that even casual UN observers would know that such a commission could not be created without America's consent.

"Let me finish explaining the idea, and then you and Mr. Saunders can destroy it!" protested Bourget.

Jordan and Saunders said that the United States might play along, provided they had assurance that the commission would lead to the hostages' release.

"There must be some balance to this," Jordan said. He explained that the president would be making a major concession.

"I understand," said Bourget, "but this same commission must win credibility with the Iranians. . . . Don't forget the political pressures in Iran!"

"Don't forget the political pressures here," said Jordan. "President Carter will have to be able to publicly explain and defend our actions to the American people. Khomeini doesn't have to run for reelection."

The second day's session lasted twelve hours. The two emissaries hammered out a detailed schedule, a formal dance that they believed would lead to the hostages' freedom. Jordan was excited; he agreed to meet with them again after they returned from another visit to Panama, where they were keeping up the pretense of pursuing the shah's extradition.

The chief of staff's enthusiasm was not shared by everyone in the White House. At Brzezinski's request, council staffer Gary Sick took a hard look at the plan and concluded that it was unlikely to succeed. He saw both Bourget and Villalon as men emotionally invested in the outcome of Iran's revolution, who knew that the continuing hostage crisis was likely to be a drag on the country for a long time and so were eager to see it end. That didn't mean they couldn't be effective, but their analysis of events in that country seemed to him full of "wishful thinking." Sick was also aware of how easily Ghotbzadeh could be left on a limb. If others decided to backtrack, the foreign minister could end up as scapegoat, accused of collaborating with the Great Satan. Sick wasn't worried about Iran's foreign minister, whom he saw as "crafty and very much concerned about his political skin." In fact, he saw Villalon and Bourget as Ghotbzadeh's hedge—he could safely back away from the agreement himself at any point claiming that he had never authorized the two. Sick recommended that to make the process work, they would need to get beyond these "well-meaning but possibly naive intermediaries," and deal directly with both Ghotbzadeh and Bani-Sadr. Brzezinski was even more skeptical. He had a better sense than most in Carter's inner circle of the emerging reality in Iran, that Bani-Sadr, Ghotbzadeh, and the rest of the "government" in Tehran were nothing more than a temporary dispensation. If Khomeini wasn't at the other end of the talks, they were irrelevant.

Jordan remained sanguine. When news broke a few days later that six of the American embassy workers, Mark and Cora Lijek, Robert Anders, Lee Schatz, and Joe and Kathleen Stafford, who had been hidden by the Canadian mission in Tehran since the day of the takeover, had been spirited out of Iran, the news there was received with dismay. "That's illegal!" one of the students at the embassy complained to a Western reporter. Ghotbzadeh had the gall to accuse Canada of "flagrantly violating international law" for helping six accredited diplomats escape being kidnapped and held hostage. The furtive presence in Iran of the six who had escaped capture at the embassy was the reason the State Department had refused from the beginning to announce the correct number of staffers there. One State Department correspondent had complained, "Goddamn it, how can you *not* know!" There was some concern in the White House that the Canadian coup would derail the secret protocol, but early reports from Bourget and Villalon were good. They had delivered the outline prepared in the White House to Ghotbzadeh and reported back that, despite his public pronouncements, privately Ghotbzadeh saw the ill will stirred up by the escape of the "Canadian Six" as a minor setback.

As the month ended, President Carter's patience seemed finally about to be rewarded. Bani-Sadr, the finance minister who had been outspokenly critical of the students, won more than 70 percent of the vote for president.

Khomeini was admitted to the hospital with heart trouble, and in the speech he gave approving the voters' choice he appeared to be preparing the people for his passing. "Be without fear, no matter whether a person comes or a person goes," he said. It appeared as though Iran was on the verge of another tectonic shift. Daily there were new reports from different sources that a solution to the hostage crisis was imminent. Kennedy had not withdrawn from the presidential race, but it looked as if things might finally be breaking Carter's way.

There was now a steady parade of Americans making unofficial visits to Tehran, ostensibly seeking some resolution of the crisis. The effect of these visits, nearly all of them by leftist activists whom the students regarded as allies, was to validate the hostage taking and legitimize the captors' allegations.

In early January one of these visitors was Native American activist John Thomas, who would participate in a student-led seminar that branded the United States the major enemy of all the oppressed nations of the world and ended up leading the mob outside the embassy in chants of "Death to Carter," urging his new Iranian friends to put all the hostages on trial. They were all spies, Thomas said.

In the days before his arrival the possibility of a meeting with the activist was offered to Rick Kupke, because of his Native American heritage. Kupke was told that he first must write a letter to President Carter explaining what he and the others and the embassy had done wrong and urging the president to take the necessary steps for their release.

Kupke was given a pen and a piece of paper. He was less than eager to meet with Thomas—he and his family had never felt much kinship with the native American political movement—but he did like the idea of something to break the monotony, and he worried about what might happen to him if he disappointed his captors, who seemed quite eager to make the session happen. At the time he was being held in the basement of the chancery with Mike Kennedy and John Graves. Kupke confessed to them, "I don't know what to do."

Graves, the embassy's press attaché, was a flamboyant man with a long graying beard, a world-weary but playful air, and a cutting sense of humor. He had worked in Vietnam and had been involved there in the interrogation of Vietnamese prisoners.

"I'll give you a trick," he said. "If you pull it off, they probably won't bother you, but if you get caught you'll probably regret the day you were born."

Graves suggested that Kupke write four or five pages of nothing, just doodle verbally, and if they got mad when they read it, tell them, "Okay, bring me more paper, I'll redo it."

"Then do the same thing again," Graves said. "I've only known you for two or three months, but if anybody can play stupid, you can."

Kupke swallowed the insult and took the advice. He decided to write like a third grader. He began his letter, "Dear Jimmy." Then he wrote, "How are you? I am fine. I find myself laying here on this floor. I'm not sure how I got here, but I sure find myself here a lot. Any way you can figure to get us out of here is good. The way I see things is that a lot of things happened . . ." It went on like this four pages.

Mailman, one of their guards, returned with the papers, flushed with anger.

"Are you joking or something?" he asked.

"No, no," said Kupke. "What's wrong?"

"This is no good."

"Can I have more paper?"

Mailman gave him more, telling him, "You do a better job."

"Okay," Kupke said. "I like doing this."

And he started another letter. "Dear Jimmy. How are you? I am fine. But there are several things that I'd like to tell you. Above all, it's just how hard this floor is that I'm sleeping on. And I think there's things that ought to be done immediately . . ."

Mailman took his pencil away and Kupke was never asked to write another letter.

Graves's advice was good, but his superior attitude grated on Kupke. The fifty-three-year-old foreign service officer had actually been held hostage briefly once before in his career, on the island of Fernando Póo off the coast of Nigeria. He saw himself as a modern Renaissance man: he was an avid tennis player, motorcyclist, skier, and scuba diver, the father of six, and an unabashed and unapologetic egotist. He was half-French and leaned toward Gallic in most things. He regarded that country's style, food, and international acumen as entirely superior to America's. His children were being raised French, he said proudly, and went on and on about their sophistication, brilliance, and accomplishment—in sharp contrast, it went without saying, to Kupke's own. Graves had nothing but scorn for the American policies that had created the situation in Iran and regarded the Iranian students' anger, if not their actions, as entirely justified. He thought Iran did deserve at least an apology from the United States, and held forth at length about the idiots in Washington who had allowed this situation to develop. Graves had other annoying traits. He smoked his pipe constantly, clouding the room with smoke, and chewed with his mouth open, loudly smacking his lips. He was routinely insulting in an offhand way. At one point in his career he had been an English teacher and he had never lost the habit of instruction. Kupke's usage was strictly rural colloquial and Graves could not curb his contempt.

Once, pacing impatiently as he waited for the single bathroom to open, Kupke complained, "Somebody must have went in there and died."

"No," Graves corrected. "Somebody must have *gone* in there and died."

"Whatever."

"I can tell you're from the Midwest by the way you're pacing," Graves said.

"Why?"

"Because you drag your heels like a midwestern shitkicker."

One day Graves came back from the bathroom and his hair and beard, which had been a graying brown, were suddenly completely white. At first Kupke thought the captivity had scared his hair white, but then he realized that Graves had been dying his hair. He'd evidently decided to shampoo in the bathroom sink.

Kupke both admired Graves and was put off by his airs. The marines Jimmy Lopez, Rocky Sickmann, and Greg Persinger loathed him. His Gallic superiority was to them simple anti-Americanism, and they didn't get his prickly sense of humor. He was less diligent than they about washing himself and his clothing, so he gave off a stench that in such constant close quarters was considered abusive. Like so many of the hostages, Graves had been immediately and mistakenly tagged as CIA, partly because of his age and senior status—the students now had access to the embassy's payroll records, so they knew how much their prisoners were being paid. Graves's check was near the top of the list. But they also assumed he was a spy because his name had turned up on a list of suspected CIA agents in a book that was published in East Germany. He had been awakened one night about two weeks after the takeover by a rough-looking Iranian whom he had not seen before. The man showed him the East German book, which had an old picture of Graves and his name.

"That's not me," Graves said, lying.

He was hauled off, certain that he was going to be shot. Instead, he was thrown into the back of a station wagon and driven somewhere off the compound, where he was kept for about three weeks and interrogated continually, always at night. He didn't have much to tell. They all wanted to know about the plot to kill Khomeini. Graves told them it was silly, which convinced them all the more that he was in on it.

Shortly before John Thomas's arrival, Bruce German, the embassy's budget management officer who, more than most of the embassy workers, had been ill-prepared emotionally for such a trial and who had spent much of his time in captivity without word from his wife or family, wrote an angry letter addressed to Ben Bradlee, the executive editor of the *Washington Post*. Thomas carried it home and delivered it. The *Post* published it after verifying its authenticity and it came as a shock in America. It voiced the fear and bewildered anger of the hostages and German's startling empathy for his kidnappers:

> Our future is very uncertain, and I am not overdramatizing when I say that our very lives hang in the balance. Needless to say, we have become rather bitter, disillusioned, and frustrated, because we are the victims of poor judgment and lack of foresight on the part of the U.S. The Shah is still in the U.S. . . . something which totally defies logic. [*He did not know that the shah had flown to Panama.*] We certainly do not agree with the methods used, such as disregarding diplomatic immunity, but we do sympathize and understand the motives of the Moslem Students. They firmly believe that the Shah was a tyrant, and guilty of despicable crimes against the human rights of his former subjects; and some of us have seen overwhelming evidence to support those charges. The majority of the hostages know that the Shah should never have been allowed to enter the U.S., regardless of the reasons given.

Certain people, political-interest groups and lobbyists, would have people believe that the U.S. owed the Shah the right to American medical care. Unfortunately, months prior to our capture, it was speculated in Washington that if the Shah entered the U.S. for any purpose, this embassy might have serious difficulties, and possibly be overrun. We wonder, therefore, why we were not forewarned, and later, adequately protected, once the decision was made.

Lending credence to the student captors' allegations of secret American plots, German, who would not have been privy to any classified American operations, suggested that the Carter administration was reluctant to return the shah "because of certain things he might reveal, things which could prove to be very embarrassing, to say the least."

5

A MARVELOUS COUP

Bill Belk's combative roommate, the army medic Donald Hohman, undertook a long hunger strike early in the year and, after several weeks, had grown so frail he lay on his mattress all day. He ignored the rule against speaking, talking loud and long to Belk. They were too worried about him to leave him alone; they couldn't withhold his food and he was too frail to beat. He'd challenge them, "What are you going to do to me? Go ahead and do it right now."

He had started the hunger strike to get away from Joe Subic, whom he regarded as a traitor and collaborator, but even after he was moved he continued to refuse food. He liked the way it worried his captors. Hohman was a mystery to the Iranian students. Like most everyone else he was considered CIA, and in his case it was a belief heightened by the fact that he had been issued two passports. Yet he was admired for his medical skill. After his dramatic treatment of Belk's allergic attack in the first days, many assumed he was a doctor. He had been mistakenly identified as such on one of the papers in his personnel file.

Hohman knew the medical conditions of most of the Americans who had been seized, and he would brief the medical students among the guards about what medications and precautions his various patients needed. Charles Jones had hypertension, so he needed his pills. Lee Holland had gout and Hohman taught them how to treat it, and what medications to deliver—"He knows the dosage," he said. His professional standing, even if he was not an M.D., accorded him a measure of status the others captives did not enjoy. He abused it freely, and because he was admired, his insults stung. When Sheikh-ol-eslam and Ebtekar tried to interrogate him he cut them short.

"I don't know anything about the CIA. I'm down here TDY [temporary duty]," he told them. "I'm medical. Period." Ebtekar was so insulted by his demeanor that she slapped his face.

Hohman's hunger strike flummoxed his guards. At first they were angry, and the medic gave the anger right back, screaming and cursing at them. In time, they were afraid to enter his room. He had hoped others would join him, that it would spread and that all the hostages would stop eating, but none of the others had his willpower. Yet Hohman persisted. He was not suicidal; he saw the hunger strike as a way of fighting back. In a letter to his father in Sacramento, Hohman wrote:

"I'll come through this no matter what they do to me or how long they keep me. Also, the longer I am held, the more I've come to despise my captors and what harm they've done myself and all my family by taking my freedom without me ever having done an Iranian any harm. What they forget is that the game can be played both ways. Mentally they can't get to me because I can go into my mind and lock them out, but physically, with my weight loss and poor diet, they could hurt me. They also, if they push hard enough, could bring on my death. But I don't think they'll do that."

Hohman was taken to see Ebtekar again; she was the resident expert on these peculiar Americans. She had spread out some fresh pistachios and small white candies.

"Try some of that," she said.

"No, I'm not going to."

"What do you want?" she asked.

"I want to go home," Hohman said.

"Well, we can't do that until the shah is returned," she said and then launched into the usual litany, starting with the sins of the shah's father and then enumerating the decades of American-sponsored crimes against simple, honest Iranians. "Don't you feel sorry for those people?" she asked.

"No," Hohman said. "You're keeping me here against my will for something I know nothing about." He was convinced that this whole ordeal had more to do with the political struggle in Iran than with the "crimes" of the United States.

She resumed lecturing. How were oppressed Iranians to gain the attention of the world when "the whole world system was subjugated to American imperatives?" Their action had forced the world's media to broadcast their grievances and demands and to realize the suffering the Iranian people had endured. "The decisions of the powerful have never benefited the oppressed," she said. "If the downtrodden want their case to be considered and their sufferings made known, they must find a new strategy, one capable of paralyzing the existing institutions and mechanisms of domination." Holding him and the others hostage was designed to do just that. She believed that many of the Americans they held were spies, and that even those who weren't—and she wasn't ready to believe that Hohman was not—shared responsibility for the acts of their government. While she admitted that holding otherwise innocent people prisoner apparently was not in accord with "human values," it was justified in this case by the larger issues involved. He needed to eat not just because his life was still terribly important to his family back home, she said, but because his life was *important to Iran*—"as a symbol of a country's legitimate demands!"

She went on and on, repeating the same material in various versions, trying to find the right way of putting it so that it would work its way into Hohman's hard skull. He listened with both boredom and wonder. She had talent, he concluded. If anyone had to listen to her long enough, he thought, they probably could be convinced of anything. While Ebtekar reasoned on, his eyes wandered to a group of young women across the room who were painstakingly piecing together shredded embassy documents.

"Do you really think there's anything important in that?" he asked, interrupting, gesturing toward the mound of shredded paper.

Ebtekar left the session convinced she had talked Hohman into ending his hunger strike, but it continued. It lasted twenty-one days. He subsisted on vitamins and drank plenty of water. His clothes hung on him, his skin was pallid and his cheeks sunken. He spent his days sleeping; it seemed to Belk that his roommate had simply turned himself off. He was slowly fading away to nothing. It was difficult for Belk, who after nearly two months of enforced silence and then a month alone chained to a chair had enjoyed having someone to talk to. A companion made captivity more bearable, and besides, Belk admired and *liked* Hohman. The medic had started him on an exercise regimen when they were first put together, and even though Hohman didn't smoke he never complained about the clouds that Belk's habit threw into the room.

One night the medic stood up from his mattress and walked over to pour a glass of water from the pitcher they kept by the window. There was a hole in the window from the break-in, and they had stuffed a rag into it, but enough cold air still flowed through to keep the pitcher chilled. On his way to the window Hohman blacked out.

"You've got to eat," Belk said, helping him back to his mattress and pleading with him. "You're scaring the hell out of me. You're going to die here and I'm going to be here by myself."

Hohman took his next meal.

Next door, Limbert had discovered a small opening where the thin partition wall imperfectly joined the more permanent basement wall. It allowed him to see enough so that he could tell when Belk and Hohman were alone. They didn't dare speak—the guard outside would have heard them—but Limbert tore blank pages from the front and back of his books and they began passing written messages back and forth, carrying on a running conversation. Limbert told them what news he had and they shared what they knew. He learned of Belk's attempted escape, and that Hohman had at last started eating. Because they had a window, Hohman and Belk told Limbert what kind of day it was outside.

One day, Limbert received the following message:

"We have a small radio. I guess you can understand Persian. Will this be useful to you?"

Limbert wrote back, "Is the pope Catholic?"

Belk had stolen the radio from one of the guards when he'd dozed off. He slid it deep in the back of a drawer at the guard's desk—that way, if it was missed and they searched rooms for it, he wouldn't be caught with it. Apparently the guard hadn't had the thing long enough to miss it, either that or he assumed another guard had taken it, because the radio's disappearance seemed to go unnoticed. After a few days, Belk retrieved it from the desk drawer and hid it someplace else. Then he offered it to Limbert.

They arranged for a drop in the bathroom. Late at night Limbert would wait until Belk had gone to the bathroom, and then immediately ask to go himself. That way he was ushered in right behind the tall State Department communicator, who had left the radio tucked behind a radiator on the floor. Limbert returned with it bundled under the waist of his pants. He unzipped the sofa cushion he used as a pillow and hollowed out a small place in the foam. With the radio nestled there, he could lay with his ear close to the speaker and play it quietly enough so that the guards couldn't hear. To preserve the batteries, he would switch it on for news reports only when he napped at two in the afternoon, at eight in the evening, and then again at midnight.

He wrote Belk a note, complimenting him on his "marvelous coup!"

6

A NEW AND MUTUALLY
BENEFICIAL RELATIONSHIP

With a secret process in place to secure the hostages' release, the Carter White House subtly changed its tone. There was no more talk of sanctions, blockades, and punitive strikes, and instead came reminders of shared interests, particularly of the danger posed by the Soviet armies just over the border. The threat of a Russian move toward Persian Gulf oil fields was of course a tremendous anxiety, not just in Iran but throughout the Western world. To reporters who knew nothing of the secret talks, the new strategy was, in the words of one pundit, "Talk softly and remind Iran of the Red Menace next door."

Privately, the pieces seemed to be falling into place. Bani-Sadr was sworn in as president in late January by Khomeini and then named head of the Revolutionary Council. The odd-looking little Iranian with the pompadour, clipped mustache, and black glasses was now, at least on paper, the most powerful figure in the country next to Khomeini. In an early speech he referred to the hostage crisis as a "minor affair," and suggested that a solution was within reach if the United States would only agree to cease meddling in Iranian affairs.

Patience was the message to the American people, who were still watching the days of captivity enumerated nightly on TV. For the time being, doing nothing was the best strategy, argued Carter's press spokesman Jody Powell.

"Iran is on the verge of disintegration," he said in a TV interview. "Nothing is the same from one day to the next. They are paying a terrible price for their fascination, their preoccupation with the hostages. The question arises of who in fact is determining the fate of Iran: Is it the Ayatollah Khomeini? Is it the Revolutionary Council? Is it this small group of terrorists who are holding the hostages? Meanwhile, the economy is in shambles. The military is in many ways nonexistent, and disorder and chaos increase every day."

In his State of the Union address, President Carter emphasized that the United States was ready to be friends with Iran again, to form "a new and mutually beneficial relationship."

"We have no basic quarrel with the nation, the revolution, or the people of Iran," he said. "The threat to them comes not from American policy but from Soviet actions in that region." Carter suggested that retribution was unlikely if the hostages were returned unharmed, but warned that "our patience is not unlimited."

Although it now seemed happily less necessary, preparations for a rescue mission progressed. "Bob," the CIA operative who had flown into Mehrabad Airport and breezed through customs a month earlier, had been in and out of the country several times in the previous month, shuttling from Tehran to Athens and Rome. Working with a wealthy Iranian exile who had volunteered to help, he had rented a warehouse and bought five Ford trucks and two Mazda vans to drive the assault force to the embassy from their hiding place south of the city on the second night of the mission. He had purchased material to form a wall of fake cargo at the back end of the truck in order to hide the force in case the vehicles were stopped and inspected at a checkpoint.

To solve the helicopter-refueling problem, Air Force Colonel James H. Kyle had arranged for three-thousand-gallon fuel blivits to be placed *inside* C-130s, instead of being dropped from them. This meant that six of the four-propeller workhorses would have to land in the desert on the first night of the mission, refuel the eight helicopters, and then fly back out of Iran. Since the plan now called for the planes to go in ahead of the helicopters, Delta Force could ride into Iran on the C-130s, camped out on top of the fuel bladders, an especially welcome development because Charlie Beckwith's assault teams had swollen from the original forty-five men to ninety-five, the new counterterrorism unit's full complement. Those numbers would have badly strained the eight RH-53D Sea Stallion helicopters that were now waiting beneath the deck of the aircraft carrier *Nimitz,* which had replaced the *Kitty Hawk* in the Indian Ocean.

Delta had been through several more full-dress rehearsals for the raid in the Utah, Nevada, and Arizona deserts. They were a mob of crusty, sunburned mountain men in blue jeans and T-shirts cadging supplies without explanation from every military unit in the region. All of the men assigned to the mission were given top priority but were not allowed to reveal what they were doing, which created confusing and sometimes very satisfying clashes with the regular military command. Major Jim Schaefer, one of the marine helicopter pilots, was told to report immediately with his crew to the *Nimitz* to inspect the helicopters. He hopped a military plane to Hawaii and then the Philippines and was preparing to board another flight at Clark Air Force Base to Guam when a naval officer somewhat dismissively told him that he would have to wait for the next plane.

"I have to get the university baseball team on this airplane," the officer said.

"No, I don't think you're going to do that," said Schaefer.

"Sir, you don't understand," the navy man said firmly. "I am the navy liaison officer, and I'm in charge of this, and I have to bounce you off. We'll get you on the next available flight."

"*You* don't understand," Schaefer said.

"Sir, the flight is closed. I'm going to have to do this."

"This flight is not leaving without me," said Schaefer.

On the airport wall was a poster with the photograph of the base's commanding general. The poster welcomed all comers to Clark Air Force Base and invited anyone with a problem to call the commanding general directly. Schaefer called.

After a series of conversations, during which certain orders and their priority were clarified, Schaefer was connected to the general at home at three o'clock in the morning.

"This is Major Jim Schaefer," he said. "I've got a little problem down here at the terminal and I saw your sign offering to help. General, would you help?"

The general drove directly to the terminal. He was wearing a flowery tropical shirt, shorts, and flip-flops. He looked, Schaefer thought, exactly as the commanding general of a Philippines air force base should look.

"Who's Major Schaefer?" the general asked.

"I am, sir."

Schaefer showed him the letter giving him his orders. The general, suddenly wide awake, told the naval liaison officer, "Lieutenant, release that airplane, now."

Training sessions in the western American deserts created their own local stir. The region was sparsely populated, and the rescue force did its best to stay out of sight during the day, but there were bound to be run-ins with the locals. Just before the holiday break, one of the helicopters on a night training run had unknowingly tried to snatch a Christmas tree from some local's roof. The pilots oriented their choppers at night with flashing infrared markers on the ground, and when the training exercise was over they were required to retrieve them. They had a pincer attached to a rope and would hover over the flashing light, grab it, and haul it back aboard without landing. One night, when a pilot searching for his last marker found a blinking light, he hovered and lowered the aircraft over it and, before he could drop the rope, the light moved.

Confused, he decided to set the chopper down for a closer look, and suddenly the landing area was flooded with light. He was about to land on a house. The light had been blinking on a rooftop Christmas tree decoration. The downdraft from the choppers created winds in the 150 miles per hour range, considerably more than any visit by Santa's nimble-footed reindeer, and the decoration had taken flight and landed somewhere out on the highway. The shocked home owner, no doubt alarmed by the sudden violent storm, had turned on the lights to investigate. The chopper pulled up and flew away. The unit sent someone out to the house the next day with a hundred bucks and an apology.

The Delta "operators," as they called themselves, were hardly timid souls, but they were terrified by the helicopter rides in darkness. All of them complained about the marine pilots' skills. The fliers were being asked to do things they had never tried. They were working hard to learn and adapt. When the ever changing plan called for them to land in a soccer stadium in Tehran, they began practicing blacked-out landings at a football stadium at Twenty-nine Palms, the marine base in California. The newfangled night-vision goggles, which enabled them to fly without any lights, were so heavy that after an hour or two it became difficult to hold their heads upright. Everyone in the unit had a stiff neck. Then one of the pilots hit upon the idea of fastening a garter belt to the roof of the cockpit just over his head and latching the goggles to it so that the belt took some of the weight. The garter's flexibility allowed him to turn and bend his head. It worked so well that the pilots cleaned out the PX at the nearest military base. To practice night flying over a city without land lights, they got permission to practice low-level flights over San Diego.

Beckwith remained skeptical about the CIA's "Bob" and was unwilling despite CIA assurances to trust his elite, handpicked force to this swarthy, slippery-seeming foreigner. He began making plans to get one of his own men into the city in advance of the mission.

The way things were shaping up, however, it appeared less likely than ever that a rescue mission would be attempted. Iran's newly elected president had turned up the heat on the students and appeared headed for a showdown with them over the hostages. Bani-Sadr publicly called them "children" who behave "like a government within a government." When they responded by condemning one of Bani-Sadr's cabinet as an American spy and had him arrested, the president intervened to have the man released and condemned the students as "lawless dictators."

The students were feeling the pressure. Near the end of January three of their star hostages were caught trying to escape. Joe Subic had cooked up a half-baked plan to make ropes and climb out of a second-floor window of the ambassador's house the next time he and his roommates, Kevin Hermening and Steve Lauterbach, were taken for showers. He had a vague notion about stealing a car and driving to Turkey. Hermening was excited about it and helped make the ropes, and Lauterbach, while filled with reservation, went along with the plan. They didn't get anywhere. On the day of their attempt, all three were caught with their ropes and marched off to stretches of solitary confinement.

Lauterbach was locked in a basement room of the chancery with his hands tightly cuffed. Sitting alone in the darkness for days, his hands aching badly, he grew increasingly despondent. His guards had given him a water glass embossed with the embassy's emblem, and it began beckoning him. In the deeper sense, he was not suicidal. He loved life and wanted to keep on living it, but not here, not in pain, alone, with no idea of when or if his circumstances would ease. He was angry. Hurting himself was the only way he had with which to lash out at his captors. On the fourth day he stopped arguing with himself, broke the glass, and slashed his wrists.

He didn't make a sound. When a guard entered his room some time later he found Lauterbach woozy and bloody. He was rushed to a hospital, startled at how alarmed and angry his captors were. There was plenty of blood but the wounds were not deep enough to have severed his arteries. A doctor patched him up, and after that Lauterbach's treatment dramatically improved. His captors were apparently afraid that word of his suicide attempt would put the lie to their claims of treating the hostages as "guests." He was given a room of his own on the upper floor of the chancery, one with a couch made up as a bed. His guards became solicitous, even kind.

SAVAK! SAVAK!

Inside Iran, the students remained extraordinarily popular. Some were offered positions in the government, others received offers of marriage in the mail. But at least some of the group's leaders wanted out. Ibrahim Asgharzadeh, the author of the takeover, felt trapped. He believed they had backed themselves into a corner by demanding the shah's return, a condition they had never seriously expected would be met. Now even if they had wanted to back down they could not, because their continued occupation of the U.S. embassy gave leverage to hard-line clerical elements opposed to the government—no mullahs had been allowed to run for office. With their hostages, the students had become pawns in the battle over the future of Iran.

Their frustration boiled over on the night of February 5, in what would be the most terrifying night yet for the fifty-three American hostages.

John Limbert and the others in the chancery basement were awakened by a sudden clamor. Guards in black ski masks moved through the rooms with weapons, shouting in English, "SAVAK! SAVAK! Everybody up and out! Up and out *now!* Everybody! Move! Hurry! Now! Now!"

Limbert was awake anyway. He was reading *War and Peace* after listening to the news on the small radio tucked inside his pillow. He was accosted by two guards in masks.

"Okay!" one of them demanded. "Come on, get out! Get up!"

He stood and was blindfolded and then led down the corridor with the rest.

The scene in the Mushroom Inn across the compound was the same. A masked guard entered the room shared by Joe Hall and the ailing Richard Queen. "Get your hands up!" he shouted, waking them. "Do not speak! Stand up!" Out in the larger room, many of the captives, similarly roused from sleep and used to the rituals of their imprisonment, obligingly tied on their own blindfolds.

Chuck Scott asked for his hands to be unbound so that he could pull on a sweatshirt. "It's cold," he said.

"You will not need a shirt or sweater again ever!" one of the masked men said, pushing him out of his room.

Hall walked with his hands up as a guard propelled him along, shouting. One of them kicked him in the buttocks and pushed at his back with a gun.

Those in the Mushroom Inn were led to a cold, empty part of the warehouse basement and ordered to strip to their underwear. Because the numbness in his hand had worsened, Queen had to be helped with the buttons of his pants. It was very cold.

Bruce German felt betrayed. The embassy's budget officer had sought assurances that Tehran would be safe before he had accepted the assignment just five weeks before the takeover, and he felt bitter about those who had encouraged him to come. Now he could hardly move he was so frightened. His legs were shaking.

In the chancery basement, the hostages stood as instructed, leaning forward with their hands extended over their heads, holding themselves off the wall by their fingertips. One by one, the guards moved down the line, forcing them to drop their pants to be searched. Bob Ode's legs weren't wide enough apart and one of the guards roughly rattled the butt of his weapon between the old man's knees. They pulled on the waist of each captive's underpants front and back to make sure they weren't hiding anything. Kupke's legs were shaking from the cold and from fright. Barry Rosen, whose nerves were shattered anyway, felt his heart pounding heavily. He assumed immediately that he and the others were going to be shot. Everyone was confused. Why were they suddenly doing this? It occurred to Roeder, one of the cooler heads, that the gunmen might be clearing everyone out so they could search the area for contraband.

Rosen heard one of the guards growl to another, "Don't speak Farsi here," warning him that the hostages spoke their language. This seemed to confirm Rosen's worst suspicions. He was shaking so badly he was having a hard time keeping his arms raised against the wall, and when he stooped to pull his pants back up he couldn't. He was both terrified and ashamed of his terror, of how he looked to the others. He put his arms back up against the wall and when one slipped down again the guard screamed at him.

Limbert thought it was unlikely they would be shot in the chancery basement. He assumed that if they were going to do it, they would take them out to the countryside somewhere, out of the city. The executions he had seen on TV in Iran had always taken place outdoors. He considered these young Iranians' flair for the dramatic and decided this simply wasn't for real. But the fear was there anyway; he couldn't reason it away.

Kupke prayed. He thought about turning around to fight, not being led like a sheep to the slaughter, but saw the futility of it. He prayed that the bullets would kill him quickly, and that he not be left alive, wounded, and maybe paralyzed. Belk just felt numb, as though he was in shock. He did what he was told. Part of him refused to believe it was true, that they might shoot him, that this was it. Hohman didn't stand close enough to the wall so one of the gunmen pushed his head hard into it. Belk was surprised that his roommate didn't raise hell. Once he had seen Hohman take off after five guards, kicking and swinging. If Hohman was afraid, then this was for real.

In the warehouse basement, German also prayed. He hadn't been particularly religious since his childhood but it seemed the only thing to do. He prayed for himself and for his wife and family. He imagined what a shock his execution would be to them.

When he and the others were told to face the wall, Navy Commander Sharer refused.

"If you are going to shoot me, you're not going to shoot me in the back," he said.

And, amazingly, the would-be executioners obliged him.

To the rest, one of the guards screamed, "Arms against the walls! Spread your legs! Don't drop your arms! Do not lower them a centimeter or you will die right now!"

Bob Englemann thought, "Negotiations must have broken down." Apparently they were going to finish this.

Because of his illness, Queen could not keep his left hand up, and one of the guards kept hitting him with his weapon.

"He *can't* get his hand up!" Hall protested.

"Shut up! No speak!" one of the gunmen screamed at him.

Scott's hands were bound so he could not spread his arms as far apart as demanded. A guard pushed his hands higher up the wall and kicked his legs wider apart. He heard the guards behind him clear their weapons for firing.

Hall was more frightened than he had ever been. *Jesus, this is it! They're going to kill us!* He asked God to take care of his wife, Cheri. He felt terrible about leaving her and then thought, *I hope I get hit in the back of the head and that it will be over quickly.* "God, take care of Cheri. God, take care of Cheri," Hall kept repeating quietly to himself, shaking. His knees were banging together and suddenly they stopped. His whole body stiffened, as if clenching to receive a final blow.

Queen clenched his teeth and said the Lord's Prayer.

Scott felt dizzy and ill and began to pray.

Jimmy Lopez wondered what it was going to feel like. He had heard about Iranian executions where they machine-gunned the victim starting with his lower legs and working their way up the body, to prolong the pain. How long would it last? Would it hurt or would it happen too fast to feel anything? He hoped that when they shot they hit his head right away.

Bill Keough stood with his hands held high, filled with disbelief. Like many of the others, his mind raced involuntarily to find some last reason to hope. For one thing, the wall they were up against was made of thin plasterboard. There were plenty of places nearby where there were concrete or brick walls. *If they are going to shoot us, wouldn't they put us in front of one of those?* Some foreign ambassadors had just come through, checking to make sure everyone was well. Why would they do that and then perform a mass execution? It didn't make sense. Still, it was a perilous moment. *If one of my colleagues panics and goes after one of them, they might start shooting and that would be the end.*

Don Cooke was as frightened as he had ever been. In the first days, when he had been taken out to a residence in north Tehran for a few weeks, he was convinced on that drive that he was being taken away to be shot, and for some reason he had been perfectly calm. Now, he was shaking so badly that he could barely keep himself upright.

"Oh my God!" he shouted. "No! No! No!"

Golacinski told Cooke to shut up. The embassy security chief didn't want these assholes to see any American buckle in his final moments. He felt curiously calm, as though he were watching himself from the outside, thinking, *So this is it.* It was not the first time he had felt this way since all this started. And he felt relieved. *At last this is over. Shoot straight.*

Greg Persinger smelled fear. He had always heard that expression and never believed it, but suddenly he detected an odor coming from himself and knew immediately what it was.

A long moment passed. Then another.

Hall relaxed a little . . . *maybe not?* Had they gotten past the moment? Maybe they really weren't going to shoot.

Jimmy Lopez turned around and sat down.

"I'm tired of this shit," he said. "If you're going to shoot me, just shoot me."

Roeder's fingers got tired, so he leaned his forearms on the wall, resting on his elbows. A guard smacked him sharply in the ribs and he pushed back out to his fingertips. He, too, looked for reasons not to believe that he was about to be shot. Beyond a certain point, he couldn't take these guards seriously. They were stupid, but not stupid enough to shoot all of them. He was convinced America would turn Iran into a parking lot if that happened. The guards were acting angry and threatening, but when they cocked their weapons, readying them to fire, one of them let his slip from his hands. It clattered to the floor.

The suspense was broken not by an explosion but by the ringing of metal on the concrete floor. They had ejected the rounds.

"Pull up your pants!" one of the guards shouted at Rosen, who stooped to the task with trembling hands.

When it was over, the shaken hostages were led back to their cubicles and rooms, which had been ransacked.

"Goddamned sons of bitches!" shouted Lopez as they left him and Kirtley back in their chancery room. "Fuck you all!"

Limbert found his room in disarray. They had obviously gone through his extra pants and shirt. They had taken a heavy water pitcher that he had scrounged, and a fork, but they hadn't taken his paper, nor had they found his hidden pencils and the radio! Kupke's hidden stash of sugar cubes was gone—he had been hoarding them, stealing one or two extra every day at teatime. The guards had also found and taken a small piece of glass he had saved and hidden, and a stub of a pencil. Their belts were confiscated. In the Mushroom Inn, Roeder's mattress was upended and a few of the little items he'd hoarded were gone. There were rumors that someone had attempted suicide, which would explain removing the belts.

In the room shared by Bob Ode, Barry Rosen, and Bob Blucker, everything had been upended and some things removed but there seemed to be no logic to it. Ode's liniment for his sore back was gone but all of his mail was left behind. Rosen's prized picture of his children was gone. Ode was given back his belt, which he had been forced to remove during the strip-search, but Rosen was not given back his.

Some of Bill Royer's clothing was missing, a second pair of pants, a shirt, and his tweed jacket! He complained enough over the next few days that they brought back the sport coat.

When it was over, Kupke felt exhilarated. He and Kennedy and Graves were in terrifically high spirits, laughing and joking with one another. They were thrilled to still be alive.

In his room, Ode lay down on his mattress and suddenly felt his heart pounding heavily in his chest. He had a heart murmur and was now certain that he was suffering a heart attack. He believed he was dying. He lay perfectly still, in a cold sweat, terrified, but believing there was nothing that could be done. Gradually, his heartbeat slowed until it felt normal again. He felt the need to urinate, and as the guard led him back from the toilet he said in broken English, "These men not ours. They are very angry."

The next morning, Hall asked Hamid the Liar.

"What was that shit about last night?"

"Oh, that was just a joke," he said.

"Some goddamn joke. Why would you do that?"

Hamid said that it wasn't him or his group, that it was a unit of exterior guards. It was just something they had wanted to do.

The mock execution marked the end of one stage of captivity and the beginning of another. It was the last time Rick Kupke felt threatened by the guards. As February wore on, the weather turned brutally cold and there was still boredom, confinement, hunger, and inactivity to cope with, but for a time things settled into a relatively comfortable routine. He, John Graves, and Mike Kennedy were moved to a room on the top floor of the chancery and were given a heater. Kupke was allowed to make a brief phone call home to his mother. The guards now let them speak. For months, "No speak!" had been the most common expression they and the others had heard from the guards, and though Kupke and his roommates had been talking for months, it had always been in whispers, and always in fear that they would be punished. Now they could talk and laugh freely.

Kennedy asked the guards for a can of coffee grounds from the commissary and proceeded to make what he called "cowboy coffee." He poured some grounds into the bottom of a pot, added water, and brought it to a boil on the heater. They scooped the coffee from the top of the pot.

Colonel Scott sensed that the mock execution had acted as a purgative, and afterward many of the guards felt guilty about it. At night, he and the others in the Mushroom Inn were allowed to resume playing checkers, something they had not been allowed to do since leaving the house in north Tehran before Christmas. The guards set up a folding table in the hallway outside the large room where the hostages could take turns playing. Scott kept telling the guards he wanted to play with Colonel Schaefer, who had been taken away weeks ago and had not returned. By asking for him, Scott was trying to learn something about what had happened to him.

"It is not possible to play with Colonel Schaefer," said a guard they called Little Ali because he was the smaller of two guards with that name—neither was very big.

"Why not?" demanded Scott. "We were allowed to play together before."

The colonel let loose a string of oaths and threats, which caused him to be carried off to a cold room and threatened with a beating. Little Ali waved a length of hard rubber hose and promised that if Scott did not behave he would use it. Left alone, he found evidence that Schaefer had been in the room. It was lined with steel lockers, and in one he found a slip of paper and a short pencil. On the paper in handwriting he recognized as Schaefer's—they had been passing notes for months—was a list of songs. Scott guessed that his air force colleague had been trying to memorize them. On another slip of paper was a rudimentary calendar, again in Schaefer's handwriting. One of the lessons they had been taught in survival school was to try to keep track of time. From the scraps, Scott determined that Schaefer had been held in this freezing room for thirteen days, and that he had been moved three days earlier.

He shook with cold. Little Ali had locked him up wearing just a T-shirt and slacks. He realized how pathetic he had become. The guards had refused them razors for fear of a suicide attempt, so his dark beard was long and unkempt and he found there was no way to keep soup drippings and chunks of food from falling into it. Without a comb or scissors he could not trim it or keep it clean. He had lost more than a dozen pounds—his clothes hung on him—and he hadn't seen sunlight for anything more than a few fleeting minutes in months. He was pale, scruffy, dirty, and his teeth were chattering with the cold.

After a few hours, Little Ali returned, standing a safe distance away from Scott in the doorway, and suggested that the colonel apologize. If he did, he would be allowed to return to his warm cubicle—Scott insisted on calling it a "cell."

The colonel refused. Whatever he had said or done was a lot less than what had been done to him in the previous months. Little Ali closed the door and left. Later that day, he was visited by Akbar, the kindly guard with whom Scott had established some rapport. The slender, mustachioed Iranian told Scott that Bani-Sadr had been elected president of Iran. Scott told him that he had no respect for a government that treated him and his fellow Americans as they had been treated, and complained to Akbar about the mock execution.

Akbar apologized for it and seemed genuinely chagrined. It had been "un-Islamic," he said. He then led Scott out of the cold room and back to his cubicle.

"Be good," he implored.

It was the first time Scott realized that Akbar outranked the other guards.

After the mock execution, mail was delivered more frequently. Most was from strangers, which remained a disappointment. Sometimes it seemed as if all of America had adopted the hostages as pen pals. Many of the letters continued to be from schoolchildren who had written as part of a classroom assignment.

"Dear Mr. Hall. Hi, my name is Jimmy. I am eight years old and I am writing this letter because my teacher says that I have to. What do you eat?" One of the letters was similarly chatty and upbeat and ended with, "I sure hope they don't shoot you." Hall received several from a man in Houston who had apparently chosen him as his hostage pen pal. These were cleverer than most and Hall actually enjoyed them. The writer always incorporated short parables that were ostensibly preachy little stories, the kind of thing his Iranian captors liked but which could be relatively easily deciphered to reveal important news developments. For instance, when the Soviets invaded Afghanistan, Hall's correspondent wrote a story about a large man, whom he likened to a bear, attacking his neighbor and insisting that the neighbor wear a bright red collar with a star on it.

The guards withheld mail to punish prisoners they didn't like. Colonel Scott rarely received anything, and when he did it was usually from a stranger. Once, Hamid the Liar surprised him by offering to escort him to the mail table.

Behind the table, stacked high with letters, was a guard named Ahmad, a squat, thick, balding, cheerfully abusive man who was at least ten years older than the other guards. He made a pretense of shuffling through the stacks.

"I don't see anything for you, Mr. Scott," he said. "Are you sure your wife has not found another man?"

A guard alongside Ahmad handed him several letters, and the colonel found a spot on the floor to sit and read them. The first two were from strangers; one was addressed to "Lieutenant Colonel" Scott, which was annoying to a man very proud of his rank. One was a letter from his sister, and another from his wife, Betty, postmarked October 26, more than a week before he was taken hostage. It was terribly disappointing. Like most of the hostages, Scott worried a great deal about his wife and children and wondered how they were coping with this ordeal. The encouraging letter from his sister also revealed nothing about his family. The last letter was from a precocious grade-school girl in Nebraska, writing as part of a class assignment, who addressed him as "Lieutenant Scott" and confided that she thought it would have been smarter for President Carter to send the shah back to Iran instead of letting him go to Panama—it was the first he had heard that the shah was no longer in the United States. The little girl concluded by noting that Scott was forty-eight and that he was a "lieutenant." She asked, "At your age, shouldn't you be higher than that?"

Multiple copies of the comics and sports pages of the *Boston Globe* were being mailed to the hostages daily by someone from that city, and though the students saw no harm in passing them along, the cartoons and stories often disclosed useful information. Garry Trudeau, the cartoonist, was spoofing the Iranian students in his popular strip *Doonesbury*, which gave a heartening indication of how intense public interest remained in their plight after six months. When a letter from Bill Keough published in the United States thanked the anonymous sender, the Boston benefactor surfaced. He was a taxi driver who was thrilled to learn that his long-shot effort to help his kidnapped countrymen in Tehran had scored. He sent a card to Keough saying that he regarded the success of his gesture as the only "great thing" he had ever accomplished in his life. He promised to keep mailing the sections, and did.

8

HAM, THEY ARE CRAZY

On the same day as the mock execution, forty-nine members of a group calling itself the Committee for American-Iranian Crisis Resolution left New York for Tehran. It had been formed by a professor of industrial relations at the University of Kansas, Norm Forer, who had been active years earlier in efforts to publicize the shah's human rights abuses and hoped that a dialogue between American citizens critical of their government and the hostage takers might help break the deadlock. He proposed that his group travel to Iran not to initiate a dialogue but simply to listen, to give the hostage takers an opportunity to vent before a group of sympathetic Americans. Many prominent leftist activists sought to be included but Forer, perhaps mindful that his own name would be eclipsed, wanted unknowns, what he called "grassroots." He polled antiwar organizations for names and selected a cross section of people who shared his political outlook. The student hostage takers, who still felt their message to Americans was being distorted by government-controlled media, smelled enough opportunity for propaganda points to put up the money for the trip. Among those in the private mission were Hershel Jaffe, a rabbi from Newburgh, New York, and the Reverend Darrell Rupiper, an activist Catholic priest from Omaha, Nebraska.

Unlike most members of the mission, Jaffe was not a political activist. He had pushed to have himself included in part because he was something of a publicity hound—a garrulous, energetic man, he was already well known in the Newburgh area as the "running rabbi," after running in the New York City marathon—and in part because he was concerned about the Jewish hostages feeling neglected. He was interviewed by Forer, who was also Jewish, and a group of furtive young Iranians in a bare room on the west side of Manhattan and explained that he had been following the story closely, and had been struck by the outpouring of Christmas cards for the hostages. It made him feel for the special isolation of Jewish hostages such as Barry Rosen and Jerry Plotkin. Reports of the Forer mission had portrayed it primarily as Christian outreach—Forer was not religious and its co-organizer, the Reverend Jack Bremer, was a Methodist minister from Lawrence, Kansas—and Jaffe felt that the group ought to include a rabbi, so he had volunteered. After Forer invited him, Jaffe arranged to be briefed by two Israeli agents about the situation he would encounter in Iran.

Rupiper, a tall, slender man with long dark hair and glasses, was a member of the Missionary Oblates of Mary Immaculate, a small order of Catholic priests dedicated to the poor and those on society's margins. He had been an activist priest for many years, and like many of those in the group he had been sharply critical of American foreign policy in Central and South America. He had been recommended to Forer by the group Nebraskans for Peace, who knew him from several trips to jail protesting at Strategic Air Command bases in that part of the country. Rupiper believed American foreign policy was often criminal and saw the CIA as a tool of oppression. He had been imprisoned in Brazil for protesting America's actions there.

Forer kicked off the trip with a press conference, at which he saluted the students for seizing the embassy and taking his countrymen hostage.

"We congratulate the students for their bold and courageous effort," he said. Forer did acknowledge the act as "illegal," as protests often were, but suggested that fact deserved to be considered "side by side with the anguish of the Iranian people." Despite the fact the United States had essentially acquiesced in the kidnapping of its embassy and personnel for three months, Forer lambasted "the wanton exploitation of the hostage situation by the warmongers and moneychangers of this country," describing his group as "the mainstream of American conscience."

In Tehran, the group spent ten days attending the standard anti-American demonstrations, lectures, and presentations about the crimes of the shah and SAVAK. They visited the martyrs graveyard and saw the wheelchair-bound "victims of SAVAK." Jaffe was appalled when the group was taken to meet Yasir Arafat, the PLO chairman, whom he considered a mortal enemy of his people. At one demonstration, protesters pounded on their bus, chanting the usual "Death to America! Death to Carter!"; and the group narrowly escaped serious injury when a rickety reviewing stand erected to hold them at one rally collapsed, crushing some of the spectators below. When in the midst of the confusion of that accident Jaffe grabbed the hand of a female Quaker minister and helped pull her from the pile, they were immediately accosted by veiled Iranian women shaking their fingers with disapproval. At first, Jaffe didn't know what was going on; then he realized the women were objecting to a man and a woman holding hands. Most of the others in the group seemed to take these things in stride. Jaffe grew increasingly alarmed, frightened, and disgusted by the reactions of his traveling companions. He was particularly struck by Rupiper, who seemed ready to join the revolution.

It was Valentine's Day when they were finally taken to see the hostages. The members of the group stopped to buy candy and flowers from street vendors on their way to the embassy. They were escorted to a room in the chancery with blankets draped over the windows and decorated with the usual posters of Khomeini and other revolutionary trimmings. The hostages were brought in to see them in small groups before TV cameras.

They spent the longest time with marines Billy Gallegos and Paul Lewis, who was delighted when he saw Rupiper. Lewis had met him before. Gallegos seemed chipper. "I had no idea what was going on," he said, referring to the embassy takeover. "I thought for sure he [the shah] would be back the second week."

Lewis said, "I don't feel that we were going to be taken out in the courtyard and shot. I think they realize that it wouldn't do anyone any good."

On his way out, Lewis stopped to chat with Rupiper and Jaffe. He told them that he had met Rupiper when the priest had visited his parish in Illinois several years earlier, soon after Rupiper had been freed from the prison in Brazil. Seeing the same priest in Tehran seemed an amazing coincidence to the young marine. He asked Rupiper to contact his parents, which the priest did not do.

As the last of the hostages left, the rabbi was disappointed because among the handful of hostages brought into the room there were no Jews. He asked the guards where the Jewish hostages were and he was told that they had declined the opportunity to meet with him and the others.

"They are asleep," another of the guards said.

When the visiting Americans were on their way out, Jaffe was stopped and accused of accepting a note from Lewis. The group had promised going in that no one would accept notes from the hostages, only the letters that had been written for the occasion. Jaffe had received nothing from Lewis and was indignant. It crossed his mind that it was a setup, that perhaps something had been planted on him, and now he was going to be arrested and held with the embassy staff.

"I am here on a humanitarian mission and I will not be treated this way!" he said.

He was escorted to a courtyard and ordered to strip. His clothing was searched thoroughly. He was glad that he had scratched the names of the two Israeli agents out of his address book before the session, because the guards pored over it very carefully. There was no note to be found. Jaffe pulled on his clothing and on his way back to the others he tipped his yarmulke to the guards—they had neglected to look under it. He wanted them to know that if he had been hiding a note, they wouldn't have found it.

When the Forer group returned home several days later, Jaffe told reporters that the situation in Iran looked bad and predicted that the hostages would be held for a long time.

In Omaha, Rupiper also predicted a long standoff, so long as "the United States refuses to acknowledge its guilt for the abuses of the past twenty-five years." He said the hostages might be stuck in Tehran "for years."

There was reason to be more optimistic than that. The White House believed it had mapped out a path for the hostages' release.

The election of Bani-Sadr by such a strong majority in Iran seemed to bode well for the secret plan, and there were other encouraging signs. Iran's new president promptly engineered the resignation of Mousavi Khoeniha, the students' "spiritual adviser," who since the takeover had been named head of Iran's Council of National Radio and TV. In an interview with *Le Monde,* Bani-Sadr said that his government was no longer demanding the return of the shah before releasing the hostages. His remarks dovetailed neatly with the secret negotiations.

In another interview Bani-Sadr said, "If the U.S. government gets away from its past policy of intervention in [Iran's] internal affairs, and if it accepts the right of the Iranian government to [pursue] the criminals ... who have plundered our wealth and accepts in practical terms to help us in that matter, that would be the grounds for deliberation on the hostages."

As far as the White House was concerned, the United States had no way to significantly interfere in Iran's internal affairs anyway. The extradition proceedings in Panama appeared to satisfy the second demand. UN general-secretary Kurt Waldheim was putting together the six-man international commission to study America's role in Iran, and Carter had agreed not to block it. The panel was virtually certain to denounce the United States for the quarter-century-old crime of overthrowing Mossadeq and for propping up the now-despised monarchy, but that was a humiliation the administration was willing to endure if it meant the safe return of the hostages.

Jordan had become fond of the two intermediaries, Villalon and Bourget, whom he had met with again secretly on February 9 in Bern, Switzerland. There they agreed to set up a secret meeting with Ghotbzadeh himself. The plan appeared to be unfolding smoothly, despite the Iranians' tendency to keep adding new demands. One called for Iran to be able to claim "victory" when the hostages were released. Carter expressed concern about that, wondering how such a joint statement could be made palatable to the outraged American people.

"We've got three languages to play with," said Jordan. "English, French, and Farsi. We can take an English word, find a French synonym that is weaker or even vague, and find a Farsi word that is even more so. We'll stick with our English word and let them give it their best possible Farsi interpretation."

"You can play with words all you want," warned Carter. "But I am going to have to be able to stand up in front of the American people and defend whatever statement I make."

Despite his misgivings, the president was willing to proceed. He was so hopeful that the process would lead to the hostages' release that he wrote a note to Jordan prior to the scheduled meeting with Ghotbzadeh:

"If, at any time, the Government of Iran desires to release the American hostages at an earlier date than called for in the mutually agreed plan, the Government of Iran has my personal assurance that the United States will abide by all the terms of that plan." Carter was fully on board.

Jordan flew to Paris on a Concorde with Henry Precht, with tickets they purchased themselves in order to keep the secret meeting off the books. Wearing a disguise—a wig, false mustache, and glasses—Jordan arrived at Villalon's luxurious Paris apartment, and shortly after midnight on Sunday, February 17, he was joined by Iran's embattled foreign minister himself, whose swarthy, thick, pugilistic features looked worn. He had dark lines under his small deep-set eyes. Jordan had been coached by the intermediaries to view Ghotbzadeh as a "rug merchant," one who liked nothing better than to haggle. The two adversaries chatted amiably; Jordan told him that he was "honored" to be meeting with him. Ghotbzadeh was curious about the Concorde, which he had never flown on.

"We must be sure to do it while we can charge it to our governments," said Jordan. "It's very expensive!"

Ghotbzadeh emphasized that the meeting remain secret. If it became public, the foreign minister warned, "First I would lose my job and then I would lose my head!"

Jordan tried to ingratiate himself by telling the Iranian, on behalf of himself and the president, that it would be "terribly helpful" if he would explain the origins of the revolution and help sort out the present situation in Tehran. He listened as Ghotbzadeh recited the familiar story of America's subversions, dividing his remarks into three periods, 1900–1953, 1953–1978, and the present. The foreign minister spoke reverently about Khomeini and the revolution, with what Jordan later called a "mystical" passion, and while he said he could not condone what the students had done, he regarded it as a small thing compared to the crimes of America and the shah. Ghotbzadeh spoke of the hostility between the United States and Iran sadly and, as Jordan would note later in a handwritten memo to Carter (in which he referred to Ghotbzadeh only as "Mr. S."), "[with] regret that things between us had gone so far and were in such a mess." Jordan tried to move the conversation past these differences. He asked for Ghotbzadeh's opinion of Carter, and when the foreign minister complained that the president seemed to poorly understand his country, Jordan defended his boss, arguing that Carter had resisted pressures to intervene in Iran during the revolution and had ignored demands to respond militarily to the seizure of the embassy. The foreign minister acknowledged that the president had shown restraint.

"Now, let's talk about the hostages," Ghotbzadeh said. "I am in a better mood to talk about them since you have heard our case."

Jordan asked about Michael Metrinko, the one American hostage who had not been seen or heard from since the day of the takeover. Ghotbzadeh said he did not know anything about Metrinko in particular but assured Jordan that all of the captive Americans were still alive. Then he confided, "Only I can solve this."

Jordan asked how, and Ghotbzadeh's big face produced a small, conspiratorial smile.

"It is easy to resolve the crisis," he said. "All you have to do is kill the shah."

"You're kidding," said Jordan, flabbergasted. After all the weeks of negotiations with his emissaries, after hammering out a complex multistepped plan to sort out this mess in a way acceptable to both sides, Ghotbzadeh suddenly introduces the idea of state-sponsored assassination?

"I am very serious, Mr. Jordan," he said. "The shah is in Panama now. I am not talking about anything dramatic. Perhaps the CIA can give him an injection or something to make it look like a natural death. I'm only asking you to do to the shah what the CIA did to thousands of innocent Iranians over the past thirty years!"

Jordan let the baseless charge against the CIA go and addressed the idea of assassination.

"That's impossible," he said. "It's totally out of the question."

Ghotbzadeh went into a long explanation of why Iran "hated" both the United States and the Soviet Union, and speculated about being killed himself by either an American or a Russian spy. He eventually came around to discussing the existing plan, and (having apparently dropped the idea of bumping off the shah) suggested that if Carter stuck to the outline drawn up by Bourget and Villalon, the hostages would be released "soon."

"What is soon?" Jordan asked.

"Weeks," he said. He assured Jordan that the Iranian government, meaning the Revolutionary Council, would abide by its promises.

"What about the Ayatollah Khomeini?" Jordan asked.

Ghotbzadeh said that the council had approved the plan unanimously, despite some objections from its cleric members, and that he had briefed the imam in Qom.

"And what was his response?" Jordan asked.

"The imam does not often respond," said Ghotbzadeh. "He listened to our explanation and nodded. . . . If he had objected to our proposal, he would have said so."

Thus the fate of this effort hung on the cryptic nod of the sharp-featured, white-bearded, black-turbaned prophet. The two men discussed at some length the future relations between their countries after the hostages were released. Ghotbzadeh promised that the new Iran would prove to be an even better ally against the Soviets than the old.

In his memo to the president about the meeting, Jordan didn't mention Ghotbzadeh's suggestion of assassinating the shah—he referred to it only as "Point #1," and wrote, "I'll tell you about this in person." In assessing the meeting, he wrote, "At best, Mr. S. is a deeply committed revolutionary, dedicated to the survival of that revolution and to the integrity and independence of Iran. His ego is enormous, but his devotion to the Imam is genuine. His commitment to the revolution makes the Soviet threat the dominant political concern in his life. At worst, Mr. S. is a devious person whose only source of power is the Imam. Now that the Imam's health is in question, he is engaged in a number of activities (hostage negotiations, anti-Soviet rhetoric) that he perceives as being in his own best interests. The truth about Mr. S. is probably somewhere in between, but either way, we should use his present attitudes to our benefit."

Jordan clearly believed the first characterization of Ghotbzadeh to be true. He made no mention in his memo of the ambiguity in Khomeini's reported response to the plan. He left Paris emphasizing to Bourget and Villalon that Carter would not "apologize" for America's actions in Iran, and that the hostages could stay in Iran "another ten months or ten years" before the president would make a statement that dishonored his country.

The meeting with Ghotbzadeh, which would have been electrifying news, remained a secret, but the mood of optimism about the hostage crisis continued to build for the rest of the month. All signs pointed to the hostages' imminent release. A Kuwaiti newspaper reported that a deal had been struck. Ghotbzadeh publicly suggested that if the hostage takers refused to cooperate with the government, then military force might be used by Iranian authorities to retake the embassy. Iran's ambassador to the UN, Mansour Farhang, said that the students had begun "to lose credibility with the Iranian people," and had "gone beyond their task." For their part, the students continued to insist that the hostages would be released only when the imam ordered them released.

Word of the solution Jordan had worked out with Bourget and Villalon began to leak. No one had the particulars, or word that the president's chief of staff had actually met with Iran's foreign minister, but the plan's general outline became public, and the expectant mood in the White House was impossible to hide. A peaceful solution to the standoff not only would bring home the American hostages, it would trump Carter's critics, particularly his Democratic challenger Kennedy, and no doubt boost both his approval ratings and his standings in the presidential race.

In keeping with the secret protocol, Carter announced on February 13 that he would support the creation of a UN commission to study the crimes of the shah, and announced at the same time that there were "positive signs" about the hostage standoff. To savvy Washington watchers, there was clearly a connection. The president's surprising retreat on the commission, which would certainly reach conclusions critical of the United States, coupled with this suddenly optimistic assessment, strongly suggested that a deal had been struck. As anticipated, the good news eclipsed criticism of the concession.

One way that would-be important men advertise their proximity to power is to predict events. In Tehran, Ayatollah Mohammed Behesti, secretary of the Revolutionary Council, declared that the crisis would be resolved soon, and Secretary-General Waldheim, after announcing formation of a five-man commission—a French lawyer, diplomats from Algeria, Syria, and Venezuela, and the former president of Bangladesh—told reporters that he had received "general assurances" that the hostages would be released soon after the group met.

Christian Science Monitor reporter Louis Wiznitzer wrote that the hostages "can be expected to return home at or near the end of the month," citing sources at the UN, and gave credit for the agreement to Waldheim. He reported that the UN secretary-general had worked out the basic outline of the agreement in January, but that his efforts to sell it to the White House had at first been "rebuffed" by an administration bent on responding to the Iranians with "pressure." No doubt the secretary-general saw it that way but, in fact, Carter's initial refusal to support creating the commission had given the United States the key bargaining point and concession. Otherwise, Wiznitzer had it right. He reported that first the hostages would be removed from the embassy and transferred to the custody of Iran's revolutionary government, probably to the Foreign Ministry, where Laingen, Tomseth, and Howland were trapped. Two days later the *Washington Post* reported that the president had obtained "a commitment in principle," and editorialized that the frustrating episode seemed to be reaching "its final chapter."

Those following the story closely saw plenty of evidence to support this optimism. The State Department asked a federal judge in Manhattan to delay legal proceedings aimed at seizing $1 billion of Iranian assets to cover defaulted loans. The government asked a publisher to delay release of a book by Kermit Roosevelt about the CIA's role in the 1953 Iranian coup.

Bani-Sadr kept insisting that the United States had to "apologize," but the White House seemed to feel it could finesse that demand with Jordan's linguistic artifice. The Iranian president formally invited the commission to Tehran and said it would be allowed to speak to all of the hostages. American TV networks latched on to the commission's trip as the likely endgame to the months-long story, and its every move led their reports. Hostage families were interviewed from all over the country and all were visibly glowing with hope. In an interview, Vice President Walter Mondale said on the nineteenth that the crisis was nearing an end.

"We think progress is being made, but I don't want to characterize the chances," he said at first, but then hinted that a release was imminent. "When they [the hostages] return, people will see the whole story, and I think they will be appreciative."

In Tehran, the student captors were still insisting that the hostages would not be freed until the shah was returned, but they seemed to be swimming against an overwhelming tide.

Then Khomeini, upon whose silent nod this whole scheme turned, finally spoke. He pulled the rug out from under Ghotbzadeh and his allies and upended the fragile agreement. In a radio speech he praised the students, and once again demanded the return of the shah. The occupation of the American embassy had "dealt a crushing blow to the world-devouring U.S.A." He said the fate of the hostages would be decided not by Bani-Sadr and the Revolutionary Council but by the *Majlis,* Iran's parliament, which had as yet not even been elected. That meant the earliest the hostages could be released was at least a month away, probably more. It also meant that the deal negotiated in secret with Ghotbzadeh was worthless.

Jordan was at home on Saturday morning when he received a call from Camp David, where he knew the president was staying that weekend. Ordinarily, an operator placed the call and the president picked up the line after a short delay. This time Carter evidently had dialed himself.

"Ham, what the hell is going on?" he demanded.

Jordan had not heard the news from Tehran.

"Well, I just got a call from Cy Vance," said the irate president, "who said that Khomeini had made a statement this morning that the hostages would be dealt with when the Iranian parliament assembles!"

"Oh, my God, no," said Jordan. "That's terrible. I don't know what to say." He promised Carter he would call Villalon and Bourget immediately.

"Please do," the president said. "And let them know they are playing with fire. The commission is probably already on the way to Tehran now, believing that we have an agreement . . . and now this! It makes us all look foolish. It's starting to look as if the only person involved is Khomeini!"

It got worse. The UN commission very publicly left for Tehran with the private deal already collapsing, and with well-informed reporters covering its every move anticipating its futility. The imam instructed the students to turn over incriminating documents seized at the embassy to the UN commission, but when the students attempted to deliver a box of the files to their hotel the commission members refused to accept it, fearing that it contained a bomb. Despite a unanimous ruling from the Revolutionary Council and the public backing of Ghotbzadeh and Bani-Sadr, the students, emboldened by Khomeini's speech and sensing that the commission was the linchpin of a plot to release the hostages, refused to allow its members to meet with the captive Americans.

Jordan summarized these events for the president in a memo, and Carter sent it back with the scribbled note, "Ham, they are crazy."

The panel lingered in Tehran, hearing testimony and getting the graveyard and cripple tour, waiting for a chance to interview the accused American spies. The commission's presence in Tehran intensified the struggle between the government and the students, with Ghotbzadeh denouncing the students as "Zionists and Communists," and paying a visit to the embassy to confront them personally. At one point TV cameras caught the embattled foreign minister locked in heated argument with the unknown Hussein Sheikh-ol-eslam, the bearded, gap-toothed student leader, who was seen pulling the collar of an army field jacket up around his neck and jabbing a hectoring finger at the older man. Accused of collaborating with the American government, Ghotbzadeh began to receive death threats, as did Bourget and Villalon. The foreign minister offered to resign, but though Khomeini would not support him in the showdown, he refused to let Ghotbzadeh go. For the first time, the shape of the ongoing struggle between moderate secularists and religious conservatives in the new Iran spilled fully into the open, with the maverick role being played by the students on full display. The sight was confusing to most. All parties swore allegiance to Khomeini, but the imam projected not leadership but ambivalence. Finally, the commission gave up its efforts to see the hostages, suspended its inquiry, and flew home. The deal had fallen through.

In his nightly roundup of events in the hostage story on ABC, which would soon evolve into the program *Nightline,* Ted Koppel summed up the diplomatic disaster, still perceived primarily as Waldheim's folly: "From the first the commission was a body born of despair, nurtured by frustration, and fueled by the absence of any alternative."

The commission members were pictured boarding a plane in Tehran. The hostage families were back on TV at home with long, worried faces.

For his part, Bani-Sadr immediately scurried back into the radical camp. The same students he had called "self-centered children" and "dictators" weeks before, he now praised as "young patriots," and argued that the label "moderate," which had been applied to those trying to compromise over the hostage issue, certainly did not apply to him. Carter's hopes were dashed and, worse, he appeared to have been snookered. All that had come of it was the creation of a UN commission that seemed certain to find fault with the United States.

"I am amazed at the naiveté of the American authorities," said Bani-Sadr.

Carter was fed up. He was an extraordinarily patient man, but in him that virtue was now nearly exhausted. The government officials he was dealing with in Iran were powerless. He felt the last chance to free the captives peacefully had failed. Polls taken immediately after this disappointment showed that a majority of Americans believed the administration's Iran policy had failed. Brzezinski sent a memo to Carter reporting this latest indignity, and the president scribbled in the margin, "The polls are accurate."

Near the end of February, a guard named Mohammed told Joe Hall and Richard Queen that he was leaving. Mohammed had always treated them well, allowing them to whisper back and forth when it was forbidden to speak and sometimes bringing them candy and extra helpings of a dinner they especially liked. He told them that he was tired of the thing. It was going nowhere, and he had lost too much time away from his studies.

"I don't believe anymore that it is the right thing to do," he told them.

And then he was gone.

9

FIE ON THEM ALL

Bruce Laingen, his deputy Vic Tomseth, and security officer Mike Howland were still walking in circles on the third floor of the Foreign Ministry, involuntary "guests" of the Iranian government. Their hair had grown long and their clothes looked worn and wrinkled. They were able to shower—Laingen noted in his diary on January 2 the first hot one since the day he had arrived. Toward the end of the month they were finally given mattresses, and now they no longer had to sleep curled up on the lumpy sofas in the reception dining hall. Both Laingen and Howland had taken up watercolor painting and stood for hours by the big third-floor windows painting the views north toward the mountains. Tomseth spent most of his time reading, grabbing for the thickest books he could find. He got lost in novels set in faraway places and times.

Howland was still secretly exploring every corner of the old ministry building. He had started sneaking around at night in the nude; knowing how squeamish Iranian men were about nudity, he figured nakedness would give him a momentary advantage if he were discovered. One night he had crept downstairs to a foyer when two guards surprised him, and he hid beneath a table just a few feet away, his heart beating so loudly he felt sure they would hear it. They had passed on without noticing him.

Gradually, Howland expanded his range, and in time he had explored the whole building. He found a phone in a VIP waiting area that he used to call friends in north Tehran and to place calls to the British and Danish embassies, which gave them a line of communications that, unlike the phone in their quarters upstairs, was probably not monitored—at least no one suspected the Americans of having access to it. With the British ambassador's office he worked out a system for passing coded messages keyed to the page numbers and lines of a book they agreed upon. This gave them another secret line of communication if they needed it. In fact, the Swiss ambassador was able to carry messages in and out of his meetings with them without being searched, and Laingen was already using that method to send private messages to Washington. Howland's girlfriend Joan Walsh, one of the women among the thirteen hostages released in November, sent him a small file buried in a packet of pipe tobacco; she also sent him a hacksaw blade hidden in the spine of a book. Howland used the file to whittle down the blade of his pocketknife into a shim, which he then used to break into the guards' key box in the kitchen and steal a key to the attic door.

There was nothing for him up there except for the feeling of having put one over on his captors. Howland did these things as much for personal amusement as for any practical reason. He thought a lot about what might happen if the American military tried to rescue them and planned for that contingency in part by disabling the pistols carried by their interior guards. One afternoon, sitting with two of the guards in their small kitchen, Howland offered to show them how to field-strip their Spanish-made pistols. He broke them down and put them back together quickly, and then set about teaching them how to do it themselves. It got so they felt comfortable enough to leave him alone with them for brief periods when they were disassembled.

Howland borrowed Tomseth's toenail clippers and cut the recoil springs on the weapons, which meant they could fire one round but then the pistol would fail to successfully chamber a second round.

They watched Iranian TV with Tomseth providing a running translation, listened to the *Voice of America* and BBC broadcasts, and devoured the local newspapers and magazines. Their hopes had soared when the UN panel arrived in Tehran and then were dashed when its mission came apart. They pored over every statement from Qom, Washington, and Tehran like runes, trying to divine what was taking place behind the scenes. Tomseth, who had met his wife during his first State Department assignment in Thailand, would speak with her in Oregon periodically on the phone in fluent Thai, a language he felt sure would not be understood by the Iranians who monitored their calls. So he had yet another unfiltered source of information about what was going on in the United States.

When Khomeini fell ill with a heart ailment in January, there were stories of Iranian zealots offering to give up their lives in order to provide the imam with a fresh heart. Tomseth wrote a letter to the editor of a

Tehran newspaper endorsing the idea, but suggesting that the wrong organ was being offered. Khomeini already had demonstrated by his behavior after the embassy takeover that he could function perfectly well without a heart, but "he could do very nicely with a new brain." He showed the letter to Laingen, and they thought better of it. Tomseth tore it up.

The ordeal was a special strain on the idealistic Laingen, who every day suffered a fresh outrage. Nothing angered him more than Americans like Thomas, the native American activist, or the Kansas activist group headed by Forer, people Laingen felt were lending sympathy to his kidnappers. In America they were free to criticize and oppose, but how could they travel to a foreign country where America itself was under attack and applaud its enemies? How long would their defiant free speech and oppositionist politics last in a country ruled by the imam? By the third month of the standoff, even Iranians were beginning to sour on the young radicals holding the embassy, with their nightly telecasts revealing "spy documents," which gave them a national platform to denounce the nation's highest officials on the basis of revealed "contacts" with the American embassy, usually casual and routine. The students were very selective in these denunciations. Laingen knew well that plenty of the top clerics in the country, heroes of the revolution, had precisely the same kinds of contacts with the embassy, some of them more than routine, but their names never surfaced in the press conference. Exposing those ties was not politically advantageous. The increasingly embittered chargé saw that the students, unable to find any evidence for the most outlandish of their theories, had found another more cynical use for their treasure of stolen paper. The documents and revelations were being used to cow and ruin moderate politicians who threatened their vision of a "pure" Islamist state.

He wrote in his diary:

> It is so degrading to Iran. Surely an intelligent Iranian watching this kind of performance must be repelled ... allowing a group of "students" to claim TV time to denigrate leaders in the present government. But beyond that, allowing "students" to continue defying all standards of conduct and decency—looting a foreign government's files ... It is so outrageous I could choke the first Iranian I see. A gang of thieves, condoned by another gang of thieves. Fie on them all ...

Former prime minister Mehdi Bazargan was quoted in a newspaper complaining, "Now the country is run by a bunch of kids, and this is regrettable. It is not correct to devote the TV screen to the most shameful accusations against people without asking the other side to defend themselves. You jeopardize the honor and nobility of the people with this."

Precisely at this moment, Forer's group appeared in Tehran seeking "reconciliation," and effectively endorsing the takeover. The Kansas professor's words were gladly reproduced in Tehran newspapers.

Laingen found Forer's use of language from the New Testament especially galling, rhetorically linking the American government and diplomatic mission to the Pharisees and venal usurers of the ancient Jewish temple and, by implication, comparing the students to an angry Jesus Christ the Lord himself, chasing blasphemers from God's house. And Forer was Jewish! Did he realize how anti-Semitic this new regime was? What could he be thinking? From his third-floor prison, Laingen wrote, "Good grief, if that is the way he interprets U.S. restraint on this issue, he isn't fit to teach kindergarten."

All pretense of keeping the three for their own protection was gone. They were now treated simply as hostages, with the doors to their living space chained and padlocked. They slept on the dining room floor and washed their socks and underclothes in the bathroom. Laingen discovered that the best way to clean his sheets was to soak them in the washbasin in soapy water and then, with the wet, soapy sheet draped over his shoulders in the shower, rinse it. The sheet could then be wrung out and hung up to dry, which didn't take long in air so free of moisture. When the weather grew warmer they were allowed outside to exercise for an hour each day in the minister's spacious garden. Laingen walked for ten minutes, jogged for thirty, and then did ten minutes of calisthenics. They were given a Ping-Pong table to help pass the time. Archbishop Hilarion Capucci, the Greek cleric, sent them a record player and a cassette player, along with some music—including the song "Tie a Yellow Ribbon," which had become an anthem of sorts to the hostages thanks to Laingen's wife Penne's yellow ribbon campaign. That and the tunes of Elton John could be heard echoing in the cavernous chambers.

It was a strange existence. On the first day of March, looking out the window across the gray city toward the mountains, Howland spotted Laingen's Italian cook and his Iranian driver on the sidewalk outside the ministry building looking up. They had evidently driven over hoping to catch a glimpse of their former employer, and when they caught Howland's eye, and he brought Laingen and Tomseth to the window, they waved back and forth vigorously for a few moments until the Americans, worried that the ministry guards would see, gestured for their friends to get back in their car and leave.

They watched and listened as Bani-Sadr and Ghotbzadeh staged a vain last-ditch effort to salvage the previous month's negotiated solution.

In a flurry of activity, the ministry staff had actually begun preparing the third floor to receive all of the hostages. President Bani-Sadr and his foreign minister Ghotbzadeh were such intense political rivals that they would not speak to each other, but in this effort they were together. They pressed to get formal custody of the hostages, realizing that so long as the captive Americans remained in the hands of the students at the occupied embassy, where they could rally public demonstrations of support that swayed Khomeini, there was no way the newly formed government could release them. It was a straightforward power struggle, and the new government was confident that Khomeini would not twice undercut them so blatantly. Ghotbzadeh told a reporter from the *Washington Post* on March 7 that "the hostages would be turned over to the Revolutionary Council in two days," and added, "Maybe they [the students] will make little obstacles, but not major ones."

Laingen watched with excitement when Ghotbzadeh, accompanied by the chief of the Revolutionary Guards and a security escort, conducted an inspection of the upper-floor rooms. It was clear they were evaluating the space as a holding area for all of the hostages. That surmise was confirmed later in the morning when Ghotbzadeh asked to see Laingen and explained what was going on. The Revolutionary Council had instructed the students to hand over the hostages. He said those Americans being held at the embassy would be sharing space with Laingen and the others within twenty-four hours. The foreign minister said that he would need Laingen's help in managing the group and caring for them, which confirmed for the chargé the wisdom of the decision he, Tomseth, and Howland had made early on—that they would stay in the ministry in the hope that they might become useful to their colleagues. Laingen was ecstatic. Ghotbzadeh did not say how much longer they would all be held. The imam had stated that the hostages' fate would be decided by the *Majlis,* which would not meet again until May, but prying the hostages from the hands of the students opened up all sorts of possibilities. Fifty cots and steel lockers were delivered to the large dining hall. The three longtime Foreign Ministry wards drew up a schedule for using the three bathrooms on their level.

But then a student spokesman announced that before handing over the hostages to the government, the hostage takers demanded a "hearing" before the Iranian people. Crowds formed outside the embassy walls, as thousands of religious hard-liners expressed their opposition to the move. As the number of demonstrators swelled, so did the students' defiance. Scrambling to save face, the Revolutionary Council agreed to give them another twenty-four hours to comply. Another day went by, and the students still refused. Then the imam spoke again.

Laingen, Tomseth, and Howland listened to the radio on March 10, as Khomeini, in his cryptic way, doused the last embers of hope for an early solution.

"The crimes of the shah and America need no proof. We fight against America until death," he said. "We shall not stop fighting until we defeat it and cut its hands in the area and lead weak people to victory. . . . We are sure of victory because right always is victorious. Be careful. There are long years of struggle ahead because the big powers scheme daily to pounce on you."

Ghotbzadeh was crushed and went on television to denounce the students for sabotaging an agreement that he said was clearly in Iran's best interests. Laingen was disappointed and angry and guessed that the same mood prevailed in Washington. The chargé's mood was darkened further by new televised propaganda statements from Joe Subic, the renegade sergeant who, by all appearances, had gone fully native in captivity. On a day when the students threatened to kill all the hostages if America took any military action, Subic appeared on a late-night Iranian TV show to confirm that the embassy had, indeed, been a den of spies. Laingen wrote in his journal:

> Why? Someday we may know, but someday, as a result, what charges face him? What burden will he carry in his own heart and mind for the rest of his life? It was a cold and chilling performance, to see a young American so clearly used by his militant captors to further their cause, whatever the cost to this man's future.

Ministry officials from time to time made a show of treating Laingen and the others as official emissaries, despite their de facto hostage status. Observing from the windows on the evening of March 22, Laingen saw a steady stream of limousines arriving at the ministry flying flags from various nations, and watched as formally dressed diplomats filed into the building. There was obviously a formal diplomatic event that evening. How could Iran and other nations maintain the pretense of diplomatic normalcy with the U.S. embassy forcibly occupied, its staff imprisoned, and the head of the mission held hostage upstairs?

Later that evening, however, Ghotbzadeh sent for the three, and they were escorted, with shaggy hair and rumpled clothes, before eight of their dapper colleagues and allowed to sit and talk about their predicament for more than an hour. Laingen later wrote in his journal:

> The whole affair is incongruous—the magnificent hall, now empty save for us and the eight, the [Iranian] chief of protocol staying discreetly out of earshot (he is a professional, too), our colleagues sympathetic but powerless to help. Diplomats in the ministry of the country to which they are accredited, "allowed" by a possibly embarrassed foreign minister to meet with fellow diplomats held hostage, in total violation of international law and practice.... Yet we conduct ourselves as if nothing had happened, sharing impressions and keeping our emotions under full control, despite our anger and frustration. After an hour or so, we bid our visitors goodbye under the enormous chandelier in the mirrored reception rotunda, acting almost as if we were the hosts of the glittering affair rather than the hostages generously allowed briefly to resume our diplomatic careers!

America's highest-ranking diplomat in Iran, still washing his socks and underwear in the Foreign Ministry bathroom every morning, assembling jigsaw puzzles, reading books, and walking up and down a closed staircase for exercise, composed yet another futile, angry letter to the president after seeing news reports of Bani-Sadr giving a speech from the outer wall of the occupied embassy.

> Dear Mr. President,
>
> As you know, it is the view of my government, a view overwhelmingly supported by world legal and public opinion, that the seizure of the Embassy in Tehran and the holding of all its personnel

hostage for political purposes was and is a flagrant violation of all precepts of international law and practice.

I must therefore record my deep sense of regret that by the use of the walls of that Embassy as a podium for yesterday's National Mobilization Week march-past, the dignity of your office was so directly and graphically linked to the situation affecting the Embassy and the personnel still held there as hostages.

He was repeating himself and he knew it. Laingen sent off the letter, signed "Chargé D'Affaires ad Interregnum," feeling like the one sane person in a world gone mad.

10

THE ATMOSPHERE
OF RESTRAINT CANNOT
LAST FOREVER

On March 13, in a hotel room in Bern, Jordan wrote out a three-page letter to Bani-Sadr in his cramped handwriting, a blend of cursive and printing. He discarded the third page and rewrote the final three paragraphs to get them right.

Dear Mr. President,

I am taking the liberty of sending you this personal and private message through a mutual friend, Mr. Hector Villalon. The only copy of this letter is in the possession of President Carter.

Because we have reached a critical point in this process of trying to peacefully resolve the differences which face our countries, I thought it was important that I convey my thoughts to you personally and in complete frankness. I would welcome your reaction to these suggestions.

... I believe that we share a single objective: to put an end to the present crisis and build a new relationship with your country and government based on equality and mutual respect. But, quite frankly, the possibility of having such a relationship in the future will not be possible unless all hostages are returned safely to our country at an early date.

From the outset, President Carter had pursued a policy of patience and restraint.... However, the atmosphere of restraint ... cannot last forever. A growing number of political figures and journalists who have supported President Carter ... are now advocating extreme measures as a result of the commission's departure from Tehran. Despite this growing frustration, President Carter has not abandoned his policy of restraint. As soon as we learned of the commission's decision to leave Iran, [he] called on the American people and the Congress to be patient. He also conveyed to the UN Commission through Secretary General Waldheim and Secretary Vance his desire that the Commission not abandon their work and be prepared to return to Tehran under the proper circumstances.

We believe the process negotiated by Misters Villalon and Bourget represents an honorable way to resolve our problems. We are prepared to renew our commitment to that process, but must have evidence of your government's willingness and ability to abide by the process. The transfer of the hostages to the custody of the government would be evidence of Iranian good will.

Beyond the present problems, I can assure you that our government will adopt a reasonable attitude in resolving the numerous bilateral issues we face.

Finally, I appreciate the opportunity to be able to communicate directly with you. Please know that we will do everything possible to bring an early and honorable conclusion to the present crisis. I hope that you will accept my frank analysis and that time is working against U.S.

I hope I have the honor of meeting you someday.

> Sincerely,
> Hamilton Jordan
> Chief of Staff to the President

It was not a bluff. The pressure was growing on Carter to act. His approval ratings had fallen sharply in polls, down to 40 percent, and Ted Kennedy had picked up several early primary victories. Indiana Republican senator Richard Lugar charged that the president was bungling the crisis and called for an immediate naval blockade of Iran and the mining of its harbors. Republican presidential candidate George H. W. Bush, a former CIA director, accused Carter of "pussy-footing around" with the ayatollah, and of "appeasement." Ronald Reagan, the governor of California and front-runner among the Republican candidates, offered his own homespun analysis of the Iranians, suggesting that it was a waste to pursue diplomacy with such faithless negotiators: "They keep slicing the salami up. They lead us to believe that if a certain thing is done, the hostages will be released, and as soon as we say, 'That's fine,' then they add another term, another condition. As long as we are willing to negotiate these additional conditions, then they've got a reason for keeping the hostages." Asked what he would do instead, Reagan said he didn't know, that he was "waiting for a miracle."

Days after the UN commission returned to New York, Brzezinski, long an advocate for more forceful measures, suggested to the president that power in Tehran was so confused there was little point in continuing to work with Ghotbzadeh and Bani-Sadr. He found the plans of both would-be leaders, despite their official titles, had "an unrealistic quality," because neither Iranian seemed to fully comprehend all the forces at work. Days later, Brzezinski complained further about Iran "diddling along" the United States, and urged the president to issue an ultimatum. The administration had considered blockading Iran and mining its harbors, but Carter was fearful that such a step would lead to a much broader conflict. So Brzezinski proposed another approach. Why not seize Kharg, an island in the northeastern Persian Gulf about sixteen miles off the Iranian coast that was the world's largest offshore crude oil plant and the principal sea terminal for Iran's oil industry? It would be a limited military strike, self-contained, and the island could be held until the hostages were released. That way, the decision to escalate the conflict would be Iran's.

Brzezinski's dramatic idea was not adopted, but clearly the mood in the White House was testy. When Deputy Secretary of State Warren Christopher worried that daring Khomeini to broaden the conflict might just feed into the Shiite "martyrdom complex," Harold Brown, the defense secretary, noted, "A man with a martyr complex rarely lives to be seventy-nine."

In a long Saturday meeting at Camp David, with participants dressed casually before a roaring fire in the stone fireplace, the president approved a secret, very risky reconnaissance trip into Iran to put the final piece in place for a rescue mission. Brzezinski and General Jones, chairman of the joint chiefs, both argued that the rescue mission could work, provided no word of it leaked in advance. When Secretary of State Vance objected to further discussion of military action, which he had adamantly opposed from the start, Carter's shifting mood showed.

"Should we wait another year then?" he asked Vance.

Vance agreed to support the reconnaissance mission because it made sense even from his perspective; if it ever became necessary to rescue the hostages, if Iran started show trials and executions, the better prepared Delta Force was, the more likely it could succeed.

On March 23, the ailing shah flew from Panama to Egypt, despite administration efforts to prevent it. President Anwar Sadat of Egypt offered the shah permanent sanctuary. The official reason for the move was that he needed surgery to remove a cancerous spleen. A Cairo newspaper reported that he had fled Panama when he learned of a secret American plot to poison him.

11

I'M NOT GOING TO ANSWER QUESTIONS FROM ANYONE WEARING A DRESS!

On March 19, Richard Queen and Joe Hall were told that they were going to be moved later that day.

"We are going to move you to a better place," the guard said. "This is a good thing. You should be very happy."

They were not very happy. Like the others, both men found that change flung them into fear and uncertainty. Both dreaded the move, especially when they were told they were going to be separated.

"You are going to be with some very important people," Queen was told.

"I don't want to go with any important people. I want to stay with Joe. We get along well. We want to stay together."

They packed up their small stash of toiletries, letters, books, and Queen's Civil War game that Hall refused to play—one look at the thick book of rules and instructions and he had backed down. Later that day they were led outside with blankets over their heads and placed in a car. They were driven around for about half an hour, mostly in circles. Both Hall and Queen knew they were still on the compound when they were let out. They were led inside a building and told to sit on the floor. From beneath his blanket Hall could see feet moving back and forth, shod guard feet and sandaled hostage feet. Then he was moved and told to sit someplace else, then someplace else. At last he was taken to a room and the blanket was removed . . . and standing across from him was Queen. They had not been separated after all. The room was on the top floor of the chancery, one that had been trashed on the day of the takeover and left that way. The smell of tear gas still clung to its walls like a bad memory.

They asked for some supplies and set about cleaning. The guards gave them two big leather chairs, perfect for reading, and a table with a lamp. But no matter how bright and clean and pleasant the room was—they were both especially thrilled to have a window and actual sunlight—the lingering tear gas continued to sting their eyes. It got worse and worse until finally the guards moved them out to another room down the hall, a nicer one, which they promptly cleaned and arranged to their liking, hanging their snapshots and keepsakes on the walls. Then they were moved again.

This time they were placed in a basement chancery office that had belonged to Bruce German, the embassy budget officer. It was an ugly space with walls that had been stained by a burst pipe. This was where marines Jimmy Lopez and Steve Kirtley had given the guards such fits months earlier. They had drawn and painted slogans all over the walls. Lopez had written out patriotic lines in Spanish and drawn a giant eagle. Hamid the Liar brought them a big gum eraser and instructed the new tenants to remove the drawing, which had been done in thick pencil. Hall went to work on it, but found that the eraser wasn't doing the job.

"Do it yourself," he told Hamid.

"If you don't remove it, you will be taken back to the Mushroom," he said.

"In the warehouse there's lots of paint and brushes," said Queen. "Could you bring us some?"

They were given buckets of white paint and they went to work. They applied several coats, and before long the room looked clean and bright. The guards gave them a vacuum cleaner. They were given back the big leather chairs and a desk with a glass top with some shelving on it. Guards got into the spirit of the redecoration and supplied a few paintings they had earlier taken off the walls. Queen asked for a poster of Alaska he had hung in his office months earlier and they even found and delivered that. A table lamp provided soft light in the evenings. They had windows to let in sunlight and fresh air. They could hear birds outside. When spring came they left the window open to let in cool air at night but discovered that Tehran bred swarms of nasty mosquitoes. Killing them became a nightly competition.

The only downside was the protesters. All light and sound had been shut out of the Mushroom Inn, but now, restored to the surface world, the protesters, somewhat less in number but with no noticeable diminution of zeal, remained outside. It was as if the students needed to have a massive audience at all times. The demonstrations were supplemented by audio-tapes of earlier gatherings, and sometimes the tape would get stuck and the sound level would drop, revealing the relatively small size of the crowd. The guards hustled to fix it as though they were all living in a balloon that had just sprung a leak.

Hall and Queen were at last allowed to speak. They spent days going over everything that had happened since the takeover and every scrap of information they had about what was happening in Iran and the world. They reviewed all the things they and the others had done, or hadn't done, and critiqued everything and everyone, including themselves.

With the holidays gone, there was nothing tangible to look forward to. The holidays had carried the hope of release, and once they were over their captivity stretched open-ended into the future. The change of scenery and the freedom to converse helped Queen rally from his post-Christmas depression, even with the worsening numbness of his left arm and side. He started an exercise program, walking around the room and doing calisthenics as well as he could, taking a cold shower afterward, and then plunging into his books.

Hall and Queen argued—no two men locked in the same room for months together could be entirely free of discord—but their disagreements never ran deep enough to last. With some of the hostages the arguments got ugly and occasionally turned into out-and-out fights and deep-rooted bitterness. Given the cramped and overall unsettling circumstances, and the constant discomfort, Hall and the gangly, bearded, ailing consular officer got along famously. After dinner each evening was the smoking hour. Hall had never been a pipe smoker, but Queen gave him one of the pipes Akbar had brought from his apartment and now Hall was hooked. When the lights went out they would switch on a soft lamp on their table and sit smoking and sipping tea and talking into the night.

Their pleasant routine was haunted, however, by Queen's mysterious illness. Ever since the day when he dropped the tea, his symptoms had gradually worsened. He lost sensation in his left hand completely, and then his legs grew weak. They would wobble when he walked. Hall had to help him button his shirt. Then his vision began to go. He was so dizzy that whenever he stood it would make him nauseous.

Queen felt himself slipping further and further into a kind of dream world. At the Christmas party he had been given a songbook, and on the back was stamped "The Brooklyn Savings Bank"—he guessed the books had once been a bank giveaway. His father had been born in Brooklyn and he had fond memories of the place. Inside the book was the hymn "We Three Kings," which he set about memorizing. He would sing the song to himself, realizing that this was not behavior he would consider normal under other circumstances. But he found himself increasingly, and with increasing comfort, retreating from the basement room, from the discomfort and uncertainty of his illness, into his own rich inner world. He stopped straining to overhear conversations and the radio. He felt better off for it. He felt calmer and more accepting, even more charitable toward the guards. He knew the situation wasn't improving; in a letter home in late January he told his parents he was living "in a timeless void of a world," but he was coping better.

He brushed aside Hall's concern for his worsening physical symptoms.

"I'll get over it," he said. "It'll go away. At least I'm still alive."

Hall thought Queen was remarkable, and was increasingly influenced by him. Queen was quietly but devoutly religious, and that, too, began to rub off on his roommate. Hall's parents had not raised him to be a regular churchgoer and he had grown up considering himself agnostic, at least as he understood the term; he did not believe in a God who listened to men's prayers or in divine justice being meted out in an afterlife. But in this openended confinement, with the threat of execution lurking offstage, he began trying to pray. He read two or three chapters of the Bible each morning. He went through the entire book once, then started a second time. He had some bad feelings about it. He knew he was only flirting with religion as a way of covering all bets—hey, if there *is* a God, maybe *He* could get him out of Iran. He assumed the traditional posture, down on his knees, and clasped his hands together as he saw Queen and the others do. He knew it would greatly please his wife, who was devout and distressed that he was not. If only for her sake, he *wished* he could believe. But Hall never felt anything or any closer to God. At night he would sometimes pull the blanket over his head and "talk" to his wife, whom he missed terribly, and there were times when he felt that he had actually made a connection with her. He definitely felt closer to her in those moments than he'd ever felt to God.

Hall was also hesitant about any visible display of religious interest because his captors were so obnoxious about their own faith. The guards would routinely call him and the others infidels, and note that America was doomed to fail in the long run because Americans did not pray to Allah and live according to the dictates of the Koran. Most of them liked to have an audience for their prayers. Hall didn't want to give them the satisfaction of seeing him undergo a foxhole conversion.

Hall ended his effort at finding God with one last prayer: "God, if you exist I will make a deal with you. You take care of my wife and family, and I will take care of myself, and won't ask anything for me. You take care of them because they are true believers."

He knew his wife would be praying for him. It seemed to him a better avenue of approach.

John Limbert was moved in Iran's New Year, March 21, to a room on the top floor of the chancery. The move came after Hohman and Belk had slipped a note into Limbert's room when he was taking a shower. Not realizing a guard had stayed in his room, they knocked on the wall to get his attention and the guard had found the note, which asked for news about Waldheim's visit. If the guards were surprised at how much they seemed to know about what was going on they never said a word. They simply moved Limbert. Again the embassy's political officer experienced the trauma of being torn from the relative security of his routines and colleagues and forced to face a new and uncertain situation. They would not let him take his pillow with him and so he lost his radio. He tried hard to keep it.

"Can't I take my mattress and pillow?" Limbert pleaded. "I've gotten used to them."

The new room had a window that had been bricked up, and the walls were thick and solid. This time he really was alone.

He fell back on his routines, eating, exercising, reading, sleeping, talking to the guards. He sorely missed the radio. He stretched out his meals as long as he could, reading old magazines, trying to savor each mouthful slowly enough to make the food last through an entire magazine. At one point he managed to accumulate a stack of old *Fortune* magazines and read one with each meal.

He made himself a deck of cards, and when he was playing solitaire with it one day the guard took pity on him and brought him a real deck.

Over the next ten months he wore out six or seven packs. He used pistachio shells to re-create football and soccer plays, and then acted out whole games, and he worked on translating some of the works of Shariati into English. The guards were pleased enough about this to bring him a typewriter. When he was finished with one set of essays he gave it to the guard.

"If anybody is interested, they can have them printed," he said. "If they make any money, just give it to charity."

He translated some of C. S. Lewis's *Screwtape Letters* into Persian.

One Monday afternoon, a TV crew swept unannounced into his room with Red Cross representatives and Ali Khamenei, the powerful cleric who had been named chief of Friday prayers in Tehran, a very prestigious position. With the cameras rolling, Limbert talked briefly to Khamenei, telling him that his own living conditions were passable and complaining jokingly that Persian hospitality was so aggressive that "they refuse to let the guests go."

When Khamenei spoke of the shah's criminality, Limbert acknowledged it dismissively, as a thing that no one disputed.

The interrogations of Michael Metrinko had ended early in the new year. The authorities had not given up their theory that he was a master spy, but they had gotten nothing out of him. Metrinko knew that any association with him, no matter how innocent, might mean a jail sentence or even execution for an Iranian. So he was alarmed in early spring when he was led from his basement cell to be questioned again and found himself in the presence of Mousavi Khoeniha, the nearsighted, portly mid-level cleric and architect of the takeover. He was wearing a turban and clerical robes. Standing beside Khoeniha was Ali Sharshar, an acquaintance of Metrinko's from better days. Metrinko had taken judo lessons arranged by Ali's brother Behrouz, a former police colonel and a well-known martial arts teacher.

Earlier in the year, the embassy political officer had helped arrange for Ali and his wife to travel to the United States with their daughter, who needed open-heart surgery. When the family had returned home afterward, Ali had brought a gift to the embassy to thank Metrinko for his help, a tie and a bottle of cologne. It was awkward for Metrinko. He was not allowed to accept gifts, so he had called his friend Behrouz and asked him to return the gift to Ali and explain that he meant no offense by refusing it. Behrouz had invited Metrinko to dinner with his brother.

The Sharshar family was a distinguished one, and both Behrouz and his younger brother, a helicopter pilot, had served the shah. They were a well-educated, Westernized family—Behrouz and Ali's sister, Fereshte, had married an American journalist and was living in Philadelphia—and they had nothing but contempt for the so-called religious leaders who had seized power. They were Muslims but they were appalled by the hypocrisy of many mullahs, who they saw as more interested in worldly wealth and power than in religion. They had been living in fear of the revolutionary government ever since the shah's departure. Behrouz had been fired from his police job. At the dinner with Metrinko, Ali had made some harshly critical comments about Khomeini and his circle. Metrinko, as he always did, had written up a report of the dinner and had included an account of the conversation. Evidently this report had fallen into the hands of the hostage takers. Metrinko's heart sank when he saw Ali in the room with Khoeniha.

The previous weeks had been a nightmare for the Sharshars. Ali had been denounced by the students at a routine press conference in the embassy, and Metrinko's "spy document" had been produced as proof. Much had been made of it in the press. Ali had been thrown in jail for nineteen days until his father, a former governor of Qom, successfully pleaded for his release. But after his release some of the mullahs complained that Ali was being let off too easily. Behrouz and Ali had been summoned before a meeting with a high-ranking ayatollah, a friend of their father's, who explained that not everyone was convinced of their innocence. Hotheaded Ali had defiantly told the cleric, "All mullahs are filth." Behrouz felt like slapping his brother and did his best to smooth over the insult, but the upshot of the meeting was that they were ordered to an interrogation session at the "den of spies," where Ali, in particular, would have to explain his comments and his relationship to Metrinko.

It was a delicate matter. The Sharshar brothers had friends and family connections that still mattered in the new Iran, but Ali's effrontery and his documented connection to one of the embassy's most notorious "spies" demanded some kind of response. On the appointed morning they were driven to the embassy in a windowless van with several of the students, along with Khoeniha.

Behrouz felt confident. He knew he had said nothing compromising, and he trusted that his clever American friend would say nothing to make matters worse. He was kept waiting in the hallway of the chancery when his brother was led inside for questioning. It was sad; the once airy and stately halls of the building were littered with trash and its walls covered with graffiti and slogans. While he waited, he saw Metrinko being led down the hallway and into the room. He could hardly believe his eyes. At first he wasn't sure the ragged, spectral figure he saw was his American friend, but then he recognized him in the gaunt, bearded face. Metrinko was wearing a green nylon shirt and oversized pants that were gathered and bunched together into a ball at the waist and clamped together with a paper clip. His flip-flop sandals smacked against the hard floor with each step. Behrouz thought Metrinko saw him but his friend made no sign of it. As soon as Metrinko was led into the room where they had taken Ali, Behrouz heard Metrinko start shouting.

"Why have you brought this guy here?" he demanded.

Khoeniha ignored the question. He glowered behind his desk, oddly digging a fork into the palm of his hand, as though working to control his anger.

"What was your relationship with this man?" Khoeniha asked. "How did you know him?"

"His brother is a judo master," Metrinko said. "His brother-in-law is from Philadelphia. I know him. And he works for a newspaper."

Khoeniha raised an eyebrow. They were getting somewhere. He asked about this brother-in-law.

"I'm not going to answer questions from anyone wearing a dress," Metrinko said, contemptuously.

"Shut up, you motherfucker," one of the students barked at him.

Metrinko exploded. "*You* are the motherfuckers! The real motherfucker is Khomeini. Fuck him and fuck you all!"

The guards beat him. Behrouz was appalled. He wanted to help his friend but knew he could not. He loathed the scruffy, bearded "students," and he felt ashamed for his country. So he sat, fighting the urge to run from the building, for as long as the kicks and blows continued and until Metrinko was dragged back down the hall, his head down, still muttering defiance.

One of the students, still clearly angry, brought Ali out of the room and then he and Behrouz and the others left. The students were concerned about what the brothers had seen. They had made a big public show of how gently and respectfully they were treating their "guests" at the embassy.

"If you talk one bit about what you have heard," one of them told Behrouz, "we'll stand you up before a firing squad."

In the coming days, both Sharshar brothers fled Iran. Both ended up in the United States. Behrouz visited Metrinko's parents in Olyphant. Of all the hostages, Metrinko was the only one the State Department had heard nothing about. There had been no pictures of him at any of the staged events, and none of the hostages who had been released knew what had happened to him. There had been no letters from him, and there was serious concern that he had been killed. Metrinko's mother sobbed when Behrouz told her that he had seen him alive. He described how he looked but didn't mention the beating.

Back in his basement cell, bruised and scraped, Metrinko worried about his Iranian friends and was pleased to have escaped from the session without further compromising them. He was confident that they would find their way to safety. And insulting Khoeniha to his face? That was simply delicious. He replayed the moment in his mind with increasing satisfaction. It was well worth the beating they'd given him. He found that as he grew leaner he was also growing tougher; the blows didn't bother him as much as they had in the past. He knew he must have presented a frightening picture to his old friends, a ragged, dirty, pale, hairy ghost of his former self, captive and pathetically vulnerable. But inwardly he glowed. All in all, it had been the most interesting thing to happen to him in months.

12

I THINK WE'RE READY

As the month of dashed hopes came to an end, a small CIA plane took off from a desert airstrip in Oman and, with the eyes of America's most sophisticated tracking system watching carefully, threaded its way through Iran's radar defense systems, flew across half the country in darkness, and set down on the spot being considered as a staging area for Delta Force's rescue mission. The president had given authorization for this reconnaissance flight only days before, along with permission for Colonel Charlie Beckwith to slip two of his men into Tehran. To the men who had been planning and practicing a hostage rescue for months, it was a sign that the White House was getting serious about sending them in.

Aboard the CIA plane, a Twin Otter, was Major John Carney, an air force combat controller known as "Coach," because he had once coached football at the Air Force Academy. He was a big, rangy man dressed completely in black—jeans, sweater, and knit cap—carrying a 9mm automatic pistol with a silencer, more to make himself feel better than out of any realistic hope it would save him if he were discovered. The pistol would do about as much good as his lame cover story, that he and the pilots were geologists. To make that work he'd have to quickly ditch the gun. Carney was stretched out in the back of the plane on a metal fuel tank that provided extra gas for the long flight—four hours in and four hours out—and between that and his Kawasaki dirt bike there was barely room for him to sit up. Beckwith had never even asked Carney about undertaking this mission; he had just volunteered him. The veteran air force man would not have turned it down, but he was surprised not to have been consulted about it. That was Beckwith's way. Carney saw it in football terms. The colonel was the kind of man who figured if you showed up with a helmet, you'd damn well be ready to play.

They landed in an empty quadrant of the vast emptiness of the Dasht-e Kavir salt desert. The nearest town, Yazd, was more than ninety miles away. There was a "road," more like a well-worn path, used very occasionally by trucks and buses traveling north from Qom to Meshad, a town on the northeastern border of Iran and Afghanistan. Ninety days of satellite surveillance had observed only two vehicles. It was here that six C-130 transports carrying fuel blivits and Beckwith's men—now nearly a hundred—would land on the first night of the two-day mission. The eight Sea Stallion helicopters from the aircraft carrier *Nimitz* would meet them here, refuel, load the Delta operators, and then fly off to their prearranged hiding places outside Tehran. But before this complex rendezvous could be attempted, the mission planners needed to know whether the soil was firm enough to enable large fixed-wing aircraft to land and take off without getting stuck in the sand.

Carney nervously disembarked into darkness suffused with moonlight, unloaded his dirt bike, and went to work. The ground seemed plenty firm enough; it was hard-packed sand as smooth and solid as a pool table. He drilled several soil samples that he would carry back to Washington for more detailed analysis. Then Carney measured out a runway and painstakingly dug holes with his K-bar knife to chip away at the soil and bury small infrared beacons at intervals to define it from the air. He set up four lights to outline the box into which the plane would land, and then planted another about three thousand feet farther on to mark the end of the runway. The beacons were virtually invisible to the naked eye but showed up brightly through night-vision goggles. He connected the lights to batteries, and attached them to a trigger he had removed from a garage-door opener he had picked up at Sears. With the garage-door remote, one of the pilots would be able to turn on the runway lights on his approach on the night of the mission. He also paced off the ground inside the lights to make sure there was no debris, stumps, dips, or bumps big enough to damage a wing or harm the plane's landing gear.

Because he had some difficulty at first orienting himself, the work took fifty minutes, ten more than he had estimated. Twice while he worked vehicles came roaring past. The landscape was so flat that he could see the headlights coming from a long way off, and Carney just lay flat, pressing himself to the ground. They passed so close by that Carney watched the truck driver casually light a cigarette as he passed. One of the pilots, Bud McBroom, had come out to help Carney align the runway lights, and as they lay flat he told a long joke about Roy Rogers, concluding with a silly punch line he sang to the tune of "The Chattanooga Choo-Choo." "Pardon me, Roy, is that the cat that chewed your new shoes?" It made Carney laugh.

Both men and the other pilot were armed, but the last thing they wanted was a confrontation in the middle of the desert. It could scotch the whole mission. Apparently neither passing vehicle had spotted them or the plane. When, exhausted and relieved, they returned to the plane with the soil samples, tools, and motorcycle, they found the other pilot, Jim Rhyne, standing at the nose of the plane with his M-16.

On the long flight out of Iran, the pilots noted an electronic indication that the plane had been picked up by radar. They were near the southern coastline, just minutes from the Persian Gulf, and fearing that one of the country's defense radar stations might have spotted them, the pilot changed his course and the indicator went off. Later analysis showed that the radar had come from a commercial vessel in the gulf, not from Iranian defenses. When they landed back in Oman, Carney immediately boarded another plane for London, where he was met at Gatwick Airport by two CIA agents who escorted him to the Concorde lounge. Feeling out of place in his dirty jeans and sweater, still ripe from his days of travel and night of work in the Iranian desert, with traces of camouflage paint still on his face and hands, he passed on the complimentary champagne and asked for a beer. Later that same day he was in the office of General James B. Vaught, the mission commander. His soil samples, analyzed at nearby Fort Belvoir, showed that the "Desert One" location was suitable. There was some concern over the trucks that had rolled past; it indicated a much busier road than surveillance had led mission planners to believe, but that was dismissed as an anomaly.

Carney's bold scout mission did more than test the soil and lay out a runway. It confirmed that it was possible to slip into and out of Iran without detection. Satellites watched Desert One carefully for several more days until wind had erased all traces of the marks left by the Twin Otter and Carney's dirt bike.

Over the same days, Beckwith's operatives had slipped separately into Tehran. Led by Major Dick Meadows, they were the Iranian-born U.S. airman and several special forces soldiers who spoke fluent German, posing as German businessmen. Meadows went under an Irish passport and had apparently summoned enough of a brogue to satisfy the customs officer at Mehrabad Airport.

Over the next few days, Meadows and the rest of the team double-checked all the arrangements put in place by "Bob," the CIA agent Beckwith didn't completely trust. They checked the hide sites and spent time observing the embassy from outside, noting the number of guards and the kinds of weapons they carried and also their habits. Nights were still cold in Tehran at the end of March, and the guards could be seen leaving their posts to duck periodically into shelter.

The German-speaking team managed to pay a visit to the Foreign Ministry building where Laingen, Tomseth, and Howland were being held. Their assessment of the security precautions there prompted mission planners to increase the size of the separate force planning to rescue the diplomats from their gilded cage on the third floor.

Confidence in the mission was now high. The planes and choppers and Delta had conducted their sixth full-dress rehearsal at Twenty-nine Palms, the Marine Corps base in California, in the last week of March, and it had gone well. Delta's operators knew their moves so well they could practically do them in their sleep. Yet Beckwith still fretted over the unforeseen. There were so many things that could go wrong that, if you let yourself think about it for too long, it induced paralysis. His men were trained to quickly scan hands when they entered a room, and to direct their fire at those with weapons. What if, in the confusion, some of the hostages jumped guards and seized their rifles? He worried about what would happen if, after his men had taken down the embassy and herded the hostages into Amajadieh soccer stadium across the street, the Iranian police or army counterattacked with armor. Delta was strictly light infantry. They could not hold out long against tanks or any kind of armored assault vehicles. The answer to those worries were the AC-130 gunships that would be flying that night over the city. They would destroy any Iranian armor that moved toward the rescue operation as well as any Iranian fighters on the runway at Mehrabad Airport.

By the beginning of April the colonel was convinced Delta Force was as ready as it was going to be. His men had been sequestered for months, training endlessly. Major Pete Schoomaker, one of the squadron leaders, had simply vanished from his fiancée's life. He had not been allowed to tell her or anyone else what he was doing, where he was going, or when he might be back. She canceled their wedding several months after he left, having heard nothing from him. At night the men would watch Ted

Koppel's new program on TV, *Nightline, America Held Hostage,* which every night would list the number of days since the embassy takeover. Somebody hung up a sign in their barracks that read "Delta Force Held Hostage" and every day upped the number of days. As spring approached in Iran the nights grew shorter, robbing the mission of precious minutes of darkness.

General David Jones, chairman of the joint chiefs, visited Fort Bragg not long after these secret surveillance trips were completed. He and Beckwith pulled off on a muddy trail near one of Delta's practice sites and had a long conversation in the car. Beckwith looked Jones in the eye and told him his men were ready.

"We've got to do it," he said.

The colonel explained how many times his men had practiced, and how often they had been told to get ready to go only to be stood down.

"Sir, I can't get these troops up one more time," Beckwith said. "If we're going to go, this has got to be it."

"I would agree with you," said Jones. "I think we're ready."

PART FOUR

ONE HUNDRED AND THIRTY-TWO MEN

Colonel Charlie Beckwith, founder and commander of Delta Force, training for the rescue mission in Arizona in December 1978. *(Courtesy: Lewis Burruss)*

Members of Delta Force prepare for the rescue mission in Wadi Kena, Egpyt. From left to right: Dick Potter, Lt. Col. Lewis "Bucky" Burruss, Fred Lewis. Background, left to right: Phil Hanson, Jimmy Knotts (with beard), Norm Crawford, Steve Wright, Moe Elmore (wearing camouflage hat), Mike Vining. The man in the foreground is Lawrence N. "Larry" Freedman, the first American killed in Somalia in 1992. *(Courtesy: Lewis Burruss)*

1

BUNNY SADR

Forcing grown men to live together in a small space day and night, month after month, is a form of slow torture.

The way one man chews his food, sniffles, coughs, farts, snores, or clears his throat becomes a torment. Bob Ode's garrulousness drove his roommates crazy. He was guilty of a failing that afflicts many men as they age, the tendency to tell the same stories over and over again. ICA chief John Graves's patrician disdain for meticulous personal hygiene—he stank —had his roommates contemplating roommate-icide. Economics officer Bob Blucker's hatred of tobacco smoke finally drove him to isolation; he would stuff toilet-paper wads under the crack of his door to keep smoke out of his space. Opinions become deadly, and anything can provoke argument—the rules of a card game, the coming American elections, the likelihood of snow in Tehran in February, the advantages of French cooking . . . anything. Rocky Sickmann and Jerry Plotkin grew intensely envious of their roommate Billy Gallegos because for some reason—reasons were hard to come by—he had been given back his shoes after the visit from Norm Forer's crowd, and his roommates had not. It engendered weeks of ill will.

The three primary beats of each day were meals. Immediately after breakfast, speculation would begin about what would come for lunch and, after lunch, what would be served for dinner. It was pathetic. Many of the hostages coped with boredom by sleeping half the day. Some of the hostages took up arts and crafts. Al Golacinski received a paint-by-number set in the mail from someone and spent hours patiently coloring in the intricate patterns, producing paintings that the guards vied to take home. At the Foreign Ministry, Bruce Laingen took up watercolors, painting scenes outside the tall windows on the third floor. Michael Metrinko drew complex geometric designs on the walls of his cell, using his food bowl and the top of his drinking cup, and then colored them in.

The main pastime was making life difficult for the guards, who obliged, many of them, by being exquisitely sensitive to slight.

Hamid the Liar stepped into Sickmann's room one night and complained about the marine's use of the word "guard" in reference to him. The term, he said, was "too cruel."

"We don't want you to feel that you are in a prison," he said. "We want you to feel that you are our guests."

Sickmann and his roommates were visited one day by an Iranian professor who encouraged them not to despair so much about going home.

"It is good to take four months off work and have a rest," he said.

Then he went home.

America's long lack of a military response to Iran's provocation prompted a popular joke; in which President Carter was visited by the ghost of Theodore Roosevelt, who wondered what was going on in the world.

"The Soviets have invaded Afghanistan," Carter says.

"Are you retaliating with conventional forces or with nuclear weapons?" Roosevelt asks.

"Uh, neither one," says Carter. "We're boycotting the Olympics in Moscow."

"What else is going on?" the former Rough Rider asks.

"Iranians have taken over an embassy in Tehran and they're holding fifty-three of our diplomats hostage."

"How many bombers have you sent over?" Roosevelt asks. "How many divisions have you committed?"

"None," says Carter. "We're using diplomatic restraint."

Roosevelt looks stunned, and then bursts into laughter.

"I get it," he says, "you're joking! Next you're gonna tell me you gave away the Panama Canal!"

Jimmy Carter's patience was not just principled forbearance, nor was his determination to end the crisis peacefully fed by wishful thinking. It was based on the belief that nations were guided ultimately by self-interest. Even in the swirling currents of Iran, he was convinced that cooler heads would eventually prevail. By any realistic calculation, sustaining the standoff hurt Iran far more than it did America. Khomeini's new Islamist state was struggling to define itself while battling ethnic separatists and Soviet-backed leftists inside its borders and fending off increasingly bold incursions by Saddam

Hussein's Iraq. Russian armies had occupied its neighbor Afghanistan. The country was imperiled by both civil war and invasion. Even as it disdained Western allies, Iran needed trading partners and military suppliers. So why jeopardize these things for the sake of holding a few score Americans captive? The move made sense only in the imaginary world of the student hostage takers and their hard-core clerical supporters, who were motivated more by symbols than by reality. In their eyes, the embassy occupation had become the revolution's defining moment, a dramatic uprooting of all American interests and values and a hopeful beacon to all the world's oppressed. The various downsides to drawing it out were dismissed by the faithful with a wave of the hand; Allah would defend and provide.

Less well understood by Carter and even the foreign service professionals who advised him were the practical political benefits to religious hardliners inside Iran of sustaining this crisis. Stories of American subterfuge undercut the efforts of popular rivals such as Bani-Sadr and Ghotbzadeh to create a more democratic, secular state. The embattled president and foreign minister made one last effort to wrest control of the hostages from the students in April. With support from the Revolutionary Council, Bani-Sadr once again demanded that the hostages be delivered to the Foreign Ministry, where Laingen, Tomseth, and Howland oversaw new preparations to receive them. For once, the students appeared to have been outmaneuvered. Instead of repeating their defiance, a spokesman for the hostage takers declined public comment, fueling hopes in Washington that at last they were prepared to submit. Carter was so encouraged that he took the unusual step of inviting reporters into the Oval Office on the morning of April 1 to share the good news. It appeared at last that this long, embarrassing, confusing ordeal was at an end.

"This morning the president of Iran has announced that the hostages' control will be transferred to the government of Iran, which we consider to be a positive step," the president told the journalists. The shift came at a propitious moment for Carter, who was facing off against Senator Kennedy that day in two primaries, in Wisconsin and Kansas.

Carter was not just preening. He had prearranged with Ghotbzadeh to make such public remarks. Bani-Sadr was to announce that the Revolutionary Council had approved the transfer, and the White House would respond by welcoming the move and promising not to impose additional sanctions. Carter made a point of repeating the promise three times to reporters. He had met the afternoon before with Ben Bradlee, editor of the

Washington Post, and several powerful national reporters and columnists to brief them, off the record, about the deal, hoping to forestall a critical response that might undermine the overture.

By the end of the day the president had carried both election primaries, but his hopes for a resolution of the hostage standoff were once again dashed. For reasons the White House did not understand, Bani-Sadr had abruptly announced that the United States had failed to fully live up to its part of the bargain. The accusation was bewildering. "We're not sure what he's talking about," said Jody Powell, the president's press secretary, when reporters asked what Bani-Sadr meant.

Sensing an advantage, the Iranian president once again had changed the rules at the last minute. He now sought various new assurances, among them official recognition by Washington that the appropriate venue for resolving the hostage question was Iran's parliament, the as-yet unformed *Majlis.* Moving the hostages to the Foreign Ministry was understood to be a step toward their rapid release, but what Bani-Sadr now asked for was, in effect, American approval of a plan that would leave the hostages in Tehran for another month or two, until after the *Majlis* was elected and convened. He also wanted Carter to refrain from making "hostile statements." In other words Iran, having kidnapped American diplomats, was entitled to imprison them until it decided upon the terms of their release, and the United States should agree not to publicly complain. Carter acquiesced to even these galling demands. A message essentially complying to them was drafted and sent to Iran but to no avail. Before it reached Bani-Sadr, the effort to move the hostages was again vetoed by Khomeini, and the slippery Iranian president gave up. He announced that he was henceforth "washing his hands" of the hostage mess. Disgusted and dismayed, Carter called Bani-Sadr "gutless."

News stories in America speculated that the president had concocted the "hostage transfer" story to boost his chances in the Wisconsin and Kansas primaries.

Carter vented to Jordan.

"He had a chance to move the hostages and he didn't do it," the president said, tossing aside a news account of Bani-Sadr's latest sidestep. "The council approved the transfer, the militants agreed to do it, and then nothing happens! I don't know what we do now. I really don't." Jordan began to describe what his contacts Bourget and Villalon now suggested, and the president cut him off. "Ham, the only people in the world who think we're going to get our people back soon are you and your French friends."

Carter said again that he had been made to feel "foolish" and doubted any hope of a negotiated solution remained. He would take the expected beating for this latest bait and switch. The Iranians, in Reagan's analogy, had sliced the salami yet again. A pattern had developed: Carter would latch on to a deal proffered by a top Iranian official and grant minor but humiliating concessions, only to have it scotched at the last minute by Khomeini. The White House was feeling pressure from both sides, from those who thought it hadn't done enough to comply with Iran's demands and those who felt the president had gone too far.

Helping to lead the charge for more conciliation were some of the hostages' families. Several had become public figures over the previous four months and, as family members will in hostage situations, they urged the White House to meet the kidnappers' demands. Bonnie Graves, the wife of hostage John Graves, and the parents of hostage Joe Hall joined former hostage William Quarles, one of the African-Americans released in November, and Congressman George Hansen at a press conference calling for a congressional investigation of America's role in "the crimes of the shah."

Such a probe would not be "appeasement," said Hansen, although he acknowledged that a probe would meet one of the students' demands.

"I think it would be very important in getting them out," said Quarles, who since his release had effectively become a spokesman for the hostage takers.

The drumbeat for a more aggressive response was also growing louder, and not just from conservatives and Republicans. So far, Carter's patience had seemed only to reward Iran for this outrage. Among other things, he had agreed to approve creation of the ill-fated UN commission, urged a judge in New York to postpone hearings on seizing Iran's assets, postponed the imposition of economic sanctions, acquiesced in Khomeini's decision to refer the hostage question to the *Majlis,* and agreed to refrain from making hostile statements about Iran . . . and what had come of it?

"There comes a time in negotiations with people of this kind that you have to say, 'No, this is our last offer,'" said presidential candidate Reagan.

The *Washington Post* editorialized:

The United States, far from earning respect for its restraint and forbearance, is increasingly seen as a country that shrinks from asserting what even its enemies recognize as a legitimate interest in protecting its diplomats from a mob. The latest sequence of negotiations between Washington and Tehran puts the issue beyond argument. The United

> States has made concessions of the sort one might expect from a nation
> that had lost a war. Each concession has been met with a demand for
> another. The divisions and disputes within Iran that are responsible for
> the impasse seem almost self-perpetuating.... The only reasonable
> conclusion is that this string of diplomacy has been played out.... Fresh
> sanctions are being weighed by the administration. Good. They should
> be applied.... They should be direct and consequential.

The newspaper mirrored Carter's thoughts. His mood had changed.
At another NSC meeting at the end of the first week of April, the president announced that negotiations were over, that he was going to act, and
that it had been a mistake not to act sooner.

Bani-Sadr had become a joke, even to Secretary of State Vance,
who continued to urge moderation. Henry Precht, the head of the State
Department's Iran desk who had worked closely with Jordan through all
the secret negotiations, walked into the secretary's office on Easter Sunday to find a large stuffed pink and yellow rabbit.

"Henry," said Vance, "I'd like you to meet Bunny Sadr."

It was the only time Precht had ever heard the earnest Vance make a
joke. One of Carter's "acts" was to finally expel Iran's diplomatic mission
and to break all formal ties, a step so unsurprising that many Americans were
startled to learn it had not been done already. In fact, Carter had deliberately delayed closing Iran's embassy because American eavesdroppers had
broken Iran's codes and considered the "secure" communications between
the Iranians in Washington and their bosses in Tehran to be a useful source
of intelligence. The task of formal eviction fell to Precht, who invited to his
office Ali Agah, the Iranian chargé d'affaires. Agah arrived with his deputy,
not knowing the purpose of the summons. Chatting with them while he
waited for the formal note of expulsion to be drafted—Deputy Secretary
Warren Christopher was supposed to arrive with it at any moment—Precht
expressed irritation over a small group of Iranians who had mounted another pro-Khomeini demonstration outside the State Department building.

"Why do you suppose these guys don't go back to Tehran and rebuild the country?" he asked. "Why are they wasting their time here when
their countrymen are mistreating our people over there?"

The Iranian deputy, whom Precht would later describe as "snake-
like," countered, "We are not mistreating the hostages. They are being very
well taken care of in Tehran. They are our guests."

"Bullshit," said Precht.

Agah stood up and declared, "I'm not going to stay here and have my country, my government, insulted by you. We are leaving."

The Iran desk chief bolted into the hallway after them. His job was to keep them occupied until they could be formally expelled.

"Ali, I apologize," he said. "I retract my statement. Come back and let's just chat a little more."

"No," said Agah.

Precht raced ahead to intercept them at the elevator door. He was now creating a scene in the fifth-floor hallway. The Iranians stepped around him into the elevator, but Precht wouldn't let the doors shut.

"Ali, let's sit," he urged.

"You are holding us hostage in this elevator," said Agah. "Get out of the way and let us out of here."

Precht relented. The last thing he wanted was to make it appear the United States had gone into the business of reciprocal hostage taking. Outside the State Department building, Agah complained angrily to Marvin Kalb, the CBS reporter, that he had just been insulted by an American official. Kalb then phoned Precht.

"Henry, what did you say?" he asked. "What did you do to Ali?"

Precht explained, and that night's lead news item became the flustered Iranian diplomats leaving the State Department in a huff. It could not have played out better in millions of impatient American living rooms. The formal message was delivered by a junior official who chased Agah's car across the city. Within twenty-four hours, after the State Department rejected several last-minute appeals from some in the Iranian mission who were especially eager to stay (including one who requested political asylum), all but one of them boarded flights in Washington, Chicago, San Francisco, and New York. The stress of returning home had provoked chest pains in one, who stayed behind under observation at a D.C. hospital.

The expulsion and the way it had been carried out were warmly applauded. Precht, who felt he had mishandled the assignment, became an overnight hero to millions of Americans who relished the idea of hurling "bullshit!" into the face of an Iranian official before kicking him and his entire mission out the door. He received congratulatory mail from all over the country, including proposals of marriage.

Even Carter applauded Precht, expressing particular satisfaction with his choice of words.

2

A BEGINNING OF THE DAWN
OF FINAL VICTORY

Easter in Tehran brought another visit from concerned American clergy. The Reverend Jack Bremer was back under the auspices of the Committee for American-Iranian Crisis Resolution, the group headed by Kansas professor Norm Forer, which had so impressed the Iranian students with its sympathies on the February visit that it was invited back, at the students' expense. Bremer brought along the activist priest Darrell Rupiper, who had visited earlier in the year. He and the others practiced what they called "moral patriotism," which condemned America for falling short of universal ethical standards. While they condemned the kidnapping of diplomats, they also acknowledged that Iran had valid grievances against the United States, and though they claimed strict neutrality their sympathies clearly leaned toward Tehran. Rupiper had kicked off the trip with a press conference at which he urged President Carter to comply with Iranian demands, admit complicity in the crimes of the shah, agree not to obstruct efforts to extradite the shah (now from Egypt), and promise not to meddle further in Iranian affairs.

The visiting clergymen presented Kathryn Koob and Ann Swift each with a plastic bag filled with gifts: a shirt, some underwear, and soaps and other toiletries. Bremer told Koob that he had delivered similar gifts to Laingen, Tomseth, and Howland at the Foreign Ministry.

Bremer then led a prayer, which asked for God's blessings on Americans and Iranians both, and for a renewed understanding and friendship between these nations. Koob was moved. She had been struggling in her prayer sessions for the right way to pray for her captors and heard in Bremer's words an approach she hadn't considered. After the service, the American women were positioned before the cameras, handed letters from their families, and told they could send messages home. Koob knew that her much-reduced frame was now so skinny and angular that her face seemed lost behind the wide plastic frames of her glasses. "The only reason I'm losing weight, Mother, is that I decided that was the only thing I could do over here." Encouraged to keep talking, Koob and Swift described their daily routines and soon fell to giggling.

"Which one of you keeps the other in good spirits?" Bremer asked.

The two women pointed at each other.

When they were finished they added nuts, candy, and brownies to their plastic bags and listened as their guards told the cameras about how their hostages were provided an exercise room with a Ping-Pong table (Koob had been there twice) and showings of American movies (Koob had seen one).

Al Golacinski and Kevin Hermening had been told weeks earlier to expect the Easter visit, so each prepared a note on a foil wrapper from a stick of Wrigley's spearmint gum. Golacinski's note said that they were sick, that the sanitary conditions were terrible, that they couldn't take it anymore, and that they were "losing it." Hermening wrote that he believed the American people were unaware of how badly he and the others were being treated. He mentioned solitary confinement, beatings, the blindfolding and handcuffs, the lack of showers, and said they all just wanted to "get the hell out."

Hermening had a tear in the cuff of his blue slacks, so he stuffed the note inside it for safekeeping.

A Mass was to be said by Rupiper. When the hostages arrived for the ceremony, Hermening, who was Catholic, asked if he could perform the ceremony's lay readings. There were bright lights and cameras everywhere and the room was decorated with posters and festive ornaments made of construction paper. Dick Morefield and Billy Gallegos, two of the other Catholic hostages, looked on. As he waited for his chance to read, Hermening slid the note out of his cuff and cupped it in the palm of his right hand. He slipped the gum wrapper into the Bible during his reading, and when he handed it back to the priest he said, "There's a note in there." Rupiper was so startled he took a step back and nearly dropped the book. He said nothing, but Hermening thought the priest looked frightened.

Golacinski took advantage of the session to whisper to one of the other ministers that he wanted to get word to his fiancée that she should not wait for him.

"I'm going to be here for a long time," he said.

Richard Queen and Joe Hall were in the last group to meet with the delegation. They sat at a table with the Reverend Nelson Thompson, an African-American Methodist preacher from Kansas City, and Rupiper. Queen was particularly grateful for the chance to receive communion. He was moved by Rupiper's kindness.

"I wish I had the strength to stay here with you," the priest told Queen. "This is a real test, a test of one's faith."

The slender, longhaired priest had been so struck by the condition of Jerry Miele, the CIA communicator who had become increasingly disturbed, that he offered to stay in Tehran and take the man's place.

"I would want no privileges the others do not have," he told Hussein Sheikh-ol-eslam and several of the other student captors. Rupiper explained that the night before he had opened the Bible at random and found a passage in Galatians about Christ's willingness to sacrifice himself to "set us free from the present age of evil."

This was language that the students understood.

"We need not say that you are good," Sheikh-ol-eslam told Rupiper. "God knows that. We have a similar way of opening the Koran and finding God's will." Nevertheless, they turned his offer down.

"We see you as a member of the American nation," one of the other student leaders told him. "But we saw them [the hostages] not as members of the American nation but as individuals who were plotting against us."

Another explained that substituting the priest for Miele would "confuse the identity of the American embassy as a center of evil activity."

Despite his concern for Miele, the priest's good impression of the hostage takers was reinforced during this visit, and he once again brought back a glowing report on their kindness and compassion.

"They [the hostages] have exercise bicycles, Ping-Pong, watch TV, see movies, videocassettes," he said. "The food is fine. They say that the students are treating them correctly."

Since they were the last to visit the clergymen, Queen, Hall, Lee, and Englemann were allowed to hoard whatever remained of the candy, cake, and fruit that had been placed out for the occasion. Queen piled a paper plate high and stuffed his shirt and pants pockets with candy. He worried as he was doing it that he might be caught on camera—how would that look, him greedily making off with a mountain of treats? Back in their room, he satisfied his urge to organize things by sorting the candies into Krackle bars, peanut butter cups, and almond bars, and stashed them in a drawer out of sight—otherwise the guards would pick at it. He and Hall ate the cake first and then portioned out the candy over days, debating every evening which kind of treat to have with their tea.

As they sorted through the goodies in their room, Koob and Swift began to second-guess their behavior at the televised session. On reflection, they felt they had behaved like schoolgirls at a sleepover. Swift felt worse about it than Koob, who figured any chance she had to communicate with her family was worth whatever downside, but they both agreed that if fate handed them another turn before the cameras they would try to maintain a more sober demeanor.

In their room, Hermening and Golacinski were congratulating themselves for slipping the note to Rupiper when a guard burst in with the note in his hand. They concluded that instead of taking it home Rupiper had handed it over.

Hermening admitted that he had passed it and braced himself for punishment.

The successful, stealthy incursions into Iran of John Carney and Dick Meadows had a big effect in Washington. Both men returned to brief their superiors on the readiness of the desert landing strip and the various hide sites, trucks, and equipment. It all awaited just outside Tehran. The ease of their success made a rescue mission seem less like wishful thinking and more like a real option. December's preposterous plan suddenly seemed doable.

President Carter's crackdown in the first week of April had proved nothing more than his futility. The break in diplomatic ties was dramatic but clearly overdue, and a decision to cancel all entry visas for Iranians was perceived as primarily symbolic, because most such travel had come to a halt anyway. His call for allies to break ties and join in a trade embargo succeeded only in exposing a distressing lack of unanimity: England's response was lukewarm; Canada promised to consult with other nations first; Japan said it would "carefully study" the idea; West Germany declined outright; Denmark announced it was "hesitant" to break ties; Italy called such punitive steps "a mistake." All of these nations, of course, publicly deplored the taking of hostages but none decided to join the United States in pressuring Iran for their release.

America's toothlessness was embarrassing. An article on the front page of the *Christian Science Monitor* suggested that Carter's new "tough" tactics "were apparently designed more for public relations than to have any real impact. They are not expected to have any immediate or tangible effect."

Khomeini scoffed. He publicly welcomed the break in diplomatic ties, suggesting that it was what Iran had had in mind all along.

"It is the one thing in all his life Carter has done in the interests of the oppressed," the imam said, noting that it marked the end of ties between "a risen country and a world-devouring plunderer. This is the beginning of the dawn of final victory of a nation against the bloodthirsty superpower which was forced to cut relations."

Ronald Reagan, now the clear Republican front-runner for president, dismissed the president's actions as "more of the same, and it's been wrong from the first. There will be no impact on Iran at all."

Richard Hermening, father of the hostage marine, was publicly underwhelmed. Asked to comment on Carter's moves, he said, "It's things he had said he was going to do, but kept backing off." It still seemed to him that the president "just seems like he says one thing but never follows through on anything he says."

The pressure to use America's military strength was becoming inexorable. The country braced for war. Carter told reporters, "We have been trying to avoid [military action] and we are still attempting to avoid that kind of action," but the "availability of peaceful measures, like the patience of the American people, is running out." An unnamed government official told the *New York Times* that it seemed as though the country were marching helplessly, "with the best of intentions," into a "Greek tragedy." Demands for action came from both sides of the political aisle. Democratic senator George McGovern, a former bomber pilot in World War II whose opposition to the Vietnam War had defined his presidential candidacy in 1972, joined conservative Republicans in calling for military action. The student hostage takers sensed something was coming. They announced that any military action by the Carter administration, or by Saddam Hussein, whose forces continued to harass Iranian forces along their shared border, would be met by execution of the hostages.

Months of careful calculation had reduced the military options to rescue or a naval blockade. Anything more violent than a blockade would invite retaliation against the hostages, and even a blockade made the prospect of public executions more likely. Rescue was enormously appealing. For the beleaguered White House, the prospect of a precise, relatively bloodless liberation from this dilemma was a joy to contemplate. Success would demonstrate remarkable daring, capability, and resolve and would in one deft stroke deprive Iran of its trump card. It was eminently justifiable in the eyes of the world, because it was a response gauged perfectly to the provocation. Americans would rejoice. Carter's second term would be virtually assured.

Yet as delightful as success was to contemplate, failure was correspondingly calamitous. The jury-rigged mission plan contrived by the Pentagon's plotters would be, without a doubt, one of the boldest and most complex military missions in American history. Potential disaster lurked at every step. What if the small armada of planes and helicopters was discovered as it moved into Iran, alerting the country's air force and armies? What if the force failed to rendezvous and refuel successfully at Desert One, a task that required elaborate choreography in darkness over unfamiliar terrain? What if the force was stumbled upon in its mountain hiding place outside Tehran on the mission's second day, or stopped and attacked on its way into the city on that night? There was a permanent checkpoint on Damavand Road on the way into the city. If the rescuers were stopped, they would try to talk their way past, but if that didn't work they planned to just grab the guards and take them along. What alarms would that raise? What other hazards awaited on the drive in? What if the guards at the embassy put up a terrific fight and began slaughtering the hostages once the raid began? What if army and police units near the embassy responded more rapidly than anticipated, or if angry crowds massed at the scene while the rescue operation was under way? What if the occupied soccer stadium was attacked by Iran's American-trained and -equipped air force or by an Iranian armored unit? What if Beckwith's men managed to chopper themselves and the freed hostages to the seized Mehrabad Airport only to face a determined Iranian assault there? What if Iranian jets attacked the American planes on their way out of Iran? Any one of these entirely plausible setbacks could mean the deaths of all or many of the hostages, and possibly the loss of the entire American force. Most failure scenarios led to a large military clash between America and Iran, with the incumbent loss of life, no doubt mostly Iranian, and not just dozens or hundreds but potentially thousands. What would happen then? It might well provoke an all-out war. What would the Soviets do? And these were just the bad consequences that could be readily foreseen. Anyone familiar with military missions knew there would be unforeseen ones. There always were.

Nevertheless, both Hamilton Jordan and Defense Secretary Harold Brown, talking on the phone on April 10, agreed that it was the right move.

"Neither the naval blockade nor mining the harbors will bring the hostages home, except in boxes," said Brown. "And if they begin killing our people, then we'll have to take punitive measures, and God only knows where that would lead. The rescue mission is the best of a lousy set of options."

Carter surprised Jordan by talking about blockade instead of rescue at the next morning's policy breakfast, but it was just because the president was hiding his bombshell. The chief of staff was on his way to the airport later that morning when he was summoned back to the White House for an off-the-books lunchtime meeting with the president, Brown, Vice President Mondale, Brzezinski, Deputy Secretary of State Christopher (Secretary Vance was vacationing), CIA director Stansfield Turner, Chairman of the Joint Chiefs Jones, and press secretary Jody Powell, whom Carter had invited to attend only if he felt comfortable keeping an important secret.

Powell had given the matter some thought. He concluded that he was comfortable lying to the press in order to protect a state secret and figured that, if the occasion demanded it, knowing the truth would make him a more effective liar.

"If you lie to the press, I may have to fire you before all this is over, you know," Carter teased his longtime friend.

"It would be doing me a real favor," said Powell.

The meeting began with the president announcing, "Gentlemen, I want you to know that I am seriously considering an attempt to rescue the hostages."

Jordan knew immediately that the president had made up his mind. The rescue option had been regarded as a last resort, a drastic step to be avoided, and all the efforts the White House had made since the embassy takeover were toward that end, but as the president launched into a list of detailed questions about how it was to be done, his aides knew he had mentally crossed into new and dangerous territory. He had met the outrage in Iran with tremendous restraint, equating national interest with the well-being of the remaining fifty-three hostages, and his measured response had elicited a great deal of admiration, both at home and abroad. Carter's approval ratings had doubled in the first month of the crisis. But as the months wore on, restraint had begun to smell like weakness and indecision. Three times in the past six months carefully negotiated secret settlements had been unilaterally ditched by the inscrutable Iranian mullahs, and each time the administration had been made to look more inept. Carter's formidable patience was badly strained. He had a long list of questions about the proposed mission, but his mind was set. Jones unrolled a big map and walked the meeting's members through the raid's elaborate course, pointing out the location of Desert One and the various hide-site locations, the embassy in central Tehran, the soccer stadium, and the airfield from which everyone would escape. Christopher said he had not discussed the rescue option with Vance, so he couldn't speak for the secretary, but everyone else in the meeting was in agreement.

"It's time to bring the hostages home," Carter said. He deferred making a final decision until he had a chance to talk directly to Vance.

"The president is going to go through with this thing," Powell told Defense Secretary Brown. "I can sense it. If we can bring our people out of there, it will do more good for this country than anything that has happened in twenty years."

"Yes," said Brown, "and if we fail, that will be the end of the Carter presidency."

"We don't really have much choice, do we?" said Powell.

In order to maintain appearances, Carter sent Jordan back to Paris for a scheduled second secret meeting with Ghotbzadeh at Hector Villalon's apartment. The Iranian foreign minister was deflated. He complained that the White House decision to break diplomatic ties had been a tragic mistake; it would drive his country into the arms of the Soviets. Ghotbzadeh confirmed the intractable nature of the impasse, predicting now that it would be many months before the hostages would be released. He was apologetic, but explained that to take a "soft" position on the hostage issue in Iran at that point was tantamount to political, if not actual, suicide.

"I just hope your president doesn't do anything rash," he said, "like attack Iran or mine our harbors."

"Don't worry," said Jordan. "He won't. President Carter is not a militaristic man."

That conversation itself, however, further hardened the decision to send Delta Force. Ghotbzadeh's prediction of "many months" confirmed the White House's grim assessment. At that point, the only things that might have averted the rescue was word that release was imminent.

Vance was alarmed when he learned of Carter's thinking. The president listened coolly to his secretary of state's impassioned argument against going, which Vance delivered in person when he returned from vacation. He pointed out that in just about any projected scenario some of the hostages would be hurt or killed and reminded the president of his pledge to the families. There were hundreds of American journalists in Tehran—they had been allowed back in after a brief period of exile. Even if the rescue mission was successful, what was to stop angry Iranians from seizing them? They might end up with more hostages and an even more volatile situation. There was some consideration given to taking a number of Iranians hostage and bringing them back as bargaining chips in the event more Americans were kidnapped in Iran, but this tack led to increasingly unseemly scenarios. What would the United States do with its captive Iranians if the radical students began defiantly executing American reporters? Brzezinski responded with the kind of joke a man makes to poke fun at himself, exaggerating his own perceived worst tendencies: "They could always just fall out of a helicopter over the Red Sea," he said.

The idea of seizing hostages was quickly dropped, but Carter was inclined to go ahead even without answers for every conceivable contingency. Diplomacy had proved useless, and he felt he was wrong to have pursued it for so long. He was responsible for State Department employees and military staffers in Tehran in a more direct way than for reporters who had traveled there on their own.

Colonel Beckwith was summoned to the White House, and the two Georgia natives swapped stories about their neighboring home counties.

The tough, gray-haired colonel gave a brisk, detailed account of the plan, and Carter was impressed. Beckwith had spent a career selling the idea of his elite unit, and now that he had created it he was eager to show what miracles it could perform. Despite his initial misgivings about being assigned such a hard task the first time out, the colonel was more convinced than ever that it could work. He was eager. Briefing the Pentagon brass the day before, he had concluded with an enthusiastic, "Hey, we *gotta* do this thing!" His enthusiasm was infectious. He and his men were going to make history, not just sever this particular Gordian knot but write their names in the annals of military glory. In a sense, Beckwith's career-long crusade to create Delta had been a rebellion against the mechanization and bureaucratization of modern warfare. He held to an older, more visceral conviction: War was the business of brave men. He loved soldiers and soldiering, and his vision was of a company of men like himself, impatient with rank, rules, and politics, focused entirely on the mission. Now he had created such a force, choosing the best of the best and training them to perfection. They were not just good, they were magnificent. In his eyes they were beautiful. And now he would lead them into battle. They were going to prove themselves on the most difficult, improbable mission in American history, moving straight into the enemy's heart, a small force of brave men hopelessly outnumbered, shouldering impossible odds. The fact that it seemed so far-fetched made it all the more appealing. It was perfect. He sold it well, projecting his own brand of brute certainty.

"On behalf of my men, sir, I hope you will let us go," Beckwith told Carter.

Eight choppers were waiting beneath the decks of the *Nimitz*. Staging areas in Wadi Kena, the abandoned Soviet airstrip in Egypt, and Masirah, an island off the coast of Oman, were being readied to receive his men and planes. Dick Meadows was packing his bags for a return trip to Tehran. It would take about two weeks to move everything into position.

Technically, Carter had not yet given the go-ahead, but when he left the White House Beckwith was certain the mission was on. He flew to Delta's stockade at Fort Bragg and immediately assembled his top men. He was elated.

"You can't tell the people, you can't tell anybody," the colonel said. "Don't talk about this to anyone, but the president has approved the mission and we're going to go on April 24."

*   *   *

One morning, for no reason he could discern, Michael Metrinko was allowed to go outside. He was taken from the basement of the chancery to a walled garden outside the ambassador's residence. It was a sunny morning, and the first time Metrinko had been outdoors since mid-November. The odors, the color, the feel of sunshine on his skin, the slight breeze . . . it was all intoxicating. It was as though he had been blind and his sight was suddenly restored. He was allowed to walk around the garden slowly, drinking it in.

He noticed that someone was using one of the embassy's sterling silver candleholders to prop open a window apparently ignorant of how valuable it was. It crossed his mind to take it, but what would he do with it? Metrinko had always been acquisitive. He loved beautiful things, and in his years of travel he had accumulated a small treasure of valuable objects, which had decorated his apartment in Tehran. The candlestick reminded him of such luxuries, which now, walking in his silly plastic flip-flops and oversized pants bunched at the waist with a paper clip, seemed to him frivolous. His instinct to grab the candlestick made him laugh.

Archbishop Hilarion Capucci was sent by the Vatican to visit with the hostages near Easter, and the occasion prompted the guards to bring Metrinko upstairs. He had met the archbishop before when he had stayed at the Greek Catholic patriarchate in Jerusalem for a week in 1969, on his first visit to Israel. They remembered each other right away. He told Capucci that he was being kept in solitary confinement and was badly treated, and the archbishop just nodded and smiled and said he would pray for him. He urged Metrinko to be patient. The hostage wondered what his other options were.

The guards were careful about what he got to read. One of the publications they judged innocuous was the *Sporting News,* and though Metrinko was not a sports fan he was so desperate for any diversion he began reading about games and athletes and teams that held no interest for him. In one of the stories about a baseball game—the season was just beginning at home—he was stunned to read that the host stadium had welcomed *the six former hostages who had escaped Iran with the Canadian ambassador!* His heart leapt with the news. The story didn't name the escapees, but he assumed that among them were Bruce Laingen, Victor Tomseth, and Mike Howland, who had gone to the Foreign Ministry on the morning of the take-over and never returned. His pleasure in the news that his colleagues had escaped was heightened by the way he discovered it. The English-speaking students who censored his reading wouldn't have had the patience to wade through all these stories about batting averages and sore pitching arms. Any small victory over them was enough to lift his spirits for days.

3

YOU'VE GOT A MOTHER

The punishment Kevin Hermening expected after the guards discovered his note to Rupiper never came. Instead, in the days after Easter the guards became suspiciously friendly toward him. Those who spoke English stopped to chat and, for some reason, asked a lot of questions about his family. They wanted to know what his father did for a living, and his mother, where he lived, about his brothers and sisters. He was happy to tell them, and although both he and Golacinski suspected that something odd was afoot, they couldn't figure out what it was. In their most optimistic moments they toyed with the idea that perhaps Hermening, the youngest of the hostages, was going to be released.

On the morning of April 21, two guards came to the room with Hermening's shoes and a clean shirt.

"You better get cleaned up," one said.

Excited, and afraid even to think that this might mean the end of this ordeal for him, he dressed. The guards returned and led him down the hall to the Ping-Pong room, where they told him that his mother had come to visit him. Hermening was flabbergasted.

His mom?

In an epic gesture of maternal devotion, Barbara Timm had traveled from the suburbs of Milwaukee to Tehran to see her captive son. Not even the fiercest revolutionary zealot could resist the story's appeal. A few months earlier, Timm could not even have found Tehran on a map. She had her hands full raising five children and working as a telephone operator. Kevin was her son from her first marriage, which had ended in divorce. She had felt no particular fears about his posting. A tall, slender woman with big eyes whose short-cropped hair gave her a boyish look, she didn't know enough about Iran to feel anything, except that it was far away and had not been her son's first choice. She was a little disappointed for him, but figured the country's embassy there was as good as any other. When she had started getting letters from him they were all upbeat and filled with assurances that he was happy and okay, so she hadn't worried about him at all. Her own mother was the worrier. From the first day that Kevin left, his grandmother had phoned every few days with an alarming story about something bad that had happened in Iran.

When her mother had called again on Sunday morning, November 4, and told one of Hermening's stepbrothers that the U.S. embassy in Tehran had been overrun by crazed Islamic radicals, Timm's first reaction was annoyance. Why wouldn't her mother just leave it alone? She figured it was something minor that would blow over. She hadn't even bothered to turn on the radio. Then there was a news break during the Packers game, an autumn Sunday ritual in the Timm household, saying that the embassy had been seized but still, she refused to worry about her son. She wasn't even sure if the embassy was the same one where he had been sent. She went bowling that night, as she usually did.

Then the media storm descended with the fury of a Wisconsin blizzard. It started the minute she walked in the door after bowling, with a phone call from a local newscaster, and her life had not been the same since. A representative from the marines called the following morning with official word that her son was among those who had been taken captive, which by then was old news. From that day forward the fate of her eldest son played out in public. Over the next three months, Timm got to know the various local TV producers and reporters and print journalists all too well, and she had agreed to be interviewed periodically. It was a curious new position to be in; suddenly the whole world seemed fascinated by every comment or insight from this working Milwaukee mom. In short order she regretted saying yes to that first interview, because it undermined her future ability to say no. Whenever a local news outlet would get a picture or an audio or videotape from the embassy they would use it to blackmail her. *Would you like to come in and see it?* Of course she would. *We just want to film you as you watch (or listen) to it.* Even during slow news periods she got four or five media requests a day. She drew the line at talking to the persistent national news figures who stalked her for interviews and appearances. The local storm was bad enough.

As much as she hated being pursued by newsmen, though, she was addicted to their reports. The TV was on every minute in her house and her ears arched at any word from Iran. The sight of those marching, chanting, fist- and placard-waving crowds outside the embassy convinced her that the country was populated by maniacs. She feared she would never see her son again.

Timm had attended the regional and national briefings held by the State Department, even though the transportation costs were steep. Because the government would pay expenses only for Hermening's mother and father, and Timm did not want to travel without her husband, Ken, she had had to foot his bill for two trips to Washington. At the first Washington session she met President Carter, who initially she blamed for the whole mess. She had disliked him before meeting him but left with her feelings somewhat mollified. She and the others had been assured that the administration was doing all it could to bring the hostages home, and that they would almost certainly be back before the end of the year. Carter had seemed genuinely concerned. But by the second Washington trip, in mid-February, Timm was completely fed up. She believed she'd been misled and manipulated.

She was not the only one. Barbara Rosen, whose husband, Barry, the embassy's press attaché, had been singled out by the students and publicly denounced as a top spy, felt that the State Department was treating her and the other families like children. They had been genuinely moved by the long standing ovation they were given when, as a group, they entered the auditorium at department headquarters for the February meeting, but in the question and answer sessions later, she and others complained about what little information they were being given. As a group, the hostages' families felt they were being deliberately kept in the dark.

There was good reason for it. Rosen had seen other family members handing over recordings of the "private" sessions to reporters. Clearly, some of the families were enjoying their long moment in the spotlight. The department had grown increasingly circumspect as a result, which aggravated suspicion.

Timm was appalled by many of the families. She regarded the second family session, when they had all been extravagantly wined and dined, as nothing more than an effort to pacify them. She watched with disgust as these supposedly suffering fathers, mothers, spouses, and siblings milked the open bar at receptions and mobbed the buffet tables at mealtime. They seemed more interested in sampling the goodies than in finding out what was really going on. As the weeks progressed and her bitterness grew, Timm found herself losing interest completely in what happened to the other fifty-two hostages. Her one concern was Kevin. She wanted to see him.

So when State Department officials urged her to have nothing to do with Carl McAfee, a Virginia attorney who wanted to fly her and her husband to Tehran, she ignored their advice. McAfee was one of a breed of attention-seeking Washington attorneys who look for ways to inject themselves into the ongoing drama of national and world affairs. He had made a name for himself almost twenty years earlier negotiating a trade for Gary Powers, the U-2 pilot who served nearly two years in a Soviet prison after his spy plane was shot down. McAfee had attended the second hostage family briefing, introduced himself around, and said that he was interested in arranging personal visits to Tehran. After that session, twenty-four of the families signed up to make the trip. Timm's husband and her ex-husband, Kevin's father, were among them. Timm and the other mothers and wives were advised that because women were second-class citizens in Iran, the men would have a better chance of success. Those planning to make the trip were waiting in Washington for visas from the Iranian embassy when the six Americans who had been sheltered by the Canadian embassy escaped. That had killed the plan.

Then Timm got a call from a woman in Canada who had received one of the Christmas cards Hermening had mailed months earlier. The ones he sent to his family had not arrived, but for some reason this letter had gotten through. In the note he had mentioned his plan to escape (the attempt had ended badly months earlier). He had also noted that he expected to be dead by the time the card reached its recipient, if ever, and asked that the recipient contact his mother. So the Canadian woman had called.

Timm was alarmed. She knew right away that the card was authentic. It sounded like her son, and she knew he would be trying to get word to her in particular. She determined then and there that even if no one else was going to Tehran, she was. She had contacted McAfee and joined up with twelve other families who had enlisted for the lawyer's second attempt at a trip. The government was reportedly cool to the idea, but the Timms had never heard anything from the State Department directly and didn't ask permission. The marines were completely supportive but warned against letting the Iranians use Timm for propaganda purposes. For weeks McAfee kept setting dates and canceling them.

Then, in mid-April, Carter announced a ban on travel to Iran. Without putting it in so many words, the decision was meant primarily to encourage American news organizations to bring their reporters home, mindful of Vance's worry about what might happen in the aftermath of a rescue attempt. Carter could not order reporters out of Iran without provoking a showdown over freedom of the press—Powell had speculated that such a direct move might actually prompt the networks and major newspapers to send *more* reporters there, simply to assert their independence—but the president did specifically ask news organizations to "minimize, as severely as possible" their presence there. Even that prompted an angry response from news editors, who accused the White House of trampling First Amendment freedoms.

"I warned him that you people would get on a high horse," Powell told CBS News executive producer Sandy Socolow, and then the president's press secretary tried to hint at the real concern. "I personally don't give a good goddamn what you people do. If I had my way, I'd ask the fucking ayatollah to keep fifty reporters and give us our diplomats back. Then you people who have all the answers could figure out how to get them out." Socolow didn't get the hint.

The travel ban was not directed at the families of the hostages, but it had the effect of dismantling McAfee's plan. One by one the other families dropped out. News reports in late winter and early spring were hopeful, and nobody wanted to do anything that might derail an agreement. Several of the wives, Penne Laingen, Louise Kennedy, whose husband Mike headed the economics section, and Katherine Keough, whose husband Bill was the school headmaster who had been trapped at the embassy with the others, formed their own organization in March, called FLAG (Family Liaison Action Group), and were given office space at State Department headquarters. They took it upon themselves to improve outreach to the others, to coordinate public statements and actions, and to keep reminding official Washington, America, and the world that their loved ones' fate hung in the balance of this dispute. FLAG conducted a mission to Europe, led by Louise Kennedy, and including Barbara Rosen, Jeanne Queen, mother of the ailing vice consul, and Pearl Golacinski, mother of the former embassy security chief who, with a gun to his head, had urged his colleagues to open the doors on the day of the takeover. The group met with French president Giscard d'Estaing, and then split up for meetings with other European heads of state. Rosen, who just months ago had been daunted by the prospect of meeting strangers, traveled to Bonn and found herself in serious conversation with German chancellor Helmut Schmidt, who told her that he thought the use of force by America would only worsen the crisis. He had more advice.

"Tell my friend Jimmy to get it off the front pages," he said. "Let him concentrate on Afghanistan or even the old Russian threat, anything to stop giving the militants what they need."

Rosen asked if he thought she should speak out against her government if it attempted to use force, and Schmidt told her no. "It is *most* important not to embarrass your own country," he said. "Do everything you can to influence it, but do not oppose it."

Opposition was precisely what motivated Timm to go to Iran herself. The government's travel ban was the final straw. It made her determined to go. She felt her son's loneliness and isolation viscerally, and believed none of her letters to him were getting through. Reports of the visits by American clergymen had infuriated her, because it was said that the ministers had carried letters from home to the hostages. Evidently at least some of the other families had known about these ministers' trip and had been provided the opportunity to give them letters. Why hadn't she? How could the authorities be so careless and incompetent?

After that, the government's sins kept accumulating. When she saw a news report that thousands of Iranians had been let into the United States since the embassy takeover, she couldn't believe it. What was happening? For the first time in her life she felt betrayed by her own government. Nothing made sense anymore, and her confusion gave birth to suspicion. The card she had heard about had been mailed to Canada. Why had that one gotten through? Kevin was a faithful correspondent, and she knew that under these circumstances, if he was writing to perfect strangers and asking them to contact his mother, then he was certainly writing regularly to her. Was she not getting his letters because the government was intercepting them? Why would it do that? The only answer she came up with was that something must be going on that the authorities did not want her to know about. She had seen Kevin on TV reading the statement in support of his captors in December. Maybe the United States was up to something in Iran that it did not want the American people to learn. In time, she was ready to believe anything that fed her conspiracy theories. The Iranians holding her son and the others insisted that the fault for everything was America's. Maybe they were right!

As the other families dropped out, Timm grew more committed. Because Iran's embassy in Washington had been closed, she and her husband Ken and McAfee left for Paris in mid-April to seek visas at the embassy there.

Milwaukee reporters followed them, demanding an interview at the airport in New York, where Timm asked the United States to apologize to Iran for its support of the shah. She assumed that she would be leaving the journalists behind, but they boarded her plane with their cameras and microphones and moved into the same Parisian hotel. Timm wasn't bothered by it; she was so accustomed to the reporters and cameras by now that as she ventured into strange lands the familiar entourage actually comforted and emboldened her. Their reports made much of her defiance of President Carter's travel ban, but Timm said she had never been informed of it personally and, unless word reached her directly from the White House, she was going. After waiting five days in Paris for a visa, the three left the reporters behind (Iran refused them visas) and flew to Germany, where they caught a connecting flight to Damascus, and then a plane to Tehran, all the while expecting the CIA to show up at the last moment to stop them. When she heard her name being called on the public address system at the German airport, she assumed it was the long arm of the law, but it turned out to be another reporter looking for a comment. She hung up on him. This was quite a dramatic stepping out for Barbara Timm. Her son's graduation from embassy guard training the year before in Quantico, Virginia, had been the first flight she had ever taken. When they landed in Damascus it hit her. They had left behind everything familiar. In Syria all of the people who looked normal to her got off the plane. Only Timm, her husband, and the lawyer stayed. When new passengers boarded, all the women were draped in chadors. Timm had a moment of terror. *What in God's name are we doing?* She suddenly wanted to get off the plane and go back home, but it was too late to turn back.

Her fear heightened when they landed in Tehran. Waiting for them was a mob of journalists; it seemed like thousands. There were armed men in green uniforms everywhere. They and their luggage were searched. Once they cleared customs the cameras and microphones closed in on them so fast Timm thought she was going to be trampled to death. She latched on to McAfee and did whatever he suggested, even though she didn't agree with most of what he said. Right away, for instance, he had urged her to step up before the cameras and answer the reporters' questions.

"We've come this far and we have a responsibility to the world," he told her.

Trembling with fear, Timm answered question after question before finally they were placed in a car. A pretty young Iranian woman got in with them to act as interpreter. At Timm's request, they drove by the embassy on their way to their hotel, and when she saw it—the walls draped with hateful anti-American propaganda, more mobs of press waiting outside the front gate—she finally broke down. *He's in there*, she thought. *I'm this close. Does he sense that I am here? Have they told him I'm coming?* When the car slowed down before the front gate, more reporters came running over and the driver stepped on the gas to speed away.

They went back late that night with their interpreter without informing anyone. The media mob was gone. Student guards stood with weapons outside as well as inside the front gate at posts formed by stacked sandbags. Their interpreter talked for a few moments with the guards, and after a short wait Nilufar Ebtekar walked out to see them. The chubby, black-clad young woman launched immediately into a rant: "You are here to see the evidence of the plotting and spying your country was doing in Iran . . . your CIA has . . . the Great Satan in 1953 . . . and it was the CIA and SAVAK that tortured and killed . . ." Timm tuned her out. She had heard it all before a hundred times on TV. Standing before this round-faced, diminutive, arrogant yet familiar young woman who was holding her son prisoner, Timm felt all her fear drop away. She felt rage. She was here to see her son. She had nothing whatsoever to do with the things

Ebtekar was going on about. She was a mother from Milwaukee who wanted to visit with her son. Timm started to cry, and then she started to scream at Ebtekar, woman to woman.

"You don't know what it's like to be a mother! What would your mother do if you—you can't be any older than my son is! And you've got a mother someplace. Underneath all that shit that you are wearing there's got to be a human being someplace. You've got a mother. How would she feel if you were locked up in a strange country someplace?"

She called Ebtekar cold and heartless.

"You don't even behave like you're human," she said. "Even these guards with their guns talk to us like real people."

Timm was so furious that she started to turn away. She didn't even know where she was going, she just had to get away from Ebtekar. She made it partway down the sidewalk before her husband caught up to her.

"She wants to talk to you," he said.

When she came back, tears still running down her cheeks, Ebtekar had dropped the hectoring tone. She spoke quietly and soothingly.

"If you want to see your boy we'll have to get a permit," she said. She said that if they met with Sadegh Ghotbzadeh, the foreign minister, and with the president, Abolhassan Bani-Sadr, and got permission, then they could come back and meet with her son. Despite the hour they drove immediately to the foreign ministry, and while the Timms waited in the car McAfee went inside. He returned a short while later with a piece of paper that he said would be all the permission they needed. They drove back to the embassy, where Ebtekar examined the paper and told them to return the next day.

Timm hardly slept that night. The following morning, Monday, April 21, they received a phone call in their hotel room. Several students from the "den of spies" were going to collect them from the hotel, she was told, and McAfee was not allowed to accompany them. This frightened Timm. Ever since she had arrived in Tehran she felt the lawyer was her shield. But she wasn't going to turn back now. At the appointed hour three young Iranians knocked on their door: Ebtekar and two men. Timm begged them to let McAfee come along and cried when they said no.

They were driven to Behest-e-Zahra cemetery, where Timm was instructed to walk among the graves before a battery of TV cameras. There were Iranian women in chadors waiting by some of the graves, and as she approached with the cameras behind her they would drop to their knees and begin to wail. It all appeared to be theater, orchestrated and narrated by Ebtekar, who explained that these were some of the many victims of the Great Satan and the shah, martyred in their revolution.

"We are friends of the American people," Ebtekar told her before the cameras, "but the American people must ask their government to return this criminal to Iran so he can be tried."

Timm got the impression that she was being sized up. They still had not promised to let her see her son. She sat with them for a long time, mostly listening and promising to take their comments and ideas home with her. They told her that they believed Congress ought to investigate and expose the years of American meddling in Iran, and she said that she would advocate that on her return. Finally, driving away from the cemetery, they told her that they had decided to let her see her son for thirty minutes. Timm was told that she and Kevin were not allowed to discuss "politics," and she readily agreed. She was driven to a rear gate of the compound at midafternoon.

She and her husband were left in a littered, dusty room somewhere on the compound, into which came a young bearded man who questioned them at length. He wanted to know where they were born, where they had grown up and gone to school, what jobs they had . . . it went on and on. Whom had they met with in Washington before coming? Did they have any special instructions? Had either ever worked for the United States government? Timm was petrified and answered as best she could. When the man urged her to make statements critical of her country on camera, angry as she was at the government, she refused.

Hermening was blindfolded and led out of the chancery to a car. He was driven in what appeared to be circles around the city for about fifteen minutes before steering back into what he felt certain was the embassy compound. He was taken into a building and up a flight of stairs. When they removed the blindfold he was seated at a dining room table with a flowerpot at the center filled with red flowers around a big microphone.

At the last minute, the man questioning Barbara Timm had refused to let her husband come along. Protesting that decision, she had been escorted down a long, scummy, trash-strewn corridor accompanied by

Ebtekar and two young men walking on either side of her so closely that she could feel their breath on her arms. She was more frightened than she had ever been in her life. Then, as they mounted a flight of stairs and went down another long corridor, with Ebtekar reminding her that there was to be no conversation about politics, nothing about the hostage situation, that she could discuss only family matters, Timm suddenly doubted that she was being taken to see her son at all. What if Ebtekar were just humoring her with these instructions, leading her along to a place where they would shoot her? She started to cry.

They stopped before a door. Ebtekar opened it and there was her Kevin, sitting on a couch, tall, thin, mop-haired, and amazed.

He stood and embraced her. She was weeping and still trembling, with happiness now, and the two just held each other for a long time. Kevin started to cry with her. Eventually they noticed that they were not alone. There were several guards in the room with rifles, as well as Ebtekar, standing before big posters of Khomeini and some with anti-American propaganda.

"Be careful," Hermening whispered to his mother. "There are bugs everywhere."

They sat on the couch next to each other and sipped tea and talked about their family and about sports. Barbara told her son about his younger brothers and sisters and some of his old high school friends. She said Bud Selig, owner of the Milwaukee Brewers, had said that as soon as he got home he could throw out the first ball for a game. Hermening wanted to know more about what was happening in the States regarding their situation, but every time he approached a banned subject Ebtekar would interject to his mother, "You cannot answer that." She was not allowed to tell him about her trip or where she had been in Tehran that day. Seeing that his questions were making his mother nervous, Hermening asked if he could tell her who his roommate was. Ebtekar said no.

Timm didn't let on, but she was shocked at how bad her son looked. He had never suffered acne, or any other skin problem, and now his face had completely erupted in what looked like some kind of rash. He looked pale and sickly.

Hermening was thrilled to see his mother but couldn't get over a feeling of awkwardness about it. Why him? Why was he getting a chance to visit his mom? Did it have to do with his having read that statement on TV at

Christmas? What would the Americans who saw this and read about it think? Would he be seen as collaborating with his captors? What would his fellow hostages think? As they talked—Hermening had to keep looking at his mother and holding her hand to assure himself she was really there—he found himself wishing almost in spite of himself that she had not come. He was worried about her safety, too. What if they didn't let her go?

"Time is up," said Ebtekar, and without ceremony Hermening was pulled up off the couch by the arm, blindfolded, and led from the room.

Timm broke down sobbing. Ebtekar sat next to her and tried to put an arm around her and Timm shoved her away, swore at her, and then sat crying for a long time. Her husband was led in then, and they were made to watch a movie about the revolution, full of grotesque images of the dead, wounded, tortured, and executed. It was horrible. It went on and on, well over an hour.

"When the hell does this end?" Timm asked.

"It never will end," said Ebtekar.

"Oh, Jesus," said Timm.

"Our revolution has not ended and it won't end until all the oppressed people of the world are free with us," said the robed young woman.

Unlike the revolution, the film did eventually end. Afterward they were led to a room where a feast had been prepared for them, steaks, vegetables, potatoes, and salad. Timm said she wasn't hungry, but Ebtekar and the others insisted that they eat.

She sat and picked at the food while her Iranian hosts stood around and watched.

"Is this not a delicious meal?" they kept asking.

The Timms nodded and ate and tried to appear thankful enough to satisfy them.

"This is a fine meal," Timm said finally. "Now I'd like to just get back to the United States."

"You can go back and let your people know that this is what the hostages are eating every day," said Ebtekar.

Ken Timm called her a liar, which did not seem to startle or bother Ebtekar. It was dark when they were finally led from the compound. They were handed blindfolds and instructed to tie them on, but once in the car the driver told them they didn't have to do so.

"Just put your heads down in your laps," he said.

They were driven away hunched over in the backseat. After a few minutes of driving they were told they could sit up again. At their hotel a mob of reporters was waiting with cameras, and they were filmed as they left the car and entered the lobby. Back upstairs, McAfee wanted them to return to the lobby to answer questions, but Timm refused. She had had enough. But McAfee waited until she cooled down and then led her downstairs. She was worried about saying anything that might prevent them from going home, but before the cameras she seemed composed and happy. In answer to one question, she said she would go home and work for a peaceful settlement of the standoff. She said that she had found her son to be "in excellent health and very, very happy to see me. He was surprised and overjoyed that I had traveled across the globe to be with him."

What was the reunion like?

"We never quit holding hands. There was a lot of hugging, a lot of touching. I kept telling him how strong he was, and he kept telling me how strong I was. He says he has not lost faith. He said, 'I've become a better person and a stronger person.' I told him I had come to give him strength and faith."

Timm portrayed the six hours inside the embassy as a happy social occasion. She and the militant students had "talked and talked and talked. I still can't understand or justify an embassy being taken over. But I had to live with one of two choices, either going on hating these people and having that destroy our family or trying to understand these people."

The captors showed her and her husband "nothing but the best of hospitality. I found human beings. . . . The government has said these people are brainwashed. I really don't know what that means, but I can't agree. What would be the sign?"

Hermening returned to his chancery room in a daze.

"You're not going to believe this," he told Golacinski.

"What?"

"I just saw my mother."

"What do you mean you saw your mother?"

"I just met with my mother."

They talked for hours, with Hermening reconstructing the dialogue as best he could. Golacinski kept pressing for more details—"Try to remember," he said. "Try to remember. What did she say?"—until it dawned on him that his young friend was embarrassed. He realized that Hermening felt bad for him and for Miele.

As she waited the next few days in a Tehran hotel for her flight home on Friday, Barbara Timm prayed that her son would be allowed to join her. She had played along with his captors in every way she could, nodding sympathetically to their stories of the abusive shah and the evil designs her country had on theirs.

Inside the chancery, the guards fed the same hope in Hermening. Several days after the meeting the guards brought him a box of photos and long letters from just about everyone in his family. One of his guards even told him it might happen. Hermening had mixed feelings. There was no question that he would go if he got the chance, but he wondered if it might brand him for life as a "mama's boy." He was prepared to live with that.

"If you let me go, I'll make sure that the American public hears about what the shah did," he promised.

He closed his eyes Thursday night nursing hope that tomorrow might be the day of his release.

Bruce Laingen composed a secret letter for his colleagues in Washington in mid-April and passed it to the Swiss emissary who visited him on occasion. It expressed his growing sense that the crisis was at a hopeless impasse, and while it was not Laingen's intent, it was received in the White House as a request from the hostage action:

> We welcome steps announced by the president this past week [the expulsion of Iranian diplomats, among other sanctions]. They can only succeed if they in fact hurt and if the prospect for further hurt looks real to those who seek to guide and influence the way the Majlis handles this issue. It is vital that we have the maximum support of our allies and friends. . . . [Iran] can now only hope to limit the damage that is being done to its own vital interests . . . that damage will increase each additional day the hostages were held.

The imprisoned chargé had in mind economic and political sanctions, not a military mission, but Carter would see in those words a call to arms.

Howland became convinced that there would be a rescue attempt. He knew that if commandos came in, they would come through either doors or windows, loud and fast. He knew they would shoot anyone who didn't comply.

"If some guys come bursting through the windows, don't get up and start yelling," he told Laingen and Tomseth. "Just do exactly what they tell you. Because they're going to pick you up and physically carry you out. They will not let you walk. They will physically carry you."

If the raiders came in downstairs, they would have to fight their way up the stairs, which would give the guards upstairs time to shoot them, so Howland started sleeping in the nude again, figuring the split-second advantage it gave him would help. He found a heavy stick that he put under his mattress. He put it next to the door every night, figuring he could jump the first guard to come through. He knew their pistols could fire only one round, so all he had to do was make a gunman miss that first shot.

The evening of April 24 was clear, and the view out the windows of the Foreign Ministry was quite beautiful. Laingen watched the mountains at sunset, admiring the blush of bright green spring growth in the gardens below. He continued watching until the Iranian sky faded into darkness.

4

WELCOME TO
WORLD WAR THREE

Through that falling darkness a lone plane was moving fast and low toward Iran over the dark waters of the Gulf of Oman. It was a big, four-propeller U.S. Air Force workhorse, a C-130 Hercules, painted in a mottled black and green camouflage that made it all but invisible against the black water and night sky. It flew with no lights. Inside, in the eerie red glow of the plane's blackout lamps, seventy-four men struggled to get comfortable in a cramped, unaccommodating space. Only the plane's usual eleven-man crew had assigned seats; the others sprawled on and around a jeep, five motorcycles, and two long sheets of heavy aluminum—which would be placed under the plane's tires if it became stuck in desert sand—and a bulky portable guidance system that would help the planes and helicopters to home in on Desert One. It had taken all the ingenuity of the plane's loadmaster to squeeze it all in. As they had been working on it, one of the air force crewmen had wondered aloud, "With all this added weight, I hope we can get off the ground," which had set off the already edgy Colonel Beckwith like a firecracker. He had to be reassured by the loadmaster that the excess cargo had been carefully weighed and was within the plane's limits. The Hercules was designed primarily to carry sixty-four paratroopers, with webbing on the sides and fold-out aluminum seats, but even those spare comforts had been stripped to make more room. The men had spread mattresses on the steel floor of the fuselage, which got frigid once airborne. Some were napping on their gear. There was the vaguely sweet smell of fuel and, other than the drone of four big propellers, mostly silence.

Just after dark they moved in over the coast of Iran at two hundred and fifty feet, well below radar, and then began a gradual ascent to five thousand feet. They were still flying dangerously low at that altitude, because the land rose up abruptly in row after row of jagged ridges—the Zagros Mountains, which looked jet black in the gray-green tints of the pilots' night-vision goggles. The plane's terrain-hugging radar was so sensitive that, even though they were safely above the peaks, the highest ridges always triggered the loud, disconcerting horn of its warning system. The plane's copilot kept one finger poised over the override button to silence it.

Since the decision to fly into Iran on fixed-wing transports instead of the helicopters, Beckwith had added still more men to Eagle Claw, as the rescue mission was now code-named, most notably a half dozen soldiers from the First Battalion (Ranger) 75th Infantry out of Fort Benning. They would block off both ends of the dirt road that angled through Desert One and man Red-eye missile launchers to protect the force on the first night in case it was discovered and attacked from the air. The rangers, who would fly out of Iran when all the planes and choppers departed, would be commanded by Wade Ishimoto, a Delta captain who worked the unit's intelligence division. Then there was the separate thirteen-man army special forces team that would assault the Foreign Ministry to free Bruce Laingen, Victor Tomseth, and Mike Howland. Also on Beckwith's lead plane was John Carney, the air force major who was making his second secret flight into Iran; he would command a small air force combat control team that would orchestrate the complex maneuvers at the impromptu airfield. Some of these men sat on and around the jeep. One of Delta's team leaders, the tall Texan Logan Fitch, who had never believed this day would come, stood in the rear with Carney and the plane's loadmaster, who informed them when they entered Iranian airspace. Fitch told one of his men, "Pass the word. We're in Iran." It didn't get much of a response. If there was one character trait these men shared, it was professional calm. After six months of practice runs this method of deployment had become so routine that it took effort to remember that this time it was for real. Their attitude for the most part was, *It's about goddamn time.*

They had taken off at dusk from the tiny island of Masirah, off the coast of Oman at the southeastern tip of the Arabian peninsula. One hour behind them would come five more C-130s, one carrying most of the remainder of Beckwith's assault force, which now numbered one hundred and thirty-two men, and four "bladder planes," each equipped with two gigantic rubber balloons filled with fuel, carrying a total of eighteen thousand gallons. One of the four bladder planes was specially outfitted for eavesdropping and communications and was capable of listening in on Iranian telecommunications.

Days earlier the entire force had flown to an abandoned Soviet airstrip in Wadi Kena, Egypt, on big air force transports. His big mission under way, Beckwith was in full-bore command mode; abrupt, decisive, and aggressively irritable.

They spent a few days at the Egyptian airstrip, which had been amply outfitted for their arrival. There were two refrigerators and pallets full of beer and soda. Much beer was consumed, the first time in any of the soldiers' memories that they had been supplied free drinks by the U.S. Army. When the refrigerators were finally emptied of beer, they were stocked with blood.

Waiting there, the men were given a new CIA briefing about the location of the hostages in the compound. The agency claimed that, by chance, a cook who had been working there all these months had left the country and happened to sit on a plane next to a CIA officer . . . none of the men believed it. Many of the men suspected that a Red Cross visit to the embassy ten days earlier had included a CIA agent. No matter how obtained, the information was specific and critically useful. A larger number of the hostages were in the chancery now than had been thought, the bulk of them on the first floor but small numbers on the top floor and basement. Delta learned which hostages were in which rooms, that there were just sixteen guards in the building, and where the guards were usually positioned at night. The other hostages were in the Mushroom Inn and ambassador's house, but not as many as had been thought. There were fifty guards posted on the surrounding grounds. Most of the information corresponded with what Delta had learned on its own, but it was much more detailed. The team leaders made some adjustments, assigning more men to Fitch's White Element, which would take down the chancery.

On the afternoon of the mission the shaggy-haired, unshaven force assembled in a warehouse, where Major Jerry Boykin had offered a prayer. Tall, lean, with a long dark beard, he stood at a podium before a plug box where electrical wires intersected to form a big cross on the wall. Behind him, taped to the wall, was a poster-sized sheet containing photographs of their countrymen held hostage. Boykin chose a passage from the First Book of Samuel about the slaying of Goliath—the small American force could see itself as the underdog on this bold thrust into the heart of Iran.

"And David put his hand in his bag, and took thence a stone, and slang it, and smote the Philistine in the forehead, that the stone sunk into his forehead; and he fell on his face to the earth. So David prevailed over the Philistine with a sling and with a stone ..." Then Bucky Burruss, with a deep, commanding baritone, led the men in singing "God Bless America." The chorus of that American folk anthem rang stirringly off the distant hangar's bare walls.

They had then flown to Masirah, where they hunkered in tents through a bright and broiling afternoon, fighting off large stinging flies and waiting impatiently for dusk. They had no replacements, so they were forbidden from playing their favorite game, "combat soccer," a full-contact no-rules version of the universal sport.

It would be a short hop over the gulf and then a four-hour flight to Desert One, crossing the southern border in darkness and hugging the mountain and desert terrain for seven hundred miles to avoid being detected by radar. The route had been calculated to exploit gaps in Iran's coastal defenses and to avoid passing over military bases and populated areas. The planes were equipped with the air force's most sophisticated ground-hugging, "terrain-avoidance" gear and navigation systems. Major Wayne Long, Delta's intelligence officer, was at a console in the front of the telecommunications bird with a National Security Agency linguist, who was monitoring Iranian telecommunications for any sign that the aircraft had been discovered and the mission compromised. There was none.

Not long after the lead plane departed Masirah, eight RH-53D Sea Stallion helicopters left the *Nimitz* and moved out over the Arabian Sea in order to reach landfall shortly after sunset. The choppers flew a different route, crossing into Iran between the towns of Jask and Konarak and flying even closer to the ground than the planes. Word of the successful launch reached the lead plane—"Eight off the deck"—as especially welcome news because they had expected only seven. Earlier reports had indicated that the eighth was having mechanical problems. Eight widened the margin of error. They expected breakdowns. In their many rehearsals they had determined that six were essential for carrying all the men and equipment from Desert One to the two hide sites. The load was finely calibrated; every assaulter had an assigned limit and was weighed to make sure he met it. They wouldn't need all six to haul the hostages and assaulters from the stadium the next night—as few as two would do in a pinch—but they expected some of the aircraft that made it all the way to the hide sites to fail the next morning. If seven was enough, eight provided comfort.

The final decision to launch had come only after Dick Meadows, Delta's advance man, broadcast a signal from Tehran earlier that day that all was ready. He had returned to the city in his disguise as an Irish businessman and met up with "Fred," his Iranian-American guide and translator—the same young airman volunteer who had helped the CIA agent code-named "Bob,"—and with two American soldiers who had entered Iran posing as businessmen, one Irish and the other German. They had spent that day personally inspecting all of the various hide sites: the embassy, the Foreign Ministry, and the soccer stadium.

As the lead plane pushed on well into Iran, Major Burruss, Beckwith's deputy, was on the second C-130, sprawled on a mattress near the front of the plane beside Major Pete Schoomaker, leader of the Red Element. Burruss was still somewhat startled to find himself on the actual mission, although there was still no telling if they were going through with it. One of the things President Carter had insisted upon was the option to call off the raid right up to the last minute, right up to the moment they stormed the embassy walls. A satellite radio and relay system at Wadi Kena had been put in place to make sure they could get real-time instructions from Washington. Another presidential directive concerned the use of nonlethal riot control agents. Given that the shah's occasionally violent methods against crowds during the revolution were now exhibit A in Iran's human rights case against the former regime and America, Carter was understandably concerned about killing Iranians, so he had insisted that if a hostile mob formed during the raid that Delta first attempt to control it without shooting people. Burruss could appreciate the political logic, but from a practical standpoint he considered it ridiculous. He and his men were going to lay siege to a guarded compound in the middle of a city of more than five million people, most of them presumed to be aggressively hostile. It was unbelievably risky; everyone on the mission knew there was a very good chance they would never get home alive. And Carter had the idea that this desperately tiny, daring, vastly outnumbered force was first going to try holding off the city with methods of nonviolent crowd control? Burruss understood where the president was coming from on this, but with their hides so nakedly on the line, shouldn't they be free to decide how best to defend themselves? He had complained about the requirement to General Jones, who said he would look into it, but the answer had come back, "No, the president insists." So Burruss had made his own peace with the requirement. He had with him one tear gas grenade, one, which he intended to throw as soon as necessary and then use its smoke as a marker to call in devastatingly lethal 40mm AC-130 gunship fire.

Burruss was so keenly aware of the risks on this mission that he had a kind of admiration for the navy pilot who had chickened out back in November, the one Beckwith had wanted court-martialed. The man had been kept isolated on an aircraft carrier ever since. He figured it took a special kind of courage to admit you were that afraid, even when the circumstances clearly warranted fear. Burruss was not built that way. Delta was made up of men who would have felt crushed not to be included on this mission, precisely because it was so hazardous. They were ambitious for glory. They had volunteered to serve with Beckwith and had undergone the hardships and trials of the selection process so that they would be included on improbable exploits like this. Men read about wildly heroic feats in history and sometimes wished they had been alive to take part, and here was such a moment, now, without question. If they pulled it off, it would go down as one of the boldest maneuvers in military history. All over America their feat would be cheered in the streets.

The fact that their countrymen would not know who they were made it all the more appealing. It made the heroism pure. *They* would not be celebrated, only their achievement. None of these men would be in the ticker-tape parades or sitting down for interviews on national TV or have their pictures on the covers of magazines, nor would they be cashing in on fat book contracts. They were quiet professionals. In a world of brag and hype they embodied substance. They would come home and after a few days off go right back to work. Of course, within their own world, they would become legends. For the rest of their lives, behind them knowing soldiers would whisper, "He was on Eagle Claw." That was honor worth having.

Some men lived for such chances. Burruss was a patriot, first, a man steeped in the rich military history of his native Tidewater, Virginia, and a man blessed with the kind of physical courage and swagger to try anything. As a boy he had talked his cousin into rowing with him in a skiff one and a half miles across the York River to reenact Alexander Hamilton's successful storming of Redoubt Number Ten at the Yorktown battlefield, then and now a national park. In broad daylight the two boys stormed and retook the fortification, hauled down the vintage British flag, and rowed it back across the river to hang on Burruss's bedroom wall. He was a rangy, cheerful man with long arms and big hands and an elongated, bony frame, a long straight nose, a mouth that was usually open, and a tendency toward physical belligerence when drunk. Burruss possessed a kind of swagger and playfulness that suggested, despite his size and athleticism, that his most powerful asset was his wit. He had not bothered like some of the men to dye his straight sandy hair, which hung down well over both ears. When they got to Tehran, *if* they got there, one of his jobs was to coordinate air support from the press box of the soccer stadium. The plan called for him to be one of the last men to leave the stadium, and he had accepted the likelihood that it was where he would die. There wouldn't be enough helicopters. There were just too many ways for them to fail. He had fought in Vietnam and knew both the beauty and the fragility of those machines. If they managed to get the required six off the ground at Desert One to the hiding places, he felt sure that at least one or two of them wouldn't restart the next night, and when all hell broke loose in Tehran there was a good chance of losing one or more of those that could fly. Even if the machines had been more reliable, like the other Delta commanders Burruss was wary of the marines piloting them; he was not sure they possessed the calm fatalism that defined this kind of dead-end special ops. A reluctant pilot meant a marginal machine was as good as grounded. At the end of this informed calculation was the probability that they would get only one or two helos into the stadium. If they were fuel-light, that meant they would be able to get all of the hostages aboard, along with a small escort force, but that would leave him and a significant portion of his men behind in the soccer stadium. He and the other men were carrying thousands of dollars worth of cash, most of it in newly minted Iranian rials, and fake passports stamped with fake visas. Burruss had paid strict attention to the E&E (Escape and Evade) classes that taught the men how to hotwire cars. He had memorized several escape routes out of Tehran. That was the plan. If they were left behind, they would commandeer vehicles and drive like hell toward the border of either Turkey or Afghanistan, a journey of three to four hundred miles, fighting their way out if necessary, possibly calling for air support. The men took this desperate possibility so seriously they had taken the trouble to locate jewelry stores on their way out of the city, where they could grab valuables with which to help bribe their way past roadblocks and border crossings. This could work, but it involved more wishful thinking than a realist like Burruss could summon. In his mind, the more likely scenario was a bloody last stand inside the stadium, where they would take a large number of Iranians with them into the next world. He and his wife had dined with Beckwith and his wife and a few of the other Delta commanders and their wives the night before they departed. Most of them, Beckwith included, had written death letters to be delivered to their spouses in the event they were killed. They were going all the way with this, to victory or to Valhalla.

The level of risk worried the unit commanders, who were concerned that such a generous prospect of not returning might compel men to tell their wives or girlfriends what they were going off to do. Delta Sergeant Major Dave Cheney had broached the sensitive topic with some of his men shortly before they left Fort Bragg.

"What are you guys telling your wives and girlfriends?" he asked.

"Depends," said Phil Hanson, one of the shooters.

"Depends on what?" Cheney asked.

"Depends on whether she's giving me any drawers. If she's giving me drawers, I'll tell her anything."

They were by appearance a motley, deliberately nonmilitary-looking bunch of young men; in fact, they looked a lot like the students who had seized the embassy. Most were just a few years older than the hostage takers. They had long hair and had grown mustaches and beards or were just unshaven. The loose-fitting, many-pocketed field jackets they wore, dyed black, were just like the ones favored by young men in Iran. Many with fair hair had dyed it dark brown or black, figuring that might nudge the odds at least minutely in their direction if they were forced to fight their way out of Iran. Under the Geneva Convention, soldiers (as opposed to spies) must enter combat in uniform, so for the occasion the men all wore matching black knit caps and had an American flag on their jacket sleeve that could be covered by a small black Velcro patch. On the streets of

Tehran the flag would invite trouble, but inside the embassy compound it would reassure the hostages that they weren't just being kidnapped by some rival Iranian faction. They wore faded blue jeans and combat boots, and beneath the jacket some wore armored vests. Much of their gear was improvised. They had sewn additional pockets inside the jackets to carry weapons, ammo, and water. Most of the men carried small MP-5 submachine guns with silencers, sidearms, grenades, and various explosive devices. Burruss had a .45, although he wasn't sure why he'd bothered. He wasn't on any of the teams taking down buildings, and if a situation arose where he'd have to use it, he doubted a handgun would save him. Beckwith had insisted on a ranger tradition: all the men carried a length of rope wrapped around their waist and clips, in case the need arose to rappel. The men who were to guard the perimeter carried M-60 machine guns and some light antitank weapons. Beckwith himself had the rapelling rope and clips and carried a pistol. With his white stubble, dangling cigarette or cigar, and wild eyes under thick dark eyebrows, he looked like a dangerous vagrant. Before leaving Masirah, the men had been joking about which actors would portray them in the movie version of the raid, and they decided that the hillbilly actor Slim Pickens, who had ridden a nuclear weapon kamikazi-like into doomsday waving his cowboy hat and hallooing in Stanley Kubrick's *Dr. Strangelove,* would be the perfect choice for the colonel.

With Delta on the planes was an assortment of Farsi-speaking volunteers from various branches of the American military (all of them Iranian-American) and two former Iranian generals. A onetime SAVAK agent who had trained with the group, and who had boasted for months of his eagerness to shoot a few Khomeini fanatics, had gotten cold feet at the last minute. The Farsi-speaking American soldiers would drive the trucks and vans that would carry the assaulters through Tehran to the embassy for the next night's raid, and the former generals were there to try to talk their way through any contacts with the Iranian military. In such instances, they would attempt to pass themselves off as a secret Iranian force on a training exercise. In fact, the contingency did not arise. Even though the second formation of planes was spotted from the ground as it moved over the coast, and a question about it was broadcast to a military station, the Iranian self-defense forces concluded without inquiring that the planes were Iranian. If the nation was alert to the possibility of an American invasion, they certainly wouldn't expect it to arrive in a small low-flying formation of propeller-driven planes.

As the lead plane closed in on the desert landing site, its pilots noted curious milky patches in the night sky. They flew through one that appeared to be just haze, not even substantial enough to interfere with the downward-looking radar. They approached a second one as they got closer to the landing site and it was noticed by John Carney, who had come into the cockpit to be ready to activate the landing lights he had buried on his trip weeks earlier. One of the pilots asked him, "What do you make of that stuff out there?"

He looked through the copilot's window.

"You're in a *haboob*," he said.

The men in the cockpit laughed at the word.

"No, we're flying through suspended dust," Carney explained. "The Iranians call it a *haboob*."

He had heard about it from the CIA pilots who had flown him in earlier. Shifting air pressure frequently forced the especially fine desert sand straight up thousands of feet, where sometimes it hung like a vertical cloud for hours. It was just a desert curiosity. The dust clouds were too insubstantial to cause a problem for the planes, but Air Force Colonel James H. Kyle, the air commander whose responsibility included all the airborne aspects of the mission, knew that the *haboob* would create much bigger problems for a helicopter. He noticed that the temperature inside the plane went up significantly when they were passing through them. He advised the copilot to radio "Red Barn," the command center at Wadi Kena, and have them warn the trailing helicopter formation. The chopper pilots might want to break formation or fly higher to avoid the stuff. This second patch took them about thirty minutes to fly through, which meant that it extended for about one hundred miles.

As the lead C-130 approached the landing area, Carney activated his buried infrared runway lights by pressing the button of his garage-door opener. The lights came on below, but the plane's newfangled FLIR (Forward Looking Infrared Radar) detected something on the road, which proved to be a truck hurtling along the dirt road that ran through the landing site, so the pilots passed over the spot and then circled back around.

On the second pass the stretch of desert was clear. They circled around for a third time and touched down—Fitch was amazed by how smoothly. The plane coasted to a stop, and when the back ramp was lowered Ishimoto and the rangers roared off in the jeep and motorcycle to give chase to the truck; word that an American plane had landed in the desert, relayed promptly to the right people, could defeat the whole effort. They were followed by Carney and his men, who would help guide in the other Hercules formation and the choppers.

One of the first things Carney noticed, stepping off the ramp, was that the hard-packed surface of three weeks prior was now coated with a layer of feathery sand, the consistency of baby powder, ankle deep in some places. It made it more difficult to taxi the planes, and the backwash from the propellers kicked up a serious dust storm, but it also accounted for the extraordinary softness of their landing.

Fitch followed with his men, walking down the ramp and stepping into a cauldron of noise and dust. His team had nothing to do at Desert One except wait to offload camouflage netting and equipment from the second C-130, which had not yet arrived, and then board helicopters for the short trip to the hiding place. The big plane's propellers were still roaring and kicked up the powdery desert floor. Fitch raised his arm to cover his eyes and face, and as he turned to his right he was shocked to see, coming toward him, a bus! Out of nowhere. The odds that the plane would intersect with both a truck and a bus past midnight on such a lonely, isolated, little-used dirt road were vanishing, but there it was, a big Mercedes passenger bus lit up like midday inside, its roof piled with luggage and filled with more than forty astonished Iranian passengers, honoring an absolute law of military operations, the certainty of the unexpected.

Then, suddenly, the night desert flashed as bright as daylight and shook with an explosion. In the near distance, a giant ball of flame rose high into the darkness. One of the pursuing rangers had fired an anti-tank weapon at the fleeing truck, which turned out to have been loaded with fuel. The thing went up like a miniature sun and kept on burning brightly. Their clandestine rendezvous spot, this patch of desert in the middle of nowhere, was spotlit like Friday night football back in Texas. The men with night vision removed their goggles. It appeared as though at least one of the men in the truck's front cab had bailed out in time, climbed into a trailing pickup truck, and escaped at high speed. A ranger on the motorcycle gave chase but couldn't catch it. The truck was a ball of fire; no one could get close enough to see if anyone had been caught inside.

In this sudden brightness the bus now rolled to a stop with a leaking radiator and a flat right front tire. Rangers had fired their weapons to disable it. Fitch, still confused, sent machine-gun teams to either side of the stalled, steaming vehicle and led a group of his men to the front. There were already rangers aboard.

"What the hell is going on?" Fitch asked a sergeant as he mounted the steps.

"I'm trying to get these people off the bus, but they won't move," he said. The passengers were obviously astonished. "Should I fire a shot over their heads?" the sergeant asked.

"No," said Fitch. "Why don't you just get off the bus and I'll get my people in here."

One of Delta's specialties was handling hostages, herding them, searching them, securing them. In the next few minutes, Fitch's men firmly and efficiently emptied the bus, searched the passengers for weapons, and deposited them on the powdery sand. They then stripped the baggage off the top of the bus, searched it, and found no weapons. The passengers appeared to be poor Iranians, simply traveling through the night from Yazd to Tabas. The bus was decorated with placards and posters of Khomeini. They had rolled into the wrong place at the wrong time. One of them spoke English and recognized the soldiers as Americans.

"It's about time," he said. He kept asking questions, which no one answered.

"How's it going, Joe? Where are you from?" he asked Captain E. K. Smith. "I'm from Pittsburgh."

They were all instructed in Farsi to remain silent, without effect. Most of the passengers were women, all of them wearing chadors and wailing eerily in their distress. Sergeant Eric Haney had trouble silencing one of the few young men among them, who insisted on loudly whispering to the others despite even their apparent desire for him to shut up. Haney put the muzzle of his automatic rifle under the man's nose and repeated, in Farsi, for him to be silent. But soon the offender was whispering again, so

Haney roughly put the muzzle of his weapon in his ear and dragged him away from the group. Fearing he was being taken off to be shot, the young man began crying and begging, holding both hands up beseechingly. Haney sat him down on the road a good distance from the others and left him there, whimpering and praying.

The question of what to do with the bus passengers was relayed all the way to the White House, where it was late afternoon. The president and his staff were deliberately going through motions of a typical workday, secretly hanging on every update from the desert. The secret had held, but just barely. The tenacious *Los Angeles Times* bureau chief Jack Nelson had sensed something serious afoot and had called Powell two days earlier to ask about it. He said he had heard that the president was about to do something that might "involve us in a war."

"You people aren't really thinking about doing anything drastic like launching a rescue mission are you?" he had asked Powell directly. The press secretary swallowed hard and lied.

"If and when we are forced to move militarily, I suspect it will be something like a blockade," Powell said. "But that decision is still a step or two down the road."

Nelson accepted Powell's word. He wrote a story citing high-level White House sources stating that military action was not pending, and that a rescue attempt was entirely impractical. It had run yesterday.

Brzezinski relayed the unexpected problem of the bus to the president, and Carter agreed that the only thing to do was to fly all the Iranians out that night on one of the C-130s, and then return them to Iran when the mission was complete. The decision was conveyed to Beckwith, who now fretted about which plane to choose. One of the Iranian generals who had flown in with them had evidently discarded his weapon, probably out of fear—if he were captured with a weapon, he would have had a harder time claiming that he had been held hostage by these Americans. Beckwith didn't want to put a crowd of kidnapped Iranians on a plane that had a loose handgun. Search parties were organized to find the general's nickel-plated revolver, without success.

The passengers had been set down on the right side of the bus, so Fitch wandered around the left side to take a look and found another Iranian hiding beside the front wheel. Fitch approached him and shouted for him to stand, and when the man didn't move Fitch fired a shot into the ground. This got him on his feet and he made a move as if to run away, so Fitch swung his weapon and clobbered him in the head with its butt. In the process, the Delta squadron commander accidentally raked the gun sight over his own nose and opened a deep cut, which in the excitement of the moment he neither felt nor noticed. Fitch led the stunned man, who turned out to be the assistant driver, back around to the others.

He had been on the ground for only a few minutes and already the veteran soldier was bleeding, coated with dust, and amazed. Three vehicles? This patch of desert suddenly seemed like a major thoroughfare.

Carney and his men better marked the two parallel runways for the following planes and set up the portable guidance device. Shortly before midnight things grew louder and busier as the second C-130 roared in for a landing, right on schedule. It taxied to a stop. Behind it came the four tankers. As Burruss and his men came down the lowered ramp of the first of these planes, they gaped at the ball of flame, the bus, and the passengers.

"Welcome to World War Three!" greeted Fitch.

Burruss looked at the bleeding face of his friend and said, "What the hell is going on?"

For the first time Fitch noticed that he was cut. He explained, shouting over the noise of all the planes. It was hot and the desert air now smelled of burning gasoline. No one seemed concerned. Their makeshift airport was lit up a lot more than they would have liked, but these were veteran soldiers; they knew operations like this went smoothly only in briefings and on paper. In a way, it felt good to have encountered the unexpected right at the outset, and coped with it.

"I think we've got everything under control," Fitch told Burruss. They would have to take their chances with the men in the fleeing pickup, who they assumed, given the time of night and method of transport, to have been smuggling gasoline. It didn't seem likely that they would go to the police, and if they did, what sense would be made of their story? A plane landed in the desert and attacked them? Even if it was investigated, the effort would take the better part of a day, at least, and by then it would be too late to interfere with the mission.

Desert One was now looking more like an airport, and Carney's men were busy directing traffic, preparing for the arrival of the helicopters.

Shortly after midnight, all four bladder birds were parked and positioned. The communications plane stayed, but the two lead planes, having delivered their cargo, took off for their rendezvous with the airborne tankers and the return flight to Masirah.

The unloading had gone pretty much as planned. The second C-130 had landed a few thousand feet farther off the landing zone than expected, so the job of hauling the camouflage netting from it was a correspondingly bigger job. The netting would be draped over the helicopters at the hide site at daylight. It was not an especially warm night in the desert, but all the men were overdressed, wearing layers of clothing and body armor, and they were sweating heavily with exertion. Moving through the loose sand made it an even more difficult task. The air force crews struggled to unfurl hundreds of pounds of hoses from the parked tankers, positioning them to receive the choppers. The bus had to be moved, so all the passengers were herded back on and it was repositioned.

"What is the status of the choppers?" Beckwith asked the commanders at Wadi Kena.

The command station at Masirah responded by relaying a request from the lead chopper for conditions at Desert One.

"Visibility five miles with negative surface winds," reported Colonel Kyle, who was with Beckwith in the desert.

Then they heard from the lead chopper. "Fifty minutes out and low on fuel."

It was a satisfying moment. The fuel crews had practiced the routine like pit crews at the Indy 500, and had the whole exercise down so well that it took only ten minutes to refill a landed chopper and send it on its way. Everything was behind schedule, however, which meant that even if the refueling and loading operations were done perfectly, the choppers would not arrive at the two hide sites before the crack of dawn. That posed only a small risk. The sites were in mountains outside the city, the choppers had been painted the same colors as Iranian army choppers, and it would still not be full daylight when they arrived. Still, if they didn't land soon, they would be arriving at the hiding places in daylight. Burruss asked one of his men to check their maps for a gully or natural depression where they might be able to sit the choppers short of the planned hide site.

There was nothing to do then but wait. Most of the force had been on the ground for more than two hours. The sandstorms stirred by the aircraft whipped around the men and stung their faces, making it difficult to see. The choppers were late and getting later. They had been late in every one of the rehearsals, too, so no one was surprised.

5

WHAT THE HELL IS THIS?

Already the eight Sea Stallions had become six.

The original formation of eight had crossed into Iran flying at two hundred feet, and then moved down to one hundred feet. They were just behind the planes, as scheduled. When they had departed the *Nimitz,* more than five thousand crew members had come on deck to salute them. It had been deeply moving. On the deck of the carrier, with the last light of the dying day splayed behind it in the direction of faraway home, thousands of American sailors stood at attention, saluting the courage and skill of these soldiers off to rescue their countrymen. Major Jim Schaefer, in the third Sea Stallion to launch, had tears in his eyes.

Their approach over water was right on target. As they crossed Iran's coast, several of the marine crews had spotted the single lead Hercules overhead moving at twice their airspeed. Two of the choppers were having difficulty with their navigation equipment, but flying that close to the ground they could steer by landmarks and by staying with the formation. They were not allowed to communicate by radio, lest they be overheard by Iranian defenses, but they had practiced flashing lights as signals; a quick one, two meant that there was a problem, and then the second sequence of lights indicated the nature of the problem. They flew in a staggered line of four pairs. Not long after crossing into Iran the marine crews spotted part of the trailing formation of C-130s, which confirmed they were heading the right way. Lieutenant Colonel Ed Seiffert, the flight leader and pilot of the lead chopper, felt relaxed enough to take a break and eat his packed lunch.

The formation made it only one hundred and forty miles into Iran, however, before one of the choppers had trouble. A warning light came on in the cockpit of the sixth in formation indicating that one of the blades had been hit by something or had cracked, a potentially fatal problem. The pilot immediately landed, followed by another, the trailing chopper, and after determining that one rotor blade was in fact cracked badly, they abandoned the aircraft, removing all of the classified documents inside and climbing into helo eight, flown by Captain Jimmy Linderman. It lifted off, gave chase, and eventually caught up with the others.

As they burned off fuel, the choppers picked up speed. They were closing in on Desert One faster and faster, 120 knots and accelerating. About two hundred miles into Iran they saw before them what looked like a wall of talcum powder. They flew right into it. Seiffert realized it was suspended dust when he tasted it and felt it in his teeth. If it was penetrating his cockpit, it was penetrating his engines. The temperature inside rose to one hundred degrees. But before it became a problem, the cloud vanished as suddenly as it had appeared. They had flown right through it.

Looming ahead was the second, much larger *haboob,* but Seiffert didn't know it. Kyle's warning had not been relayed; radio blackout conditions and the necessity for transmitting everything in code had defeated the C-130 flight crews' efforts, that and the assumption that the hazy patches did not pose a severe problem.

This may have been the most serious miscalculation of the night, because the formation passed into the second cloud assuming that it would dissipate as quickly as the first. This one grew thicker and thicker, and soon Seiffert could no longer see the other choppers in the formation or on the ground. The choppers had to turn on their outside red safety lights, and off in the haze there were now indistinct halos of red strung out at varying distances. When the fuzzy beacons themselves vanished, Seiffert and his wingman made a U-turn, flew back out of the cloud, and landed. None of the other five choppers had seen them go down. Seiffert had hoped they would all follow him down to confer and decide on a strategy. Now he had no choice but to take off and wade back into the soup trying to catch up.

Seiffert's manuever had placed Schaefer in the lead position. One moment Seiffert's aircraft had been in front of him, and the next moment it was gone. One by one, the indistinct red suns in the milky haze had grown dimmer and dimmer and then they were gone. *How could I lose them?* Schaefer thought. He could see nothing and he heard nothing but the sounds of his own engines. All around was a smothering cloak of whiteness. He executed a "lost plane" maneuver, turning fifteen degrees off course for a few minutes, and then turning back on course, hoping to pick up the formation again. Even as low as two hundred feet he could not see the ground.

"Is this fog?" he asked his crew.

His crew chief said, "Lick your finger and stick it out the window." He did. When he pulled his hand in, it was covered with white dust. "What the hell is this?" he said.

He climbed to one thousand feet and was still in the cloud. Inside the chopper it was hot and getting hotter. They descended, this time below two hundred feet. Schaefer could see the ground only intermittently. For three hours they flew like this on instruments, a series of small blue panels alongside the dials. In training for instrument flying, the pilots always flew in teams, with one aircraft blacked out and the other not. And there was always the option, when things got hairy, of removing the blackout screens. Now Schaefer had nothing to go on but the glowing blue panels, and his faith was being sorely tested. The cockpit was overheated and the men in it were both hot and increasingly tense.

"Is there anything in front of us?" Schaefer asked his copilot, Les Petty.

"Well, there's a six-thousand-foot mountain in front of us," he said.

"How soon?" asked Schaefer.

"I don't trust the machine," said Petty, "and I don't trust my map. I ain't seen the ground in three hours. I'd say right now."

So they started to climb. They climbed to eight thousand feet, and abruptly the dust cloud broke. Inside the chopper it was suddenly very cold. Off to one side, Schaefer saw the peak of a mountain.

"Good job, Les," he said. "I love you."

Desert One was still about an hour away, so they plunged right back into the *haboob*. This time, Schaefer leveled off at six hundred feet. He didn't know it, but the remaining six choppers were doing the same. The lack of visibility made the crews woozy. It was especially hard on the pilots, who wore night-vision goggles, which distorted depth perception and exaggerated feelings of vertigo. The men were becoming dehydrated in the extreme heat. They knew that some more tall peaks were between them and Desert One and could only hope that visibility improved in time for them to steer around or over them. One of the choppers lost its backup hydraulic system, which under ordinary circumstances would have required it to land immediately, but the pilot pressed on.

It was a tense, difficult struggle for all of them, and finally one gave up. Lieutenant Commander Rodney Davis had watched the control lights in his cockpit indicate a number of failures. His electrically powered compass was not working, and his other navigation devices, while working, were being affected by the heat. His copilot was feeling sick. When he lost sight of the nearest chopper, Davis was alone in the cloud. He tried the lost plane manuever, but he didn't see the other choppers and could not get a clear fix on anything below that would allow him to know his exact position. Davis took it up to nine thousand feet but was still in the milk. He might try flying higher, but that would burn more fuel and there was no telling how high up he would have to go; there was also the fear of being picked up by radar. He was at a critical point in the flight. To press on meant there would not be enough fuel to make it back to the carrier. Because they couldn't see, ahead or down, it meant they could steer off course or collide with a mountain on their way to Desert One. He conferred with Colonel Chuck Pittman, the ranking officer of the entire helicopter contingent, who was riding in back. With the other seven choppers still presumably en route—they did not know that one had already been lost—they assumed that turning back would not fatally compromise the mission.

So they turned back.

At the desert airfield, Delta waited anxiously as precious minutes of darkness passed. It was an enormous relief, just before one o'clock, when the distinctive *whoop-whoop-whoop* of the first two was heard in the desert night sky.

In the lead helicopter, Schaefer saw a giant pillar of flame, and his first thought was that one of the C-130s had crashed and exploded. He flew over Desert One and counted four planes on the ground, exactly what he expected. *Thank you, Lord,* he said to himself.

He turned to land on a second pass, and as he came down he clipped a rut so hard that he knew he had damaged his aircraft. The tires on his landing gear were blown and knocked off the rims. He had been in the air for five hours. He was tired, relieved, and had to piss. Like the planes, the choppers kept their engines running to lower the risk of a mechanical failure; most problems showed up stopping and restarting. Schaefer and his crew got out and walked around behind his aircraft to urinate, which is what he was doing when he was confronted by the eager Beckwith, trailed by Burruss, Kyle, and the other commanders.

"What the hell's going on?" asked the colonel. "How did you get so goddamned late?"

"First of all, we're only twenty-five minutes late," said Schaefer. "Second of all, I don't know where anyone else is because we went into a big dust cloud."

"There's no goddamned dust cloud out here," said Beckwith, gesturing at the open sky. He had not been told about the *haboobs* on the way in.

"Well, there is one," said Schaefer. He said that the flying conditions coming in had been the worst he had ever flown through. His men were badly shaken. His chopper still flew but may have been damaged. He wasn't sure they could go on.

This is not what Beckwith wanted to hear.

"I'm going to report this thing," he said angrily. He thought the pilot looked shattered, as though the pressure of this thing had completely broken him down. He slapped Schaefer on the back and told him that he and the others were going to have to suck it up.

The refueling crew went right to work on Schaefer's chopper. Lyle Walton, one of the airmen helping with the hose, was approached by one of the helicopter crewmen.

"Where are you from, airman?" he asked.

"Little Rock, Arkansas," said Walton.

"No shit, I'm from Pine Bluff," said the crewman. They had not met during any of the training runs. He said his name was George Holmes, and it turned out they had grown up just thirty miles apart. They talked a little about that, and Holmes said, "I guess we're going to have to go show this ayatollah you don't mess with Arkansas boys."

Burruss was surprised by how rattled the first two pair of chopper pilots looked. It occurred to him that it might have less to do with *haboobs* than the dangers of this mission. Maybe these guys never believed they might actually be called upon to fly it. Training was one thing. He had known men before who were superb in practice but shrank from a real fight.

Two more choppers arrived, and there was trouble with one of them. The helicopter flown by Captain B. J. McGuire had been flying with a warning light on in the cockpit, indicating trouble with his backup hydraulic system. Fitch was the first person to him on landing.

"I'm so happy you're here," the Delta squadron leader said, shouting to be heard. "Where are the rest of the guys?" Fitch asked.

"I don't know," said McGuire. "We don't have any communication."

McGuire told the Delta squadron commander about the problem with his helicopter. He said he thought the working hydraulic system was sufficiently trustworthy for him to continue.

When at last the final two choppers landed, it was cause for quiet celebration. It was one-thirty in the morning, which gave them just enough time to get everything done and hidden before full daylight. They had the required six. Some members of the assault force exchanged high fives. Seiffert soon had them maneuvering into position behind the four C-130s to refuel. Their wheels made deep tracks in the fine sand and the turning rotors whipped violent dust storms. It was deafening with all the rotors and propellers running. The truck fire was still burning brightly.

Beckwith, impatient to get going, climbed into the cockpit of the last chopper to land and tried to get the attention of Seiffert, who was coordinating these maneuvers on the radio with his pilots.

"Request permission to load, skipper," said Beckwith. "We need to get with it."

"Hey, remember me?" he asked.

Seiffert either didn't hear him or ignored him. The colonel slapped his helmet.

Seiffert took off his helmet and confronted Beckwith angrily.

"I can't guarantee we'll get you to the next site before first light."

"I don't care," said Beckwith.

Seiffert told him to go ahead and load his men.

Because they were transferring from the plane to choppers, Fitch and his men had been carrying all their own gear as they hauled the camouflage netting. In some cases men were carrying well over eighty pounds— Fitch himself was hauling ninety-five extra pounds of gear on his two-hundred-pound frame. They were eager to get settled on the choppers. When he got word, the major told his team to begin loading the camouflage netting and themselves on the choppers and went off to retrieve the men he had left guarding the bus passengers. Supervision of the Iranians was given to Carl Savory, the Delta surgeon. Doc Savory, a less experienced shooter than his Delta comrades, had been guarding the passengers for some time before one of the other men pointed out that he had forgotten to put the magazine in his weapon.

Beckwith was moving from chopper to chopper, urging things forward, when another of the marine pilots stepped out and said, "The skipper told me to tell you we only have five flyable helicopters. That's what the skipper told me to tell you."

Looking around, the colonel could see that the rotor on one of the Sea Stallions had stopped turning. They had shut it down.

It was precisely what the Delta commander had feared: *These pilots are determined to scuttle this mission.* It had not been lost on the other commanders working with him, most of whom outranked Beckwith, that the pugnacious colonel regarded them all as inferiors, as supporting players. The pilots, the navigators, the aircrews, the fuel equipment operators, the rangers, the combat controllers, the spies in Tehran, even the generals back at Wadi Kena . . . they were all ordinary mortals, squires, spear-carriers, water boys. Their job was to serve Delta, to get his magnificent men in place for their rendezvous with destiny. All along he had been impatient and suspicious of the other services and units involved; they lacked experience, nerve, and skill. They were screwups. He had little appreciation of the heroic difficulties they faced—indeed, most of the mission planners regarded getting Delta in and out of Tehran as the hardest piece of the job—so now, when things began to go sour, Beckwith felt not just disappointment and anger, but contempt. These piddling, gutless amateurs—the colonel was a master of the blunt, insulting adjective —were stepping on his glory. *They weren't getting him there!* He oozed scorn.

When he found Kyle, he bellowed, "That goddamn number two helo has been shut down! We only have five good helicopters. You've got to talk to Seiffert and see what he says. You talk their language—I don't."

Beckwith didn't see mechanical problems; he saw faltering courage in the pilots. He said as much to Kyle, grumbling that the flyers were looking for excuses not to go.

The comment burned the air force officer, who had been contending for months with Beckwith's gruff hauteur. He knew better than to argue with him. The helo captains had the same kind of responsibilities as Beckwith, and Kyle better understood their concerns. They were responsible for getting their own crews in and out safely, not to mention themselves. No one knew their machines as well as they did, because they literally bet their lives on them every time they flew. Seiffert had made his decision. One of the hydraulic pumps on McGuire's chopper was shot and they had no way to fix it. Kyle asked if it would be possible to fly with just the remaining one, and Seiffert had told him emphatically, "No! It's unsafe! If the controls lock up, it becomes uncontrollable. It's grounded!"

When Fitch returned from rounding up the rest of his men, he was surprised to find that his second in command, Captain E. K. Smith, was still waiting with his squadron in the dust. He told Smith to get the men on the choppers.

"The mission is an abort," said Smith.

"What do you mean, it's an abort?"

"Colonel Beckwith said it's an abort," said Smith. He explained that McGuire's chopper was damaged and couldn't fly. This contradicted what McGuire had told Fitch, that the chopper was damaged but flyable. Beckwith was such a hothead that it was entirely possible he had said something like that with only half the story.

"E.K., I'm not doubting your word, but I'm going to see Beckwith about this," he said.

The abort scenario, which they had rehearsed, called for Fitch and his men to board not helicopters but one of the fuel birds. The choppers would fly back to the carrier and the planes would return to Masirah. He told Smith to prepare the men to get on the plane but said to wait until he returned.

It wasn't easy finding the colonel in the noise and swirling dust. One of the things they had failed to build into the plan was some kind of clearly defined rallying point or command center. It took some wandering, but Fitch eventually found Beckwith, huddled with Burruss, Kyle, and the other mission commanders, outside one of the C-130s with a satellite radio.

"What's going on?" Fitch shouted over the din.

"Well, Seiffert said that helicopter can't fly, that it's not mission capable, and we're down to five," Beckwith said, disgusted.

Kyle and the chopper crews said they were ready to proceed with five helicopters, but that would require trimming the assault force down by twenty men. Beckwith refused. "We all go or nobody goes," he said.

The decision was passed up the chain to Washington, where Secretary of Defense Brown relayed the bad news to Brzezinski in the White House. The national security adviser, who only minutes earlier had been told all six choppers were refueling and the mission was proceeding as planned, was stunned. He quickly assessed what he knew and engaged in a little wishful thinking. He imagined Beckwith, who had been so gung ho in his visit to the White House, fuming in the desert, eager to proceed but stymied by more cautious generals in the rear. He wanted Brown to ask the commanders on the ground if they were prepared to go ahead with fewer than six choppers. Brzezinski urged Carter to have Brown at least raise the question.

In the din of Desert One, Beckwith, Kyle, Burruss, and the other commanders received Brzezinski's request and reconsidered. It angered the colonel even to be asked; he felt as if his judgment and commitment were being questioned. Nevertheless, he asked Fitch, Burruss, and the others, "Can we make it with fewer aircraft?"

"Sir, we have been through this in rehearsals," said Fitch. "Who are we going to leave behind?"

Some felt that they could trim the package and proceed. The new, more specific intelligence about the location of the hostages in the compound had eliminated the need for some of the searching they had planned to do, so maybe they could do it with fewer men.

But Beckwith didn't like the odds. If they left behind the translators, who would talk them past the roadblocks in the city? If they got five choppers to the hide site, how likely was it that all five would restart the next day? If one or two refused to start, and another got hit—all likely scenarios that they had built into the plan—how were they going to airlift out all the hostages and his men? His plan was too finely wrought, too carefully calibrated between risk and opportunity to risk leaving *anything* out. It meant shifting the odds too greatly against his men, his beautiful creation, which he was not prepared to do. That was the conclusion they had reached in advance after repeated, calm deliberation. They had predetermined these automatic abort scenarios precisely to avoid having to make life-and-death decisions on the spur of the moment. This was clearly an abort situation. On their written mission schedule, just after the line "less than six helos," was the word ABORT, and it was the only word on the page written in capital letters. Still, so much was at stake it was tempting to disregard their own prior assessment. To quit now might mean giving up on their only chance to carry out the mission. That was what many of them thought.

"If we don't go now, we're fucked," said Major Long. "This is the last chance."

But that might not be true. If they loaded up and left now, destroying the broken chopper with an incendiary grenade and scattering diversionary material that would make it appear to be a crashed Soviet chopper—they had brought some along—it was possible that their presence in the desert would go unnoticed, or at least be misunderstood, which meant they might be able to come back and try again in a few days. They could take the bus passengers back with them and hold them until the second try. Their disappearance would just be an unsolved mystery for a few days. The prospect of coming back and trying again argued for caution. Both Beckwith and his deputy commander, Burruss, concurred.

"I need every man I've got and every piece of gear," said Beckwith finally. "There's no fat I can cut out."

As the dusty soldiers were making this decision in the Iranian desert, Brzezinski was breaking the news of the setback to Carter. Standing in a corridor between the Oval Office and the president's study, Brzezinski whispered the news. Carter muttered, "Damn. Damn."

Behind his study desk, Carter called the defense secretary. Brzezinski debated what to say. Having come this far, he didn't want the mission scratched out of bureaucratic timidity. He sensed a historic chance and was inclined to urge the president to push his generals to proceed with only five helicopters. Convinced that Beckwith, out in the desert, would be feeling the same way, Brzezinski leaned across the desk and looked squarely at the president.

"You should get the opinion of the commander in the field. His attitude should be taken into account."

Moments later, Brown received Beckwith's final decision.

"Let's go with his recommendation," the president said. Carter then lowered his head and rested it on his arms for a few long seconds. The failure was catastrophic.

He and Brzezinski were then joined by a larger group of advisers, including Mondale, Jordan, Christopher, and Powell. Standing behind his desk in his small study, his sleeves rolled up, hands on his hips, the president told them, "I've got some bad news. . . . I had to abort the rescue mission. Two of our helicopters never reached Desert One—that left us six. The Delta team was boarding the six helicopters when they found out that one of them had a mechanical problem and couldn't go on."

"What did Beckwith think?" asked Jordan, thinking along the same lines as Brzezinski.

Carter explained that they had consulted Beckwith and that the decision had been unanimous.

"At least there were no American casualties and no innocent Iranians hurt," Carter said softly.

6

TWO LOUD, DULL *THUNKS*

At Desert One there wasn't time to dwell on the decision, no matter how disappointing. Paul Zeisman, Delta's radio operator, raised Dick Meadows by satellite radio. Meadows was waiting at the hide site. Zeisman and Meadows had worked out a code. Meadows was "Test Alpha," Zeisman was "Test Bravo," the hide site was "antenna," the helicopters were "trucks," and Delta Force was "antenna parts."

"Test Alpha, this is Test Bravo," said Zeisman, speaking into the radio on the flight deck of one of the C-130s. "We can't get the antenna parts to you because we had a lot of trucks break down. We're going to go ahead and cancel the contract. You should come back."

The decision left Meadows and his crew hanging. If the American intrusion were discovered, it would imperil their trip out of Iran. The authorities were likely to take a strong interest in every caucasian foreigner who had recently entered the country. Meadows was greatly disappointed but he didn't sound worried.

Fitch went back to his men and directed them to board one of the fuel planes. As he saw it, they weren't dead yet. This might just mean as little as postponing the mission one day. With Meadows and their trucks and local help poised and ready, they could not delay long. He and his men piled in on top of the nearly deflated fuel bladder, which rippled like a giant black waterbed. Everyone was weary and disappointed. Eric Haney stripped off his gear and his black field jacket, balling it up behind him to form a cushion against the hard metal angles of the plane's inner wall. He and some of the other men wedged their weapons snugly between the fuel bladder and the wall of the plane so they would be secure and out of the way. Some of the men fell immediately asleep.

Lyle Walton, one of the members of the refueling crew, had no idea that the mission was scrubbed. He and his fellow crew members were in the back of the same plane as Fitch's men, congratulating themselves for having so efficiently refueled their chopper. It was still dark outside. So far as they knew, everything was going as planned.

Fitch told his sergeant major, Dave Cheney, to make sure everyone was accounted for. The sergeant shouted out the roster and ticked off the team members and came up short. It wasn't surprising, in their haste, and on a patch of desert roaring with the propellers and rotors of four big planes and five helicopters, it would have been easy for one man to get on the wrong plane or to somehow have gotten hurt and now be lying alone just out of eyeshot. Their plane was supposed to take off first and the pilots were eager to depart.

"Don't let them take off until I make sure we find this guy," Fitch told Cheney and then took off to search for his missing man. He checked all the other aircraft, without success, and then saw what appeared to be a figure lying on the desert floor a short distance away. He ran over to look and discovered a heap of camouflage netting. He returned to the C-130 that held his squadron.

"He's got to be here," he told Cheney. Their search located him curled up in the front of the plane, right where he was supposed to be, fast asleep. Either he had never heard the sergeant major call out his name or, in the general clamor, no one had heard his response.

"We're all set, let's go," Fitch told the plane's crew chief.

Just behind their plane, a combat controller in goggles, one of Carney's crew, appeared outside the cockpit of chopper three and informed the pilot, Major Schaefer, that he had to move his aircraft out of the way. Schaefer had refueled behind that tanker, and he now had enough fuel to fly back to the *Nimitz,* but first they wanted to get the C-130s off the ground. The tanker needed to turn off to the left to clear the runway, and they needed Schaefer's helicopter out of the way.

Schaefer lifted the nose of his craft. His crew chief Dewey Johnson jumped out to straighten the nose wheels, which had been bent sideways when they'd landed. Straightened, they could be retracted so they wouldn't cause drag in flight. Johnson climbed back in and Schaefer lifted the chopper into a hover at about fifteen feet and held it, kicking up a wicked storm of dust that whipped around the combat controller on the ground. He was the only thing Schaefer could see below, a hazy black image in a cloud of brown, so the pilot fixed on him as a point of reference.

To escape the dust storm created by Schaefer's rotors, the combat controller retreated toward the wing of the parked C-130, but seeing only a blurry image of the man on the ground, and concentrating on his own aircraft, Schaefer didn't notice that he had moved. He kept the nose of his blinded chopper pointed at him, and as the combat controller moved, the helicopter turned in the same direction.

"How much power do we have, Les?" asked Schaefer, performing his usual checklist.

"Ninety-four percent," said his copilot Les Petty.

Then Schaefer heard and felt a loud, strong, metallic *whack!* It sounded as if someone had hit the side of his aircraft with a large aluminum bat. Others in the desert heard a cracking sound as loud as an explosion but sharper-edged somehow, more piercing and particular, like the shearing impact of giant unmoored industrial tools. The marine pilot's rotors had clipped the top of the plane, metal violently and loudly cracking into metal in a wild spray of sparks, and instantly the helicopter lost all aerodynamics, its cushion of air whipped out from beneath, and it fell with a grinding bang into the C-130's cockpit, an impact so stunning that Schaefer briefly blacked out. Both aircraft were engorged with fuel and the sparks caused by the collision immediately ignited both with a powerful, lung-emptying *thump!* that seemed to suck all the air out of the desert. It formed a huge blue ball of fire around the front of the C-130 and then rocketed a pillar of white flame three hundred feet or more into the sky, in a split second turning the scene once more from night into day.

Beckwith pivoted the moment he felt and heard the crash and started running toward it. He pulled up short the length of a football field away, stopped by the intense heat, and thought immediately with despair of his men, Fitch's entire White Element, trapped.

Inside the C-130, Fitch had felt the plane begin to shudder, as though the pilots were revving the engines for takeoff. There were no windows and he couldn't tell if they were moving yet. Then he heard two loud, dull *thunks*. He thought maybe the nose gear or landing gear had hit a rock or a divot, but when he looked toward the front of the aircraft he saw flames and sparks. His first thought was that they were under attack.

He had removed his rucksack, and leaning against it was his weapon, an M203. He grabbed it and stood in one motion. Beside him the plane's loadmaster, responding wordlessly to the same sight, pulled open the troop door on the port side of the plane. It revealed a solid wall of flame. Fitch helped him slam it down and push the handle in to lock it. He and the men were sitting and standing on a thousand gallons of fuel, and they appeared to be caught in an inferno.

"Open the ramp!" Fitch shouted, but it lowered to reveal more flames. The plane was going to explode. Loaded as it was with fuel, it was an enormous bomb, and it was enveloped in fire. The only other way out was the starboard troop door to the rear of the plane above two-thirds of the distance to the tail, which had been calmly opened by three of the plane's crewmen. That doorway proved blessedly free of flames. Men were piling out of it before it was completely opened.

One of them was the Hercules crewman Walton, who had been trying to walk to the front of the plane to get a cup of coffee, picking his way through the crowd of men while keeping his balance on the shifting fuel bladder, when he heard the collision and felt the plane tilt forward and then shake from side to side. He fought his way out of the door and dropped six feet to the desert floor. Men were raining on top of him so fast he couldn't stand up. He rolled until he found himself under the plane, surrounded by fire. Then a marine grabbed him beneath both arms, hauled him into the clear, and shouted, "Haul ass, brother!"

Still inside the plane Cheney, a bull of a man with a big deep voice, kept shouting, "Don't panic! Don't panic!" as the men crowded toward the only escape. Flames spread rapidly from the ceiling of the plane and were wrapping down on both sides. Fire ignited a primitive flight instinct that none of the men could control. One of the junior air force crewmen was knocked down and was being trampled by the aggressive, fleeing Deltas, when Technical Sergeant Ken Bancroft fought his way to the man, picked him up, and carried him to the doorway and out. Cheney's natural authority and clarity helped avoid a complete mad scramble and kept a steady flow of men out the door. They were used to filing out this way on parachute jumps, so the line moved fast. Still, it was torture for the men at the rear of the line. "Don't panic!" Cheney kept screaming. Fitch stood opposite him in the doorway, regulating the flow. In their haste, many of the men stumbled when they hit the ground, which created pileups just outside the door. They scrambled to get to their feet, run, and clear the way.

Ray Doyle, a loadmaster on one of the other tankers standing more than a hundred feet away, was knocked over by the force of the initial explosion. Jesse Rowe, a crewman on another of the tankers, felt his plane shake and the temperature of the air suddenly shoot up. Burruss saw the plane erupt as he stepped off the back of his C-130. He was carrying incendiary explosives to destroy the disabled Sea Stallion, coming down the ramp, and the sight of it buckled him. He sat down, watching the tower of flame engulfing the plane, and thought, *Man, Fitch's whole squadron gone, those poor bastards.* But then he saw men running from the fireball, as if they were fleeing hell itself.

Pilots quickly spread the word to their crews that they had not been attacked, which eased some of the initial confusion.

Still inside the burning plane, Haney was near the end of the line of men trying to get out. He and the men around him had been jarred alert by the noise and impact outside the plane and saw blue sparks overhead and toward the front. Then the galley door at the front of the plane blew in and flames blasted out along the ceiling.

"Haul ass!" shouted the man next to him, leaping to his feet. Captain Smith, who had dozed off, woke up to see men trying to gain footing on the shifting surface of the fuel bladder and at first thought it was amusing, until he saw flames. He and the others at the front of the plane began running as well as they could, fearing they would never outrace the flames around them, acutely aware that beneath their feet were thousands of gallons of fuel. Ahead, men were jammed in the doorway. Haney threw himself out when he finally reached the door and dropped down hard on the man who had jumped before him. They both scrambled up and ran until they were about fifty meters away, then turned to watch with horror.

One of the soldiers, Frank McKenna, had fallen asleep before the commotion and awoke to flames and to men lining up to jump from the plane. He ran to join them, assuming they had been attacked in the air and were now evacuating a burning plane. He looked around frantically for a parachute, didn't see one, and when it was his turn to jump he just flung himself out the door belly-first, in arched skydiving position, and collided hard with the earth a split second later. It had all happened so fast he didn't have time to consider the folly of free-falling without a parachute. As he later told his buddies, "One problem at a time."

Fitch felt it was his duty to stay until all the men were off, but it was hard. As the flames rapidly advanced he realized that not everyone was going to make it. Instinct finally won out and both he and Cheney leapt out the door, falling when they hit the ground. Other men crashed on top of them. They helped each other up and out to where the others were now watching, brightly illuminated by the enlarging fire.

Staff Sergeant Joe Byers was one of the last struggling to escape. He was a radio operator on the plane's crew and his seat was in the front of the aircraft behind the cockpit. As soon as he realized the plane had been hit by something, he started moving toward his evacuation door, which happened to be the starboard troop door in the rear, the only way out. When he dropped down the small flight of stairs from the flight deck, he was shocked to see the inside of the cargo hold ablaze and nearly empty. He started crawling across the fuel bladders toward the door, scarcely able to breathe. He thought he was going to die. The door looked miles away, fire was all around him, and he was crawling across tons of fuel. But he kept going.

Fitch ran to what appeared to be a safe distance, then turned around, lifting his weapon, still assuming they were under attack, looking for the enemy and instead seeing an awesome and ugly sight. Crouched like a huge dragonfly, its rotors still turning, a helicopter was mounted on top of the plane. He realized it wasn't an attack, it was an accident.

He saw two more men jump out, one of them Byers, whose flight suit was burning. Other men rushed to put out the flames and to drag him clear. Then ammunition started cooking off—all the grenades, missiles, explosives, and rifle rounds—causing loud cracking explosions and throwing flames and light. The Red-eye missiles went off, drawing smoke trails high into the sky. Then the fuel bladder finally ignited. A huge pillar of flame shot skyward in a loud explosion that buckled the fuselage. All four propellers dropped straight down into the sand and stuck there, like somebody had planted them. One last man came flying out of the open troop door, Sergeant James McLain, blown out by the force of the blast. He hit the ground so hard it damaged his back. His flight suit was in flames. Sergeant Paul Lawrence ran back toward the fire to grab him and pull him to safety. McLain was badly burned.

In the cockpit of the chopper, set now on top of the C-130, Schaefer had blacked out on impact. He awkened from his blackout sitting crooked in his seat, the chopper listing to one side, with flames engulfing his cockpit.

"What's wrong, Les? What's wrong?" he said, turning to his copilot, but Petty was already gone. He had jumped out the window on his side.

Schaefer heard a scream behind him and turned to grab the arm of Dewey Johnson, his crew chief, who had been with him since Vietnam. He took his helmet off and pulled on Johnson's arm again, and then heard his friend scream once more in agony and drop away from him.

The pilot shut down the engines and sat for a moment, certain he was about to die. Then for some reason an image came into his mind of his fiancée's father—a man who had always seemed none too impressed with his future pilot son-in-law—commenting during some future family meal about how the poor sap's body had been found cooked like a holiday turkey in the front seat of his aircraft, and something about that horrifying image motivated him. His body would not be found like an overcooked Butterball; he had to at least try to escape. He ejected the window on his side and, as fire closed over him, burning his face, he threw himself into the flames.

He dropped a good distance to the ground, landing hard, and he lay stunned for a long time, badly burned and half blind. When he saw pillars of flame shooting up around him—patches of fuel-saturated sand were catching fire—he forced himself to his feet and ran from the erupting wreckage.

He and Petty escaped, badly scorched. One of the backup C-130 pilots got out, but the two main pilots, two navigators, and one crewman were not so fortunate. They and all three of Schaefer's crewmen, including Arkansas-born George Holmes, perished.

The exploding plane and ammo sent flaming bits of hot metal and debris spraying across the makeshift airport, riddling the other four working helicopters, whose crews promptly began climbing out and moving to a safe distance. Most of the men had no idea what was going on, just that a plane and chopper had exploded. The air over the scene had been heavy with the odor of fuel, and it wasn't hard to imagine that all the other aircraft were going to burst into flames as well. The three remaining C-130s began taxiing in different directions away from the exploding wreckage. There was chaos on the ground. One of the Delta medics kept shouting over the engine noise and wails of the wounded, "Look in your E and E kit and get me some Percodan!" which was misheard by one group of men who huddled over a map on the ground.

"What are you guys doing?" they were asked.

"Didn't you hear? We're going to E and E to Percodan," one said.

Word of the calamity reached the command center in Wadi Kena with the following hurried report: "We have a crash. A helo crashed into one of the C-130s. We have some dead, some wounded, and some trapped. The crash site is ablaze. Ammunition is cooking off."

Jerry Uttaro, piloting one of the tankers, started taxiing away from the blaze when he heard debris raining down on top of his plane. Desert One was lit up like a homecoming bonfire rally, complete with fireworks. He got only a few feet when some of the Delta operators, fearing that he was leaving without them, ran out in front of his plane to stop him. Uttaro told his radio operator to go down and explain to the idiots in front of his airplane that he was just trying to avoid being the next log on the fire and that he wasn't going to strand them.

Fitch saw one of the other C-130s move away and then turn back. He ran to it and began banging on its starboard troop door. It taxied on a bit farther and then came to a stop. The door slid open.

"I've got to get some people on here," he shouted. The crewman objected at first that they were already full but quickly relented.

"Load as many as you can," said Fitch. Some of his men climbed into that plane, then it taxied on and took off.

He turned to look back and saw two of the helicopters with their rotors turning. He was impressed. He figured they had stayed on the ground to see if anyone else needed to be picked up. The only people he saw remaining on the ground were Carney and his combat controllers, which was reassuring, because clearly they had some way out. He assumed the helicopters had stayed behind to do that.

Then Jessie Johnson, another member of Delta, pulled up in the jeep.

"What are you doing?" he asked Fitch.

"Well, I'm making sure everybody is out of here and then I'm going to get on this helicopter," Fitch said.

"Look up in the helicopter, dummy," said Johnson. Fitch did and saw immediately that it was empty. After the collision the pilots had hastily abandoned ship and boarded the C-130s. Fitch thought all the planes had taken off, but with Johnson and Carney and his men still on the ground he realized he must be wrong. Johnson pointed out the last C-130, waiting for them.

"Get in the jeep, we're pulling out," he said.

Beckwith was in the cockpit of the last plane, talking to Vaught at Wadi Kena, explaining the new calamity. There was thought given to leaving a small force behind in some low hills to the north to keep an eye on the scene—there was still a small chance all this would go unnoticed and they might be able to return and complete the mission—but that idea was quickly nixed. The only answer now was to clear out, and fast. The plane was low on fuel and they were running out of darkness. Burruss took charge of making sure everyone was accounted for, the able-bodied and the injured. There was some thought given to retrieving the bodies of the dead, but the fire was still raging and there wasn't time. After consulting with Vaught, Burruss was told to turn loose the Iranian bus passengers. The Delta officer ordered one of his men to rip some wires from the bus engine to make sure it was disabled and, after locating one of the Farsi speakers, he boarded the bus and addressed the passengers.

He told them that they were leaving some snipers behind, and that if anyone tried to leave the scene before morning they would be shot.

"So make sure you stay on the bus until daylight," Burruss said.

As he left and headed back to the plane, he took one last look at the flaming ruins of the plane and chopper and felt a stab of remorse over leaving behind the dead. But there was nothing to be done about it.

John Carney was the last man to leave Desert One. He climbed into Uttaro's tanker and said, "Everybody is out of the desert now."

There were so many men inside the last plane that they had to throw some of their rucksacks, mattresses, and equipment out to make room. The injured pilots and air force crewmen were being attended to by the Delta medics, who administered morphine and dressed their burns. As the plane accelerated across the desert floor it hit the lip of the road at full speed and with a frightening jolt was airborne. Inside it felt like Iran had delivered one last kick to the rear as they reached the sky, but then the plane hit the ground again hard. It didn't have enough speed to stay airborne. Fitch managed to stay on his feet as the plane kept surging forward and then slowly urged itself off the ground. One of the propellers had clipped the rise by the road and had been bent, so the overloaded C-130 flew off toward Masirah with just three engines. Behind them on the desert floor was a giant flaming wreck surrounded by four intact helicopters, an amazed bus full of Iranian pilgrims, and the still-burning ruins of the fuel truck. It was hard to imagine that such a spectacular series of calamities had not caught the attention of any Iranian authorities, but there was no indication that the intrusion had been noticed.

As they got in the air, Fitch told Boykin. "We need to get some fighters over." He was assuming that with all the commotion at Desert One the Iranian air force would be on them soon. They would not be out of Iranian airspace by daylight, and the overburdened, wounded, and unarmed C-130 would be a fat and easy target for a jet fighter.

"It's already done," said Boykin.

No fighters were necessary. All four C-130s limped out of Iran without being challenged by Iran's air defenses—fighters on the *Nimitz* were ready to intervene if necessary. The planes flew back the same way they had flown in, unescorted and unseen by Iran's air defenses. It was the one part of the mission that had gone right.

America's elite rescue force had lost eight men, seven helicopters, and a C-130 and had not even made contact with the enemy. It was a debacle. It defined the word "debacle." Meadows and his crew would be stranded in a very tight spot in Tehran as the country woke up to this hamhanded invasion. Still, the men in the departing planes clung to the hope that the disaster scene in the desert would remain a mystery long enough for them to try again.

What they didn't yet know was that there would be one more disaster to add to the mortifying list. In their haste to clear out immediately after the collision, the marine crews and pilots had left behind in their Sea Stallions classified documents describing their failed mission in detail. It would all be there for the Iranian authorities to inspect, a veritable play by play. Kyle called for an air strike to destroy the choppers and the papers in them, but concern for the bus passengers, who had been so sternly instructed to stay put, ruled out that option. There would be no mystery, and there would be no second chance.

Word reached the White House at about that time, just before the force left the ground. Still in his study, surrounded by his advisers, absorbing the shock of the abort decision, Carter received a call from General Jones.

"Yes, Dave."

Jordan watched the president close his eyes, and then Carter's jaw fell and his face went pale.

"Are there any dead?" Carter asked.

The room was silent. Finally, the president said softly, "I understand," and hung up the phone.

He calmly explained to the others what had happened. The men took in the awful news quietly. Then Secretary of State Vance, who had submitted his resignation earlier that day because he objected to the mission, said, "Mr. President, I'm very, very sorry."

Jordan ducked into the president's bathroom and vomited.

Iran found out about the failed rescue attempt the same way the rest of the world did; the White House issued a statement at one o'clock in the morning (nine-thirty in the morning in Tehran). It began, "The president has ordered the cancellation of an operation in Iran which was under way to prepare for a rescue of our hostages. The mission was terminated because of equipment failure."

It went on to briefly explain without details that there had been "a collision between our aircraft on the ground at a remote desert location in Iran."

> This mission was not motivated by hostility toward Iran or the Iranian people, and there were no Iranian casualties . . . Preparations for this rescue mission were ordered for humanitarian reasons, to protect the national interests of this country and to alleviate international tensions. The president accepts full responsibility for the decision to attempt the rescue. The nation is deeply grateful to the brave men who were preparing to rescue the hostages.

PART FIVE

HAGGLING WITH THE BARBARIANS

Released hostages arrive at Rhein-Main Air Base in West Germany. Top to bottom: Michael Metrinko, David Roeder, and Tom Schaefer. *(Courtesy: AP)*

President Reagan listens to Bruce Laingen at the official welcome ceremony at the White House, Tuesday, January 27, 1981. *(Courtesy: AP)*

1

A PRISON-LIKE PLACE

On the day after the failed rescue mission most of the hostages were moved from the embassy and scattered around Iran. Stunned by the audacity of the American rescue effort, and alarmed by how vulnerable they had been, the student hostage takers quickly corrected the major mistake of keeping all of the hostages in the same place.

Without knowing why, the Americans were hustled out of Tehran in cars and vans, bound and blindfolded, sometimes taken for drives that went on straight through the night. Bill Keough, Bill Royer, Cort Barnes, and Charles Jones were driven to an airport and flown to a southern city on a commercial airliner. The hostages, who had grown accustomed to being shuffled around for no apparent reason, sensed that something important had happened. The guards were all wearing gas masks and seemed especially skittish. They carried more weapons than usual and seemed unwilling to look the hostages in the eye. Kevin Hermening guessed that his chances of going home with his mother were dashed. His roommate, embassy security chief Al Golacinski, wondered if there had been an attempted coup d'état.

After a long drive through the night, CIA station chief Tom Ahern was deposited in an empty room in what appeared to have once been a large private residence or a small school. There was a giant bush outside filled with birds, hundreds of them. At first the chirping of this mob entertained him, but gradually it became annoying. He still had his music sheets and one or two books and resumed his solitary routines. He would be there for more than a month.

Speeding along in the back of a different van, John Limbert could tell that the landscape was flat, which indicated he and the others with him were being driven south, since to the north were mountains. He knew that part of Iran well from many drives he had taken back and forth between Tehran and Shiraz during his years as a teacher, so he could picture the small towns and open spaces even though he couldn't see. They drove for seven to eight hours. He was glad he had eaten and gone to the toilet not long before they'd left. When he could see the light of dawn glowing at the edges of his blindfold, they came to a stop in what he figured was Isfahan.

Limbert was left in a room by himself again, which he did not like, but there was a bay window in which he could sit and look out into a large garden. He was doing that on his first evening when he saw Colonel Lee Holland standing in a window across the way. Holland didn't see him and Limbert didn't dare call out. But it was the first American he had seen since February.

Michael Metrinko bounced blindfolded in the back of a van for two hours, and was then led up some stairs and left in a prison cell with, to his delight, two other Americans, CIA technician Phil Ward and army Master Sergeant Regis Regan. It was the first time the embassy political officer had been out of isolation since the previous November. Metrinko recognized Regan, although he didn't know him well. They had been together once escorting a group of visitors on official embassy business. He had no memory of Ward and thought he might be a plant. But Regan vouched for him, and soon the pleasure of having company overcame any sense of caution. The three men sat up all night talking. It was the first time Metrinko had spoken more than a few words of English in almost six months and it felt wonderful. The cell was very hot and had iron cots with thin, soiled mattresses on them. They knew they weren't in the mountains because it was too warm, and they concluded that they had been driven south. The taste of the water was extremely sour, which was peculiar to just a few places, and they heard the whistle of a train. They finally concluded with certainty that they had been driven to the holy city of Qom, the Ayatollah Khomeini's home base.

When one of the guards asked if they knew where they were, Metrinko told him, "Of course."

"Where are you?" the guard asked.

"I will tell you if you will go out and get us some *sohan* [an oily and brittle yellow candy peculiar to Qom]."

The guard laughed and confirmed the deduction.

Ward was taken away without explanation soon after they arrived. Metrinko and Regan were moved to better quarters, an old art school. They were given a bigger room that had mattresses on the floor and a new room-mate, Dave Roeder.

CIA officer Bill Daugherty was one of the last to be moved after the rescue attempt. Late in the afternoon that day he noticed a peculiar quiet had fallen over the embassy. Usually things picked up before dusk, when the day-shift guards were replaced by the night shift. When he pounded on his door to be taken to the toilet no one came. In the hall outside he could hear only what sounded like a news broadcast on the radio. He sensed that something had happened, or was about to happen, and in his experience such changes were almost always for the worse. Instead of his usual well-rounded dinner he was brought just a thin bowl of chili. In the middle of the night, guards entered his room, cuffed his hands, and slipped a canvas bag over his head. He was led to the back of a van, where he joined several other American captives similarly bound and hooded, and taken on a silent drive that lasted only a half hour. Daugherty was escorted into a building—he had the sense that he was passing through a huge room—up several flights of metal stairs, and into a room, where he was told to remove his hood.

It was a prison cell, an oddly shaped room about six by eight feet, with a stainless steel toilet in a corner. The entrance to the room was a steel door with a slot at the bottom big enough for a food tray and a small window at eye level that was closed by a sliding panel on the outside. Some light filtered in from a small window high above, but otherwise the cell was lit by a single lightbulb hanging from the ceiling, fifteen feet up. Daugherty was furious. One of his persistent fears was of being hauled off for trial and execution, and being placed in a prison cell seemed a big step closer to that fate. No one responded when he banged on the door, so he began pacing back and forth—three steps forward, turn, three steps back. About the only reassurance he had was that he had arrived with other captives, and he had heard other doors slamming nearby, so at least he wasn't here alone.

One of the student leaders paid him a visit the next morning. He seemed calm and he assured Daugherty that he and the others had been moved "for their own safety." He told Daugherty that he was not in a prison but "a prison-like place." He would learn later that he was, in fact, in Evin Prison, the most notorious of the jails in Tehran. Set in the foothills of the snowcapped peaks north of the city, Evin was an ugly, self-contained city of incarceration, a sprawling complex of older, dungeon-like buildings and more modern administrative ones surrounded by high stone walls that climbed and dipped with the steep contours of the landscape. The color and construction of the walls varied from brown to brick, reflecting the patchwork nature of the place, which had been expanded, renovated, and rebuilt over its seventy-five-year history.

On his second day there, for the first time since being taken hostage, Daugherty got a cellmate. Bruce German, the embassy's budget officer, introduced himself. The two men had seen each other in the embassy but had never been acquainted. German had spent much of the previous night sobbing and weeping in a cell in another part of the same building, which may be why the guards decided to put him in with someone else. The two men compared notes about where they had been and who they had been with. Daugherty had precious little to contribute to the conversation. He had been held alone for nearly the entire time and had not been able to communicate with any of his former colleagues, much less anyone at home. German shared some of his experiences, but not all. He had been allowed to send letters home and had received mail and had even been allowed to speak on the phone with his family in the Maryland suburbs of Washington. He didn't mention this to Daugherty, and even after the CIA officer said, "I heard somebody talking on the phone with their wife," German didn't mention that it might have been him.

Daugherty noticed that German still had his watch, which surprised him. All of his own possessions except the clothes he wore had been taken on the first night, along with those of everybody else as they sat around the big table in the ambassador's residence. The two men were together very briefly. German was taken away after only four hours, and Daugherty did not see him there again. He had felt uneasy about German—he wondered if he was helping their captors—and the episode reinforced his preference for solitude.

It was early spring, but the mountain altitude was chilly. Several times Daugherty was taken out to a tiny enclosed space for "exercise." It was no bigger than a large dining room table, surrounded on four sides by brick walls reaching up nearly twenty feet. He was allowed to stand in this space for about a half hour. He was so cold that he followed a small patch of sunlight around the space.

Kathryn Koob and Ann Swift were told to pack on the day after the rescue attempt, but when they were finally moved, after waiting anxiously all day, they were simply taken to another room in the chancery. It had been home to three male hostages, one of whom had written on the wall "Khomeini Hilton, 176 days." It was so dirty the women immediately asked for buckets, mops, scrub brushes, and a vacuum.

They had no sooner cleaned it than they were moved again, across the hall. They pleaded with Hamid to let them stay in the room they had laboriously scrubbed and improved, but to no avail. They were marched across the hall to a room that was just as dirty as the first. They scrubbed and vacuumed this one, too.

The women were not the only ones who stayed behind. In another room in the big, now mostly vacant office building was Bob Ode, who when he heard the demonstrations and saw the other hostages being taken off assumed that an agreement at last had been reached between Iran and the United States. He and Bruce German had packed expectantly, but when only German was taken away Ode's disappointment and anger erupted. He swore a blue streak at the guards, dredging up language he hadn't used since he was a sailor in World War Two. It was a full-fledged temper tantrum, pointless and probably self-destructive, which Ode understood but could not contain. He screamed at them until a senior guard named Akmed came into his room and upbraided him.

"Older men should have more dignity," he said.

Dignity was the last thing on Ode's mind. His disappointment ached. He assumed that German was being taken home, and he was not, because he had misbehaved. The notion seemed confirmed when the next morning he was taken from the room but not even out of the building. He was moved down the hall into a room with Don Hohman, the embassy medic. The rest of the building had grown quiet as a tomb. When Ode complained that the new room wasn't as comfortable as the old one, where he had everything set up, Hamid told him, "It is because you cursed at the students." Besides, said Hamid, the new room was larger.

"But the other room had a desk with drawers where we could keep our things, and two chairs, and was brighter," Ode pleaded.

"This will be your room from now on," said Hamid.

"How long is 'from now on'?" Ode asked.

Hamid told Ode that he complained too much.

2

ANY POSSIBILITY OF FAILURE
SHOULD HAVE RULED IT OUT

Barbara Timm was awakened at the Intercontinental Hotel Friday morning in Tehran by a team of angry students, who accused her and her husband of having come as part of the "secret invasion." That was how the mission was being portrayed in Iran. The United States had attempted a military invasion of Iran but had been dealt a crushing defeat. One of the students suggested that the Timms and their lawyer had been sent by the U.S. government as a distraction.

"You tricked us," one of them accused her. "You lied to us. We believed that you were just a mother coming to see her son."

She had seen Kevin on Monday, and the days between then and the rescue mission had unfolded like absurdist theater. First they had been visited by, of all people, the comedian and civil rights activist Dick Gregory, who had come to Tehran threatening to fast outside the occupied embassy until the hostages were released. Timm had also met and lunched with a freelance American journalist named Cynthia Dwyer, who had come to Tehran to research an article. They had met at a restaurant in the huge hotel lobby. To further complicate matters, the young Iranian woman who was acting as their interpreter had taken them to meet Iranians who were opposed to Khomeini and the taking of the embassy. They had also attended a prayer service and heard calls of "Death to Carter" and "Death to America." It was all so strange it was hard to know what to think. What sustained Timm was the hope that she might get another chance to visit with Kevin and perhaps even rescue him from this place. She had passed the long days of that week filled with anxiety, confusion, and hope.

Now this, some kind of American attack. The Timms were dismayed. She knew any hope of taking Kevin home was gone and began to fear arrest and detention herself. She had long opposed any use of force to resolve the standoff. Why had Carter done this while she was in Tehran? What if the hostage takers now blew up the embassy and killed the hostages, something they had threatened to do if the United States attacked? Ken Timm had seen what looked like plastic explosives at various places around the outside of the chancery. In this state, Timm got a panicked international phone call from Bonnie Graves, the wife of hostage John Graves, who was angry and distraught and who urged an immediate public apology to Iran. In hopes of sparing her husband what was to come, Bonnie urged Barbara to specifically mention the "family of John Graves." McAfee also urged her to make the statement, as a way of clearing any suspicions about her and her husband and as a way to head off a possible bloody response by the hostage takers.

So Timm went before the TV cameras in the hotel lobby and read a statement drafted by McAfee.

"On behalf of my family and the family of Bonnie Graves, we deeply regret there has been military action taken," she said. She was more vehement in answer to reporters' questions. "I am very angry that the president of our country would do something so stupid, something that we've been told for five months could be so disastrous and could not in any way bring about good results. As a result of trying to make a military move I believe it is time the American people see that President Carter and his advisers are not capable of handling this crisis and that it should be turned over to the people, turned over to the Congress." She lied and told reporters that she did not fear for her son.

On the same day, as Iranian army investigators pored over the wreckage at Desert One and gathered the charred remains of the eight dead members of the failed rescue mission into plastic bags, Timm attended a presidential press conference in Tehran, where Bani-Sadr lambasted her country. Rumors ran high in Iran, and Iranians of course did not believe President Carter's statement about the nature and scope of the mission. The passengers on the arrested bus were quizzed repeatedly about their miraculous escape from peril. Some claimed to have seen at least a dozen helicopters and four hundred to five hundred American soldiers. There were reports that at least forty Iranians, some of them former students of the U.S. Air Force Academy, had been allied with the plot, which was not just a rescue mission but a full-scale invasion and an attempt to murder Khomeini and destroy the revolution.

At Bani-Sadr's side, a sobbing Timm addressed the world press.

"I am going to tell you and the people of Iran that our family and another family of one of the hostages, the Graves family, deeply regret the action our president took yesterday. We'd like to apologize for that action."

Gloating over the American "defeat," Khomeini chastised Carter for his "foolish maneuver" and warned that any further military action by the United States would prompt the immediate execution of all hostages. His threat actually came as a relief to the White House and hostages' families, who remembered earlier such threats by the student captors. It appeared to mean that, perhaps because of the complete ignominy of the mission's failure, there would be no executions this time.

A cruel and macabre press conference was held the next morning at the embassy, where remains of the dead crewmen were put on display. Attended by the imam's son and grandson, it was orchestrated by Ayatollah Khalkali, the hanging judge, who opened the session by expressing condolences to the families of the dead and then unzipped one of the plastic body bags and withdrew a blackened severed hand and forearm to show off its military-style wristwatch. He insisted that twenty-nine Americans had perished, and then claimed to have nine skulls in the bags before him, not eight—one might have belonged to the driver of the exploded fuel truck, who had not escaped the blaze as was thought. Khalkali joked, "I can show you nine skulls. Perhaps Carter can explain how some American soldiers have two heads?" He said evidence recovered from the site— they had found a driver's license in a wallet left behind by one of the mission participants, Stanley E. Thomas—showed that at least one of the invaders had been African-American, which proved, said the ayatollah, that the American invaders had been compelled to participate since no black would volunteer for such a thing.

Barbara Rosen had been in Bonn for her meeting with Chancellor Schmidt when news of the rescue attempt broke. She closed herself in her hotel bathroom and cried. She was terrified about what might now happen to her husband Barry and the rest, appalled at the display of American military ineptitude, and felt personally betrayed by Carter's decision; did he still have the photos of her and Barry's daughters she had given him in that first meeting with the families in December? But when she faced a large crowd of reporters later at the American embassy she took Schmidt's advice and bit her lip. She declined to criticize the president or the military. She met up with the other members of the FLAG European mission in Paris the next day and together they went to Rome for an audience with Pope John Paul II. They had hoped to talk with the pope and solicit his aid in resolving the crisis, but instead they were put in a long line of ceremonial visitors and were ushered before the pope only for a few moments. He told them he would pray and work for the hostages' release and gave each a set of rosary beads.

The Timms were not allowed to leave Tehran on Friday as scheduled. Barbara spent a long and difficult Saturday wondering if she and her husband would ever be permitted to go. She was further shocked to learn that an angry reception now awaited them at home. Phone calls from Milwaukee revealed that her "apology" had set off a furor in the United States. Threatening phone calls had come to their house and there were police stationed outside it. Timm felt that she was at the center of a colossal worldwide misunderstanding, and whatever she did or said just seemed to make it worse. She kept playing over in her mind the moment Ebtekar had said, "Time's up," and her son had been pulled from the room.

Permission to depart came on Sunday, and when their plane lifted into the air Timm collapsed into tears. She felt helpless and angry and guilty and terribly relieved all at the same time. As she cried, a journalist on the same flight took a picture of her. McAfee lost his temper, grabbing the camera and tearing the film out of it.

They stopped in London and ignored the press there, and when they landed in Chicago the next day there was another press mob waiting. It was not friendly.

Most Americans heartily approved of the rescue attempt, and were saddened and disappointed by its failure, but they did not condemn the president. Polls taken in the days afterward showed that while a substantial majority disagreed with the handling of the hostage crisis overall—Ronald Reagan called it "a national disgrace"—a full 66 percent agreed with the president's decision to launch the mission. His approval ratings for handling the hostage crisis fell, but not precipitously, from 47 percent to 42 percent. Overall, Carter still led Reagan in the polls.

In the final meeting before Carter had given the go-ahead to the mission, Brzezinski had brought up the possibility of failure. He had suggested, in keeping with his aggressive posture, that the military draw up a plan that would, in a way, cushion the blow. If it became apparent that the mission was going to fail, then the United States should attack Iran from the air, destroying key oil facilities. The president could then go on television, Brzezinski said, and announce that his patience with Iran had been exhausted by its blatant disregard for international law and its refusal to negotiate in good faith and, as a result, he had authorized a hostage rescue mission and a variety of retaliatory air strikes.

"Then you could say, 'I regret to say that the rescue mission has failed, but we have struck and destroyed the Abadan oil refinery,'" Brzezinski offered. "You could then warn Iran that if any harm comes to the American hostages, 'This is just a foretaste of what is coming.'"

Carter had dismissed the suggestion. "We'll discuss that later," he told his national security adviser and had not followed up. Now there was just the cold fact of failure to report, and the president's stolid, grim face appeared on television screens to deliver the news straight.

Across a wide, disappointed nation, the president took a predictable beating from the pious second-guessers of the nation's editorial pages.

The *News-Tribune* of Tacoma, Washington, boldly concluded, "It may be too early to make a judgment, but first impressions are that the U.S. badly bungled the rescue mission. Further, although Carter certainly deserves the benefit of the doubt at this point, it appears he failed miserably in judgment and leadership."

The *St. Louis Post-Dispatch* predicted that the mission's failure would deepen Iranian distrust of the United States, and that it "cannot have beneficial consequences for ending the hostage situation. To be sure, they now know that Mr. Carter is capable of rash action, but America's failure is more likely to strengthen the Ayatollah's hand than to persuade him to bring the crisis to an end."

The *Phoenix Gazette* accused Carter of undermining the mission by trying to manage it himself from Washington instead of leaving decisions to men in the field. The *Baltimore Evening Sun* offered the remarkable opinion that authorizing the mission had been wrong because there was a chance it might not succeed: "Any possibility of failure should have ruled it out.

We remain unconvinced . . . that the decision to resort to military action was in fact a wise one. On the evidence thus far, it was not." The paper presumably remained solidly behind missions entailing no risk whatsoever.

The *San Diego Evening Tribune* objected to the unilateralism and secrecy of the mission: "Military action may ultimately become necessary. But it should not be undertaken without full consultation with Congress, with our allies, and with other nations in the Middle East."

The *Daily Mail* of Charleston, West Virginia, was bewildered: "It is incredible, in the first place, that the president ever supposed that a commando raid into downtown Tehran would ever have a chance. . . . How could Mr. Carter, who for nearly six months has done virtually nothing to obtain the hostages' release, attempt such a foolhardy operation as this? Having failed to consult with Congress, as the War Powers Act would appear to require, he can scarcely share the responsibility with anyone else. . . . Mr. Carter has contrived to make matters worse."

The *New York Daily News* complained that the mission "entailed risks out of all proportion to the likelihood of success." In Chicago, the *Sun-Times* editorialized, "In his aborted effort . . . President Carter shockingly overcame the charge that he is super-cautious. He is exposed instead as a crap-shooter, willing to gamble away the lives of Americans and the security of the country and its allies to reassert U.S. power against long odds. Before the failure, the U.S.—in the eyes of our friends as well as our enemies—was merely frustrated. . . . Now it has been demonstrated to be impotent."

The *Chicago Tribune* was one of the only newspapers to offer unqualified words of support: "We believe, and the nation must believe, that President Carter made the right decision in sending the rescue team to Iran. It is wrong to criticize him now for making the decision. It is wrong to criticize him for failing to consult in advance with Congress or with the allies. . . . There are but three proper emotions for Americans in the tragic aftermath of the mission's failure: gratitude to the brave volunteers who undertook it; grief for the eight who died in it; and intense disappointment over the bad luck that aborted it."

There was a mixed response from the families of the hostages. Those who had become outspoken critics of the administration, like Timm and Bonnie Graves, were publicly appalled. "Eight deaths for what?" said Bonnie Graves. "I hope to God the Iranians are capable of restraint."

"It's a bumbling error by the president," said Zane Hall, the father of Joe Hall. "We didn't approve of it. We don't know what this could lead to."

Richard Hermening, Timm's former husband and Kevin's father, who just weeks earlier had lamented Carter's slowness to act and lack of follow-through, now criticized the president's "timing."

However, most of the families, who had a ready and waiting press audience for their every utterance, were sympathetic to the president and respectful of the courage and sacrifice of those who had made the effort.

"I understand why he [Carter] had to go to this point in time," said John W. Limbert, the hostage's father. "He had to take action."

A grieving but proud George N. Holmes, father of the Pine Bluff, Arkansas, marine crewman who had perished at Desert One, told reporters, "I think it was fine. It was a risk worth taking. That's what I thought beforehand. I don't change it now."

It was a dejected group of Delta soldiers who reassembled at Wadi Kena after the mission, and none was more depressed than Beckwith, who treated his pain with booze. The colonel realized that the chance of his lifetime had been blown, badly, and he was liberal and unsparing in apportioning blame. He let it be known that he never again wanted to work with the mission's commanding general, James Vaught, and in one tirade he placed the primary responsibility for the mission's failure on the marine pilots, whom he called "cowards." He was particularly scornful of Colonel Chuck Pittman, the ranking officer on board the relatively undamaged chopper that had given up in the second *haboob* and returned to the *Nimitz*. For some reason—it was not immediately clear why—Beckwith also regarded the Iranian-American drivers and translators as "cowards."

Dick Meadows, the courageous Delta point man in Tehran, weighed his options the day after the mission failed. He could try to drive across the Turkish border, or drive down to Abadan on the Persian Gulf coast and use his satellite radio to request pickup by helicopter. He chose a third, less dramatic course. He simply drove to Tehran's international airport on Sunday, the same day as the Timms' departure, and while the country was still in an uproar over the American "invasion," he presented his Irish credentials, fully expecting at any moment to be stopped. He was allowed to board a commercial flight to Ankara. The false passports of the other agents also held up; they were able to fly out of the country in the days after the disaster—one, the young Iranian-American airman code-named "Fred," slipped out weeks later.

Given the uproar in the media at home, it was decided to fly the rest of Delta Force from Egypt to the Farm in Virginia, keep them sequestered there for a few days, and then allow them to fly home to Fayetteville and enjoy a vacation. Alert reporters spotted some of the men arriving at the airport in North Carolina days later, but the only public comment they got was one from an unnamed arriving passenger, probably not a member of the rescue force, who grumbled about not being allowed to "finish the job."

The men who had taken part knew that "finishing the job" had not been an option. Their humiliation had already felt complete when, before they departed Egypt, Beckwith gathered both squadrons in a hangar. Apparently drunk, at first it seemed he had just wanted to console them and buck up their spirits. He began by telling them how proud of them he was, and how professionally they had prepared for the mission, and how in his mind no part of the blame was theirs for the debacle.

As he spoke he grew more and more worked up and emotional, and his remarks began to wander, until he was telling the men that he was disappointed in them for only one thing, for having left their weapons behind when they scrambled out of the burning C-130. Technically, of course, he was correct. A soldier is taught from day one that his weapon is his life, that to lose it or misplace it or leave it behind is a cardinal sin in soldiering. Most of the men had left their weapons and their gear, including the thousands of dollars in American and Iranian cash they had been issued in case they had to find their own ways out of Iran. But given the circumstances—some of the men had been asleep when the accident happened, and had only seconds to evacuate in an inferno—it was certainly understandable.

"You guys, as you came off, should have reached up and grabbed something," Beckwith said angrily. "Goddamn, a lot of money burned up in there."

The men took it badly. They were just getting used to this disappointment, one that they knew well they'd wear for the rest of their lives, which many had escaped with only narrowly. They had felt the flames and had seen men on fire. Many were injured. They were in no mood to be chastised by someone who had watched the inferno from a safe distance. A sergeant major interrupted Beckwith.

"Sir, we were lucky to get off with our asses," he said.

"Well, some of you picked up your weapons. Why in the hell didn't all of you?" Beckwith asked.

The sergeant major began, "Sir—," but the colonel lost it. "Shut up!" he shouted. "You're all just a bunch of goddamn cowards."

"That's not true, sir," Fitch said sharply, grabbing the colonel by the arm and hustling him out of the hangar before things got uglier.

Beckwith would later regret this outburst and asked Fitch to convey an apology to the men, but he never softened his assessment of the other service branches involved in the fiasco.

The mood had been glum on the long flight home. When Fitch's squadron landed at an airport outside Washington, they transferred to a C-130 for a short flight to Virginia. Welcoming them into the plane was a veteran air force sergeant who, having no idea who this motley assortment of hairy apparent civilians were, assumed that they were unfamiliar with the C-130 and so, upon takeoff, launched into an especially spirited performance of the standard safety briefing for passengers—something ordinarily abbreviated or forgone entirely for military passengers. The plane was virtually identical to the one the mission members had flown into Iran just days before. They sat obediently through the meticulous and thorough safety presentation, then stood up (against instructions) and gave the bewildered sergeant a spirited ovation.

3

S-E-N-D-N-E-W-S

After the rescue attempt, Bruce Laingen noticed a change in his keepers
on the third floor of the Foreign Ministry building. Gone was the easy
banter that had characterized his relationship with most of them, and
some of the guards had become outright hostile. There were accusations
that the chargé and his roommates, Mike Howland and Vic Tomseth,
had known in advance about the mission, given their occasional phone
calls and telex contacts with Washington and visits from foreign ministers. In the garden below their balcony, the army unit assigned to the
ministry still spent every spare moment playing pickup games of soccer, but they no longer waved and joked with the Americans looking
down from the high windows. Some glared up at them with what was
clearly hatred.

Unlike the other hostages, the three in the Foreign Ministry learned
of the rescue mission in breathless local press reports as soon as the rest of
Iran did. Laingen wrote in his diary on the evening of April 27:

> Our minds and hearts are filled with thoughts and emotions that
> leave us confused and perplexed. Had there been no mechanical fail-
> ure, where would we be now? On board an aircraft carrier, stranded
> in the desert, still here in the ministry, injured, or even dead? Who
> can say? And who can say now what might have happened to our
> colleagues, to their captors, and to personnel guarding us in this
> ministry? In a sense, we are, in the aftermath, less fortunate than our
> 50 colleagues, since they will not know, presumably, what happened,
> while we do and must now live with the emotions and frustrations
> that are the consequence. . . . So we are filled with an enormous sense
> of sadness. Grief for those eight courageous men who volunteered
> and were ready to give their lives for their country and for the prin-
> ciple we represent here—the nation should be forever grateful to
> them. A sense of compassion for a president who made this difficult
> and lonely decision and who now suffers this bitter disappointment

and must bear the full responsibility of failure. Concern for the hostage families whose worries are now deepened. Regret for our country that it should suffer this blow to its self-esteem and pride. Sorrow for the Iranian people whose future is so jeopardized by the continuation of this whole tragic affair. Anger at those who perpetrate this crisis here, when the simple act of decency of releasing the hostages would turn this whole thing around . . . and finally, pride in our country for this demonstration of resolve in our efforts to get the hostages released.

It was galling for the three to watch the gleeful press coverage in Tehran, where the failure of the rescue mission was seen as nothing less than divine intervention and a heavenly blessing on the *gerogan-girha*, the hostage takers. Allah had dealt the Great World Devouring Satan a terrible blow. At night, to celebrate the "victory," thousands of Iranians had again taken to their rooftops to shout over and over, *"Allahuakbar!"*

Laingen spent long portions of his days now watching the pigeons that roosted in small gaps in the brickwork of the ministry garden walls. They lived on the ledges of the windows outside the third floor and roof, periodically swooping down to the large fountain in the middle of the courtyard and then back. He also watched the swallows, which appeared at dusk to flit crazily around the sky catching bugs. They reminded him of the barn swallows he had watched as a boy on the family farm in Minnesota. He worried about becoming lazy, after so many months of idleness. Laingen was an energetic and ambitious man, and having little to do besides eat, sleep, read, and work crossword puzzles ate away at his sense of himself. He worried that he would find it hard to resume the pace of work and family and wondered admiringly at the industry of his wife Penne, who had for so long now managed everything at home by herself and yet had emerged as a leading activist and voice of the hostage families.

At long last the *Majlis* convened at the end of May, fanning faint hopes that the hostage issue would be resolved. Laingen noted in the local press that his old friend Ibrahim Yazdi, the foreign minister on the day of the takeover who had resigned with the rest of the provisional government when it was clear their authority had been usurped by a gang of students, was now a member of the legislature calling for public trial of the hostages as a way of taking the United States to task for its "interference" in Iranian affairs. Laingen wondered if his friend ever thought of him locked away where he had left him six months before.

John Limbert enjoyed his garden view for only three days before being taken to a villa more in the center of Isfahan, near a river that he knew to be the Zayandeh. His new room had no view nor any good light, but he could overhear bits of radio reports that drifted in from somewhere outside, and it was here that he first caught snippets of a broadcast about a rescue attempt. The sound faded in and out, and he heard only bits, but that's what it had sounded like. A mission, unsuccessful, and American casualties. This was confirmed when, on a visit to the bathroom, he found a week-old newspaper that one of the guards had used to line the top of a shelf. It carried a wire service story about the mission, so Limbert became the first of the hostages other than the three at the foreign ministry to learn that his government had tried a daring rescue and had failed. He wasn't sure how to feel about it. On the one hand, it showed that he and the others had not been forgotten by President Carter and their countrymen, which lifted his spirits and filled him with hope and pride. On the other hand, it had failed, which meant that the prospects of being saved by military action, always remote, were now nil. He also felt a pang of sorrow and gratitude for his countrymen who had tried, especially those who had died in the effort.

As the long summer dragged on, Limbert was beset with boredom, loneliness, and despair. Occasional letters from his wife and two children helped sustain him. The children mailed their school report cards, and the fact that they were doing well heartened him enormously. He received, months late, a Valentine the children had made at school. Just to know that they were safe and thriving eliminated one of his biggest worries. He had been concerned early on that his wife Parvaneh might try to come to Iran to lobby for his freedom, which, given the present atmosphere in her home country, might well have landed her in jail. He worried whether his daughter and son would recognize him when they saw him next, whether they would remember him and whether he would be the same person he was when he had left. In his own letters (most of them never made it home) he left coded messages in the text. Counting on the students' generally poor English, he constructed sentences with strings of words that barely made sense, but which, if you took the first letter of each, spelled out his message. For instance, he wrote, "Shervin [his son] every new defenseman needs energy with savvy." The first letters of each word spelled out "s-e-n-d-n-e-w-s." When Parveneh received the letters she knew that there was a code embedded but could not figure it out. She turned it over to the State Department and the CIA and neither of these agencies figured it out either.

Limbert was not the only one whose code scheme failed. In dozens of letters to his wife, Navy Commander Don Sharer spelled out secret messages, choosing the first letter of each paragraph so that when put together they would read, "TORTURE," or "STARVING," which wasn't exactly true but which conveyed the message that things weren't all hunky-dory. Years earlier he had told his wife about that code, which had been employed by some prisoners in Vietnam, and was sure she would be looking for it. Once, just to throw his captors off, he reversed the pattern, spelling out the hidden message backward. This, as it happens, was the only letter his wife received from him. She looked for the code, but because it was backward, she didn't find it.

Eventually Limbert discovered that Malcolm Kalp, one of the embassy's three CIA officers and the one he knew least, was in a room separated from his by a shared bathroom. Limbert tore the top off a paper box of raisins one day, wrote the word "hide" on it, and left it in a conspicuous spot on the toilet. He figured that if one of the guards found it they wouldn't know what to make of it and if the person on the other side of the bathroom found it he could know what it meant. Kalp found it and understood immediately. He wrote, "Inside the Ajax container" on it and left it where he had found it. There was a box of powdered soap in the bathroom. Kalp figured that an American who left the note would know what "Ajax" was but that an Iranian would not. Sure enough, when he used the bathroom next there was a note from Limbert in the soap box. Later they found that there was a space between the washbasin and its pedestal that would serve even better. They passed messages four times a day. Limbert informed Kalp of the failed rescue mission, and it was Kalp who told him that Bill Belk, Kevin Hermening, and Joe Subic were also in the villa. In one of his notes Kalp wrote that he had not been mistreated but that he had been kept alone for a long time.

*   *   *

Summer turned suffocating in the windowless room in Qom where Michael
Metrinko, Dave Roeder, and Regis Regan were imprisoned. They spent
hours each day exercising, three pale, shaggy, bearded men in ill-fitting
clothes bouncing up and down, running in place for hours at a time, then
dropping down to do push-ups. The downside was that they would sweat
heavily and, because they could shower only occasionally, their room
reeked like a dirty gym locker. Regan was withdrawn, but Metrinko and
Roeder hit it off. Metrinko admired Roeder's sly military sense of humor,
and Roeder admired the political officer's intelligence and unyielding
toughness. Metrinko taught Roeder how to swear in Farsi, more particularly, how to grievously and obscenely insult the guards. He still missed
no opportunity to aggravate his captors.

One day they were visited by Ahmad Khomeini, the imam's son, who
greeted the three as "guests." The false hospitality disgusted Metrinko, who
had bottomless contempt for all of Iran's new "spiritual" rulers; to him
Ahmad just seemed a fat, greasy young man in robes and a black turban.
The guards, however, were awestruck. Clearly anxious about hosting such
an august figure, they had urged their three captives to say nice things about
them.

"What can I do for you?" the cleric asked beneficently. "We want to
make you more comfortable."

Metrinko told him that they wished to be released. They were being
treated worse than animals, he said, and their captivity was an insult to
Islamic values and Iranian traditions.

"I haven't been outside for several months," Metrinko told him. "I
want to see the sun. We need air. We would also like to have some meat
with our food."

Khomeini seemed shocked and the guards were chagrined.

"They haven't been outside?" he said, turning to the guards, who
looked panic-stricken. "They must go out every day!" he said.

"Oh, yes, your Excellency," the nearest guard said. "Yes, sir, we will
arrange it immediately."

After that, Metrinko was taken to a courtyard, a standard feature
of an Iranian house, and for the first time he had a better sense of where
he was imprisoned. It was a fairly large building that had once been some
kind of art school. The walls were covered with propaganda, mostly

drawings of Khomeini and others in the new pantheon of Islamist leadership. Metrinko had no knowledge yet of the attempted rescue mission, but it was apparent that his guards had been spooked by something. After months of growing more and more lackadaisical, suddenly they were vigilant out of all proportion. They had been holding him now for six months and he had not made the slightest move to escape, yet in the small courtyard where he was permitted to stroll he was surrounded by more than a dozen armed guards who eyed him so warily it was comical. He ignored them and gave himself over to the rare pleasure of being outside. He basked in the sunshine, smells, and sounds. Metrinko had never considered himself a great lover of the outdoors, but in his captivity he discovered in himself a deep need for it. He had begun to fantasize about taking long walks in the woods, watching sunsets, drinking great gulps of glorious fresh air. In the little courtyard he walked back and forth aimlessly inside the circle of armed guards. It occurred to him that if he made a sudden move in any direction and they opened fire, they would probably all inadvertently shoot each other. It might be worth getting shot himself just to see it happen. His outdoor stroll lasted ten minutes. Despite the admonition of the imam's son, he and the others got to go outside once more in the next two months.

It was sometime in July when the three were taken back to Tehran and placed in a cell at Qasr Prison, another of the shah's notorious lockups. It was modeled after the nineteenth-century "panoptican" prisons, a central hub with arms that projected outward. They were placed in a large cell, the first genuine prison cell they had inhabited. It was concrete and clean, with a thin carpet stretched over the floor from wall to wall. It had one barred window, too high on the wall for them to look out. The door was made of solid iron and had a transom with a barred window that they could reach by gripping the top of the door and pulling themselves up. It afforded nothing more than a view of the empty hallway. Given a mattress and a pillow, they chose their spots and unpacked their few belongings.

It was summer but the concrete walls and floor were cool. The guards allowed them to listen to music. Every few days they would bring in a portable tape player with cassettes of classical music and they were permitted to listen for an hour. On occasion they were led down the hall to a room with a television, where they watched videotapes. One of the tapes was of a press conference in the United States by Darrell Rupiper, the radical oblate missionary who had visited Iran in the spring and come away favorably impressed by the revolution and the embassy takeover. Metrinko and the others were appalled. The hostages, Rupiper said, were being treated well by their captors, whom he believed were justified in their action. America, he said, owed Iran a big apology.

4

MORAL SADNESS

At home during the late spring and summer of 1980 the hostage drama went flat. Jonathan Schell, writing in *The New Yorker*, wrote of "a numbness, an emotional fatigue" that seemed to settle over the nation in the weeks after the failed rescue mission. Throughout the previous winter and spring there had been dramatic developments to keep the story moving, the takeover itself, the threats, the secret negotiations that, in the words of ABC's Ted Koppel, would come "so tantalizingly close" again and again, only to repeatedly collapse. In the weeks before the rescue mission there had been a mounting expectation of war; the crisis was like a festering boil, and the prospect of ending it violently engendered not so much dread as relief. The spectacular failure at Desert One had lanced the boil. It had a peculiar and unanticipated effect: the fever seemed to lift. For a few days afterward the hostages' families, the Carter administration, and the rest of the country waited anxiously to see if the Iranians would make good on their threat to retaliate by killing hostages, which would have provoked a furious American military response, and when they did not it was as though Iran had earned, for a time, a respite. Both sides backed away from the precipice. The angry rhetoric from Washington cooled. Word got back that the hostages were being scattered around Iran, which killed any prospect of a second rescue effort. Congress settled in to investigate Beckwith's disaster and to assign blame for it, but the hostages themselves receded from television and the front pages. The story had exhausted itself. It seemed there was simply nothing to be done about it or, perhaps, that too much had been made of it.

Commenting in the June 2 issue of *The New Yorker*, Schell speculated that the abrupt change had more to do with the news media itself than world events. "In an instant, the frantic urgency about [the hostages'] release dissipated, and they seemed to disappear from the face of the earth," he wrote. "Gone were the interviews with their friends and relatives, gone the impromptu delegations of clerical would-be peacemakers, and gone the sideshow of freelance meddlers. . . . Gone, too, were reports of the 'rising impatience' of the American people which was thought to have so much to do with the decision to launch the rescue mission." Schell noted the tendency of television news to leap from one short-lived obsession to the next, in "obedience to a rhythm . . . which seems to have more to do with the world of entertainment than the world of international affairs," and concluded, "In part, however, the news media may have abandoned the hostage issue because of a well-founded if largely unarticulated suspicion that their own disproportionate coverage of it, together with the presidential campaign, had generated a terrifying vortex of political pressure that brought on the tragic rescue mission and came near to dragging the nation into a catastrophe."

Some of the hostage families had reached similar conclusions, which helped explain why they suddenly vanished from television. All had grown savvy about news coverage, particularly about cameras, and so became more wary. Barbara Rosen was annoyed with herself for not having caught on sooner. Like most of the other spouses, parents, and siblings, she had assumed that the more attention given the plight of their loved ones the better, but her conversation with Helmut Schmidt in Bonn had stayed with her. "Get the story off the front pages!" he had said. She now saw the wisdom in that advice. The great swirl of media attention in the months after the takeover had fed the crisis. She had fed the crisis. She regretted having allowed TV cameras into her home over the Christmas holidays the year before, and winced at the memory of her children telling America how much they missed their daddy. Those snippets of family life had tugged at the heartstrings of her fellow countrymen and people of goodwill everywhere, which, she now realized, was precisely what her husband's kidnappers wanted. Now she refused to go on TV. When reporters showed up she would sometimes agree to talk, but declined to do so on camera. When a New York studio lured her with an offer to see the latest film released from Tehran, she went to the studio but refused to allow them to film her watching it. When a producer insisted, Rosen picked up her bag and started out of the building. The producer chased her down and let her watch the film in private.

In light of the obvious heroism of the men who attempted the rescue, it was predictable that efforts were made to hang the mission's failure on the White House. Some reports suggested that Delta Force had been pressured to launch against its will by an overeager president, or that it had been prevented from going all out by presidential timidity. Colonel Beckwith stepped forward to bluntly deny both claims. He said that he and his men had been eager to launch and still believed they might have succeeded. He dismissed speculation that the raid had been undermined by micromanagement from the White House, that Carter had aborted it in an excess of caution over the objections of the men in the desert. Beckwith said he had aborted the mission himself and would do so again, and called reports that said otherwise "pure bullshit."

"I'm not about to be party to a half-assed loading of a bunch of aircraft and going up and murdering a bunch of fine soldiers," he said, indignant, his eyes blazing under his dark eyebrows. "I'm not that kind of man."

Carter himself pushed the hostages out of the news by abandoning his strategy of camping in the White House and looking presidential. He declared world events more "manageable" and hit the campaign trail, failing even to mention Iran in two major speeches.

Americans took grim satisfaction in May when Iran's own embassy in London was seized by six Iraqi-trained Khuzestan separatists, who took hostage two dozen Iranian diplomats and staffers. The situation, according to Iranian president Bani-Sadr, was "in no way comparable" to the seizure of the U.S. embassy in Tehran. This was "an unjust hostage taking," he said, because Iranian diplomats, unlike American, "had no other duties but to represent their country." They had been kidnapped by "a group of hired and deceived terrorists," as opposed to the patriotic heroes who had kidnapped American diplomats in Tehran. But the parallel was obvious and there for all the world to see. The British government demonstrated how responsible nations protect foreign missions on their soil by storming the embassy and rescuing fourteen of the sixteen hostages—two Iranian diplomats were killed by their captors, and five of the six terrorists were killed by the British SAS forces, several of them apparently executed on the spot. Without a trace of irony, Bani-Sadr praised the British government for upholding its obligations as a host government under international law.

It did nothing to alter the standoff in Tehran. A "Crimes of America" conference kicked off there in June, attended by representatives of many small nations and by a ten-person delegation of Americans led by Ramsey

Clark, who had failed to win permission to enter Iran as a special emissary of the president the previous November, and who now attended in defiance of President Carter's ban on American travel to Iran. The TV networks showed the tall, lean former U.S. attorney general listening and lecturing at the conference, faulting both sides of the dispute. He admitted the imperiousness of America's foreign policy—"The United States still clings to the idea that it can control the government and destinies of other people," he said—and he denounced the embassy takeover and the holding of hostages. Clark's public criticism of the hostage takers in Tehran was courageous, but his presence there conferred a trace of legitimacy to an event designed for only one purpose, to embarrass and insult his own country. When Khomeini addressed the conference, he suggested that Carter's travel ban showed how much he feared what Americans might learn. He urged those attending to return to their homes in the West and tell the truth, because the mainstream press portrayed Iran "as a jungle filled with crazy people."

He wasn't far from the truth. Months into the crisis there was still very little effort, particularly on television, to dissect either the Iranian revolution or the American policy that had preceded it. The typical American saw images almost daily of angry Iranians waving their fists and denouncing the United States, but with few exceptions—Ted Koppel's *Nightline* program each evening was one—saw little to explain what had prompted such anger and hatred. Clark's willingness to speak unpopular truths to both sides earned him little praise or admiration. He was condemned as a traitor at home and many called for him to be prosecuted. Radio Tehran called him "the vilest of CIA spies."

Neither Clark's trip nor any of the other news out of Iran suggested hope for a resolution. As summer wore on, the presence of fifty-three captive Americans scattered throughout Iran had become a fact of life. Bani-Sadr pronounced the crisis "unsolvable," and suggested that the responsibility for drawing it out rested with the United States.

"America has not changed its hostile policy and has not changed anything in it," he said. "The Americans think Iran is their private property . . . and that it should remain American property forever. If they can't have it today, they want to take over Iran tomorrow, and they are using [the hostage crisis] to add on pressure in order to topple us from inside. So we are going to live here and resist. We will live with the hostages."

Despite the dearth of news, the months of intense coverage on television had made many of the hostages' families into national figures, even patriotic icons. Dorothea Morefield, wife of the captive American consul, had become a regular on television news shows in San Diego and was often featured on national news programs. Always meticulously coiffed and groomed, well spoken, calm, and cheerful, this prim middle-aged housewife in oversized glasses was steadfast in her support of the administration's handling of the crisis. When their son had been murdered in Washington, D.C., years earlier, she and her husband had been impressed by some of the reporters who had covered the tragedy with compassion and dignity. So when the embassy was seized she had decided to open her cheerful home to reporters. She was motivated initially by a desire to counter some of the maudlin, weepy scenes in the homes of other hostage families, and in the ensuing months she had developed an easy rapport with a whole group of local and national reporters. She presented the patriotic, smart, determined image that Washington felt would be most helpful in the long run. She was, in fact, angry with the State Department for many things, first for not closing the embassy and evacuating the staff prior to admitting the shah into the United States, and also for doing so little to keep the families informed. She thought the family outreach effort of the Iran Working Group was laughable, a clutch of untrained, gossipy spouses. But she kept those feelings to herself in public, working to represent her husband and the others as professionals and kidnap victims. Her resolve rarely wavered, but as the crisis became more and more noticeably a back-burner issue for the White House, now fully engaged in a reelection campaign, it wobbled ever so slightly. She did not share the view that publicity only made matters worse and worked hard to keep the story in the news. She bristled publicly at Carter's use of the word "manageable."

"It may be manageable, but I don't know in what way," she told a TV interviewer. "One hopes that there is something more going on behind the scenes." It was a subtle criticism, more like a plea. She proceeded to defend the president's decision to get out and campaign, and said that it would be wrong for the nation to be held captive to every new twist and turn of the story. Yet she clearly felt more needed to be done.

"Do you know where your husband is?" she was asked.

"I have no idea," she said. "I haven't heard from him since the rescue attempt."

"Do you have any reservations about the way it's being handled?"

"Well, we don't know what's going on behind the scenes," she said. "I would like to see a little more publicity about the hostages themselves." She said the attention helped keep the pressure on Iran, because the more Iranians understood how much all of America cared and was watching, the less likely they would be to harm the captives. She faulted the world community for not doing more to help the United States put pressure on Iran, but unlike Barbara Timm, who had gone to ground after returning from her controversial apology in Iran, and the outspokenly critical Graves family, Morefield presented a concerned but stoical face. She was the honored guest at that year's municipal Fourth of July celebrations and asked a crowd at an air show at Miramar Naval Air Station to "say a prayer" for their countrymen who were being deprived of their God-given freedom.

The Fourth of July flushed more of the hostage families into the limelight. Marine Rocky Sickmann's parents were the featured guests at an Independence Day ceremony in their hometown of St. Louis, and Harry Metrinko, Michael's father, appeared at the ceremonies near their home in Hermitage, Pennsylvania, where a new flag was added to a growing forest of Stars and Stripes for each day of his son's captivity. The rhetorical thrust of these events and others like them was that America would never forget or forsake its kidnapped diplomats, but it had been a long eight months, and the very need to so publicly pledge mindfulness showed that the issue was dimming in the American mind.

By August the "crisis" had faded almost completely away. There was a rote, unexceptional tone to the nightly reminders on network news shows of the days of captivity, which was nearing three hundred.

Even the death of the shah in Cairo failed to produce the slightest change in the standoff. The former ruler succumbed in late July to pneumonia that had set in after another round of chemotherapy for liver cancer. An extended ABC News review of Pahlavi's life referred briefly to Mossadeq, and even showed a black-and-white film clip of the old political figure, but only to say that he had angled to remove the young Pahlavi from power. There was no mention in the program that Mossadeq had been an elected figure, which left the impression that his efforts had just been part of a typical Third World power struggle, decided in favor of the shah by American intervention. The exiled monarch was buried in a state funeral in Egypt, a ceremony to which the United States sent only its ambassador. Carter, who just three years earlier had effusively toasted the dictator in Tehran, dared not send a more prominent representative for fear of aggravating the hostage situation.

The president remained unsparing in his criticism of Iran's leadership, whom he called "kidnappers and international terrorists." When he characterized its government as divided and its politics as "chaotic," it just underscored his bewilderment. Carter was, in so many words, agreeing with Bani-Sadr. The matter appeared unsolvable. As August turned to September, the crisis had not so much disappeared from public consciousness as it had become simply a fact of life, a chronic, low-level annoyance. Near the end of summer, ABC correspondent Peter Jennings concluded, "The United States and Iran are on different wavelengths . . . no better able to understand each other than on the day of the takeover."

Eventually even family members who shunned the media began to feel that no news was as bad as too much. Worried that her husband and the rest of the hostages were slipping off the country's political agenda entirely, Penne Laingen and Dottie Morefield wrote a public letter to both the Republican and Democratic Parties urging them to mention the hostages in their platforms, to refrain from making their captive family members an issue during the campaign, and to oppose any agreement that called for the United States to apologize to Iran. A group supporting the hostages began a billboard campaign to remind the American public that their countrymen were still trapped.

The billboards read, "Have you thought of the hostages today?"

The obstinacy of their plight wore hard on the hostages. Imprisoned chargé d'affaires Bruce Laingen was amused in midsummer when he received the results of a Red Cross medical assessment conducted months earlier. Delivered by a Swiss emissary, the report found all three of the Foreign Ministry captives otherwise fit but afflicted with "moral sadness." In Laingen's case, it was "moral sadness, with some nervousness."

His moral sadness had been aggravated by the participation of Ramsey Clark and other Americans in the "Crimes of America" conference. How could Clark, who had long been a respected figure in the

United States, participate in such a propaganda pageant at any time, much less while his hosts were holding dozens of his countrymen hostage?

All summer long, dry, hot desert winds blew through the open windows of the stuffy third-floor of the ministry building, giving little relief. Despite the cramped, uncomfortable circumstances, Laingen, Tomseth, and Howland still got along with one another remarkably well. They had lived together in the same rooms for months now, day and night, and in all that time Laingen could not remember an angry word being spoken. This he attributed to their temperaments; all three were polite and by nature easygoing and friendly. None of them was overbearingly opinionated. They also shared a sense of victimhood, which made them each more tolerant of the others. The fact that they were being held in such spacious quarters helped. They came together when they wished and whenever one of them wanted solitude, the size of the reception area and dining room enabled them to effectively get away for hours. They spent their long days writing, reading, exercising, or working crossword puzzles, which arrived in the mail and as gifts from diplomatic visitors in a steady stream.

"How do you spell 'chaos'?" Howland asked one day.

"I-R-A-N," deadpanned Laingen.

The cockroaches that invaded their quarters came in two sizes, large and extra large. The three called the smaller ones "mullahs" and the larger "ayatollahs," and took some pleasure in crunching them underfoot.

Chocolates, books, and occasional packages from home were delivered by their most faithful visitor, the Swiss envoy. On one call he passed along, laughing, an official request from the home office in Washington. It was standard procedure for the heads of embassies to produce annual employee evaluations for the department's files. Even though the entire Tehran staff was detained under fairly remarkable circumstances, the efficient bureaucracy of Foggy Bottom still wanted its annual "fitness reports."

For the next few days, Laingen and Tomseth worked up assessments of their colleagues. At the end of each they wrote, "This is being written in Tehran. The recipient of our report is not here because he's being held hostage. So he cannot have any direct input."

They sent the reports back with the Swiss envoy on his next visit.

It was more apparent every day that the one unmistakable consequence of the embassy seizure had been to tilt the balance of power in Iran toward the clergy. At the time of the revolution it was unclear how the new Iran would shake out, but voting for the *Majlis* in May had produced an overwhelming victory for religious hardliners and had further isolated such secular leaders as Bani-Sadr and Ghotbzadeh, whose powerlessness had been fully exposed by their failure to get all the hostages transferred to government custody. The new leader of the Iranian legislature, Akbar Hashemi-Rafsanjani, dismissed the hostage issue as a low priority, and stated that it would not even be discussed until July.

The only contact between an American and Iran's leadership that summer occurred when an audience with the imam was granted to Dick Gregory, who had dropped forty pounds fasting for the hostages' release. The comedian/activist advocated a solution that would bring the majority of the Americans home, leaving only the most "suspicious" behind to stand trial as spies. Bani-Sadr, for his part, believed that President Carter was still plotting to destroy the revolution and saw conspiracies everywhere. Despite their political differences, both the embattled Iranian president and his radical religious opponents imagined a White House completely obsessed with Iran. Since they considered the United States not just amoral but evil, they developed stunning hypotheses of American deceit. Bani-Sadr accused the United States of sending teams of assassins to find and kill its own captive countrymen in an effort to bring further ignominy on Iran. Increasingly, he blamed America for the whole mess, and, in time, would convince himself that the United States had actually planned and instigated the takeover of its own embassy, and that the Muslim Students Following the Imam's Line were either dupes or directly employed by the CIA.

When Bani-Sadr had said, "We will live with the hostages," it alarmed Laingen. With religious authority clearly entrenched, there were regular reports of sweeping executions—dozens of "coup plotters" or "spies" were dispatched at a time. Ayatollah Khalkali held multiple public executions on the streets of Tehran, and boasted that he had personally dispatched to Allah in just three months a thousand "counterrevolutionaries" and four hundred common criminals for drug violations. Victims were put to death for homosexuality, adultery, and drug dealing as well as political crimes. Troops opened fire on thousands of leftist demonstrators as they marched in the street toward the U.S. embassy on June 12, killing five and injuring three hundred. These vicious excesses went well beyond the crimes of the shah, and the purges were just beginning. Khomeini issued an ominous call for a "cultural revolution" to rid Iran of remnants of monarchical and Western influence. Iranians from all walks of life were denounced as spies or collaborators, and many were shown "confessing" their crimes on television prior to their executions. Laingen wondered what possessed a clearly doomed man to do such a thing. Why would even a real enemy of the regime give his captors the satisfaction of admitting everything before execution? Did he do so in the hope that it would earn him clemency or protect his family and friends from arrest or persecution? It was a subject of more than just casual interest to him. Many in the *Majlis* were still calling for trials of the American "spies." What would he do when his turn came?

All this was accompanied by increasing talk of putting at least some of the hostages on trial. Ever since the failed rescue attempt, spy fever had seized the country. Dozens of military men were executed for their alleged role in aiding the planned American "invasion." One woman turned in her husband, who she said had confessed to her that he worked for the CIA. There was new outrage in Iran in June when a young man walked into a Tehran police station and announced that he had just hung his twenty-three-year-old younger sister, Amaz, because his family had discovered that she was five months pregnant by Sergeant Mike Moeller, one of the embassy marines being held hostage. Moeller had been questioned in detail about the woman on Easter Sunday and admitted he had known her. Amaz was a regular at parties the marines had held in the small house Moeller was renting—they were not allowed to have alcohol on the embassy grounds, and the marines had not yet been moved to the Bijon apartments behind the complex. Moeller knew that several marines had engaged in sex with Amaz but denied that he was one of them. The authorities claimed that the unfortunate woman had specifically mentioned Moeller in her diary, and the marine suggested it was only because the parties had been held at his house. The brother who killed Amaz received an outpouring of public sympathy; Moeller faced charges for engaging in an "illegal sexual affair."

The episode fed the predatory image of Americans, and thus served an important political purpose. Facing increasing opposition from ethnic minorities and secular factions, and having discovered an apparently well-organized military plot to overthrow the revolutionary government, Khomeini resorted to a familiar tactic. He blamed all opposition and betrayal on secret American meddling and whipped up anti-American displays. On July 4, hundreds of thousands of Iranians marched in Tehran to protest continued American efforts to undermine their revolution.

Countrywide celebrations marked the death of the shah three weeks later, but for the hostage takers his passing was irrelevant; indeed, for most of the students the demand for his return had been purely rhetorical from the beginning. "Larger issues have taken his place in the negotiations that have yet to begin," Laingen wrote. More than a year after overthrowing the shah's government because of its brutality, an even more brutal boss was on the throne, proclaiming his own version of divine right. Laingen wrote:

> There is no doubt that the clergy are now in the saddle, and they are determined to exploit their current opportunity to entrench themselves as deeply and firmly as possible, all this out of that group's genuine conviction that Iran's problems stem from its failure to follow the precepts and practices of Shia Islam in all aspects of life. Hence the drive for "purity" and "cleansing" of the body politic of all contrary tendencies, not least the exterior manifestations of aping Western ways and the pernicious (in their view) penetration of Western cultural influences that have exposed Iran to weakness and that threaten the Islamic way of life.

It seemed clear to Laingen that this consolidation of power was not just happenstance, and because the embassy takeover had so strengthened the hands of the mullahs, it must have been engineered, or at least steered, by them.

> The Tehran *Times* of the past two days has carried excerpts from an interview with the celebrated cleric Mousavi Khoeniha, the clerical link with the "students" at the embassy since the day of the seizure and, as it is now much clearer, the link before that, too, in the planning of the seizure. Khoeniha's insistence that the ARK [Ayatollah Ruhollah Khomeini] had not been informed before the seizure of the students' plans. Said he: "We knew it would have been incorrect for the leader of our revolution to know in advance what we were going to do." That, he said, would have been "politically unwise." Later, "We simply did not think that our action would have such grave international consequences." (Obviously not. The gentleman is obviously too shallow to have any such comprehension.)

> It is old stuff, but it raises the question anew: Khoeniha was the link between these "students" planning the act, and who else? Who else among the clerics, and in the ARK's entourage, knew about it in advance? It is too much to expect me to believe that there were not others.

Laingen still struggled to keep up appearances. He was, after all, the highest ranking American official in Iran. From time to time, in his official capacity, he hand-printed letters to Iran's officials, if only to remind them that he and the other hostages were still there.

At the end of June he wrote Bani-Sadr.

Dear Mr. President,

> Today's press had reported you as deploring what you describe as the fundamental hostility of the United States toward you.

> With all respect, Mr. President, this can only reflect a complete misunderstanding of the American government and its people.

> There is no hostility toward Iran that one single act will not remove. That is the release of the American diplomats held hostage for the last eight months. . . . The United States has only one other interest in Iran, that is the maintenance of Iran's independence and territorial integrity by a people and government pursuing policies of their own choosing and without outside interference.

> Sincerely,
> L. Bruce Laingen
> Chargé d'Affaires

For all his anti-American pronouncements, Bani-Sadr and his foreign minister, Ghotbzadeh, remained publicly opposed to further holding hostages. Laingen figured that in their position they saw every day the damage being done to Iran's standing in the world and to its internal security. All the ambitious construction projects under way when the shah fled were still suspended—the great empty cranes on the city's low skyline were rusting—and all forms of international credit had virtually dried up. The true believers didn't care, of course; Allah would provide. The imam said he would rather see the country return to donkey transport than make the smallest concession to the Great Satan. And Allah *was* providing. The great dragon of anti-Americanism loose in the land was devouring all the enemies of the turbaned class. Practical men concerned about Iran's place in the world, and who looked to more earthly solutions, ran the risk of being branded traitor or incompetent. Cherished Western ideals became subversive, and no one criticized the emerging regime without fear. Ghotbzadeh had been attacked in the government-controlled press and had been summoned to appear before the *Majlis* to explain his "mishandling of the ministry." Khomeini himself blasted Bani-Sadr for failing to adequately cope with the country's mounting economic difficulties. The president, of course, blamed America, which, by refusing to resolve the hostage crisis, was trying to "sink me in trivial issues so that I fail to battle against U.S. economic pressure." Still, the Iranian president reserved some ire for the student captors. At the end of August, he was quoted in the newspapers two days in a row speaking critically of the hostage takers. He said the Americans ought to be released, that the continuing standoff had, in effect, "made Iran a hostage of the United States," because American influence around the world ensured that the new Islamic republic was seen as a pariah. Whatever their reasons, these two primarily secular men were taking a huge risk opposing the hard-liners.

Still, nothing changed. The death of the shah, the seating of the *Majlis*, the opposition of the president and his foreign minister . . . the hostage issue bobbed like a cork in a restless sea of change. Laingen had come to suspect that they might not see the end until after the coming American elections and what looked increasingly like Carter's eventual defeat.

> It makes one wonder sometimes . . . whether the objective is to hold the hostages through the elections in hopes of seeing Carter defeated. You will ask, ah yes, but surely [they] realize that Reagan would be more difficult? I don't think that matters. The hatred of Jimmy Carter among some of the fundamentalists is so intense as to regard his defeat as an end in itself, an end or objective that if it can be achieved would be hailed as one more example of the justice of Iran's cause—Allahuakbar. God is great, and He is on our side. That is not a very pleasant prognosis as to intentions here, but, among some of them, I do not exclude it at all.

After all these months of isolation in the ministry, the three Americans were still regarded as a threat. On the first day of July, one of the guards barged into their room with a soldier and the two men stood scrutinizing one of the windows overlooking the garden, apparently convinced that a coded message had been written there by the captives. What they had seen were just a few random splashes of bird droppings.

In mid-August, the ministry guards suddenly delivered a big plastic bag filled with Valentines that had been mailed almost six months earlier. Most were from schoolchildren.

One suggested, " I hope you can sneak out of Iran when the people go to bed. Then you can go back home."

A girl wrote Laingen, "Hi, Dream Boat. I wish you a lot of luck. I am going to give you a plan to get out. Number one: Cry for food, then hit them in the face and run out. If this isn't a good plan, hear [*sic*] is another one. If there is a key by there, all of you should each get a sock and try to throw the sock and get the key. Try your own [idea] if it doesn't work."

5

I'M GOING

Others responded to the continuing ordeal of captivity very differently. The irrepressible CIA officer Malcolm Kalp had always been a man whose motor ran fast, and being confined to a small space made him increasingly desperate to escape. Confined to the same villa in Isfahan as John Limbert, with whom he regularly passed notes in their shared bathroom, he tried to enlist the gentle embassy political officer in his plans. His first involved overpowering a guard and taking his weapon.

"Then what are we going to do, shoot our way out?" Limbert wrote back, to which Kalp responded, "Is that something you are willing to do?"

Limbert wasn't. He didn't think he could. Besides, there were many armed guards, not just one or two. If they knocked down a guard and took his weapon, they would soon have to use it. On reflection, Kalp agreed that trying to shoot their way out would be suicidal, but he continued to scheme. Perhaps they could sneak out. Limbert noted that even if they were able to slip outside the villa, the area immediately surrounding it was patrolled by a guard dog and encircled by a wall. Beyond the wall were floodlights that turned night into day. Assuming they made it over the wall and across the floodlit area beyond, what would they do then, without money, ID, or proper clothing? Kalp suggested looking for a foreign consulate, or perhaps finding someone sympathetic on the street. Limbert wondered how many people like that there were in Isfahan, Iranians so sympathetic they would risk their lives to help them. None of these entirely sensible obtacles deterred Kalp in the least. He was going, Limbert was not. The political officer admired his colleague's determination and ingenuity but wondered at his sanity.

Kalp had a nine-inch-long hacksaw blade he had scrounged from the chancery basement and kept hidden in his shoe, and he had been using it to saw through the iron bars over his window. Whenever there was a loud demonstration or the lawn mower started outside, Kalp sawed furiously.

It took some time, but eventually he cut completely through one of the bars before his guards, inspecting his room, noticed. Then they bricked over his window.

"No more windows for you," the guard told him.

A lesser man would have given up.

One morning in June, Kalp was led out and placed in the back of a station wagon with Bill Belk and Joe Subic, who had been kept in another part of the same villa. He knew Belk was sitting in front of him because the State Department communicator had asthma and wheezed. Kalp recognized the sound. He didn't learn until later that the other American was Subic. There were three Iranians in the front.

All he could think about, sitting in the back, was that this was the perfect time to escape. There were just three Iranians and three Americans, and Kalp liked the odds. He didn't know if the guards had weapons but he felt that, if the three of them moved fast, it wouldn't matter. Without the cooperation of his colleagues it wouldn't work, and he had no way to enlist them without alerting the guards. As soon as they got to the new place, again with a shared bathroom, this one painted and decorated totally in pink, Kalp wrote a note saying that, if they were moved like that again, he would cough and that would be the signal to attack.

On the way, the guards had promised them that the new place would be cooler, but it wasn't true. The air-conditioning units were shot. The days were brutal. Kalp immediately went to work on the locks on his room's windows. He might have been a spy, but he had never learned to pick a lock. It was something he had always wanted to know how to do but he'd never gotten instruction, and whenever he had tried as a boy he had failed. Now, with nothing but time on his hands, he spent hour after hour probing the mechanism with a pin until, much to his delight and surprise, he popped it open. He eased the window up and looked out. They were three stories up in what looked like a middle-class neighborhood. There were no guards in sight, but chained beneath the window again was a big dog. Beyond the dog was a wall that he could easily climb.

Kalp placed a note in the pink bathroom announcing his intention to break out.

"We have to be careful not to hurt any of the guards, because if we hurt them they are going to shoot us for sure," Kalp wrote.

Belk's previous escape attempt in the first days of the takeover had ended badly. He remembered the beating and punishment he'd suffered after he was caught, and he had determined that if he ever saw the chance to run again he would not be taken alive. He had stolen a heavy metal drain stop, which, wrapped in his fist, could do serious damage. Kalp, however, had taken Limbert's caution to heart and had reverted to his earlier position, he had ruled out attacking any of the guards. So Belk told him no. If attacking the guards was not part of the plan, he would stay put and wait for an opening that suited him.

Belk's roommate Joe Subic, on the other hand, whose days of cozying up to his captors had long since stopped paying dividends, told Kalp he was game. The CIA officer now had the knack of picking locks, so when he was allowed to visit Belk and Subic he unlocked their window. To prepare for his break, Kalp kept careful watch out of his own window through the night. One problem was a floodlight that illuminated the yard outside all night. Kalp pulled out a wall socket in his room and played with the wires, crossing this one and that, until all the lights in the house suddenly went black. This was not unusual. There were frequent blackouts in Isfahan so the guards weren't surprised. When they realized the short had occurred only at their location they reset the circuits. That, Kalp noted, was a trick that would come in handy.

The next problem was the dog, but he had an answer for that. He convinced the guards that he had a nervous condition that required regular treatment with Librium and Valium, and then hoarded the pills. He was not allowed to eat meat—a punishment from some earlier transgression—but Belk and Subic were, so Kalp got a hot dog from them. His plan was to stuff the hot dog with his pills and then throw it to the dog about half an hour before going out the window. With any luck, the animal would be unconscious, or at least mellow.

Still exchanging notes in the pink bathroom, Kalp and Subic decided at last that all was ready and set the time for their break at three o'clock the following morning. Kalp would tie the sheets from his bed into a rope, lower himself to the ground, check around to see if the coast was clear, and then, using a red lens he had scrounged, signal Subic to climb down. Kalp opened his own window a crack early that evening to check out the yard, and for the first time he saw a guard walking underneath. He quickly shut the window, asked the guard in the hallway to take him to the bathroom, and left a note for Subic that said, "Cancel."

Another week of discussion ensued. By now it was late June, and the news—mostly what Kalp had learned from Limbert at the other house—was that the *Majlis* planned to vote on the hostage question in July. Subic wanted to wait for the vote but Kalp was through with waiting.

"To hell with it," he wrote. "The 27th of June I'm going."

Subic reluctantly agreed to go along. Kalp would throw the spiked hot dog out, then wait for the dog to eat it and fall asleep. Then he would drop to the ground, signal Subic, wait for him to climb down, and the two of them would cross the yard, scale the wall, and drop down into the neighborhood outside. They would hide nearby until morning and wait for someone to start the motor on his car—neither knew how to hot-wire a vehicle. They would jump the driver, hit him over the head with a brick or stone, and drive the car in the direction of the Persian Gulf, hundreds of miles away, where they would steal a boat and row or motor themselves out to where American warships patrolled. Kalp figured he had about a fifty-fifty chance of getting over the wall and about a five percent chance of making it to the gulf. After eight months, it was chance enough.

At the last moment he decided not to use the rope he had painstakingly made. He could tie it down inside his room and it would serve nicely for descending, but he couldn't figure out a way to then pull it down behind him. If it were left hanging, a guard might spot it and alert the others before he and Subic had a chance to scale the wall and find a good hiding place outside. Their best chance was to slip out without anyone noticing until the guards came for breakfast. That would give them a good four hours of darkness to flee the house and hide. Instead of climbing down, Kalp decided he would simply hang from the window, which was about eighteen feet from the ground, and drop. He figured he was five-ten, and his arms extended fully gave him another two feet, which meant about a ten-foot drop, which wasn't too bad. He saved himself some of the pills just in case he hurt his ankle or legs in the jump.

On the night of June 26, he threw the stuffed hot dog down to the dog, but it landed in a place where the tethered animal couldn't reach. Again he wrote "cancel." He asked for another hot dog and left the note in the bathroom for Subic.

On the following night, he asked the guard to shut his door. Usually they left it open but the guard obliged. Kalp threw out the new spiked hot dog, and this time the dog gobbled it up and appeared to fall immediately asleep. Kalp stuffed all the things he wanted to take with him into his pillowcase—his pills, a bottle of water, some food he had scrounged, a change of clothes, and some letters from his family. He was doing this when a guard abruptly reopened the door to his room. Kalp was crouched in a far corner of the room with his bag, the mattress on the floor stripped and empty, but the guard just took a quick look, shut the door, and did nothing! Kalp couldn't believe it. The best he could figure is that the guard was so bored with making bed checks he no longer actually looked.

At the last moment he decided not to carry the stuffed pillowcase. He worried it might throw off his balance, so using a long piece of string —Kalp collected things all the time in hopes they would come in handy —he gently lowered it out the window. When it touched ground he hesitated for a moment. Once he let go of the string and the bag was outside, he had to go. He knew his chances were slim, but he had been a soldier and CIA officer for a long time without ever having taken any truly big risks. *You've been training for this for twenty-odd years, you gonna do it or not?* He let go of the string. Then he opened the window fully and eased himself out. Hanging from the window ledge the eighteen-foot drop looked a lot more daunting than he had convinced himself it would be. He saw a ventilation ledge about two feet below him to one side and he managed to swing himself over there and lower himself farther. Still, it was quite a fall.

It was at this point that the dog suddenly sprang fully to life, lunging up at him from its chain, barking furiously. Kalp let go and landed hard on the balls of his feet. He rolled quickly away from the dog, badly scraping his elbows and knees. Bleeding now, with the dog raising holy hell, Kalp got to his feet. He had been lucky. His decision to move over the two feet to the ventilation ledge meant he had landed just out of the dog's reach.

With the animal still making a racket, he sprinted down to peer around the corner of the building, where he saw no one, and then ran back the other way, beneath Belk's and Subic's window. Subic wasn't there. The army sergeant had been waiting by the window, fully dressed, but when he heard the dog start to bark he had run back across the room, peeled off his shirt, and crawled back under the covers.

"I told you. I told you," said Belk bitterly. "Now you're going to get us both in trouble."

Kalp was beneath their window, reaching in his pocket for the red lens, when a guard appeared, leveling a gun at him and shouting angrily in Farsi. Kalp jerked his hands up, but noticed that his pants were falling down. He instinctively reached to hike them up, then realized that a move like that could get him shot. He jerked his hands back into the air. The guard with the gun was screaming, the dog was raising a racket, his pants were falling down, and he was soon surrounded by irate Iranians.

He smiled sheepishly. "Good morning," he said. "Good morning."

Bound and blindfolded, he was led first up a long winding staircase, and then the guards changed their minds and brought him back down to the first floor and placed him in a bathroom. They stripped him, screamed at him, and then two began beating and kicking him.

When Kalp pleaded and protested the guards told him to shut up and kept up the beating. Subic and Belk could hear his cries and figured they were next, but the guards never came for them. Their room was checked, but no one took notice that Subic was fully dressed and that he had several full water bottles in a bag by his mattress. They also didn't notice that the window was unlocked.

When they had finished beating Kalp, he was led back upstairs and placed in a chair with his hands cuffed behind its back. Then they tied his elbows together and bound his feet. Two strips of cloth were tied over his eyes and pulled so tight that a corner of the lower one dug painfully into his left eye. Kalp spent a day and a half like this with no food or water. Guards led him to the toilet at long intervals. They finally removed the outer blindfold, which eased the painful pressure on his eye. Sometime later they untied him, cuffed his hands in front, and took him to the basement. He felt that the worst was over. They probably wouldn't shoot him. How mad could they be at him? He hadn't hurt anyone and even the Geneva Convention, he thought, recognized that prisoners of war were entitled to try to escape.

In the basement he was questioned about the note-passing system, which he denied. Then he was beaten again. His head was smacked against the concrete wall and he was kicked in the groin. They showed him a note he had left for Subic and Belk. He denied that he had written it, even though it was clearly his handwriting and on paper he had brought with him from the embassy in Tehran. Next he was asked about his escape plan.

"I was going to go into Isfahan and find a Westerner," he told them.

"Why did you think there would be Westerners there?" he was asked.

"I don't know," he said. "I haven't been out of here. I don't know who is in Isfahan."

They brought him back upstairs and kept him tied to a chair for a few more days, and then they threw him into a car and returned him to the villa where he had been staying before the move. They took away his knife and fork.

Kalp went quietly to work with the spoon, scraping away the mortar between the bricks.

Both Belk and Subic were punished for Kalp's attempted escape. When the guards found braided sheets in their room they were separated.

Belk responded by refusing to eat. When they brought him tea on the first day there was no sugar. He asked for some and was told no. So he refused the tea and everything else. He took only water for nine days, and then decided to stop even that. He soon discovered that it is a lot harder to stop drinking than to stop eating. Inside of one day his mouth was like cotton. He gave up and started eating his meals again.

All John Limbert knew was that one day Kalp had disappeared, and then, about a week later, he was back, with a note describing his adventure. Kalp had hidden a ballpoint pen in his room months ago and was delighted to find it still there when he returned. His escape had ended as Limbert thought it would, but he admired Kalp for trying.

Limbert said he had wondered what happened to him, whether he had been moved to a different place or just to another part of the villa, and Kalp promised that in the future he would make a small soap mark on the mirror whenever he used the bathroom. If the mark was gone, he was gone. In the next few days they exchanged notes about the possibility of another rescue attempt. Kalp knew more about the military's capabilities than Limbert and corrected him when the diplomat speculated that the United

States could not reach far into Iran on helicopters. Kalp explained that there were many different ways to refuel en route.

Clearly, another American raid was on the minds of their guards. Limbert overheard a number of them discussing the possibility one night. He heard one say, "Well, if something happens, make sure the explosives are placed right."

He had seen no explosives at the villa and figured if they were around, he would have noticed them. He suspected the conversation had been staged for his benefit, although for what reason exactly he could not fathom. Apparently the guards still feared their captives were secretly communicating with Washington.

For three days after his return Kalp was kept handcuffed in his room and was denied reading material. He easily picked the lock on the cuffs, refastening them quickly when a guard approached. To pass the time, he began trying to count to a billion. He had read somewhere that if a person tried counting to a billion, his whole life would pass before he finished. He was up somewhere around 20,000 when, on the night of the third of July, a guard gave him a tranquilizer to swallow, removed his glasses, and then took him, blindfolded and cuffed, to a van, where five or six other Iranians and a group of hostages were already waiting. He was handcuffed to Belk—he heard the wheeze. They had agreed that the next time they were together on a move, they would jump the guards and try to escape, and on the long drive he felt Belk trying to pick the lock on the cuffs, though by this time Kalp knew they didn't have a prayer. They were outnumbered, the guards probably had weapons, he was woozy from the tranquilizer, and without his glasses he couldn't even see. He patted Belk's hand gently and whispered, "No, no, no."

The drive took ten hours. The guards played loudly a tape of their revolutionary songs, which to Kalp felt like torture.

The logistics of moving the captives around the country strained the resources of their student captors, who had to arrange guard shifts, food delivery, and other services wherever their charges were housed. In the month after the rescue attempt they shuffled hostages from place to place, trying to get the makeshift new system to work, but by midsummer they had begun driving them all back to Tehran, to several of the city's old prisons, which were designed to hold captives and could be heavily fortified against assault. The students took pains to disguise these shifts, mindful of how vulnerable they had been in April when the rescue mission was attempted. When marine Jimmy Lopez was taken from a country house, where he had been kept all summer, the guards kept his guitar, and every evening at the same time Lopez normally practiced one of them stayed behind to pluck at the strings so that anyone listening from outside would think the hostages were still there.

Among the first to be moved were Joe Hall, John Graves, and the marines Greg Persinger and Steve Kirtley. On June 18, they were being driven from Isfahan when their transport van had a severe accident.

The four were blindfolded and handcuffed in the back—Hall to Persinger and Graves to Kirtley—and had ridden for hours through the night when they were awakened by violent bumping, and then were suddenly thrown wildly into the walls of the van as it left the road at high speed and rolled several times before coming to a stop. They were tumbled inside like markers in a Bingo hopper. Hall blacked out. He came to with his blindfold off, lying in thick dust at the bottom of the van, staring at Persinger. Both had bloody faces and were twisted in awkward positions. They untangled themselves slowly, checking for cuts and broken bones, and then crawled outside. Surveying the battered remains of the vehicle, Hall noticed a leg that looked bent in a peculiar position, and his first thought was, *Somebody has lost a leg!* Then the leg moved and was followed by the intact body of Kirtley, who pulled himself from the van and dragged Graves out behind him. Graves had hurt his back and the marine's shoulder ached.

There was no sign of the guards. All four had been riding for so long that they had to urinate urgently, so the two shackled pairs ran off a short distance to do that. When they returned, neither guard nor driver had emerged from the battered front of the van.

Kirtley's first thought was, *Now's our chance!* But they were standing in the middle of nowhere. Nothing but sand stretched off in all directions. They all turned slowly in a complete circle, thinking the same thought. Which way should they go? The van was going nowhere.

They were gaping at it, wondering at their good fortune in having escaped with only minor injury, when the guard they called Big Ali, who had been riding shotgun in front, emerged slowly from the wreckage with his gun. He had apparently just come to. It was the first time Hall had seen Big Ali with a weapon, and the Iranian gruffly ordered them to do what they had already decided.

"Stay here," he said.

Not long afterward an ambulance arrived; it had been coming along the same road a distance behind them. Big Ali told them to climb in, where they were surprised to find hostage Jerry Miele on a stretcher. They were squeezed in around him, and when Big Ali told them to put their blindfolds back on, which he had retrieved, they all refused. He and the other guards were too shaken and distressed to push the issue—the hostages learned later that the driver of the van had been killed—so the hostages had an opportunity to talk freely for the rest of the drive.

Miele's head was bandaged. He was particularly surprised to see Kirtley again. They had been together until a few days earlier, when Miele had made a bizarre and futile attempt to kill himself. He was known to be CIA—he was a communicator, a technician—and the guards constantly harassed him about it. They had told him repeatedly since the day of the takeover that, once the trials began, he would be the first to be killed. A short, bald man with a long hooked nose and protruding eyes with deep dark circles under them, Miele looked ill, old, tired, and broken. He was naturally withdrawn, and over months of captivity he had grown increasingly silent and sullen, convinced his life was over. The method most frequently mentioned was electrocution, and on one occasion the guards had rigged a chair with wires to drive home the threat. Occasionally Miele would mutter fearfully, "They were going to plug me in." Before the rescue attempt, Miele had regressed to an extent that was alarming to his fellow hostages. Sometimes he would just curl up in the corner and shake. Kathryn Koob had been shocked one evening to see Miele, whom she did not know, sitting curled up like a child, asking meekly, "Bathroom? My turn? Bathroom?"

In the dispersal after the failed rescue, he had been placed with Kirtley in Isfahan, where one afternoon, when Big Ali was bringing lunch into the room, he became agitated and started pacing rapidly.

"I hope when this is all over the real truth comes out," he said, and then ran himself head first, with as much speed as he could muster in such a small space, into the edge of the opened door. The blow knocked him cold and carved a deep eight-inch cut in his scalp. Kirtley ran to him and tried to wake him up. Blood poured out over Miele's face. The marine put his head to Miele's chest and heard his heart still beating.

"Call an ambulance, Ali!" he shouted.

Kirtley inspected the wound carefully, looking to make sure that there were no visible pieces of dirt or stone inside, and then folded the loose flap of scalp back over Miele's slick, bleeding forehead. He took a towel, one that he had washed and hung to dry, and pressed it against the top of his roommate's head. He leaned on it, applying steady pressure.

Miele awakened. He opened his eyes and looked around the room and said nothing.

"Jerry! Jerry! Wake up! Say something!" urged Kirtley.

Miele didn't speak. An ambulance came quickly, but then it sat for a long time while the two attendants debated about what to do. Kirtley kept shouting at them to get Miele to a hospital, but they ignored him. Finally they wrapped some gauze around his head. Kirtley retrieved Miele's Bible and gave it to the ambulance men to take with them. After what seemed like hours, they drove off.

This was the first Kirtley had seen him since then, and Miele seemed better, no worse off than the four of them. Graves was the most severely injured; his back would trouble him for the rest of his life. Hall had noticed blood in his urine and presumed he'd bruised his kidneys. He also had a gash on his right ankle. Persinger and Kirtley had deep cuts. When they arrived at Qom, just a fifteen-minute drive from the site of the accident, Hall washed the cut on Persinger's back and asked the guards for a disinfectant, but they didn't have any and refused to find some, so he used toothpaste. Fluoride was supposed to kill germs; at least that's what all the commercials said. Nobody knew for sure. Persinger said it stung when it was applied, which they figured was a good sign.

Kathryn Koob and Ann Swift were given a remedy for tedium in late June when Akbar, their new guard supervisor, asked them if they knew how to cook. They were brought to the chancery kitchenette, where they proceeded to take charge. They were told to cook for six, which meant somewhere in the cavernous building were four of their male colleagues. There was a working oven, two burners, and a hot plate. They thoroughly scrubbed down the kitchen and threw themselves into making creative dishes out of the ingredients at hand. There was a huge store of frozen vegetables, cheese, and canned food. The students kept them supplied with fresh eggs. The women captives put cans of flour and grains in the freezer and then sifted out the frozen bugs and larvae.

One night they found a tiny message of thanks under a dish on a returned tray, signed "The Boys in the Back Room." That set them searching for clues to who their mystery diners were. Swift ran into Bob Ode on one trip to the bathroom, and on another they found discarded wrapping in the waste bin from a package addressed to Don Hohman. Eventually they were able to determine that the remaining two diners were Richard Queen and Jerry Miele, who had been returned to the chancery after his suicide attempt.

Koob knew that Hohman was a vegetarian and worked hard to provide him with interesting dishes, including an attempt at *huevos rancheros*. The empty dishes now routinely carried notes of thanks and requests. Chocolate chip cookies? Peanut butter cookies? Pumpkin pie? Most of the ingredients came from the vast stores in the embassy commissary, but occasionally the students were talked into making shopping trips to local markets. They provided a steady assortment of fresh fruits.

On Independence Day Koob and Swift baked a chocolate cake and decorated it with four fake firecrackers they had fashioned out of cardboard covered with brightly colored paper and topped with a piece of silver tinsel for a fuse. The feast included fried chicken and potato salad. In the bathroom, a few days later, they saw three of the four firecrackers lined up in a row on the floor behind the wastebasket. It was a message. One of their diners was gone.

Queen, Miele, and Ode were placed with Hohman so he could keep an eye on their health. Queen's mysterious symptoms had worsened, Miele was on suicide watch, and Ode's condition was worrisome just because he was the eldest and seemed so frail. At first, Queen and Ode had hit it off, but in time their personalities clashed. Ode was bitter and angry about his circumstances, while Queen tended toward irrational optimism, and because he spoke a little Farsi and could eavesdrop on the guards he tended to rush to conclusions about things that were later proved wrong. As

Queen's optimistic predictions failed to pan out again and again, Ode wrote him off as a Pollyanna. In time, the older man couldn't be around him without arguing with him.

More and more, the lanky, bearded vice consul retreated into himself. The numbness on his left side had spread to his right, which both troubled and confused him. If his problem had been caused by a slight stroke, that explained why the loss of feeling and strength affected only one side of his body, but why was he now experiencing it on the other? He noticed that he was having trouble hearing with his right ear and with keeping his balance. What did that mean? Hohman told him that it was possible he had suffered another slight stroke on the other side of his brain, but the medic said it was unlikely and confessed that he was out of his depth. Queen explained his symptoms to Akbar, who was also baffled. Hohman guessed that the dizziness and hearing loss might indicate an ear infection, so Queen began taking antihistamines to dry out his ear. It had no effect.

The dizziness worsened until it was so bad that Queen couldn't stand without getting sick. He tried turning off his air conditioner, thinking maybe something he was breathing was making him nauseous, but that made no difference. The vomiting grew worse. Even when he didn't eat he could not stop retching. By the Fourth of July, as nearly a million Iranians were outside marching in protest against the United States, Queen was literally flat on his back, unable to move without growing dizzy and throwing up.

His roommates were alarmed and angry. His condition was bad enough to intrude even on Ode's typically self-obsessed diary entry.

> I presume our great and glorious President is enjoying himself over the weekend at Camp David as well as all our other hard-working government officials who are certainly not going to let a little matter of 50 hostages spoil their long holiday weekend.... Now that the Fourth of July has come and gone I guess our hopes of ever getting out of here within the foreseeable future are practically nil. I had so hoped that some arrangement could be made to free us by our 'Freedom Day.' Just wishful thinking, I guess.... Hopefully, even the Iranians are getting tired of this state of affairs, but again that is probably wishful thinking.... Queen has been very ill for the past several days with some sort of ear trouble that is causing him considerable dizziness and nausea.

Hohman was worried. He believed Queen was dying and complained bitterly to Akbar about the lack of medical care. He told Akbar that he personally was "killing" Queen, and that unless he did something quickly they were going to have a dead hostage on their hands. "How's that going to play?" Hohman asked. Akbar agreed to send for help, and the next day Queen was visited by both a student doctor and an ear specialist. When the student doctor walked in, Queen turned his head to look at him and that slight movement made him so dizzy he vomited. The ear doctor quickly surmised that the problem was not an ear infection. He promised Queen a visit to the hospital the next day.

Ode noted:

> It is about time. In his condition he should have been released immediately and sent home or at least taken to a local hospital months ago. Now, I'm afraid he is going to suffer for the rest of his life because of the neglect during his period of captivity. It is a miracle that others have not taken seriously ill and it is a national scandal and a national disgrace, as far as I'm concerned, that our government hasn't done something long before this to obtain our release. The medical student took an EKG of me today. Said that everything is normal! Considering my heart condition, I don't see how that could be!

That night, Ode and Hohman sat up beside Queen until late, talking to him and trying to cheer him up. When it was time to sleep, Ode gave him a broom handle and told him to hit the door if he needed anything. Queen lay awake that whole night. He was afraid to fall asleep for fear he might try to turn over, which would make him vomit again. The retching had bruised his insides and become extremely painful.

The next morning he was half carried to a passenger van. Queen felt he was dying. He lay supine in the vehicle's backseat, his long, skinny legs bent at a sharp angle. After being locked up for eight months it was his first trip off the compound, and he lacked the strength or will even to lift his head and look out the windows. Inside the hospital he was helped to a bed. His head was swimming and the heat and odors of the place aggravated his nausea. The hospital, renamed Martyr's Hospital after the revolution, was not up to Western standards. The bathroom in his room was unclean. Cockroaches ran on the walls. There were flowers alongside his bed, and when Queen asked Akbar about them he was told that they had been sent to the Ayatollah Sadeq Khalkali, the revolution's notorious hanging judge, who had been treated in that same room earlier in the day for injuries from an auto accident. Queen noticed that Akbar had a .45 shoved under his belt, the first time he had seen him armed. He asked what they were worried about, since he couldn't even sit up. Akbar said they weren't worried about him trying to escape, they were worried that a rival group might kidnap him.

Queen observed that Akbar and the other guards were despised by the hospital workers, especially the women. When one of Queen's armed student guards sat in a chair in his room, a nurse tending Queen snapped at the young man angrily, "Can you get rid of that thing," pointing at his weapon. "This patient is not going anywhere." The guard took a towel and wrapped it around his weapon. The nurses complained to Akbar about the white head scarves they were now required to wear, arguing that they interfered with their ability to work.

"Why do you torture us with these new requirements?" one nurse asked.

Queen was surprised by their anger and by the fact that they saw Akbar as responsible, which meant they saw him as an important man. The afflicted young American amused himself by softly singing old marching songs he had learned in the military. There was nothing else he could do. The doctors tried several treatments, which just made him feel worse. One set of shots caused violent spasms of the muscles in his head, causing it to turn violently from side to side. He began grinding his teeth uncontrollably.

"Akbar! Look what's happening!" he cried fearfully. When he put his tongue between his teeth to stop the grinding, he involuntarily bit into it.

Five days of tests and various treatments led finally to the surprising announcement, by Akbar, that Queen was going home. The hostage assumed he meant back to the chancery.

"With all this?" he asked, horrified, nodding at the tubes plugged into his arms.

"No, you are going home. To your home," said Akbar.

Queen still looked mystified.

"America," said Akbar. "Ayatollah Khomeini has decided to release you to your parents."

Later that day Gaptooth, Hussein Sheikh-ol-eslam, the student captors' black-bearded leader, came into his room for a last political harangue.

"My people and the American people get along well," he said, "but the government . . . the CIA is trying to destroy our revolution. No one tried to harass or kill the Americans who were leaving Iran at the time of the shah's overthrow. The people had nothing against America, but the United States is trying to destroy the revolution. When you go back, speak the truth." He apologized for any misbehavior by Queen's guards, particularly in the first two months. "We tried to treat you well. The first two months were chaotic here—it was so disorganized."

Hours later, Richard Queen was being carried off a plane in Zurich, Switzerland.

6

THE BRAYING OF DONKEYS

On the night of July 27, John Limbert heard car horns honking all over Isfahan. At first he thought it was a wedding. Iranians often celebrated by honking horns, but it was Ramadan, and there usually weren't weddings during the holy season. Besides, the horns seemed to be sounding not just in one place but all over the city. Out in the yard the students had a television in a tent, and at night sometimes they would sit around it and turn it up. Limbert could stand by his window and pick up bits and pieces of the report. He heard the phrase, "vampire of the age," and "bloodsucker." Later, when one of his guards came in, a young man named Mohammed, Limbert asked about the car horns.

"It's a wedding," Mohammed said.

"Really? A wedding during Ramadan? These people must have been in an awful hurry to get married."

Mohammed spent a lot of time talking to Limbert. He was twenty-two, and Limbert judged him to be a pretty good student. He was thoughtful, well spoken, and eager to learn. Most important, he didn't seem to have a completely closed mind as so many of the other young Iranians did. They had struck a deal: Mohammed would play chess with Limbert in exchange for English lessons. They discussed religious ideas, and Limbert asked Mohammed to tell him about some of the characters in Iran's long history. Once the guard asked a question that intrigued Limbert.

"Whenever you leave us here and go home, what are you going to say about us?"

"I will tell people that some of you were decent human beings and that some of you are filth," he had said and then explained that, no matter how many decent individuals were involved, their action would be remembered in the latter category.

The offhand assumption behind the question intrigued Limbert, however, and gave him a sense of hope and relief at a time when he desperately needed it. It showed Mohammed was concerned that Americans not get the wrong idea about him and the other hostage takers, because he hadn't given up hope of visiting and studying in the States.

"After all this is over, do you think I could get a visa?" he asked.

Not a chance in hell, Limbert thought, but said, diplomatically, "Well, Mohammed. All you can do is apply."

Mohammed caught his captive's drift and seemed crestfallen. That suited Limbert fine. He hoped he would worry about it.

On reflection, Limbert realized that he knew why horns were honking, and why Mohammed had been thinking about an end to this ordeal. His mind had assembled the clues—celebration, "bloodsucker," "vampire," and Mohammed's unexpected question. The shah was dead. But what did it mean? That had been the pretense for holding them, but it had been apparent for months that the shah wasn't coming back. Still, his death removed an important obstacle. The students would have had a harder time releasing him and the others if the shah were still lounging on a beach somewhere.

There was another demonstration in Isfahan during Limbert's long summer. It was a Friday, the day of communal prayers in Iran, and after the usual chanting and singing outside, a group of young people, some portion of a local *khomiteh,* gathered to read off a windy umpteen-point political statement. Limbert was surprised to hear in this one a call for Type A blood for loyal soldiers hurt during fighting in Kurdistan.

"I understand you need Type A blood," Limbert told the next guard to come by his room. "I am Type A, and I'd be perfectly happy to donate some if your soldiers in Kurdistan need it."

His offer upset the guard. Limbert was not supposed to know of the fighting in Kurdistan or the need for blood. He was concerned about a breakdown in their security system at the villa.

"How did you know?" he asked.

"I just know," Limbert told him unhelpfully. What he wanted was for the guard to think that one of his own had been talking. He kept renewing his offer to donate blood but was ignored.

Mohammed brought him a fresh towel, some comfortable Iranian-style pajama pants, and a small cassette tape player with recordings by Gordon Lightfoot, classical Iranian music, recitations of classical Persian poetry, and, for some reason, music by Mikis Theodorakis from the sound track of the movie *Serpico*. Limbert especially liked the old Iranian songs, which had been pronounced passé by the new regime, so were out of favor, but which had an irresistible pull even for the young guards. He noticed how they drifted in when he was playing them.

Eventually Limbert was moved to another room with its own bathroom, so he lost his message drop and all communication with Kalp. Each afternoon at about two, the guards would turn up their radios and listen to a broadcast sermon from a zealous cleric who ranted on and on, usually for nearly two hours, spouting bizarre revisionist history, spreading lies and distortions, condemning the late shah and denouncing everything about America and the West. It called to Limbert's mind an old saying, "Against stupidity the gods themselves labor in vain." For many weeks he had no contact with anyone other than his guards. He began to worry that something had happened. Had everyone else been released? Had he been left behind? Had the others been killed?

Then one day a guard asked him to define some English words that he didn't understand.

The words were "raghead," "bozo," "motherfucker," and "cocksucker." Limbert laughed. It warmed his heart. Someplace nearby his captors were still coping with the United States Marine Corps.

Limbert made it a point to get along with everyone, but for some of the hostages it was a trial just getting along with each other. Colonel Chuck Scott found it difficult to share space with the sullen, white-bearded Bob Blucker. The colonel had initially been thrilled months ago at the chancery when, after a month in solitary, the middle-aged budget officer was led into his room. Blucker immediately told the guard that he didn't want to stay. He said he preferred his own room across the hall, where it was cooler and there was no smoke. The guard refused to reconsider and Blucker stayed, but right from the start Scott was offended and disappointed. Though from time to time his new roommate had made an effort to indulge the colonel's need for conversation, most of the time he was distant and sullen. Now, forced again to cohabit, their relationship worsened. Little things Blucker did or refused to do irritated Scott. For instance, after eating, if the colonel used the bathroom first he would scoop up all the dirty dishes on the way out and wash them in the bathroom sink. When

Blucker went out, he took only his own dishes. If a guard dropped a treat, nuts or dates, into Scott's bowl, the fussy Blucker declined to take one—he would eat only out of his own bowl, as if the colonel's had not been adequately cleaned.

One morning, after months of being locked indoors, a guard announced as he served breakfast that they must eat it quickly because in fifteen minutes they would be allowed to exercise outdoors. Scott was delighted. He ate fast and donned his slacks and shirt. Blucker continued to pick slowly at his food.

"Bob, you better hurry," Scott said. He was worried that if they both weren't ready, neither of them would get to go outside. Blucker said he couldn't care less.

"I'm not going to hurry through my breakfast just to go outside."

They argued for a few moments, and Scott pleaded, "Come on, Bob, we're in this thing together. I know you prefer to be alone, but give me a break."

Blucker refused to hurry and Scott lost his temper. He grabbed hold of his roommate's shirt and pulled him to his feet. He was going outside if he had to drag Blucker with him. They were arguing loudly when the guards intervened. Blucker claimed that Scott had hit him. Scott denied it.

As punishment, the colonel was left alone in a small, dark room, where he sat stewing over his roommate's lack of basic consideration. He was angry at himself for losing both his temper and the trip outdoors, where the weather had turned warm. After an hour of cooling off, Akbar came to retrieve him.

"Mr. Blucker is afraid that if he is left with you that you will kill him," he said. "He says you are crazy."

Scott was placed in a new room with different roommates, which he found a vast improvement, and soon afterward he was summoned to an unusual session with Ayatollah Ali Khamenei, one of the state's most powerful clerics (and the eventual successor to the imam as supreme leader). In his capacity as military liaison, Scott had met Khamenei almost a year earlier. The ayatollah was in charge of Iran's military, and the colonel had sought him out to discuss outstanding defense contracts. As the colonel saw it, no matter how hateful its bluster, Iran had an overwhelming interest in opening such discussions because there were still billions of dollars of Iranian money deposited in trusts to pay off military purchases, money that was earning interest in American banks. It was not unusual for payouts from these accounts to total $750 million per quarter. Evidently ignorant of the trust fund, Khamenei initially told Scott that he was wasting his time; Iran was not interested in doing business with the United States anymore, under any circumstances, and that any outstanding debts would not be paid.

"So, let me get this straight," Scott had said. "If after all the contracts are paid out the fund still has a few hundred million dollars in it, we should just donate it to the U.S. Treasury?"

At that point the ayatollah became interested. This was the work Scott had been doing when taken hostage. It turned out that if Iran wanted to keep its air force flying, it had to continue doing business with the United States. In the weeks before the takeover, Scott had arranged for the first official purchase by revolutionary Iran from the U.S. military, a $10 million order of tires for their fleet of F-14s and F-5 fighters. All that now seemed like it had happened in a different world.

In the months since he had last seen Khamenei, Iran's geopolitical position had grown more precarious. Saddam Hussein had become increasingly belligerent along its western border and just weeks before had executed a revered Shia leader. Ever since, Iran had been both mourning and girding for war. So it came as no surprise to Scott that Khamenei's interest in American parts would be stronger than ever. He had come looking for the American colonel who had sold him aircraft tires. Delivery of that order had been frozen, along with the rest of Iran's considerable assets in the United States, since the takeover of the embassy.

Sitting cross-legged on the rug, puffing on a pipe, wearing a fat gold Rolex on his wrist, Khamenei asked the colonel, "If we were to release all of you now, without any conditions, how long would it be before you could begin to supply us again with spare parts for our military forces?"

"You're asking the wrong man," said Scott. "I have had no contact with either my government or the American people since I became a hostage. I've been kept in the dark by your people."

"But you have served in your army for many years. What do you think? How long would it take?"

"Frankly, my guess is that it will be a long time before you get any cooperation on spare parts from America, after what you have done and continue to do to us."

Khamenei insisted that neither Scott nor any of the other hostages had been harmed; they were being "protected," he said, and then explained how the United States had just sent commandos to Iran in a failed attempt to assassinate them. Scott quickly scrutinized this remark through a well-honed rhetorical filter—what Iran called an "assassination squad" would have to have been . . . yes, a rescue force! So there had been a rescue attempt! Scott now understood why they had all been so suddenly moved. He told the ayatollah that he doubted American troops would have been sent to kill him and the others. If Carter was that cavalier about their fate, he would have leveled Tehran months ago.

"You are lucky to be alive, don't you know that?" Khamenei said, annoyed.

When the ayatollah departed he left instructions that the prisoners' diets be improved, but despite this concern all three men fell ill with dysentery. On July 12, still weak from the illness, Scott, Don Sharer, and navy petty officer Sam Gillette were driven back to Tehran and locked in Komiteh prison. A single lightbulb dangled from the ceiling of a room about fifteen feet square, furnished with three Styrofoam mattresses, three wooden chairs, and a table. Their guard turned out to be Ahmad, the squat, balding man who in the Mushroom Inn had taken such pleasure in tormenting them. He told them that they were being placed in prison for their own safety.

"You know about the mission that was sent to kill you?" Ahmad asked.

They said they had heard the whole bullshit story, and then complained about being locked in a prison, reminding the guard of the repeated assurances that they were not "prisoners" but "guests."

"This is not a prison," said Ahmad. "It is only a place to keep hostages."

By the end of summer all of the hostages were in Tehran prison cells.

John Limbert's at Komiteh was about fifteen feet wide and twenty feet long, with two mattresses on the floor and a high window that admitted some light. It reminded him of Jack Benny's "vault"—a standing joke on the famous comic's TV program was that he was so miserly he kept all his money in a vault, which he would visit periodically on the show, passing through a series of huge, clanking doors draped with chains and locks. Komiteh was like that; it was so prison-like that it seemed over the top to Limbert, complete with echoing stone walls, and creaking steel doors with a lip on the bottom like those on naval vessels.

There was a center courtyard and outside the cell door was a long hallway. He could hear other American voices talking in cells up and down. The bathroom was at the end of the hall, and other prisoners were frequently escorted down it past his door. One of them was obviously a marine, because he invariably whistled "The Halls of Montezuma." At all hours of day and night Limbert could hear from somewhere else in the prison the voice of an Iranian woman singing patriotic songs and talking loudly to herself. He imagined it was some poor prisoner who had lost her mind.

Despite the gloominess of the new place, Limbert was happy. He was surrounded again by his colleagues, which was reassuring, and there were two mattresses! He had a roommate, Lee Holland, the embassy's army attaché. Holland was a small fireplug of a man who was nicknamed "Jumper" because he had enrolled and passed jump school at Fort Bragg relatively late in his career. He was more than a decade older than Limbert, with thinning straight hair that now hung limply around his broad forehead. He had grown a gray beard. Holland had also spent some time in Tehran before the revolution, so both he and Limbert remembered the country in what they considered better days. They dubbed their new home the "Hitler Hilton."

After seven months of being alone, Limbert was thrilled to have company, and he found Holland to be especially pleasant. The first few days they were thrown together they sat up until the wee hours every morning conversing—so much that a guard came in and complained, "Don't you people ever sleep?" They talked about their lives, their families, their children, and what they knew about their situation. Holland had not heard about the rescue mission and had not learned of the shah's death. Holland told Limbert about his experiences since the day of the takeover, and about his past, about his service in Vietnam and in Germany. They played cards. Holland taught Limbert to play euchre, and Limbert taught him to play casino. Limbert was impressed by Holland's imperturbability. He was a gruff, steady man, not easily impressed or frightened, who treated his captors with steadfast contempt without deliberately courting trouble. A little of Holland's defiance rubbed off on the pliant political officer.

Limbert recognized that small acts of defiance preserved the prisoner's sense of self-worth and remembered how good it had felt when he had been listening at night to his stolen radio, putting one over on the guards.

He began practicing this new, measured belligerence on their guard, a young man named Gholam Reza, who was so perpetually glum that he had been nicknamed "Smiley." He was one of the true believers, someone who in Limbert's eyes embodied Iran's "New Man," appalling ignorance combined with absolute conviction. He found Reza too high-strung and impassioned to argue with directly, so he began leaving him mocking messages on the walls. In one, he wrote in Farsi:

> I am foaming at the mouth
> With violence and curses.
> I'm a rabid dog
> And I desire a bad name
> And a bone.
> I am tired of the voices of human beings
> All I want now is the braying of donkeys.
> I have disregarded the law
> Of God and man
> I desire the jungle
> And the characteristics of the wild animal.

Limbert made posters and drew cartoons. In one, he contrasted in Farsi the perfect Muslim state described in the Koran with the kind of system created by the radical students, comparing the generous historical acts of Muhammad with the students' authoritarian methods. Muhammad, for instance, had freed all of the prisoners after one battle, had not bothered the people of Mecca after his conquest, and treated foreigners in his country as honored guests. The students, on the other hand, had attacked defenseless people, harmed those in their protection, and had stolen from them. Reza began writing responses on the wall when Limbert went to the toilet. It got so that every time Limbert left for the bathroom he would return to find something new Reza had added to his wall drawings. The guard never spoke to him about it. For instance, in response to Limbert's point about visitors being treated as honored guests, the guard wrote, "Islam protects diplomats, not spies." Limbert then wrote, "For example, a businessman and a nurse are spies, like those you have taken hostage." This went on until his posters were so defaced that Limbert put them in a corner, hung clean paper in another part of the room, and labeled it "Free Speech Area." Reza continued the dialogue there. They never spoke to each other but carried on this written exchange for weeks.

In the hallway, the guards often played revolutionary songs. Limbert was a lover of old Persian folk music and regarded the new songs as dreadful. The words to one tune just repeated the familiar "*Magbar A'mrika*" (Death to America).

He teased Reza by replacing the lyrics with a loud singsong, "Hee-haw! Hee-haw! Hee-haw!"

7

BUY IRAQI WAR BONDS

Summer is long in Tehran. It was still sunning weather in early October when Mike Howland, stretched out on the balcony over the ministry garden one afternoon, was approached by a new guard named Isfahani, who asked the embassy security officer if he would show him how to field-strip his Spanish pistol. Howland had done so for some of the others. The big embassy security chief liked Isfahani. He was a slender reed, a slight, inoffensive man whose commitment to the pieties of Islam was suspect—he had asked Howland once if he could get him special American sunglasses that would enable him to see through women's robes.

They sat together on the third-floor balcony, just under the eave of the roof, and Howland broke down the weapon, explaining as he went. The hardest part about putting the .45 back together was holding down the recoil spring cap as you locked it back beneath the gun barrel. More than one trainee had injured himself by letting the spring cap slip and having it fly up into his eye or forehead. Howland demonstrated the tricky maneuver with his thick thumb pressed hard on the spring cap. Then he handed the pistol to the guard to try it himself.

"Isfahani, you've got to be careful or that thing will fly off and hit you," Howland warned him.

"*Bali, bali, bali,*" the guard said ("Yes, yes, yes!").

Isfahani's thumb slipped. The cap missed him, flying high into the air and landing on the upper roof, where it rolled down and came to rest in the gutter high overhead. The young guard went white with panic. How was he going to explain breaking his own gun or letting his hostage take his weapon apart? He was so beside himself that Howland took pity on him.

"Okay, Isfahani," he said. "Come with me."

The other guards were sleeping. Howland led the panic-stricken Iranian quietly into the kitchen and, much to the guard's amazement, slipped open the key box and removed the key to the attic.

"Shhh," Howland told him, a finger to his lips.

There was a dormer near the point on the roof where the spring cap had landed, and Howland led the amazed guard up the stairs and into the attic. He took him to the window and pointed down to the place in the gutter where he would find the cap.

The guard said he was too afraid of heights to climb out on the roof. Howland looked down. There were guards in the garden below.

"Bullshit, Isfahani, I'm not going out there," he said. "Those guards down there see me, they're liable to start shooting. You're going to have to go out there."

He showed him how he could hang on to the dormer on his way down and use it to help pull himself back up when he had retrieved the spring cap. Howland promised to stand in the window the whole time and direct him.

He was standing in the window, encouraging the trembling guard as he eased his way down toward the gutter, when suddenly they both heard explosions in the distance. Howland was shocked. He knew the sound; he remembered it from Vietnam. It sounded like an air strike, coming from the direction of Mehrabad Airport. Off to the west he saw rising columns of smoke. Isfahani looked back up at Howland, stricken and confused.

Just then a MiG-23 fighter bomber flew right past the window. Howland was at eye level with the pilot. The jet turned, hit its afterburners, and shot away from them. Howland braced himself for a bomb to hit but nothing happened. The startled guards below, looking up, saw Isfahani on the roof.

"Isfahani, get the goddamn cap and get back in here!" Howland shouted. Suddenly spry, the guard eased himself down to the gutter, scooped out the cap, and made it back to the window. He was so happy that he hugged and kissed Howland when he got back inside. Then the American helped him put the pistol back together. Isfahani had a perfect excuse for being on the roof. He told his comrades that he had reacted quickly when he heard the jets and had climbed out to shoot at it. His fellows were tremendously impressed with his alert and fearless response.

Laingen saw two jets. While Howland was watching Isfahani out on the attic dormer, the chargé had been sitting at an open third-floor window below, painting. The explosions to the west turned his head and at once he saw two low-flying MiG-23s with Iraqi insignia move directly over the ministry. They were less than a thousand feet from his window, and the angle of their approach made them seem to be moving slowly. One was trailing a drag chute, presumably deployed in error. They seemed bigger than Laingen imagined they would be and, in their apparent leisure, appeared to be flaunting their presence in enemy skies. "As they crossed over us, they swung to the west slightly and then gunned their speed as we watched their afterburners," he wrote later in his diary.

Holland and Limbert were together at Komiteh prison when they heard the roar of jet engines pass low overhead, a powerful *swoosh!*, which Holland recognized as the sound of two fighters on a shooting run, and then the burp of their electric cannons. In the distance a bomb exploded, followed by a second much larger *boom* that vibrated the floors and walls. The guards were shouting angrily outside.

"Goddamn, John! They're playing our song!" Holland said gleefully.

"What is it?" Limbert asked.

Holland explained that Tehran had just been attacked from the air. A siren began to scream just outside their window.

In a nearby cell, Chuck Scott and Don Sharer went right to work on the sounds. The jet engines sounded like something Sharer had heard once at an air base in Nevada.

"Chuck, I think those were air-dropped bombs, and that jet was a MiG," he said, referring to the Soviet-built fighter.

Five minutes later two more jets passed over.

"What were they?" asked Scott.

"J-79 engines, must be F-4 Phantoms," said Sharer. The Iranian air force's F-4s were one of the models he had come to Iran to discuss with the new government. "Somebody has attacked somebody."

Then all the lights went out. Antiaircraft guns opened up loudly nearby.

"That was a hundred-twenty millimeter," said Scott.

Sharer beat on the door, shouting, "I have to go to the head!"

"Can't go, can't go," the guard answered through the door.

"I have diarrhea!" Sharer lied.

The door was opened and he was taken to the bathroom, where he could stand on the toilet and look out a window. It confirmed Scott's assessment. He could see tracers arcing skyward from nearby rooftops.

They deduced that the likely culprit was Iraq, because other than the Soviet Union it was the only country close enough with MiGs. If the Soviets were attacking it wouldn't be just two fighters streaking over Tehran. It had to be Saddam Hussein.

In his cell, Daugherty arrived at the same point by a different route. The distant explosions and jets made him believe for a moment that President Carter had launched an attack . . . then he thought better of it. He sat on the floor of his darkened cell watching the flashes of what he assumed were antiaircraft guns in the small window overhead, trying to figure out what was going on. If Carter were going to attack Iran, it would have happened months ago. The Russians would have no reason to bomb Tehran. The most logical conclusion was Iraq. Saddam Hussein had always been at odds with Iran, even under the shah. Maybe now he sensed weakness and realized he could get some support—under these circumstances, even the United States might be helping him.

Daugherty felt good about it. He wasn't frightened. He reckoned that if he was going to sit through an aerial assault, few places were better than a prison. Its walls were many times thicker than a normal building. It was probably the safest spot in all of Tehran. At one point the guards opened the door and poked their heads in his room. They looked terrified. Daugherty figured they were checking to make sure he wasn't secretly communicating with the planes. They were watching when the large *whump!* of an explosion sounded in the distance. Daugherty smiled at them and clapped.

In a nearby cell, Metrinko and Roeder heard bombs falling close enough to rattle the walls.

"That's incoming," said Roeder.

Metrinko asked what was exploding.

"I can't tell," Roeder told him.

"You must know," said Metrinko. "You were in Vietnam all those years."

"Yeah, but all I ever heard was the sound from the top going down, not on the ground listening to them coming in. I've never been on the receiving end."

Roeder knew his jets, and listening intently to the sounds overhead he told Metrinko that they were MiG-23s, Soviet-built fighters. It took him just a few seconds to figure Saddam was behind the assault.

A panicked guard burst into their cell and asked if they were "weapons trained." Both men said they could handle a weapon.

"You might be issued weapons to help defend the prison," the guard told them.

Metrinko was shocked at the suggestion that he and Roeder might be asked to help their guards defend the prison.

"Please give me a gun," Metrinko said. "I'll use it all right."

Blaring loudspeakers spelled out the story for Limbert, who translated for his roommate Holland. Iraq had invaded Iran. Thirty-five people had been killed at the Iran National Works, where the bombs had exploded. The broadcasts urged citizens to postpone going to hospitals except for emergencies.

Suddenly, Iran was at war. At the various prisons guards began enforcing strict blackout rules and distributed candles. On the first night of the blackout, looking out the large windows that had framed his world for so long, Laingen had never seen such blackness since the moonless nights of his boyhood in rural Minnesota. There seemed to be universal compliance with the new blackout regulations. The city was not just black but silent, dead. Nothing was moving. The events of the day shook the chargé d'affaires out of hostage mode and back into gear as a foreign service officer. He recorded his analysis of the situation in his journal.

> In a series of simultaneous strikes against Tehran's Mehrabad Airport and air force facilities in six other cities, Iraq has suddenly escalated what has been for several weeks a low-level border conflict into a full-scale invasion. Saddam Hussein's purpose appears to be to demonstrate, by a quick and successful military assault, that Iraq is now the dominant military power in the Persian Gulf region—taking advantage of Iran's weakened military strength and its self-imposed political isolation intentionally to accomplish that purpose.

Laingen went on to describe the 1975 Iran–Iraq border accord, which Saddam Hussein had signed with the shah, and surmised correctly that, with Pahlavi dead and with Iran having cast off its alliance with the United States to pursue its divine destiny, Saddam had seized the moment to grab contested lands along the Shatt al-Arab (the Arab River) and possibly steal some of Iran's oil-rich territory in Khuzestan. The attacks prompted a surge of patriotism and calls for glorious martyrdom from Khomeini—"Everything we are doing is for Islam. What matter if we die? We shall go to Paradise." The imprisoned American, even with his professional objectivity, couldn't help but express a little satisfaction over Iran's predicament.

> Not a few Iranians, we suspect, recall that during the Shah's period, whatever his faults, such an attack by Iraq would have been out of the question, given the sheer preponderance of Iran's military power, real or imagined (in any event, untested).... To what degree did Iran's international isolation, itself certainly a consequence of the hostage affair together with the other internationally perceived excesses of the Revolution, figure on the timing and degree of the Iraq attack? As a speaker in this week's Friday prayers in Tehran reportedly said, "Oh, Blind World! There is not a single country which defends us. It is a veritable crime." Indeed, it is, but self-imposed.

There was evidence that at least some Iranians recognized this. One of the kitchen workers delivering a meal told Tomseth, "All this mess is Khomeini's fault."

"Yes, and someday the people will recognize that," said the American.

"Ha!" scoffed the Iranian. "The people—they are cows!"

What Iran lacked in military force it was making up for with its zeal. One night early in the war, Tomseth translated a plea heard on the radio:

"Heroic people of Tehran, especially those living in the vicinity of Mehrabad Airport. Please allow the aircraft to land. The aircraft is one of ours. Stop shooting at it!"

None of the hostages guessed that this outbreak of war might prolong their captivity. In Komiteh prison, John Limbert knew that Iran's relations with Iraq had been deteriorating, and that its new isolation made it vulnerable, so he felt a certain satisfaction in knowing that the country had finally paid a price for thumbing its nose at the rest of the world.

When there was an air attack, the guards at the Evin prison would run from room to room shouting, "Turn off your candles!" Bill Belk wondered, *How do you turn off a candle?*

After the first few days the attacks tapered off, then stopped. Several days and nights had passed with not a sound from the sky when one afternoon a lone jet streaked in low over the city and launched a rocket. It was a daring assault; a single aircraft had penetrated the city's air defenses by flying close to the ground to deliver a single large weapon, which exploded somewhere near the prison with enough force to shake its walls. From up and down the gray corridor on the hostage wing of Komiteh came sounds of delight. There was clapping, cheering, and shouting.

"Give 'em hell!" said one.

"Buy Iraqi war bonds!"

At the near-empty chancery, Kathryn Koob and Ann Swift were terrified when they heard the eruption of ground fire that accompanied the first raid, thinking that the guards were fighting off angry mobs who were coming after them. They were reassured by one that the shooting was only "practice air raid drills." The immediate assumption was that they were anticipating an American assault. Koob and Swift had learned months earlier about the failed rescue attempt in a letter that had slipped past the censors from a Vermont schoolgirl, who had written, "Dear Kathryn, How are you? My name is Jennifer Wilcox. I am ten and in the fourth grade and I'm writing this letter to cheer you up. I'm sorry that the rescue attempt didn't succeed. I hope they try again. I have no pets . . ."

During the night they could see shell bursts in the air and hear bombs dropping. There was a rhythm to it. The sounds of jets, antiaircraft fire, and then the guards unloading their weapons into the air for long stretches.

"You have to understand," one of the older guards explained. "These kids have been carrying guns for a long time with no excuse to use them."

During the day their windows were now draped with black plastic, which blocked the view of the snowcapped northern mountains. Outside there were air-raid sirens and the broadcast of martial music. Koob and Swift were delighted one day when a rousing rendition of John Philip Sousa's "Stars and Stripes Forever" blasted out over Tehran.

They didn't learn what was going on until the chief hostage spokesman Nilufar Ebtekar inadvertently informed them. She stopped by to chat in her flawless English and complained that the "Iraqis" had stooped to an all-time low. They were dropping fancy table napkins over the city contaminated with a virus that would cause cancer. Swift and Koob were shocked that she would believe such a thing, which was both wildly impractical and technically impossible, but delighted with the information. So Iran was at war with Iraq.

The window to the cell at Evin shared by Al Golacinski and Dick Morefield was painted black, but whoever had done the job had applied the paint on the inside, so Golacinski could scrape a little from one corner to peek out. Morefield wasn't that interested in looking out, but Golacinski spent hours with his eye pressed to that tiny portal, peering out over a gray stone courtyard and at the sky. At night he saw antiaircraft fire.

One morning there was a commotion below. A group of armed guards assembled and formed themselves into a line, and a bedraggled, bearded prisoner was dragged out and left standing alone against a wall before them. He was a young man, very thin, wearing what looked like rags. He was blindfolded and his hands were tied behind his back. He was violently shaking.

Then he was shot. It happened just like that, no final words, no ceremony, no swell of music like in the movies. The weapons cracked sharply and their echo bounced around the enclosure for a few moments. The victim slumped lifelessly to the ground and the firing squad walked off. Blood pooled on the pavement beneath the lifeless form. Golacinski watched dumbstruck. It had happened in less than a minute, a loud crack and a life abruptly ended. He could see it happening to him, just like that.

A few hours later two men in gray clothes came into the courtyard, one of them pushing a cart. They lifted the body and tossed it on the cart and rolled it out. The blood on the pavement dried black.

Tom Ahern was being kept in an administrative building of some kind on the outskirts of the Komiteh prison. In the next room were Don Sharer and Chuck Scott, who tried to communicate with him using a tap code. Ahern didn't know the code.

One day, to the CIA station chief's amazement, his guard began allowing him to visit with his military colleagues. He spent the week playing cribbage with Sharer, whom he especially liked. His relationship with Scott was testier. Scott was surprised when Ahern told him about the information he had given up in interrogation. The ramrod army colonel had endured what he considered great hardships trying to protect Ahern, Daugherty, Kalp, and whatever he knew about their efforts. That Ahern himself had, as he saw it, "rolled over" came as a shock.

Ahern felt very conflicted about how he had handled himself, but he did believe he had done the best he could, and he felt sure he had held out long enough to allow his Iranian agents to flee. The old name-rank-serial-number approach to interrogation was unrealistic, he felt, and he was gratified when both Sharer and Scott reassured him that he had done fine—Scott kept his reservations to himself. They agreed that his interrogation had been the worst, and Ahern took comfort in it.

The hiatus ended abruptly about a week after it had started. An older Iranian guard appeared one day in the open doorway staring at the three of them. He turned without saying a word and walked away. After he left a guard came and removed Ahern from the room and placed him back in solitary.

One sweltering night in late September, Bill Keough banged on his cell door in Komiteh because he had to use the toilet, or what the hostages called the "Khomeini Hole." No one answered. He banged again more loudly. Nothing.

"Esspeak more esslowly," one of the marines called out, imitating the guards who would say "slowly" when they meant "softly" and would not accept correction from American devils.

"Who's that?" Keough asked.

"Where in the hell is the guard?" called out the marine.

"He's right outside the door," Keough answered, apparently having pulled his tall frame high enough to look down into the hall, "but he's dead."

Everyone laughed. This got everyone's attention, and prisoners began pulling themselves up to the transom to see into the hall.

"Christ, he's fallen asleep out there!" someone else said.

The guard, one of the youngest and smallest, was sprawled with his head down on a table in front of his chair. Suddenly the hallway was alive with conversation. Each of the prisoners knew only who was locked up with them in their own rooms. Some had heard no news of their friends and coworkers since the day of the takeover. Questions and information started flying back and forth.

"Hey, what do you know?"

"Did you hear that the shah died?"

"Did you hear about the rescue attempt?"

CIA officer Bill Daugherty was alone in his cell, standing on a chair and looking out the open vent over the steel door. When he whispered out there was a momentary hush. Everyone was surprised to hear his voice. Some thought he might have been executed.

"How are you, Bill?" several shouted happily.

"I'm okay," he said. "Keeping myself very busy. The only thing is the food. Is there still something in the world to eat besides bread?"

Barry Rosen heard his old roommate Dave Roeder's voice and they exchanged greetings.

Information was pooled in those minutes of hurried, hushed conversation. Limbert explained to those who had not figured it out that the jets dropping bombs were Iraqi, and that Iran was now at war with Saddam Hussein. In overlapping whispers hostages compared notes about whom they had seen, what they had heard. Daugherty was delighted to find his friend Colonel Schaefer in the cell directly across from his. Schaefer told Daugherty all about the failed rescue attempt, which explained why they had been so suddenly moved and scattered in April. He told about Richard Queen's serious illness and his release. Daugherty was enormously pleased to hear that at least one of them had gotten home, and was both stunned and heartened by news of the rescue effort.

One of the men asked, "Hey, did any of you guys see that film of Rupiper, the one that priest did?"

Everyone had. The guards were especially proud of it and showed it repeatedly.

"They must have given him a blow job before he made that film," the voice said, and everyone collapsed into laughter.

Then the guard woke up.

"No speak!" he shouted, and silence returned. Moments later, Keough started banging on the door. He still had to use the toilet. For some reason everyone up and down the hall started to laugh.

The guard Abbas liked to debate with his captives and instruct them in language borrowed from the common rants about the evil practices of the United States.

Vice consul Donald Cooke looked up once from his book and said, "You know, Abbas, you're right. Even before I was born my parents decided that what they wanted me to do was to become a ruthless exploiter of the oppressed people of the third world. And from the time I was small I can remember them teaching me how to be a ruthless exploiter of the oppressed people of the third world. And when it came time for me to decide what kind of job I was going to get, I said to myself, I know what I want. I want to become a ruthless exploiter of the oppressed people of the third world. And here I am. I got a job with the United States government as a ruthless exploiter of the oppressed people of the third world and my parents, they're so proud of me they thank God every day. They get up in the morning and say thank you Lord for making our son a ruthless exploiter of the oppressed people of the third world."

Even Abbas was laughing by the time he was finished.

"I see we are being facetious today, Mr. Cooke," he said.

When Abbas lectured about racial, ethnic, and religious oppression in the United States, Cooke went off.

"Abbas, you have got to be kidding me," he said, and asked the guard, "In your embassy in London, how many Jews do you have serving there? How many Christians? How many Baha'i?" In contrast, Cooke noted the ethnic and racial mix among the embassy employees they had kidnapped. "My embassy looks like my country," he said. "Do your embassies look like that overseas?"

Abbas had to admit that they didn't.

Wound up now, Cooke described the fear he had seen in the eyes of visa applicants who had lined up by the thousands before the embassy seizure to apply for visas to escape Iran. "These were people trying to escape," he said.

"Tell me there's a long line outside of the Iranian embassy in Washington of blacks and Indians or Hispanics and whatever, seeking to try to escape the United States in order to come to Iran, you know, for their protection. Well, by God, there was a line half a mile long outside of my embassy the day we opened, of people who were just that. Religious and ethnic minorities trying to escape your government. Real oppression. Firing squads, executions."

As time wore on in the prison, Abbas was among those guards who became openly disgusted with their role in this hostage taking. He admitted that the whole standoff had gotten tiresomely bogged down. He said he and the others who had been involved from the beginning were weary of it and powerless to end it. He complained that the students had lost control of the protest right at the start, and that ever since they had become nothing more than jailers, trapped in a crisis of their own devising.

Not long after the attacks, Michael Metrinko was taken away from Dave Roeder and again placed in solitary in a basement cell at Qasr prison. The combative embassy political officer was always picking fights with his captors. Every time things started to feel a little bit too chummy, Metrinko would lash out. One night, after several had lingered in his cell for a long time lamenting how badly the war with Iraq was going, Metrinko suddenly announced: "You know, the imam is not a man."

The words immediately stilled the conversation. After a stunned moment, one of the guards asked, "What?"

"The Ayatollah Khomeini, he is not a man," said Metrinko.

"He is a man," said one of the guards.

"He is not a man," said Metrinko. "He does not have a wife."

"He does have a wife."

"No, he doesn't," Metrinko said. "The Ayatollah Khomeini does not have a wife."

"He does have a wife," one of the guards insisted. "There are pictures."

"The only pictures I have ever seen of the ayatollah with anyone else are always pictures of him with a small boy beside him," said Metrinko.

The guards caught his drift; he was suggesting that their imam was a pederast. Metrinko was grabbed by the hair—it had grown quite long—

and dragged from the room. The angry guards took turns kicking and punching him. He was thrown into a cell at the end of the hall where a blanket was draped over him and he was beaten some more. Then they locked the door and left him there and refused to bring him food for three days. Then he was driven to Qasr, where he was placed alone in a "punishment" cell. They took away his watch and his glasses and left him. The room was dark and cold. At first he upbraided himself for provoking the guards, but he also felt good about standing up to them. He would pay a heavy price.

When they saw how much time Metrinko spent reading, they took away his books for days at a time. For two weeks he was left alone in the cell, freezing. They fed him bread and water. He spent his days and nights shivering in his blanket, pacing or jogging in place to keep warm, and brooding. After some time, he was visited by several of the student leaders.

"You have insulted the guards, who have complained that they can no longer bring you food or take you to the toilet," the head of the group explained.

Metrinko was eventually taken back to Evin and placed again in a cell by himself. Now and then he was let out into a small courtyard to exercise. He walked in circles in the yard, just like prisoners in old Hollywood movies. Sometimes there were others walking in circles with him. That was how he discovered which hostages were being kept in that part of the prison, a discovery he found disconcerting. They were all embassy workers with the most sensitive jobs. There was Swift, the second-ranking political officer; Thomas Ahern, the CIA station chief; CIA officer Bill Daugherty; Lee Holland, an assistant defense attaché, and his boss, Tom Schaefer, the military attaché; and others. If the students were planning to put any of the hostages on trial, this would be the group.

He still lived with the guards' special enmity. One day one of them entered his cell with a stack of letters.

"These are from your family," he said. Metrinko had received mail from his family only a handful of times since the day of the takeover. Sometimes the letters he received seemed to have been chosen at random. One had appeared out of the blue from an old girlfriend whom he had not seen for eight years. He had devoured the letter, and was glad to get it, but had no way to respond. He wrote letters to his mother and father frequently but suspected they were not being sent (he was correct). So the sight of a pile of letters from his family was a thrill.

Then the guard tore the letters in half and walked back out of the cell with them.

Akbar was the only guard who took pity on him. When he took over at Evin, the mood of the place lifted. Even Metrinko grew to like him; he found him well educated and kindhearted. Akbar spoke some English and was fluent in Turkish and Farsi. He was not an innocent. He had taken part in the assassination of a government official ten years earlier, and at one point had been arrested by SAVAK and thrown in jail. He and Metrinko often conversed in Turkish, which few of the other guards understood. Metrinko found him to be a true believer in the revolution but not a fanatic. He would actually listen in conversation and carefully weigh what was said.

Akbar told Metrinko that he, too, had been trapped by the embassy takeover, caught up in events that he could no longer control and which he no longer agreed with. He shared some of the prisoner's contempt for his jailers; they, after all, were warm and comfortable and still basking in praise from the great mass of Iranians. For many of them this would be the most important accomplishment of their lives, and they delighted in remaining at the center of such worldwide attention. But what kind of attention? It pained Akbar to know that because of what they had done they were considered thugs all over the world, and he admitted to Metrinko that even in Iran there was now a growing criticism of the ongoing standoff. He and many others now believed the effects of taking and holding diplomats hostage were bad for his country and were going to get worse. He stayed, he said, because he felt partly responsible for putting the Americans in this position and felt obliged to do what he could to ease their captivity. When Metrinko told him he had not been able to communicate with his family, Akbar brought him a letter from his parents and offered to hand-carry his own letter out of the prison and mail it for him. Metrinko sat down right then, filled with skepticism about Akbar's promise, and wrote a typically uncompromising one-page letter in a tight but clear script.

Dear mom and dad—this is another futile attempt at a letter—futile because the Iranians won't send this one just as they have never sent any of the others I've written. Their so-called spokesmen lie about it, of course, just as they lie about everything else. But what else can one expect? If nothing else I can now fully understand what the old regime jails were like, since I am presently incarcerated in my third different one ... the type of jailer hasn't seemed to have changed much either ... only the name of the regime. Certainly standards of conduct remain barbaric, but there's no reason for me to belabor the point. Anyone who has had any contact with the "new government" knows exactly what I mean. It's just that now crimes are committed under a different imprimatur. There are exceptions to this generalization, even among the guards, but even the exceptional few refuse to accept any personal responsibility for the poor (very) conditions—"Orders are orders." One wonders if all this present and past idiocy and ill treatment of the hostages/prisoners stems from Persian paranoia, xenophobia, simple malice or just typical and all-pervasive incompetence ... but then trying to figure it out is hardly worth the effort. Enough. Rather obviously I am not in a good mood. Chalk it up to my eight months of solitary confinement (not even SAVAK did that to prisoners), my lack of news of what's happening and my general weariness of all the local lies and ranting and raving. It's safe to say that I have spent the last 13 months being angry and "pissed off," and my own emotions have tired me out. Your last 2 letters were dated 10 July and 1 October. So much for the freedom of receiving mail. Yesterday I got birthday cards from Debbie and Aunt Mitzi—Please give them my best. Since most of my mail is destroyed I have no idea how many other cards I would have gotten. The birthday itself was uneventful. I did my usual three hours of calisthenics (mostly jogging in place) as well as 2 hours of pacing the 4-pace length of my cell. Enough already. You can see what kind of mood I am in. Someday all of this will be funny ... God knows it's already ridiculous. Take care of yourselves, and I hope you have a pleasant Thanksgiving, Christmas, etc. All my love, and regards to everyone—Michael.

Akbar kept his word. The letter arrived a week later in Olyphant, Pennsylvania, the first his family had heard from him in more than a year. His parents read the letter out loud over the phone to an official at the State Department, and it further confirmed their fears that at least some of the hostages were not being treated well.

One day, without explanation, Metrinko was handed several new paperback science-fiction books. He was a big fan of science fiction and the books were like manna. Then, in the TV room, he discovered a box with dozens of similar volumes, all of them new, published in 1980. Adding to the mystery, as he poked through the box, he discovered one of his own books, which had evidently been removed from the shelf of his apartment—the first proof that his apartment had been invaded and looted. Looking with even more interest now, Metrinko found that one of the new paperbacks was inscribed, "Hope you enjoy the books, Michael," and that they had been sent from Cooperfield's Bookstore in Scranton, Pennsylvania. He had no idea how the box had found its way to Evin prison. He never asked, and no one explained, but Metrinko felt an enormous debt of gratitude toward the bookshop. He plunged into the books.

Reading was only a partial cure for the boredom, however. At times, Metrinko's spirits sank. The worst prior moments for him had been the two weeks in the chancery basement, handcuffed day and night, and then, more recently, the two weeks of cold, dark, and loneliness in the punishment cell. In those circumstances Metrinko's despair was salvaged by the pride he took in defying his captors. But time and tedium eroded even the defiance that sustained him.

One fall night, alone in his cell at Evin, the moist walls peeling paint, Metrinko listened to the muffled booms of bombs exploding in the distance. Then the walls and floor of his cell began to shake. It had announced itself first as a great rumbling sound that grew louder and louder as it approached. It was an earthquake. The shaking lasted only a few seconds, and after that he could hear sirens and horns outside. It made him feel small, hopelessly alone, stranded, vulnerable, and insignificant. Part of him wanted to laugh out loud. It was such a travesty of disasters. Here he was a pawn in a great struggle between nations over matters that neither Iran nor the United States fully understood, trapped on a battlefield between two nations fighting over something else, and in an instant all of it could be rendered irrelevant by some blind, unthinkably powerful tectonic shrug. The futility of his predicament mirrored the absurdity of life itself. He was going to sit in this miserable cell until the day he died and it didn't matter to a soul, his life was forgotten and meaningless, all his dreams were illusions, and when he was dead and gone the great idiot pageant would keep on rolling right along, heedless, pointless, and cruel.

8

IT HAS BECOME A QUAGMIRE

Iraq's invasion of Iran was a direct consequence of Khomeini's revolution and of the embassy seizure, and it would take a horrendous toll on both nations over the next eight years.

It was hard to disguise the tone of satisfaction in American TV reports on the outbreak of the war, just as the hostages had cheered the pounding of Tehran. But Saddam's aggression had derailed, at least temporarily, an agreement for their release.

Two weeks before the bombs started falling Sadegh Tabatabai, a mid-level official in the collapsed Bazargan provisional government and the brother-in-law of the imam's son Ahmad, had initiated secret talks with the United States to resolve the crisis. A chain-smoking dandy who wore expensive suits with colorful matching silk ties and pocket handkerchiefs, who combed his brown wavy hair into a pompadour and had more than one hundred varieties of tulips in his personal gardens, Tabatabai was a highly unlikely figure to be a member of Khomeini's inner circle. He had run unsuccessfully for president in the last election. For almost two decades before the revolution he had lived in Germany—indeed, documents seized at the embassy suggested that the CIA regarded him as a German spy—and he had the appearance and manner of a sixties-era Western playboy. But his marital connection and kinship with Ahmad Khomeini gave him a unique opportunity to speak unpopular truths.

There had been a number of worldly, well-educated, well-placed Iranians who considered the hostage taking to have been a mistake from the beginning. Tabatabai was a veteran diplomat and knew well that the documents seized at the U.S. embassy revealed nothing more than the routine, prudent espionage conducted at diplomatic missions everywhere. Now, as the one-year anniversary of the embassy takeover approached, as Soviet troops built up in Afghanistan, as world opinion continued to condemn Iran, as economic sanctions, although hardly crippling, began to have a noticeable effect, and as Saddam Hussein's military might massed on the nation's western border and increasingly menaced Iranian forces inside their own country—a helicopter carrying President Bani-Sadr would nearly be shot down by Iraqi fighters in mid-September—it was all too clear that Iran would only become further isolated and vulnerable if the hostage standoff continued. While popular opinion still responded enthusiastically to anti-Americanism and calls for trying the hostages as spies, more practical elements in the country's leadership, including some in the clergy, realized they could no longer afford to indulge in this warm bath of popular anger. Unlike the most devout of the mullahs consolidating power, these men were not entirely willing to leave their future in the hands of Allah. Iran had, for instance, started buying those desperately needed parts for their American-made jets from Islam's presumed archenemy Israel.

Speaking with his brother-in-law Ahmad Khomeini one evening early that fall, Tabatabai again expressed his impatience with the hostage crisis. He admitted storming the embassy had had its purposes, but that "it has become a quagmire. I would like to try and end it," he said.

"What is your idea?" Ahmad asked.

"If you endorse me, if you support me, I can find a way."

Tabatabai said that he was friends with Hans-Dietrich Genscher, the West German foreign minister, and that through him he could arrange for private talks at the highest level of the American government. It was critical that the talks remain secret, because any public move toward an agreement with the Great Satan would trigger the wrath of Iran's religious conservatives and could bring down catastrophic reprisals. Only someone with connections like Tabatabai's would dare to initiate such discussions. Even he was frightened.

"What do you want?" Tabatabai asked his brother-in-law. "What should we expect America to do for us in return for releasing the hostages?"

Ahmad said that his father would be satisfied if the United States would express remorse or apologize for its historical role in Iran, unlock Iranian assets in America and withdraw any legal claims against Iran arising from the embassy seizure, and promise not to interfere in the future. This represented a significant retreat from the long-standing demands for the return of the shah and all his wealth. Tabatabai invited the West German ambassador to his house in Niavaran, an affluent suburb in north

Tehran. The Iranian host dismissed his bodyguards early so that there would be no one to note the coming and going of the Germans. He asked the ambassador to quietly convey the new list of demands through Genscher to the White House.

Ever since the failed rescue mission, Carter had been at a loss about how to approach Iran. The debacle had, in the peculiar logic of this crisis, placed the United States on the defensive. There was little or nothing for Iran to gain by holding the hostages, especially with the shah dead and buried. Most of the monarch's wealth had been moved from American banks, so the demand for the return of his wealth was moot. Secretary of State Cyrus Vance was replaced by Senator Ed Muskie, and the United States waited for Iran to make the next move. Even the slightest hint of a feeler got immediate and serious White House attention.

As Carter would note in his diary on September 10, "Ed Muskie called, and said he must see me immediately and alone. I told him to come over. He brought Chris [Deputy Secretary of State Warren Christopher] and I called in Zbig [Zbigniew Brzezinski]. We had a message through Genscher from Iran, to which I responded affirmatively."

The proposal seemed to Carter designed to succeed. It represented a significant shift in Iran's position, and other than the insistence on an apology the demands really did nothing more than undo the steps taken by the United States in retaliation for the hostage-taking. But who were they dealing with? Who was this Tabatabai? Even if the Germans vouched for him, what did that mean? Their earlier dealings had been with the elected president of the country and its foreign minister, neither of whom, it turned out, had any real power over the situation. Hard experience had demonstrated that there was only one Iranian in a position to deliver the hostages, and that was Khomeini. If Tabatabai could prove he spoke for the imam, the United States would take the proposal seriously.

In Tehran, the brothers-in-law knew they had Ayatollah Khomeini's support, but even with that there was still the chance that the newly empowered *Majlis* would dig in its heels. In an effort to forestall an ugly public battle, they set about building a quiet consensus for the initiative. They visited Akbar Hashemi-Rafsanjani, the speaker of the *Majlis,* and found that he was delighted by the idea.

"Can you give me a guarantee that you can sell these things to the *Majlis*?" Tabatabai asked.

Rafsanjani said he could.

So Tabatabai met again with the West German ambassador inviting him once more to his home at night and dismissing his security guards, and told him that the Americans should listen to a broadcast speech by Khomeini scheduled for three days hence. In the speech, the imam would mention the same four conditions Tabatabai had conveyed.

Three days later, Khomeini gave a long, rambling speech, at the end of which he enunciated Tabatabai's four conditions for ending the hostage crisis. Journalists around the world correctly interpreted Khomeini's conditions to be a major shift on Iran's side of the impasse, but the White House played down the importance of the remarks. America was suffering a kind of hostage fatigue. Dick Gregory had just returned from Tehran, fifty pounds lighter from his months-long fast, and after outlining his own solution to the crisis, which essentially called for Carter to capitulate to every one of Iran's demands, he began a doctor-supervised one-man march on Washington. His skeletal frame—he was down to under one hundred pounds—symbolized the country's exhaustion and sense of futility over the matter. According to polls, Carter and Reagan were running neck and neck in the upcoming election, where the country's attention was increasingly focused. Carter dispatched Deputy Secretary of State Christopher to meet secretly with Tabatabai in Bonn at Schlock Gimmick, a private palace owned by the West German Foreign Ministry.

Christopher was shocked to discover a tall, slick, urbane man in a well-cut tweed jacket who spoke with none of the overheated rhetoric they had come to expect. Nothing about the encounter with Tabatabai was what he and his entourage had expected. This emissary was pleasant, agreeable, and unfailingly polite. As they moved into a room for formal discussions, both Christopher and Tabatabai offered to let the other go first, and then the Iranian noted that the room they were about to enter had a Persian rug and took Christopher's hand, "Let us step on this Persian carpet together, hand-in-hand. . . . Let us forget the past, start from now, and go into the future."

His German was fluent, and he spoke to Christopher through a German translator because he had not dared bring a Farsi interpreter with him from the Foreign Ministry in Tehran—there was too much risk of a leak. It was hard to believe that this man with manicured fingernails, who held his cigarettes gingerly in the old theatrical manner, between the thumb and first two fingers, was a representative of the fierce mullahs governing Iran. There didn't seem to be an ideological bone in his body; he was strictly pragmatic. Tabatabai was particularly interested in opening the gates for spare military parts and wanted that to be part of the deal. Over the next two days they hammered out an agreement to end the crisis, one that met all the new demands save one: the United States would not be issuing an apology. Both men agreed to take the proposals home for approval.

Tabatabai was excited. He prepared an eight-page account of the agreement in preparation for the flight home. He had flown to Bonn on a private plane owned by Iran's Foreign Ministry, but when he arrived at the airport for the flight back to Tehran he was told his plane could not leave. War had broken out.

Saddam's bombs crushed Tabatabai's initiative. Iranian officialdom immediately blamed Iraq's aggression on the United States. For nearly a month, the Carter White House waited for word from Tabatabai but there was none. It started to look as if the hostages would have to wait out this war.

As the American presidential campaign moved into the home stretch, it was watched with great interest from Iran, by both guards and hostages. Early on, the public had rallied around Carter, and his poll numbers were high, but they had begun to decline in early 1980 and, following the rescue attempt, they had plummeted. People seemed to feel sorry for him, which translated into respect but not support. His stewardship took on a sickly cast, with a number of events and issues combining to make the humble engineer from Plains, Georgia, seem well intentioned but yielding and ineffectual. His concern for human rights and his willingness to reevaluate foreign policy on those terms rankled those who believed that containing the larger evil of communism occasionally demanded unsavory acts and alliances. The decision to cede the Panama Canal back to that tiny Central American nation was both pragmatic and inevitable, but it gave America-firsters the charge that Carter was a pushover and an apologist for the nation's power. Rising oil prices throughout his tenure dramatically revealed the United States' growing dependence on oil imports from the Middle East and a vulnerability to decisions over which Washington had only limited influence. Ever since the 1973 OPEC embargo the world's markets had been jumpy, and Iran's decision to bar oil exports briefly in 1978 had panicked investors globally, even though the country accounted for an insignificant portion of oil supplies. The seizure of the embassy created more concern, and then OPEC raised oil prices 50 percent in 1979. Carter's perfectly sensible call under the circumstances for Americans to conserve oil and gas, reasoning in his button-front sweater before a White House fireplace, produced one of those iconic images that permanently brand public figures. Here was a critical natural resource that the United States could no longer cheaply supply, controlled by suppliers it could no longer direct or even influence. It was an admission of impotence. When the Soviet Union invaded Afghanistan at the end of 1979, it aggravated the sense of American weakness. The hostage crisis confirmed the impression. It was a prolonged national humiliation, painted in ever worsening detail by the majority of the news media, from the parading of blindfolded American diplomats before angry crowds to a series of failed diplomatic initiatives to the military ineptitude at Desert One. The previous three and a half years seemed marked with Carter's sad, puffy face on a TV screen, earnestly administering another dose of bad news.

Ronald Reagan, whose familiar chiseled features recalled an era of seemingly limitless American potential, skillfully played off Carter's powerlessness. The Gipper's broad-shouldered, cinematic swagger alone was anodyne to Carter's "malaise." America had received enough doses of bitter medicine from the peanut-farmer president and was eager to sail off into a dreamworld of patriotic bliss. Reagan deliberately dithered when pressed for specifics, but his well-articulated dreams were rooted in the country's fondest fantasy of itself. Arriving in a blizzard of brilliant red, white, and blue, the Republican convention was a restorative to the country's sagging spirits, and it gave Reagan a big enough boost to overtake the president in most polls. Carter gained ground during the Democratic convention in late summer, but Reagan's appeal and the stubborn presence of Representative John Anderson in the campaign, whose small percentage of the vote would come primarily from former Carter voters, kept the Republican candidate on top. In the final months of the campaign, Reagan refused to debate the president on television unless Anderson was included, which would likely broaden the third-party candidate's exposure and pull.

In Tehran, the guards at Evin prison took a straw poll one evening to see who the hostages would elect for president. Limbert selected Carter. Most of his colleagues wanted Reagan, as did the guards, who considered the hated Carter's electoral woes a great victory for Iran and glowed with satisfaction that their actions were shaping big events in the United States. They were convinced that anyone other than Carter would understand their reasons for seizing the embassy and would admit the great wrongs America had committed in Iran.

Lieutenant Colonel Dave Roeder asked one of them, "Do you know who Ronald Reagan is?"

"He was a movie star," the guard said.

"Do you know what will happen to Iran if Reagan wins the election?" Roeder asked. The white-haired prisoner with the deep-set eyes and heavily lined face leaned forward dramatically, made a sudden expanding gesture with his hands, and said, "Boom!"

All through October, as Election Day in the States approached, rumors swirled about the hostages' imminent release. The *Majlis* finally took up the issue toward the end of the month, and after days of private debate there were strong signs that the country was ready to give up the hostages. In what the Associated Press termed "rampant worldwide speculation," there were reports from a variety of sources about a secret deal to free the hostages before Election Day, the first anniversary of the takeover. Ever since the coincidence of the Wisconsin primary, when Carter was unfairly accused of having deliberately stirred expectations for a breakthrough in the crisis to improve his chances, the White House had been under suspicions that Carter found particularly wounding. His critics made mutually contradictory accusations, that he was powerless and incompetent but also that he was somehow manipulating the crisis to his benefit. The Republican campaign all but conceded that the president was likely to produce an election eve solution to the crisis. Suspicion went both ways. There were also rumors, although less widespread, that Reagan's campaign was somehow conspiring to prevent a hostage release before Election Day. For his part, Carter and his staff repeatedly stated that rumors of a secret deal were baseless.

They were not entirely so. Early in October, the amateur botanist Tabatabai had employed a horticultural metaphor in a secret message to Warren Christopher, reporting that the terms they had worked out in Bonn before the outbreak of the Iran–Iraq war "had fallen on fertile ground." This message had been conveyed to Carter at a campaign stop in Winston-Salem, North Carolina.

After a secret debate in the *Majlis,* Rafsanjani had made good on his guarantee, winning a 100–80 vote in support of the agreement despite last-minute minority efforts to scuttle it by walking out. In a speech at the end of the month, Khomeini announced that the conditions under consideration were "just," and no less a figure than the hanging judge Ayatollah Khalkali, who only a few months back had toyed on TV with the charred corpses of American airmen killed in the rescue attempt, predicted that the hostages would soon be released, citing Iran's desperate need for the hundreds of millions of dollars worth of military contracts that the country had purchased before the embassy seizure—the same contracts that imprisoned American military men had brought to the revolutionary government's attention more than a year earlier.

"We want to free the hostages before the election," Khalkali said. "We know the war with Iraq will be long. Many will die if the United States doesn't give us the weapons we have already bought. We need the reserve parts now."

On the last day of the month, Radio Tehran tried to put the best face on this change of heart. It announced that a "just method" for the hostages' release had been worked out by the *Majlis,* emphasizing that the conditions would force the United States to make "concessions." Iran, it seemed, was ready simply to declare victory and send the American hostages home wrapped in great clouds of cant.

> The bitter struggle waged by Islam against the greatest tyrannical force in the world to raise the word of right and obliterate the signs of falsehood and aggression is the best example for humanity to follow in its journey towards right and justice. The seizure of the spy hostages was a bold human act by the heroic Iranian people, undertaken with confidence and loyalty, in order to rid the world of the vicious hand which had played havoc with the people's dignity, freedom, and independence. The detention of these spies for a year is an unforgettable lesson for those who let themselves be seduced into working in this ill-fated field. It is also a good lesson for the tyrants who rely on such unethical methods to carry out their oppression against the people.

Matters reached a head in the days before the American elections In Tehran, buses were parked outside the U.S. embassy, a Swedish plane poised to fly the hostages out, and medical teams assembled to receive them at the American military base in Wiesbaden, Germany. For their part, the student captors informed the Iranian government that this time they were prepared to comply with the agreement and release the hostages.

If the hostages came home, it might provide Carter the margin of victory. The hostage crisis was now all over television again as reporters got wind of a possible settlement. There were pictures of the waiting buses and plane, interviews with the hostage families, and long recapitulations of the whole sorry story as the first-year anniversary of the takeover approached. Poised, ever cheerful Dorothea Morefield, wife of the captive embassy consul, was everywhere. "They [the Iranians] want to resolve it want to bring it to an end," she told one reporter, gazing out softly behind her big-rimmed glasses. "I think they [the hostages] are coming home and I don't think it will be too much longer."

A half-hour-long special on the hostage crisis, "A Year in Captivity," punctuated by passages from letters written by Dick Morefield to his wife and children, aired on CBS just days before the election. The special suggested that an end to the crisis was at hand, perhaps too much at hand with moderator Dan Rather commenting, "There are questions whether the deal is being rushed too hastily for election campaign purposes."

Suspense over the election and the hostages rose toward a crescendo on election eve. Once again the nation was poised for a happy ending . . . and nothing happened. The Iranian leaders had apparently expected Carter to grab at the chance to save his presidency; they had demanded that he simply announce his acceptance of the deal on television. To his credit Carter didn't bite. He coolly issued a statement calling the proposed deal "a good and constructive move," but said that his actions would not be governed by the press of the campaign or his desire for a second term. There was still a filament of hope that the Iranians would go through with the release and complete the negotiations afterward. The president would note in his memoirs, "Now my political future might well be determined by irrational people on the other side of the world over whom I had no control."

There were complex legal issues involved. Probably the most difficult conditions were the requests that Iranian assets be unfrozen and that legal claims against the country be dropped. There were about $10 billion in assets at stake, which included securities, gold deposits with the Federal Reserve, and money in the U.S. Treasury and in American banks both at home and abroad. At least $500 million was being held by American companies. Lodged against that fortune were lawsuits over debts incurred by the shah's government that had gone unpaid after the revolution, including a $175 million bill from Sedco, a Texas oil equipment firm, a $93 million bill owed the E. I. Du Pont Corporation for a synthetic textile plant it had built in Iran, and an unpaid $85 million bill to the Xerox Corporation. The most hopeful part of the proposal was Iran's suggestion that Algerian diplomats mediate final discussions.

Instead of a breakthrough, however, Carter's beleaguered face appeared on TV to announce yet another in a long series of disappointments. The result was immediate. With typically cold calculation, Carter wrote in his diary that evening, Monday, November 3:

> Pat [Cadell, his pollster] was getting some very disturbing public-opinion poll results, showing a massive slippage as people realized that the hostages were not coming home. The anniversary date . . . absolutely filled the news media. *Time, Newsweek, U.S. News*—all had cover stories on the hostages. And by Monday only a tiny portion (I think Pat said 19 percent) thought that the hostages were going to be coming home any time soon. This apparently opened up a flood of related concerns among the people that we were impotent . . . Strangely enough, my favorability rating went up—the way I handled the Iran situation went up, and the percentage that thought it was used for political purposes went down . . . [but] prospects had faded away for us to win.

On Election Day, Carter returned to his home in Plains, Georgia, to cast his vote. He told reporters, coyly, "I asked my wife who she was voting for, and I voted the same way." When reporters asked him what he planned to do in the event that he lost, he demurred, saying that he expected to win, but he already knew the truth. In a moment rare for him, the president lost his composure thanking the gathered friends and family from his hometown. He said he felt "more encouraged than I have in the past" about winning the hostages' release, and, asked about the impact the hostage crisis had on his reelection campaign, Carter said with conviction tinged by a trace of wistfulness, "I'd have to say it was a negative factor, but we acted properly."

In the end, the third-party candidate Anderson wasn't even a factor. American voters making up their minds at the last minute decided in favor of the Republican candidate, giving Reagan and his party an overwhelming victory. The former movie star and California governor took almost 10 percent more of the popular tally and a landslide of electoral votes—489 to 49. He carried forty-four of the fifty states.

There was widespread rejoicing in Iran over Carter's defeat. It was regarded by many as another sign of Allah's hand in world affairs, although no less a local hero than Mousavi Khoeniha, spiritual adviser to the student hostage takers, was less sanguine. Referring to Reagan, he told a reporter, "The yellow dog is brother to the jackal."

On the first anniversary of their captivity, some of the hostages were awakened in Evin prison by radio broadcasts in English. Apparently the students wanted to spread the news, and had tuned in to a BBC station and cranked up the volume. Some of the report concerned the Polish uprising against its Soviet masters, and then came the news that Ronald Reagan had defeated Jimmy Carter in the American election.

Most of the hostages were delighted. They assumed that Reagan's election meant something was going to happen. They had done such a good job convincing their guards that the "something" would not be good for Iran that Joe Hall felt the need to reassure a fearful Big Ali that nothing would happen right away.

"In the American system, Reagan will not take office until the end of January," he explained.

Even those hostages who preferred Carter were heartened. They had known nothing of the deal for their release that had seemed so close as the election approached, so this news was the first in months that suggested change. Everyone, hostages and guards, started counting down the days until Reagan's inauguration, January 21, 1981.

After Reagan's victory, talks over the hostages cooled. For Laingen, Howland, and Tomseth, the only captives who were in a position to follow the process closely, it was maddening. Perhaps most distressing was the absence of continued American outrage. Somehow during the year of captivity, the threats and counterthreats and the failed rescue mission, the capacity for anger seemed to have exhausted itself. Negotiations proceeded through November, with overtures and responses, as though America were hammering out a trade agreement, not dealing with a criminal regime. Carter welcomed the conditions demanded by the Iranian kidnappers. Reagan, after the election, pledged to abide by whatever solution was reached. It seemed that American blood could no longer boil. Clare Boothe Luce, the elderly former journalist, ambassador, and conservative congress-woman, commented sarcastically, "The United States will end up apolo-gizing to Iran for its having declared war on us."

The passion had also drained out of Laingen's writings. In the early months of captivity, his journal and long letters home were filled with repetitive railing against the flagrant injustice and folly of Iran's policies. But he had emptied that well. Like a man who wakes up to a green sky, he had worn himself out trying to get other people to notice that something was wrong and now had given himself over to simple observation.

He wrote in his journal:

> How do I feel about Iran? It has gone on so long that I think I have overcome most of the anger and bitterness I felt earlier. It is behind us now; we are alive and well and physically no worse for wear—only a year older! I could not feel good toward the leadership, certainly not the hard-liners, certainly not the clerics and the "student" militants. I think I feel scorn for them but not hate. They will suffer—are suffering—for what they did. They have brought Iran to the point of collapse, to a war that they encouraged in the sense that they weak-ened Iran to the point where Hussein felt he could attack—or felt angry enough to attack because of [Khomeini] and his constant call for Hussein's overthrow. . . . There is the hard reality of our country's interest. It is not in our interest to see Iran defeated or dismembered by war, or to see it weakened so that extremist political elements of another persuasion take over. On balance, our long-range interests are Iran, not Iraq.

Still, there was that "scorn." Most revolutions are driven at least in part by fantasy, the belief that a certain class or tribe of people is special or chosen, that some idea represents the permanent apex of human thought, if not God's own. Never was this more evident than in Iran. The rhetoric of the revolu-tion was arrogant and self-righteous to the point of parody, and from his third-floor perch, monitoring the local TV, radio, and press, Laingen had heard about all he could stand. "Sanctimonious" was the word he used for it in his journal. It resembled the doublespeak of Orwell's *1984*, where the word "freedom" was simply assigned a new and opposite meaning—religious oppression was true freedom, a twist that could be appreciated only by donning the green-tinted glasses of Islam. "It is not freedom of the kind known in Western countries and termed liberalism," explained his holiness the Ayatollah Ali Khamenei at one Friday prayer meeting. "Freedom in that liberal sense is license to follow any sort of desire, passion, or corruption. Freedom under Islam lies within the framework of Islamic principles," as determined of course by him and the other mullahs.

Month by month the clerics' double-talk was becoming more institutionalized, more the official vocabulary of the state. If it were not totally clear that the religious extremists were in control, it became so when Sadegh Ghotbzadeh, the dapper official who had stepped down as foreign minister to make way for an appointee more acceptable to the ruling clerics, was briefly arrested in mid-November. Among other heresies, he pronounced in a TV interview, "Iran is governed by a group of fascist extremists who are driving this country to disaster."

It sounded like something Laingen himself had written a year earlier.

9

WEREN'T YOU FED AMPLY?

In the interregnum, as Reagan began putting together his administration and Carter and his team prepared to move on, it appeared as if the hostage crisis was hastening toward some kind of ending, but it wasn't clear what sort. Negotiations through Algeria had continued with Carter after his defeat, and once or twice more hopes of a settlement were fanned by news reports only to vanish again. Washington and Tehran traded final offers, and shortly before Christmas it appeared as though the talks had failed. Ayatollah Mohammed Behesti, Secretary of the Revolutionary Council, held a press conference in which he answered many questions in calm, correct English. He said that it was likely the hostages would be brought to trial, and those convicted of spying would be dealt with accordingly. Stansfield Turner, the CIA chief, advised the president on the first of December that the talks "offered little prospect of success."

As the hostages entered their second year of captivity, the rain and cold had come again to Tehran, and the jubes once more were filled with swift-flowing mountain water. Another year of rust had formed on the great cranes poised on the skyline over now forgotten construction projects. The hostages had become little more than an afterthought. The country was at war. Iraq was raiding the pipelines and refineries of the country's oil industry. It had set fire to the great works in Abadan during a siege of that city, doing precisely the kind of damage that American warplanes might have a year earlier if Carter had yielded to calls for punitive air strikes. Kurdish rebels backed by Saddam Hussein were fighting pitched battles against Iran's Revolutionary Guards. The death toll that would ultimately reach a million had begun to grimly accumulate, and the country wore the gray pallor of hardship. Internally, the religious rulers continued their bloody purges of political opponents; any criticism of the regime was now treason. Gasoline and kerosene were being rationed. Many of the students involved in the takeover had left to defend their country against Saddam, a more urgent and tangible threat than the Great Satan.

Those who remained behind to supervise the hostages were no longer the darlings of the revolution and were weary of the task. The shah was dead and buried. All but the most ardent true believers had long ago concluded that the assassinations and countercoup they had imagined forming behind the embassy walls didn't exist. Study of the "Spy Den documents" had revealed details of the considerable influence the United States had had over the shah—the embassy's files contained records that went back decades—and showed that after the revolution the CIA and American military had tried to cultivate spies within the new regime, but this was hardly surprising. Such was the work of embassies the world over, including Iran's. Still, the protest had served a purpose. It had helped leverage the mullahs into long-term power, a result that not all of the student planners had desired or foreseen, and it had, as public theater, spectacularly underscored an end to the nation's old vassalage. As a show of defiance, it had been a yearlong, televised Boston Tea Party. If the past twelve months had proved anything, they had demonstrated how powerless the United States was to influence anything in the new Iran; if the embassy takeover had done nothing else, it had broadcast Iran's total independence to the world. It had produced unforgettable images of America humbled: blindfolded hostages, burning flags, and the charred remains of airmen and helicopters in the desert, dead even before striking a blow. But Iran was now paying a terrible price in the real world for its symbolic triumph.

Of what use were the hostages now?

Carter had tried to conduct his handling of the hostage crisis from the beginning without concern for his political future, and now there was no future even to consider. It gave him solid footing for the next ten weeks of offers and counteroffers. When one of the many voices from Iran's leadership at one point demanded a one-word answer from the president to its latest offer, Carter obliged.

"No," he said.

They could deal with him, or they could wait and deal with President-elect Reagan, who publicly scorned the process. Reagan said little about the standoff, except to repeatedly deplore the taking of hostages, and he even refused to be briefed on the secret negotiations. Here was a man with none of Carter's fluency on policy details, but who intuitively understood the role of theater in world politics. When he did speak, in an interview shortly before Christmas, standing with his wife, Nancy, before a Christmas tree, his face became a steely mask of contempt, the virtuous cowboy confronting Black Bart. He said that like most Americans he felt, deep down, "anger" at the very idea that demands were being made of America by "criminals and kidnappers." Days later he said, "I don't think you pay ransom for people who have been kidnapped by barbarians." Both the president and the president-elect made it clear that Reagan would not simply pick up the process when Carter left office. His term would start with a clean slate, and in the brutal calculus of popular concern the hostages were an old and tired story. Throughout the campaign the Republican candidate had expressed nothing but disgust for the whole travesty, hinting that were he president nothing of this sort would be allowed to happen. With Carter it was taken for granted that he would do nothing rash, but there was no such certainty with Reagan, who with a large popular majority behind him might well consider swiftly ending the standoff. Many Americans would applaud a bold, punitive move by the new administration, even if it was a bloody one. By any calculation, most of the blood spilled would be Iranian. Thus the election results imparted a new urgency to the talks.

Carter had accepted Algeria as intermediary. Deputy Secretary of State Christopher led a delegation there after the election to present America's formal response. It accepted all four of Iran's demands in principle: 1) stop interfering in Iranian affairs; 2) unfreeze Iranian assets frozen after the embassy was seized; 3) remove sanctions and block legal claims resulting from the takeover; 4) block remaining assets of the shah from leaving the United States. The United States countered with a fifth demand that all of the above was contingent on the hostages' safe return. Christopher then outlined to the Algerians the major sticking point: Iran had overestimated the shah's missing fortune by a factor of a thousand—Iran put the figure at between $20 to $60 billion and the United States said it was closer to $20 to $60 million. There were also legal constraints on what an American president could do about the shah's private holdings and to what extent he could interfere with the courts.

Christopher pointed out that although America could not legally seize the Pahlavi family fortune, Iran might sue for its return. The United States government also could not bar corporations from suing to recover money owed on unpaid contracts. To avoid having to convince American judges to rule in their favor, Iran responded by suggesting that the United States simply repay from its own Treasury money looted from the Iranian people. The White House acknowledged this line of reasoning, but it was unwilling to concede that the shah's fortune was lawfully Iran's. Carter had immediately rejected it.

In mid-December, Iran added a new demand, one that was particularly revealing and that amounted very nearly to an admission of wrongdoing. It wanted indemnity. It wanted the United States to forfeit any future claims against Iran by the hostages or their families. Since private lawsuits against foreign countries very rarely succeed, it was not a major concession, but Carter knew that such a step would close for the victims of this outrage their only legal avenue for redress. Carter directed that the hostage family organization, FLAG, be consulted, but the families were hardly inclined to hold up a deal that might bring their loved ones home. The White House accepted the demand.

What followed over the next month in Algiers was like haggling over a rug in the Tehran bazaar. The bargaining eventually boiled down to the amount of Iranian wealth deposited in American banks that Carter had locked in place the year before, weighed against the country's outstanding debts, most of them for military hardware. Iran first demanded $14 billion in frozen assets and $10 billion in cash guarantees, then a day later suggested that the United States could expedite the release by depositing $24 billion in Algeria as a guarantee against whatever the assets proved to be, a sum that the president called "ridiculous." Iran was, in effect, demanding $640 million per hostage. A few days before Christmas, it appeared as though the talks had broken down, until State Department officials with experience in the Middle East encouraged Carter to make a lowball counteroffer.

Christopher secretly proposed $6 billion.

And that's where negotiations stalled. Cornered by a pack of reporters outside a grocery store in Plains, where the Carters were paying a pre-Christmas visit, the president didn't sound hopeful.

"We explained our position very clearly through the Algerians," he said, "and either they [the Iranian authorities] decided to ignore what we said or they have deliberately decided to make demands that they know we cannot meet."

The Carters then climbed on a tandem bike, a Christmas gift from their hometown, and pedaled off down Main Street, looking positively carefree for the first time in more than a year.

At the end of November, the student captors began relocating the hostages to the Tehran mansion of onetime SAVAK chief Teymour Bahktiari, who had been assassinated by Iranian agents in Iraq after a falling-out with the shah in 1970. His extravagant home had been converted by the shah into a sumptuous guesthouse, and though it had fallen into disuse and some disrepair after the revolution it was, to the hostages, sheer luxury. There were working bathrooms with tubs and showers and hot and cold running water. Many of the rooms looked out over spacious gardens, which, while bare and sometimes snow-covered as winter closed over the city, and while the windows had been fitted with wire mesh or bars, it afforded for many of them the first steady view of the outdoors in over a year.

As usual, they didn't know why they were being moved, but there was a growing sense even among the hostages that the long drama was nearing its end. They had very limited access to news, but there were subtle signs of a breakthrough everywhere, and the hostages missed none of them. In early December, still at Evin, Colonel Chuck Scott and his roommates had not seen the kindly guard supervisor Akbar for several weeks when one day he showed up with a bag of fresh pistachios. He announced that he was no longer involved with supervising hostages, that he had taken a job with PARS, the Iranian news agency. The whole situation, the standoff, the shah's death, the war, had grown so complex and difficult that he said he no longer wished to be involved.

Scott was angry with him. The two had developed a friendship over the yearlong ordeal, and he was the one Iranian whom the colonel felt he could trust and even respect. Ever since the previous summer, Scott had seen Akbar's enthusiasm for the exercise waning. The young Iranian still defended the action but acknowledged that nothing had worked out the way he and the others had planned. Scott had told him once during the previous summer in Tabriz that if he helped him and his roommates escape, he would see to it that Akbar would be paid for his efforts and set up in America or wherever he wanted with a new identity. He had been surprised by the guard's response. He did not get angry nor did he dismiss the idea out of hand. "Be careful of what you say," he had advised the colonel. It had always been reassuring to know that Akbar was there; many times he had interceded to pull Scott out of solitary or to calm tensions with guards and fellow hostages.

"Now you tell me that you're tired of it?" Scott said.

His disgust wounded Akbar, who acknowledged a trace of betrayal in his departure. But after a few moments of conversation Scott's anger melted. No one could understand better than he the desire to escape this dismal ordeal, and the fact that Akbar had stayed with it for so long despite his ambivalence started Scott thinking that there might be more behind his young friend's departure than he was free to tell.

"Do you still think I will ever get home?" he asked.

"In my heart, I am sure you will live to see your family again," Akbar said. "When you are released, if it is possible, I will come to say good-bye."

Still alone, CIA station chief Tom Ahern delayed taking off his blindfold when he was first brought to the guesthouse. He had been placed in a very cold room in an overstuffed chair. He had a powerful sense that what he saw would finally reveal his fate. Was release near or death? He was certain that if the surroundings were worse than those he had left then he would never get out of Iran alive.

The upholstered chair was a good sign. He began reaching around and felt some kind of soft wallpaper, something fancy with padding behind it. He finally inhaled deeply, untied the blindfold, and discovered that he was sitting in an elegantly furnished room, and for the first time in fourteen months he was filled with the conviction that this ordeal was going to end well. He felt it in his bones. He was going home.

As part of the general improvement, his guards were now encouraging him to write letters. He thought it unlikely that any letter he wrote would actually be mailed, but he was certain that his captors would read it, so primarily for their eyes he wrote a long letter to his wife. It was a contingent good-bye letter. He wrote that Reagan's election made it certain the United States would attack Iran and destroy the revolution. "If

Reagan comes and gets them," he wrote, "I won't survive it. So let me say good-bye and I love you just in case."

He hoped that would make them think.

Laingen, Tomseth, and Howland were finally moved from their spacious quarters at the Foreign Ministry, but not without a scuffle. When a group of students first showed up to take them, Howland got in a shoving match with the leader, kicking him in the groin, and the three had been escorted back upstairs at gunpoint. They were left alone in their rooms and, after a few minutes, a deputy foreign minister appeared looking shaken.

"This is not Iran," he said, as if trying to convince himself. "This is not Iran. What has happened to us?"

"This is the first time in my diplomatic career that I have had a pistol pointed at my head," said Laingen.

The three were successfully removed some days later and locked in prison for several weeks before being moved to the guesthouse.

Kathryn Koob and Ann Swift could scarcely believe their eyes when they arrived. They had been brought to what appeared to be a large, luxurious hotel room suite with a fifteen-foot ceiling. It was clean, with a closet, beds, a bathroom with hot and cold water, and a tub! At the center of the room was a large, gleaming mahogany table with two straight-back chairs, and hanging from the high ceiling was a pewter chandelier. The walls were papered with a textured material, and one whole wall was a floor-to-ceiling window covered with pale blue drapes. Koob and Swift were astonished. The suite was so large they could now actually run from room to room instead of running in place, as they had for most of the year. They jogged for almost an hour late that night, waiting for their bedding and possessions to arrive. Both were fit and had lost a lot of weight. Koob especially. She had dropped so many pounds that she had made Christmas presents out of the wide strips of material she had cut from the seams of her blue slacks. She used them to make bookmarks, on which she embroidered small designs. Reed thin for the first time since she had been a little girl, Koob was now virtually unrecognizable to those who had known her only as big, soft, and wide-hipped. She was now all sharp angles, the hard lines of her face ill suited to her wide-framed plastic glasses.

She and Swift counted this as their thirteenth move since the day they were taken prisoner. Koob took out her Christmas ornaments, some of them saved from the previous year, and set about decorating the enormous space. When the sun came up they were allowed to pull back the blue drapes and their rooms were flooded with sunlight. What a pleasure! They looked out over a snow-covered garden with a backdrop of mountains, a thrilling view after their months of close confinement. Koob marveled at the simple things, the feel of sunlight on her skin as she sat near the window, the way the tinsel and foil in her Christmas decorations twinkled. Yet the new home was harrowing in the evenings, as Iraqi air assaults on the capital continued. When the planes came over they moved to the entryway of the suite, as far away from the broad window as they could get.

The guards asked them to prepare their room for a holiday party. They received an artificial tree and strips of bright red and white ribbons and—of all things—yellow bows. The women wondered if their guards knew the significance of yellow ribbons back home and decided to put one big one front and center, where the cameras would not miss it. When it came time for the party, to their disappointment, they were led out. Women were forbidden to worship with the men, the guards explained. So they sat forlorn in a chilly room down the hall and listened to chorus after chorus of "Silent Night" as the male hostages were led into their suite in groups.

For the hostages' second Christmas in captivity, the students and the Iranian government decided against allowing a visit from American clergy. Instead they arranged for ceremonies at the Foreign Ministry guesthouse to be conducted by priests and ministers from Tehran's small Christian community.

Film of the celebrations, which resembled the one made a year earlier, was shown throughout the world.

Joe Hall stuffed his pockets with candy and pastries and asked if he could say something to the cameras for his wife Cheri.

"I'm still out here, honey, and I can hold on if you can, kid."

Greg Persinger told the camera, "Mom, Dad, I just want to say Merry Christmas and I send you my love. . . . Take care. I hope I see you soon."

When his turn came before the camera Bob Ode said, "I would like to send a message to my wife, Rita Ode, who is living in Sun City West, Arizona. I want to tell her how much I miss her, especially now at Christmas, and I love her very much." He also sent greetings to his brothers and sister.

Barry Rosen sent his love to his wife and children and parents, and added, "I'd like to thank all the people in the United States who have written to us and sent books and other materials. I'm sure I speak for the other hostages when I say that the support and concern shown toward us by our fellow Americans has been of immeasurable value to all of us . . . God bless all of you and God bless America."

They were given gifts. Hall got some clean underwear and a green sweatshirt, which he felt went nicely with his lime green pants, the ones he had worn every day now for nearly fourteen months, and packages from both his wife and his sister filled with goodies. Hall particularly prized a pair of new insulated slippers.

Michael Metrinko decided to attend this year's Christmas party, if only to make trouble. The night before, he had been brought to the guesthouse and had been placed again with Dave Roeder, this time in a large room with real furniture, even real beds. There was wall-to-wall carpeting, a beautiful chest of drawers with ornate inlaid woodwork, a crystal chandelier, damask wall coverings and drapes, and—luxury of luxuries!—their own bathroom. Metrinko stood for a long time beneath the flow of hot water, basking in it. It was heaven. They were given new clothes, blankets, and even the food was tolerable. The guards were acting strangely. They had become warm and friendly, joking with the hostages as if this whole ordeal had just been a great adventure they had shared. They complained about how much time they had to spend caring for them, and talked about how much they would love to someday visit the United States. Something clearly was up.

The next day they were taken to the party. One of the guards showed up at the door wearing a fancy cowboy shirt with pearl buttons and intricate stitching.

"Where did you steal that?" Roeder asked him.

The guard protested that the shirt had not been stolen.

"It is a Christmas present gift from my sister who lives in Texas," he said.

Roeder didn't know which was stranger to believe, that the man had stolen it from the belongings of a fellow hostage or whether this devoutly Islamic young Iranian who had helped hold him and the others prisoner for more than a year to protest the Great Satan United States had a sister who chose to live in America and send her hostage-taking brother a cowboy shirt for Christmas, a holiday that wasn't on the Islamic calendar.

At the ceremony, Metrinko confronted in Farsi the Iranian clergyman who was there to conduct the service.

"It's disgusting that you would collaborate with these people," he told him. "How could you do it?"

The clergyman was insulted.

"I don't have to be here," he said. "I could be at home celebrating the holidays with my wife. I had to go through a lot of trouble to arrange this for you . . ."

Metrinko was openly ungrateful. He found the man obnoxious, a fraud who was there in order to be photographed being a "good Christian." After a round of dispirited carols—the camera caught the Americans singing "O Come All Ye Faithful"—Metrinko, Roeder, and the others were instructed to pour all the candy and goodies they had scooped up on their plates back into the big bowl. They were, however, given gifts that they were allowed to keep. Some of the other embassies had sent over presents. Metrinko got an exercise warm-up suit. There was also mail from home. Metrinko received a small package sent by a woman in North Carolina with vitamins, candy, and some books. Roeder was given a Christmas package from his wife. It had been opened and rifled. Some of the contents had been removed, including clean underwear, which he very much would have liked to have had. There was candy in the box, a toothbrush, and eight dinner mints, a private Christmas joke from his wife—a little tradition they honored. There were new socks, a Christmas ornament that his daughter had made at school, and a picture of his daughter with her arm in a cast. There was no explanation of how his daughter had broken her arm.

When Metrinko and Roeder were back in their room, two Algerian diplomats were shown in, the ambassador and an aide. They explained that an agreement for their release was very near, and the two hostages began to entertain a flicker of hope.

Kathryn Koob and Ann Swift forbade their guards to speak of their imminent release. They had heard such stories so often that they no longer dared to get their hopes up. One morning in mid-January a guard entered their room and announced, very pleased, that they were to have a "special visitor."

Into the room walked the familiar, short, round, draped figure of Nilufar Ebtekar. Koob wondered how the guards had ever gotten the idea that they would be happy to see her again. They regarded her as a liar and something of a dupe, and disdained the way she and the other educated Iranian women showed such reverent deference to the men. When they coolly exchanged the standard greetings in Farsi, the two hostages invited Ebtekar to sit down.

Ebtekar had no sympathy for the rumpled, frail-looking women before her. She still suspected Swift of being a spy, and even though she knew Koob was not, in her mind the American cultural emissary shared the collective guilt of all Americans for her country's sins against Iran and for that reason alone was a suitable candidate for revolutionary justice. Ebtekar was not an empathetic woman. She saw the whole episode through the lens of her own difficulties; even though it had turned her into a national hero of sorts and a notorious international figure, to her it had meant hardship, even though she had met during the previous year the man she would marry, one of the leaders of this action, Mohammad Hashemi. She thought that the women especially had been treated with heroic restraint in captivity, with genuine Islamic kindness. She and the other student captors had worked long and hard to ensure their safety and relative comfort. The business of housing, guarding, and feeding them had been a huge undertaking, all the more difficult for having been unforeseen. Even during the hardship of war, the students had held faithfully to their assigned mission. If she expected anything from the hostages, particularly these two relatively coddled women, who had been treated throughout with all the appropriate Islamic concern for modesty and respect, it was gratitude, especially for the news she was bringing.

"We are not one hundred percent certain that you will be released, but let me tell you that it has never been so close and so real," she said. "Negotiations are under way, and the possibility exists that you will be released."

Koob and Swift listened in polite silence and thanked Ebtekar for the information as she left. Later that same morning they were led out of their suite, waited in the same chilly room where they had sat out most of the Christmas celebrations, and then were brought back to the suite, which had been rearranged and equipped with a camera and microphone. Two chairs behind a small table with one of their small Christmas trees at the center had been moved in front of the camera, and Ebtekar sat with her back to the camera facing the table. The two women sat in the chairs.

"We'd like to talk to you about your treatment while you were here," said Ebtekar. "We want you to tell us about the food, about the care you received, and how you were treated, what your feelings were like."

Ever since the giggly Easter interview, which both Koob and Swift immediately regretted, they had prepared themselves for another propaganda session like this. They were determined to be truthful, but to project nothing but the grim reality of their predicament and to utter nothing that would give Ebtekar and the other students satisfaction.

"Physically we have been treated quite well," said Swift. "We have had plenty of food to eat, we are warm. But we have been afraid the entire time we've been here. We have not always had the mail from our families that you told us we would have. Sometimes months have gone by without letters from our parents."

Both women complained of their constant confinement, the weeks of not seeing sunlight, the inability to regularly exercise, the poor access to bathrooms and infrequent opportunities to bathe, and the isolation from their colleagues.

"You are being very negative," Ebtekar scolded them as a new tape was put in the camera. "You might talk about some of the positive things that happened."

"Can you tell me one positive thing about being locked up?" asked Koob.

Ebtekar shrugged. This was a thing that could not be helped.

"But what about the treats?" she asked. "What about the nuts? What about the goodies?"

The interview went on for forty-five minutes. Both women felt confident they had given Ebtekar nothing she could use to make the case that they had been happy "guests" of the ayatollah.

One by one, the hostages were led in to be questioned by Ebtekar before the camera. Informed that their release might depend on their answers, most of the hostages tried to play along amiably without giving Ebtekar the satisfaction of praising their captors. Ahern just glared at her contemptuously. Regis Regan waited until the camera was turned on and then lewdly insulted her. He was hauled out and beaten. Metrinko glared at her and refused to speak. Ebtekar asked Dave Roeder, "Weren't you fed amply? We know this was a bad situation, but didn't everyone try to work together to make the best of it?"

"Turn off your camera," Roeder told her. "I'm not going to say anything like that."

The camera was turned off. Ebtekar suggested to Roeder that they do it again.

"If you do not cooperate, you will not be released with the rest of your colleagues," she said.

Roeder refused.

Dick Morefield, the embassy consul whose wife Dorothea had become such a public figure at home, enjoyed the chance to talk politics with Ebtekar.

"We have made a decision that we are going to release some of you," she said. "Wouldn't you like to be released?"

"I understand that I will be released no sooner or later than when you come to the conclusion that it's to your advantage. There isn't much I can do that will either speed it up or delay it."

"Have you been mistreated?" she asked.

"Do you mean, have I been tortured?" he asked. "No. I've been held in very close confinement under very difficult stressful conditions for a very long period of time. I have been through mock executions. But have I been beaten or tortured? No."

She asked him what he had learned from the experience, and with the camera rolling he lectured her.

"One of the things that I didn't learn was what you were trying to accomplish," he said. "You were the first social revolution in history that didn't have to compromise from the very first moment for lack of money. When you took over, you had all the money you needed to make Iran back into part of the fertile crescent. If you wanted to do reforestation, if you wanted to reinstitute the underground irrigation systems you once had . . . anything at all. Anything was possible because you had the money, and you threw that away."

Ebtekar argued that all revolutions required a period of cleansing, of wiping away corrupt influences, such as Iran's ties to the United States.

"All I've got to say is that nothing we could have done to you in our wildest dreams is half as bad as what you've done to yourselves," Morefield said. "Your children and your grandchildren are going to curse your name."

Bruce Laingen recorded his session in his diary.

I am shown to a chair behind a low table, on which is a microphone and a small plastic Christmas tree. My "interviewer" is none other than the celebrated "Mary," the woman militant who is so often on Iranian TV interviewing my colleagues. She is in her usual Iranian dress, heavy scarves over her head, and with a trace of a smile. She tells me that she will ask me questions about my treatment and asks if I am prepared to respond. I answer that I assume I am. Sitting and standing around the room are perhaps 20 to 25 young Iranians, men and women; their purpose is not clear, but all of them seem by their manner to feel that they have a right to be present. I assume they are the veterans of the embassy seizure and are present tonight because they, too, sense that the climax of their operation is about to be reached, whether they like it or not.

Their manner is not hostile or friendly. We—I—seem to be regarded, as we always have been, as mere pawns in their larger purposes. Some look quizzically at me; most seem to ignore me. I make a determined effort to ignore them, and I am determined not to smile. I am angry, reflecting my frustration and anger over all these long months—now to see these "students" assembled for this final act in the drama arouses all my irritation from that long stretch of time. One wonders what is in their minds, how they really feel now, and how they regard the settlement that is probably near.

Mary begins her questioning, the exercise lasting only five minutes at most. The questions are about our treatment in the foreign ministry; my answers are as factual as I can make them, as terse as I can be without being rude. I am determined to keep my dignity and to make sure they understand that I haven't lost it and don't intend to do so now. The gist of my answers is that my treatment at the ministry had been reasonably fair, but that, like all my colleagues, I had suffered from the deprivation of my most fundamental human right, freedom. Answering questions about my experience in prison, I note that life there had been Spartan at best and cold. But I add that I had been glad in a sense to be taken there, since it gave me a chance to see what my colleagues had suffered.

Mary does not persist with her questions. There is no attempt to sermonize or to try to get me to acknowledge any Iranian grievances. She seems to conclude that I am not very interesting or useful, and so she coldly thanks me and terminates the conversation.

10

WE DON'T DO
STUFF LIKE THAT

Before Laingen and his roommates were removed from the Foreign Ministry, where they could listen to news broadcasts and receive visitors, he had learned enough to be convinced that the impasse had been broken. He had heard with pleasure the refreshingly blunt statements of the president-elect, whose use of words like "criminals," "kidnappers," and "barbarians" stood in marked contrast to Carter's measured public comments. Reagan's tough talk set off a scornful crescendo of renewed anti-American rhetoric from the pulpits of Tehran and alarmed Tomseth and Howland, who felt it didn't help with the delicate negotiations they all knew to be under way, but Laingen felt it was a dose of exactly what was needed. Carter and Reagan, perhaps intentionally, were working a classic good cop/bad cop routine. Reagan's words would make the powers in Iran think hard about blowing the remaining weeks they had to make a deal with the very reasonable Jimmy Carter.

This was more of the chargé's constitutional optimism, to which he clung even now when he had lost all sense of what was going on. For the first time since the day of the takeover he was cut off from all sources of outside information and from any sense of why things were happening, but his instincts were solid.

If the students believed the televised Christmas greetings they had allowed many of the hostages to make would earn them goodwill in the United States, they had miscalculated. The images of scrawny, unkempt American diplomats, held prisoner for more than a year, once again inflamed American anger and put the hostages back on the front pages. The Christmas tree at the White House remained unlit for the second year, although Carter allowed it to be illuminated briefly for a ceremony that remembered the hostages. There was renewed pressure on Washington to *do something*, and speculation flared over what military steps Reagan might take when he assumed office in less than a month. There was blood on the horizon. More than 60 percent of Americans polled at the end of the year said they expected Reagan to attack Iran in some way. When all the lights were turned off in Times Square for a full minute on New Year's Eve in honor of the hostages, the darkness and quiet seemed ominous.

At first, Radio Tehran seemed to welcome the coming clash. In a broadcast on the first of the year, it reported that Iran would be rid of the hostages soon. Either the United States would accept the country's demands for their return or they would be tried as spies and executed. Carter took the threat seriously. He instructed his staff to prepare a declaration of war if trials began. Iran's assets would be permanently frozen and some form of military action would proceed.

Despite the gathering clouds, or perhaps because of them, the bazaar-style haggling had resumed behind the scenes. Although he'd tendered a "final" offer weeks before, toward the end of December Carter dispatched a new initiative. In a Camp David meeting the week after Christmas with the Algerians, the president made another counterproposal that still fell way short of paying up the $24 billion Iran had demanded but that offered something new: "All claims by American institutions and companies against Iran in U.S. courts will be cancelled and nullified." The immediate effect of that provision, which Carter once again labeled a "final offer," would be to free Iran of the almost $3 billion in claims by Sedco, Du Pont, Xerox, and other corporations. The proposal also contained a new wrinkle, which proved to be key in surmounting opposition from Iranian hard-liners: Any agreement ending the crisis would be made with the country of Algeria, and not directly between Iran and the United States. After a weeks-long silence, Tehran responded favorably, and by January 6 the talks in Algiers had resumed.

Now, as the countdown to Reagan's January 20 inauguration proceeded in the United States, television reports about the change of power competed with news about a hostage agreement. Reagan announced that he was setting up a special team to take over the talks, but that he might decide to keep Warren Christopher and several other members of Carter's team in Algiers for a time to ensure continuity.

Iran countered with some modifications to Carter's "final" offer, but Christopher and the head of the *Majlis*'s special negotiating committee, Bezhad Nabavi, were ironing out the details of an agreement that still essentially followed the outline achieved by Sadegh Tabatabai and the American emissary months ago in Germany. The United States would promise not to interfere with Iran; it would return $9.5 billion in Iranian assets frozen after the embassy takeover; it would freeze the shah's assets in the United States to enable Iran to mount a legal effort to reclaim them; and it would nullify all lawsuits presently filed against Iran (referring the large corporate claims to binding arbitration before an international tribunal) and bar any such actions in the future.

With neither side trusting the other, a complex scheme of money transfers was worked out to trigger the hostages' release. The United States would wire money to a bank in England, and only after it was safely deposited would the Iranians release the hostages. The British bank would not release the funds to Algeria until the hostages had departed Iran. The deal was all but done.

"Iran is not getting one dime of U.S. money," said State Department spokesman James Trattner, explaining the deal to reporters. "The basic exchange is we're getting back what they took from us and giving back to them what we took from them."

In the final hours of his presidency, Carter had become obsessed with finishing the matter before stepping down. He believed he had lost his office because of his determination to preserve the hostages from harm, so securing their release and safe return before leaving office was on some level a satisfactory bargain. He feared that the negotiations under way in Algiers might not survive the transition, and what Reagan would do was anybody's guess. It might be many months before the hostages came home, if they ever did. To lose the presidency only to see all his efforts on their behalf unravel was a disappointment he dreaded.

The Iranians were deliberately stalling. They had agreed to accept the deal and to send the hostages home, but they had also decided to deny Carter the satisfaction of seeing it happen on his watch. Such pettiness didn't enter the president's thoughts. He pushed Christopher to finish the deal and made plans to fly to Germany to greet the hostages on their return as the final act of his presidency. Then he would fly back to Washington and take his place on the inaugural stand behind Reagan with a sense of completion and accomplishment.

Two days before the inauguration, there was a knock on Bill Daugherty's door in the Tehran guesthouse basement. He was startled. He couldn't remember the last time that had happened—his guards always just burst in. Even his friend Mehdi, when he came by with food or to chat, just walked right in. When Daugherty overcame his surprise and opened the door, he found himself face-to-face with a young man wearing a white jacket and carrying a tray. Had a waiter come to take his order for dinner? The tray held a hypodermic needle, and Daugherty submitted to having blood drawn from his arm. He took this as proof that he and the others were actually going to be released, and, indeed, just after midnight he was blindfolded and taken to a large room for a medical exam. Two of his embassy colleagues were already on tables, men he had not seen in more than a year. They did nothing more than exchange silent hellos and hopeful smiles. An Algerian doctor gave him a quick once-over and pronounced him fit.

It was only the first in a cascade of signs that they were at last going home.

Back in his room, Daugherty was visited by the black-bearded, gap-toothed Hussein Sheikh-ol-eslam, who said he had come to say goodbye. The tall, slender young Iranian slipped to the floor and leaned against the wall. He was wearing his usual sweater and dirty blue jeans, his feet thrust into a pair of unlaced athletic shoes that he wore like sandals, with the back ends crushed under his heels. To Daugherty he seemed weary but pleased with himself. Iran, he told the CIA officer, would at last be free of outside interference and Iranians would build the country based on their own culture and values. Daugherty told him that he foresaw more trouble for Iran, years of oppression and isolation. For any country to thrive, he argued, it had to give its citizens room to breathe. Any government that did not was ultimately doomed. Sheikh-ol-eslam said that an Islamic government had great respect for the rights of its citizens, provided they obeyed the rules. For instance, he said, a newspaper would be free to publish whatever it wished so long as it didn't say anything "prohibited." Daugherty was amazed at how this intelligent, sincere young man could so blithely embrace such a striking contradiction.

If Sheikh-ol-eslam had hoped for an amicable parting, he wasn't going to get it. He wished Daugherty well, then hesitated before leaving, waiting for a response. Daugherty just shrugged and his former interrogator departed.

Sheikh-ol-eslam also had one more session with Tom Ahern. The CIA station chief was led into a room where his old interrogator was seated alone behind a desk. Stretched across the desk was a long piece of cord.

Sheikh-ol-eslam lectured Ahern about how well he and the other hostages had been treated, and explained why it had been necessary to shame the United States and to reveal the insidious plotting that had been going on. Ahern listened silently. He had heard it all before. He was eyeing the rope. The best he could figure, Sheikh-ol-eslam was going to use it on him again. Instead, Sheikh-ol-eslam started explaining that the beatings Ahern had received were really not indicative of his own values or those of Islam.

"As a token of my sincerity in this, I invite you to use this rope to do to me what I did to you."

Ahern looked at the rope and then at Sheikh-ol-eslam.

"We don't do stuff like that," he said.

John Limbert fought a losing battle against his rising hopes. He had heard snatches of a report on TV when he had been taken for his physical, and the announcer had been talking about an agreement, about money and conditions, so he knew that something important was afoot. But he also knew that any number of things could happen at the last minute to abort all this. Months earlier there had been talk of turning all the hostages over to the government, and that had come close and then fallen apart. Limbert was aware of the time difference between Tehran and Washington and knew that it was drawing close to Reagan's inauguration.

The guards told everyone to expect to leave on the nineteenth, and throughout the guesthouse the anxious hostages waited through the entire day and night. Nothing happened. Limbert and his roommates then sat expectantly through another long day on the twentieth, and again nothing happened. At dusk, he decided that the deal must have fallen apart. It was already approaching noon in Washington, which meant Carter's term, and his power to make the deal, would soon expire. If it fell through, it seemed fairly likely to Limbert that they would never go home.

Then, just as the sound of evening prayers began to crackle through loudspeakers in the neighborhood, came the roar of big guns. It wasn't the usual sound of antiaircraft fire, which the hostages had grown accustomed to hearing. It sounded more like heavy artillery, and it was going off at regular intervals, like a salute. Holland said that it sounded like they were celebrating some great victory.

Only then did a guard appear.

"Pack up," he said. "We're going. One sack."

Koob and Swift were instructed shortly before six to "Get ready. We are going."

"Going where?" asked Swift.

"To the United States. Get your things ready."

Neither woman assumed it was true. They pulled on several layers of clothing, because they had learned that the things they packed were often lost in transit. They packed their possessions in bags and waited. When the guards came they were led blindfolded down a hall and some stairs and then outdoors.

"Be careful," said Koob's guard. "There is ice underfoot."

They were ushered into a van with rows of seats and sensed immediately that it was full of people. Koob slid over next to a man.

"How are you?" the man asked quietly.

"Fine. Who is it?"

"Kalp."

"It's Koob."

For the first time since the morning of the takeover, Al Golacinski heard the voice of his assistant, Mike Howland. Golacinski was shocked. He had assumed long ago that Howland, Bruce Laingen, and Vic Tomseth, whom he knew had been at the Foreign Ministry on the day of the takeover, had gotten out. On that day a year ago, Howland had accompanied Laingen instead of Golacinski. The embassy security chief had no idea where his assistant had been for the previous year, but he assumed it had not been spent in prison.

"Mike, that's the last time you and I are going to have a shift change," he said.

Kevin Hermening was sitting on the bus when the guards pushed Bob Ode down to the floor. The youngest hostage stood and gave the eldest his seat.

Laingen argued with the guards who tried to take away his small blue bag.

"Don't you trust us?" one of the guards asked.

Laingen laughed scornfully, but sensing that now was not the time to mount a struggle over insignificant possessions he handed it over.

Marine guard Rocky Sickmann was squeezed into a small place that turned out to be some kind of radiator. He had a hole in the seat of his pants—he had spent most of the past year sitting on a mattress—and suddenly felt a sharp pain in his rump. There was no place for him to move. So he fidgeted on the hot plate. If the bus was taking him home, he could cope.

Michael Metrinko heard people behind him whispering.

"Shut up!" shouted Akmed in English, and then cursed all of them in Farsi.

Metrinko responded in Farsi, "You shut up, you son of a Persian whore."

The bus ground to a halt. Metrinko was grabbed by the arm and felt himself being pulled from the bus.

He shouted in English, "This is Metrinko and they are taking me off the bus!" Outside he kept bellowing loudly as he was beaten. Metrinko wanted everyone on the bus to know what was happening. The blows didn't hurt much. The past fifiteen months had toughened him up.

State Department communicator Rick Kupke felt angry at Metrinko. Here he was thinking that he might live through this after all, and this hard case has to pick a fight! He prayed that his colleague would just shut up.

Hermening had to smile. Metrinko was still giving them shit, but then he worried about him. It was the wrong time to rock the boat. The young marine kept trying to tilt his head and see out the bottom of his blindfold. All of them were hopeful but still a little worried. They wanted to believe that this was it, but wouldn't do so until they were at least in the air on their way out of Tehran.

Golacinski heard the voice of Ann Swift. Feelings were running high. Golacinski could tell this was it and suggested loudly, "Let's take off our blindfolds."

He and a number of the others did. Golacinski looked around and saw a large number of his embassy colleagues for the first time in more than a year, and what a worn-out, hairy, ill-clad group they had become! The sight filled him with joy.

"What are you doing?" asked a guard they called Bozo, who was carrying a pistol in each hand.

"Fuck you," said Golacinski, feeling brazen. "You're not going to screw this up. We're on our way."

He was dragged off the van by Bozo and several other guards and thrown up against a wall. He stood there for a few minutes and then heard the motors start. All of sudden his brazenness drained away.

"I'm sorry! I'm sorry! I'm sorry!" he shouted, pleading. He was placed back aboard.

Limbert's bus was so crowded that he had to sit in the toilet stall. When it started to move he was surprised that it didn't stop. In Tehran's insanely congested traffic, with mobbed traffic circles and jams at every intersection, driving through the city was always stop and go. The smooth movement of this bus suggested that it had some kind of escort, which implied government authority. They were on their way.

Carter had reluctantly abandoned his plan to fly to Wiesbaden before the inauguration in order to greet the returning hostages, but as the final hours of his presidency ticked away he remained determined to bring the crisis to a satisfactory end on his watch, to exit the White House announcing that the hostages were on their way home.

Christopher and Nabavi finally initialed the agreement very early in the morning on Tuesday, the twentieth. Carter and his staff had been up all night in the Oval Office, its walls stripped bare and the outgoing president's books and papers in boxes that were being removed, waiting for word that it was done. The Federal Reserve Bank was to transfer the first portion of Iran's frozen assets to an account in London as soon as the banks opened for business there, and then the Bank of England would move that money into an escrow account controlled by the National Bank of Algiers. When the White House received word about the agreement shortly after five o'clock, Carter immediately placed a call to Reagan. The president-elect, he was informed, did not wish to be disturbed.

The president took the news to the American people. He appeared behind the podium in the White House press room—"looking tired," as the CBS correspondent noted—to make the announcement. The signatures had just put the release process in motion and, given the dramatic reversals of the previous fifteen months, nobody was going to celebrate yet. Until the hostages were actually aboard the Algerian commercial jets waiting for them on the runway of blacked-out Mehrabad Airport in Tehran, winging their way home, there was still a chance it would all fall apart again.

As a sunny, cold inauguration day dawned over the temporary stage set up in the back porch of the Capitol building, the two stories unfolded simultaneously. Carter maintained a vigil at his desk, fretting to his aides that some last-minute glitch might still derail the process and leave the sensitive matter in his successor's hands. "I can just see the Iranians delaying for another day, Reagan saying something inflammatory, and our deal going down the drain," he said. Reagan did call after seven to ask for an update and Carter explained exactly what was going on. When he hung up, Hamilton Jordan asked, "What did he say?"

"What hostages?" Carter quipped.

The departing first couple met the Reagans on the front porch of the White House a few hours later. Carter had cleaned up and sat for a haircut. "We think the Reagans will enjoy their new home," he told the reporters on the front steps. The two couples sat together for the traditional inauguration morning tea, and Carter was surprised that the president-elect didn't ask him a thing about the tense situation that had kept him up for the past forty-eight hours. It was as though Reagan wanted nothing to do with it, as though the whole mess belonged to Carter and was going to be swept away with the change of administration. As they rode together in a car to the Capitol, Reagan told jokes.

Carter sat wrapped in a tan trench coat through the pomp of the swearing in, as Reagan stepped out on a bright red carpet and looked out over a sea of spectators, to the grand promenade of the East Mall and the Washington Monument.

"No arsenal, or no weapon in the arsenals of the world, is so formidable as the will and moral courage of free men and women," Reagan said in his address. "It is a weapon our adversaries in today's world do not have. It is a weapon that we as Americans do have. Let that be understood by those who practice terrorism and prey upon their neighbors."

Carter wasn't listening. He was waiting for news from Tehran.

Mehrabad Airport was blacked out because of the Iraqi air raids, but the tarmac where the buses stopped shone under the glare of television lights. The hostages were led one by one off the buses and through a jeering gauntlet of students who had formed two long parallel lines from the buses to the plane.

"Magbar A'mrika!" they shouted, and then, something new, *"Magbar Reagan!"*

Sickmann was grabbed from behind by one of the guards and pulled toward the plane. One of his sandals slipped off, and the marine resisted for a moment, stooping to adjust it, then ran toward the plane. He was the first one up the steps. A pretty stewardess greeted him with a smile at the top and he choked up with emotion.

"Yankee go home!" one of the Iranians screamed in English at Hermening. He thought, *From your lips to God's ears.*

When they let go of him at the foot of the stairs, Hermening ran up into the plane. It crossed his mind that someone might take a shot at him as he went up, and he practically flew up the stairs.

Bill Royer in his rumpled tweed sport coat felt a sense of pride and satisfaction as he was escorted to the airplane down the jeering corridor. Whatever the arrangements had been, and he didn't know what they were precisely, he was confident that his captors had not gotten what they'd wanted. They didn't get the shah back, for one thing, and that had been their primary demand.

Farsi-speaking Vic Tomseth toyed with the idea of shouting out his own slogan as he was led through the gauntlet, something along the lines of "*Magbar Khomeini*," but he thought better of it. I get to leave, he thought, these poor suckers have to stay here. So he walked silently and happily through the gauntlet to the plane.

Koob was frightened but made an effort to walk through the gauntlet with her head up. She was led up the stairs of the plane and steered down the aisle, where she saw Laingen and, beside him, her boss John Graves. Before them sat Barry Rosen and her assistant Royer. She slipped into the empty seat between them and they both recoiled with surprise to find her just a slender remnant of her former hefty self.

John Limbert heard the doors of the bus open and he was led out into the night air, where his blindfold was finally removed. The guards took the sack he had packed and searched and removed everything from his pockets.

"Steal, steal, and steal again," Limbert said, and kept repeating the phrase.

Stripped of even this small horde of possessions, skinny and shaggy, Limbert walked happily across the tarmac toward the plane. The insults shouted at him were more disappointing to him than threatening. *They have no sense whatsoever of decency or style.* If they had any class at all they would have sent him and the others off with a human gesture, some flowers, a handshake, a "Nothing personal" or "No hard feelings." Just this ugly, meaningless display, beyond all reason.

Laingen saw Limbert's face first when he reached the top of the stairs. To him, the political officer looked like he hadn't changed a bit. They embraced and laughed with joy on seeing each other again.

Joe Hall just ignored the crowd. He kept his eyes fixed on the stairs leading up to the plane, and once he was on board he took a seat and held on for dear life.

Bill Belk raised his middle finger and responded to cries of "*Magbar A'mrika!*" with "*Magbar Khomeini!*"

Colonel Chuck Scott made a point of marching through the gauntlet. He had come to Iran as a soldier and he was going to leave it like one. He regretted that Akbar, the guard he had come to admire, had not been able to say good-bye.

Jimmy Lopez looked down at the watch on his wrist. It was the self-winding kind and it had worked perfectly through the entire captivity. He wondered if he might get to make a commercial for Timex watches when he got home.

On the bus, awaiting his turn to leave, Dave Roeder sat wondering what was happening to his friend Metrinko. Had he been taken off the bus?

Was he being left behind? He felt helpless and angry, at both the Iranian guards and his friend and roommate. Didn't the man know when to keep his mouth shut? He admired his friend's constant pugnacity, but there were times when it crossed over into pure stupidity.

Metrinko had had much the same thought when he heard the bus move off. His heart sank. *How stupid can I be?* But then an apparently higher-ranking guard approached and angrily demanded of the others, "Why did you take him off the bus?"

It was explained that he had shouted an insult.

"You have to get him to the airport," the guard said angrily. "He has to get out of here with the others. They all have to go."

Metrinko had been placed in a car with Lee Holland, a white Mercedes. His blindfold was removed. Evidently they did not want to attract attention on the roads by having a blindfolded man in the backseat. Metrinko watched with fascination as they drove off through the city. It was the first time he had been able to see Tehran in over a year.

At the airport, waiting for his turn, Metrinko watched as his colleagues were led through the gauntlet. To him it all seemed rote, like a summer camp initiation ritual. The guards no longer had their hearts in it. Everybody was exhausted by this game.

Metrinko finally walked through the jeering crowd in a cloud of joy and disbelief. He felt none of the slaps or jabs and heard none of the insults. More than a year of near constant abuse coated him like a shell. As he reached the end he was pleased to see armed, uniformed Algerian guards. He mounted the steps and entered the plane and there, arrayed in seats on either side, were all the embassy workers he had barely known and the few, like Roeder, Regan, and Ward, whom he had come to know well in captivity. Everyone looked skinny, poorly dressed, and shaggy—long hair and long beards. It felt wonderful to see them, all of them. People reached out and touched him as he passed down the aisle. It was like a reunion he had just happened upon, and for the first time in more than a year he felt surrounded by countrymen, by warmth and friendship.

For all the joy of reunion, the plane stayed silent. People sat together not in the groups that might have formed according to the hierarchy or job descriptions at the old embassy, but in the random groupings of their imprisonment. This was partly because the various roommates had grown close during their captivity, but also because they did not yet feel free. So long as they were still in Tehran, they were still hostages.

Only when the plane taxied down the runway and its wheels left the ground did the great weight of fear begin to lift for the fifty-two Americans on the plane. There was still some disbelief. Billy Gallegos thought it entirely possible that the Iranians would let them take off and then hit them with a surface-to-air missile.

Real celebration didn't begin on the plane until the Algerian pilot announced they were out of Iran. The freed hostages went wild with happiness. Shouting, cheering, crying, clapping, falling into one another's arms. Hall fell into an embrace with Jerry Plotkin, whom he didn't know and had never seen before. Champagne corks popped and half full plastic cups were passed around the plane.

There was something more complicated than joy in the hours of celebration that ensued. There was a sense that they had weathered an extraordinary adventure, had all involuntarily participated in an historic ordeal, but they had not done so together. Many of them had not known one another before the takeover, and were strangers still. Yet they would always be tied together now. Those who had been forced to live together in close quarters for months and months had seen each other at their best and at their worst, and they would forget neither. Colonel Scott, who still burned over the time his onetime roommate Bob Blucker had refused to hurry his meal so that they could go outside for a walk, was not the only one who harbored anger toward the prickly economics officer. Dave Roeder hung a sign on the back of Blucker's seat that read, "I'm an asshole." Many of the passengers eyed Army Sergeant Joe Subic with scorn and made resolutions to report his behavior when they got back. Nearly all of them had done or said things over the past fifteen months that made them feel proud, or that made them feel ashamed. How would their behavior in captivity be assessed? Few felt heroic. The experience had been in many ways humiliating. Some of them were ashamed of things they had done or said, secrets they had named, weaknesses they had revealed. There was no sense yet of the frenzied national welcome that awaited them at home, the reunions with families and friends, the crush of press, the ticker-tape parades, the speeches, the gifts, the great smothering embrace of American sympathy fully aroused.

Rick Kupke finally had a chance to confront Tom Ahern over something that had been bugging him ever since the day of the takeover, when he had been soundly beaten after being stranded on the roof of the chancery.

"Why did we surrender?" he asked the CIA station chief. "I wanted to stay there in the vault for two weeks and force the United States government to make a decision—we still had a phone line open—whether to come save us or not."

Ahern said that the decision was his responsibility, his best judgment at the time.

"So why did you open the door when I was on the roof?" Kupke asked. "When I came down, they just kicked the hell out of me!"

Ahern explained that they had Golacinski outside the door with a gun to his head.

"Tom, couldn't you have at least taken a head count?" complained Kupke. "You left me. I had guns scattered around. I was on the roof by myself, only to find out there was a bunch of Iranians down there when I decided to come down."

"Well, Al convinced me they were going to shoot him," Ahern said, "and Al promised me that they wouldn't hurt anybody."

Metrinko was at peace with his own behavior. He had fought his captors and insulted them every day, right up to the ride to the airport, and he had fresh scrapes and bruises to show for it. His fifteen months in captivity would be summed up many years later by Ebtekar: "We thought [him] to be deranged; [he] hated everyone and was hated in return." Always the loner, he sat quietly and contentedly in the midst of the celebration taking long swigs of champagne. He felt different, and he tried to define to himself how. It was partly the champagne, but that alone didn't account for the luxurious sensation that seemed to settle him deeper into his seat. Then he realized what it was. It was a feeling he had almost forgotten. For the first time in four hundred and forty-four days, he felt relaxed.

President Reagan made the announcement. He stood up in the Capitol Rotunda, where he was the guest of honor for a congressional luncheon, and raised a glass of champagne.

"The plane bearing our prisoners has left Iranian airspace," he said to the cheers of the revelers. Then he took a long gulp of bubbly.

Carter made the same announcement in soft rain on a platform erected to welcome him home to Plains, disappointed not to have been able to make the announcement to the whole nation but relieved nevertheless.

He said, "Just a few moments ago on Air Force One, before we landed at Warner Robins, I received word officially for the first time that the aircraft carrying the fifty-two American hostages"—and then his voice broke and tears choked his words; he took a second to swallow and continued—"has cleared Iranian airspace. Every one of the fifty-two hostages is alive, well, and free."

After that Carter smiled, the crowd cheered, a band started playing, and the former president slipped his arm around his wife's waist and they started to dance.

EPILOGUE

Iranian President Mahmoud Ahmadinejad.
(© *Vahid Salemi/AP*)

Mohammad Mousavi Khoeniha, "spiri
adviser" to the students who seized the
embassy. *(Courtesy: Wild Eyes Production*

Barry Rosen and Kevin Hermening protesting the visit of Ahmadinejad to the
United Nations in 2005. (© *Tina Fineberg/AP*)

LOOKING FOR AKBAR IN
AYATOLLAHVILLE

Nowadays the grand old embassy in Tehran looks forlorn, like a hostage left behind and long forgotten. The chancery, a solid battleship of an office building in orange brick, two stories high and more than a block long, was once the symbol of America's formidable presence in Iran. Today it remains standing in the heart of the capital, facing a wide, busy thoroughfare renamed Taleghani Avenue, after the murdered cleric whose sons Michael Metrinko was waiting to meet on the morning of the takeover. Although more crowded with structures, the grounds are still a large, leafy oasis, a haven from the noisy hustle of this city of now more than twelve million. Long ago dubbed by its invaders and occupiers the "den of spies," this old symbol of America's friendship with Iran is festooned with hateful garnish: anti-American graffiti, banners, and propaganda displays to remind people of the nation's undying disdain. The compound is now home to the Revolutionary Guards, an elite military unit that reports to the black-turbaned elite of Iran's authoritarian mullahocracy, and to the *Basij,* Islamic brownshirts, the civilian goon squads who turn out in large numbers at a moment's notice to demonstrate on behalf of the regime and to help put down public displays of dissent and "immorality," such as women whose scarves do not fully cover their hair or young people holding hands. The chancery itself now serves as an anti-American museum, with a grim, ugly, permanent display called the "Great Aban 13th" exhibition. The takeover is remembered as one of the founding events of the Islamic "republic," for better or worse, and one whose repercussions are still being felt throughout the world.

The museum is supposed to be an official shrine to that bold act of national defiance, but in the four times I went there in 2003 and 2004 it was empty of visitors. A bookstore just outside the entrance that was once known for selling anti-American literature and reprints of the infamous

"Spy Den Documents" was vacant when I first saw it, its racks empty, and when I visited again nine months later it appeared ready to reopen as a bookstore for children. The anti-American slogans and spiteful artwork that had been spray-painted on the embassy's outer brick walls by angry crowds during the fourteen-month crisis had faded, including an image of the Statue of Liberty with a death mask for a face and a sign in English that said "Death to the USA." The official shield of the United States on the front gate has been chipped or sandblasted away beyond recognition.

Even the guardhouse on the southeast corner, where visitors enter, was in shambles. On my first visit, two friendly, unshaven Revolutionary Guards stood behind the counter in a small marble-veneered reception area that looked like a frat house on Sunday morning, with battered furniture, an old swivel chair leaning precariously on its stem with cushion stuffing hanging out, dirt caked on the floors and walls, and muddy boot prints everywhere. I pointed quizzically at a complete boot print on the ceiling and, grinning, asked my guide and translator, Ramin, to tell the guards that as an American citizen, I protested the abuse of what could arguably be called American property.

"Tell them that if they are going to steal it, the least they could do is take care of it," I said.

When Ramin relayed my comments, the guards laughed, looked around sheepishly at the mess, and shrugged happily. They were conscripts serving out the last few months of their duty at a gravy post. "It's great here," one said. "Nothing ever happens."

It took some doing and a few bribes to the guards' higher-ups to get inside. The exhibit is amateurish, as if put together by a group of high school students with a bad attitude. On the front steps are two cartoonish statues that appear to have been fashioned out of papier-mâché and thickly coated with bronze-colored paint. One is of a surrendering marine—apparently based on a photograph of Sergeant Steve Kirtley—with his arms up and his hands clasped behind his head; the other is a replica of the Statue of Liberty with a white bird (a symbol of Islam) caged in her abdomen. Inside was more of the same: displays illustrating America's "role of evil" in the world over the past several decades; lots of gory photographs of wounded children presented as victims of American bombings; and a framed copy of an important-looking "spy document," stamped "Classified" and "Top Secret," but which on closer inspection turned out to be a memo requesting additional drivers for the embassy's motor pool. There were also pieces of the helicopter engines recovered in the Iranian desert following the failed rescue mission, photographs of the hostages themselves, and somewhat dated propaganda showcasing America and Saddam Hussein as partners in crime. In its preoccupation with American symbols, the whole exhibit is more a defacement than an indictment, like drawing a big nose and mustache on a poster of someone famous. That such a gloating, adolescent display has endured in the heart of Tehran for a quarter century says more about Iran than it does about America.

The taking of the embassy in Tehran was a crime. The argument of the hostage takers that it was engaged in a massive spy operation intent on stopping the revolution, killing Khomeini, and restoring the Peacock Throne was false. None of the thousands of documents they seized and published supports it, and a close look at the hostages themselves reveals only a handful who were engaged in spying, and those by their own admission ineffectually. The strongest argument in defense of the takeover is that Iran had legitimate grievances against the United States, which was true, but what two nations with long histories do not have grievances? They are a fact of international life. Diplomacy exists because it offers a chance of rising above them.

Indeed, the hostage crisis, an assault on diplomacy, itself ultimately depended on diplomacy for resolution. A quarter century later Iran's stature in the world community remains diminished, and will remain so until the act itself is renounced. Diplomats serve at the pleasure of the host nation, and when they are no longer welcome they can be readily expelled. Holding America's emissaries hostage was a crime not just against those held captive and their country but against the entire civilized world. President Carter deserves credit for his restraint, and the world community deserves blame for failing to respond adequately to the insult. Apart from pronouncements, the United Nations and most of our allies were content to leave the captive American mission to its fate. Anyone who believes in the importance of diplomacy as an alternative to war ought to regard that failure as significant, and those who see the UN as an answer to the world's conflicts ought to take note.

The failure of the rescue mission spurred the U.S. military to place a greater emphasis on special operations. The tactical issues that confronted mission planners in 1979 would pose little problem for today's more flexible and multifaceted force. Veterans of the rescue mission remain bitterly disappointed about the loss of life and their failure to reach Tehran but regard the mission as a vital step into the modern age of warfare. Those familiar with the details of their audacious plan are amused by the perception of Carter as a timid commander in chief.

The Iran hostage crisis was for most Americans their first encounter with Islamo-facism and, as such, can be seen as the first battle in that ongoing world conflict. Iran's hatred of the United States was in part a consequence of heavy-handed, arrogant, and sometimes criminal twentieth-century American foreign policy, but it was also rooted in something that has nothing to do with that. It grew out of anger over the erosion of tradition. The modern Western world does not recognize revelation and divine right as the root of government authority. The trend of history has long been away from strict tribal authority grounded in one holy book or the other, whether the Koran, the Torah, the Bible, or any other ancient text, and toward those strictly human values distilled so well in the Declaration of Independence as "life, liberty, and the pursuit of happiness." The murderous terrorism that has become a fact of modern life is part of the death throes of an ancient way of life. The glorious Islamist revolution in Iran, which a quarter century later has produced a despised, corrupt, and ineffectual religious dictatorship, will wind up little more than a footnote in the long and colorful history of that nation, and probably an embarrassing one, judging by the disgruntlement of many Iranians, including at least some of the old hostage takers.

In that sense, the hostage crisis is a case study in the futility of governing a country by fantasy. The stirring symbolism of the embassy takeover excited the nation, and in that sense served the political goals of the mullahs as they skillfully maneuvered for power. Indeed, even as the hostages were flying home in 1981, Iran's chief negotiator was proclaiming a great victory, and gloating, "We rubbed dirt in the nose of the world's greatest superpower." But glee over that symbolic triumph had given way months earlier to real-life concerns, namely, the urgent need for military supplies to fend off the armies of Saddam Hussein. In the quarter century since, the fever of revolution in Iran has given way to a deep and widespread resentment of religious figures who presume to dictate the smallest, most personal details of people's lives. Extremism, religious or otherwise, is by definition the province of a small minority.

God speaks to very few, if any of us. The great majority of those who are not so blessed hold beliefs tinctured with doubt and basic decency.

The ordeal of the American hostages is easy to minimize in retrospect. All of them were released, most of them physically unharmed. Given the tragic and brutal progress of the Islamo-fascists in the years since, the video-taped beheadings and horrific mass slaughters, the embassy takeover seems almost polite. But as Philip Roth noted in the brief passage quoted at the front of this book, the "terror of the unforeseen is what . . . history hides." The Americans taken prisoner on November 4, 1979, did not know if they would ever come home. Every day they lived with the threat of trial and execution, of becoming victims of Iranian political violence or an American rescue attempt. They lived with the arrogance of Islamist certainty, which prompts otherwise decent men to acts of unflinching cruelty. My goal was to reconstruct their experience as they lived it. The men and women held hostage in Iran survived nearly fifteen months of unrelenting fear. They were the first victims of the inaptly named "war on terror."

Today a number of them are trying to sue the Iranian government for damages but are blocked by the agreement the United States signed to secure their release. It seems wrong to me that any country should be bound by an agreement signed under duress, yet the administration of President George W. Bush continues to oppose the hostages' action.

The sorry course of Iran's revolution suggests a pattern for the whole retrograde Islamist movement currently terrorizing the world. Driven by a vague goal of establishing a Koranic utopia, a fanatical fringe allies itself with mainstream political disaffection, but instead of opening the doors to liberty and prosperity it succeeds only in creating a closed and stunted society under the thumb of so-called spiritual leaders who prove, in the end, to be merely human, subject to the same temptations of power and wealth as rulers everywhere and always. The only political system that serves the majority is one that respects true human spirituality, something deeply personal and almost infinitely various.

THE HOSTAGES

The returning American hostages stepped off a plane in Wiesbaden, West Germany, into a whirl of unexpected and, for many, unwanted celebrity. Few of them felt heroic—indeed, some wrestled with feelings of shame—but they were heroes to their countrymen whether they liked it or not, complete with fan mail, flashing cameras, unceasing demands for interviews, honors, and even ticker-tape parades. The Miami Beach Convention Bureau donated a free weeklong vacation to all the hostages; Bill Royer was given a yellow Cadillac by wealthy admirers in Houston; Kevin Hermening was awarded a free lifetime pass to Milwaukee Brewers baseball games. Major League Baseball then awarded similar lifetime passes to all the hostages. There was much discussion over whether their treatment had amounted to "torture," with divisions among the hostages themselves. Asked about it, one marine commander took a gentle swipe at the civilian foreign service. "Torture is a subjective term," he said. "What some soft-living State Department types might consider torture is just normal living conditions for a marine." The ever cantankerous and blunt Bob Ode knew that nothing about his experience was heroic, "unless there is a new definition of hero as being in the wrong place at the wrong time." Nevertheless, President Reagan invited the lot of them to the White House, where he pinned small American flags to their lapels and thanked them for their service. The State Department employees were given the prestigious Medal of Valor; Michael Metrinko got two, one for his time as a hostage and another for his daring rescue of the young Americans who had been jailed in Tabriz months before the embassy takeover. The CIA employees received both the State Department award and the agency's Exceptional Service Medallion. All of the military hostages were awarded meritorious service medals except Joe Subic, "Brother Subic," the army sergeant whose self-serving behavior in captivity had earned the undying scorn of most of his fellow hostages, but not all.

"I think Joe has gotten a bum rap," says Al Golacinski, who now works as a consultant in Ponte Vedra Beach, Florida. "He was a young man who was just more eager than most to be the center of attention and to please whoever was in charge. He is guilty of poor judgment in a difficult situation, that's all. Nothing he did really harmed anybody." Golacinski feels that Subic's public mistakes were less harmful than some of the capitulations behind the scenes of other high-ranking hostages.

They all had stories about returning to their country's smothering embrace. My favorite was Metrinko's, the man in love with distant lands. He was accustomed to deliberately low-key homecomings after his frequent travels. Once, after being away for two years in the Peace Corps, he had come home to Pennsylvania without announcing his arrival, taken a cab from the bus station in Scranton, entered the big old family house in Olyphant quietly through the cellar door, taken a seat in the kitchen, and just said hello to whoever walked in. It was fun watching the startled, delighted reactions. But there would be no understated return this time.

On the then emerging (now prevailing) popular notion that those who have experienced any sort of trauma need professional help to cope, he and the rest of the hostages were subjected to a daunting series of medical and psychological examinations in Wiesbaden. Waiting with noses pressed to the window were American and international reporters. They would impose a different kind of captivity. When Metrinko phoned home for the first time he felt a little sheepish; it was the middle of the night in Olyphant. His parents not only didn't mind, they had been waiting with a TV crew for his call. His mother explained that they had been deluged by the press.

"This one is particularly nice," she said. "Would you talk to him?"

In Germany he was given a free satellite phone with an answering service, and once the number got out to family and friends, messages began to pile up. It seemed like everybody in the world was waiting in line to talk to him.

One call was from an Iranian professor in Bonn, a man he had met when he was in Tabriz, who had an unusual invitation. It seemed a daughter of Imam Khomeini was visiting in Germany and wanted to meet with Metrinko and discuss what had happened. He turned her down. He wanted nothing further to do with the Khomeinis and Iran.

Some old friends living in Germany had a more welcome suggestion. They offered to pick him up and take him touring through the country by car, just to get away from everything. His minders in Wiesbaden were appalled. They had a full agenda of activities planned, more tests, meetings, debriefings. They said he couldn't possibly go.

"Am I a prisoner?" Metrinko asked.

The question brought looks of horror.

So he went touring, eating, drinking, and talking his way down the Rhine.

In the months and years that followed, some of the freed captives became, in effect, professional hostages, writing and lecturing and popping up whenever events called the crisis to mind. Most just got on with their lives. When I interviewed Greg Persinger, who now works in Roanoke, Virginia, for a company that makes electronic devices for the military and law enforcement, he said that few of his friends or coworkers had even been aware that he was once one of the hostages in Iran until the company newsletter ran a small feature story about him several years ago. Some of the hostages have never spoken of their ordeal and refused to do so with me, and when I started working on this book in 2001, ten of the hostages were dead: Malcolm Kalp, Bill Keough, Richard Queen, John Graves, Bob Blucker, Lee Holland, Bert Moore, Jerry Plotkin, Bob Ode, and John McKeel. Ann Swift was killed in a horseback riding accident while I was working on the book.

I heard a story about Kalp from Keith Hall, a fellow CIA operative, who said he spent a long night with the former hostage in Tegucigalpa, Honduras, in 1989, on the tenth anniversary of the embassy takeover. Kalp was drinking and had a tube-shaped grenade launcher in the backseat of his car. He and Hall and another agency man went off in search of the Iranian embassy, into which Kalp announced his intent to mark the occasion by lobbing a grenade. It turned out, fortunately for all concerned, that there was no Iranian embassy in Tegucigalpa.

Metrinko came home and completely renovated his family's sprawling home in Olyphant along the lines of the meticulous plans he had made in his head during all those months alone. Today he is officially retired from the U.S. State Department, but he is busier than ever putting his language skills and experience in that part of the world to work for the United States. During his long career in foreign service, in addition to his seven years of service in Iran, he spent four years in Turkey, four in Israel, over a year in Yemen (on two separate tours), six months in Syria, even months in Afghanistan, and years at Department headquarters, where he served as deputy director of Iran and Iraq affairs. He served as consul general in Tel Aviv, and then spent three years as a director in the refuge bureau. His small home in the Virginia suburbs is furnished with mementos of his travels, and he is still frequently gone. During the years I worked on this book, Metrinko was away for months at a time on government contract work in Afghanistan and Iraq. He still has the bowl and spoon he used in captivity and the collection of poetry that he took from the chancery library.

In answer to an e-mailed question in July 2005, he sent me the following:

> This response comes to you from my military base at Farah in southwestern Afghanistan, a *Beau Geste* cement fort that sits in the middle of a vast expanse of sand and rock under what we expect to be 120 degrees of heat by noon time. I share my abode with about 100 guys from East Texas, and I am the Political Officer here. In a very few more days, I will be transferring to the Lithuanian Army base (Think NATO) in Chaghcheran, Ghor Province. Chaghcheran is noted for its inaccessibility for several months a year because of heavy snow and VERY BAD roads through some of the most difficult mountain terrain in Afghanistan. I get to live in a tent there until next spring. Do you remember *The Man Who Would Be King?* The origin of that story was an adventurer from the USA going to Ghor in the 1830s . . . and he was from Pennsylvania too. All in all, retirement is a hell of a lot of fun!

John Limbert spent a long and distinguished State Department career in the Middle and Near East, including tours in Algeria, Djibouti, Saudi Arabia, and the United Arab Emirates. He served as U.S. ambassador to Mauritania. He also taught political science at the U.S. Naval Academy and was a senior fellow at Harvard University's Center for International Affairs. After the U.S. invasion of Iraq in 2003, he went to Baghdad with the Organization for Reconstruction and Humanitarian Assistance, where he was responsible for trying to restore the looted Iraqi Museum. When I interviewed him he was serving as president of the American Foreign Service Association, a group that represents the interests of career diplomats.

Tom Ahern retired from the CIA in 1989, having spent the bulk of his career in Southeast Asia, and accepted a contract with the agency's Center

for the Study of Intelligence. When I met him he was working on the sev
enth in a series of classified books on both the operational and the analytica
aspects of the CIA's participation in the Vietnam War. He lives with his wif
in a Virginia suburb, where he kindly agreed to discuss with me his experi
ences in captivity for the first time, and did so with remarkable candor. Bil
Daugherty served out his career for the agency and then made real the imagi
nary classes he had taught in his long months of solitary confinement. He i
a professor of political science at Armstrong Atlantic State University i
Savannah, Georgia, and is the author of a book about his hostage experi
ence, *In the Shadow of the Ayatollah,* and a book of CIA case studies, *Executiv
Secrets, Covert Action and the Presidency.*

Dave Roeder retired from the air force in 1989 as a full colonel and
from his home in Alexandria, Virginia, has on occasion served as an in
formal leader and spokesman for the hostages' ongoing effort to su
the Iranian government for damages related to their captivity. As lea
plaintiff, Roeder won a default verdict in federal court that would awar
each of the hostages $4.4 million. Iran declined to defend itself, but n
payout appears likely. The judgment was vacated, and appeals have bee
fruitless. Lawyers for the former hostages continue to pursue remed
through legislation. The damages theoretically would be paid out of mil
lions of dollars of Iranian assets still tied up in litigation before an inter
national court. Contesting the awards, as I have said, is the America
government.

"It never occurred to me when I was getting the crap beat out of m
in a Tehran jail cell that I would have to one day fight the same govern
ment that I was defending," said Roeder. "It's just so demoralizing. S
discouraging."

Colonel Chuck Scott retired from the army when he returned fron
Tehran and wrote a book about his experience, entitled *Pieces of the Gam
which tells both his own story and that of the guard he knew as Akba
Housseini, the most sympathetic of the students who held him and th
others captive. He received a letter from Akbar some years ago but ha
since lost track of him. Scott travels to make motivational speeches and t
talk of the Islamist threat.

Joe Subic, the man so many of the former hostages regard as a turn
coat, was back in the army and serving in Iraq where my friend the journal
ist and author Christina Asquith interviewed him on my behalf in the summe

f 2004. Subic said he was a different man today than he was twenty-five years ago, and acknowledged that under duress he occasionally cooperated with his captors, but not to the extent some of his fellow captives have alleged, and no more, he says, than did others. He was in Iraq with a National Guard unit from Florida, where he is the police chief in a small town.

Kathryn Koob, who had a religious awakening in captivity, is now a part-time professor at her old school, Wartburg College, in Waverly, Iowa. Joe Hall, who pined so for his wife, Cheri, through all those months in captivity, split up with her when he returned. They had grown apart during the fourteen months and could never completely reconnect. Hall, who is now a lobbyist in Washington, D.C., cites the breakup of "a good marriage" as one of the lasting consequences of the ordeal.

Among those who wrote books about their experiences was Morehead "Mike" Kennedy, who now makes a living as a writer and lecturer. His book, *The Ayatollah in the Cathedral*, describes his own religious awakening in captivity. Kathryn Koob wrote *Guests of the Revolution* about hers. The late Richard Queen, the hostage released early because of multiple sclerosis, wrote a dramatic account of his ordeal called *Inside and Out*. Barry Rosen, an administrator at Columbia Teachers College in New York, wrote a book with his wife, Barbara, entitled, *The Destined Hour*, which tells both of their stories during the ordeal; Rocky Sickmann, the ever cheerful marine, married his girlfriend Jill when he got back home to St. Louis. He was allowed to return with his diary, which was published as *Hostage, A Personal Diary*. Bruce Laingen, the long-suffering chargé locked on the third floor of Iran's Foreign Ministry, published his diary under the title *Yellow Ribbon: The Secret Journal of Bruce Laingen*. I have learned much from them all.

Laingen is now retired from a long career in the foreign service. When he returned from Iran he was named vice president of the National Defense University, where he stayed until his retirement in 1987. He was executive director of the National Commission on the Public Service (the Volcker Commission) from 1987 until the commission completed its work in 1990. He became president of the American Academy of Diplomacy in 1991. He still frequently lectures on the hostage crisis. Victor Tomseth, his old roommate, served a variety of posts in the State Department, and was U.S. ambassador to Laos from 1993 to 1996. Mike Howland, who prowled the Iran Foreign Ministry nude, now runs his own security company in Virginia and is married to former hostage Joan Walsh.

Kevin Hermening became a financial adviser and formed his own firm in Wausau, Wisconsin. He's still enjoying his free seats at Brewers baseball games. His mother, Barbara Timm, lives in Phoenix.

On round-numbered anniversaries, most recently the twenty-fifth, the hostages are accustomed to being tracked down by local and national news reporters, and often when there are major events in Iran their insight and comments are sought. The surprising Iranian election in June 2005 of Mahmoud Ahmadinejad as president brought several of the former hostages back to the front pages. Some claim to remember the new Iranian leader as one of their former jailers and interrogators.

THE LAND OF *BORDBARI*

The Muslim Students Following the Imam's Line had taken part in a grand experiment that ought to be familiar to Americans. They were out to build a new world, a utopia, their own version of a "City on the Hill." Their vision borrowed from both sides of the Cold War. They would blend American democracy with a Soviet-style state-run economy, a system they believed to be both revolutionary and ancient. In their view, the perfect society had been described centuries ago in the Koran. Inspired by the vision of Ali Shariati, one of the ideological fathers of their revolution, they were striving toward the *umma,* the perfect Muslim community, a classless, crimeless community infused with the "spirit of God."

Twenty-five years on, what does the experiment look like?

Tehran today is a bland, teeming, gray-brown sprawl swimming in a miasma of smog and dust that coats everything with a patina of grit, especially in the summer, when you can literally taste the air. It is a remarkably colorless city, except for occasional patches of faded green, apparently the only color that pleases Allah. Spreading down the southern slopes of the towering brown Alborz Mountains, it is a metropolis of low, dense construction cut into irregular squares by busy streets and expressways with only occasional isolated patches of open space. There are a few tall buildings of ten stories or more, and here and there the onion dome of a mosque, but otherwise the architecture is singularly uninspired. Most of the structures are shaped like building blocks, sometimes elongated and stacked on end. There's a lot of dirt-streaked prefab concrete. Trees and bushes are plentiful, but they tend to be stunted, pale, and hanging on for dear life. Streets are bordered on both sides by the open canals called jubes, which, in lieu of an underground water and sewer system, channel flowing water downhill to every corner of the city. The farther south one goes the more clogged the canals are with litter and garbage. The only large structure in the city that grabs your eye is the graceful Azadi monument, a towering concrete arch just outside the airport supported by four sweeping buttresses, which was designed and built in the time of the shah.

The city is choking in traffic, a galaxy of small cars rushing everywhere pell-mell. The good news is that apparently everyone in Iran can afford a car and gasoline, and they all seem impressively busy, all the time, judging by the hurry. A downside is that the city smells like the back end of an old bus. Road manners are mad in most Third World cities, but in Tehran recklessness rises to the level of a cultural statement. It is said that an Iranian dies every twenty-two minutes in an auto accident, which is an impossibly low figure. The truth must be closer to twenty-two seconds. Traffic signals are purely ornamental. Most intersections have flashing reds or yellows, but neither color has any discernible effect. Drivers in Tehran see only one color behind the wheel, a pure Islamic green. Rules of the road are strictly optional. I was sitting once in an outer office in Tehran where they had a picture book on the coffee table, a collection of "pretty" photographs of the city, a challenging concept. Most of the pictures were taken at night (which hides the dirt), and the one on the cover was a time-lapse aerial shot. In it, a divided three-lane highway bends through downtown forming two distinct rivers of light, one white, formed by headlamps, and the other red, formed by taillights. If you looked closely, however, there are thin, wavy red lines inside the white river. It is subtle, and you might dismiss it as some anomaly in the printing of the photograph, but no, these are the taillights of motorbikes braving the onslaught and driving the wrong way on the busy interstate. It is something hard to believe until you actually see it.

Efforts are under way to ease this madness. In recent years, Tehran has completed a modern subway system consisting of two wide tunnels that form a crooked X pattern under the city's streets. The stops along this system—Taleghani Station is just outside the southeast corner of the former U.S. embassy—are amazingly wide, clean, well ventilated, and well lit, with smooth granite walls inlaid with decorative red stones. The underground offers a striking refuge from the madness at ground level. The enormous engineering and construction contract for this massive project went, of course, to the son of then-president Akbar Hashemi-Rafsanjani. Tehranis are clearly thrilled to have it; the trains are jammed day and night.

For a visiting American, Iran is like an inverse world. Bad is good and good is bad. In Tehran patriotic symbols of the United States are everywhere, but always as images of violence, evil, and defeat. The American flag is shown in the shape of a gun; a bald eagle is shown going down in flames. In the West we are bombarded with advertising images of youth, beauty, sex, and life; in Tehran the preponderance of advertising images celebrate death. There are murals everywhere honoring martyrs—primarily those who died in the eight-year Iran–Iraq War, in the 1980s, but also more recent Islamic martyrs, including Sheikh Ahmed Yassin, the spiritual leader of Hamas, who was assassinated by Israeli forces in Gaza in 2004. Billboards in the West often feature scantily dressed, provocatively posed teens, but in Tehran the gigantic wall murals tend to depict robed grandpas and grumpy-looking white-bearded clerics, especially common are the bespectacled face of Supreme Leader Ayatollah Ali Khamenei, and the more imposing, threatening visage of the late Imam Khomeini.

This inverse nature is pervasive. In August of 2004, when I left on one of my visits to Iran, a media blitz at home was trumpeting a more or less nonstop parade of American triumphs in the Olympic Games in Greece. When I arrived in Tehran, I was greeted with pleased accounts of American defeats. The *Tehran Times* reported an "anguished reaction" in Washington, D.C., over three losses by the U.S. men's basketball team and its failure to win a gold medal (it won the bronze), and when American boxer Andre Ward advanced toward a gold medal, it ran the headline "Saves U.S. Team from Historic Failure." Coverage of the Iraq War in Tehran's newspapers cheers the savage insurgent violence there and portrays the Iraqi Shia Ayatollah Ali Sistani—not the American and British armies that actually toppled the tyrant Saddam Hussein—as the real force for democracy and independence.

And just when one seems to have the place in full *inverse* focus, there comes some wildly discordant note—such as the blocks-long open-air drug market in the center of Tehran, where dealers hawk Viagra, ecstasy, and opium at rock-bottom infidel prices. In this pious city where women are forced to cover their bodies and heads, even in stifling summer heat, it is common to see prostitutes—duly scarved and draped—freely patrolling the streets, sending with a slightly heavier application of makeup, flamboyant jewelry, and a few straying strands of hair the same message sent by spike heels and a G-string in Atlantic City.

Nowhere is the inverse nature of Iran more evident than in its memory of the *gerogan-giri,* the "hostage taking." The different ways this event is remembered in Iran and in the United States illustrate how nations invent their own pasts, and how the simplification of history can create impossible gulfs between peoples. To Americans, for whom the incident has become little more than an embarrassing historical footnote, it was an unprovoked kidnapping carried out by a scruffy band of half-crazy Islamist zealots driven by a senseless hatred of all things American. It was a terrifying ordeal for the hostages and their families, fatal for eight of the would-be rescuers and some of the Iranians who had taken American money to spy, and a political disaster for Jimmy Carter—perhaps the single most important factor in making him a one-term president. It was a protracted public humiliation.

For many Iranians, however, the hostage crisis was an unalloyed triumph. From the earliest moments of the takeover, artists, poets, journalists, politicians, mullahs, and historians began wrapping it in the cloak of legend, shading the actual incident with historical and mystical significance. It remains for the true believers a keystone of the national mythology, the epic tale of a small group of devout young *gerogan-girha* who, armed only with prayer and purity of heart, stormed the fortress gates of the most evil potent empire on the planet, faced down the infidels' rifles and tear gas, and secured it without shedding a drop of blood, reclaiming the heart of Iran from the clutches of the devil himself. The poignant and poetic story continues, telling how these innocent servants of Allah treated their often crude and abusive captives with kindness and respect even as they pieced together shredded embassy documents to expose and thwart their plots to destroy the revolution and reinstate the criminal shah. And when the Great Satan dispatched its deadly commandos to slay these young heroes (this is the part that fires the blood of the faithful), Allah stirred *haboobs* in the desert to down the infidel helicopters and turn back the invaders. This is the story taught to schoolchildren who are bused in to see the "Great Aban 13th" exhibition, where they can measure the reality of the miracle for themselves by touching remains of the aircraft that Allah scorched while the innocent *gerogan-girha* slept.

Apart from the fantasy, and aside from the heavy price the country continues to pay, the embassy takeover served an important purpose during revolutionary days. For those Iranians who were waiting for the Islamist fervor to die down and for the forces formerly allied with the United States to reassert themselves, it crushed any hope for a return to Western-style normalcy. The standoff and the allegations of American plotting purveyed by the students undermined every political faction in Iran except the Islamists and, as we have seen, carried them firmly into power. It also was a wildly popular assertion of national pride, a symbolic casting-off of colonial subservience and a reassertion of that nation's greatness and distinction.

In this sense, the fairy tale of the *gerogan-giri* may still manage to stir a piece of the Persian soul, but many (if not most) Iranians today aren't buying it. When I was posing before a Khomeini mural for a snapshot one afternoon in the winter of 2003, a young Iranian passerby asked me in English, "Why do you want a picture of that asshole?"

On arriving at the airport in Tehran, my American passport—unusual in Iran these days—provoked a grimace and an annoyed grunt from the customs agent. My traveling companion, the filmmaker David Keane, and I were both waved back into the waiting area while various officials argued spiritedly in Farsi over the correct protocol for ushering two vipers of iniquity across their borders. We sat while extra forms were prepared, inspected, signed, and stamped, and we were fingerprinted, every finger. Everyone was polite but we passed through customs hours after the rest of our flight had departed.

Traveling to Iran isn't really hard, just expensive. Early in 2002 I applied for a visa to the Iranian UN mission in New York, then waited for months. When I learned that sometimes years are spent in limbo following this procedure, I sought other means. In Iran there is no such thing as a bribe, but happily there is something called *reshveh*, or a "success fee"—just as in Iranian banking there are *karmozd*, or "banking fees," because usury is forbidden by the Koran. It turns out that in the right hands, a *reshveh* can generate a visa application within hours. The engineer of this miracle in our case was one Kamal Taheri, an oily gentleman with a great soft belly and perpetual week-old gray stubble who directs something called *Reseneh Yar*, the "Foreign Media Guide Centre." For roughly five thousand dollars (Taheri will dicker), he will produce a perfectly valid visa and, to facilitate reporting in Iran, an able fixer and translator (who does all the actual work). On arrival, a few hundred dollars more is extracted for the mandatory "press pass," a laminated photo ID decked with elaborate Farsi that is good for startling cops in rural Pennsylvania but which serves no purpose whatsoever in Iran; in my two trips, no one ever asked to see it.

Taheri is a former mid-level intelligence ministry official with friends in high places, hence he gets to run this "business," which has effectively privatized the ministry's tradition of assigning a "minder" to visiting journalists. All our requests for interviews went through Taheri, and taped copies of them must be turned over to him. Privatization is a big deal right now in Iran, but it just serves as an excuse for flagrant cronyism. Taheri and a few smaller, less well connected rivals operate as gatekeepers and babysitters for all foreign journalists in Iran.

The country is governed in a way that differs fundamentally from any conventional Western power structure. Most hierarchies can be diagrammed in a pyramid; Iran's is more like a string of prayer beads suspended vertically. The beads are of various sizes so that one's rank in the descending row does not necessarily indicate one's power. Nepotism and friendship count for a lot in Iran, and even if someone holds a relatively unimportant office, or none at all, he may wield disproportionate clout. Many areas of authority overlap. Plotting the overall design is a little like trying to trace the pattern on a Persian rug.

The use of the term "republic" is double-talk. The elected government is run by a small group of privileged clerics who decide what candidates and what laws are acceptable, who control the military and the secret police, and whatever else they wish, and who stifle dissent, beating up or locking up those they don't like. The ruling clerics are led by Khamenei, who in the years since he made periodic visits to the hostages has become an avuncular old ayatollah with big glasses and the mandatory long white beard. He was appointed by an "assembly of experts" after the death of the Imam Khomeini in 1989 and, by all accounts, is comfortable seeing himself as the hand of Allah Himself in Iran. All laws and candidates for any public post must be approved by him and the Guardians Council, a twelve-member body of clerics and judges that he appoints. The elected government of Iran is a kind of toy democracy that serves at his pleasure. It consists of an elected president, currently the populist ultraconservative former mayor of Tehran, Ahmadinejad, the *Majlis,* and a judiciary. The mullahs tolerate just enough of a semblance of democracy and freedom to maintain the pretense of democracy.

It is a clever despotism, a combination of full oppression leavened with an appreciation for appearances. Iran's leaders have learned from the mistakes of past dictators. Stalin and Mao were brutal and unapologetic;

hey saw communism as the wave of the future and were molding a so-called new man. Those who opposed or disagreed were dealt with summarily. Saddam Hussein, who ruled Iraq next door for decades through sheer error, was unapologetically in business for himself and his family. The mullahocracy is kinder and gentler. Iran is the land of *bordbari,* or "toleration." If you are not a true believer, or even if you are but you disagree with official policy, you are tolerated by the regime provided you don't make too much trouble. Indeed, certain kinds of criticism from certain quarters, so long as it does not deal with religion or politics, are duly licensed and authorized and are "well tolerated."

Bordbari is something the government takes seriously, as with the case of a literary scholar who sought to publish a Farsi translation of James Joyce's *Ulysses.* The story was told to me by an Iranian friend, and is so delicious that it must be apocryphal, but it illustrates a point. A censor predictably objected to some of the steamier passages in the novel, which offended Islamic moral standards. The scholar refused to cut the passages. "The book is a classic," he told the censor. "I refuse to publish it with pieces cut out." He was prepared to leave it at that but the censor persisted. "This is a great book, let's find a solution," he said. The scholar then proposed publishing the objectionable passages, exactly as Joyce wrote them, in English. But the censor objected again, saying that too many Iranians could read English. It was decided that the sexy bits would be printed in Italian, an oddly appropriate solution that I suspect would have especially amused the novel's famously multilingual author.

Flexibility and compromise make this system palatable for the educated upper middle class, and nurtures hope among the more liberal-minded that real change will eventually come. Meanwhile, they cope by getting out. Iranians are free to travel, if they can afford it. Many well-to-do citizens spend large portions of their year overseas, free of petty religious dictates, and when they return home they live in relatively unharassed enclaves on the mountain slopes at the north side of the city. Inside shopping malls and food courts in this part of town the only obvious difference with the West is the reduced number and variety of retail shops. The same products and brand names—clothing, electronics, sporting goods—line the shelves. The women in these places turn *hijab* into a fashion statement. They wear sheer, colorful head scarves and sleek, clinging *roupoosh,* or "manteaus," that mock the intent of vice laws. In one

popular food court I observed a rainbow of lovely *roupoosh* in pink, white
orange, turquoise, and powder blue. The merchants pay a *reshveh* to the
local morality thugs to keep them at bay, but if a camera crew record
such excesses, perhaps catching pictures of couples actually holding
hands, then the *Basij* in their "Mobile Units of God's Vengeance" descend
with long sticks and fines and restore Islamic order. This usually last
for just a few weeks, when divine vigilance relaxes and, for the usual fee
standards are allowed to quietly slip again.

There is a similar pattern to *bordbari* on a larger scale. Near the end
of his two-term presidency, Rafsanjani was permitted to loosen the politi
cal bonds countrywide in 1996, when the ruling mullahs decided to allow
the relatively liberal Mohammed Khatami to run for president with a slate
of reform-minded *Majlis* candidates. By all accounts, the balloting wa
allowed to proceed unmolested; Iran held an honest election. It produced
a walloping landslide for Khatami and reform, and the newly elected leg
islators and president felt emboldened enough to seek real change. There
was a brief blossoming of free speech and debate, opposition newspaper
sprang up, and Iran began to smell the prospect of real freedom. There
was heady talk of Iran "evolving" peacefully toward democracy. Khatam
encoded the hopes of many in legislation that would have freed Iran's law
makers from the veto power of the Guardians Council.

The mullahs stopped that fast. Ayatollah Khamenei vetoed the leg
islation, which provoked some rioting on college campuses in 2003 and
some spontaneous heretical pro-American displays, but such outburst
were quickly subdued. Early in 2005, the Guardians Council simply crossed
all reform candidates off the ballot. The conservatives were back in the
saddle. The elevation of the blunt true believer Ahmadinejad, who as of
this writing had called the Holocaust a myth and urged the destruction of
Israel, has for a time stripped the kindly mask from the face of the regime

Writers and artists must be licensed to work for any of the majo
news outlets, or for their work to be published or shown. A jury repre
senting the ministries of information and culture weighs applicants and
decides which pass political and religious muster. To be "authorized"
supposedly means that you have the talent, the skills, and the experi
ence to be taken seriously in your field, and to the extent that a broad
range of journalism, literature, and art are tolerated, it lends credibility
to the link between "authorized" and "qualified." An unauthorized write

might even have some things published here or abroad and be tolerated for a time. Nothing might happen to him if the climate is right, or if he or she has important enough friends to be "well tolerated." But if the climate changes, as it has recently, licensed publications live in daily fear of being shut down. In the current crackdown more than a hundred reform newspapers and magazines have been banned. Many formerly tolerated journalists are out of work. To attempt any unlicensed work means risking being hauled in to chat with a polished but unyielding middle-management Information Ministry zealot with the power to fire, arrest, torture, and even execute enemies of the state, although in the Land of *Bordbari,* such measures are no longer frequently required. Some writers are silenced by threats to keep their children from acceptance at universities, a critical path to future success.

Without a free press it is hard to know how most people feel about progress toward the *umma.* There are without doubt many true believers in Iran who see their nation as the seed of future worldwide salvation. David and I visited a small retail mall adjacent to Tehran University filled with shops selling pro-regime literature and Islamic fundamentalist knick-knacks, cassette tapes of inspirational sermons and chants, and paintings of the familiar whitebeards and martyrs—the rough Iranian equivalent of Elvis portraits on black velvet. One of the merchants stepped out and handed us a small sample of what looked like holy cards, which they were, but of a different sort than I was familiar with. The Catholic holy cards I had seen often enough depicted saints and martyrs, but in romantic, classical paintings. These were grisly little battlefield snapshots, one showing a young martyr with half his head blown away, another with just a gory severed foot in a high-topped tennis shoe—"American" atrocities, we were assured.

Then again, later that day, when we stopped to buy cans of cold orange juice from a small store, the two men behind the counter asked our translator, Ramin, who we were. He told them we were American journalists.

"Why are they here?" one of the men asked.

"They are writing about the *gerogan-giri,*" Ramin said.

The men nodded appreciatively. Then one said, "Tell them that the thieves that did it are now in power, robbing all of us blind. Tell them we love America."

Ramin passed this along and we thanked them for the kind words. Both men bowed, pressing their hands to their chests in a gesture of sincerity.

We Americans would like to believe that such sentiments are in the majority, and that, given time, Iranians will shrug off the smothering hold of religious dogma. But there is no way to tell. A determined tyranny can last for many lifetimes no matter how unpopular. I did note that on both flights out of Tehran (admittedly an affluent sample), *all* of the women aboard quickly shed head scarves and *roupoosh* the moment the plane left the ground.

THE *GEROGAN-GIRHA*

The complicated role the hostage crisis plays in current Iranian politics was suggested after Ahmadinejad's election in July 2005. News reports from the United States linked him to the embassy takeover. Former hostages Roeder, Scott, Daugherty, and several others claimed that they recognized the president-elect from still and moving pictures and named him as one of their captors. Roeder was particularly adamant, saying that Ahmadinejad was one of those who, in an effort to get him to talk, threatened to kidnap his disabled son in suburban Virginia and begin cutting off his fingers and toes. The diminutive, bearded former appointed mayor of Tehran promptly denied it, and members of the Muslim Students Following the Imam's Line, clearly encouraged by the regime, held press conferences to help him put distance between himself and the takeover.

The denial itself was revealing. There was a time in Iran when any association with the *gerogan-giri* would have been a tremendous boon to a politician. In the past, a politician might be expected to exaggerate his connection rather than downplay it. Instead, Ahmadinejad admitted, as I have reported in this book, that while he was one of the original five members of "Strengthen the Unity," the student coalition led by Ibrahim Asgharzadeh that initiated the embassy takeover, he identified himself as one of the two members who preferred directing political action against the Soviet Union and who had backed away from the protest when he was voted down and the United States embassy became the target. He said he subsequently supported the takeover when Khomeini blessed it, which took place shortly after the embassy was seized, but denied personally invading the grounds or holding and interrogating hostages. An old photograph showing a bearded student resembling him was widely reprinted, but it's impossible to tell if it is the same man. Without any doubt Ahmadinejad was one of the central players in the group that seized the embassy and held hostages.

The new president's prompt disavowal was a tacit acknowledgment that the episode today comes with distinct political liabilities, both foreign and domestic. This despite the fact that many of those involved in the take-over have risen to the highest positions in Iran's government. Supreme Leader Ayatollah Ali Khamenei and Akbar Hashemi-Rafsanjani, the former president and losing candidate in the most recent election, were directly involved in endorsing the *gerogan-giri* and in supervising negotiations for its eventual end. Habibullah Bitaraf, Iran's minister of energy, was one of the leaders of the takeover and lists his connection proudly on his Web site. Nilufar Ebtekar, the notorious spokesman for the students who has since changed her first name to Massoumeh, now serves as a vice president of Iran and minister for the environment. Her husband, Mohammad Hashemi, another of the primary architects of the takeover, rose to become deputy minister for information, Iran's second most powerful intelligence official. Mohsen Mirdamadi was serving in the *Majlis* before he and other reformers were crossed off the ballots by the mullahs. Mohammed Reza Khatami, speaker of the *Majlis* and brother of Iran's former two-term president, was one of the original planners of the takeover, and among other student leaders who have served in the *Majlis* are Asgharzadeh and the infamous guard and interrogator known to the hostages as "Gaptooth," Hussein Sheikh-ol-eslam, who was primarily responsible for translating the seized documents and is the man who took a rubber hose to Ahern and Daugherty. Sheikh-ol-eslam reportedly blames the United States for his inability to pursue a career in diplomacy. It seems the only country that would accept him as ambassador was Syria. It may well be that America has had a hand in this, but pursuing a career in diplomacy after seizing and holding any diplomatic mission hostage for more than a year would be like trying to join an exclusive club after first urinating on its front steps.

We tried to approach Sheikh-ol-eslam through his brother, a psychiatrist, who reported back that there was no point in talking to American journalists. He said his brother believed that I could never comprehend the "mysticism" of the event, which is probably true.

Once celebrated as national heroes, the *gerogan-girha* are today viewed critically from both ends of Iran's political spectrum. Those on the left, who want to topple the mullahs and create a true democracy, rightly blame the students for turning their revolutionary dreams into a religious autocracy. On the right, religious extremists attack the old students as opportunists and celebrate only the "pure" *gerogan-girha* who after the takeover heeded the imam's call to the martyr brigades and perished with most of the rest of their generation in the war with Iraq. Conspiracy buffs on both sides suspect today that the *gerogan-giri* itself, which helped prompt the disastrous Iran–Iraq War and twenty-five years of international troubles for Iran, was a secret CIA plot, which makes the students either stooges or, at worst, American agents. To Americans this is laughable, but in Iran it is taken seriously by many, even well-educated people.

Reza Ghapour, a young fundamentalist "scholar" who recently compiled a book illustrating this theory of the takeover, told me with a straight face and strong voice that the CIA was responsible for installing and preserving the shah, for engineering his overthrow *and* secretly planning his return, for propping up the provisional government that followed the coup *and* fomenting the national unrest that ultimately undermined and toppled it, and for secretly engineering the seizure of the "den of spies" and keeping fifty-two Americans imprisoned for more than a year.

"Aren't some of these things mutually contradictory?" I asked. "For instance, why would the CIA wish to foment trouble for a provisional government it was secretly supporting?"

Ghapour smiled sweetly.

"You must view the world through the lens of Islam to see the logic of these things," he said.

I heard the same idea several times. Once from Abolhassan Bani-Sadr, the former president of Iran who was elected during the hostage crisis and who eventually fled to Paris—accused of being a CIA agent himself—where he lives today under protection of the French police. (His foreign minister Sadegh Ghotbzadeh, who had warned Hamilton Jordan that he was sticking out his neck by engaging in secret talks with America, was convicted of plotting against the state and executed in 1982.) Bani-Sadr is of the school that believes earth-shattering events generally do not happen spontaneously, and finds it hard to accept that a group of college students cooked up by themselves a protest with such profound consequences for Iran, not to mention his own life. "There needs to be a person who is the intermediary who receives the project and can transform that project into a revolutionary one that is passed on to the students," he says, naming as his prime suspect Mohammad Mousavi Khoeniha, the relatively un-known cleric who served as the so-called spiritual adviser to the *gerogan-girha*. Bani-Sadr thinks Khoeniha was put up to it by the CIA.

I also heard the theory from a liberal magazine editor and critic of the current regime, a worn-looking man with a concave face and tobacco stains on his fingertips, who argued vigorously, "If you consider the event backwards, from where we are today to the point twenty-five years ago when the takeover took place, and you consider who was hurt most by it and who most benefited from it, then you would have to conclude that the answer is Iran in the first place and America in the second place."

He went on for a while, outlining the details of his hypothesis, and then waited with a pleased look on his face as the whole torrent of Farsi was translated to me. I said nothing in response, so he asked, "What do you think?"

"I think you're crackers," I said.

My translator looked at me quizzically.

"Just use the word 'crackers,'" I told him.

The editor seemed confused by my response but nodded sagely.

The wild conspiracy theories suggest a recognition that the embassy takeover was a mistake but an unwillingness to admit responsibility for it. Some, though, are ready to do that.

"To my mind, the taking of the embassy was emotional but ill con-sidered," said Alizera Alavitabar, a professor of public policy who did not take part but who enthusiastically supported the takeover when it hap-pened. "I personally was very naive at that time. For example, sometimes I thought that if I would get a chance to have an interview on American television, I could tell them what their administration had done to us and soon we would have all the American people behind us. . . . In those days I thought you can build a paradise out of the world. My utopia was a society of mysticism, Sufism, and love, in addition to brotherhood and equality. I never thought of equality only for religious people. I also never believed in discrimination against women. I always thought men and women are equals . . . [The takeover] strengthened and endorsed the radical movements and ideas in Iran instead of liberal ones. . . . It promoted fundamentalism. Fun-damentalism was not the main drive behind our revolution. Modernism was. Bear in mind that all of this impact was not foreseen. If you want my opinion today I should say that if I had the same mind I have today, I would not support that action, but if you take me back to the same time, same social environment, same age, and same views, I would be supportive of the takeover again. I am not the same age with the same ideas and the conditions are different therefore I am not happy with what happened."

"Do you ever wish it had never happened?" I asked.

"You know, I am not sure if that would be a good wish. As I said, if you take me back to the same time and condition I would say go ahead and attack the embassy. In those conditions it was inevitable. There would have been an emotional reaction toward America anyways. . . . The society was so ready for it. . . . But considering the things that happened afterward, it wasn't to our benefit. . . . It kept us unified and together in a time when there were conflicts in the society, but the cost of it was high."

So ambivalence and conspiracy-theorizing have left the *gerogan-girha* themselves well known, but hardly cultural heroes.

"At the time, I was so happy my friends and I went three nights in a row to the embassy and stayed up all night long," said a bookseller who operates a street stand in central Tehran. "It was fun. There was food and chanting and marching, boys and girls. Now, I don't know. I'm not sure why it happened, or who planned it. I do not see the hostage takers as heroes."

Mohammad Hashemi, one of the student leaders, who recently stepped down from his powerful position in the Intelligence Ministry to become an entrepreneur developer, dismisses such talk with an impatient wave of his chubby hand. Seated before a big color map of the world in his office several flights up from a wet, busy street in downtown Tehran, he served small glasses of tea and chatted jovially. Today he is an animated middle-aged fat man, dark, short, thick, and wide, with great round cheeks, a goatee framing voluptuous pouting lips, aviator-style glasses tinted faintly orange, and a wild spray of bushy gray hair that widens from his ears down to his round shoulders. He was talkative, imperious, animated, and proud.

Hashemi was eager to put the episode in the past but breezily unapologetic.

"One of the characteristics of the Iranian people is that they are strongly against oppression and injustice," he said. "Second, our pride is very important to us. We might die from hunger, lose many advantages, but we will never sacrifice our dignity." His role in the takeover was just an early step on a path to respect and power in his country. He is proud not only of what he and the others did but how they did it. "We knew that there is an end to everything, like there is peace after every war," he said. "We wanted it to be a hostage taking without any kind of harshness and scuffle, unique in history, a hostage taking that represented a nation and its concerns, and that is what we are proud of."

This, he believes, was the essence of the embassy seizure, an emotional act by angry young idealists who felt wronged by decades of U.S. policy. The action shaped not only his career but his personal life. During the fourteen-month takeover, he courted and eventually married Nilufar Ebtekar. Of all the *gerogan-girha*, none have achieved such high-ranking roles in the ruling regime as this couple. Not surprisingly, they are its most prominent defenders. Which explains in part why both were willing to meet with me.

Yet they had, it seems, another motive. The Iranian power couple was looking for publicity. They were heavily invested in an ambitious new vacation resort on the Caspian Sea called Cham Paradise. On my first visit to Tehran in December 2003, Hashemi showed me slick brochures and advertisements for the venture printed in both Farsi and English, clearly designed to help attract foreign visitors as well as Iranians. Hashemi predicted that soon there will be a significant thaw in relations between Iran and the Western world, including the United States. The project seemed to rest in part on that supposition, and in the hope that English-speaking tourists would be drawn to the beauties of the Caspian shore despite the forbidding piety of its regime. Hashemi was obviously excited. He showed me a detailed model of the project, a cluster of modern apartment buildings, hotels, villas, lakes, restaurants, and other features arrayed on the tip of a peninsula that juts into the sea. Then he had an idea.

"Perhaps, in a few years, we might invite back the Americans we held hostage, and they can all stay at the resort as our guests!"

"This time, can they go home when they want?" I asked, then waited for my question to be translated to him.

Listening to the Farsi, Hashemi first scowled and then reeled with laughter. He said to me in English, "You make a joke!"

On my trips to Tehran I made efforts to meet all of the original hostage takers. What I discovered was a group of graying politicians and intellectuals with a broad range of views about the event. How they felt about the *gerogan-giri* tended to define where they stood on Iran's wide political spectrum. Some remain true believers and have prospered in the mullahocracy they helped create, and even as they acknowledge that the embassy seizure permanently stained their nation in the eyes of the world, they defend it as necessary and just. They see the problems of modern Iran as growing pains and are heartened by the upsurge in Islamist fundamentalism around the world. Some of these true believers refused to speak to an American reporter, who they suspected would misunderstand or distort their words. Other *gerogan-girha* are ambivalent about what they did, weighing the pride and satisfaction of their youthful defiance against a more mature understanding of world politics. These people tend to stay in the shadows, afraid of getting into trouble or drawing attention to themselves. But a surprising number of *gerogan-girha*, constituting a third group, are outspokenly embarrassed by their role and regard their actions as a monumental mistake—a criminal act that disrupted not just the lives of the American hostages but ultimately the structure of their own country, which has yet to live down its outlaw status among nations.

Some of the *gerogan-girha* have gone into exile and taken up arms against the religious rulers; others have been harassed, denounced, beaten, or imprisoned for advocating democratic changes. In some cases they have been persecuted by their former colleagues. "None of us in the revolution believed Iran would ever have an autocratic regime again," said Mohsen Mirdamadi, a leader of the *gerogan-girha* who is today a controversial reform politician, in an interview with a Knight Ridder correspondent earlier this year. "Yet here we are."

Ibrahim Asgharzadeh was a reed-thin, intense engineering student with a neatly trimmed beard when he came up with the idea, in September of 1979, of seizing the American embassy. "The initial idea was mine," he told me in an interview in December 2003 at the office of his newspaper, *Hambastegi,* off an alley in Tehran. "Ever since high school I had been outraged by American policies."

In addition to his terms in the *Majlis,* Asgharzadeh has been president of the Tehran City Council and ran unsuccessfully for president in 2001. In his politics and journalism he has strongly urged the mullahs to adopt democratic reforms, such as freedom of the press and the elimination of the veto powers they wield over political candidates and legislation. He has been banned from seeking public office and, in 1992, served a term in solitary confinement. When I interviewed Asgharzadeh, he looked entirely different from the images I had seen of him in the hostage-crisis days; he looked much too prosperous and at ease for his outlaw status. Despite appearances he has become the most prominent of the *gerogan-girha* who have turned against the mullahocracy. He chose his words carefully (to denounce the takeover is, in a sense, to debunk one of the founding myths of the regime), but his feelings about the episode were clear:

"Hostage taking is not an acceptable action under international norms and standards. The hostages underwent severe emotional difficulties. Prolonging it affected both countries in a negative way. The chaos caused such tension between Iran and the United States that even now, after two decades, no one knows how to resolve it. We failed in enforcing it the way it was meant to be. We lost control of events very quickly—within twenty-four hours! Unfortunately, things got out of hand and took their own course. The initial hours were quite pleasant for us, because [the protest] had a clear purpose and justification. But once the event got out of its student mold and turned into a hostage taking, it became a long, drawn-out, and corrosive phenomenon."

Asgharzadeh and his fellow planners knew at the time that seizing the embassy would be dramatic and popular with large portions of the Iranian people; they had even thought it might lead eventually to the fall of Bazargan's provisional government. But he and the others had not anticipated how explosive the public response would be. Hundreds of thousands of jubilant Iranians jammed the streets around the embassy to celebrate and rant against the evil U.S. plotters. He said the students spent much of their first day on the embassy grounds fending off these rivals who they feared would muddy the purity of their protest with ideological cant, or even harm the Americans. In the confusion, Asgharzadeh recalled, they failed to fully control even their own members.

"American hostages were not supposed to be paraded blindfolded in front of the press," he told me. "The blindfolding was done only for security reasons. In order to control the hostages we used strips of cloth to blindfold them. Unfortunately, our humane objectives were really distorted. We objected strongly to this behavior, and the people who did this were reprimanded, but the damage had been done. These things did happen, ever

hough we tried very hard to prevent the operation from being manipu-
ated and abused by political groups and factions." Asgharzadeh and his
ellow students eventually chased the other political groups out of the
ompound and locked the gates.

How would President Carter respond? Would there be military ac-
ion? Sanctions? A blockade? This was an unprecedented event, amplified
y around-the-clock global television coverage, and it seemed to herald
omething completely new and unpredictable in international affairs. The
hing began to take on a life of its own. With the provisional government
n tatters, the United States had no one with whom to negotiate a solu-
ion, and the students, locked inside the embassy compound with their
ostages, unprepared for a drawn-out ordeal and with no plan for ending
t, watched the great storm swirling outside the embassy walls and began
o see themselves as captives too.

Still, the episode remained thrilling for them, romantic even. During
he long occupation, Asgharzadeh met and proposed to his wife, Tahereh
Rezazadeh, one of the guards, at the embassy compound.

Asgharzadeh realizes that he cannot change the past. But knowing
vhat he knows now he would not do it again. "If today I was to devise a
lan or political action, for myself personally or for the team of com-
ades that we were, it would certainly not be an action along the lines of
he takeover of the American embassy," he said. "Five years ago I had a
peech in front of the American embassy, in which I mentioned that this
ig wall between us should be demolished. I was attacked and criticized
y my own friends and accused by the opposing parties. In that speech I
aid that we were concerned then that some of the diplomats were work-
ng for the CIA. Some of the documents we found were in favor of this
pinion. They were working beyond regular tasks of a diplomat. Many
f them were simple diplomats and had nothing to do with these activi-
ies. Five years ago in my speech I mentioned that we should invite back
hose hostages to make up for what they went through, and to show that
ve had good intentions.

"I think that the revolution was like a big earthquake. We know that
very earthquake has some aftershocks, which could be almost as strong.
n an atmosphere like that I think the situation with the American embassy
ould be viewed as an aftershock, especially with that atmosphere of anti-
mericanism. For students who were nationalists or some that were

religious, we were in an environment where even the air you breathed wa
anti-American. So this was not a strange event to take place. We shoul
have stayed with the plan. We failed in enforcing it the way it was mean
to be. If everything was going by plan, the mass media, our society, an
the whole world would have helped us to pass on our message."

Instead, the takeover poisoned ties between the two countries an
created a situation that benefits neither.

"All this is like a dysfunctional cycle which needs to be stopped a
some point," Asgharzadeh continued. "I do not like to bring back all thos
bitter memories because it will not help the situation. Instead I think tha
both countries need to change their policies and behavior. Changing poli
cies and behavior is accepted and understandable in international law, bu
if one wants to exterminate the other, it is the right of the other to take an
kind of action for defense and survival. . . . I hope that the people of th
United States, intellectuals and politicians, understand the situation tha
we were involved in during those days and what caused us to take suc
action. We know that an event like the hostage taking could not and shoul
not be repeated again and we are willing to come to a better understand
ing and relationship today."

Among the old hostage takers, Asgharzadeh is not the only one wh
has found himself at odds with the current regime. On the day before
was supposed to interview Mirdamadi, another of the students' foundin
members, he was beaten by stick-wielding *Basij.* The slightly built, bald
ing man was delivering a speech at a university when his assailants storme
the lecture hall and attacked him. A photograph on the front pages of th
next morning's newspapers in Tehran showed his head and chest blood
ied and bandaged.

Abbas Abdi, another *gerogan-gir* who became a journalist, has bee
jailed repeatedly for criticizing the regime and for advocating renewed talk
with the United States. He spent eight months in solitary confinement i
1993, and on both of my visits he was serving a four-and-a-half-year term
in the notorious Evin prison—where some of his former hostages wer
kept—for publishing poll results showing that 74 percent of Iranians fa
vored renewing ties with the United States. The newspaper for which h
served as editor in chief, *Salam,* was banned in the late 1990s, and sever
years ago Abdi got into trouble with the government when he attended

much publicized meeting in Paris with one of his hostages, Barry Rosen, the embassy's press attaché, in an attempt to begin what Abdi described as a "healing process." The meeting of the two men fell well short of a warm and fuzzy reunion, however. Rosen condemned the seizure of the hostages and Abdi refused to apologize for it. Indeed, Abdi's old captives feel little sympathy for his current plight. Dave Roeder told me, "It couldn't happen to a nicer guy."

Perhaps the treatment of reformers like Mirdamadi and Abdi explains why some of the *gerogan-girha* tend to speak in stilted euphemisms, even when they are discussing events now a quarter of a century old. Mohammad Naimipoor, a friend and political ally of Abdi's who was also one of the *gerogan-girha*, would say, "What happened overall between Iran and the U.S. could have been handled much better. Even the taking of hostages, in my opinion, could have been handled much better."

When we interviewed Naimipoor, in December of 2003, he was an elected member of the *Majlis*, but both he and Mirdamadi had been crossed off the list of eligible candidates by the Guardians Council. Thickset and graying, Naimipoor at forty-eight regards himself as "an old man."

"Because of all the stress and pressures we have had to live with, we have all aged well beyond our actual years," he told me. Several months after our interview, he suffered a debilitating stroke. "The taking of hostages could have alerted everyone—the world, the Americans—about what had taken place in Iran. I don't think American politicians really care about ordinary people and nations, and do not want to be troubled by them. Instead they would rather deal with governments and rulers. That is why I think after the taking of hostages the Americans did whatever was in their power against Iran.

"For example, I cannot conceive of the war with Iraq without the American role and involvement [in support of Iraq]. This attitude has only deepened the sense of hostility and concern among our people. I think a solution to the U.S.–Iranian relations requires rather delicate methods, which are beyond the reach of the rough and harsh methods used by politicians, who much too readily resort to power and to force. I think even now that the U.S. is [the sole superpower]. All the evidence shows that if they continue in their present course they will only create further resentment among third world people, and especially among Muslims.

Under such circumstances, even with normal diplomatic relations in place
the relations between people and the U.S. will not be normal and appropriate. In effect the U.S. will not have a place in people's hearts. In an era
when we all agree we are living in a global village and in the age of communication, in my opinion, staying on this course is politically short-
sighted."

Naimipoor was hopeful that some of the initiatives proposed by
former President Khatami would renew a dialogue between the United
States and Iran, but he has been disappointed by America's more confrontational pose under President Bush. At the same time, he welcomed
the U.S. invasion of neighboring Iraq and the toppling of Saddam.

"Let me say something unambiguously. The Iraqis used to live under
absolute terror during Saddam's reign," Naimipoor said. "During a trip
made to Iraq I could clearly sense and detect the fear in the very fiber of
ordinary Iraqis. I had lived under the shah, and had been a political prisoner of the SAVAK. I had experienced [torture] with my own body. But
my impression of Iraq was far more bitter and disturbing. The vast majority of Iraqis are certainly happy that the Americans have come and saved
them."

The former hostage taker would like to see ties between America and
Iran reestablished.

"I do not see the U.S.–Iranian relations as a taboo at all," he said. "I
think this taboo should be broken, and I have done whatever was in my
power to do this. I think nations should have relations with each other. Even
now I believe it is in our national interest to establish this relationship in
a reasonable manner."

If anyone at the time had a clear vision of what the embassy takeover's
full consequences would be, it was Mohammad Mousavi Khoeniha, the
man Bani-Sadr believed engineered the whole thing. Khoeniha was the
black-bearded young cleric to whom the students took their plan in October of 1979. He has long been a somewhat mysterious figure, the clerical
hand behind the scenes. His criticism of the regime in recent years has
pushed him to the periphery—his newspaper has been banned—and when
I sought an interview with him he sent word, "Consider me dead." He had
resurrected himself enough by the time I returned to Tehran to meet with
me, and we did so in his spacious, sunny office two flights up in a leafy

neighborhood in the north of the city. His long black beard had turned white. He was a small, precise man dressed in an elegant gray tunic and wearing a white turban.

"We didn't foresee [the provisional government's] resignation," Khoeniha said. "We merely had thought that it would oppose us, and that the imam either would decide to accept the interim government's request, and in that case would order the students to evacuate the embassy compound, or support us. But that the interim government, as a sign of opposition, would go to the degree of resigning, we hadn't thought of that. We had so many bitter memories from the government of the United States that such actions seemed absolutely legitimate and reasonable to us."

If there was concern about activities at the embassy, why wasn't the diplomatic mission simply asked to leave?

"Our goal was not expelling the Americans from Iran, but [because] in those days, when the shah was allowed to enter the United States supposedly for medical treatment, our analysis was that this was nothing but an excuse and America would make the shah an axis for all the people who had fled Iran, both military personnel and civilians. With the shah an axis for those fugitives, America would organize some measures against the Islamic Revolution there. We made our move in order to prevent such an action."

In 1999 Khoeniha was charged with publishing lies and classified information and was found guilty by a special court for the clergy. He was given a three-and-a-half-year prison term and was sentenced to be flogged, but because of his sterling revolutionary credentials the penalty was reduced to a fine. Despite his feelings about the current regime, Khoeniha remains a staunch defender of the embassy takeover, and he still thinks the United States owes Iran an apology for meddling in its affairs. As I was leaving his office, located over the former offices of his newspaper, I noticed a gray four-drawer metal filing cabinet in the corner with a combination lock on the front. It bore a plate with the inscription "Property of the General Services Administration."

Khoeniha smiled when I asked where it had come from. It was a souvenir from the U.S. embassy.

He dismissed as immaterial the popular American theory of an "October surprise," the theory mounted most compellingly by former

Carter adviser Gary Sick in a book by that name. Sick shows that several of Reagan's advisers, most notably his campaign manager William Casey (later CIA director), intervened through Iranian friends in the summer and fall of 1980 in an effort to prolong the hostages' ordeal until after the November elections. Sick makes a strong case that such contacts were made, and the efforts were confirmed by Khoeniha, several of the other hostage takers, and also Sadegh Tabatabai, the former provisional government official who instigated the talks with Warren Christopher that eventually led to the hostages' release. Like the cleric, they found the Reagan campaign's efforts a revealing peek at the cynical underside of American politics but said they had little bearing on Iran's decision to hang on to the hostages until Carter officially left office.

Despite Carter's image at home of being conciliatory to a fault, and the most human rights–conscious president in modern times, during the 1978–79 revolution he had come to personify for Iranians the Great Satan and, as we have seen, where the *gerogan-giri* was concerned, symbols mattered more than reality. Reagan may have been perceived as more of a hard liner, but to Iran he merely represented a change, and a triumph. Carter's defeat was tangible proof that the hostage takers had changed history; they had brought down the leader of the free world. It didn't take any push from Reagan's minions for them to see an advantage in waiting until after the elections to free the hostages.

Still, despite that obvious advantage, Iran was desperate enough in its need for military parts by the fall to consider releasing the hostages early. Thus Tabatabai's efforts in September, blessed by the imam himself, which he believes would have borne fruit before the U.S. Election Day were it not for the outbreak of war with Iraq. Even with the distraction of the war, Iran's leadership made one last effort to tempt Carter just days before the vote, floating a complex new offer and urging the president to respond immediately via a press conference. It seems apparent to me that neither of these efforts would have been made if Iran had already struck a deal with the Reagan campaign. Likewise, if such deal had been made, and if Iran had already gotten what it wanted from the president-elect, why keep the hostages after Carter's defeat for almost three months more? The nation was in desperate need of its military parts, and the students themselves were weary of serving as jailers

In this case the most likely explanation seems the obvious one. The deal to release the hostages was complicated, and it took three months of difficult negotiations to achieve.

All of the hostage takers I interviewed said that the decision to wait until Carter officially left office was deliberate, a final insult to the man they had propped up as the representative of the devil on earth.

That's the memory of the most famous of the hostage takers, Nilufar Ebtekar, whom I met on my second trip to Tehran in a conference room upstairs in the Ministry of the Environment. In the six months since I had met with her husband, Mohammad Hashmei, their ambitious resort venture had gone bankrupt. They had sold their home to pay off their debts and, according to Ebtekar, were living with her mother.

The Iranian vice president is a plump middle-aged woman with a soft round face and pretty smile, who was wrapped from head to toe in the same manner of the Sisters of Mercy who'd taught me in grade school. Most of the hostages hold a special scorn for "Mother Mary," or "Screaming Mary," which may be undeserved. She has written a book about the episode called *Takeover in Tehran,* which is the best explanation I have seen of what motivated her and the other students, and evokes the naive, heady romanticism of the time. Harsh feelings about Ebtekar seem to stem in part from her fluent, American-accented English, which casts her perhaps undeservedly as a "Tokyo Rose" figure, as though anyone with such clear familiarity with America who would take part in denouncing it was somehow a traitor. During the hostage crisis, she was often encountered by the hostages with cameras in tow, trying to elicit comments from them that would frame their ordeal in favorable terms. She would ask leading questions, such as, "You have been treated well, haven't you?" Michael Metrinko summed up his feelings about Ebtekar in this way: "If she were on fire on the street I wouldn't piss on her to put it out." She has a smarmy, self-certain manner that anyone would find annoying. And she has not moderated her views of the United States one bit.

"Did you know that no American publisher would publish my book?" she asked me.

I had purchased it at a bookstore in Pennsylvania without any difficulty, and hadn't noticed that the book had a Canadian publisher. She was convinced this was a result of U.S. government censorship.

"I originally intended to publish the book in the United States," she said. "And we approached fifty major American publishers through a well-respected literary agent in New York." She was very confident that the book would be published. Then, after two or three years, she felt there was something that prevented the book from getting published.

"There are publishers in the United States who specialize in publishing tracts against the United States government," I said.

"Not big publishers," she said.

"No, they're not. Big publishing houses tend to buy books that they think will sell well enough to make a profit. I suspect they didn't think yours would."

She wasn't buying it. The notion of government censorship made more sense to her than the idea that a self-serving book by a generally despised Iranian about a twenty-five-year-old incident would lack commercial appeal.

Ebtekar seems to have missed the uglier parts of the Iranian revolution. She still has a warm feeling about the *gerogan-giri* and talks of it in dreamy, idealistic tones.

"It was more or less clear for all of us that this action would prevent further interference of the Americans in Iranian affairs," she said. "At least it would for some time delay the different plots that they had against the Islamic Revolution. This was clear in our minds. This action would serve as an impediment to American policy in Iran. As it took longer and as different developments took place, both in Iran and at the international level, the students understood how important and how decisive this action was after changing the direction of affairs in Iran and in the region, and also how inspirational it was for many other freedom-seeking movements in the world. Because at that time, the general idea was that either governments have to be under American influence or under Russian influence, Soviet influence at that time. So either the East or the West, nothing in between. Freedom-seeking movements were usually just somehow affiliated with the East. Socialist or communist, I suppose. But what happened in Iran was affiliated to the East and the West. And I think this event, the actions the students took, was in a sense quite inspirational for many freedom-seeking countries in the world and for many nations who were looking for a sense of identity."

She lectured me further about the universal principles of democracy. She still feels that the reason why the American public did not rise up as one to support holding scores of its fellow citizens hostage was U.S. government censorship: "The government, the American administration, was keeping the American public unaware of what happened in Iran." If the truth had been reported, she believes, things would have gone differently.

"Because if you go back to the basics, if you go back to the principles, if you go back to the Declaration of Independence of America, the Constitution, what the students were speaking about were common values, values that are appreciated by people in America, in Iran, in Europe," Ebtekar said. "And I think that many of the ideas and the concepts that the students, Iran, the Islamic Revolution had in mind were concepts very close to the concepts inherent in the American Constitution, the Declaration of Independence. What were we after other than independence? We were after the right to determine our future. We were after the right to decide about our destiny. That's all. And we were after religious principles, which are highly regarded in American society."

Just days after this conversation, when I was in London, I turned on the TV in my hotel room and was startled to see Ebtekar's wrapped face. She was being interviewed on a split screen with a BBC announcer and Iran's new Nobel Peace Prize winner, Shirin Ebadi, talking about how proud everyone in Iran was of her, even though Ebadi was awarded the prize for work opposing the oppressive regime Ebtekar so ably represents and defends.

The announcer asked the Iranian vice president how she, as a woman, could defend a regime that forbade Ebadi to travel to Stockholm and receive her award without permission from her husband.

If Ebtekar squirmed, it was only for a split second. She smiled and segued smoothly into a recitation of the gains women had made under Iran's Islamic regime.

YEAH GEORGE BUSH!

In my search for the hostage takers I was particularly eager to find and interview the guard known as Akbar, whose open-mindedness during that time was such a surprise and comfort to many of the hostages. I wasn't even sure of his name. It had been reported by Scott and others as Akbar Housseini.

There were more than four hundred young Iranians involved in the takeover, the bulk of whom worked as guards or performed other menial tasks. Akbar was by all accounts a significant player. He was a few years older than most of the students, and unlike the others he is remembered with a touch of fondness by his former captives, a well-educated young man with mixed feelings about what he and his comrades were doing, who seemed troubled by the fact that this prolonged piece of dangerous political theater, so thrilling to his young comrades, was toying with the lives of scores of people in a way that was painful for them and in some cases deeply unfair. Akbar treated his prisoners with kindness and understanding, sometimes even defying the leadership of his own group to hand-carry letters out of the embassy from particularly isolated hostages and post them himself. When Colonel Scott wrote his own account of the ordeal, he devoted nearly half the book to Akbar, writing out the stories his friendly captor had told him about prison and torture under the shah, and detailing their running dialogue during the long ordeal. There is a picture of him in the book, a slender modish-looking young man in bell-bottom jeans and army jacket, clean shaven except for a neatly trimmed mustache, carefully styled hair, and side-burns, and holding a rifle while posing rakishly on the hood of a jeep before one of the embassy gates. Scott had received one letter from him not long after his release, but had not heard from him since. He did not believe the name "Akbar Housseini" was a pseudonym but didn't know for sure. The last he had heard, sometime in the late 1980s his former jailer was working for the PARS news agency.

I checked with the news agency and they had never heard of him. None of the hostage takers I interviewed seemed to know who he was. With his central role in the takeover and his long career in intelligence, I figured Mohammad Hashemi was a good bet, but when I asked he twisted his bullfrog features into a look of bewilderment.

"Who?" was the answer relayed by my translator.

"Akbar Housseini." I spelled it.

Hashemi shrugged.

"Is a pseudonym," he suggested, ignoring the translator and suddenly speaking directly to me in English. "No one used real names. I don't know him. If he was with us, I would know."

I finally got a lead on Akbar on the day before I had to leave Iran. It turned out that Kamal Taheri, the fellow who, for a fee, procured our visas, had been involved himself in the embassy takeover, as a young intelligence agent working for Hashemi. He examined the photograph of Akbar and said, "It looks like Lavasani. He became an ambassador and now nobody knows where he is."

I quickly did a Google search on the creaking dial-up Internet connection at Tehran's Laleh Hotel and found two Lavasanis. There was a Hassan Lavasani, who was foreign editor of IRNA (Iran National News Agency), and there was a Mohammad Hussein Lavasani, who had served as Iran's ambassador to Canada and to Turkey. Scott remembered that Akbar had worked for a news agency years ago, so that lent credence to him being Hassan, and Taheri remembered that he had been an ambassador, which suggested Mohammad.

It was a national holiday, so Hassan Lavasani wasn't in at the IRNA offices. A man at the front desk eyed the photograph carefully and shook his head.

"No," he said. "It isn't him. Not even close."

There was an interesting story about Mohammad Lavasani, which, if he was one of the hostage takers, hinted at a kind of brutal poetic justice—even if visited upon the wrong former hostage taker. In 1993, when he was serving as ambassador to Canada, agents of the militant Iranian MKO climbed the walls of the Iranian embassy, broke into the ambassador's residence, and beat Lavasani brutally, breaking an arm and several ribs. Even though the assailants videotaped the beating, the men subsequently arrested and charged with the crime were later acquitted in Canadian courts. Lavasani had more recently served as Iranian ambassador to Turkey.

The Canadian embassy in Tehran had no knowledge of Lavasani's whereabouts, and he was no longer at the post in Ankara, so we went looking at the Iranian Foreign Ministry. It is a complex of buildings constructed in the traditional, ornate Persian style, a rare sight in the city today.

We stopped some officious young men on the sidewalk and they directed us to a reception desk in one of the buildings. Sure enough, Lavasani had an office in that building but had not been in it for some time.

"He's a grouchy man," said the receptionist, which didn't sound like the man the hostages remembered as being so kindly and cheerful, but then, twenty-five years and a good hiding in Ottawa could sour a man. The receptionist looked hard at the photograph and shook his head.

"It doesn't look like the same person," he said.

We tried one more building in the complex, where a man said that Lavasani was out of the country.

"We don't know where," he said.

At that, the trail went cold. I'm still looking for Akbar.

I also tried to reach Amir Entezam. Other than the two Iranians—the Education Ministry official Victoria Bassiri and the journalist Simon Farzami—who were executed as a direct result of the embassy takeover, Entezam is the man who has arguably suffered the most from it. A respected diplomat in 1979, his name cropped up in some of the documents seized in the embassy. The CIA had approached Entezam in Stockholm during the postrevolutionary period to see if he was willing to provide information. By all accounts, Entezam refused. But in the furor of anti-Americanism after the embassy seizure, merely having met with someone identified as a CIA officer was tantamount to treason. Entezam was sentenced to prison and he has been locked up ever since.

Today he is elderly and infirm. For the past year he has been confined at home, although he is still technically a prisoner. He reluctantly declined to talk. A friend said that Entezam would like nothing better than to tell his story, but several years ago, when he had been let out on probation, he attended a memorial service for an Iranian poet and was briefly interviewed by a reporter. He offered some innocuous comments about the state literature and sports in Iran. He was put back in prison for three years.

Ramin, our interpreter, explained that any interview would have official authorization.

"You live in Iran, right?" the friend asked him. "Then you know that just because you receive permission from one official, it doesn't mean that another official won't object and punish him. His back is bad and he can no longer use the Iranian squat toilets they have in prison. We are afraid he will not survive if he goes back."

The standard practice of journalists writing about a foreign country is to assume a commanding overview, offer important insights, and arrive at impressive conclusions. I can offer only these observations, experiences, and conversations, which amount to nothing more than random pieces of an unsolvable puzzle. My impression, for what it's worth, is that Iranians today are conflicted and ambivalent about the embassy takeover. Despite all the flamboyant rhetoric, the great show of resolute anti-Americanism, and divinely sanctioned purpose, the "Great Aban 13th" exhibition is at some level an enduring embarrassment.

On our last day in Tehran, we visited the "den of spies" one more time. David wanted to shoot some film inside the compound and chancery. We stopped in at the guardhouse on the southeast corner and saw that it had been spruced up! There were no more boot prints on the walls and ceiling, which looked to have been given a new coat of paint, and the old busted furniture had been replaced. Another bored team of young Revolutionary Guards sat behind the marble-veneered reception counter. We had stopped by the "den" three days before, unexpectedly, and had been turned away—the empty exhibit hall was off-limits. This time we had made an appointment. The guard rang an official to announce our arrival and we sat down to wait for an escort inside.

Hours later, a mid-level official in an open-collared pale blue shirt stopped by to say that we could walk through the exhibit but that no filming would be allowed.

"It's an exhibit," I argued. "The whole idea is for people to see it. If we film it, millions of people will."

On our previous visit, we had gotten through initial resistance with a small *reshveh*, at which point we were given a bang-up tour. But David had not brought a movie camera that day. We suggested that Ramin offer a similar incentive. No, Ramin said, this group of officials was new to the job—management of the grounds had turned over since our last visit—and too nervous to bend the rules. Blue Shirt disappeared, and we waited for another hour. He came back with exciting news. We would be allowed to film inside the exhibit hall but David would have to use their camera. This prompted further discussion. What kind of camera did they have? Would it be compatible with the digital cassettes David used in his camera? He left with those questions, then returned to report that they could not find their camera.

"You will have to hire a camera," he said.

"But I have a camera!" shouted David, holding up his impressive Sony model. "You can inspect it if you like."

Even the Revolutionary Guards behind the counter felt our frustration. They joined in the argument—"What's the big deal? Let them take pictures with their camera." No, a camera would have to be rented. As a car pulled away to find a rental shop, another official came running with the news that they had located their own.

After a long day of waiting, David and I were finally escorted through the small pine grove at the east end of the compound, past the old two-story white ambassador's residence where most of the hostages had spent their first days in captivity tied to chairs, and into a small new office building at the rear of the site where the tennis courts had once been. The "official" camera turned out to be exactly the same as the model David was carrying. After exchanging a round of thank-yous and handshakes, he clipped a cassette in it and we set off at last for the chancery building to film the exhibit.

We got about ten steps. Blue Shirt came running back out.

"No, it has been decided that you can only take still pictures, no moving pictures," he said.

We gave up. We had taken still pictures on the first visit. As we left crossing the sidewalk out on Taleghani Avenue to hail a cab, the three young Revolutionary Guards from the guardhouse came running out after us. We thought for a minute that the rules had changed again.

They all spoke to Ramin in Farsi, smiling and gesturing toward us, and then he relayed their comments.

"They want me to tell you that they are embarrassed. That they think this is silly. They want to apologize on behalf of their country."

Ramin grinned as the soldiers kept pulling at him.

"They want me to tell you that they love America. And to tell you, Yeah George Bush!'"

And right there in front of the "Death to the USA" sign, in front of the faded banners denouncing the Great Satan, one of the soldiers stuck his thumb into the air, and said in halting English:

"Okay for George W. Bush!"

APPENDIX

Fifty-two Americans were held hostage in Iran for the full 444 days. They were:

Thomas L. Ahern, Jr., 48, McLean, VA. CIA station chief.

Clair Cortland Barnes, 35, Falls Church, VA. CIA communications specialist.

William E. Belk, 44, West Columbia, SC. State Department communications and records officer.

Robert O. Blucker, 54, North Little Rock, AR. Economics officer specializing in oil.

Donald J. Cooke, 26, Memphis, TN. Vice consul.

William J. Daugherty, 33, Tulsa, OK. CIA officer.

Lt. Cmdr. Robert Englemann, 34, Hurst, TX. Naval attaché.

Sgt. William Gallegos, 22, Pueblo, CO. Marine guard.

Bruce W. German, 44, Rockville, MD. Budget officer.

Sam Gillette, 24, Columbia, PA. Navy communications and intelligence specialist.

Alan B. Golancinksi, 30, Silver Spring, MD. Security officer.

John E. Graves, 53, Reston, VA. Public affairs officer.

Joseph M. Hall, 32, Elyria, OH. Military attaché with warrant officer rank.

Sgt. Kevin J. Hermening, 21, Oak Creek, WI. Marine guard.

Sgt. 1st Class Donald R. Hohman, 38, Frankfurt, West Germany. Army medic.

Col. Leland J. Holland, 53, Laurel, MD. Military attaché.

Michael Howland, 34, Alexandria, VA. Security aide; one of three held in Iranian Foreign Ministry.

Charles A. Jones, Jr., 40, Communications specialist and teletype operator.

Malcolm Kalp, 42, Fairfax, VA. CIA officer.

Morehead "Mike" C. Kennedy Jr., 50, Washington, D.C. Economics and commercial officer.

William F. Keough, Jr., 50, Brookline, MA. Superintendent of American School in Islamabad, Pakistan.

Cpl. Steven W. Kirtley, 22, Little Rock, AR. Marine guard.

Kathryn L. Koob, 42, Fairfax, VA. Embassy cultural officer.

Frederick Lee Kupke, 34, Francesville, IN. Communications officer and electronics specialist.

L. Bruce Laingen, 58, Bethesda, MD. Chargé d'affaires; one of three held in Iranian Foreign Ministry.

Steven Lauterbach, 29, North Dayton, OH. Administrative officer.

Gary E. Lee, 37, Falls Church, VA. Administrative officer.

Sgt. Paul Edward Lewis, 23, Homer, IL. Marine guard.

John W. Limbert, Jr., 37, Washington, D.C. Political officer.

Sgt. James M. Lopez, 22, Globe, AZ. Marine guard.

Sgt. John D. McKeel, Jr., 27, Balch Springs, TX. Marine guard.

Michael J. Metrinko, 34, Olyphant, PA. Political officer.

Jerry J. Miele, 42, Mount Pleasant, PA. CIA communications officer.

Staff Sgt. Michael E. Moeller, 31, Quantico, VA. Head of marine guard unit.

Bert C. Moore, 45, Mount Vernon, OH. Counselor for administration.

Richard H. Morefield, 51, San Diego, CA. U.S. consul general in Tehran.

Capt. Paul M. Needham, Jr., 30, Bellevue, NE. Air force logistics staff officer.

Robert C. Ode, 65, Sun City, AZ. Retired foreign service officer on temporary duty in Tehran.

Sgt. Gregory A. Persinger, 23, Seaford, DE. Marine guard.

Jerry Plotkin, 45, Sherman Oaks, CA. Private businessman visiting Tehran.

MSgt. Regis Regan, 38, Johnstown, PA. Army noncom, assigned to defense attaché's officer.

Lt. Col. David M. Roeder, 41, Alexandria, VA. Deputy air force attaché.

Barry M. Rosen, 36, Brooklyn, NY. Press attaché.

William B. Royer, Jr., 49, Houston, TX. Assistant director of Iran-American Society.

Col. Thomas E. Schaefer, 50, Tacoma, WA. Air Force attaché.

Col. Charles W. Scott, 48, Stone Mountain, GA. Army officer, military liaison.

Cmdr. Donald A. Sharer, 40, Chesapeake, VA. Naval air attaché.

Sgt. Rodney V. (Rocky) Sickmann, 22, Krakow, MO. Marine guard.

Staff Sgt. Joseph Subic, Jr., 23, Redford Township, MI. Military policeman (army) on defense attaché' staff.

Elizabeth Ann Swift, 40, Washington, D.C. Chief of embassy's political section.

Victor L. Tomseth, 39, Springfield, OR. Senior political officer; one of three held in Iranian Foreign Ministry.

Phillip R. Ward, 40, Culpeper, VA. CIA communications officer.

Freed on July 11, 1980, because of an illness later diagnosed as multiple sclerosis, was:

Richard I. Queen, 28, New York, NY. Vice consul.

ix Americans escaped the embassy and were hidden and ultimately
muggled out of Iran by the Canadian and Swedish embassies. They were:

obert Anders, 34, Port Charlotte, FL. Consular officer.

ark J. Lijek, 29, Falls Church, VA. Consular officer.

ora A. Lijek, 25, Falls Church, VA. Consular assistant.

enry L. Schatz, 31, Coeur d'Alene, ID. Agriculture attaché.

seph D. Stafford, 29, Crossville, TN. Consular officer.

athleen F. Stafford, 28, Crossville, TN. Consular assistant.

hirteen women and African-Americans were released November 19 and
0, 1979. They were:

athy Gross, 22, Cambridge Springs, PA. Secretary.

gt. James Hughes, 30, Langley Air Force Base, VA. Air force administrative manager.

llian Johnson, 32, Elmont, NY. Secretary.

gt. Ladel Maples, 23, Earle, AR. Marine guard.

izabeth Montagne, 42, Calumet City, IL. Secretary.

gt. William Quarles, 23, Washington, D.C. Marine guard.

oyd Rollins, 40, Alexandria, VA. Administrative officer.

apt. Neil (Terry) Robinson, 30, Houston, TX. Air force intelligence officer.

erri Tedford, 24, South San Francisco, CA. Secretary.

gt. Joseph Vincent, 42, New Orleans, LA. Air force administrative manager.

gt. David Walker, 25, Prairie View, TX. Marine guard.

an Walsh, 33, Ogden, UT. CIA secretary.

pl. Wesley Williams, 24, Albany, NY. Marine guard.

ight U.S. servicemen lost their lives in the attempt to free the hostages.
hey were:

apt. Richard L. Bakke, 34, Long Beach, CA. Air force.

gt. John D. Harvey, 21, Roanoke, VA. Marine corps.

pl. George N. Holmes, Jr., 22, Pine Bluff, AR. Marine corps.

aff Sgt. Dewey L. Johnson, 32, Jacksonville, NC. Marine corps.

apt. Harold L. Lewis, 35, Mansfield, CT. Air force.

ech. Sgt. Joel C. Mayo, 34, Bonifay, FL. Air force.

apt. Lynn D. McIntosh, 33, Valdosta, GA. Air force.

apt. Charles T. McMillan II, 28, Corrytown, TN. Air force.

SOURCE NOTES

Although I have drawn from a large collection of work about the Iranian hostage crisis, most of the information in this book is based on interviews with the participants. I owe a great debt to the many in-depth hostage interviews conducted by Tim Wells in preparation for his book *444 Days,* material that Wells donated to the Duke University library and graciously allowed me to pillage. In the case of some of the hostages who have died, Wells's interview was my only source for that person's experience. Included in his collection was the unpublished diary of the late Bob Ode. I reinterviewed most of the hostages, but even in those cases the Wells interviews, which were conducted so soon after the events, were invaluable.

In the notes that follow, the reference to "news reports" refers to a fifteen-volume collection of newspaper articles printed out, collated, and bound for me by Terrence Henry, my tenacious researcher. The articles consisted of reports from the *Washington Post,* the *Christian Science Monitor,* Associated Press, and United Press International and abstracts from the *New York Times* and the *Wall Street Journal.* I have not noted in every case the exact date and title of each article, because often the stories on given days were very similar and, frankly, I drew on so many that sorting it all out at this point would be tedious and (I think) unnecessary, especially with the easy search capabilities of electronic databases.

The Carter Center in Atlanta provided me with copies of dozens of videotapes, almost forty hours of news programming (local and national) through the fifteen-month standoff. Again, I have not in each instance referred to the exact date, time, and source of each report, because the timing of the report in the context of the larger story is obvious, and the same material was broadcast on all of the networks and local stations. In certain instances, where the report or comment was particularly noteworthy, I have indicated the reporter and network in the text of the story. Some of the interviews for this book were done on my behalf by Terrence Henry, Aaron Bowden, David Keane, Arcadia Keane, Kaveh Ehsani, and the intrepid Christina Asquith, who tracked down former hostage Joe Subic in Baghdad.

INTERVIEWS

Hostages: Tom Ahern, Bill Belk, Don Cooke, Bill Daugherty, Billy Gallegos, Al Golacinski, Joe Hall, Kevin Hermening, Don Hohman, Joan (Walsh) Howland, Mike Howland, Charles Jones, Morehead "Mike" Kennedy, Kathryn Koob, Rick Kupke, Bruce Laingen, Steve Lauterbach, John Limbert, James Lopez, Michael Metrinko, Mike Moeller, Dick Morefield, Greg Persinger, Dave Roeder, Bill Royer, Chuck Scott, Don Sharer, Rocky Sickmann, Joe Subic. **Tim Wells**

interviews: Cort Barnes, Belk, Cooke, Bob Englemann, Gallegos, Bruce Ger man, Golacinski, John Graves, Hall, Hermening, Hohman, Lee Holland, Charle Jones, Malcolm Kalp, William Keough, Steven Kirtley, Bruce Laingen, Gary Lee Paul Lewis, Mark Lijek, Limbert, Lopez, Metrinko, Morefield, Paul Needham Bob Ode, Richard Queen, Barry Rosen, Royer, Thomas Schaefer, Scot Sickmann, Victor Tomseth.

Rescue mission: Ken Bancroft, Joseph Byers, Bob Brenci, Fred Brook Zbigniew Brzezinski, Bucky Burruss, John Carney, Dave Cheney, Dave Dorosk Ray Doyle, Logan Fitch, Eric Haney, Jim Hughes, Reed Hughes, Wade Ishimote Rod Lenahan, Wayne Long, Bob Mingo, Keith Nightengale, Chuck Pittman, Jod Powell, Tim Prater, Frank Rotundo, Jesse Rowe, Taco Sanchez, Carl Savory, Jir Schaefer, Jim Scurria, Pete Schoomaker, E. K. Smith, Gerald Uttaro, Jim Vaugh Lyle Walton.

Iran interviews: Abbas Abdi, Alizera Alavitabar, Ibrahim Asgharzadel Abolhassan Bani-Sadr (in Paris), Massoud Dehnamaki, Nilufar (Massoumel Ebtekar, Reza Golpour, Mohammad Hashemi, Taha Hashemi, Morteza Kavake bian, Mousavi Khoeniha, Mohsen Mirdamadi, Mohammad Naimipoor, Farou Rajaeefar, Saeed Razavi-Faqih, Hossein Shariatmadari, Sadegh Tabatabai, Mosta Tajzadeh, Hossein Valeh, Ibrahim Yazdi.

Other: Cynthia Dwyer, Hershel Jaffe, Stephen Kinzer, Penne Laingen, Darre Rupiper, Behrooz Sharsar, Zena Sheardown, Stansfield Turner, Richard Valerian **Tim Wells interview:** Cheri Lee, Parvaneh Limbert, Dorothea Morefield, Rita Ode Barbara Timm.

Official State Department interviews: John Graves, Bruce Lainger Richard Morefield, Henry Precht, Harold Saunders, Ann Swift.

BOOKS AND PUBLICATIONS

Hostages

In the Shadow of the Ayatollah: A CIA Hostage in Iran, William Daugherty. Nava Institute Press, 2001.

The Ayatollah in the Cathedral: Reflections of a Hostage, Morehead Kennedy. Hi and Wang, 1986.

Guest of the Revolution, Kathryn Koob. Thomas Nelson Publishers, 1982.

Yellow Ribbon: The Secret Journal of Bruce Laingen, Bruce Laingen. Brassey' 1992.

Iran, At War with History, John W. Limbert. Westview Press, 1987.

Inside and Out: Hostage to Iran, Hostage to Myself, Richard Queen, with Patric Haas. G. P. Putnam's Sons, 1981.

The Destined Hour, Barbara and Barry Rosen, with George Feifer. Doubleda 1982.

Iranian Hostage: A Personal Diary, Rocky Sickmann. Crawford Press, 1982.

Diplomacy

Day-by-day chronology of the U.S. hostages crisis in Iran, The Associated ress, January 8, 1981.

The Eagle and the Lion: The Tragedy of American-Iranian Relations, James Bill. ale University Press, 1988.

Power and Principle: Memoirs of the National Security Adviser, 1977–1981, Zbigniew rzezinski. Farrar, Straus and Giroux, 1983.

Keeping Faith: Memoirs of a President, Jimmy Carter. Bantam, 1982.

Chances of a Lifetime: A Memoir, Warren Christopher. Scribner, 2001.

American Hostages in Iran: The Conduct of a Crisis, Warren Christopher et al. ouncil on Foreign Relations, 1985.

U.S. Foreign Policy and the Iran Hostage Crisis: Cambridge Studies in International elations, David Patrick Houghton. Cambridge University Press, 2001.

The Iran Hostage Crisis, a Chronology of Daily Developments: Report, U.S. Congress, ouse Committee on Foreign Affairs and Library of Congress. Foreign Affairs d National Defense Division. Government Printing Office, 1981.

Crisis: The Last Year of the Carter Presidency, Hamilton Jordan. G. P. Putnam's ns, 1982.

No Hiding Place: The New York Times *Inside Report on the Hostage Crisis,* Robert McFadden et al. Times Books, 1981.

Freeing the Hostages: Reexamining U.S.-Iranian Negotiations and Soviet Policy, 1979– 81, Russell Leigh Moses. University of Pittsburgh Press, 1996.

Microfiche Collection: Iran, the Making of U.S. Policy, 1977–1980 (Spy en Documents), National Security Archive. George Washington University, 90.

The Other Side of History, Jody Powell. William Morrow, 1984.

America Held Hostage: The Secret Negotiations, Pierre Salinger. Doubleday, 81.

All Fall Down: America's Tragic Encounter with Iran, Gary Sick. Random House, 86.

Inside the Iranian Revolution, John Stempel. Indiana University Press, 1981.

Embassies Under Siege: Personal Accounts by Diplomats on the Front Line, Joseph . Sullivan, ed. Brassey's, 1995.

Nest of Spies: America's Journey to Disaster in Iran, Amir Taheri. Adler & Adler, 88.

Hard Choices: Critical Years in America's Foreign Policy, Cyrus Vance. Simon and huster, 1983.

Rescue Mission

Delta Force, Charlie Beckwith and Donald Knox. Harper Collins, 1983.

No Room for Error: The Story Behind the USAF Special Tactics Unit, John Carney d Benjamin Schemmer. Presidio Press, 2003.

The Holloway Commission Report, Department of Defense, 1982.

Inside Delta Force, Eric L. Haney. Delacorte Press, 2002.

The Guts to Try: The Untold Story of the Iran Hostage Rescue Mission by the O Scene Desert Commander, James Kyle. Crown, 1990.

Crippled Eagle: A Historical Perspective of U.S. Operations, 1976–1996, Rod Lenaha Narwhal Press, 1998.

"Inside the Rescue Mission," David Martin. *Newsweek,* June 12, 1982.

The Master of Disguise: My Secret Life in the CIA, Antonio J. Mendez. Pere nial, 1999.

The Iranian Rescue Mission: Why It Failed, Paul B. Ryan. Naval Institute Pre 1985.

Terrorism and Democracy, Stansfield Turner. Houghton Mifflin, 1991.

Hostage Takers

The Takeover in Tehran, by Massoumeh Ebtekar, as told to Fred Reed. Talo books, 2000.

The Spy Den Documents, National Security Archives.

The 444-Day Crisis in Tehran, Amir Reza, Sotoudeh Hamid Kaviani, tra Nikki Faratsatpour.

Other

Iran and the United States, Richard W. Cottam. University of Pittsburgh Pre 1988.

Nationalism in Iran, Richard W. Cottam. University of Pittsburgh Pre 1979.

The Longest War: The Iran-Iraq Military Conflict, Dilip Hiro. Routledg 1991.

All the Shah's Men, Stephen Kinzer. Wiley, 2003.

The Unthinkable Revolution in Iran, Charles Kurzman. Harvard Universi Press, 2004.

Reading Lolita in Tehran, Azar Nafisi. Random House, 2003.

An Islamic Utopia: A Political Biography of Ali Shariati, Ali Rahnema. I. B. Taur 2000.

Prophets Without Honor: A Requiem for Moral Patriotism, William M. Straba and Michael J. Palecek. Algora, 2002.

444 Days, The Hostages Remember, Tim Wells. Harcourt, 1985.

DOCUMENTARY AND VIDEO

The Carter Center Library collection

444 Days to Freedom: What Really Happened in Iran, directed by Les Harris. Vi Video, 1998.

NOTES

Part One
The "Set-in"

The Desert Angel   *Before dawn . . . secret meeting,* Hashemi. *Hashemi was opposed . . . "the United States is next!"* Hashemi, Ebtekar's *Takeover in Tehran* (TT). *w of the hundred . . . siege to the place,* Hashemi, Asgharzadeh, Ebtekar, *The 444-Day isis in Tehran* (T444DCT). *A CIA analysis . . . "prerevolutionary situation,"* Carter's *eping the Faith* (KF), p. 438. *When the embassy opened . . . no imperial designs.* Taheri's *st of Spies* (NS), p. 92. *By the fall of 1979 . . . like a fort,* Howland, Golacinski, Laingen, *mbert, Metrinko.

Would the Marines Shoot?   *A big demonstration . . . larger crowd,* Laingen, *mbert, Golacinski, Hashemi. For a discussion of the tendency to inflate the *mbers of "martyrs" at anti-shah demonstrations, see Kurzman, *The Unthinkable *volution* (UR). Referring to the most notorious of the "massacres," Black Friday, *urzman writes: "Estimates of casualties on this day . . . range from fewer than one *ndred to many thousands. The post-revolutionary Martyr Foundation could *entify only seventy-nine dead, while the coroner's office counted eighty-two *d Tehran's main cemetery, Behesht-e-Zahra, registered only forty" (p. 75). *Shortly *fore . . . cars and on foot,* Hashemi, Asgharzadeh, Ebtekar, TT and T444DCT. *he plan had been hatched . . . would die,* Asgharzadeh, Hashemi, Mirdamadi, Abdi, *aimipoor, Khoeniha, T444DCT. *When Asgharzadeh . . . Islamic Republic,* Rajaeefar, *gharzadeh, Ebtekar, Khoeniha, T444DCT. *The mullah's ideas . . . source of all *il,* Golpour, Kashani, Khoeniha, Tajzadeh, Rahnema's *An Islamic Utopia* (IU). *In *sions . . . blindfold that many,* Hashemi, Asgharzadeh, Ebtekar, TT, T444DCT. *The *nners had . . . traitorous administration,* Mirdamadi, Asgharzadeh, Ebtekar, TT. *The *dents had also . . . a statement,* Asgharzadeh, T444DCT. *Days after the plan was *tched . . . knew nothing of takeover plan,* Asgharzadeh, Khoeniha, Ebtekar TT; *nomeini quoted on p. 58. *Now, as Hashemi moved . . . what would happen then?* *ashemi, Asgharzedeh, Naimipoor, Ebtekar, TT.

The Morning Meeting   *Walking down the wide corridor . . . feel for the place, *hn and Parvaneh Limbert. *The morning meeting . . . voting with their feet,* Laingen. *omeini had . . . "the nation,"* The Iran Hostage Crisis, a Chronology of Daily Develop- *nts,* p. 35. *John Graves . . . his staffing,* DOS/ICA cable, Tehran 11376, 10/28/79. *ingen had . . . case basis,* Laingen's *Yellow Ribbon* (YR), p. 9. *The decision . . . cata- *ophic,* Laingen cable ref: State 256811, 9/30/79. *It was . . . had answered,* Jordan's *isis* (C), p. 32. *The embassy . . . for decades,* Laingen, Golacinski, Morefield, Scott, *haefer. *Kalp, a CIA officer . . . not everyone could rise above it,* Kalp. *Some of those *peacefully resolved,* Golacinski. *Limbert then . . . report of the trip,* Laingen, Golacinski, *owland, Limbert, Tomseth. *Michael Metrinko . . . across the front yard,* Metrinko, *an (Walsh) Howland, Limbert.

4 We Only Wish to Set-in   *Kevin Hermening . . . closed and locked,* Hermenin
Inured to months . . . thin, vertical strips, Ahern, Laingen. A few of the Iranians w
seized the embassy continue to argue, twenty-five years later, that they unco
ered an American plot to overthrow the revolution, but nothing in the volun
nous "Den of Spies" documents they seized, pieced together, and published in mc
than forty volumes makes their case. The documents do offer a fascinating look
clandestine American activity in Iran going back to the mid-twentieth century a
dramatically illustrate the failure of the spy agency to accurately understand t
forces leading up to the revolution. Just six months before the shah was forced
flee the country, CIA deputy station chief Jack Miklos wrote from Tehran, whe
he had been stationed since 1974, "Iran has now reached the position of a stal
and moderate middle-level power well disposed to the United States, which h
been a goal of our policy since the end of World War II." In appendices to h
book *Takeover in Tehran,* which she judged too hot for American publishers
handle, Massoumeh Ebtekar had all of the seized documents from which to choc
her bombshell revelations and, out of the mass of material, chose two cables. T
first is a portion of a letter by John Graves, attempting to analyze the revolutio
in which he concludes that it was primarily a revolt against privilege. Graves's a
sessment is dubious, and Ebtekar would disagree, but there isn't the slightest h
of spying in it. The second document records a CIA meeting with Abolhassan Bar
Sadr in Tehran after the revolution, in which Bani-Sadr is revealed to be worki
long hours—"until after midnight on a regular basis"—and somewhat less th
eager to meet with Americans (he stood up the officer at their first scheduled me
ing, and kept him waiting for hours for the second). The Iranian official confess
he was concerned about making arrangements to bring his family back to Iran a
offered his guest—there is no indication that Bani-Sadr knew he worked for t
CIA—some broad and entirely innocuous insights into how the emerging go
ernment was taking shape. Hardly the stuff of a coup d'état. *In his office . . . ou*
his office, Rosen's *The Destined Hour* (DH). *Inside the front door . . . take more ti*
Golacinski, Howland, Sickmann, Gallegos, Moeller, Joan (Walsh) Howlar
Laingen, Tomseth.

5 Michael, I'm Really Sorry   *Inside the consulate . . . on the roof,* Lopez, Mor
field, Queen's *Inside and Out* (IO), Ode. *In his second-floor . . . felt set up,* Metrin
Golacinski was . . . situation needed, Golacinski, Gallegos, Lopez, Sickmann, Limbe
Persinger, Joan (Walsh) Howland, Belk, Hermening.

6 Hostage to Whom? For What?   Golacinski, Lee, Lopez, Morefield, Coo
Queen, Lijek.

7 Shoot Me, Don't Burn Me!   *On the top floor . . . nobody else was,* Kupke, Be
Barnes. *At the foot . . . "them away!"* Gallegos, Moeller, Hermening. *Looking do*
. . . "burn it down!" Hermening, Golacinski. *After seeing . . . everyone else,* Limbe

8 Ann, Let Them In   *On the other side . . . open the door,* Laingen, Scott, Schaef
Swift. *The stash . . . locked it,* Kupke. *One of the marines . . . were there,* Belk, Scc
Kupke. *Golacinski was hustled . . .* "Allahuakbar!" Golacinski, Roeder, Shar
Kennedy, Belk, German, Sickmann, Hall, Limbert. *President Jimmy Carter . . .* "gre

...y for football!" Beckwith's *Delta Force* (DF), Burruss, Jordan, C, Brzezinski's *Power ...d Principle* (P&P).

I Told You So *Farouz Rajaeefar . . . she hung up.* Rajaeefar. *Other excited oc-...piers . . . "the Imam's Line,"* Ebtekar, TT. *A few miles . . . embassy returned,* Laingen, ...azdi, Tomseth, Precht.

I'm Going to Cut Out This Eye First *Inside the chancery . . . to the roof,* Ahern, ...rnes, Kupke, Hermening, Howland. *The phone lines . . . he said,* Howland, Koob, ...oyer, Englemann, Jones, Golacinski.

Gaptooth *Kupke's pockets . . . evident disbelief,* Kupke. The description of ...eikh-ol-eslam is drawn from several of the hostages who came to know him ...ell, among them Daugherty, Ahern, Kupke, Scott, Metrinko, and Limbert, as ...ell as from photographs taken at that time. *With men grabbing . . . walked away,* ...hern memo to CIA director, from National Security Archive.

Go and Kick Them Out *By midafternoon . . . swish of fabric,* Joan (Walsh) ...owland, Limbert, Rosen. *Ibrahim Yazdi . . . out of their hands,* Laingen, Yazdi, ...hoeniha.

Wheat Mold *Before he was . . . than they themselves did,* Limbert. *Throughout ...e residence . . . and never returned,* Cooke, Hall, Queen, Scott, Sickmann, Subic, ...ersinger, Sharer. *After the moment . . . just a nightmare!* Belk, Jones, Hermening, ...upke, Queen, Limbert, Hall.

Okay, Go Ahead and Shoot *There was to be little . . . smoking cigarettes,* ...augherty—both my interviews with him and his *In the Shadow of the Ayatollah* ...SA).

An Island of Stability *Across a continent . . . Delta's first mission,* Beckwith, ...F, Burruss, Fitch. *Beckwith was northbound . . . Kennedy interview,* Brzezinski, P&P, ...arter, KF, Jordan, C, Precht, Powell, Kinzer, *All the Shah's Men* (ASM), Cottam's ...ationalism in Iran* (NI) and *Iran and the United States* (IUS), Turner, press ac-...ounts (*New York Times, Washington Post*), Valeriani.

Two Minutes of Hate *Monday morning brought . . . heavy sleep,* Limbert, ...sgharzadeh, Rajaeefar, Hashemi, Hall, Parvaneh Limbert. *Through that long . . . ...xty-six hostages,* Koob, Royer, Lijek.

Obviously, We Don't Want to Do This *Two days after . . . its response,* ...rzezinski, P&P, Jordan, C, Beckwith, DF, Burruss, Lenahan, Nightengale, Vaught. ...a meeting of the National Security Council . . . "Islamic thugs?"* Powell's *The Other Side ...History* (TOSH). *Any hope of the higher powers . . . and so fast,* Yazdi, Tabatabai, ...hoeniha. *Ibrahim Yazdi left his office . . . had the imam's ear last,* Yazdi. *In his speech ...at day . . . willing to negotiate,* news reports, Jordan, C, Brzezinski, P&P, Valeriani. ...- Hamilton Jordan . . . angry Americans,* Jordan, C.

18 Yes, and This Is for You   *The hostages at the embassy . . . save his life,* Bel
Hohman. *As the students scrambled to organize themselves . . . if it came to that,* Morefiel
Hashemi. *Bob Ode, the eldest of the hostages . . . "this is for you,"* Ode, Sickmann. *In*
first week of confinement . . . they were being interrogated, Limbert. *Bruce Laingen . . . maki*
circles, Laingen, Tomseth, *New York Times, Washington Post* accounts, TV news tap
from the Carter Center.

19 George Lambrakis   *Having accomplished . . . significant enough?* Hashen
Scott (interview and *Pieces of the Game*), Keough, Sharer, Ebtekar, TT, T444DC
Overview on embassy operations was provided primarily by Laingen. The ro
played by Captain Neil Robinson emerged from many interviews. Now an air for
general assigned to the NSA, Robinson declined to be interviewed. *Vice con*
Richard Queen . . . given a raise without being informed, Queen (interview and IC
Kathryn Koob walked . . . she told them, Koob (interview and *Guest of the Revolution* [GR
Al Golacinski was questioned about his watch . . . torture and interrogation, Golacinski. *Jo*
Limbert *was questioned . . . "ten years old at the time,"* Limbert. *Those interrogated . . .*
the takeover, Hall. *Many of those sessions . . . suited him fine,* Golacinski. *Air Force Lie*
tenant Colonel Dave Roeder . . . led him back upstairs, Roeder, Ebtekar, Hashemi. *If th*
had a hard time . . . where he would spend the next five months, Metrinko, Joan (Wals
Howland.

20 "R" Designation   *Despite their clumsy and sometimes comical methods . . .*
pleaded, Daugherty, National Security Archive. *The students realized soon enough . . .*
was told, Ahern.

Part Two
Den of Spies

1 We Don't Have the Shadow or Superman   Videotapes of TV news co
erage from the Carter Center Library, news reports.

2 Forgive Me, Oh, Imam   *On a chilly Thanksgiving . . . a long time,* Quarle
Maples, news reports. *Quarles, Maples, and Gross . . . certain as a spy,* Ebtekar (i
terview and TT), T444DCT. *Joan Walsh . . . to freedom,* Joan (Walsh) Howlan
The release . . . "determined to avoid," videotapes of news reports, including the
Minutes interview with Khomeini from the Carter Center Library, news repor
Powell.

3 Only Whores Go Without Underwear   *As winter settled over . . . an irreg*
lar schedule, the Mushroom Inn description and changing of the guards is draw
from my interviews and the Wells interviews, Queen, IO, and Scott, PG. *Golacinsk*
group . . . moved to a new spot, Golacinski, Roeder. *Richard Queen . . . claim of impo*
tance, Queen (interview and IO), Hall, Lijek. *The two remaining female hostages .*
Swift was taken away, Koob.

World-Devouring Ghouls *Perhaps because . . . "Richard Owen,"* Queen (in-
~view and IO). *Thirty-three hostages . . . five days after the takeover,* news reports,
zezinski, P&P, Carter, KF, Vance's *Hard Choices* (HC). *The first big session . . . photos
his pocket,* Rita Ode, Dorothea Morefield, Penne Laingen, Barbara Rosen, DH,
aplen (*The New Yorker,* June 2, 1980). *For his part . . . pure capitulation,* Brzezinski
erview. *At a foreign policy breakfast . . . the response would be swift and harsh,* Brzezinski,
, Jordan, C, TV news tapes from the Carter Center, Carter, KF, Moses's *Free-
g the Hostages* (FTH).

Davy Crockett Didn't Have to Fight His Way In Burruss, Fitch, Schoo-
ker, Beckwith, DF, Ishimoto, Kyle's *The Guts to Try* (GT), Nightengale, Holloway
ommission.

The Corrupt of the Earth Limbert, Kupke, Graves, TW, *The Spy Den
cuments.*

The Largest Thefts and Exploitations in History *It would be hard to tell
he would never recover,* news reports. *Carter was considering . . . said Brzezinski,*
oses, FTH, National Security Archive, TV news tapes from the Carter Center
d the Morefield family. *Carter was furious with the network . . . dare to assert control,*
well, Lenahan, Nightengale. *House Speaker . . . "horseshit,"* news reports, Nighten-
le, Burruss. *Given the bewildering variety . . . condemn Carter and the American gov-
nment,* AP. *When the shah attempted to . . . political weight, The Iran Hostage Crisis, a
ronology of Daily Developments,* Jordan, C. *At the White House . . . underscore his im-
ence,* Carter, KF, Jordan, C, Brzezinski, P&P, memo obtained from the Carter
nter Library. *In a series of speeches . . . toward military action, Tehran Times. The presi-
t was briefed daily . . . left dark,* Carter, KF.

The Cure Is an Airline Ticket Out of Here *On the embassy grounds
"out of here,"* Queen (interview and IO), Hall. *The Mushroom Inn . . . three
es a day,* description of Hamid from Koob, Queen (the list of library rules
from IO, p. 130), Scott, Roeder, Golacinski, Rosen, DH, Sharer, Persinger,
yer. *They were beginning . . . across the room,* Golacinski, Roeder, Scott (inter-
w and PG).

Escape *Bill Belk had been moved . . . Christmas holidays,* Belk (my interview and
ells interview). *The approach of Christmas . . . on her "tree,"* Koob.

Captivity Pageant *On Christmas morning . . . entirely at ease,* Hermening,
bic, Lauterbach, videotape from the Carter Center Library, Ebtekar, TT. *In
at the students . . . cut into her skin,* news reports, videotape from the Carter Cen-
 Library, Kupke, Ebtekar, TT, Keough, Scott, PG, Koob. *Several days . . . as
captives,* Laingen, Tomseth. *Vice consul Bob Ode . . . "not prayers,"* Ode (interview
d his diary), news reports. *Despite its obvious . . . he was crushed,* Limbert, Scott
terview and PG), Hall, Golacinski. *Michael Metrinko . . . for two weeks,* Metrinko,
tekar.

11 Invasion and Opportunity *Charlie Beckwith decided . . . everyone arou*
them understood, Burruss, Fitch, Beckwith, DF. *Two other things happened . . .*
president's ear, news reports, Jordan, C, Associated Press chronology, Brzezins
P&P, Salinger's *America Held Hostage* (AHH). *In the second week . . . dangerous bu*
ness in Iran, news reports, Jordan, C.

Part Three
Waiting

1 They Started It, We Ended It *After his questioners . . . eyes fell shut,* Ahe
Some background information about Simon Farzami came from http://ho
.online.no/~hhakimi/album/abolhassan/abh.htm, National Security Archiv
news reports. *Ahern's colleague Bill Daugherty . . . ended the interview,* Daugher
Schaefer, National Security Archive, TV news tapes from the Carter Center I
brary, Ahern, newspaper reports.

2 We Know What Route That Bus Takes *CIA officers . . . "That's it,"* Limbe
Precht. *Lieutenant Colonel Dave Roeder . . . should he take it?* Roeder.

3 Happy New Year *After more than . . . several times,* Kirtley, Lopez (Wells int
view and my interview), Gallegos, Sickmann, Royer, Persinger, Cooke, Golacins
Roeder, Sharer, Koob, Scott (interview and PG), Queen (interview and IO), Be
Hall. *Queen's condition . . . whatever it was,* Queen (interview and IO), Hall.

4 That's Illegal! *On January 25 . . . might finally be breaking Carter's u*
Jordan, C, Sick's *All Fall Down* (AFD), Associated Press chronology. *Th*
was now . . . he was in on it, Kupke, news reports, Lopez, Sickmann, Persing
Graves.

5 A Marvelous Coup *Bill Belk's combative . . . his next meal,* Belk, Hohm
Ebtekar, TT. *Next door, Limbert . . . "marvelous coup!"* Limbert, Belk.

6 A New and Mutually Beneficial Relationship *With a secret process . . . "la*
less dictators," news reports, videotapes from the Carter Center Library, Burru
Fitch, Beckwith, DF, Kyle, GT, Schaefer. *The students were feeling . . . even kr*
Subic, Hermening, Lauterbach.

7 SAVAK! SAVAK! *Inside Iran . . . future of Iran,* Hashemi, Asgharzadeh. *Th*
frustration . . . wanted to do, Limbert, Hall, Queen (interview and IO), Scott (int
views and PG), German, Ode, Kupke, Rosen (interview and DH), *444 Days to Fr*
dom, Belk, Sharer, Englemann, Lopez, Keough, Cooke, Golacinski, Persing
Roeder, Royer, Kennedy. After being assured repeatedly by Mohammad Hashe
and other former hostage takers that their captives had been treated gently a
with respect at all times, I asked him about the mock execution. He said it nev
happened, that such stories were "lies." "I have been interviewing former hosta

ll over the United States, dozens of them," I told him. "And their memories about he incident are all in agreement, and agree with accounts they gave in interviews wenty years ago. They are all lying?" Hashemi said that he couldn't vouch for very guard who took care of the hostages and every moment. "So now you are aying it might have happened?" I asked. He shrugged off the question. *The mock xecution . . . other guards,* Kupke, Scott (interviews and PG). *After the mock execu- ion . . . and did,* Hall, Scott, Keough.

Ham, They Are Crazy   *On the same day . . . "for years,"* news reports, Jaffe, Rupiper, Lewis, Gallegos. *There was reason to be more optimistic . . . "polls are accurate,"* ordan, C, Carter, KF, memo from Carter Center Library, TV news tapes from he Carter Center Library, *The Iran Hostage Crisis, a Chronology of Daily Developments,* Associated Press chronology.

Fie on Them All   Laingen, Howland, Tomseth, news reports, *444 Days to Freedom.*

0 The Atmosphere of Restraint Cannot Last Forever   *On March 13 . . . to oison him,* Jordan, C, Carter, KF, letter from the Carter Center Library, *The Iran Hostage Crisis, a Chronology of Daily Developments,* Sick, AFD.

1 I'm Not Going to Answer Questions from Anyone Wearing a Dress!   *On March 19 . . . avenue of approach,* Queen (interview and IO), Hall. *John Limbert was noved . . . no one disputed,* Limbert. *The interrogations . . . him in months,* Metrinko, harsar.

2 I Think We're Ready   *As the month . . . Carney's dirt bike,* Carney (inter- iews and *No Room for Error* [NRE], . . . with some e-mail assistance from Bud McBroom). *Over the same days . . . "I think we're ready,"* Burruss, Fitch, Schoomaker, Beckwith, DF.

Part Four
One Hundred and Thirty-Two Men

Bunny Sadr   *Forcing grown men . . . he went home,* Queen (interview and IO), Hall, Ode, Sickmann, Lopez, Gallegos, Golacinski, Laingen, Metrinko. *Jimmy Carter's patience . . . his choice of words,* Jordan, C, Carter, KF, Associated Press chro- ology, Precht.

A Beginning of the Dawn of Final Victory   *Easter in Tehran . . . for pun- shment,* news reports, Rupiper, Strabala's *Prophets Without Honor* (PWH), Koob, Golacinski, Hermening, Morefield, Gallegos, Queen, Hall. *The successful, stealthy . . seemed doable,* Burruss, Fitch. *President Carter's crackdown . . . had traveled there on heir own,* Christopher's *Chances of a Lifetime* (CL), Vance, HC, Jordan, C, Carter, KF, Brzezinski (interview and P&P), Powell interview, newspaper reports. *Colonel*

Beckwith . . . April 24, Beckwith, DF, Carter, KF, Brzezinski, P&P, Jordan, C, Burrus
Fitch, Schoomaker. *One morning, for no reason . . . spirits for days,* Metrinko.

3 You've Got a Mother   *The punishment . . . His mom?* Hermening, Golacinsk
In an epic gesture . . . misled and manipulated, Timm. *She was not . . . aggravated susp.
cion,* Barbara Rosen, DH. *Timm was appalled . . . canceling them,* Timm, news report
Then, in mid-April . . . "how to get them out," Powell, McFadden's *No Hiding Pla
(NHP). The travel ban . . . "do not oppose it,"* Barbara Rosen, DH, Penne Laingen, new
reports. *Opposition was . . . she refused,* Timm, Ebtekar, TT. *Hermening was blind
folded . . . day of his release,* Hermening, Timm, Golacinski, Ebtekar. *Bruce Lainge
. . . sky faded into darkness,* Laingen (interviews and YR), Carter, KF, Howland.

4 Welcome to World War Three   Burruss, Beckwith, Uttaro, Fitch, Carne
Holloway Commission Report, photos taken by mission members, Cheney, Smith
Savory, Schoomaker, Kyle, GT, Sanchez, Brenci, Bancroft, Byers, Rowe, Doyle
Long, Ishimoto, Carter, KF, Jordan, C, Brzezinski, P&P, Powell.

5 What the Hell Is This?   *Already the eight . . . they turned back,* Schaefer, Kyle
GT, *Holloway Commission Report. At the desert . . . Carter said softy,* Schaefer, Burrus
Beckwith, DF, Kyle, GT, Walton, Fitch, Smith, Schoomaker, Long, Brzezinsk
(interview and P&P), Jordan, C, Carter, KF, Christopher, CL, Vance, HC, Marti
(*Newsweek,* "Inside the Failed Mission" [IFM]), *444 Days to Freedom.*

6 Two Loud, Dull *Thunks*   *At Desert One . . . no second chance,* Haney's *Insi
Delta Force* (IDF), Martin, IFM, Fitch, Walton, Cheney, Schaefer, Beckwith, DI
Bancroft, Doyle, Rowe, Smith, Byers, Uttaro, Burruss. *Word reached . . . rescue th
hostages,* Jordan, C, Vance, HC; theWhite House statement was reprinted in th
Washington Post.

Part Five
Haggling With the Barbarians

1 A Prison-like Place   Hashemi, Asgharzadeh, Keough, Royer, Barnes, Jone
Ahern, Limbert, Metrinko, Daugherty, German, Koob, Ode.

2 Any Possibility of Failure Should Have Ruled It Out   *Barbara Timm . .
was not friendly,* Timm, news reports, videotapes of TV news from the Carter Cente
Library. *Most Americans . . . steady months-long decline,* Associated Press–NBC New
poll. *In the final meeting . . . "I don't change it now,"* Barbara Rosen, DH, Timm
Brzezinski (interview and P&P); the roundup of newspaper editorial reactions wa
compiled by AP in the week after the mission. *It was a dejected . . . spirited ovatio
news reports, Fitch, Burruss, Beckwith, DF, Martin, IFM.

3 S-E-N-D-N-E-W-S   *After the rescue attempt . . . six months before,* Laingen
news reports. *John Limbert . . . alone for a long time,* Limbert, Sharer, Kalp. *Summe

urned . . . a big apology, Metrinko, Roeder, news reports, videotape from the Carter Center Library, *444 Days to Freedom.*

Moral Sadness *At home during . . . "into a catastrophe,* Schell (*The New Yorker,* ine 2, 1980). *Some of the . . . in private,* Barbara Rosen, DH. *In light . . . "live with the ostages,* news reports, videotapes from the Carter Center Library. *Despite the dearth . "you thought of the hostages today?,"* Carter, KF, Jordan, C, *Washington Post,* McFadden, JHP, Associated Press chronology, Sick, AFD, TV news tapes from the Morefields, *44 Days to Freedom,* Dorothea Morefield, TV news tapes from the Carter Center ibrary, *New York Times. The obstinacy . . . "if it doesn't work," The Iran Hostage Crisis, Chronology of Daily Developments,* news reports, Laingen (interviews and YR), Howland, Bani-Sadr.

I'm Going *Others responded . . . like torture,* Limbert, Kalp, Belk, Subic. *The gistics . . . a good sign,* Lopez, Hall, Kirtley, Persinger, Koob. *Kathryn Koob . . . was one,* Koob. *Queen, Miele . . . Zurich, Switzerland,* Queen (interview and IO), Ode (in-rview and diary), Hohman.

The Braying of Donkeys Limbert, Scott (interviews and PG), Holland.

Buy Iraqi War Bonds *Summer is long . . . fearless response,* Howland. *Laingen w . . . for emergencies,* Laingen, Holland, Limbert, Scott (interview and PG), Sharer, Daugherty, Metrinko, Roeder. *Suddenly, Iran . . . "Stop shooting at it,"* Laingen, YR. *Jone of the hostages . . . war with Iraq,* Limbert, Belk, Koob. *The window to the cell . dried black,* Golacinski, Morefield. *Tom Ahern . . . back in solitary,* Ahern, Sharer, cott. The question of who told what to the Iranians continues to be a source of onfusion and dissension among the hostages twenty-five years later. *One swelter-ig night . . . started to laugh,* Keough, Daugherty, Roeder, Rosen, DH, Schaefer. *The uard Abbas . . . own divising,* Cooke. *Not long . . . pointless, and cruel,* Metrinko, news eports (Metrinko gave me a copy of the letter).

It Has Become a Quagmire *Iraq's invasion of Iran . . . have to wait out this war,* abatabai, Christopher, CL, Associated Press chronology, Carter, KF, Jordan, C, P, Sick, AFD, McFadden, NHP. *As the American . . . exposure and pull,* news reports, V videotapes from the Carter Center Library. *In Tehran . . . "Boom!"* Roeder. *All rough October . . . January 21, 1981,* Carter, KF, Associated Press chronology, Jor-an, C, Christopher, CL, UPI, AP, TV news tapes from the Morefield family and ie Carter Center Library, McFadden, NHP. *After Reagan's victory . . . other mullahs,* aingen (interviews and YR), Tomseth, Howland, news reports. *Month by month . . written a year earlier,* McFadden, NHP, TV news tapes from the Carter Center Library, *444 Days to Freedom.*

Weren't You Fed Amply? *In the interregnum . . . for the first time in more than year,* Turner's *Terrorism and Democracy* (TD), McFadden, NHP, Associated Press hronology, Carter, KF, Jordan, C, TV news tapes from the Carter Center Library, ick, AFD. *At the end . . . suite in groups,* Daugherty, Scott, Ahern, Laingen, Tomseth, lowland, Koob. *For the hostages' . . . flicker of hope,* Hall, TV videotapes from the

Carter Center Library, Metrinko, Roeder. *Kathryn Koob and Ann Swift . . . terminat* *the conversation,* Koob, Ebtekar, TV videotapes from the Carter Center Librar *444 Days to Freedom,* Metrinko, Roeder, Morefield, Laingen, YR.

10 We Don't Do Stuff Like That   *Before Laingen . . . were solid,* Laingen. *If t students believed . . . sense of completion and accomplishment,* McFadden, NHP, Carte KF, Christopher, CL, Associated Press chronology, Sick, AFD, TV news tapes fro the Carter Center Library. *Two days before . . . interrogator departed,* Daugherty. *Sheik ol-eslam . . . he said,* Ahern. *John Limbert . . . on their way,* Limbert, Koob, Golacinsk Howland, Hermening, Laingen, Sickmann, Metrinko, Kupke. *Carter had reluctant abandoned his plan . . . waiting for news from Tehran,* Carter, KF, Christopher, Cl McFadden, NHP, Sick, AFD, Brzezinski, P&P, TV news tapes from the Carte Center Library, Jordan, C, AP. *Mehrabad Airport . . . he felt relaxed,* videotapes fro the Carter Center Library, Sickmann, Hermening, Royer, Tomseth, Koob, Limbe Laingen, Hall, Belk, Scott (interviews and PG), Lopez, Roeder, Metrinko, Gallego Ahern, Kupke, Golacinski. *President Reagan made the announcement . . . they started dance,* TV news tapes from the Carter Center Library and the Morefield famil *444 Days to Freedom.*

ACKNOWLEDGMENTS

I have never had so much help in writing a book, and I'm afraid now I have been permanently spoiled. I would like to thank Morgan Entrekin, David Bradley, and Scott Rudin for their enthusiastic and generous support of this project. Michael Oreskes and Vivian Schiller of *The New York Times* (and Discovery-Times) made the companion documentary possible.

My research assistant Terrence Henry has been invaluable. He joined me in this project soon after I started it, and over the years I came to lean on him more and more. I might have been able to write this book without him, but it would have taken me twenty years and it would still be missing bits and pieces of information he cleverly unearthed from the National Archives and the Carter Center in Atlanta. My cousins David and Arcadia Keane, and my son Aaron Bowden (along with the rest of the talented folks at Wild Eyes Productions) signed on early to make the companion documentary for the Discovery-Times channel, and effectively became my collaborators. David and Arcadia made one reporting trip to Tehran, and David accompanied me on my two trips, and I owe them a great debt for their help, companionship, and a terrific place to stay in Hermosa Beach. Aaron wrote the documentary and chipped in on a lot of the interviewing, traveling all over America, and my gratitude toward him is mixed with a huge helping of fatherly pride.

I would also like to thank Tim Wells for the extraordinary early reporting he did on this story, all of which is deposited in a special collection at the Duke University Library, where my own notes, transcripts, and files will be donated. Wells was gracious and extraordinarily generous in sharing his work. Ramin Mostaqim was our guide and translator in Tehran, and he threw himself into the work like the talented journalist he is. I would also like to thank Michael Hornburg for his careful and patient copyediting, Ron Bernstein, Christina Asquith, Jennie Dunham, Scott Manning, Jamison Stoltz, Kaveh Ehsani, and Nikki Faratsatpour.

Lastly, I would like to thank the participants in this story who worked hard to make sure I told it accurately, most of all John Limbert, Michael Metrinko, Bill Daugherty, Dave Roeder, Mike Howland, Bruce Laingen, Bucky Burruss, and Logan Fitch.

INDEX